Italian Culture in America
The Immigrants 1880 to 1930
From Discrimination to Assimilation

By:
Ralph G. Giordano

With Contributing Contemplative Essays by:

**Mandy Tuttle, Janice Therese Mancuso,
and
John Bemelmans Marciano**

Italian Culture in America
The Immigrants 1880 to 1930
From Discrimination to Assimilation

By:
Ralph G. Giordano

With Contributing Contemplative Essays by:

Mandy Tuttle, Janice Therese Mancuso,
and
John Bemelmans Marciano

ACADEMICA PRESS
WASHINGTON - LONDON

Library of Congress Cataloging-in-Publication Data

Names: Giordano, Ralph G. (author)
Title: Italian culture in america : the immigrants, 1880 to 1930 – from discrimination to assimilation | Giordano, Ralph G.
Description: Washington : Academica Press, 2023. | Includes references.
Identifiers: LCCN 2023940828 | ISBN 9781680538380 (hardcover) | 9781680538397 (e-book) | 9781680538403 (paperback)

Copyright 2023 Ralph G. Giordano

Contents

ACKNOWLEDGMENTS *Riconoscimenti* xi

PREFACE – *Prefazione* xiii

INTRODUCTION – "*INTRODUZIONE*"
A CULTURAL HERITAGE of ENRICHING HUMANITY 1

CHAPTER 1
NATIONALISM, INDUSTRIAL REVOLUTION, AND IMMIGRATION... 17

CHAPTER 2
ITALIAN IMMIGRANTS: THE GREAT ARRIVAL OPENS The DOOR .. 51

CHAPTER 3
ANTI-IMMIGRATION, DISCRIMINATION, AND LYNCHING 93

CHAPTER 4A
AN INNOCENT, A DIPLOMAT,
BOOKER T. WASHINGTON, AND A TRAVEL EXPERT IN ITALY 135

CHAPTER 4B
CONSTANTINO BRUMIDI,
GIUSEPPE GARIBALDI, AND ANTONIO MEUCCI 155

CHAPTER 5
WHERE DID THEY GO? AND WHAT DID THEY DO? 175

CHAPTER 6
AMERICANS PLAY - ITALIANS WORK – HULL HOUSE
– A FACTORY FIRE - MARGARET SANGER
– AND ITALIAN LEISURE 209

CHAPTER 7
BIRTH OF AMERICAN VAUDEVILLE AND SHOW BUSINESS 249

CHAPTER 7A
ITALIAN OPERA AND ENRICO CARUSO.. 265

CHAPTER 7B
JAZZ AND ITALIAN ORIGINS 323

CHAPTER 7C
CALIFORNIA (AND TEXAS) HERE THEY COME............................. 343

CHAPTER 7D
ITALIANS IN HOLLYWOOD AND RUDOLPH VALENTINO.............. 371

CHAPTER 8
THE 20TH CENTURY:
HEROES, VILLAINS, AND CULTURAL NOTABLES.......................... 397

CHAPTER 9
BIOGRAPHIES OF ITALIANS SHAPING AMERICAN CULTURE 429

CHAPTER 10
THE 1920S: THE DOOR CLOSES 469

CHAPTER 11
ITALIAN FOOD SHAPING AMERICAN CULINARY CULTURE 509

CONCLUSION
A SCENARIO FOR A FINALE.. 525

APPENDIX
HISTORICAL ITALIAN IMMIGRATION DOCUMENTS 531

SELECT BIBLIOGRAPHY... 533

INDEX 547

Dedication - "*Dedizione*"

For all those brave Italians who crossed the Atlantic Ocean
including my four Immigrant Italian Grandparents

Domenico Giordano   Antonio "Anthony" Dattilo
Filomena Finelli   Annina "Anna" Colacino

Our Grandchildren
Madison Paige Giordano   Lucas Harry Giordano
Henry Thomas Giordano   Audrey Ann Giordano

And Always to my Wife and Partner-in-Life Thelma Lynn Olsen

Other Publications by Ralph G. Giordano

Italian Culture In America: How A Founding Father Introduced Italian Art, Architecture, Food, Wine, And Liberty To The American People

Pop Goes the Decade: The Fifties

The Architectural Ideology of Thomas Jefferson

La Danse Country & Western (French Translation)

Country & Western Dance - The American Dance Floor Series

Satan in the Dance Hall: Rev. John Roach Straton, Social Dancing, and Morality in 1920s New York City

Social Dancing in America: Fair Terpsichore to the Ghost Dance, 1607-1900

Social Dancing in America: Lindy Hop to Hip Hop, 1901-2000

Fun and Games in Twentieth-Century America: A Historical Guide to Leisure

Editor: *The American Dance Floor Series*

Latin Dance

Disco Dance

Folk Dancing

Swing Dancing

Hip Hop Dance

Country & Western Dance

Rock 'n' Roll Dances of the 1950s

ACKNOWLEDGMENTS

Riconoscimenti

My first and foremost acknowledgement is for the encouragement and support from my wife and partner-in-life Thelma Olsen. As such, I am also always grateful to our children Matthew Giordano, Jonathan Giordano, and Laura Schubert. My formative research was fundamentally shaped by three prominent historians and professors at the College of Staten Island Fred Binder, David Nasaw, and David Traboulay, each deserves a grateful thank you. A significant gratitude is due to author, educator, and researcher Janice Therese Mancuso for establishing "Thirty-One Days of Italian American Heritage Month" as an integral part of The National Italian American Foundation (NIAF). Another supporter through many years is Joseph Scelsa of the John D. Calandra Italian American Institute. As is some valuable Italian translation by Nicholas Pellegrino of many documents from my family archives.

Acknowledgement of research support goes to the valuable resources of the U.S. Library of Congress and Curator of the U.S. Senate with a heartfelt thanks for these and many other well-organized U.S. Government research agencies. Others providing just as much equal assistance and valuable contributions include:

- Benedetto Youssef
- Phil Rokus, Office of the Senate Curator
- United States Office of the Historian
- The Library Company of Philadelphia
- The New York Public Library
- Claudia Timossi, Museum of Santa Croce Opera in Florence
- Will Crutchfield, General Director, Teatro Nuovo
- John Bemelmans Marciano
- Lou Del Bianco
- Richard Migliaccio and the Migliaccio Family
- Mandy Tuttle and Robert Shimp, Research and Program Directors Paul Revere House
- Keeley Tulio Archivist and Collections Coordinator at The Union League Legacy Foundation of Philadelphia
- U.S. Library of Congress Prints and Photograph Division

xii Italian Culture in America:
The Immigrants 1880 to 1930 From Discrimination to Assimilation

- Wikipedia Commons
- Garibaldi-Meucci Museum Staten Island, New York
- Jennifer Navarre and The Historic New Orleans Collection
- Ellen Engseth at Immigration History Research Center Archives, University of Minnesota Libraries
- The Migliaccio Family
- Caroline Yeager and the George Eastman Museum
- Lisa Werner and Rick Steves
- B. G. Firmani
- Aldo Mancusi and TJ Borriello

As a reference, I have encountered some criticism on the Web-based source of information Wikipedia (www.wikipedia.org). As a free online encyclopedia, Wikipedia was created and edited by volunteers around the world and hosted by the Wikimedia Foundation. It can, and is, a valuable resource for research and information. I have learned *not* to simply take the entries at "face value." During my research, when information is not readily available, I try a Wikipedia search. In reading through, I always look to the footnotes and work my way through to those references to provide a pathway to verifiable sources. The simple technique provides access to verifiable citations and exciting compilation information.

It is imperative to state, I am a 40-year research veteran who fondly remembers paging through library volumes and loading microfilm reels on readers. Many hours were devoted to books and magazines on microfiche, inter-library loans, and many personal visits to both libraries and historical sites. As the years have progressed digital source information has made the research process more efficient; yet more than ever requires a critical eye of verifying the source for factual content. During the 21st century, we are all hindered by an era of "fake news," mis-information, and "seat-of-the-pants" social media blogs where it seems like everyone has an opinion (but not supported by fact) to disseminate information "for all the world to see."

Thankfully we still have many historians who are factually trustworthy. In compiling a social, cultural, and historical journey such as this from the formative Italian immigration years of 1880 to 1930, I am thankful for the archival resources of the many academic and scholarly individuals who fill the pages of my very long bibliography. For all those who are un-named and have ever provided valuable assistance; and especially for those who read my work, I offer a very humble –

Grazie mille a tutti!

PREFACE – *Prefazione*

This publication is not an attempt to drive a proverbial "Square Peg" of Italian culture into the "Round Hole" of American culture. I contend the reverse is true, easily placing an Italian "Round Peg" into an American "Square Hole." Therefore, an understanding is carefully presented throughout this work revealing the presence of Italian culture as one significant part of a larger whole contributing a unique historical blend to an ever-expanding American culture.

My own Italian-American heritage stems from an unbroken lineage of four grandparents, namely, Domenico Giordano, Filomena Finelli, Antonio Dattilo, and Annina Colacino, who each emigrated separately from southern Italy during the 1920s - settling in Brooklyn - as immigrants enticed by a promise offering a better life in *L'America*. My father Tomaso "Thomas" Giordano (one of ten children) and mother Felice "Phyllis" Dattilo (one of five) were born in America. In looking to my own Italian heritage, the focus of this publication is to identify so many of the "taken for granted" aspects of innovations and creative ideas of American life. Some with those distinct Italian roots include aeronautics, banking, communications, education, entertainment, music, radio, the Lincoln Memorial, Mount Rushmore, the Statue of Liberty, and even a Little Red Wagon, Mr. Peanut, and a Jacuzzi, among dozens of others.

INTRODUCTION – "*INTRODUZIONE*"

A CULTURAL HERITAGE
of
ENRICHING HUMANITY

A definitive work *Italian Americans: A History*, proposes separating of the "myth from reality and uncover a more complicated story and deeper truths." With this publication, I offer a similar theme centered on the Italian immigrant experience in America from the years 1880 to 1930. An analysis of the overt severe discrimination has delved into the subliminal, overshadowing many positive Italian cultural contributions to America which are intertwined with the changing public perception of Italians. The American cultural admiration for Italy is not new. Prior to the American Civil War, Italian affinity, can be placed among "things," rather than people. The Italian *things* established within American culture include art, architecture, law, liberty, music, macaroni, tomato sauce, wine, and democratic political ideals. For the most part are as indelible, tangible, and important as those items are within American Culture, they can also be discovered as an intangible abstract.[1]

The *Merriam-Webster* dictionary defines *abstract* as an adjective; as "relating to or involving general ideas or qualities rather than specific people, objects, or actions." A secondary definition as a verb is to "consider (something) theoretically or separately from something else." In either, the individual experience would not necessarily be thought of as an Italian contribution; rather as an established part of American culture without any real knowledge of the original source. Similar comparison is the vast contribution to the establishment of the American nation due to the Italian Renaissance and French Enlightenment. In 1989, notable Art historian Irma B. Jaffe in *The Italian Presence in American Art 1760-1860* exclaimed,

> "It would be impossible to overstate the debt of insight and inspiration that the Western world owes to Italian culture. Can we even begin to

---

[1] Maria Laurino, *Italian Americans: A History*, New York: W. W. Norton & Company, 2015, p. 1. Ralph G. Giordano. *Italian Culture in America* (Academica Press, 2020).

2   Italian Culture in America:
The Immigrants 1880 to 1930 From Discrimination to Assimilation

estimate how much our aesthetic and intellectual expectations have been nourished by the literature, the music, the painting, the sculpture, the architecture of Italy? The United States as much as any nation in the world, has been enriched by the mysterious Italian genius, and indeed before [America] had achieved nationhood, we had already found our way into the fountain."[2]

With the continued advent of many mass-media outlets as newspapers, magazines, Hollywood movies, and the Internet mainstream, Americans could physically *see* the Italian people. Images, more often than not were of poor peasants, as stereotypical, contemptable, fictious, and misleading.

In 2022, Ferdinando Cotugno writing for *Smithsonian* magazine explained some basic cultural disinformation regarding Italy with the addition of some of the varied differences as,

> "The world tends to think of Italy as the modern inheritor of ancient Rome, the national home of pizza, espresso, and Leonardo da Vinci. But long before it was a unified nation, the boot-shape peninsular was a loose collection of towns and villages, *borghi* in Italian, with wildly varied architecture, topography, and the cultural histories. In picturesque towns in the north, Italian is often the third language spoken after German and *Ladin*, a surviving Latin dialect with roots in the Roman conquest of the Alps. Until the [start of the] 20th century, most Italians lived in such rural hamlets, which were often rich in history and natural beauty but short on economic opportunity and social services. As industrialization drove migration to cities thousands of *borghi* [villages] were left behind. Populations plummeted. Whole towns fell into disrepair or worse, further pummeled by floods, earthquakes, landslides, and wildfires."[3]

By 2022, over 2,000 Italian towns were in a state of "abandonment;" with an additional 5,000 or more "at risk of depopulation." Prior to the Great Wave of Italian immigration that began in 1880, a significant amount of Italian influence was well-entrenched into American culture. A full discussion is provided within my publication with the self-explanatory title, *Italian Culture In America: How A Founding Father Introduced Italian Art, Architecture, Food, Wine, And Liberty To The American People* (Academica Press, 2020). The "Founding Father" was none other than Thomas Jefferson (1743-1826) a lifelong *Italophile*. The synopsis for that publication describes,

> "At the onset of the American Revolution, Britain's North American

---

[2] Irma B. Jaffe, ed. *The Italian Presence in American Art 1760-1860*. New York: Fordham University Press, 1989, p. vii.
[3] Ferdinando Cotugno and Francesco Lastrucci. "Italian Renaissance." *Smithsonian* April-May 2022, Vol. 53 No. 1.

colonies sought political independence but remained culturally dependent upon Europe. Among the many vast contributions of Thomas Jefferson, one of the most celebrated Founding Fathers, was a continuing admiration and lifelong affinity for all things Italian. Jefferson believed that the genesis of liberty followed a path from Ancient Rome, through the Italian Renaissance and Enlightenment, toward a progressive future for the new American nation. While Jefferson's affinity for Italy is well known, studying his role in assimilating Italian culture into the American project is a new venture. Surveying Jefferson as an Italophile reveals a wide spectrum of cultural appreciation."

Often, Italian cultural influence came from northern regions celebrating the glories of the Renaissance, such as Florence, Venice, Milan, and Rome. Early influences from the southern peninsular regions is Mr. Jefferson's introduction of macaroni to America. A fact evidenced by a hand-sketched and eventual purchase of a macaroni machine from Naples obtained in 1789. A few years earlier, Mr. Jefferson claimed, "The best pasta in Italy is made with a particular sort of flour, called Semola, in Naples."

In 1934, an article by Vassar College located in Poughkeepsie, New York reviewed a lecture by Theodore Fred Kuper, at the time serving as director of the Thomas Jefferson Foundation. Kuper summed up American culture as one that has "taken from the best all other nations have to offer." In his talk, Mr. Kuper stressed the often untold fact that Thomas Jefferson "was a strong force in bringing to America, Italians, Italian art, and Italian literature, which have been molded into the make-up of American life."[4]

In 1992, art historian Irma B. Jaffe writing a 2nd volume as a continuation of *The Italian Presence in American Art 1860-1920*, added,

"Like a magic potion, *Italianità* [the essence of being Italain] has seeped through the stream of American aesthetic conciousness ever since [American artist] Benjamin West [1738-1820] stepped onto Italian soil in 1760."[5]

As history has often obscured the abundance of the multitude of varied contributions of Italians to all aspects of cultural development in America; a continued disparaging image has buried the overwhelming positive attainment behind the negative. The "negative" is obviously a criminal association placed upon all Italians within, or as known associates of, the "Mafia." Many sources cite the 1891 mass lynching of Italians in New Orleans as the first use of the word in America to describe an associated criminal element with the newly arriving

---

[4] "Italian Influence Great in Life of Thomas Jefferson: Title of Estate is Evidence." *Vassar Miscellany News*, Vol. XVIII, No. 29. February 1934, pp. 1, 4.
[5] Irma B. Jaffe, *The Italian Presence in American Art 1860-1920*, p. vii.

Italian Culture in America:
The Immigrants 1880 to 1930 From Discrimination to Assimilation

immigrants. The New Orleans travesty was only one of dozens of examples of the growing national anti-Italian prejudice throughout the nation. As the years progressed, with no end in sight to the millions of immigrants entering the United States, hostile discrimination continued to escalate. Maria Laurino provided thoughtful insight to the age-old discrimination in a well-researched work *Italian Americans: A History*. One thesis explained by Laurino involves,

> "Myths about Italian-American culture run deep into the fabric of American life, obscuring the complicated, nuanced, centuries-long story of the Italian-American experience that demands to be told."[6]

In paraphrasing Laurino, this publication separates that myth from reality, thereby uncovering a more complicated story with deeper truths."

On many occasions, I have been subject to similar comments that should have been left behind a century or two in the past. The most troublesome often came from academic colleagues. One example came in the year 2000 at an academic conference in Houston, Texas. One attendee blurted, "Wow you're from New York. Do you know the Godfather?" Ironically, the conference was sponsored by the National Association of African-American and Latino Studies focused on racial stereotyping. A very similar comment occurred during a meeting among colleagues at the City University of New York (CUNY) asking of my relationship with "concrete or the Godfather." Another occurred during my tenure at CUNY when a University Dean asked if I ever knew anyone who "slept with the fishes?" All derogatory terms derived from the Hollywood movie *The Godfather* (dir. Francis Ford Coppola, 1972) culled from the novel by Mario Puzo.

In contrast, Mario Puzo (1920-1999), widely known for the iconic 1969 novel *The Godfather*, provided an excellent portrait of the real-life experiences of Italian immigrants in a prior 1965 novel *Fortunate Pilgrim*. The novel might be fictionalized, but as Puzo explained within *Fortunate Pilgrim* is not of the mob or organized crime. Rather the story is about his own mother Maria Le Conti Puzo (1888/9-1974) as an Italian immigrant living in America. Despite wide literary acclaim, *Fortunate Pilgrim,* did not sell many copies. In contrast, *The Godfather* became one of the bestselling American novels of all time. Puzo might also be responsible, along with directors such as Francis Ford Coppola and Martin Scorsese, for providing the great double edge of the Italian-American conundrum. Two movies of *The Godfather* saga rate as possibly the best made films in the long history of Hollywood. The original is often rated by the American Film Institute (AFI) as the top movie of all-time. In turn, directors such as Coppola and Scorsese rate as top artists of their genres. Yet their subject matter, providing fictionalized entertainment, has unfortunately further perpetrated the Italian-

---

[6] Maria Laurino, *Italian Americans: A History*, p. 1.

INTRODUCTION   5

American stereotype of gangsters and mobsters. Those stereotypes in American Culture fall under the best descriptive statement this author has ever heard, "Images linger in the mind and Facts languish in books."[7]

One scene within the fictional movie sequel, *The Godfather: Part II* (dir. Francis Ford Coppola, 1974), does serve as a factually illustrated account of the trans-Atlantic Italian immigrant experience. In a 4-min. sequence of almost 4 minutes, Coppola provides one of the most accurate film portrayals of the Italian immigrant arrival experience at Ellis Island. The scene opens in the year 1901, as the bow of the *Moshulu* sailing ship passes the Statue of Liberty. (The real-life Moshulu, built in 1904, survives anchored at Philadelphia's Penn's Landing. Despite the inaccuracy of a three-year time span; the visual is an excellent accurate example.) As the scene progresses, all the tired immigrants, including a young Sicilian orphan named Vito Andolini, slowly rise to catch sight of the "Lady Liberty." Each face is panned by the camera, each is obviously contemplative of their possible future in *L'America*. The scene changes to scan the Ellis Island Main Hall filled with immigrants of many nationalities. The historical interior of the Ellis Island processing station reveals an inspector checking the eyes, ears, and nose of a multitude of immigrants. Upon Vito's turn, a quick decision by an inspector places a white chalk mark of an undesirable "X" on Vito's lapel.[8]

The scene moves to young Vito ushered before another inspector questioning the mute boy: "What is your name? C'mon son, what is your name." No response - as a translator reads a tag, "Vito Andolini from Corleone," thereby the inspector enters the name as "Vito Corleone" – a name retained for the remainder of his life. A doctor, via an Italian translator, tells Vito he "has smallpox and will be quarantined." The scene closes as "Vito Corleone" is placed in a 3-month quarantine hospital. For the first time, Vito speaks, actually sings a familiar Sicilian folk song "*Lu Sciccareddu*," while gazing through a window at the Statue of Liberty. As easily the most recognizable icon of the entire history of the United States (and possibly the world) the Statue of Liberty ("Liberty Enlightening the World") with a multitude of Italian connections is only one of countless instances of the influence of Italian culture upon America.

In 1989, journalist Roger Piantadosi writing for *The Washington Post* reminded Americans of the historical naming of the United States capital city of Washington D.C.; stating "the city is named after both fathers of our country." The "fathers" reference was, and still is, George Washington and Christopher Columbus. Often forgotten is the added "D.C." as the "District of Columbia" is a direct reference and honor to Columbus as the famous explorer. Piantadosi

---

[7] See: Mario Puzo. *The Godfather*. New York: G.P. Putnam Sons, 1969.
[8] "Godfather Ellis Island. Ship Moshulu," *YouTube*, Accessed February 24, 2021. 3:45min.

continued citing the legacy of the multitude of "Italian Imprints" found among all facets of America society.[9]

Above Right: Original title: "The Statue of Liberty from Ellis Island, U.S. immigration station in New York Harbor, a small boy shows his parents the Statue of Liberty," c. 1930. Library of Congress Prints and Photographs Division Reproduction No. LC-USZ62-50904.
Bottom Left: Author and wife recreate a similar experience, c. 2018.

Historian Alan Kraut writing *The Huddled Masses: The Immigrant in American Society, 1880-1921*, related the dual George Washington and Christpher Columbus connection as "the ones who shaped the nation's capital, embodying in its monuments and institutions the nation's most sacred values, such as equality and democracy." Prof. Kraut also related the "imprint" legacy [before 1880] when Italians in America "were welcomed or imported." One example within the long history of Italian emigration to the United States was creating Washington D.C. as the "New Rome." In doing so, among the many "welcomed" were "Italian painters and sculptors, military men and politicians, architects and artisans, lawyers and teachers, masons and stone-cutters."[10]

---

[9] Roger Piantadosi. "Italian Imprints." *The Washington Post*, October 6, 1989.
[10] Alan Kraut, *The Huddled Masses*. See also: Luca Molinari and Andrea Canepari, Eds. *The Italian Legacy in Washington, D.C. Architecture, Design, Art and Culture*. Milan, Italy: Skira Editore, 2007, pp. 171-172.

INTRODUCTION

Kraut and Piantadosi each replaced the storied myth of millions of Italian immigrants entering America from 1880 to 1930 as only poor unskilled laborers of southern Italians and Sicilians as a misnomer. This simple fact certainly has a focus of truth, however, often forgotten, or overlooked, was the total number of skilled individuals in agriculture, artistry, culinary, inventors, performers, and trend setters, among many other craftspeople and artisans. Opera historian Will Crutchfield offered, "The diaspora left its mark on commerce, manufacturing, sports, religion, education, crime, government, and all forms of the arts."[11]

Prof. Norman Simms writing in the journal article "The Italian-American Image During the Twentieth Century" described an unheralded aspect towards the acceptance of Italian culture in America during the years of the Great Migration of 1880 to 1920. Prof. Simms reminded us of the most basic principle of Italians as,

> "Few serious attempts were made to discuss how the Italian culture made the source of a man's pride his family and his honor, not his job. Despite the strong prejudices of this era, the Italian-American would face increasing prejudice in the years to come."[12]

This cultural attribute by Italians was in stark contrast to the existing American cultural norm of defining "the source of a man's pride" as the job he does. Therefore, as posited by other Italian Scholars, such as Dr. Anthony Tamburri of the John D. Calandra Italian American Institute,

> "We need to take Italian American culture more seriously. We simply cannot continue to engage in a series of reminiscences that lead primarily to nostalgic recall."

Therefore, an account of Italian Culture in America during the period of the Great Migration of 1880 to 1930 is quite different than the previous standards of the transformative years of the industrialized United States.

Unlike the Renaissance, Enlightenment, or any other historical imprints, the inspired aspects derived from Italian culture include Art, Architecture, Law, Liberty, and Religious Freedom emanating from the northern regions of Italy before 1880. Thorough assimilation of Italian culture in later years was mostly gained from the southern *Mezzogiorno* regions of the peninsular. In contrast to the northern "Highbrow Culture," the "Lowbrow Culture" from southern towns and regions, including Sicily, was often criticized, and dismissed by the use of discrimination, and sometimes with violent retribution.

---

[11] Will Crutchfield. "Pioneer: Ferruccio Giannini." *Teatro Nuovo*, October 17, 2020

[12] Norman Simms, "The Italian-American Image During the Twentieth Century," *The Histories*: Vol. 5:1, Article 4 (2019). La Salle University Digital Commons.

Italian Culture in America:
The Immigrants 1880 to 1930 From Discrimination to Assimilation

One discriminatory reason was derived from the dominant white American Protestant Nativists who "looked down" upon foreigners of different cultures and religion, especially dark-skinned southern Italians and Sicilians. Another was due to the low view of the menial work performed across the nation by Italian immigrants. A significant number were often discounted as uneducated unskilled "pick and shovel men" or farm workers. Menial labor by immigrants was often discounted and frowned upon; yet the work was indispensable for America to continue as a functioning society in the profitable age of a Second Industrial Revolution.[13]

Any individual walking or travelling on the roads, railways, or tunnels, across America, or in the vast underground of the New York City subway system represent the labor of Italians. A significant amount of the strenuous labor required was often provided by Italian immigrants. As such, many men came without family; many returned to Italy. Others earned enough money to arrange transport for their family to reunite in America. A descriptive article, "What Sets Italian Americans Off from Other Immigrants?" for *The National Endowment for the Humanities*, by historian Vincent J. Cannato states,

> "Italian immigrants began arriving in large numbers in the late 1800s as relatively unskilled labor that helped fuel a booming industrial economy. These Italian workers seemed unlikely new Americans. Most of those early arrivals were young men leaving a semifeudal Italian South that held little in the way of opportunity. Nearly half of Italian immigrants would eventually return to Italy, but today's Italian-American community is descended from those who decided to remain in America. They brought over their families and created ethnic enclaves in Northern cities and small industrial towns of Pennsylvania and Ohio."[14]

Historians applied the term "Birds of Passage" to those immigrants who returned home permanently, or who traversed the Atlantic more than once for employment. While many others always returned to their homeland, a significant numbered permanently made their new lives in America.

To examine Prof. Cannato's term of "What" set immigrants apart, not just Italians, was an evident self-protective desire to hold onto their own language and customs. A factor perceived by mainstream Americans as the lack of desire for the Italian immigrants in obtaining naturalization as American citizens. The often-overlooked fact had a lot to do with the status of those Italians (over two-thirds male and often single) who traveled to America with the sole intent to earn money

---

[13] "Italian Immigration," *Digital History* 2019. Accessed September 12, 2020.
[14] Vincent J. Cannato, "What Sets Italian Americans Off from Other Immigrants?" *The National Endowment for the Humanities*, January/February 2015, Volume 36, Number 1.

INTRODUCTION

and return home to Italy. Estimates vary widely as to the actual number who returned.[15]

Exploring the Italian cultural connection to America from 1880 to 1930 is vastly different than the early Italian cultural influences introduced by the likes of Thomas Jefferson. As a point of reference, the Italian Culture in America can be viewed in three distinct eras. The first period began with the first Italian immigrant named Pietro Cesare "Peter" Alberti (1608–1655) arriving in New York in June of 1635. From that point until 1880, or so, estimates place less than 25,000 Italian born people immigrated into the Colonies. Most were northern Italians skilled in the arts of sculpture, painting, stone masonry, and horticulture, among others. The second period of the years 1880 to 1930 produced over 4.5 million Italians entering into America, an historical era known as the "Great Migration." Among the overwhelming number were poor peasants, most from the southern "Mezzogiorno" portion of the Italian peninsular and Sicily. The direct translation of "Mezzogiorno" is "lunch time" or "twelve o'clock" – the term also denotes the geographic region of the southern half of the peninsular. *Italy* magazine offers the following explanation,

> "When asking a friend what time, you should meet for lunch, she may say '*a Mezzogiorno*' [meaning] at midday, at noon, or 12 p.m. However, when Italians use the word '*il Mezzogiorno*,' they are not always talking about lunchtime. Instead, they could be referring to the [most] southern area of Italy, including the regions of Abruzzo, Basilicata, Molise, Campania, Puglia, Calabria, Sicily, and Sardinia. The expression is thought to refer to the intensity of the midday sun in the south of the Italian peninsular."[16]

Significant research reveals a similar number of northern Italians left Italy during the same time periods. However, during the years 1880 to 1930, almost all of the northern Italian emigrates settled in other areas of Europe or different parts of the world, such as South America. The large number of *Il Mezzogiorno* in America were somewhat self-segregated, although most had little or no choice. Housing opportunities were often limited to overcrowded squalid tenement buildings in urban areas known as "Little Italy." As such, Italian immigrants, did not have many other employment opportunities beyond low-wage labor-intensive jobs.

The third period during and after World War II represented limited immigration; influence was from first- and second-generation American born children of Italian immigrants. The new ancestry was a lineage with roots clearly tracing back to Italy, but born as American citizens. The new "Italian-American" was less influenced by the rigid traditions of the Old World; rather a blend of

---

[15] "Italian Immigration," *Digital History* 2019. Accessed September 12, 2020.
[16] "Il Mezzogiorno," *Italy* magazine, March 20, 2020. Accessed September 12, 2020.

assimilation in a multi-cultural American society. Prof. Joseph S. Pechie, writing on the Italian Immigrant assimilation into American Culture, explains the unique phenomena,

> "As Italians immigrated and assimilated into America, so did their culture and native traditions. Over time, the Italian culture turned into a staple of American life and can be seen integrated into communities across the United States."

All three periods of Italian cultural contributions to the United States was acknowledged as the U.S. Congress designated 2013 "The Year of Italian Culture." A unique series of articles, symposiums, and exhibits appeared highlighting various national events. However, we are not sure how many Americans actually took part, or were even aware of the event?[17]

Italian-American culture is as common in daily life as aeronautical engineering, architecture, branch banking, chocolate, cowboy boots, food, Hollywood, ice skating, an ice cream cone, a Jacuzzi, macaroni, musical instruments, Jazz, national monuments, opera, painting, peanuts, Disney's Pinocchio, pizza, show business, vaudeville, wine, and even a little red wagon, to name a few. All are iconic in American culture; sadly the known Italian origins and contributions are not.

If any one item is indicative of the extent of Italian culture in America, it is pizza. Naples is widely held as the birthplace of the modern pizza. In America, Pizza has morphed into all sorts of shapes, ingredients, and toppings. The most common, pizza remains the *Margherita*. If one was to promote an American culture contest, it would be hard to top (no pun intended) the extent that pizza has attained above all others. As of the year 2022, the United States Census counted 61,269 pizzerias –another 78,029 classified as pizza restaurants. As a point of levity, but as another example, are those "pizza loving" *Teenage Mutant Ninja Turtles* named after the great Italian legends of the Renaissance of Donatello, Leonardo, Michelangelo, and Rafael - need I say more?

There are so many other items which have assimilated and become ingrained into American culture. For many the Italian connection is not even known, sometimes ignored, or conveniently forgotten. To apply the word ubiquitous, some are tangible items such as the aforementioned pizza; leading to the somewhat obvious abundance of Italian food recognizable throughout the nation in the vast array of restaurants (some created by Italians, others hint at pseudo-Italian connections.) Of the over 800,000 restaurants in America; over 100,000

---

[17] Anne Midgette. "Coming to the U.S.: 'The Year of Italian Culture 2013." *Washington Post.* October 17, 2012. Joseph S. Pechie, "The Italian Immigrants' Assimilation into American Culture." Spring 2015, College at Brockport.

INTRODUCTION 11

are classified serving "Italian Food." This author would boldly venture to guess within the other 700,000 we could probably find an Italian connection of pasta or pizza in almost all.

A walk through any open-air market or a leisurely stroll down just about any American supermarket chain or grocery stores contains dozens, if not hundreds of Italian items. Some are true Italian imports; others have capitalized by simply adding the word "Italian" to their food product. Many food stores routinely stock Olive Oil, Mozzarella, Ricotta, or "Italian style" items such as tomatoes; once again to suggest only a few as recognizable household names. Macaroni fills the shelfs in abundance, the proper term which is sometimes called "Pasta" in America, come in many shapes and sizes. Yet, pasta is the ingredient of which when shaped such as Ziti, Elbows, Linguini, and of course Spaghetti, to almost all ancestors of Italians who arrived during the great migration of 1880 to 1930 it is "Macaroni."

Hardly a child does not partake in the favorite food choices of the "big three" (as I have termed) of pizza, spaghetti, and chicken fingers; most parents know a finicky child will respond to these food items. Granted, chicken DNA traces to southern Asia and possibly China; yet spaghetti and pizza, should be obvious. By now the Italian cultural picture should be developing quite clearly. In fact, one of those Italian items was introduced to America by none other than Thomas Jefferson. While in Europe, Mr. Jefferson sketched a "Maccaroni (his spelling) Machine," requesting from his personal secretary William Short to obtain one such device from Naples, Italy. The transposition into America was as "Macaroni and Cheese;" combined with the proprietary Italian Parmesan Cheese. Simply called "Mac and Cheese" it has become one of the most common food staples, especially among children, young adults, and college dorm students.

The curators of Jefferson's home at Monticello (an Italian word for "little mountain") acknowledge, "Many aspects of Thomas Jefferson's home, work, and personal tastes were influenced by Italian people and culture." The architectural style of Monticello was derived from the greatest of all Renaissance architects the Italian Andrea Palladio (1508-1580). A lasting visual legacy of Italian culture contributed via the Jefferson conduit added the classical architectural style of ancient Rome and the Italian Renaissance reflected in the buildings in Washington D.C. and thousands of others throughout the nation.[18]

The lineage of American popular culture so ingrained in the public sphere, such as musical entertainment genres of Opera, Jazz, and Classical have distinct Italian roots. Among the easily recognizable are such ageless legendary luminaries as Enrico Caruso and Arturo Toscanini. Musical instruments such as the violin, piano, cello, and bass are well rooted throughout all American music

---

[18] "Italy." *The Thomas Jefferson Encyclopedia.* October 22, 2017. n.p.

genres. Each of these instruments are strongly rooted within the Italian legacy; as is the basic American language terminology of music.

Other cultural icons developed during the time period of 1880 to 1930, which are a major portion of the American fabric, include such nationwide household names as the Bank of America, Chef Boyardee, Contadina, Ernest and Julio Gallo Wine, Ghirardelli Chocolate, Mondavi Wine, Italian Swiss Colony Wines, Pastene, Planter's Peanuts, Prince Pasta, Progresso, Carlo Rossi, Tropicana Orange Juice, and the Waffle Ice Cream Cone. Many a health spa offers a Jacuzzi; ice skating and hockey rinks know the importance of a Zamboni. Of one of the most recognizable items from American childhood is the adorable Little Red Wagon and companion Red Tricycle by the Radio Flyer Toy Company founded by Antonio Pisan.

The art world acknowledges the first director of the world-renowned Metropolitan Museum of Art as an Italian. The spiritual world was well-received from the missionary work of Mother Frances Cabrini; as was educational methods introduced by Maria Montessori. Science and technology offered innovators as Guglielmo Marconi, Antonio Meucci, and Enrico Fermi. Higher education has benefitted greatly from the famed Farleigh Dickinson University in New Jersey. The birth of the American nation is celebrated each year with stunning pyrotechnics and fireworks in Washington D.C. by the Grucci Family and Zambelli Fireworks. Another in the nation's capital city that does not need a photograph to conjure an image is the massive sculpture of Abraham Lincoln seated within the Lincoln Memorial. The statue carved by the Italian born Piccirilli Brothers was one of their many public sculptures throughout the nation. Another is Mt. Rushmore in South Dakota under the direction of master stone carver Luigi Del Bianco.

Prior to the massive wave of Italian immigrants from 1880 to 1930, a distinct tradition of Italian art and architecture was well-established with frescoes by the likes of Constantino Brumidi in the halls of the U.S. Capitol Building. The foundation of American Architecture was established by Thomas Jefferson introducing the Italian Renaissance style of Andrea Palladio. Speaking of Mr. Jefferson, the association with Filippo Mazzei introduced the Italian wine-making tradition; more importantly the American concept of liberty through their mutual association in developing the Declaration of Independence. Regardless of 21st century cancel culture, there is no undeniable fact attributed to the discoveries of such famous Italian explorers as Christopher Columbus, John Cabot, and of course, Amerigo Vespucci from which "America" derives its name.

The full depth and complexity of the Italian immigrant experience is covered in many publications and documentaries. Two authors Jerre Mangione and Ben Morreale in *La Storia: Five Centuries of the Italian American Experience* (Harper Collins, 1992) and *Italian Americans: The History and Culture of a People*,

INTRODUCTION

13

(ABC-Clio 2017) edited by Eric Martone provide an excellent overview. Regardless of the time period or class status, Martone's compendium asserts, "Virtually every aspect of American culture has been influenced by Italian immigrants and their descendants." In another publication, I responded, "A bold statement – yes – an unattainable task to explain in any one publication – also yes.[19]

A documentary account is told in a 2015 PBS documentary *The Italian Americans: La Famiglia*. The storyline on the Internet Data Base IMDb.com summary reads,

> "At the turn of the 20th century, many Italians immigrants came to work, earn money to support their families, and eventually return home. Nearly half of the first-generation Italian immigrants did return to Italy, but for those that made America home, their struggle to maintain a distinct Italian culture was guided by remarkably powerful ideals of family that had always been at the center of their lives. While the power of the Italian family became a source of strength, it also bred suspicion, [mainly as] popularized in popular media as a dark, criminal element. This clash of culture echoed through generations of Italian Americans as they entered positions of political, social, and cultural influence."[20]

The documentary overview provides a succinct summation of the Italian immigrant. A careful reading provides a thoughtful analysis for both the past and future existence.

Looking ahead to the post 2020 years, Italian assimilation is often considered complete. In the world of politics, Italian Americans are well-represented. Overlooked is the assimilation of Italians such as Speaker of the House Nancy Pelosi, first lady Dr. Jill Biden, or the former Rhode Island Governor Gina Raimondo as 40th United States Secretary of Commerce. Much more was made of their historic first as females, yet those in the cultural community recognized each accomplishment as important "firsts" for Italian Americans. During a tumultuous election leading to the 2021 inauguration of Joseph R. Biden (b. 1942) as the 46th President of the United States, the Italian presence was in full view. On the steps of the Italian inspired U.S. Capitol Building world-renowned Lady Gaga (born 1986 as "Stefani Joanne Angelina Germanotta") strutted her international fame down the steps singing the American National Anthem. A fanfare of media ballyhoo attention offered an inordinate number of comments (both positive and negative) focusing on her stylish fashion attire rather than background of Italian American heritage.

---

[19] Eric Martone, ed. *Italian Americans, The History and Culture of a People* (ABC-Clio, 2016).
[20] "The Italian Americans," *IMDb.com*. Accessed September 12, 2020.

As my most personal note – I often wrote a number of these pages while enjoying a "Delicious Manhattan Special" founded in 1895. For those growing up Italian in New York, *Manhattan Special* is a coffee soda of carbonated espresso "Hand Brewed from Freshly Roasted Coffee Beans." As Journalist Michael Wilson writing, "A Modern Comeback for a Taste of Brooklyn" in *The New York Times* on July 7, 2008, "*Manhattan Special* was created by an Italian immigrant named Michael Garavuso, who dreamed up the soda with the help of Dr. Teresa Cimino, an osteopath, and Mr. Garavuso's friend, who treated people with bone deformations." This tidbit of information provides significant insight within this work of personal affirmation to continue a discovery of the varied legacy of my Brooklyn born Italian-American heritage.

During the writing of this project, the social, cultural, political, and historical world was overshadowed by the worldwide COVID-19 Coronavirus pandemic. During the crisis rising to worldwide fame was Dr. Anthony Fauci (b. 1940). Born in Brooklyn, all of Fauci's grandparents immigrated during the Great Migration, paternal grandparents from Sciacca in Sicily, his maternal grandmother was from Naples, Italy, and maternal grandfather born in Switzerland was an artist who studied and worked mainly in Italy. Dr. Fauci's grandparents, as with so many of the millions of Italians, entered America through the processing center at Ellis Island in New York Harbor. For all those comments and individuals of all ethnic backgrounds cherishing the thought of Liberty as citizens of the United States a very important introduction by an American cultural touchstone *The U.S. Library of Congress* reminds us,

> "When Christopher Columbus set foot on American soil in 1492, he launched a flood of migration that is still in motion, and that transformed the continent completely. Although Italy as a unified nation did not exist until 1861, the Italian peninsula has sent millions of its people to the shores of North America. These new arrivals thought of themselves as Neapolitans, Sicilians, Calabrian's, or Syracuseans. They might not have understood each other's dialects, but on arrival in the United States they became Italian-Americans. By the turn of the 20th century, they would be ready to change the continent once more."[21]

With the sanction of this official statement by the *U.S. Library of Congress* a jump from the year 1492 to the late 19th century brings clear focus to the contributions of the millions of Italian immigrants who entered as part of the "New Immigration." It is with that benchmark from the *U.S. Library of Congress* that begins our journey.

---

[21] "Italian Immigration." *The Library of Congress,* December 31, 2018.

INTRODUCTION 15

Author stands in front of the original torch on display in the Statue of Liberty Museum. In 1986, during a complete renovation of Lady Liberty an exact replica was installed upon the statue – the original was placed in a museum located on Liberty Island. (Photo by Thelma Lynn Olsen).

CHAPTER 1

NATIONALISM, INDUSTRIAL REVOLUTION, AND IMMIGRATION

"I see no reason why anyone should justly object to calling this part ... America, after Amerigo Vespucci, an Italian discoverer, a man of great ability."

Italy, as a country or culture, as we know it, is not as easily defined as the other nations of Europe or the world. Geographically, Italy is comprised of many unique natural features. As described by *Encyclopædia Britannica*,

> "Italy comprises some of the most varied and scenic landscapes. At its broad top stand the Alps, which overlook a landscape of Alpine lakes and glacier-carved valleys that stretch down to the Po River and the Piedmont. Tuscany, to the south is perhaps the country's best-known region. Running down the length of the country, radiates the tall Apennine Range, which widens near Rome. South of Rome the Apennines narrow and are flanked by two wide coastal plains, the lower Apennine chain is near-wilderness, hosting a wide range of species such as wild boars, wolves, asps, and bears. Southern Apennines are also tectonically unstable, with several active volcanoes. At the bottom of the country, in the Mediterranean Sea, lie the islands of Sicily and Sardinia."[22]

Italy is comprised of 20 regions, with vast cultural distinctions, dialects, and history. The regional difference, due to geography of the mountain ranges, seas, and islands, creates natural borders which has mostly isolated the peninsular for centuries. Unlike the north, with large cities emanating centuries of culture such as Rome, Florence, Venice, and Milan, among others, the areas of the south contain mostly agricultural towns, with only a few larger cities such as Naples and Palermo. Each of the areas maintained a sense of self-sufficiency with minimal reliance, or even basic trust, with the other regions. This basic difference is one, if not the only, reason for the political "dis-unity" of Italy after 1861. Language is

---

[22] Melanie F. Knights, et al. "Italy," Encyclopædia Britannica.com. September 23, 2020.

another regional barrier as the spoken word is called "Italian," but many regional dialects are spoken throughout. As Melanie F. Knights of *Encyclopedia Britannica* states, "Italy seem less a single nation than a collection of culturally related points in an uncommonly pleasing setting."[23]

In an article "Italian Culture: Facts, Customs, & Traditions," freelance writer Kim Ann Zimmermann provided a succinct thorough definition of Italy as, "Steeped in the arts, family, architecture, music, and food. Home of the Roman Empire and a major center of the Renaissance, culture on the Italian peninsula has flourished for centuries."[24]

Nationalism as a Unifying Factor

The official history of the United States published by the *Office of the Historian* provides a description of the "Unification of Italian States" as, "By the late 19th century, as Nationalism was sweeping Europe, the peninsula of Italy had finally been brought under one flag, but the land and the people were by no means unified."[25] Nationalism was a unifying concept for a common geographic area developed in Europe in the late 18th century; extending into, and coming to fruition in the late 19th century. Nationalism as a credence among people to come together as a single nation under one flag is loosely defined with five basic traits of: 1. Geography, 2. Language, 3. Customs, 4. Culture, and 5. History. The earliest rallying of a nation under a single flag might be credited to the reign of Napoleon Bonaparte (1769-1821) in France from 1804 to 1814.

The conflicting idea in Italy exists among people who identify with their local regions rather than common geography. The first countries to unify under nationalism with various forms of parliamentary governments and constitutional monarchies were Germany in 1871 and Italy in 1861. (An argument can be made for the United States signing the Constitution in 1787; but the divisions among the states were vast, as evidence by the American Civil War.) Geographically, Italy appears natural for unification. As a unique peninsular it is almost as geographically defined as an island. Bordered on the east by the Adriatic Sea; the west by the Tyrrhenian and Ligurian Seas; the Mediterranean and Ionian Seas to the south; and the northern plains by the snow-capped mountains of the Alps. Culturally and economically an equal divide existed between the northern and southern portions roughly divided above and below Rome. Official unification (known as the *risorgimento*) was not an easy transition nor orderly. Although 1861, is listed as the "official" date of Italian unification the process lasted until 1871 when

---

[23] Melanie F. Knights, et al. "Italy," Encyclopædia Britannica.com.
[24] Kim Ann Zimmermann. "Italian Culture." *Live Science* September 13, 2017.
[25] "Issues Relevant to U.S. Foreign Diplomacy: Unification of Italian States," *Office of the Historian*. Note: the *Office of the Historian* dates to 1789.

Rome and the Papal states were annexed. The cultural differences of the various regions continued as cause for internal strife; often chaotic, sometimes violent.

Elegant Italians strolling leisurely in St. Mark's square in Venice, Italy, ca. 1890-1900. Detroit Publishing Company Library of Congress, Prints & Photographs Division. (Public Domain).

Line Drawing Map of the Italian Peninsular and companion Islands.

Despite the unification, widespread areas, especially among the southern regions and the island of Sicily, remained in poverty. Whereas the northern regions, including the Piedmont and Sardinia regions, that led the original unification remained wealthy. As the *Office of the Historian* serving as the official history of the United States noted,

> "Yet, the idea of the Risorgimento continued to gain adherents after 1848. The final push for Italian unification came in 1859, led by the Kingdom of Piedmont-Sardinia (then the wealthiest and most liberal of the Italian states), and orchestrated by Piedmont-Sardinia's Prime Minister, Count Camillo di Cavour."

The primarily poor, mostly rural southern peoples of Italy and Sicily had little hope of improving their life. Diseases and natural disasters often swept through the new nation with little help from the new government.[26]

History declared Italy as a unified nation in 1861; yet prior to unification it was home to Ancient Rome, modern Western Civilization, and the Renaissance to the world from 1450 to 1650. As the massive immigration of southern Italians began arriving in America it coincided with the 19th century unification of the Italian peninsular. At the time, a combination of political uncertainty in Italy without better prospects for the future existed. For those in the southern half of Italy and Sicily, there was growing unease about a unified government catering only to the needs of the wealthier north while ignoring the needs of the poor peasants in the south. The promise for a better life – meaning gainful employment – only came due to the burgeoning need for labor fostered by the Industrial Revolution; eventually for millions of immigrants that meant America.

Christopher Columbus – Italian Explorer

In the late 19th century America exhibited a culture derived mainly from northern Europe, with some distinct uniqueness developed in the former colonies. The existence of Italian cultural influence upon America is traced from colonial times beginning with the European exploration of the North and South American "New World" continents. "New Immigration" of the migratory period of 1880 to 1930 trace to the founding of the nation. According to the United States Library of Congress,

> "It was an Italian who began the story of immigration to America. . . The Genoese navigator Cristoforo Colombo, known to us now as Columbus,

---

[26] "Issues Relevant to U.S. Foreign Diplomacy: Unification of Italian States," *Office of the Historian.*

CHAPTER 1   21

was only the first of many Italian explorers who would come to shape the Western Hemisphere as we know it today."

That statement remained an uncontested fact, taught to school children from the early 20th century forward. The significance of Columbus began an unprecedented migratory wave of millions of immigrants, the first northern European; eventually, millions of immigrants from all parts of the world; including forced migration of millions of enslaved Africans. As it applied to the large number of Italians, the Library of Congress tells us,

> "Although Italy as a unified nation did not exist until 1861, the Italian peninsula has sent millions of its people to the shores of North America. They might not have understood each other's dialects, but on arrival in the U.S. they became Italian-Americans. By the turn of the 20th century, they would be ready to change the continent once more."[27]

The *U.S. Library of Congress* provides a jump from 1492 to the late 19th century as the years which brings focus to the contributions of the millions of Italian immigrants who entered as part of the "New Immigration." Before 1861, the total number of Italian immigrants, mostly from the north, totaled around 25,000. During and after the American Civil War years, the numbers ticked up a little; after 1880, millions entered from the years 1890 to 1930. As for the misconceived notion of the new wave of Italians in America, historian Thomas Frascella provides an accurate statement, "the perception of Italians went from being recognized in leadership roles in the earliest colonial period to being little more than human cargo in the early 20th century." The first Italian immigrants in North America are listed in early English records of 1619 of a husband and wife with the last name of Lupo purchasing a 400-acre tract of land in the Virginia colony. Frascella's research noted, around 1622, the Virginia colony recorded "several men from Venice were invited and arrived to start a glass works in Jamestown [Virginia]."[28]

In 1635, Venetian, Peter Caesar Alberti was the first Italian to enter and settle in New York City. Alberti as the first Italian to arrive in New York did not set off a wave of immigration, only a few others followed in the years after. By 1657, another 300 or so Italians arrived in New York with only a limited number added in the ensuing decades. The event has since been documented and commemorated by the Italian Historical Society of America with a bronze in lower Manhattan on Battery Place. Unfortunately, the original plaque disappeared; but a replacement plaque was rededicated in 1985, as,

---

[27] "Italian Immigration." *The Library of Congress,* December 31, 2018.
[28] Thomas Frascella. "Italian Influence in Colonial North America 1500-1700." *San Felese Society of New Jersey.*

Peter Caesar Alberti
First Italian Settler
Landed in N.Y. June 2, 1635
Through Efforts of
John N. Lacorte Founder of
The Italian Historical Society of America
June 2, has been Proclaimed "Alberti Day"[29]

The author visiting a plaque on Battery Place between Greenwich Street and Washington Street recognizing Peter Caesar Alberti as the "First Italian Settler" to New York City in 1635. (Photo by: Thelma Lynn Olsen.)

By 1850, the total recorded number of Italians in New York was 850. In contrast, during the end of the 19th century the city processed millions of Italian immigrants passing first through Castle Island and later Ellis Island. Some stayed in New York, others ventured westward. After 1880, over 500,000 Italian immigrants claimed New York as a permanent home.

Nationalism and Nativism in Response to the "New Immigration"

In a reactionary response to the "New Immigration" of the 1880s onward, an American Nativist movement increased in both popularity and hostility. Nativism led a rallying cry against the continued influx of foreigners. Thereby, an America as only those born as a "Native American." The irony, or hypocrisy, of the term

---

[29] Text: "Peter Caesar Alberti Marker."

CHAPTER 1

did not consider indigenous native American Indian tribes who inhabited the Americas for centuries before the Europeans. Nativist believed in only a linear heritage from white Europeans who settled in the Colonies beginning in the early 1600s. One major difference among arriving immigrants was religion. The prevailing religious beliefs was devout Protestantism. In contrast, arriving immigrants were mostly Catholic and some Jewish. Some instances of Catholic oppression in America can even be traced to colonial times.[30]

Nativists were an extension of the newly emerging 19th century creed of Nationalism - often confused with Patriotism; yet the two are different. A definition of *Patriotism* is described as "a love of or devotion to one's country." Patriotism is not blind loyalty to a nation or a leader – which would serve as a better definition for "Nationalism." A simple summary is the definition by *Merriam-Webster* as,

> **Nationalism** *noun:* "exalting one nation above all others placing primary emphasis on promotion of its culture and interests as opposed to those of other nations."[31]

Nationalism and Patriotism sometimes overlap, based on prejudice, bigotry, subjugation, and very often political machinations. Nativism provided strong control over American politics. Political discourse as promoted by elected representatives led to sharp divisions among the American people. One of the most well-known examples in history was the American Civil War.

Civil War, The Ku Klux Klan and *The Birth of a Nation*

A motion picture release of historical importance looked to the American Civil War. The movie is not obscure; rather influencing the Hollywood film industry for well over a century. Cited as the most notorious film of the time period *The Birth of a Nation* (original title: *The Clansman*, 1915) directed D. W. Griffith (1875-1948), was the first Hollywood blockbuster of the grand Hollywood movie spectacles. The movie grossed over $20 million at the box office (over $500 million adjusted for inflation in 2022) as crowds lined the streets to see the film. The success of *The Birth of a Nation*, fueled the factual "rebirth" of the Ku Klux Klan. Historian David Nasaw recalled a *Variety* magazine review devoted exclusively to *The Birth of a Nation*, stated an obvious fact that the film "knew just what kind of a picture would please all white classes." Violent hateful retribution by the "white classes" of American society perpetuated against African Americans and was soon extended toward recent immigrants as the cultural

---

[30] *See*: Ray A. Billington. *The Protestant Crusade, 1800–1860: A Study of the Origins of American Nativism* (Quadrangle Books, 1964); first published 1938.
[31] "Nationalism," *Merriam-Webster Dictionary.*

attitudes against African Americans passed on to the newly arriving Italian immigrants after 1880.[32]

The Ku Klux Klan numbering more than 4 million members nationwide. Pictured here is a legal openly accepted 1926 rally in Washington, D.C. Credit: Library of Congress Prints and Photographs Division (Public Domain).

D. W. Griffith and Italian Melodramas

Prior to full length features, such as *The Birth of a Nation*, D. W. Griffith directed dozens of short melodramas with themes of contemporary Italian culture. All the actors and screenwriters involved were usually non-Italian. Another troubling factor presented the films as portraying prevalent negative Italian stereotypes of the time included,

- *Italian Blood* (1911) 18 min. silent short.
  - A tale of a wife who feels distant from her husband and concocts a plot to arouse his jealousy resulting in him "rushing home in a towering rage."
- *The Italian Barber* (1911) 17 min. short.
  - "Tony the Barber" passes a news girl named Alice each day on the street on the way home from work. The two become engaged to marry, however Tony becomes infatuated with older sister Florence "a vaudeville artist."
- *In Little Italy* (1909) 10 min. short.
  - A tale of violence as Marie is faced with two suitors named Victor and Tony. Upon accepting Victor's marriage proposal "Tony stabs Victor in a fit of jealousy."

---

[32] David Nasaw, *Going Out: The Rise and Fall of Public Amusements*, p. 202.

CHAPTER 1   25

- *The Violin Maker of Cremona* (1909) 12 min. short.
  - Character names such as Taddeo Ferrari, Giannina Taddeo, Sandro, and Filippo the Cripple. Plot takes place in Cremona, Italy (film stage) as "a violin maker and student of Andrea Amati" named Taddeo has a daughter Giannina "beloved" by a deformed apprentice. The plot focuses on the attempt to secure a yearly prize of the best made violin. The catch, unlike previous years with the prize of a "chain of gold" this time the prize would include "the hand of Giannina [in marriage] bestowed upon the most proficient craftsman."[33]

D. W. Griffith's fame is heralded in the history of American film making. In 1936, an honorary Oscar was bestowed upon Griffith at the 8th Annual Academy Awards. The first Academy Award for Best Director, however, went to Frank Borzage (1894-1962) for *Seventh Heaven* (1927). A second Oscar was awarded to Borzage a few years later for *Bad Girl* (1931). Born in Salt Lake City, Utah (birth name "Borzaga") Borzage, was one of 14 children, to an Italian stone mason father born in Ronzone, Italy and a Swiss mother. Borzage carries an impressive legacy as a film director in the early years of Hollywood through its golden age with 107 directorial credits from 1913 to 1961. To dismiss the Hollywood film making process as purely fictional is completely wrong. Imagery, rather than any written fact, is a powerful force in American culture as the stereotypical images of Italian immigrants have persisted through the current day. As evidence of the power of Hollywood films reverts back to Griffith's *The Birth of a Nation* and the rebirth of the Ku Klux Klan.

The American Second Industrial Revolution

The Second Industrial Revolution in America is also part of the story of Italian immigrants in major cities as New York, Boston, Chicago, New Orleans, and Philadelphia, to name a few. Some Italian immigrants, in much smaller numbers, dispersed throughout the nation working as migrant laborers on farms, railroads, and mines; many known as "pick & shovel" men. The period between the Civil War and First World War of 1870 to 1914 is often termed the "Second Industrial Revolution." Prof. Ryan Engelman summarized the economic growth after 1870 as, "The U.S. was awash in an abundance of natural resources from its newly acquired territories, a growing supply of labor immigrating from Europe, and the migration of emancipated African Americans North and West."

---

[33] "Italian Blood." Plot (1911), and other plot summaries from *Internet Movie Database* ImDb.com. See also: "The Violin Maker of Cremona." Plot (1909).

Grand Central Terminal New York City, c. 1880. Evident are horse drawn taxi cabs waiting to transport disembarking passengers. Courtesy of the Irma and Paul Milstein Division of U.S. History, New York Public Library **Digital Collections.**

The Second Industrial Revolution produced advancements in electricity, steel, and the internal combustion engine, among others. Historian Richard White said, "[The railroad] sped the bounty of farms and factories across the land, spawned hundreds of towns and cities along its routes, pioneered in marketing and managerial organization, and employed a huge and growing labor force." A few years before, American nationalism was on full display in Chicago celebrating 400 years since the founding of America as Christopher Columbus was revered – but not as an Italian.[34]

The World's Columbian Exposition of 1893

As America prepared to celebrate the 400th Anniversary of the discovery of the New World, a massive undertaking was planned in Chicago, Illinois for opening of the World's Columbian Exposition. The Congressional expenditure and allocation of over 600 acres in Chicago's Jackson Park was not to honor the explorer as an Italian; rather to celebrate Columbus as an American icon responsible for the founding of the nation. Congress, awarded the exposition to the city of Chicago, planned as a showcase of American industrialization.

From opening day May 1, 1893 until closing day October 31, 1893 the fair averaged 150,000 people each day. Fair goers witnessed pavilions of 46 countries and over 65,000 exhibits. Many of the buildings reflected ancient Rome

---

[34] Dee Brown, p.158; and *This Fabulous Century* (1970), p. 30.

modernized as "temples to industry and civilization." The exposition was nicknamed the "White City" due to the appearance of its white Neo-Classical styled buildings. (Actually, all the buildings were built from wood painted to appear as white marble). The *Chicago Architecture Center* likened the architecture of the "grand Neo-Classical buildings of the White City" as "templates for banks and public buildings across the country." Neo-classicism became a trend throughout the nation for museums, civic, and public buildings. The grand architectural style reflected the Neo-Classical revival sweeping the nation; a prevalent style set down in America by Thomas Jefferson (1743-1826) in collaboration with the greatest of all the Renaissance architects the Italian born Andrea Palladio (1508-1580). As magnificent and successful the Chicago World's Columbian Exposition proved, it was not without the underlying prejudices of the era.[35]

The Columbian Exposition coincided with the start of a massive wave of Italian immigration to America. Yet, the new immigrants were not revered as descendants of Columbus, rather as a necessary nuisance to fulfill the menial labor jobs required during the Second Industrial Revolution. Italian labor added to the immense growing wealth of Americans of northern European heritage. One offshoot, was celebrating Columbus Day as an unofficial annual "American" holiday.[36]

Palace of Mechanic Arts and the Lagoon at the World's Columbian Exposition, Chicago, Illinois, c. 1892. Photo by: Frances Benjamin Johnston (1864-1952).

---

[35] "World's Columbian Exposition of 1893," and "How did the 1893 World's Fair impact Chicago and its architecture?" *Chicago Architecture Center,* accessed September 7, 2020.
[36] Clark. "What Happened to Nina, Pinta, and Santa Maria that sailed in 1892?"

Celebrating the *Niña*, *Pinta*, and *Santa Maria*

A similar Columbus celebration was held honoring the 500th anniversary of the Italian from Genoa crossing the Atlantic; replicas of the *Niña*, *Pinta*, and *Santa Maria* were built for a tour of America. These were not the first replicas built acknowledging the historic 1492 voyage. Journalist James C. Clark informed the readers of a similar venture a century earlier, citing,

> "In 1891, William Curtis, an official with the U.S. State Department in Spain, came up with the idea to build replicas of the Nina, Pinta, and Santa Maria. A commission was established in Spain to build the ships and sail them to Chicago, site of the World Columbian Exposition marking the 400th anniversary of Columbus' voyage."[37]

One significant inclusion were full-size replicas of the three ships of the historic 1492 voyage for display at the 1893 fair; the carrack *Santa María*, and the caravels of the *Niña* and *Pinta*.

Construction of the Columbus ship replicas was a joint project of the governments of Spain and the United States. The ships were built in Spain and sailed to America for display at the exposition. Each of the replicas were built as close to available records, which were scant. The original *Santa Maria* ran aground during the first voyage and never returned to Europe. The original *Niña* and *Pinta* returned to Spain. Records do not indicate the future of the *Pinta*, historians say the ship "returned home only to vanish." The *Niña* survived as a Columbus favorite for all four voyages to the Americas; (1492-1493; 1493-1496; 1498-1500; and 1502-1504), the date of its demise is unknown.

By 1913, all three ships were in terrible condition. As a promotion, the ships were proposed to celebrate the Panama Canal opening in 1914. The *Niña* and *Pinta* encountered problems on the Great Lakes and were beached (later towed back to Chicago). The *Santa Maria* stopped along the east coast as "the backers thought that curious sightseers would buy tickets in droves to tour the ships;" almost no one showed up. Each remained on display in Chicago; in 1919 the *Pinta* sank and the *Niña* "caught fire and sank." The *Santa Maria* fared a bit better; in 1920, it was rebuilt and attracted tourists until 1951, when it too was destroyed by fire.

---

[37] James C. Clark. "What Happened to Nina, Pinta, and Santa Maria that sailed in 1892?" *The Orlando Sentinel,* May 10, 1992.

Top: Replica of the *Santa Maria* a "Carrack." **Bottom**: Replicas of the Caravels *Niña* (left) and *Pinta* (right) All three ships were on display at the World's Columbian World Exposition of 1893. (Public Domain)

Columbus Day – An Italian Holiday?

Columbus Day was first celebrated as an American – not Italian – holiday. The holiday did not intend to honor his birth (his exact date of birth is not known); rather the commemorative day is based from his journal dated October 12, 1492. In history, Columbus is credited as the first European exploring, at the time, the unknown continents of North and South America. The Columbus exploration led to colonial settlement; first by Spanish Conquistadors in the southern portion and the southwest of the modern-day United States. In quick succession, settlements followed by the French in the Midwest regions and the British along the east coast.[38]

In 2013, journalist Lakshmi Gandhi writing "How Columbus Sailed into U.S. History, Thanks To Italians," reports "Though he sailed in 1492, Christopher Columbus was not widely known among Americans until the mid-1700s." Throughout his four journeys from 1492 to 1506, Columbus never actually set foot on any of the modern-day continental United States. Gandhi explains the change as,

> "This began to change in the late 1700s, after the United States gained independence from Britain. The name 'Columbia' soon became a synonym for the United States, with the name being used for various landmarks in the newly created nation (see the District of Columbia, Columbia University, and the Columbia River)."[39]

Gandhi cites Washington Irving's 1828 *A History of the Life and Voyages of Christopher Columbus*, as the source of "the glorification and myth-making related to Columbus." Later historians researched and chronicled the exploration proved Irving's writing more fictional than factual.[40]

Mythical misconceptions provided many extreme fictional images of Columbus. One painting in The Metropolitan Museum of Art in New York City is "Portrait of a Man, said to be Christopher Columbus (born about 1446, died 1506), c. 1519," by Venetian artist Sebastiano del Piombo. The title and date imply it is not the actual image of Christopher Columbus. As the curators of the Met Museum explain,

> "Painted in Rome by one of the outstanding Venetian masters of the High Renaissance, this badly damaged portrait purports to show Christopher Columbus. The inscription identifies him as 'the Ligurian Colombo, the first to enter by ship into the world of the Antipodes 1519,' but the writing is not entirely trustworthy and the date 1519 means that it cannot have been painted from life, as Columbus died in 1506. Nonetheless, from an early date our picture became the authoritative likeness."

In 2016, the painting was prominently displayed at the Second Floor European Gallery, however, has since been removed.[41]

---

[38] Lakshmi Gandhi, "How Columbus Sailed into U.S. History, Thanks To Italians," October 14, 2013.

[39] Lakshmi Gandhi, "How Columbus Sailed into U.S. History, Thanks To Italians."

[40] The entire text is available at GoogleBooks.com: Washington Irving, *A History of the Life and Voyages of Christopher Columbus*, G&C Carvill, Broadway, New York, 1828.

[41] Metropolitan Museum of Art Collections Search.

Above Left: Author stands before a portrait of Christopher Columbus Titled: "Portrait of a Man, said to be Christopher Columbus (born about 1446, died 1506), c. 1519" in the Metropolitan Museum of Art. **Above Right**: The figure is most likely not painted from the actual Columbus. Artist: Sebastiano del Piombo (Sebastiano Luciani 1485/86–1547) Oil on canvas. Metropolitan Museum of Art Gift of J. Pierpont Morgan, 1900. Accession Number:00.18.2 Public Domain.[42]

The idea of a nationwide celebration was first announced by President Benjamin Henry Harrison (1833-1901). The celebration of the Italian discovery was not in apology for the growing American disdain over Italian immigrants; rather it was promoted in preparation for the 400th anniversary of the Columbus 1492 event – translation the "Discovery of the American continent." Harrison's proclamation did not mention Columbus, Italy, nor Italian immigrants at all. Instead, he proclaimed the American creed of hard work and greatness, as he said,

> "On that day let the people, so far as possible, cease from toil and devote themselves to such exercises as may best express honor to the discoverer and their appreciation of the great achievements of the four completed centuries of American life."

As for an actual celebration of Columbus Day, some accounts date the earliest to 1792 in New York City. Later, the day was often conceived as a celebration of Italian-American heritage. Editors at *History.com* state,

> "As Italian-Americans were struggling against religious and ethnic discrimination in the United States, many in the community saw

---

[42] At the time of this writing, the painting was removed from public display.

32 Italian Culture in America:
The Immigrants 1880 to 1930 From Discrimination to Assimilation

celebrating the life and accomplishments of Christopher Columbus as a way for Italian Americans to be accepted by the mainstream."

Colorado was the first state in the nation to establish Columbus Day as a legal holiday on April 1, 1907. Conflicting claim exists for the first person to lobby for an official state holiday between two Italian immigrants Hector Chiariglione and Angelo Noce, both residents of Pueblo, Colorado. Upon his death in 1940, newspapers across the country, including *The New York Times* and *The Los Angeles Times*, cited Hector Chiariglione, as the "Father of Columbus Day as sponsor of the bill that established Columbus Day as a federal holiday in 1937."[43]

As Italians, Chiariglione and Noce were not unique as immigrants in Colorado. Italians settled in the Colorado territory in the early 1850s. Historian Marianna Gatto, executive director of the Italian American Museum of Los Angeles writes, "Although you are unlikely to have heard of Chiariglione, there's a good chance that the Columbus monument or statue erected in your city or town generations ago traces its history in part to this Italian immigrant."

In 1920, over 187,000 residents of Colorado were counted of Italian ancestry; numbering almost twenty percent of the total state population.

As America sought cultural independence from Great Britain, its founders sought heroes devoid of any British association. As Gatto states,

"Columbus provided the perfect symbol for the young nation. As he was incorporated into the nation's founding myth, Columbus was transformed into an "American" icon, a man who, like the colonists-turned-Americans, shunned the Old World in favor of the characteristic of the new."

Early references to the young American nation often included the word "Columbia," as a mythical figure displayed as a Roman goddess. Instances applying the word "Columbia" abounds all over America; such as the future capital city of the United States at Washington in the District of Columbia. Other cities, towns, and areas all across the nation exist such as Columbus, Ohio and Columbia University in New York. Included is an infamous NASA Space Shuttle and a steamship *SS Columbia* built in 1902; as of this writing the last remaining ship of its kind located in Buffalo, New York. Throughout American history Christopher Columbus was honored and revered; however, his legacy has since been tarnished.[44]

---

[43] Lakshmi Gandhi, "How Columbus Sailed into U.S. History, Thanks To Italians," October 14, 2013. See also: "Columbus Day 2020," *History.com Editors* January 4, 2010.
[44] Marianna Gatto. "An Unknown 'Father of Columbus Day' and the Colorado City Embroiled in One of the Most Intense Standoffs Surrounding Its Columbus Monument." *Italian Sons & Daughters of America*, 2020. September 13, 2020.

CHAPTER 1

"Blaming Columbus for Every Evil since 1492 is Easy but Wrong"

Much of the contemporary blame for all the ills of American society against indigenous peoples of America have since placed all of the blame upon Christopher Columbus. Much of that criticism surfaced in a call for historical revisionism during the 1970s by historians such Howard Zinn and James Loewen, among others. In essence, the individual Italian explorers were not representing any of the regions or kingdoms of Italy. In that same historical fact, it was the Spanish, Portuguese, and English, among others who established the cruel systems of slavery. The Spanish, as one example, instituted the Encomienda system forcing Native American Indians into a lower social echelon of indentured servitude combined with genocidal cruelties. The English on the other hand displaced Indians from many of the soon to be settled lands within the North American continent. Therefore, throughout the Age of Exploration, we can easily claim Italy was innocent.

In contrast, many historians, cultural researchers, commentators, journalists, and others have defended Columbus. One 2017 article in a in a Port Huron, Michigan newspaper *The Times Herald*, "Blaming Columbus for every evil since 1492 is easy but wrong."[45] In another, Patrick Mason argues "Blaming Columbus Misses the Lessons of History." In an article written in October of 2017, Mason presented a credible defense.

> "We should not tear-up the Declaration of Independence on the grounds that Thomas Jefferson [1743-1826] was a slave-owner. We should not tear down the statutes and memory of Christopher Columbus on the grounds that some people in the New World committed heinous acts, or on the grounds, with little evidence, Francisco de Bobadilla [1448-1502], a man with suspect motivations, accused Christopher Columbus of brutality especially since that "brutality" was manifested in Columbus' execution of several Spaniards for their mistreatment of the Indians."[46]

Dozens of rebuttals can be cited; yet the criticism reveals deep-seeded 21st century political motives. Not often posited in the debate is the continued misinformation and stereotyping of Italians. If we fast-forward 400 plus years from the Columbus 1492 encounter, a question posed: Considering the mistreatment of Italian immigrants from 1880 to 1930; is Columbus the scapegoat figurehead for

---

[45] "Blaming Columbus for every evil since 1492 is easy but wrong." *The Times Herald*, October 9, 2017.
[46] Patrick Mason. "Blaming Columbus Misses the Lessons of History," *Catholic News Agency*, October 9, 2017.

all the anti-Italian discrimination so prevalent at that time and continuing well into the present day?

Columbus and the Quest for Jerusalem

Early 21st century research by Stanford anthropology professor Carol Delaney provides valuable evidence in defense of Columbus. In the 2011 publication *Columbus and the Quest for Jerusalem*, Delaney revealed, "An extraordinary new examination of Christopher Columbus that shows him to have been a man of deep passion, patience, and religious conviction, a man determined to save Jerusalem from Islam."

Prof. Delaney asserts, Columbus was not seeking personal fame or fortune; rather on a personal crusade "that Jerusalem needed to be back under Christian control before the end of days." Wealth was a factor as Columbus wished "to obtain enough gold for the Spanish Crown to finance a new crusade to Jerusalem to regain total control of the holy city from the Muslims." Not achieving the goal, Columbus suffered personal humiliation in his quest to secure a new Crusade. Columbus died without his wish fulfilled, yet before he died, revised his will providing "money to support the crusade he hoped would be taken up by his successors."[47]

Colorado and Anti-Italian Sentiment

Colorado resident Ettore "Hector" Chiariglione (1856-1940) is a typical representation of one of the many Italian immigrants of the "New Wave of Immigration." In 1880 at age 24, Chiariglione left home in Alba of the Piemonte region of Italy. He briefly worked in New York before heading to Pueblo, Colorado in 1887. In Pueblo, he began publication of an Italian-American newspaper *L'Unione*. Marianna Gatto tells us Pueblo became known as "Steel City" and the "Pittsburgh of the West," as home of "the largest steel mill west of the Mississippi River." By that time, Pueblo was also the nation's top refiner of gold, silver, zinc, and lead creating the need for an "extensive campaign to recruit a labor force and Italian immigrants, primarily from Sicily and Abruzzo, came to the region en masse."

Another was Angelo Noce (1847-1922) born in Coreglia, Italy. Unlike the recognition for Chiariglione, as the "Father of Columbus Day;" *The Denver Post* credits Angelo Noce for the official Colorado state holiday of Columbus Day. As co-founder of the Italian newspaper *La Stella*, Noce and Italian-American Siro Mangini (1839-1907) lobbied the Colorado state senate for five years as an acknowledgement connected to Columbus would be a chance to garner respect for their ethnic heritage as Italian immigrants in America.

---

[47] Carol Delaney. *Columbus and the Quest for Jerusalem*, 2011, p. xvi.

At the time, all association with Columbus was attached as demonstrating pride in America. Added to the name was a physical representation of monuments and statues of Christopher Columbus. Siro Mangini offered a physical building proudly associated with the Columbus name. Fellow Pueblo resident Hector Chiariglione lobbied for a town monument to honor the explorer. Marianna Gatto explained the reason as,

> "During the age of American imperialism and an era marred by anti-Catholicism and xenophobia, Chiariglione envisioned the monuments would foster solidarity among the diverse peoples of the United States."[48]

In a strange twist of guilt by association all things honoring Christopher Columbus radically changed over time especially as it applied to statues. After 1893, statues honoring Columbus were erected all over the nation (and the world). The impetus for the statues was noted in Chiariglione's obituary. *The Los Angeles Times* cited him as "the leader of movements for the erection of statues to Columbus throughout the nation."[49]

Detail of Pueblo's Columbus monument, erected in 1905.

---

[48] Marianna Gatto. "An Unknown 'Father of Columbus Day' and the Colorado City Embroiled in One of the Most Intense Standoffs Surrounding Its Columbus Monument."
[49] "Columbus Day started in Colorado," *The Denver Post*, September 23, 2010.

The city of Pueblo unveiled its own Columbus statue on October 12, 1905. Located within one of the most prominent locations, it remained for over 115 years. By the 21st century all statues of Columbus (numbering in the hundreds), even the one in Pueblo, located in an area named Christopher Columbus Piazza faced removal from the public sphere. Many were physical removed, while many others were defaced.[50]

Columbus Ohio – Leave the Name, Take Down the Monuments

In April 2021, a century old statue listed on the U.S. National Register of Historic Places in Pueblo was "one of two remaining public Columbus commemorations in Colorado." The other in Greenmount Cemetery in Durango was described as "a simple memorial to explorer, Christopher Columbus;" a bust of the explorer upon a stone pedestal, in the midst of a burial site of "proud Italians." A description for the monument explains,

> "Not surprisingly, the monument stands among the graves of many Italians and Italian-Americans who were proud of one of their own, even if [Columbus'] discovery was more news to the Europeans than it was to those already living here in North America."[51]

Durango (pop. 18,600 in 2020) is located near the New Mexico border about 330 miles (530 km) southwest of Denver.

Throughout the United States, protests called for the removal of all statues and monuments of Columbus. In Colorado, the state legislature eliminated Columbus Day as a state holiday renaming as "Cabrini Day." In a bit of irony, the day was named after an Italian Roman Catholic nun Frances Xavier Cabrini (1850-1917); bestowed sainthood in 1950 by Pope Pius XII; as "the patron saint of immigrants."

An ironic removal occurred in Columbus, Ohio. No plan existed to rename the city, but removal of two statues of Columbus; one on the campus of Columbus State Community College. The other as noted by the U.S. Library of Congress, at City Hall "the 20-foot-tall bronze statue of Columbus, by Italian sculptor Edoardo Alfieri, was a gift to the city from the citizens of Genoa, Italy, and was dedicated in 1955."

In the late 20th century, many Indigenous American groups pushed for a "rethinking" of Columbus as a national hero. In the 21st century many municipalities replaced the Columbus Day holiday with an "Indigenous

---

[50] "Veteran Italian Leader Dies." *The Los Angeles Times*, April 23, 1940, p. 28.
[51] "Christopher Columbus Greenmount Cemetery Durango, CO," *WayMarking.com*, January 3, 2022.

Americans Day." The pushback against Columbus might be two-fold; first as anti-Italian, second as anti-Catholic. A conflict existed well into the 21st century as "Columbus Day remained a celebration of Italian-American pride." Lost in the discussion is the significance of Christopher Columbus (born as "Cristoffa Colombo" in Genoa, Italy) as an Italian of historical significance and the continued mistreatment of Italian immigrants from 1880 to 1930.[52]

"Statue of the city's namesake, explorer Christopher Columbus, in front of City Hall" gift in 1955 from the residents of Genoa, Italy; removed in July 2020.
Carol M. Highsmith, c. 2016. Library of Congress (Public Domain)

ESSAY: The Plight of Columbus and Italian Americans
By: Janice **Therese** Mancuso

As we approach another Columbus Day, some Italian Americans look forward to celebrating their heritage by honoring the man who opened the old world to the new. Other Italian Americans maybe with reasonings of remorse, guilt, or self-righteousness dread the day; and some Italian Americans just don't care. In this age of instant news, social media, and the aftermath of being politically correct, Columbus Day, like Italian American culture, is tattered; although Columbus landed generations before the waves of Italian immigrants arrived, each mirrors the other.

---

[52] "Christopher Columbus Statue," *Choose Chicago.com*. Roger Piantadosi. "Italian Imprints." *The Washington Post*, October 6, 1989. Alan Kraut, *The Huddled Masses*.

Columbus sailed for Spain (Italy was not a country then, but fragmented into several city-states, the Papal States, and the Kingdom of Naples), and he bumped into the islands of a continent that was not fully known to Europe. He was an outsider to the Spaniards, but he persevered in his dedication to his beliefs and was utilized by Queen Isabella and King Ferdinand to find treasures for their kingdom: a trade route, religious recruits, precious metals, more territory. Columbus's mission was rocky from the start, and although he was an accomplished navigator and sailed with the spirit of adventure, the uncharted waters brought the beginnings of rebellion and uncertainty. After five weeks at sea the sight of land brought joy and hope.

Beginning in the late nineteenth century, massive waves of Italian immigrants most from southern Italy traveled to a new world because they felt abandoned by their country. The unification of Italy offered little hope for their survival, so they sailed for self-preservation, seeking, as all immigrants do, prosperity. Although traveling by steamship on a journey that took about ten days, the immigrant's path to America was also rough. Mostly confined to dark and dingy compartments deep in the bowels of a ship, they endured crowded unsanitary living conditions, tainted water, and barely edible food; similar to Columbus the sight of land brought joy and hope.

Columbus encountered a different civilization than what he had known; and according to his writings, he was mesmerized by the land and the people of this different culture. He continued to seek a passage to what he thought was Asia, attempted to bring Christianity to the inhabitants of the islands, and searched for gold. The relationships among Columbus, the Spaniards, and the Natives turned hostile, and years of enslavement, cruel deaths, disease, and anarchy followed. The Italian immigrants were poked and prodded. Those who stayed found an entirely different culture then what they had known: uninhabitable living conditions, sickness, and a system of forced labor. They did not find the streets paved with gold.

During governing the Spanish settlement, Columbus was scorned and maligned. He was stripped of his powers, wrongly accused, and sent back to Spain in shame. Still, he believed his dream and was exonerated. Italian immigrants who made America their home often faced discrimination and often stereotyped. They were different in appearances, language, customs, religion, and way of life. They endured the hardships of a new land and pursued dream of better life for their families.

Columbus is an enigma. By the majority of accounts, he was born in Genoa, but his life before 1492 is somewhat obscure. Because of rampant discrimination, many Italian immigrants shunned their heritage and claimed to be of another nationality. Italians are a mixture of numerous ethnic groups, and after arriving from Europe, it was easier to claim another country as their own. Additionally,

CHAPTER 1

Italian immigrants were (and continue to be) stereotyped as being associated with mobsters.

Sometime around the 500th anniversary of Columbus's landing, questions about his voyages and motives started to emerge. About 60 years before the quincentenary, during the administration of Franklin Delano Roosevelt, Columbus Day was made a federal holiday. Martin Luther King, Jr. and Christopher Columbus are the only people who were not presidents recognized with a federal holiday. During the past 25 years, the American celebration of Columbus Day has been tarnished. In schools and colleges, teachings of Columbus blame him for the exploitation of the natives, with written words taken out of context and misinterpretations by those who judge fifteenth-century events using twenty-first century values. The attacks on Columbus are indirectly an attack on Italian American culture and heritage. Children of all nationalities are at risk of being misinformed, but from the Italian immigrants who turned their backs on their heritage and with limited teaching of Italian American history, children of Italian heritage are being taught to lose their cultural identity. Italian Americans need to reclaim their heritage.

Janice Therese Mancuso is a writer, author, and researcher of Italian-American Culture and founder of Thirty-One Days of Italians, e-newsletter Tutto Italiano, and the Italian American Heritage Project Email at: JTMancuso@Earthlink.net. Web: http://italamerheritage.com/being_italian-american.htm.

©1998-2020 Janice Therese Mancuso

Emma Stebbins and "Drop the Hate Seek the Truth"

During an early 21st century nationwide onslaught demanding removing, destroying, and desecrating statues of Christopher Columbus, some small stopgap victories occurred. In 2022, an ironic situation argued by the Columbus Heritage Coalition spearheaded by its president Angelo Vivolo organized a counter campaign focused on a pursuit to "Drop the Hate. Seek the Truth." A straightforward mission, providing factual information to stop the flood of misinformation concerning Columbus caused by the inaccurate campaign known as "Take Down Columbus." In one, a 162-year-old statue in New York was preserved from removal.[53]

Prior to the immigration of the 1880s, nationwide tributes for the 400th celebratory anniversary of Christopher Columbus were underway such as the World's Columbian Exposition of 1893. An early recognition arose in Brooklyn

---

[53] Angelo Vivolo. "Victory in Brooklyn: The Christopher Columbus Memorial Stays in Place in Front of Borough Hall," *Primo Magazine*, 2023, OnlinePrimo.com.

40 Italian Culture in America:
The Immigrants 1880 to 1930 From Discrimination to Assimilation

for a Columbus statue made of Italian Carrara marble. Sculptor Emma Stebbins (1815–1882) received the commission for the artwork which was completed in 1869. Justification for the commission, as explained on the Official Website of the New York City Department of Parks & Recreation, cited the honor for Columbus was the result of, a popular reputation,

> "Of the bold, courageous adventurer who enabled American civilization. The inspiration has been described as representing the navigator standing upon the deck of a ship alone before the West Continent burst into view, ship's tiller in hand, as his mutinous crew have all deserted him."

Upon completion, Stebbins statue was put in storage; encountering more "voyages" than the actual Columbus (removed for restoration, lost twice, rediscovered, and moved twice). Recovered in 1934, it was placed in Mulberry Park in Little Italy in the renamed "Columbus Park." Later, in 1971, during a resurgence of Italian pride occurring in New York City, it was once-again relocated. *The New York Times* praised the public display as, "Brooklyn Recovers a Great Discoverer." The location, in Brooklyn's Cadman Plaza in front of the New York State Supreme Court Building.[54]

By the 21st century, Stebbins iconic Columbus statue was targeted for removal as part of a growing "Woke" movement spreading throughout America (also known as "Cancel Culture"). The movement spawned from in part of the "Black Lives Matter" campaign calling for social justice for African Americans. In 2022, *Merriam-Webster* defined "woke" as,

> **Woke:** /wōk/ **adjective.** First known use was in 1972; did not gain nationwide use until the second decade of the 21st century.

> **1.** "Aware of and actively attentive to important societal facts and issues of racial and social justice)."

> **2.** "Politically liberal especially in a way that is considered unreasonable or extreme."

"Woke" quickly spread in American society; backtracking upon history. In Brooklyn, a "Take Down Columbus" campaign (to "tear down" and "eliminate" all references) targeted the art of Emma Stebbins. A request to Brooklyn Community Board 2 favored removal. After a two-year campaign by the Columbus Heritage Coalition, Angelo Vivolo, writing for *Primo* magazine reported, "Emma Stebbins and her Columbus memorial in Columbus Park have prevailed, thanks to a coalition of activists and their appeal to drop the hate and seek the truth." Vivolo added, Stebbins "might well have been the latest victim of the irrational frenzy that seeks to wipe away all memory of Christopher

---

[54] "Columbus Park." *Official Website of the New York City Dept of Parks & Recreation.*

Columbus." A contradictory caveat by Vivolo stated, "We represent supporters of pioneering gay sculptor Emma Stebbins pushing back against a campaign to take down her celebrated 162-year-old Columbus statue in downtown Brooklyn."[55]

Christopher Columbus statue by Emma Stebbins cast in 1869; base by architect Aymar Embury II (1880-1966) located in front of New York State Supreme Court Building at Montague and Court Streets in Brooklyn, New York. Photo: Courtesy of New York Department of Parks & Recreation.

---

[55] Angelo Vivolo. "Victory in Brooklyn: The Christopher Columbus Memorial Stays in Place in Front of Borough Hall," *Primo Magazine*, 2023.

Preserving the 162-year-old artwork did not sway the Community Board based on historical fact. Rather justification was on Stebbins gender and sexual orientation. The caveat of a cautionary detail revealed preserving the statue might very well emanate from two important facts held dear to the "woke generation." Of supreme irony, Stebbins was the first woman to receive a public art commission from New York City. Second, and possibly the most important, it was revealed Stebbins was a lesbian. It would be hard pressed to have any of the Board members justify any negative association of a female and gay artist. A conflicting "woke" contradiction might have "out-woke" itself realizing the importance of a female and gay individual despite the subject matter.

Above Left: Photo of actress Charlotte Cushman (seated) and Emma Stebbins (standing) possibly while living as a married couple in Rome.
Above Right: Artist Emma Stebbins, c. 1875 (Public Domain).

An additional factor, but not part of the decision for Stebbins artwork, nor in consideration for preventing any of the removals, rewriting, or desecrations of the Columbus legacy was the historical "Italian" influence upon the American art world. Stebbins, born and died in New York, as like so many artists, traveled to Rome; living for 12 years as an "expatriate artist." Art historian and Stebbins biographer Elizabeth Milroy, explained, "Art-making was not regarded as a practical occupation in America, so going over to the Eternal City [Rome] was a way of finding a cultural community that did admire art." Those 12 years, provided the addition of living with life-partner the well-known actress Charlotte Cushman. (1816-1876), as the two "became a couple." In an 1858 letter, Cushman

CHAPTER 1

described herself "as married to Stebbins [wearing] the badge [ring] upon the finger of my left hand."[56]

In 2019, *The New York Times* said, "Stebbins and Cushman lived together in Rome for 12 years, until Cushman learned she had breast cancer. They returned to the United States in 1870, abandoning several of Stebbins's unfinished pieces." Unfinished pieces may have been left in Rome; yet upon return to New York, Stebbins unveiled one of the most famous works of art in American culture. *Angel of the Waters*, designed in 1868, best known as the Bethesda Fountain, located on Bethesda Terrace in Central Park, New York. New York City Department of Parks & Recreation cite, "It is one of the most well-known fountains in the world; [and] the only sculpture as a part of Central Park's original design."[57]

As a Neoclassical sculpture influenced by Italian history, *Angel of the Waters* is an eight-foot-high bronze upon a fountain pedestal hovering over "four small cherubim (angelic beings attending to God) representing health, purity, temperance, and peace." The outstretched arm represents an angel blessing the life-giving water source entering New York City as a result of the 1842 completion of the Croton Aqueduct Reservoir system. (Aqueducts traces its roots of origin to the ancient Romans.)[58]

In a similar focus of many misconceptions, myths, and revisions throughout American history, the truth of Stebbins gender orientation was not publicly revealed during her lifetime. As noted in a belated obituary,

> "By the time the Bethesda Fountain was unveiled three years later, Stebbins had stopped working in order to care for Cushman, who died in 1876. Stebbins's name did not appear in her partner's obituary in *The Times*, which said that Cushman 'never married, but lived and died a virgin queen of the dramatic stage.'"

An 1879 letter to a companion artist sculptor Anne Whitney (1821-1915) revealed Stebbins private grief of Cushman's death. Stebbins wrote, "I lived with the embodied principle of love so many years that it became a part of being and has grown intensive more and more since it was taken away from me." On October of 1882, Stebbins died of a lung disease possibly due to years of inhaling marble dust and other contaminants.[59]

---

[56] Angelo Vivolo. "Victory in Brooklyn," *Primo Magazine*, 2023.

[57] E. Milroy. "The Public Career of Emma Stebbins."

[58] "Bethesda Fountain." CentralPark.com, January 15, 2023. See also: "Bethesda Fountain, History." New York City Parks & Recreation.

[59] Jennifer Harlan. "Overlooked No More: Emma Stebbins, Who Sculpted an Angel of New York." *The New York Times*, May 29, 2015.

The Bethesda Fountain *Angel of the Waters* at Bethesda Terrace in Central Park, Manhattan, NYC. Photo by: Ahodges7, c. 2009 (Wiki Creative Commons).

The Bethesda Fountain is quite easy to find - just about any New Yorker would know where it is. Others might have seen the fountain featured in dozens of Hollywood movies and television shows. In contrast, familiarity was not so common with a Stebbins statue of Christopher Columbus; saved due to the historical correctness of the 21st century. Some erroneous reports placed the Christopher Columbus statue outside of Brooklyn Borough Hall. An adventurous traveler to Brooklyn Borough Hall would not find Columbus, they would find however, a monumental building oozing in the tradition of Italian Culture in America.

Brooklyn,[60] known throughout the world, is home to large numbers of Italians. A design commision for a City Hall was awarded to architect Calvin Pollard (1797-1850) and completed by architect Gamaliel King (1795-1875) in 1848. The building reflects the Italian Renaissance and Ancient Rome. Examination of the design reveals a striking resemblance to the Bethesda Fountain – without Emma Stubbins *Angle of the Waters*.

---

[60] At the time Brooklyn was its own city and not incorporated within the Five Boroughs of New York City.

Brooklyn Borough Hall completed in 1848.
Reflective of the Italian Renaissance and Ancient Rome.
(Photo by: Ad Meskens - Wiki Creative Commons).

The Pledge of Allegiance, God, and "Justice for All?"

Arising from the Columbian World's Exposition was the creation of the American Salute to the Flag (known as "The Pledge of Allegiance"). Written by Francis Bellamy in 1892, the "Pledge," was a brief 23-word statement to complement the 400th Anniversary of the Columbus voyage. Bellamy hoped "a unified salute to one flag might heal some of the wounds from the catastrophic divisive Civil War." As such would also provide a means of assimilation for recent immigrants. The 37-year-old Bellamy was assigned the task by editor Daniel Ford (? - 1899) for "arranging a patriotic program for schools around the country to coincide with opening ceremonies for the Columbian Exposition." A description for the proper observance during the forthcoming 400th Anniversary Columbus Day celebration added a unified salute to accompany the recital of the Pledge was proposed by another editor named James B. Upham.[61]

---

[61] *The Youth's Companion,* 65 (1892), p. 446. *See also*: Excerpt from: Ralph G. Giordano. *Pop Goes the Decades: The Fifties*, Greenwood, 2017, pp. 278-281.

Caption: "Rev. Francis J. Bellamy, American minister and author of the U.S. Pledge of Allegiance," c. 1894. Published in *Campbell's Illustrated History of the World's Columbian Exposition* (1894).
(Wiki Commons)

In response, Bellamy wrote the 23-word Pledge of Allegiance published in *The Youth's Companion* on September 8, 1892 as,

I PLEDGE ALLEGIANCE TO MY FLAG,
AND TO THE REPUBLIC FOR WHICH IT STANDS:
ONE NATION INDIVISIBLE,
WITH LIBERTY AND JUSTICE FOR ALL.

Bellamy provided directions for the proper salute during recital of the pledge. Upon a signal, all the students would face the flag; first with their hands at their sides. In ordered ranks, they would begin "with a military salute. Right hand lifted, palm downward, to a line with the forehead and close to it hand held at forehead." After the words "to the flag" (and as signaled by the principal or person leading the recital) it was proposed that the right arm would be "extended toward the flag [remaining] till the end of the affirmation; whereupon all hands immediately drop to the side."[62]

A 1923 revision took out the arbitrary term of "my flag" to read as "the flag of the United States." The reason was so "immigrant children" would know

---

[62] Excerpt from: *The Youth's Companion*, 65 (1892), p. 446.

exactly "which flag they were saluting." The following year, the words "of America" were added; the salute remained unchanged. The Pledge went through revisions, but the "Bellamy Salute" remained consistent. Sometimes known as the "Olympic Salute" with references to Ancient Rome. (Although, the Olympic harken back to Ancient Greece.)

Above Left: Pledge of Allegiance, "Schoolchildren pledging allegiance to the flag," c. 1908. Reproduction Number: LC-USZ62-30276. **Above Right**: "Southington, Connecticut. School children pledging their allegiance to the flag, c. 1942. Reproduction No. LC-USW3-041733-E Library of Congress Prints and Photographs Division Washington, D.C. 20540 USA.

During the 1936 Olympic Games in Berlin, Germany, the American flag salute caused some controversy. The raised right hand of the "Olympic Salute" was like the "Bellamy Salute" -- also the official salute of the Nazi Party under Adolf Hitler. American Track & Field athlete Jesse Owens (1913-1980) who earned four Gold Medals, aware of Hitler's racial policies, gave an American military salute. Long Jump Silver Medalist, German athlete Luz Long standing alongside Owens displayed the salute, but it was "Heil Hitler." (Long was killed during World War II.) In 1942, due to the obvious "Nazi connection," U.S. Congress authorized a "hand-over-the-heart" approach; as did adding the words "under God" as a means of differentiating from atheistic Soviet Union Communism.[63]

---

[63] Richard J. Ellis, *To the Flag*, pp. 65-67.

"Berlin, Olympiade, Siegerehrung Weitsprung," c. 1936. Left to right, Naoto Tajima (Japan - Bronze); Jesse Owens (USA -Gold); Luz Long (Germany - Silver). The German athlete and members of the German Olympic Committee are in a "Heil Hitler" salute. Owens opted to salute the flag; Tajima of Japan stood "at attention." This image was provided to Wikimedia Commons by the German Federal Archive (Deutsches Bundesarchiv) as part of a cooperation project.

(Note: In February 2022, "doubts about the oath" were raised as possibly written by a "13-year-old Kansas schoolboy named Frank E. Bellamy." In 2022, Sam Roberts for *The New York Times,* wrote, "Bellamy's authorship was reaffirmed during the 20th century by, among others, the American Flag Foundation, the Smithsonian Institution, and the Library of Congress. In 2021, the elder Bellamy was credited in a resolution by the United States Senate and cited by the "New Yale Book of Quotations.")[64]

Exploration of the American Colonies

After World War II, some of the most loyal and patriotic of Americans were of Italian ancestry - firmly assimilated into the Cultural fabric. That was not the situation during the immigration years of 1880 to 1930. Prior to the massive wave of Italian immigration, a small number of Italians had traveled to the colonies. According to The U.S. Library of Congress,

---

[64] Stephen J. Whitfield, *The Culture of the Cold War*. p. 92.

CHAPTER 1   49

"Throughout the colonial and early national periods, immigrants from the Italian peninsula maintained a small established presence in North America. Italian craftsmen were renowned the world over, and many traveled to the New World to help build its new institutions, working as sculptors, woodworkers, and glassblowers."[65]

Regardless of discovery of North America leading to formation as the United State of America, it all began with an Italian explorer Christopher Columbus; followed by other significant Italian explorers. In 1497, Venetian John Cabot (1450-1550, born as Giovanni Caboto), sailed under the English flag following the path of Columbus and soon "discovered" the northeast coast of America. Cabot's path encouraged Spain to sponsor Florentine Amerigo Vespucci (1454-1512), to explore the east coast of the new continent around 1500. In 1507, German geographer Martin Waldseemüller (1470-1520), wrote of the Vespucci voyages, "I see no reason why anyone should justly object to calling this part ... America, after Amerigo [Vespucci], its discoverer, a man of great ability." It is from him that the continent, both North and South earned its name.[66]

Despite both the founding and name of the American nation owe homage to an Italian heritage, the years 1880 to 1930, represented a drastic attitudinal change towards Italians. America forged through a previous century marred by the Civil War and westward expansion with the nation effectively eradicating an indigenous Indian population. By that time, a stable race population of white northern European Protestants effectively dominated all of the political, economic, social, and cultural aspects of American life. By the 1890s as the convergence of the American Industrial Revolution with unbridled capitalism opened a floodgate of "New Immigration" to the American shores – many of them peasants from southern and eastern Europe – none more so than Italians. Those same factory products were churned out by American factories staffed with poor and immigrant labor most susceptible to contracting the often debilitating Tuberculous due to impoverished living conditions.[67]

---

[65] "Italian Immigration." *The Library of Congress,* December 31, 2018.
[66] Toby Lester. "The Waldseemuller Map." *Smithsonian Magazine.* December 2009.
[67] See: Risjord, *Jefferson's America,* 1650-1815, pp. 6-7.

CHAPTER 2

ITALIAN IMMIGRANTS:
THE GREAT ARRIVAL OPENS The DOOR

A key objective of the experience is the exploration of the long-standing cultural ties between Italy and the United States through themes of art, architecture, liberty, poetry and the human condition."

From the early American colonies to the immigration surge after 1880, only about 25,000 Italians immigrated to America. Most from north Italy were skilled artisans, stone masons, woodworkers, glassblowers, sculptors, musicians, and vinters, among other skills. Over the course of some 250 years, it was only a mere "trickle." A significant attachment to the skilled artistry was due to one famous American. The *Library of Congress* notes,

> "Thomas Jefferson had a particular affinity for Italian culture; he recruited Italian stonemasons to work on his home at Monticello, and brought musicians from Italy to form the core of the Marine Band. In addition, he invented his own hand-operated pasta machine."

Jefferson introduced into the young American culture many Italian styles of architecture, art, liberty, law, wine, and food. Throughout his lifetime, Jefferson consulted and interacted with many Italians. Some relocated to the colonies such as Philip Mazzei. The point of entry was any of the major port cities such as New York, Boston, or Philadelphia.[68]

Castle Clinton: The First Immigration Station: 1855-1890

The first "official" immigration processing station in America opened at Castle Clinton at the southern end of Manhattan Island on August 3, 1855. The history

---

[68] "Early Arrivals," *The Library of Congress*, Immigration and Relocation in U.S. History. September 24, 2020.

of the location dated to the American War of 1812 serving as a series of forts in defense of New York Harbor. Entry to the harbor passes through a narrow inlet bordered by Brooklyn and Staten Island. The two boroughs of New York City were later connected by the Verrazzano Narrows Bridge named in honor of the Italian explorer.[69]

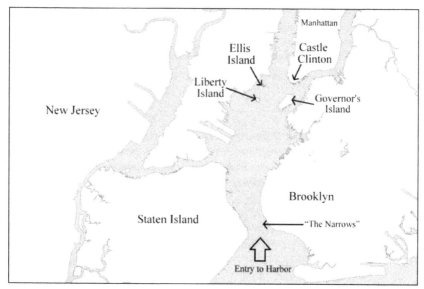

Map of New York Harbor indicating location of Castle Clinton site of New York City's first immigration processing center; Ellis Island which replaced Castle Clinton; Liberty Island home of The Statue of Liberty; Governor's Island and the entry point known as "The Narrows" between Staten Island and Brooklyn.

New York as one of the busiest natural harbors was a direct entry point from the Atlantic Ocean, therefore, it was a natural geographic location for processing the arrival of immigrants. With the upsurge Second Industrial Revolution requiring a large number of laborers immigration numbers swelled. The pressing need for the processing and determining legal entry of immigrants prompted the need to adapt nearby Castle Clinton as an immigration station administered by the State of New York.

As early as 1820, administration was by the US Customs Service. While open from August 3, 1855 to April 18, 1890, Castle Garden was wrought with corruption. Historian Thomas Pitkin in *Keepers of the Gate: A History of Ellis Island*, explained, It was discovered when the immigration process was left to the

---

[69] When first opened in 1964, the bridge was named "Verrazano," in 2019 it was renamed to match the explorers name with two "r's" and two "z's," as Verrazzano.

individual states legalities were often compromised by "jurisdictional disputes [and] serious differences."

Treasury Secretary William Windom (1827-1891) recommended full control of the immigration process by the U.S. Government. As a result, "In order to ensure a safe, controlled, and regulated entry process," and to oversee and secure all ports of entry to the United States, a Federal order warranted relocating the processing to a nearby island. Approval was granted for "the selection of Ellis Island as the site for the new immigration station." The official history of the United States added, "For most of this generation of Italian immigrants, their first steps on U.S. soil were taken in a place that has now become a legend Ellis Island."[70]

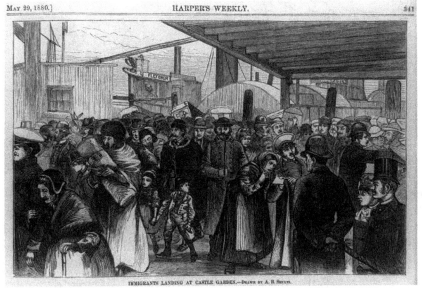

Immigrants landing at Castle Garden. Drawn by A.B. Shults, artist for *Harper's Weekly* magazine May 29, 1880, p. 341. Photograph. Retrieved from the Library of Congress, <www.loc.gov/item/90707732/>. (Public Domain)

---

[70] "Castle Garden: America's First Immigration Center," *The Battery Conservancy*. Thomas Pitkin, *Keepers of the Gate: A History of Ellis Island,* (New York University Press, 1975), pp. 12-13.

The former immigration center Castle Garden. As it appeared in 1923 housing the New York City Aquarium. During the late 20th into the 21st century, it served as a departure point for tourists to board a ferry to Ellis Island and the Statue of Liberty. (Public Domain Wiki Commons).

The STATUE of LIBERTY *"is born from an Italian idea."*

Immigrants entering New York Harbor upon seeing *Liberty Enlightening the World*, knew the "Statue of Liberty" meant they had finally arrived in *L'America*. Appropriately nicknamed "The Immigrant's Statue" Lady Liberty represented conflicting and opposing view by immigrants and Nativist Americans. Information about the statue is readily available – very few provide the totality of the "Italian Connection." Millions of Italian immigrants welcomed sight of Lady Liberty. It is highly unlikely any of the newly arriving Italian immigrants, nor modern day visitors, were aware of the multiple Italian connections with the Statue of Liberty.

1. Lady Liberty is a Roman Goddess;
2. Sculptor Bartholdi may have had Italian ancestry;
3. Bartholdi served in a military commanded by Giuseppe Garibaldi;
4. Lady Liberty shares heritage with an Italian Sculpture in Florence;
5. Lady Liberty shares heritage with a colossal statue in Arona, Italy;
6. The *tabula ansata* referencing the Declaration of Independence is connected to an Italian statesman Philip Mazzei.

The idea for a statue arose in 1865 at the end of the American Civil War. Édouard de Laboulaye (1811-1883) proposed for France to "give a statue representing liberty to the United States for its centennial." Laboulaye reasoned honoring

America would strengthen the cause for democracy in France. Laboulaye envisioned a visual representation of the alliance of the French and American people sharing the ideal of providing Liberty for all people. Approval for Bedloe's Island was given by the U.S. Congress, signed by President Ulysses S. Grant. The following year French sculptor Frédéric Auguste Bartholdi (1834-1904), began the process to build and assemble the colossal statue. The *African American Ancestry* cites, "Frederic Auguste Bartholdi was born in Colmar, France, to a family of Italian and German Protestant heritage." Another, claimed "Bartholdi had Alsatian [German] and Italian heritage and acted as liaison officer to [Giuseppe] Garibaldi during the Franco-Prussian War."[71]

The Palais du Champ-de-Mars and the head of the Statue of Liberty, Exposition *Universelle of Paris* (1878). Public Domain – Wiki Commons.

A portion of the Lady Liberty's hand holding the torch was sent to America for display at the 1876 Centennial Exposition in Philadelphia (celebrating the 100th anniversary of the Declaration of Independence). The torch was later sent to New York placed on display in Madison Square Garden until 1882. The cooperative venture between France gifting the statue paired with the United States providing the pedestal. However, money was not authorized by Congress, rather a fundraising campaign by the American Committee for the Statue of Liberty raised funds; who commissioned American architect Richard Morris Hunt to design the pedestal. Lady Liberty's head and shoulders were complete by 1878

---

[71] "The Immigrant's Statue." *National Park Service*, February 26, 2015. See also: "Frederic Bartholdi." *African American Ancestry*, September 30, 2020. Padraig Rooney, "Frederic Auguste Bartholdi: Lady Liberty." November 17, 2018.

for display at the Paris Universal Exposition; yet was dwarfed by the Eiffel Tower. Designed by engineer Alexandre-Gustave Eiffel (1832-1923) the tower has since become the defining iconic symbol of Paris. Whereas Eiffel's engineering is in full view in Paris the structural iron framework supporting Lady Liberty is hidden under the copper skin.[72]

The Eiffel Tower did not receive anywhere near the love by Parisians as they displayed for Lady Liberty. Many notable Parisians were appalled by the tower and petitioned its dismantling. Added to the dismay, authorities of the city of Paris ordered a dismantling within 20 years. The tower received a reprieve as a radio antenna was installed, due to Italian Giuseppe Marconi's invention which revolutionized communication. Bertrand Lemoine writing a history for *Tour Eiffel* stated,

> "From very early on, Gustave Eiffel knew he needed to find a use for his Tower beyond its function as a symbol of progress and a fair-time spectacle. He immediately started looking for a scientific justification for its existence. A new technique in signal transmission called wireless telegraphy was emerging in the 1890s thanks to the combined efforts of various thinkers."[73]

In 1884, work for Lady Liberty in Paris was complete; the structure disassembled for shipment to the U.S. onboard a French navy ship arriving on June 17th. Immediate placement did not occur in New York Harbor; rather placed in storage for one year – simple reasoning the pedestal was not finished.

The iconic symbol of Paris "The Eiffel Tower." The tower was designed by Gustave Eiffel who also designed the hidden structural skeleton for the Statue of Liberty. (Photo by Author c. 2018)

---

[72] "Liberty Island Chronology." *National Park Service.* February 4, 2018.
[73] Bertrand Lemoine. "How Did Radio Save the Tower." *TourEiffel.com*, 2020.

Architect: Richard Morris Hunt

The pedestal for the Statue of Liberty was designed by architect Richard Morris Hunt (1827-1895), on commission from the American Committee for the Statue of Liberty. After many rejected design schemes, Hunt completed an acceptable design in 1884 consisting of a massive stone pedestal base at 154 feet (47 meters) slightly taller than the statue at 151 feet (46 meters). The combined height of pedestal and statue measured a colossal 305 feet (93 meters). The *National Park Service* cites, "Hunt's granite pedestal became an architectural monument in its own right, yet exists in harmony with the colossus above it." Prior to working on a base for Lady Liberty, Hunt was well-known in America as an architect and also active in social causes. In 1857, he endorsed the founding of the American Institute for Architects (AIA) and supported the Union cause and Abolition of Slavery during the American Civil War.[74]

Upper Left: Portrait Architect Richard Morris Hunt. **Lower Right**: Hunt's sketch for the pedestal base. Library of Congress, LC-USZ62-107792.

---

[74] "Richard Morris Hunt." *National Park Service* June 7, 2018.

An artist rendering of the celebration dedication
of the Statue of Liberty on October 28, 1886.

Without official financial support, an American committee undertook a fund-raising campaign for the pedestal. In 1883, Emma Lazarus (1849-1887) composed a poem titled, "The New Colossus" in support of the fundraiser for the pedestal. Emma Lazarus (last name derived from the Hebrew "God has helped") provided an ideological poem of humanity attached to symbolism of Italian heritage. Lazarus did not live to see her immortal words inscribed on a bronze plaque and placed inside at the base of the Statue in 1903. The words eventually became world famous echoing as a rallying cry for the American ideal of acceptance for all.[75]

Portrait Emma Lazarus (Public Domain).

---

[75] David Garrard Lowe. "The Man who Gilded the Gilded Age," *City Journal*, Autumn 1996. "The New Colossus: Statue of Liberty." *National Park Service*, accessed October 2, 2020. Lazarus wrote the poem on November 2, 1883.

CHAPTER 2

The New Colossus

Not like the brazen giant of reek fame,
With conquering limbs astride from land to land;
Here at our sea-washed, sunset gates shall stand
A mighty woman with a torch, whose flame
Is the imprisoned lightning, and her name
Mother of Exiles. From her beacon-hand
Glows world-wide welcome; her mild eyes command
The air-bridged harbor that twin cities frame.
"Keep, ancient lands, your storied pomp!" cries she
With silent lips. "Give me your tired, your poor,
Your huddled masses yearning to breathe free,
The wretched refuse of your teeming shore.
Send these, the homeless, tempest-tost to me,
I lift my lamp beside the golden door!

Dedicated in 1886, the statue, as a collaboration designed by French sculptor Frédéric Auguste Bartholdi (1834-1904), internal structure by Gustave Eiffel (1832-1923) and Norwegian engineer Joachim Goschen Giaever, (1856-1925); with base designed by Richard Morris Hunt has numerous Italian connections to Ancient Rome, Thomas Jefferson, Philip Mazzei, and within Italy.

The figure of Lady Liberty placed atop the pedestal is derived from *Libertas* (Latin for "liberty"), the Roman goddess of freedom and liberty. As noted in the 2020 "Sisters in Liberty" exhibit, in Ancient Rome the goddess Libertas was "widely worshipped, especially among emancipated slaves." The logical connection to Thomas Jefferson, a lifelong Italophile, is found in his Declaration of Independence; referenced on the *tabula ansata* (Latin for tablet with handles) held by Lady Liberty inscribed in Roman numerals "JULY IV MDCCLXXVI" (July 4, 1776) as the birth of liberty. The genesis for the Declaration of Independence is documented in U.S. History from the friendship between Thomas Jefferson and Philip Mazzei. As noted in the *Thomas Jefferson Encyclopedia,*

> "These two Renaissance men spoke often on the state of society and government. Jefferson was an educated man with a great deal of interest in Italian culture, and as seen at Monticello Italian architecture. He and Mazzei discussed the idea of democracy, and how one's government should uphold it. Mazzei firmly believed *"Tutti gli uomini sono ugualmente liberi e indipendenti"* ["All men are by nature equally free and independent"]."[76]

It was the likes of Philip Mazzei and Thomas Jefferson who sought to break free from "the chains" of tyranny imposed upon them by the monarchs of Europe. In

---

[76] "Mazzei, Philip." Thomas Jefferson Encyclopedia.

a symbolic sense, the U.S. National Parks Service tells us, "A broken chain lies at her feet. The statue became an icon of freedom and of the United States, and was a welcoming sight to immigrants arriving from abroad."[77]

Both the Statue of Liberty and the Eiffel Tower achieved iconic worldwide status. Each designated as a UNESCO World Heritage Site -- Lady Liberty in 1984 and the Eiffel Tower in 1991. UNESCO described *Liberty Enlightening the World* as "a masterpiece of colossal statuary drawing on classical elements and iconography, a towering monument to liberty a masterpiece of the human spirit." It is not a stretch to recognize the direct influence of a "masterpiece" derived from the classical inspiration and humanism from the Italian Renaissance.[78]

Liberty Island home to the Statue of Liberty as it appeared in 2015 is basically the same first seen by millions of Italian immigrants entering into America.
Photograph by Thelma Olsen.

Sisters in Liberty and COLOSSUS of San Carlo Borromeo

The famous statue in New York harbor bears a striking resemblance to *The Liberty of Poetry*, sculptured by Pio Fedi (1815/16-1892) in the Basilica of Santa Croce in Florence. The Florentine Basilica located in the Tuscany Region of Italy, built from 1294 to 1385, was consecrated in 1443. As one of the most visited places in Florence the Basilica houses the tombs of iconic Renaissance figures such as Michelangelo Buonarotti, Galileo Galilei, and Niccolò Machiavelli, among other Italian notables. Each tomb is distinctive with sculptured funerary monuments crafted by some of the greatest artist of all-time such as Donatello (1386-1466), Giorgio Vasari (1511-1574), Antonio Canova.

---

[77] "The Immigrant's Statue." *National Park Service*, February 26, 2015.
[78] World Heritage Sites are designated by the United Nations Educational, Scientific and Cultural Organization (UNESCO) for having cultural, historical, scientific or other form of significance . . . considered to be of outstanding value to humanity."

Pio Fedi's *The Liberty of Poetry* sits atop the tomb of Giovanni Battista Niccolini (1782-1861) a noted hero of Italian Unification. The name does not resonate in the same worldwide historical importance as Garibaldi, Cavour, or Mazzini. To the Italian people, he was monumental; evident by his tomb in full view near the Renaissance giants. The Museum Text describes the connection to Lady Liberty is not coincidence, stating,

> "The possibility that this statue, sculpted by Pio Fedi, was the inspiration, or one of the sources of inspiration, for her bigger sister cannot be dismissed: a plaster cast of the Santa Croce statue identical to the final statue had already been completed in 1872, after the preparatory drawings been in circulation in contemporary [publications] for some time."

Bartholdi might have visited Florence in the 1860s and saw the *maquettes* [sculptor's preliminary sketch] by Pio Fedi. Bartholdi served in the Franco-Prussian War (1870 - 1871) with a volunteer force led by the Italian patriot Giuseppe Garibaldi. Earlier in 1870, Bartholdi traveled to New York to surveying the statues location. In 1872, Fedi completed a model of *The Liberty of Poetry* to sit atop Niccolini's tomb.[79]

Above Left: *The Liberty of Poetry*, sculptured by Pio Fedi located within the Basilica Santa Croce in Florence, Italy.
Above Right: Exterior of the Basilica of Santa Croce, c. 2009.

---

[79] Helen Farrell and Anna McGee. "Santa Croce and the Statue of Liberty to Become Partners," July 8, 2016.

The intersection of the ideal of American liberty upon Italy is evidenced by Pio Fedi's 1865 sculpture of "Abraham Lincoln." According to the *Abraham Lincoln Foundation of the Union League of Philadelphia*, Fedi did not visit the U.S., but, worked from photographs after the assassination. The end of the Civil War coincided with the Italian unification; each with hope for the future of liberty.[80]

Statue *Abraham Lincoln* marble bust by Pio Fedi c. 1865.
Courtesy of The Union League Legacy Foundation.
(2004.46.1).

As for Lady Liberty, the connection between the two statues was officially recognized in 2016, between the U.S. National Park Service and the Opera di Santa Croce. Helen Farrell and Anna McGee, in "Santa Croce and the Statue of Liberty to Become Partners" stated, "A partnership is being planned to celebrate the sculptural and symbolic connections between Manhattan's Statue of Liberty and Santa Croce's *The Liberty of Poetry* funerary monument." The planned exhibit, "Sisters in Liberty, From Florence, Italy to New York, New York," opened in 2019 at the Ellis Island National Museum displayed the two related statues together in the same place. Unlike Lady Liberty's transatlantic voyage,

---

[80] "Bartholdi, Frédéric-Auguste." *National Gallery of Art*, August 5, 2016. See also: "Abraham Lincoln." *Foundation of the Union League of Philadelphia*.

CHAPTER 2

Liberty of Poetry would not leave Florence; rathe "traveled" the Atlantic by 21st century technology. Kent State University sent a team from Ohio to create a replica employing digital technology and 3D printing. (The connection is not by chance; Kent State maintains the largest American university campus in Florence.) A press release by *Opera Santa Croce* stated,

> "The exhibition features two distinct sculptural personifications of liberty: New York City's Statue of Liberty Enlightening the World and Florence's Liberty of Poetry The exhibition "Sisters in Liberty" explores the intersection between the ideas that inspired two monumental statues . . . The visitors will discover and interact with the symbols, voices and heroes of liberty and free-thinking. A key objective of the experience is the exploration of the long-standing cultural ties between Italy and the United States through themes of art, architecture, liberty, poetry and the human condition."[81]

Opened in May 2019, the museum text cited, "the reproduction enables visitors to see the Italian predecessor to the U.S. Statue of Liberty." Diane Pardue, Director of Museum Services at Ellis Island said, "It's important that Americans learn about Italian history and Italian connections."[82]

An article by research historian Simona Aiuti, writing for *Italiani l'Italia nel cuore*, cited a not so obvious truism, "The Statue of Liberty is not entirely original and unique in the world as many believe it is born from an Italian idea." Aiuti explained Bartholdi visited the Italian town of Arona on Lake Maggiore, "to study the structure of the Colossus of San Carlo Borromeo." More so than direct symbolism, or a Roman goddess, Aiuti cites "a statue dedicated to San Carlo Borromeo stands out; built with the same technique;" of the American Statue of Liberty as a large colossal metal copper statue of a "human figure visible from the inside."

At Arona, visitors enter inside the large statue to "climb up to the top of the statue" for a majestic view of "the surrounding landscape." Also known as "San Carlone" it was designed by the painter Giovan Battista "Cerano" Crespi (1573 - 1632) began in 1614 and completed by artists Bernardo Falconi (1620-1697) and Siro Zanelli (b. ? – 1724?). A plaque at the base of the Statue of Liberty in New York references the Italian statue of San Carlo of di Arona. Aiuti concludes the obvious,

> "Therefore, the statue of the 'San Carlone' was not simply a source of inspiration, but rather a true model to trace for a unique and colossal work; the symbol of the United States. The Statue of Liberty, which

---

[81] "Sisters in Liberty: From Florence, Italy to New York, New York." *Santa Croce.*
[82] Abigail Napp. "Ellis Island: Finally, Lady Liberty Meets her Italian Twin 'Libertà della Poesia.'" *VNY La Voce di New York.* October 20, 2019.

represents the country of opportunities where everything is possible, the first thing our emigrants saw; born as the story tells, certainly from the Colossus of Rhodes, but above all from the statue of San Carlo di Arona."[83]

Colossus of San Carlo Borromeo – a copper statue in Arona, Italy is the second largest in the world at 75 feet high (23 meters) atop a stone pedestal 38 feet high (11.5 meters). (Public Domain)

The U.S. National Park Service provided a few postscripts in the Liberty Island Chronology. The Statue of Liberty was designated a National Monument in 1924 by President Calvin Coolidge; the very same year the U.S. Congress legislated "The Immigration Act of 1924" limiting the number of immigrants allowed into the United States. In 1952, planning was approved for the American Museum of Immigration inside the base of the pedestal. The late 20th century restoration committee joined with Ellis Island under the National Park Service.[84]

---

[83] Simona Aiuti. "The Statue of Liberty is born from an Italian intuition." *Italiani l'Italia nel cuore*, April 7, 2019.
[84] "Liberty Island Chronology." *National Park Service.* February 4, 2018.

ELLIS ISLAND: *The GREAT ARRIVAL*

History.com cites "Ellis Island is a historical site that opened in 1892 as an immigration station, it served for more than 60 years until closed in 1954. Millions of newly arrived immigrants passed through its doors. It has been estimated that close to 40 percent of all current U.S. citizens can trace at least one of their ancestors to Ellis Island." The concise summary does not tell a complete story as applied to the millions of Italians arriving during the "New Wave." Historian Alexandra Molnar added the distinction between the "Old" and "New" immigration periods as,

> "Italian immigrants to the United States from 1890 onward became a part of the "New Immigration," which is the third and largest wave of immigration from Europe and consisted of Slavs, Jews, and Italians. This 'New Immigration' was a major change from the 'Old Immigration' which consisted of Germans, Irish, British, and Scandinavians and occurred throughout the 19th century.

During the years from 1880 to the beginning of World War I, the largest number of Italians came from the southern impoverished rural areas. The overwhelming majority from the Italian provinces of Sicily, Abruzzo, Campania, Calabria, and the regions of Naples. A vast majority of those Italian immigrants arrival in America was at Ellis Island in New York. As the *Library of Congress* states, "Most Italian immigrants took their first steps on U.S. soil in a place that has now become a legend Ellis Island.[85]

Ellis Island Immigration Station, c. 1900-1910. The Library of Congress Prints and Photographs Division LC-USZ62-37784. (Public Domain)

---

[85] Becky Little. "U.S. Immigration History," *History.com,* 2020.

Immigrants arrived at the small island (once an Indian fishing settlement) located 1/4 mile (0.4 km) off New Jersey and 1 mile (1.6 km) south of Manhattan. In 1794, New York City deeded Ellis Island to New York State to build "fortifications by the U.S. War Department."

By 1833, the geographic location of Ellis Island and Bedloe's Island directly off the coast of New Jersey led to disputed claims of ownership. An "inter-state compact" between New York and New Jersey resolved the boundary disputes. In 1834, Congress decreed "both Bedloe's Island (later changed to Liberty Island) and Ellis Island part of New York State." From 1835 to 1865 the island was occupied by the U.S. Army until the end of the Civil War. Complete military withdrawal did not happen as the U.S. Navy added fortifications and assumed control.

In 1892, the U.S. Immigration Station on Ellis Island opened as an Irish immigrant named Anna "Annie" Moore (1874-1924) is recorded as "the first alien to be processed." Within one year an additional 400,000 immigrants joined Annie Moore passing through Ellis Island; beginning an almost unimpeded flow. Over the course of 40 years in operation, over 12 million immigrants (averaging 5,000 per day) were processed. (For Italians, each entering ship created "a passenger manifest document" at the Italian port of departure.)[86]

New York. Ellis Island, c. 1909 to 1920. Immigrants walking across pier from bridge. National Photo Company Collection. Reproduction Number: LC-USZ62-95433. Library of Congress Prints and Photographs Division.

For immigrants, the trans-Atlantic crossing endured a two-week journey of cramped conditions in Third-class steerage. According the Ellis Island museum historian Barry Moreno,

"Before the ship was allowed to enter into New York Harbor, it had to stop at a quarantine checkpoint off the coast of Staten Island where

---

[86] Nicholas P. Ciotola "Ellis Island." In *Italian Americans: The History and Culture of a People*, pp. 15-17. See also: "Ellis Island Chronology," *National Park Service,* NPS.Gov.

CHAPTER 2

doctors would look for dangerous contagious diseases such as smallpox, yellow fever, plague, cholera and leprosy."[87]

About 700 to 1,000 was the typical number of immigrants arriving on each steamship. Passengers identified with a disease were transported a nearby quarantine island of either Swinburne or Hoffman. Immigrants deemed healthy endured a process described as,

> "When the first group of immigrants disembarked on Ellis Island in 1892, they found themselves in the grip of a bewildering, though still orderly, regime of bureaucratic procedures. Newcomers were numbered, sorted, and sent through a series of inspections, where they were checked for physical and mental fitness and for their ability to find work in the U.S. The consequences of failing an eye exam, or of seeming too frail for manual labor, could be devastating; one member of a family could be sent back to Italy, perhaps never to see his or her loved ones again, because of a hint of trachoma or a careless inspector. Although less than 2 percent of Italians were turned away, fear of such a separation led some immigrants to rename Ellis Island *L'Isola dell Lagrime*—the Island of Tears."[88]

Statistical details and numbers does not provide the plausible reasons for native Italians leaving the land of birth and ancestry. The U.S. Library of Congress explains the "complex" and "unique" reasons as,

> "What brought about this dramatic surge in immigration? The causes are complex, and each hopeful individual or family no doubt had a unique story. By the late 19th century, the peninsula of Italy had finally been brought under one flag, but the land and the people were by no means unified. Decades of internal strife had left a legacy of violence, social chaos, and widespread poverty. The peasants in the primarily poor, mostly rural south of Italy and on the island of Sicily had little hope of improving their lot. Diseases and natural disasters swept through the new nation. Its fledgling government was in no condition to bring aid to the people. As word of American prosperity came via returning immigrants and U.S. recruiters, Italians found it difficult to resist the call of "L'America."[89]

Historian Nicholas P. Ciotola in an article "Ellis Island," claimed the reason many southern Italians left was due to a "push and pull factor."

The ***push,*** is attributed to numerous factors including the political, economic,

---

[87] Becky Little. "U.S. Immigration History," *History.com,* 2020
[88] "*L'Isola dell Lagrime,*" Immigration and Relocation in U.S. History.
[89] "The Great Arrival," *The Library of Congress*, Immigration and Relocation in U.S. History. September 24, 2020.

social, and natural disasters occurring in Italy. One example, was the large number of southern Italian farm laborers who "toiled for long hours on large landed estates owned by absentee landlords, leaving little chance for upward economic mobility." Another cited reason came after the unification, as the newly formed government did little to offer any opportunities for the poor southern laborers. As the years progressed, the newly formed Italian government continued to favor the wealthy northern inhabitants. A revealing account came from an American and former slave Booker T. Washington (1856-1915). In 1910, Washington traveled throughout Italy and Sicily as a free American; publishing his first-hand view in *The Man Farthest Down: A Record of Observation and Study in Europe* (see Chapter 4A); providing the simplest, direct, and truest explanation for the massive Italian emigration. He explained,

> "Italy has not done well by her lower classes in the past. She has oppressed them with heavy taxes; has maintained a land system that has worn out the soil at the same time that it has impoverished the labourer; has left the agricultural labourers in ignorance; has failed to protect them from the rapacity of the large landowners; and has finally driven them to seek their fortunes in a foreign land."[90]

Additional concern was "an unpredictable environment characterized by droughts, floods, and natural disasters such as volcanic eruptions and earthquakes also had the effect of pushing Italians from their homeland." As Nicholas Ciotola added, one instance in 1908, of "a devastating earthquake between Sicily and Calabria caused a tidal wave that killed an estimated 100,000 people and devasted local infrastructure."[91]

The Messina Earthquake and *Maremoto* of 1908

For over 3,000 years, Italy experienced its undue share of natural disasters. History records one of the earliest volcanic eruptions from Mount Vesuvius destroying Pompeii in 79 CE. The entire city was completely buried beneath volcanic ash; which remained undiscovered until the 16th century. Jumping ahead by centuries, on August 24, 2016, an earthquake hit Italy killing hundreds. *The New York Times* chronicled dozens of devasting earthquakes over the past century. Journalists Caryn A. Wilson and Patrick Boehler recapped the unique geographical conditions,

> "Over the last century, Italy has suffered a series of deadly earthquakes. The Eurasian and African tectonic plates meet in central Italy; the Apennine Mountains, which form the country's spine, witness frequent

---

[90] Booker T. Washington. *The Man Farthest Down*. P. 122.
[91] Nicholas P. Ciotola. "Ellis Island." In *Italian Americans*, p. 16.

seismic activity. The consequences of this geologic activity can be tragic."

Volcanic eruptions occurred; none as destructive as December of 1908. Historian Amy Tikkanen, indicated it "was likely the most powerful recorded earthquake to hit Europe," a magnitude lasting over 20 seconds, struck a few days after Christmas on December 28th. The epicenter was located at the narrow Strait of Messina – between Sicily and Calabria. At the southern end, the strait is about 10 miles wide (16 km) and narrows quickly to only 2 miles (3 km). The quake devasted Messina on the island of Sicily and the Reggio Calabria mainland both along the coast.[92]

The story of the earthquake was carried in dozens of newspapers internationally. Unlike previous anti-immigrant comments about Italians in America, *The New York Times*, under new ownership of Adolph Ochs (1858-1935), was sympathetic to the victims of earthquake. A page 1 headline on December 29, 1908 in *The New York Times* read,

ITALY SHAKEN; THOUSANDS DIE;
Earthquake Destroys Great Part
of Messina in Sicily and Tidal
Wave Sweeps It.

SHIPLOADS OF THE INJURED
These Carried to Catania, Which
Also Is Inundated by
Tidal Wave.

CALABRIAN TOWNS WRECKED

Reggio Said to Have Shared
Messina's Fate -- Pope Eager
to Go to Sufferers.

Two Villages Near Messina Disappear

---

[92] Caryn A. Wilson and Patrick Boehler. "*Italy's History of Deadly Earthquakes*," August 24, 2016. See also: Amy Tikkanen, "Messina Earthquake and Tsunami of 1908," Encyclopædia Britannica.com. January 29, 2020.

The 7.5 magnitude earthquake (comparable to the 1906 San Francisco earthquake) resulted in widespread death and destruction. Within a few minutes, a tsunami, ("*maremoto*" or "sea quake") causing a series of waves estimated at 40 feet high (13 meters), brought more devastation to the coasts of northern Sicily and southern Calabria. *The American Experience* called it, "Undeniably the most destructive to ever hit Europe. Most of southern Italy's cities lost as many as half their residents. The population of the city of Messina at 150,000 was reduced to only hundreds; the total Italian death toll was estimated at nearly 200,000." Devastation of the "double catastrophe" was difficult to put in words; photographs provided graphic images of death and devastation.[93]

Aftermath of Messina Earthquake and Tsunami. "Clearing away the ruins on route to Catane, Messina, Italy. Library of Congress Number: LC-USZ62-73718.

The December 1908 earthquake remains "as the most lethal natural disaster in European history." As with many other earthquakes numerous aftershocks, and violent shaking "were reported throughout Sicily." The quake was so intense seismology equipment in the United States "picked up signals of the disaster." *The New York Times* reported "thieves at work setting fires at various points and stealing everything they could lay their hands to, not stopping at robbing the injured as they lay helpless and the dead." Added reports told of looting and

---

[93] "Messina Earthquake," *The American Experience, PBS.org*.

widespread panic. After the earthquake towns were uninhabitable requiring relocation of many of the survivors. The Italian government responded by sending three battleships with military troops "sent to various points to keep down lawlessness." The military was also employed with the unsettling tasks of tearing down unstable buildings in danger of imminent collapse as well as aiding locals in shifting through the debris searching for survivors. In many cases only the dead were recovered from the rubble.[94]

"Corpses of victims of the earthquake in Messina," December 1908, Photo by: Luca Comerio (1878-1940). Public Domain Wiki Commons

For almost all survivors their homes were destroyed along with personal belongings. At the bequest of the Italian government many were relocated to other towns. Refuge was sought anywhere some were reported seeking shelter in the "grottos and caves." For some of the towns, the Italian government authorized erecting dozens of temporary wooden shelters – amounting to nothing more than "shacks;" none of which conducive to any long term recovery. Most remained in place as permanent housing for close to 30 years; some even longer. The inadequate response by the Italian government left many in Calabria and Sicily in contempt; another factor contributing to immigration for many years after the disaster.

---

[94] "Italy Shaked; Thousands Die," *The New York Times*, December 29, 1908, p. 1.

Residual Health Problems and the Coronavirus Pandemic

In 2021, journalist Emma Bubola traced complications of the century old earthquake of broken promises and residual health problems compounded by the Covid-19 pandemic. Bubola stated, "The Messina earthquake might be a thing of the past or thought to have been forgotten. For over 6,500 Italians, the devastation of 1908 was compounded by the Coronavirus Pandemic over 100 years later." Bubola whose grandparents lived through the earthquake recalled the original promises, "more than a century later, about 6,500 Italians still live in makeshift hovels [shacks] scattered around Messina." Large areas of Messina remained an impoverished rat-ridden assemblage of ramshackle shacks, locals knew it as "the slums of the Sicilian city of Messina." With another disaster in 2020-2021 the century-old situation was compounded and "ravaged by a coronavirus (Covid-19) outbreak in December (2020) as the virus spread across the narrow alleys and through the close quarters." As a result, caused by the Coronavirus, sickness and death was much higher in Messina than other areas.

The 1908 earthquake and the worldwide 2020-2021 Covid pandemic literally placed an unimaginable "bookend" of a "pre-existing health emergency of high rates of cancer, asthma, and pneumonia." A study of the 100-year time span revealed the unhealthy conditions lessened the average life expectancy of residents by seven years compared to other non-slum residents of Messina. In 2021, resident, Domenica Cambria age 66, said years ago the government reassurance of the temporary housing made to her grandparents was "Stay for a couple of days." That promise was grossly misleading according to Cambria - "It was for eternity."[95]

L'America

For many of the survivors of the 1908 earthquake, remaining in their place of birth with ancestry dating back centuries was not an option. As historians at *The American Experience* explained, "Others were forced to emigrate to America." In January of 1909, about 850 "survivors" were placed aboard an Italian cargo ship *S.S. Florida* in Naples sailing to Ellis Island. ("Florida" is a town within the Syracuse Province in Sicily.) Some to reunite with family – others with little prospect other than a promise of rebuilding their lives – hopefully, the "American Dream" in *L'America*.[96]

Most likely a sense of hope, wonder, excitement, worry, nervousness, and thankful prayers occupied the minds of the unlikely immigrants during the long Atlantic voyage. About two weeks into the voyage was another tragic occurrence.

---

[95] Emma Bubola. "In Sicily, New Hope for Denizens of Century-Old Shacks," p. A4.
[96] The *S.S. Florida* is not to be confused with the American Battleship *USS Florida* (BB-30) launched in 1910.

While sailing in a "dense fog," the *SS Florida* collided with a British luxury liner *RMS Republic* near the shores of Massachusetts. The *Republic* carrying over 700 passengers was hit broadside by the *SS Florida*; causing six deaths, many injuries, and pandemonium. Some of the *Republic's* passengers were transferred to the damaged *Florida* which stayed afloat. After receiving a radio messenger from the distressed ships, a liner the *SS Baltic* was sent as a rescue ship, successfully removing the remaining passengers. The *Republic* sank as both the *Baltic* and *Florida* made their way safely to New York.[97]

The tragic accident was not without many ironic coincidences. The rescue was made possible by a radio message sent from the luxury liner *Republic* delivered on a newly installed wireless device invented by the Italian Guglielmo Marconi (1874-1937). The radio call was considered the first time any such device of its kind was employed for rescue at sea. For those in America, who soon heard of the disaster (most likely by wireless transmission), a relief program was undertaken in New York City for collection of clothing and supplies. The "relief supplies for the survivors of Italy's Messina earthquake" were in the cargo hold of *RMS Republic* sailing west from America heading towards the Mediterranean and sunk with the supplies onboard its cargo hold.[98]

The *RMS Republic* which collided with the *SS Florida* and eventually sank. Public Domain under Wiki Creative Commons. Author: Conklinj.

---

[97] "Messina Earthquake," *The American Experience, PBS.org*.
[98] See also: "Messina Earthquake," *The American Experience, PBS.org,*

Photo of the *SS Florida* built by Martin & Ottaway, a New Jersey marine consulting firm, after the two ships collided. (Dated July 28, 1915).

Italians on the *RMS Titanic* and Marconi's Wireless Transmission

The *RMS Republic* was built only a few years earlier in 1903 at the Harland & Wolff shipyards in Belfast, Ireland. Two months after the tragic sinking, in the same Harland & Wolff shipyard, on March 31, 1909 the keel was laid for the ill-fated *RMS Titanic*. During its maiden voyage, the *Titanic* struck an iceberg, sinking on April 15, 1912. Of the 2,207 passengers and crew only 712 survived. About one-third of the passengers (over 700) were immigrants in third-class steerage. An estimated 530 immigrants perished; most in lock-down of the lower level ordered by a ship steward. Many of the immigrants were from the United Kingdom, however, Italians were also on board that fateful voyage.

Despite a lost ship passenger, possibly a dozen Italians were below among the third-class passengers. Other Italians were employed above deck as staff the elegant First-class restaurants; and a few others. As noted in *Italics* magazine, Andrea Angelini described the "tragedy within the tragedy" as,

> "The total number of Italians on the Titanic was 43, but only 11 of those were passengers. The remaining 32 were crew members, all part of the

CHAPTER 2

restaurant staff. None of them survived the disaster. Considering that the Titanic's restaurant *À la Carte* employed 66 workers, half French and half Italian, and only three of them survived, we can say that it was a tragedy within the tragedy. The White Star Line, owner of the Titanic, chose the Italian Luigi Gatti to manage its restaurant aboard, both for the great tradition of Italian cuisine and his esteemed skills as a restaurateur. Luigi Gatti, born near Pavia in Lombardy, owned two popular restaurants in London and, for Titanic's maiden voyage, the right manager to delight the discerning palates of first-class passengers."[99]

Andrea Angelini discovered of the 11 Italian passengers only 5 survived the unthinkable disaster. Two other Italians survived by a twist of fate, one a restaurant worker arrived too late. Another decided not to board the ship.

Another famous Italian was on board, although in name only; Guglielmo Marconi who created a workable wireless radio communication system. As described by *RF Café*, a tech news website,

"Marconi played a critical role in without actually being aboard, since his company Marconi Wireless Telegraph Company, owned the radio equipment aboard the *Titanic* and also employed the two radio operators."[100]

Unlike the wireless distress calls from *RMS Titanic*, which were mostly ignored, the wireless transmission on *RMS Republic* in 1909 was picked up and credited with saving at least 1,500 passengers. Added to the ironic twist of fate, Marconi was scheduled for the fateful *Titanic* voyage, opting out before the ship departed. Instead, Marconi chose to cross the Atlantic to America on the *RMS Lusitania* an ironic twist of fate as the *Lusitania* was torpedoed and sunk in May 1915.

In January 1915, another deadly earthquake hit Italy at Abruzzo. As journalists Caryn A. Wilson and Patrick Boehler recalled,

"A devastating temblor destroyed the town of Avezzano, killing 30,000 people. Only 5 percent of the town's residents survived. Many died in the bitter winter cold. Because of World War I, the country declined offers of foreign aid, complicating the response to the disaster."[101]

The stories of death and destruction such as in Abruzzo in 1915 are often lost in history. Some lived on through the ancestry of Italian immigrants. On the 100th

---

[99] Andrea Angelini "How Many Italians Were on the Titanic?" *Italics Magazine*, May 16, 2020. Note: Full name of the restaurant manager was Gaspare Antonio Pietro "Luigi" Gatti (1875-1912) born in Montalto Pavese, Italy.
[100] "Titanic Radio, Compliments of Marconi Wireless Telegraph Company," *RF Café.com*, March 15, 2020.
[101] Caryn A. Wilson and Patrick Boehler. "Italy's History of Deadly Earthquakes," *The New York Times*, August 24, 2016.

anniversary of the tragic 1908 earthquake John Bemelmans Marciano recalled how the Messina earthquake was cause for his birth in America. Marciano's grandfather Lorenzo often spoke of the tragic path to America. Marciano recalled the irony of the earthquake only a few days after Christmas, but on December 28; an important Catholic holiday the "Feast of the Slaughter of the Innocents." The day when Herod's men were sent out to kill the first born.

ESSAY: A Deadly Wave, A Lucky Star
By: John Bemelmans Marciano

One hundred years ago, the life of my grandfather Lorenzo took a tragic and extraordinary turn. December 28th marks the Feast of the Slaughter of the Innocents on the Catholic calendar. Once the final day of the Christmas season, it signaled, by 1908, a return to normal life, as children were headed back to school and parents to work for the first time in weeks. Alarm clocks were set the night before, at the end of a Sunday that had been uncommonly cold and gloomy across southern Italy, so much so that people forsook the traditional visits to friends and family and stayed home. My grandfather's family would not have ventured out in any event, because that night they welcomed a new addition, another sister for 10-year-old Lorenzo his sixth to go along with his little brother, Giuseppe.

My grandfather lived in Pellaro, a small town just south of Reggio di Calabria on the Strait of Messina. His family lived alongside that of his uncle, aunt and five cousins in the Via Madonella, a road that dead-ended into a sandy beach. His childhood was idyllic: the sea right outside his door to play in, Mount Etna rising fantastically across the blue-black waters. That late-December morning, Pellaro smelled strongly of perfume; it was harvest time for the bergamot, the small citrus fruit that is the principal ingredient in all manner of cologne and grown only on this narrow strip of the Calabrian coast.

Lorenzo was awakened shortly before the dawn, not by his alarm but by the loud low rumble of the earth and the awful crashing that followed. Living in an area recently wracked by earthquakes, most people immediately knew what was happening. During seismic events the majority of deaths are caused by people's homes collapsing in on them a fate suffered by few in Pellaro, which was a sparsely built farming community.

People gathered near the water, thinking it the safest place to be, but 10 minutes after the main shock the sea began to recede from shore. Boats at anchor tottered and hit bottom. There were two words in Italian to describe what was happening, one native (*maremoto*) the other

CHAPTER 2

borrowed from Japanese (*tsunami*). There was no time to outrun the water, but someone pushed my grandfather up into an olive tree along with his little brother, whom Lorenzo held onto with all his strength. The roar of the sea was deafening the tidal wave crested at more than 40 feet and fight though Lorenzo did, the impact broke his clutch on Giuseppe.

No one will ever know how long my grandfather wandered the ruined coast, calling out the names of his brother, of his family. Everything Lorenzo had ever known was destroyed. The land beneath his neighborhood collapsed and fell, Atlantis-like, into the sea. The Church of the Madonella was open to the sky, a boat docked in its altar. Farther up the beach, a crack in the earth revealed ancient Greco-Roman tombs, still intact.

Across the straits, Messina one of the most ancient cities in Europe had been annihilated. More than 50,000 were dead. It took only a few hours for civilization to break down among the survivors. Looting ran rampant; thieves cut fingers from the dead rather than waste time prying their rings off. Marconi's new radio transmitter at the mouth of the strait had gone silent, and many believed themselves to be the only people left alive, anywhere.

The 1908 earthquake is the most lethal natural disaster in recorded European history. Nearly 100,000 people perished, including all 16 of my grandfather's relatives in Via Madonella. The response of the royal Italian government makes FEMA's effort in New Orleans look like a model of efficiency. Most disgracefully, the shacks built as temporary shelter for the homeless would remain occupied for 30 years while the reconstruction dragged on. My grandfather himself was shuffled among relatives in Calabria before boarding the steamer Europa in 1921 to seek a better life in America.

Grampa, who died in 1990, always said he had been born under a lucky star. I assumed this belief was the sign of an earlier, more stoic generation. In fact, it was not. People went insane with grief over the events of Dec. 28, 1908. But a few survivors came away from the experience with the knowledge that they had stared apocalypse in the face and found the strength to come through it. And, having done so, they could endure anything including arriving in America with little money and even less English, and raising eight children through a Depression and a war against their home country. Grampa's lucky star was in fact mine, and my brothers,' and all our cousins.'

Italian Culture in America:
The Immigrants 1880 to 1930 From Discrimination to Assimilation

John Bemelmans Marciano is the author and illustrator of "Madeline and the Cats of Rome." Originally published as an Op-Ed in *The New York Times*, December 27, 2008.

In the aftermath of the 1908 earthquake, Pope Pius X (1835 -1914) spoke of a recent earthquake occurring in the same region only three years before. Caryn and Boehler's article did not include the earthquake which also struck Calabria on September 8, 1905. A recap by the *BBC News* in "Italy's Earthquake History," cited, "An earthquake obliterated 25 villages in the Calabria region, killing about 5,000 people." The natural disaster at Calabria registered at 7.2 magnitude was "the first major earthquake of the 20th century." The quake also caused damage in nearby Messina and the Lipari in the Aeolian Islands in the Tyrrhenian Sea north of Sicily. A significant disaster in its own right with reports of widespread destruction and death obliterating at least 25 villages in the Calabria Region alone. The *BBC News* placed the total death toll closer to 5,000. Even the worst natural disasters in Europe overlooked, it can be understandable why earlier earthquakes would be lost to modern memory.[102]

Similar to Marciano, my grandparents suffered under the similar circumstances; none as directly as my maternal grandma Annina "Anna" Colacino; born on that fateful day of September 8, 1905 in Catanzaro in Calabria. My grandma was only one who endured years of poverty after the earthquake, eventually heeding a call to America. On August 31, 1920, "Grandma Anna," with mother Maria Paone departed Italy, passing her 15th birthday enroute to Ellis Island to settle in Brooklyn with family. Italians such as Anna Colacino, and thousands of other earthquake survivors, joined millions of their *paisans* who emigrated to America. Many others left very soon after the tragedy, while others such as Anna Colacino's family attempted to endure. Eventually many immigrated years later. Regardless of the circumstances, whether it was tragedy, poverty, or simply hearing of the "American Dream," all anxiously awaited their arrival at Ellis Island and a cherished glimpse of the Statue of Liberty.

---

[102] *"Italy's Earthquake History." BBC News. October 31, 2002.*

CHAPTER 2

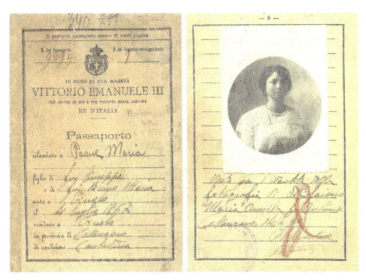

Copy of original Italian passport issued in 1920 to 15-year-old Anna Colacino (author's maternal grandmother) accompanied on the voyage by great grandmother Maria Paone.

The author reliving a scene remembered by millions of immigrants, including all four of his Italian grandparents, as their ship passed the Statue of Liberty enroute to disembarking at nearby Ellis Island. The sight of "Lady Liberty" confirmed they had reached America. (Photo: Thelma Olsen c. 2018).

Lady Liberty, *European Garbage Ships,* and William Windom

Not all Americans welcomed the iconic image of Lady Liberty as did the immigrants. Nativists viewed immigrants as literal *"wretched refuse"* as in the Lazarus poem. As the U.S. National Park Service revealed,

> "Connections drawn between the Statue of Liberty and immigration were not always positive. Nativists linked the Statue to immigration most starkly in political cartoons critiquing foreigners' threats to American liberties and values. They portrayed the monument as a symbol of a nation besieged by pollution, housing shortages, disease, and the onslaught of anarchists, communists, and other alleged subversives."[103]

In the years leading up to the official dedication of Bartholdi's statue on October 28, 1886, Lady Liberty was widely publicized and anticipated. Information was disseminated through daily newspapers published as a morning, afternoon, and evening edition. Within the national realm were weekly illustrated news magazines including *Frank Leslie's Illustrated* and *Harper's Weekly.* Each followed Lady Liberty's progress publishing updated detailed images awaiting arrival of the gift from France.

A sample of illustrations traced the progress of construction. Examples included the widely circulated and popular *Harper's Weekly* and *Frank Leslie's Illustrated Newspaper*, among others. Each were well-established chroniclers of contemporary American popular culture. Some of the illustrations included the statue in scaffolding, flame, foot, and a portrait of Frederic Bartholdi published in 1884. Another in 1885 reported on, "The torch of the Statue of 'Liberty,' as it will appear when completed." An 1886 updates included, "preparing the Statue of 'liberty' on Bedloe's Island, for the formal unveiling on October 28th - Present condition of the work."

---

[103] "The Immigrant's Statue." *National Park Service*, February 26, 2015. Accessed September 30, 2020.

CHAPTER 2

Many news outlets publicized the pending arrival of the Statue of Liberty. Shown here is the widely circulated *Frank Leslie's Illustrated* of June 13, 1885, Vol. LX No. 1,551. The caption reads: 1. Official presentation of the Statue of "Liberty enlightening the world," Paris, July 4th, 1884; 2. M. Frédéric-Auguste Bartholdi [head and shoulders]; 3. Sectional view of statue, showing iron core and braces. France, - America – The Gift of the French Republic to the United States. (Library of Congress Prints and Photographs Division. Reproduction Number: LC-USZ62-60764.)

Not all American magazines praised the French gift. As the U.S. National Parks Service described, "When a new immigrant processing station was proposed on Bedloe's Island in 1890, a cartoon in *Judge* depicted the Statue as 'the future emigrant lodging house.'" The illustration promoted "fears about the immigrants' threat to the liberty it represented." The cover of the *Judge* image of March 22, 1890 portrayed Liberty as "The Proposed Emigrant Dumping Site;" of the Statue raising her robe in protection as newcomers from "European Garbage ships" dumped at her feet."[104]

A political cartoon, "The Proposed Emigrant Dumping Site" *Judge* Magazine Cover, March 22, 1890 (Public Domain).

---

[104] "The Immigrant's Statue." *National Park Service*, February 26, 2015.

CHAPTER 2   83

In the image, two ships are shown delivering – literally "dumping" – new immigrants onto the United States. One ship named "Refuse;" with flag flying reads "European Garbage Ship." In the background is a building labeled "U.S. Treasury;" looking out over the water to Lady Liberty is William Windom. Another ship is also labeled "European Garbage Ship." Both ships are employing a Scoop and Dump machine dropping boatloads of undesirable immigrants at the feet of Lady Liberty who appears displeased; lifting her robe as to not get soiled by the refuse and garbage. The sarcastic caption has the her saying – "Mr. Windom, if you are going to make this island a garbage heap, I am going back to France." The reference to "Mr. Windom" is lost to all but a few in American history; at the time William Windom (1827-1891) was a well-known national public figure as the 33rd U.S. Secretary of the Treasury, a former member of Congress and Senator from Minnesota.[105]

William Windom is less a trivial item as a major figure connected with the history of U.S. immigration. Under Windom's guidance, the system was revamped as Castle Clinton was closed; with a proposed relocation to Ellis Island. The issue often placed him as the subject of parody and sarcasm in political cartoons such as in *Judge*. The common political satire theme "cast him as their primary villain, and evil threat to American economic and ethnic integrity." A review of all Windom cartoons in *Puck* and *Judge* were "inherently vicious and fundamentally dishonest." The historical "fear" throughout American history was always concern with a "loss of jobs" taken away by immigrants. The reality placed immigrants at the lowest stratum of American society, employed at low-paying jobs and labor others refused.[106]

Italians "the filthy, wretched, lazy, ignorant, and criminal dregs."

As a massive influx of new Italians immigrants entered America, a large majority settled in Industrialized cities. As the 20th century began, cities throughout the nation experienced a population boom. New York was most populous and densely crowded. In 1898, as with the five boroughs incorporated into the city of New York the total population was 3.4 million people. Chicago numbered 1.7 million and Philadelphia at 1.3 million. The next three most populated cities were St. Louis, Boston, and Baltimore that each numbered over 500,000.[107]

---

[105] *Judge* magazine, March 22, 1890. Vol 17, No. 440. Accessed October 3, 2020.
[106] Roger A. Fischer. "William Windom Cartoon Centerfold 1881-91," pp. 107-108.
[107] U.S. Census Bureau. *Statistical Abstract of the United States: 2000*. Washington D.C., 1999, Tables, 10, 12, 13.

"Anti-Italian cartoon published in *The Mascot* (New Orleans newspaper), September 7, 1889. **Upper Left**: "A Nuisance to Pedestrians;" Middle: "Their Sleeping Apartments;" **Upper Right**: "Afternoon's Pleasant Diversions;" **Bottom Left**: "The Wat to Dispose of Them;" **Bottom Right**: "The Way to Arrest Them." (Public Domain)

After Italian unification a social division was more evident between the prosperous and "cultured north" of Renaissance tradition in contrast to the rural peasants of southern Italy and Sicily. A division easily noticeable by visitors such as the prominent African American Booker T. Washington. In 1910, Washington toured Italy and Sicily; an account published in his memoir *The Man Farthest Down* stated,

> "I learned in Italy was that the people in northern Italy look down upon the people of southern Italy as an inferior race. In fact, nothing that I have known or heard about the Negro people in America compares with what I heard about the superstition of the Italian peasants."[108]

That division was not only evident in Italy, but also in the United States. One example in 1880 of the American perception of impoverished Italian immigrants appeared in *The New York Times*. A critical Op-Ed concerned an incoming steerage ship the *Italia* carrying over 750 Italian immigrants held in port due to a

---

[108] Booker T. Washington. *The Man Farthest Down: A Record of Observation and Study in Europe*, New York: Doubleday, Page & Co. 1912, pp. 109-10.

CHAPTER 2

suspected onboard infection of tuberculous. The editors sought to ask "authorities" empowered to "have power" to refuse port of entry to such cargo which *The New York Times* described as "the filthy, wretched, lazy, ignorant, and criminal dregs of the meanest section of Italy, and infected with a terrible disease into the bargain." More accusations claimed Italians "stab and murder on so slight provocation." Derogatory words were routinely applied such as "degraded beings," and free use of calling all Italians "criminals."[109]

Despite the Negativity –
They Came – Over Four Million Strong

Prior to 1880, Italian immigration from southern Europe was almost non-existent. The *Statistical Abstract of the United States* from 1820 to 1859 listed only 13,289 Italian immigrants (a low of only 3 in 1832 and 9 in 1830 – the high number was 1,699 in 1833). The 20-year period of 1860 to 1879 numbered 56,149. The numbers steadily increased with Italians leaving their homeland in record numbers. The total American immigration soon numbered over 4.6 million.[110]

ITALIAN IMMIGRANT POPULATION TO AMERICA[111]

YEARS	NUMBER
1880 - 1889	270,000
1890 – 1899	700,000
1900 – 1914	3,000,000
1915 – 1919	125,000
1920 – 1930	550,000
TOTAL	**4,645,000**

Immigration tapered off during the First World War as immigration from all nations was severely limited. One consistent, discrimination and anti-immigrant sentiment continued. Historian Lesley Kennedy explained, "Most immigrants came from Europe, and many white, Protestant Americans feared these immigrants couldn't "assimilate." Catholic immigrants from southern and eastern Europe were supposedly too culturally different." Discrimination focused on immigrant "foreign" culture leading to concerns of Italian anarchists and fascists supposedly permeating among working class people. In 1919, President Woodrow Wilson, added to the discriminatory rhetoric, proclaiming, "Any man who carries a hyphen about with him, carries a dagger that he is ready to plunge into the vitals of this Republic when he gets ready."[112]

---

[109] "Undesirable Immigrants," *The New York Times*, December 18, 1880, p. 4.
[110] "Italian Immigration," *Digital History* 2019.
[111] U. S. Census Historical Statistic of the United States 1789 to 1945, pp. 18-19. Numbers are rounded to the nearest 10,000.
[112] Lesley Kennedy. "U.S. Immigration History," *History.com,* April 19, 2109.

Many others in America associated the Italian cultural aspect of drinking wine with alcoholism and crime. Another false myth for the call for national Prohibition as explained by Prof. Kennedy said,

> "White Protestant men in the Anti-Saloon League—many of whom would go on to join the new Ku Klux Klan [KKK] after 1915—argued that the U.S. needed to pass a Prohibition amendment before these new immigrants acquired more voting power. During the 1920s, the KKK [Ku Klux Klan] gained millions of members by advertising itself as a vigilante police force that would keep Catholic immigrants from countries like Italy in line."[113]

Those who entered Ellis Island experienced upon entry into the main floor for processing immigrants alone, in groups, or with family were split into two sections – women and children under 16 to one area – men to another. A large majority (about 98 percent) of immigrants passed through without experiencing delay. Any immigrant examined having a disease or medical condition was transported to a quarantine facility. Through it all, immigrants of all nations realized they were in a foreign land therefore, uncertainty was always a concern. As noted, "Regulations were confusing, the crowds disorienting, the officials rushed. The moment of departure, when successful immigrants boarded ferries for New York City or destinations further west, came as a tremendous relief." The transfer for those immigrants heading to parts of the United States "further west" boarded a ferry to nearby Jersey City, directly accessing a railroad station for travel to other parts of the nation. Some estimates indicate about half of all Italian immigrants who passed through Ellis Island eventually returned to Italy – some temporarily others permanently. The *U.S. Library of Congress* reports, "Within five years, between 30 and 50 percent of this generation of immigrants would return home to Italy, where they were known as *ritornati*." For Italian immigrants who remained in America, almost all maintained "close contact with their family in the old country, and worked hard in order to have money to send back home."[114]

---

[113] See: Woodrow Wilson. "Address at the city Hall Auditorium in Pueblo Colorado," September 25, 1919. Becky Little. "How the Immigrants Who Came to Ellis Island in 1907 Compare to Arrivals Today," *History.com* April 22, 2019.
[114] Nicholas P. Ciotola. "Ellis Island." In *Italian Americans: The History and Culture of a People*, p. 16. "*L'Isola dell Lagrime*," Immigration and Relocation in U.S. History.

"U.S. inspectors examining eyes of immigrants, Ellis Island,
New York Harbor," c. 1913. Number: LC-USZ62-7386. Library of Congress.

One of the most often published photos of the immigrant experience The
caption read: "Italian Immigrant at Ellis Island – 1905" by Lewis Hines
(1874-1940). Public Domain.

Immigrants completed the processing and awaiting a boat for transfer to either Jersey City or New York, c. 1912. Published: New York: Underwood & Underwood. Library of Congress Reproduction No: LC-USZ62-11203.

Central Railroad Terminal of New Jersey Station City (now Liberty State Park) waterfront extension in Jersey City. Built in 1889, estimates range as high as 12.5 million immigrants traveled to distant parts of mainland America heading "further west" through this portal. (Photograph by: Thelma Olsen c. 2017).

The Lazaretto in Philadelphia

Ellis Island in New York is the most famous immigration station in America; it was not the only one. Less than 100 miles to the south along the same Atlantic coast was the "Lazaretto" serving as an immigrant point of entry to the city of Philadelphia within the Tinicum Township along the Delaware River. "Lazaretto" is an Italian word for a maritime quarantine station "designed to protect ports from seafaring pathogens."

In simpler terms, defined as "an isolation hospital for people with infectious diseases, especially leprosy or plague." In 1403, in response to the ravages of the

Black Death, a quarantine hospital named for Saint Lazarus was built on a small outlying island of Venice in Italy. The word "lazaretto" is derived from the Biblical Lazarus as the patron saint of the poor and sick. Located on another of the smaller outlying islands of Venice was the *Santa Maria da Nazareth*, "most likely the first of the quarantine Lazaretto's." (The Tinicum Township cites the history of the Lazaretto as an "official" quarantine station dating to 1423 in Italy.) The first restrictions placed a 40-day isolation period for any individual "suffering from a plague, disease, or possible contagion." The number "40" in Italian is *"quaranta"* which translates directly as the root derivative of the word "quarantine."

The main building of the Philadelphia Lazaretto built in the Georgian architectural style remains "the oldest surviving quarantine facility in the Western Hemisphere, and the sixth oldest in the world."

Aerial view of the Lazaretto located in the Tinicum Township of Philadelphia, alongside the Delaware River, c. 1929. Note: Arrow indicates location of main building. (Aero Services, negative #11578) Philadelphia Free Library Print and Picture Department (The Library Company of Philadelphia).

Peter Sammartino, Sister Margherita Marchione, and Philip Mazzei

Ellis Island transitioned from a government agency processing immigrants to one of the most difficult transitions as an American cultural center, tourist destination, and valuable resource for Americans to trace their ancestry. After Ellis Island closed it was abandoned and fell into disrepair. During the early 1970s, a restoration project for public tours was initiated by Dr. Peter Sammartino, president and founder of Fairleigh Dickenson University. In 1976, a committee chaired by Sammartino secured an important contribution to the Restore Ellis Island Committee allowing a partial reopening to visitors. Added to Sammartino's biography, "Today, this beautiful national shrine serves as a tribute to not just those who journeyed to this country, but to the ideals of the nation itself."[115]

Peter Sammartino (1904-1992), born in New Jersey son of Italian immigrants, was a life-long educator. In 1942, with wife Sylvia ("Sally") they founded Fairleigh Dickinson University (FDU) in Rutherford New Jersey. A tribute by *FDU Magazine* on the occasion of his death recounted his involvement in the restoration of Ellis Island, citing Sammartino "was the personification of the American Dream as a leader of the restoration project whose parents passed through Ellis Island as immigrants."

Professor Walter Savage said, Peter and Sally were "one in deed and dream." The dream started within an experimental school at Columbia University's Teachers College." Included were the innovated ideas of students gaining real-life "hands- on" experience "by working in business, about social concerns by working in the community and about global issues by studying abroad." Peter and Sally Sammartino combined the experimental teaching concept "with a strong liberal arts education" as the central focus in the founding of Fairleigh Dickinson University (FDU). Added within Sammartino's FDU obituary, "Few men of this modern era could be said to have had more impact on the life of this state [New Jersey], and even the nation, than this man who created Fairleigh Dickinson University, instigated the saving and restoration of Ellis Island, [and] provided a haven for scholars."

At FDU, Sammartino published 25 books on wide ranging topics; some on his Italian heritage. Farleigh Dickinson University was preceded by others founded by Italians. In 1877, Italian Jesuits established Regis University in New Mexico. Earlier, in 1886, a Sephardic Jewish Italian immigrant Rabbi Sabato Morais was among the founders of the Jewish Theological Seminary of

---

[115] Nicholas P. Ciotola "Ellis Island." In *Italian Americans: The History and Culture of a People*, Eric Martone, editor (ABC-Clio 2017), pp. 15-17.

America in New York. Another Jesuit Giuseppe Cataldo in Spokane, Washington founded Gonzaga University in 1887.[116]

An important colleague to the Sammartino's at FDU was a devoted nun and author Sister Margherita Marchione (1922-2021) who published a series of significant books of Italian culture. Among those, Marchione authored seven important books on Philip Mazzei, including,

- *My Life and Wanderings: The Story of an Eighteenth-Century World Citizen (1980);*
- *Philip Mazzei: World Citizen (1994); and*
- *The Adventurous Life of Philip Mazzei (1995).*

Philip Mazzei, (1730-1816) born in Tuscany, Italy; emigrated to America in 1773. The relocation was to join Thomas Jefferson in a wine making venture. Mazzei, in support of the American Revolution, became, in Jefferson's words, a "Zealous Whig." The pair became close life-long friends; often consulting on many issues from wine making to envisioning a unique version of American liberty. The most poignant collaboration came in 1774 in an article published in *The Virginia Gazzette* newspaper worded in Italian. Mazzei, using the pen-name "Furioso" wrote,

> *"Tutti gli uomini sono per natura egualmente liberi e indipendenti. Quest'*
> *eguaglianza è necessaria per costituire un governo libero.*
> *Bisogna che ognuno sia uguale all' altro nel diritto naturale."*

Thomas Jefferson provided the translation underneath Mazzei's as,

> "All men are by nature equally free and independent.
> Such equality is necessary to constitute a free government.
> Everyone must be equal to the other in natural law."

The English translation is not exactly "all men are created equal." Yet, in this entry we find the inspiration for the Declaration of Independence.

In 2013, Sister Marchione donated over 2,500 items on Philip Mazzei to The Thomas Jefferson Foundation at Monticello. Among the collection was *Americans of Italian Heritage*, described as, "This volume memorializes the accomplishments of key figures among the Italian-Americans of the twentieth century. They are the descendants of Italian immigrants and, through their achievements, bear witness to the sacrifice and valor of their forefathers." Marchione's autobiography *The Fighting Nun: My Story* recounts her birth in New Jersey as one of eight children born to immigrant parents from Campania, Italy. In 1935, Marchione joined the Religious Teachers Filippini; earned a PhD

---

[116] Vincent A. Lapomarda, "Higher Education," in *The Italian American Experience*, p.286. See also: "Peter Sammartino: A Tribute." *FDU Magazine*. Winter/Spring 2005.

from Columbia University and joined Farleigh Dickinson University as Professor of Italian language and literature.[117]

Left to Right: – Sister Margherita Marchione, Peter Sammartino, and Sally Sammartino (Courtesy of Fairleigh Dickinson University Library)

---

[117] Sister Margherita Marchione, "Book Summary," Google Books. Katharine Q. Seelye. "Sister Margherita Marchione, 99," *The New York Times*, May 31, 2021, p. B7.

CHAPTER 3

ANTI-IMMIGRATION, DISCRIMINATION, AND LYNCHING

"Those who know statistics about lynching are aware that the victims are Black people. Europeans have not been lynched except for Italians only." Il Progresso Italo-Americano, 1910

The U.S. Library of Congress cites Italian immigrants during the 1890s as "Under Attack." Situations involving violence increased against Italian immigrants. Struggles during the years of immigration came with an onslaught of "virulent prejudice and nativist hostility." The Library of Congress explained the historical significance as,

> "During the years of the great Italian immigration, they also had to confront a wave of virulent prejudice and nativist hostility. As immigration from Europe and Asia neared its crest in the late 19th century, anti-immigrant sentiment soared along with it. The U.S. was in the grips of an economic depression, and immigrants were blamed for taking American jobs. At the same time, racialist theories circulated in the press, advancing pseudo-scientific theories that alleged that "Mediterranean" types were inherently inferior to people of northern European heritage. Drawings and songs caricaturing the new immigrants as childlike, criminal, or subhuman became [all to] sadly commonplace."[118]

Historian Norman Simms writing a journal article "The Italian-American Image During the Twentieth Century," provided a poignant aspect in the acceptance and non-acceptance of Italian culture in America. A detailed analysis from 1880 to 1920, of the arriving Italians was explained as,

---

[118] "The Great Arrival," *The Library of Congress*.

"Few serious attempts were made to discuss how the Italian culture made the source of a man's pride his family and his honor, not his job. Despite the strong prejudices of this era, the Italian-American would face increasing prejudice in the years to come."[119]

"Sticks and stones may break my bones. But words will *always* hurt me"

In a reversal of a popular children's taunt, which claimed "Stick and stones may break my bones. But words will never hurt me" – at least for Italians, both were particularly damaging. "Words" continually hurt the Italian image and permeated a false imagery for well over a century. As for the "sticks and stones" – the violence was beyond mere "hurt" – amounting to lynching of many innocent Italian and Sicilian immigrants. As the Library of Congress added,

"Attacks on Italians were not limited to the printed page, however. From the late 1880s, anti-immigrant societies sprang up around the country, and the Ku Klux Klan saw a spike in membership. Catholic churches and charities were vandalized and burned, and Italians attacked by mobs. In the 1890s alone, more than 20 Italians were lynched."[120]

Anti-Immigrant Sentiment and "Dagoes"

Historical documents often used the phrase "anti-immigrant sentiment" to describe oppression against recently arrived "foreigners." It would take many volumes to discuss, or even list, the dozens – hundreds – and thousands of uses; as just another example of American cultural "sugar-coating" of legal atrocities perpetrated upon a different cultural or ethnic group. So-called "patriotic" organizations as the Ku Klux Klan and White Nationalists, for example, were often described with *nicety* words as "militia" or "fraternal group." They were never described as "domestic terrorists," "hate mongers," or truly demonstrating the essence of "anti-American." Images of the day often portrayed the KKK as "saviors" against immigrants, Catholics, Jews, among other "undesirables."

By the 1880s, many Italian cultural aspects were firmly established within the American ethos; yet the arrival of the large masses of supposedly "non-cultured" Italian immigrants – along with their Catholic faith was cause for discrimination. In retrospect, very few (even among Italian Americans) are aware of the mis-treatment and atrocities against Italian immigrants during the period of 1880 to 1930. One simple example is provided from the collection of the *Italian*

---

[119] Norman Simms (2019) "The Italian-American Image During the Twentieth Century," The Histories: Vol. 5: Issue 1, Article 4. La Salle University Digital Commons.
[120] "Under Attack." Immigration and Relocation in U.S. History, Library of Congress.

CHAPTER 3

American Museum of Los Angeles. A Public Notice of daily wages for workers on New York City's Croton Reservoir, 1895, listed the following wage scale,

Common labor, **White:** $1.30-$1.50
Common labor, **Colored:** $1.25-$1.40
Common labor, **Italian:** $1.15-$1.25

One newspaper, *The Pacific Commercial Advertiser* in Honolulu (at the time the Hawaiian Islands were a territorial possession) recapped a series of Louisiana lynchings of Italians and Sicilians during the 1890s. In an 1899 article on the discrimination, the editors discovered, in Louisiana,

"The position of the Italian in Louisiana is very anomalous because of the race, or, rather, the negro, question. Neither the whites nor the negroes know how to class him, he is, as it were, a link connecting the white and black races."

Despite the attempt to classify the Italian immigrant population as "white," the editors explained the population of Louisiana held a view of three distinct classifications of race. "The average man will classify the population as whites, dagoes, and negroes."[121]

Another on display in the Los Angeles Museum of a brief transcript on discussing Italian immigration within the U.S. Congress.

"During a Congressional hearing in the 1890s, a member of the committee asked a construction boss, "You don't call an Italian a white man?" "No sir," the boss replied, "An Italian is a dago."[122]

As common public usage, derogatory names attached to various ethnic immigrant groups are damaging in many ways. Wanton usage of words such as "*dago*" should not necessarily be routinely dismissed as innocent. A search of *Merriam-Webster* defines the word as,

da·go | \ ˈdā-(ˌ)gō \ *plural* dagos *or* dagoes

Definition of *dago offensive* used as an insulting and contemptuous term for a person of Italian birth or descent

The first recorded use of the derogatory word dates to 1832, in the same meaning as defined by *Merriam-Webster.*

Congressional response to derogatory references of immigrants was quite common. Brent Staples, writing an article "How Italians Became White" for *The New York Times*, analyzed,

---

[121] "Experience on Louisiana Plantations." *Pacific Commercial Advertiser.* 22 Aug. 1899. *Chronicling America: Historic American Newspapers.* Library of Congress.
[122] Marianna Gatto. "Dago! A History of Anti-Italianism."

> "Congress envisioned a white, Protestant and culturally homogeneous America when it declared in 1790 that only 'free white persons, who have, or shall migrate into the United States' were eligible to become naturalized citizens."

For the duration of the first 100 years the vision of the United States remained as planned with legal slavery; the second 100 years or so by legal segregation.[123]

In 1906, John Carr writing a sympathetic article "The Coming of the Italian," for *Outlook* magazine summarized the discrimination and stereotyping endured by Italian immigrants as,

> "In common with Mexicans and Jews, the Italians are pilloried by insulting nicknames. They are charged with pauperism, crime, and degraded living. These short and sturdy laborers, who swing along the streets with their heavy stride early in the morning and late at night, deserve better of the country. He comes because the country has the most urgent need of unskilled labor."[124]

The Pacific Commercial Advertiser reasoned Italians grouped among the "negro" class was due to an Italian ambivalence to adherence of the legal rules of segregation. Explained in the newspaper as,

> "On the other hand, they [Italians] are willing to live in the same quarters with the negroes and to work side by side with them, and seem wholly destitute of that anti-negro prejudice which is one of the distinguishing features of all the white races in the South."

In stark contrast to the United States views, Hawaii, which viewed Italians as "white" could not understand the discrimination against the Europeans was "difficult to understand." More so than others, Hawaiians understood discrimination by white colonial occupation. White plantation owners in Louisiana, saw Italians as cheap labor; not equal in social class. As *The Pacific Commercial Advertiser* noted, "The Italians seem to be the only race that can labor successfully and compete with the negro in the semi-tropical climate of Louisiana."

During the 1890s, Italian immigrants numbered as "the largest foreign element in the population of Louisiana." With a willingness to work the fields and a tolerance to the "semi-tropical" climate conducive to malaria conditions, Italians were a natural replacement. The largest number of settlers into Louisiana and the Mississippi Delta area was comprised mainly of Italian immigrants mostly from

---

[123] Brent Staples. "How Italians Became White." *The New York Times,* October 12, 2019.
[124] Jane Addams. *Hull House Maps and Papers* (1895), cited in "Italians – The Great Arrival – Immigration," *U.S. Library of Congress*, Accessed December 5, 2020.

CHAPTER 3 97

Sicily. In total contrast to the published accounts of Italians, an analysis by *The Pacific Commercial Advertiser* of Honolulu stated,

> "They make good laborers and give Italian perfect satisfaction to the planters, being infinitely superior to the negroes. The Louisiana planters have been for years trying to get some substitute for the negroes. The Italians come nearest to fulfilling all conditions. They are well satisfied with their wages and save money where the negro cannot. They do not drink, and cause little trouble. They are willing to live in the same cabins as the negroes and to work with them in the fields on equal terms, and they work hard and faithfully. In spite of the prejudices that exist, the mob out-breaks and the lynchings, the Italian is rapidly solving the negro problem in Louisiana."[125]

In contrast, Italian immigrants who settled within the larger cities work was found in the produce business, grocery shops, shoe making, or as push cart peddlers, among other ventures. All Italian and Sicilian immigrants possessed an insatiable desire to work; no matter how hard the physical task. Many found work as day laborer's known as "pick and shovel men" digging tunnels for the New York City Subway system, or the many roads, and railroads, across America. A significant number of Italian immigrants settled in rural areas. In one specific reference of Italians of New Orleans,

> "The status of the Italians has been very much improved of late, they dropped the hand organ long ago, and they never took to barbering, shoe-cleaning or street work, as in New York. The fruit, vegetable, and fish trades they have absolutely controlled since they first came. They are rapidly crowding into the corner grocery business, formerly monopolized by Irishmen and Germans, and into nearly all lines, even the learned professions."

Working the fields did not provide much more wealth from the comparative poverty and misery each left behind in Europe. For those who opened shops such as shoe making, grocery stores, or the vegetable, fruit, meat, or fish trades, such as the Italian Market in New Orleans, it was the beginning of a slow assimilation, process. Yet, in all areas of the nation, prosperity was envied and all sorts of political machinations were created to prevent Italians from any control of businesses or assimilation as equals within the "white" social class.[126]

Often grouped as one definition of "Italian," especially in 1880, is a misnomer. Regional differences were extreme. Italians from Sicily were "Sicilian;" others from southern Italy related their heritage to their region such as

---

[125] "Experience on Louisiana Plantations." *The Pacific Commercial Advertiser.* August 22, 1899. *Chronicling America: Historic American Newspapers.* Library of Congress.
[126] Brent Staples. "How Italians Became White." *The New York Times,* October 12, 2019.

"Calabrese" or "Neapolitan." Within the Italian peninsular those of the North, from the wealthier cities and regions of Renaissance culture such as Florence, Milan, Rome, and Venice, among others, held a long-standing belief that the poor peasants of the south were inferior. Upon arrival in America, beginning in 1880, those southern Italians and Sicilians faced similar prejudices. Historian Jennifer Guglielmo in *Are Italians White? How Race is Made in America* writes of all sorts of printed mass-media outlets including newspapers and popular nationwide magazines "bombarded Americans with images of Italians as racially suspect;" while coupled with all sorts of derogatory names [127]

In an article of March 5, 1882 discussing the "Future Citizens" of the United States, the editors at *The New York Times* wrote,

> "There has never been since New York was founded so low and ignorant a class among the immigrants who poured in here as the Southern Italians who have been crowding our [New York] docks during the past year." [128]

Almost 140 years after the "Future Citizens" article, Brent Staples writing as a "future editor" of *The New York Times* reminded readers of the vile language applied to Italian and Sicilian immigrants. He added,

> "The editors reserved their worst invective [insulting abusive] for Italian immigrant children, whom they described as "utterly unfit — ragged, filthy, and verminous as they were — to be placed in the public primary schools among the decent children of American mechanics." [129]

New Orleans

New Orleans offered work on the ship docks loading and unloading cargo. By 1890, New Orleans docks were second only to New York in the amount of imported fruit to America. Another immigrant opportunity was working in the fields on the sugar plantations, work previously done by African slaves. By 1890, of 242,000 New Orleans city residents at least 20,000 were Sicilian immigrants from Palermo, Corleone, and Trapani. It was not that all the Sicilian immigrants had vast experience in Sugar Cane plantations; they did have centuries of agricultural experience. Unlike the lush northern Italian plains of the Po Valley, Sicilian soil was unforgiving requiring a dedicated austerity for even the smallest plot of land to be viable. Jerre Mangione and Ben Morreale in *La Storia: Five Centuries of the Italian American Experience* explained in Louisiana, "Owners had come to rely heavily on Italians to work their cotton and sugarcane fields."

---

[127] Guglielmo and Salerno. Are Italians White? How Race is Made in America.
[128] "Future Citizens," *The New York Times*, March 5, 1882, p. 6.
[129] Brent Staples. "How Italians Became White." *The New York Times,* October 12, 2019.

Immigrant Italians in Louisiana appeared at first to provide an answer to the unique shortage of labor, due to the end of slavery.[130]

Italian-Americans labor on the docks of New Orleans. (Library of Congress)

In New Orleans, as in most cities, Italian immigrants settled in common neighborhoods among *paisans* from the same region of Sicily or Italy. The opportunity to live among those who spoke the same native dialect offered security and comfort. Living conditions were less than ideal; yet the Italian customs and traditions were prevalent. Many developed successful local businesses, such as selling produce and wares from pushcarts or small stores; mostly confined to a singular area known as the "French Market." The area soon changed over to a new European cultural influence.

The "French Market" since 1812, was mainly Sicilian by 1890; earning a new nickname as the "Italian Market." The market sold all sorts of meat, fish, vegetables, fruit, and produce; a significant amount of the New Orleans food supply. Most of the vendors were Sicilian, some sold dry goods; while others opened storefront shops offering services for shoe repair, barbershops, tailoring, and bakeries, among others. Living in less desirable areas of the city, the Sicilian merchants also served African-Americans; fraternization often occurred and sometimes intermarriage.

---

[130] Gambino, *Vendetta*, pp. 52-55. See also: Mangione and Morreale, pp. 185, 203.

The French Market in New Orleans, Louisiana, came to be known as the "Italian Market," c. 1906. Detroit Publishing Co.
(Library of Congress Prints and Photographs Division No. LC-D4-34323.)

With immigration, a twofold resentment problem developed among the dominant white Louisiana population. Many Sicilians were of a much darker complexion than northern Europeans, which visually placed them closer to African Americans in appearance. Sicilian merchants did not discriminate against customers; creating resentment from whites who did not provide services to Blacks in accordance with a segregation policy. Society was clearly separated between the "white only" and designated "colored only" places of establishment as the law of the land. In 1898, the Louisiana Constitutional Convention set the forward the brazen statement,

> "Our mission was, in the first place, to establish the supremacy of the white race in this State to the extent to which it could be legally and constitutionally done."

In Louisiana, Sicilians were not deemed "white," therefore, legally subjected to the same "legal" discrimination as African Americans. Italian immigrants from regions such as Abruzzo, Calabria, and Sicily, were routinely described in New Orleans as "dagoes." As such, susceptible to the same treatment as African Americans. Unfortunately, that same "similar treatment" included vigilante lynching.

Lynch: A Transitive Verb

The Italian American Museum of Los Angeles states "in the American South, Italians were the second-most common targets of lynching and [often] semi-segregated." *Merriam-Webster* dictionary provides,

> *Lynch* transitive verb: to put to death (as by hanging) by mob action without legal approval or permission. The accused killer was *lynched* by an angry mob.

Listed as "second" behind African Americans – yet the distinction of the single largest mass-lynching of any one specific ethnic group in American history belongs to the Italians. As noted in *Vendetta: The True Story of the Largest Lynching in U.S. History*, historian Richard Gambino provides a detailed account of the New Orleans travesty. In the preface, Gambino expands on the definition explaining,

> "As measured by the number of people illegally killed in one place at one time . . . Lynching here is distinguished, as is usual, from race riots and other forms of civil disorder in which victims are chosen without regard to their individual identities and no specific offense . . . is alleged."

In 1891, one of the most horrific instances of anti-Italian hatred occurred in New Orleans as stereotyping, discrimination, lies, and violence were routinely directed at Italians. Of no surprise, there are no reprisals against those who openly slandered and abused Italians. Richard Gambino added,

> "In regard to Italian-Americas, the New Orleans lynching was at once both a means of limiting their position, participation, and possibilities in the American community, and one of the first major stimuli of the stereotype of inherently criminal Italian-American culture, a common defamation which still limits the ethnic group's position, participation, and possibilities in today's America."[131]

The stereotyping emanated from a perceived image of an Italian criminal element of the "mafia." Frank Viviano writing, "Atrocities America Forgot" said the perceived "mafia" existence in New Orleans "in 1890 [the mafia's] existence and reach were more fantasy than fact."[132]

---

[131] Richard Gambino. Vendetta: The True Story of the Largest Lynching in U.S. History. Guernica, 1998, p. ix.

[132] Frank Viviano. "Atrocities America Forgot." *The New York Review*, June 6, 2019.

The Single Largest Lynching in American History

On March 14, 1891, residents of New Orleans woke up to the early morning edition newspapers throughout city, as all the publications, carried the following statement as a "call to action."

MASS MEETING

All good citizens are invited to attend a mass meeting on Saturday, March 14, at 10 o'clock A.M., at Clay Statue, to take steps to Remedy the failure of justice in the Hennessy case. Come prepared for action.

New Orleans residents were riled up over a recent murder trial involving nine local Italian residents. The previous day six were acquitted; three were deemed a "mistrial." The presiding judge dismissed two others without trail. By all historical accounts "the evidence was distressingly weak" for the arrest of eleven Italian immigrants accused in a plot which resulted in the murder of local New Orleans Police Chief David C. Hennessy; near midnight of October 15, 1890 as he was walking home. [133]

A former police officer Bill O'Connor claimed he heard shots. Running to the dying Hennessy O'Connor said, "Bending over the Chief, I said to him: 'Who gave it to you Dave?' He replied "Dagoes." The Chief lived into the night engaging in some coherent conversations with doctors, a judge, and his own mother – none accused local Italians of the shooting. Regardless of the lack of evidence, Mayor Shakspeare issued orders to "arrest every Italian you come across." Acting quickly, "hundreds of raids upon Italian homes and shops, and the wholesale arrest of Italians was accelerated." A "Call to Action" was encouraged by New Orleans Mayor Joseph A. Shakspeare (1837-1896) who said "the emigrants from the worst classes of Europe, Southern Italians and Sicilians and we find them the most idle, vicious and worthless people among us." One of the instigators, John M. Parker (1863-1939) later elected Governor of Louisiana, said publicly, "Eye-talians" as a race are "just a little worse than the Negro, being if anything filthier in their habits, lawless, and treacherous." The following day, Newspapers across the nation responded. *The New York Times* page one story blared,

CHIEF HENNESSY AVENGED

ELEVEN OF HIS ITALIAN ASSASSINS
LYNCHED BY A MOB.

AN UPRISING OF INDIGNANT CITIZENS
IN NEW-ORLEANS – THE PRISON
DOORS FORCED AND THE ITALIAN
MURDERERS SHOT DOWN.

---

[133] Erin Blakemore. "The Grisly Story of America's Largest Lynching," *History.com.*

The editorial language was not directed just at the lynching victims, but all Italian immigrants in New Orleans or New York or anywhere.[134]

Various newspaper articles sensationalizing the murder
or possible "assassination" of Chief Hennessy.

---

[134] Richard Gambino. *Vendetta*; pp. 2-7, 17, 142; See also: Brent Staples. "How Italians Became White." *The New York Times,* October 12, 2019.

The historical indignation of newspaper editors is typical of the continued rhetoric barrage against Italians. Despite the undisputable fact that an overwhelming majority of Italian immigrants were hard-working, family-orientated, law-abiding, and religious, they were not endeared by New Orleans residents; nor Americans nationwide. Historian Erin Blakemore writing of the account for *History.com* tells us,

> "When news spread that the [Hennessy murder] trial had resulted in six not-guilty convictions and three mistrials, the city went wild. They assumed that the Mafia had somehow influenced jurors or fixed the trial and that justice had not been served. 'Rise, people of New Orleans!' wrote the [New Orleans] *Daily States* newspaper. 'Alien hands of oath-bound assassins have set the blot of a martyr's blood upon your vaunted civilization.'"[135]

In response, a lynch mob of New Orleans residents formed outside the Parish Prison where the accused were held. (The innocent defendants were not released after the verdict.) The mob, estimated at 12,000 to 20,000 -- many armed with clubs and weapons -- stormed the gates, broke into the jail; racing through the prison halls seeking out the Sicilians. Unable to provide protection, the warden unlocked their cells; offering the men a chance to hide elsewhere within the prison. A determined contingent of the lynch mob canvassed the prison, soon finding the innocent victims.

Richard Gambino's research revealed all eleven of the jailed immigrants "were riddled with bullets [as] more than a hundred rifle and shotgun blast were fired into the men, tearing their bodies apart;" One report detailed one of the animalistic mob calmly walking up to a still breathing victim and literally "blew off the man's head" with a shotgun blast. Two other Sicilians, who were also still breathing, were dragged outside as the frenzied mob beat the bodies before stringing them up – hanging them by their necks from streetlight poles.[136]

In contrast to editorials such as *The New York Times*, the real "bandits and assassins" were the citizens of New Orleans. The vigilantes were quickly denounced by the Italian government, which demanded the lynch mob be punished. A grand jury was convened, to no surprise, as was typical of the time, accusatory charges were ***not*** brought forward. An incredulous statement issued by the grand jury claimed the "crowd" was comprised of "the first, best, and even the most law-abiding, of the citizens of this city."[137]

---

[135] Erin Blakemore. "The Grisly Story of America's Largest Lynching: Innocent Italian-Americans got caught in the crosshairs of a bigoted mob." *History.com*. Oct. 25, 2017.
[136] Gambino, *Vendetta*, pp. 83-87.
[137] Lipkis and Steeby, "Sicilian Lynching's at the Old Parish Prison."

In a recurring fact of thousands of lynchings throughout America no one held accountable. Despite overwhelming publicity, Hennessy's murderer was never determined. *New Orleans Historical*, summarized it as,

> "This lynching, generally considered to be the largest in U.S. history, was part of the larger phenomenon of white Southern mobs that targeted African Americans, but which also murdered dozens of Italians. In New Orleans, white elites sought to limit the control the new Sicilian working class immigrants gained over the docks in their cross-racial labor organizing with African Americans, and, for a few established Italian-American upper-class men, in the shipping industry as well. White [citizens] of varying political factions sought to consolidate their power by condemning recent Sicilian immigrants and citizens of Italian descent with the stereotype of "killer dago," leaving them with an unprotected status."[138]

Contemporary illustrations of the lynch mobs outside of Parish Prison.
(Public Domain)

War with Italy, Italian Stereotyping, *Two Bits*, and Mario Puzo

Some historians cite the New Orleans incident for prompting President Benjamin Harrison (1833-1901) to issue a proclamation in 1892 for a nationwide celebration

---

[138] Henry Lipkis and Elizabeth Steeby, "Sicilian Lynching's at the Old Parish Prison," *New Orleans Historical.*

of Columbus Day. The statement read in part, "Recommending to the people [of the United States] the observance in all their localities of the 400th anniversary of the discovery of America." Harrison cited, Columbus as "the pioneer of progress and enlightenment." The proclamation was not responding to the vigilante actions in New Orleans. Harrison's proclamation attempted to ease diplomatic tensions with the Italian government who demanded reparations due to the New Orleans lynching. In 2019, journalist Brent Staples rightfully said,

> "President Harrison would have ignored the New Orleans carnage had the victims been black. But the Italian government made that impossible. It broke off diplomatic relations and demanded an indemnity that the Harrison administration paid. Harrison even called on Congress in his 1891 State of the Union to protect foreign nationals — though not black Americans — from mob violence."[139]

The entire situation can only be described as an inherent pattern of systematic racism firmly entrenched in the cultural fabric of the United States. It is difficult to find credible scholarly sources disagreeing over systematic racism within America. In comparison, many of those same scholars are often guilty of dismissing (sometimes with a snicker) the continued stereotyping of Italians.

The discussion continues well into the 21st century stereotyping as a result of widely successful movies and television shows such as *The Godfather* (movie 1972), *The Sopranos*, (HBO TV series 1999-2007), and the *Jersey Shore* (MTV series 2009-2012), among hundreds of other negative contemporary examples. It is difficult to find many popular culture references of the Italian immigrant struggles or contributions to America. Some documentaries exists, but are mainly obscure. In 1999, HBO released *Vendetta* (dir. Nicholas Meyer, 1999) based on the Richard Gambino book. The tag line stated, "Based on a true tale of power, corruption and murder . . . the story of the largest lynching in American history." The movie was quite accurate, yet the "go-to" 21st century movie review page Rotten Tomatoes has little information, stating, "Sicilian emigrants find themselves exploited by powerful men and indicted for a police chief's assassination."[140]

One excellent example is the PBS Documentary four-episode series titled: *The Italian Americans*. The plot summary of Episode 1 titled *La Famiglia* (dir. John Maggio 2015) was described by IMDb.com as,

> "A brief history of the Italian Risorgimento provides the context for the great flight from the Mezzogiorno region. By the late 19th century,

---

[139] See: Gambino, *Vendetta*, pp. 4-5. See also: Brent Staples. "How Italians Became White." *The New York Times,* October 12, 2019.
[140] "Vendetta." *IMDb.com* October 12, 2020. https://www.imdb.com/title/tt0162735/ "Vendetta." *RottenTomatoes.com,* https://www.rottentomatoes.com/m/1094103-vendetta

CHAPTER 3

Italians begin to put down roots and 'Little Italy's' spring up in urban areas throughout the U.S. But the first generation, holding onto language and culture, is branded 'outsiders' and mistrusted by non-Italians. In New Orleans, this mistrust explodes into violence and 11 Italian Americans are murdered by an armed mob. . . in San Francisco [an] Italian American saves his community from disaster while creating one of the greatest financial institutions in America."[141]

The reference to the "financial institution" is the Bank of America founded by A.P. Giannini (see Chapter 7C).

Another excellent movie is *Two Bits* (dir. James Foley, 1995) a positive heartwarming story very indicative of a real-life Italian immigrant grandfather living in Depression-era South Philadelphia with his widowed daughter and grandson. By movie standards it was miserable at the Box Office earning less than $30,000. As a result, *Two Bits* remains regulated to obscure status despite the multitude of streaming platforms. The most plausible reason-- it is not a stereotypical Italian mob movie. Added to the mystery is the cast is led by Al Pacino (b. 1940) one of the greatest actors of all-time born. Additional cast members included an acclaimed Italian American actress Mary Elizabeth Mastrantonio (b. 1958) as the daughter, and Jerry Barone (b. 1981) as the 12-year-old grandson.

Al Pacino, as a full-blooded Italian, represents a typical example of an individual ingrained within American popular culture. Father Salvatore Pacino (1922-2005) was from San Fratello, Sicily, mother Rose Gerardi (1919-1962) was born of Italian immigrants from the small town of Corleone, Sicily. The coincidence of Pacino's connection to the factual Sicilian town of Corleone in the province of Palermo relates to an iconic portrayal as "Michael Corleone" in *The Godfather* trilogy of movies. Many sources, such as AFI, often rate *The Godfather* (dir. Francis Ford Coppola, 1972) as within the top three greatest American films ever made. *The Godfather* novel written by Mario Puzo (1920-1999) in 1969 remains in the Top-10 best-selling fictional books in America selling an estimated 20-30 million copies. Fictional is the key word as the downside of *The Godfather* totally ingrained an image within American popular culture as many believe the story as portraying real-life Italians.

Lost among the violent world of *The Godfather* is most credible movie critics understand *The Godfather* movie is a story of an Italian "family." Traveling to America as an immigrant orphan, Vito Corleone did what he had to do in a society not welcoming to Italian immigrants to not only survive, but provide and protect his family. In contrast, is a novel listed as fictional that reveals the real-life Italian

---

[141] Plot Summary, "*La Famiglia: The Italian Americans. PBS at *IMDb.com*.

experience written five years before *The Godfather*. Puzo's earlier novel *The Fortunate Pilgrim* is often considered by critics as his best literary work.

The novel was intended as a fictionalized version of Puzo's own upbringing. Mother Maria Puzo, (1889-1974) living as an immigrant in New York, was left to raise seven children after her husband was committed to an insane asylum when Mario was only 12. The experience certainly hardened Maria, who is essence was basically "widowed." Journalist Camille Paglia, writing a *New York Times* book review of the 1997 reissue of *The Fortunate Pilgrim*, aptly titled, "It All Comes Back to Family," said, "Mr. Puzo reveals that his mother, Maria (called Lucia Santa in the book), was the model for Don Corleone, the Mafia chieftain of *The Godfather*." As noted in the preface of the 1997 reissue of *The Fortunate Pilgrim*, Puzo revealed, "Whenever the Godfather opened his mouth, in my own mind I heard the voice of my mother."[142]

As such *The Fortunate Pilgrim* falls into the same relationship as the movie *Two Bits*. Puzo's novel is based on his own mother's singular real-life struggles as an Italian immigrant living in America. A reality brought forward indicative of many American born children living of Italian immigrants, Puzo like so many other Americans born of Italian immigrant parents wanted to distance himself "to show my rejection of my Italian heritage and my callow disdain of those illiterate peasant from which I sprang." In time, however, Puzo grew to understand,

> "Through my writing, those immigrant Italians who worked twelve hours a day in gray, sweat-soaked fedora, wearing great handlebar mustaches, had the dignity of heroes. I heard the voice of my mother. I heard her wisdom, her ruthlessness, and her unconquerable love for her family and for life itself, qualities not valued in women at the time."[143]

Puzo came to understand his mother epitomized the millions of Italian immigrants who did whatever was needed to "take care" of the family.

It is difficult to find any factual statistic that does not place Italian immigrants on the lowest social rung, or in this instance positive, in the way of any minimal criminal activity. Demographic crime statistics in the 140 years, or so, since the new wave of immigration in 1880 factually places the incarceration rate and criminal activity of Italians as one of, if not, the lowest percentage of the overall American population. Unfortunately, due to negative stereotyping, the opposite was believed in America. As such it is just another in a long list of negative associations that continues to exist into the present day. Historian Barbara Botein in *The Hennessy Case: An Episode in Anti-Italian Nativism*, correctly stated,

---

[142] Camille Paglia. "It All Comes Back to Family," p. C1. "Mother of Mario Puzo Dies," *The New York Times*, January 25, 1974, p. A36.

[143] Mario Puzo. *The Fortunate Pilgrim*, New York: Ballentine Books, 1997, pp. ix-x.

CHAPTER 3

"Most historians have overlooked the subject of anti-Italian feeling during the Gilded Age. The Nativist pattern became all too typical with the experience of Sicilian immigrants. Italians suffered the worst abuse of any European group during the Gilded Age. In addition, the widely held views of Sicilians as degraded, criminal, and unassimilable made them targets of popular scorn as well as national laws intended to prevent their continued migration."[144]

Irony of the Louisiana Purchase and the American Ice Cream Cone

In 1904, a World's Fair in St. Louis celebrated the 1803 Louisiana Purchase and the city as the launching point for the Lewis and Clark expedition. At St. Louis, a variety of American cultural traditions were based on mass production and industrialization. The fair also introduced the "fast food" concept; able to purchase a hot dog or ice cream cone and walk through the entertainment zones; both of which became American cultural icons.[145] Unbeknownst to many are the Italian origins of the ice cream cone. According to the *International Dairy Foods Association,*

"The first ice cream cone was produced in 1896 by Italo Marchiony. . . who emigrated from Italy in the late 1800s, invented his ice cream cone in New York City. He was granted a patent in December 1903."[146]

Marchiony (born "Italo Marchioni" 1868-1954), immigrated in 1895 from the Dolomite Mountains in northeast Italy about 102 miles (165 km) north of Venice entering Ellis Island settling in Manhattan. As explained by Pia Antonucci, writing for the *Mt. Carmel – St. Cristina Society,* "[Marchiony] changed his name from the 'i' to a 'y' because back then Italians suffered from discrimination so the 'y' made the name appear French."

In New York, Marchiony operated a single push cart in the Wall Street area. At first, he sold "lemon ice in oversized whiskey shot glasses." The cleaning of the glasses, however, "was time consuming" and costly. Antonucci's discovered, "One day [Marchiony] folded a paper cone and put the [lemon] ice in it. The word spread and lines formed at his cart, for the new way eliminated the need to return the glass." The innovative profitable product resulted in the purchase of additional pushcarts and hiring employees eventually numbering at least 45-50 push carts. As the sales increased, so did the refuse of paper collection. Around 1903, Marchiony came up with the idea of having an edible cup formed from a twisted

---

[144] Barbara Botein. "The Hennessy Case: An Episode in Anti-Italian Nativism," pp. 261-279. John Higham. "Origins of Immigration Restriction, 1882-1897, p. 82.
[145] Matthew J. Bruccoli and Richard Layman, eds. *American decades: 1900-1909,* p. 308.
[146] "History of the Ice Cream Cone." *International Dairy Foods Association.*

baked waffle. Antonucci added, by applying "mechanical genius [Marchiony] developed a machine to bake the cones." In turn, a patent was secured later in the same year for a waffle-type ice cream cone.[147]

At the 1904 St. Louis World's Fair a similar product was touted as the first ice cream cone "independently introduced by Ernest A. Hamwi, a Syrian concessionaire." Hamwi engaged a successful profitable endeavor at the St. Louis fair. Yet, it is not known the status of any of his clientele, since the St. Louis Fair did not officially segregate or discriminate, yet the fair was "unofficially" segregated. As historian Angela da Silva explains,

> "[Discrimination] didn't need to be sanctioned by organizers; plenty of volunteers and businesses were happy to discriminate on their own recognizance, refusing to serve black patrons' food, souvenirs, [or] even water."[148]

Marchiony later abandoned the New York pushcart idea. As a means to expand business, a factory was opened in Hoboken, New Jersey only for production of ice cream cones. By 1924, the output was an astounding 150,000 cones a day.

 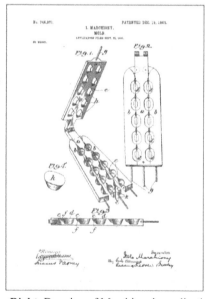

Above Left: Italo Marchiony. **Above Right**: Drawing of Marchiony's application for an Ice Cream Cone baking iron. Patent filed September 22, 1903. No. 746,971 Patent approved December 15, 1903.

---

[147] Pia Antonucci. "Italo Marchiony, Inventor of the Ice Cream Cone."
[148] "History of the Ice Cream Cone." *International Dairy Foods Association.*

"Rags to Riches" stories of Italian immigrants such as Marchiony were common. History does not tell us, if Marchiony was aware of the similar product sold by Hamwi. We do not know if the Italian was deprived of the notoriety and profits due to discrimination which was obviously prevalent, not just in St. Louis, but throughout the United States. Many Italian immigrants and entrepreneurs added to the cultural fabric of American culture despite political attempts to stop them, such as from an Italian xenophobe in the U. S. Senate named Henry Cabot Lodge.[149]

Henry Cabot Lodge: Italian XENOPHOBE

Henry Cabot Lodge (1850-1924) from Massachusetts remains as one of the most volatile and remembered U.S. Senators in American history. The "official" Senate biography listed on the United States website proclaims a glowing litany of various legal appointments and accomplishments. Not included in the "White-washed" bio was a continued fanatical xenophobia of anti-immigrant legislation for over 30 years. Through American history a pattern described by historian Barbara Botein explains an unsettling discriminatory reality as,

> "Although most Americans are the products of immigration, they have been ambivalent about allowing foreigners to enter the country. While desiring immigrants labor skills, they have expected newcomers to conform to American ways. When immigrants resist Americanization and retain ethnic lifestyles, Americans sometimes become suspicious and hostile. This nativism an "intense opposition to an internal minority on the ground of its foreign (i.e., 'un-American') connections has manifested itself in verbal abuse, physical assault, and enactment of elaborate immigration restrictions."

Significant evidence exists of continued discrimination against Italians was not limited to violent acts. Verbal assaults were common, but it was the politicians which proved insurmountable. Despite the non-criminal achievements of millions of Italians, political machinations by Nativist opposition remained dogged in the pursuit of preventing a continued trend of immigration. The most vocal and prominent proponent of anti-immigration laws was Republican U.S. Senator Henry Cabot Lodge.[150]

---

[149] Paul Friswold. "The Forgotten History of Racism at the 1904 World's Fair in St. Louis." *Riverfront Times*, May 2, 2018.

[150] Botein. "The Hennessy Case," pp. 261-279. Note: The word "white-wash" is in context, defined by *Encyclopedia Britannica* "to gloss over or cover up vices, crimes or scandals or to exonerate by means of a perfunctory investigation or through biased presentation of data."

"Mr. President: This bill is intended to amend the existing law so as to restrict still further immigration to the United States."
– Henry Cabot Lodge, 1896

Above Left: Portrait of Henry Cabot Lodge painted in 1890 by John Singer Sargent (1856-1925), Oil on canvas. National Portrait Gallery, Accession No. NPG.67.58. **Above Right**: Photograph of Lodge, c. 1901. Library of Congress Prints and Photographs Division. Digital ID: cph.3a38855. (Public Domain)

Applying words such as "xenophobia" might easily be bypassed by readers; yet reading of its definition reveals a sad and discriminatory dark truth. *Merriam-Webster* dictionary (which has been the definitive "go-to" source within American Culture since 1828) defines "xenophobia" as,

> **Xenophobia / noun** xe·no·pho·bia | \ ˌzen-ə-ˈfō-bē-ə, ˌzēn- \
>
> **Definition of** *xenophobia*: fear and hatred of strangers or foreigners or of anything that is strange or foreign.
>
> **Synonyms**: Nativism, chauvinism, jingoism, nationalism, super patriotism, prejudice, racism.

The first known use of the word in America dates to 1877. The origin dates to the Ancient Greeks, further explained by *Merriam-Webster* as,

> "Xenophobic individuals are stranger fearing. Xenophobia, that elegant-sounding name for an aversion to persons unfamiliar, derives from two

CHAPTER 3   113

Greek terms: *xenos*, which can be translated as either 'stranger' or 'guest,' and *phobos*, which means either 'fear' or 'flight.'"[151]

Some might dismiss the multiple-PhD Senator Lodge as possessing powerful knowledge as not "unfamiliar" with anything. In reality, the Senator wisely crafted anti-immigrant rhetoric appealing to Nativist sentiments. In contrast, Richard Gambino called Lodge as "Italian-hating." With growing discontent of the changing American social demographic caused by the massive number of new immigrants from southern Italy and Sicily, Nativists seized upon the nationwide media attention given to the 1891 New Orleans incident. Historian John Higham writing in *Strangers in the Land: Patterns of American Nativism, 1860-1925* discovered,

> "Anti-foreign sentiment filtered through a specific ethnic stereotype when Italians were involved; for American eyes they bore the mark of Cain. They suggested the Mafia, the deed of impassioned violence."

Richard Gambino's in-depth research of the 1891 New Orleans lynching of the eleven Italians, added, "the New Orleans affair gave birth to the American stereotype of Italian Americans as criminals."[152]

Fact, however, would not prevent a nationwide anti-immigrant crusade for the likes of Senator Lodge and American Nativists. Lodge seized upon the New Orleans incident and newspaper stereotyping to fan the flames of continued Nativist anger towards Italian immigrants; while laying a path for his own political future. As a member of Congress, Lodge often launched long tirades of anti-immigrant rhetoric gaining nationwide notoriety and strong support. In May 1891, during a campaign leading to election as a U.S. Senator (serving from 1892 to 1924), Lodge wrote "Lynch Law and Unrestricted Immigration." He said the mob who committed the lynching as "led by men of good standing in the community; affirming, "Americans are a law-abiding people, and an act of lawlessness like the lynching of these Italians is sure to meet with their utmost disapproval." As a solution, Lodge proposed the need to enact legislation curtailing immigration. In his own words, "Surely the time has come for an intelligent and effective restriction of immigration."

Lodge presented a summation of facts justifying the immigrant restriction with a simple explanation for Nativist Americans. He wrote,

> "We have, therefore, three facts here of the gravest import. <u>First,</u> an outbreak of lawlessness which resulted in the death of eleven men; <u>Second,</u> a belief that juries could not be depended upon to administer

---

[151] "Xenophobia," *Merriam-Webster*. Accessed October 21, 2020.
[152] John Higham. *Strangers in the Land: Patterns of American Nativism, 1860-1925*, Rutgers University Press, 2000. See also: Gambino, *Vendetta*, p. 138.

justice and protect the lives of the citizens; <u>Third</u> the existence of a secret society [the mafia] which was ready to use both money and murder to accomplish its objects, even to the point of perverting the administration of the law. I believe [the solution] is to be found in the utter carelessness with which we treat immigration in this country."[153]

Lodge said the "good" people [lynch mob] of New Orleans believed "these men were guilty of the crime." He insinuated Hennessy's murder was actually a plot planned and organized by "the work of a secret society known as the Mafia." Lodge fueled the xenophobic paranoia claiming the jury wanted to provide a guilty verdict. Unfortunately, the acquittal, he said, was not the result of any lack of evidence, rather Lodge claimed, "the failure of the jury to convict was due either to terror of this secret organization or to bribery by its agents." Lodge claimed "Of the existence of such a society no reasonable person can, I think, have any doubt."

At the time, it was not Sicilians who were corrupt; nor members of any alleged "secret society." It was the administration and residents of New Orleans that existed as a corrupt city, with an established, "secret society." As Jerre Mangione and Ben Morreale explained the Xenophobia in *La Storia: Five Centuries of the Italian American Experience*,

> "The men who cried "mafia" became wealthy by replacing Italian American businesses in New Orleans. This 'lynch squad' was made up of top members of the city's press, political, and business establishment."[154]

The real "lynch squad" were political lackey's such as Senator Lodge, who continually offered lies providing unsubstantiated accusations against Italians, while covering up with slander, false imagery, and stereotyping.

The continued barrage of negative associations, supported by the dominant Nativist white media outlets made it easy for false statements to permeate into the American psyche. Almost 130 years later, Brent Staples an editor at *The New York Times* wrote,

> "The New Orleans lynching solidified a defamatory view of Italians and Sicilians in particular, as irredeemable criminals who represented a danger to the nation. The influential anti-immigrant racist Representative Henry Cabot Lodge of Massachusetts. appropriated the event. He argued that a lack of confidence in juries, not mob violence, had been the real problem in New Orleans."

---

[153] Henry Cabot Lodge, "Lynch Law and Unrestricted Immigration." *The North American Review*, pp. 602-604, 611-612. Note: Underline in quote added by Author.
[154] Mangione and Morreale. *La Storia*, pp. 201, 211.

CHAPTER 3   115

Senator Lodge, in a pattern of apparently denouncing the action, but in a clever ploy laid blame of the problematic nature of lynching was due to the court verdict. He wrote, "Lawlessness and lynching are evil things, but a popular belief that juries cannot be trusted is even worse."[155]

In a presentation justifying the actions of "good" citizens of New Orleans against "bad" immigrants of a supposed "criminal organization," Senator Lodge successfully planted the idea of the lynching as a justified act. He injected a unique form of apologetic *intelligentsia* claiming,

> "In the present state of things, not only are we doing nothing to protect the quality of our citizenship or the wages of our workingmen from an unrestricted flood of immigration, but we are permitting persons so ignorant and criminal to come among us that organizations like the Mafia are sure to rise in our midst."

Lodge's well-timed warning to all Americans came as xenophobia was heightened against the massive new wave of immigration. Lodge was not opposed to immigration; his opposition was only against the "wrong kind of immigrants." He claimed Scandinavian and German immigration as "one of the best" and the French, Belgian, and Dutch immigrants have "proved valuable to this country." Of course, those immigrants were from northern Europe, distinctly white, and overwhelmingly Protestant.[156]

Historian John Higham writing in *Strangers in the Land: Patterns of American Nativism, 1860-1925*, stated Nativism as a national policy "is distinctly American." Nativism, as championed by individuals such as Lodge, was reluctance of Italians not assimilating to the American culture. Rather, keeping with European traditions, religion, and culture, including language of regional Italian dialects as causing "harm to the country."[157]

Lodge's anti-immigration stance propelled him to a U.S. Senate seat, yet his Italian xenophobia did not stop. On March 16, 1896, Senator Henry Cabot Lodge delivered a blistering speech before Congress aimed at convincing President Grover Cleveland (1837-1908) to sign an anti-immigration bill. Lodge's speech, in excess of 6,800 words, came two months before the Supreme Court decision of *Plessy v. Ferguson*. The time was ripe for segregation *within* the United States and segregation of "undesirables" from foreign nations. A call for immigration restriction was an almost word-for-word reading resurrected from *The North American Review* the Honorable Henry Cabot Lodge, Senator from Massachusetts, delivered his explanatory opening remarks,

---

[155] Brent Staples. "How Italians Became White." *The New York Times,* October 12, 2019.
[156] Henry Cabot Lodge, "Lynch Law and Unrestricted Immigration," "pp. 604,606, 612.
[157] John Higham. *Strangers in the Land: Patterns of American Nativism, 1860-1925*. New Jersey: Rutgers University Press, 2000, p. 7.

"Mr. President: This bill is intended to amend the existing law so as to restrict still further immigration to the United States. By this bill it is proposed to make a new class of excluded immigrants, and add to those which have just been named the totally ignorant. The first section excludes from the country all immigrants who cannot read and write either their own or some other language. The second section merely provides a simple test for determining whether the immigrant can read or write."

As a clever subterfuge, Lodge did not directly state his "Italian hating" (as historian Richard Gambino termed). The remarks intended to counter the economic recessions of the preceding years. As the Harvard University PhD graduate, Lodge changed his oratory rhetoric as, "It concerns us to know . . . whether the quality of our citizenship is endangered by the present course and character of immigration to the United States."

Closing remarks from the xenophobic fear-monger warned of an inherent threat to American society. Lodge's "fear factor" warned,

"The danger has begun. It is small as yet, comparatively speaking, but it is large enough to warn us to act while there is yet time and while it can be done easily and efficiently. There lies the peril at the portals of our land; there is pressing the tide of unrestricted immigration. The time has certainly come, if not to stop, at least to check, to sift, and to restrict those immigrants. In careless strength, with generous hand, we have kept our gates wide open to all the world. If we do not close them, we should at least place sentinels beside them to challenge those who would pass through. The gates which admit men to the United States and to citizenship in the great republic should no longer be left unguarded."

The remarks referenced back ten years to the 1886 dedication of the *Statue of Liberty* as immigrants viewed Lady Liberty welcoming all entering America offering a better life. In contrast, American Nativists came to view the statue with disdain as a representation of opening the floodgates to a "foreign invasion" of immigrants.[158]

In contrast to the 1883 Emma Lazarus poem "The New Colossus" offering a "world-wide welcome," Senator Lodge closed his oratory with a rebuttal poem of his own choosing, "Unguarded Gates" by Thomas Bailey Aldrich (1836-1907); a self-proclaimed white nationalist, termed Liberty as a "white goddess." The poem read as,

---

[158] Henry Cabot Lodge, "Lynch Law and Unrestricted Immigration," "pp. 604-605.

Unguarded Gates

O' Liberty, white Goddess! is it well
To leave the gates unguarded? On thy breast
Fold Sorrow's children, soothe the hurts of fate,
Lift the down-trodden, but with hand of steel
Stay those who to thy sacred portals come
To waste the gifts of freedom. Have a care
Lest from thy brow the clustered stars be torn
And trampled in the dust. For so of old
The thronging Goth and Vandal trampled Rome,
And where the temples of the Caesars stood
The lean wolf unmolested made her lair.

———

The choice of the poem reeks of prejudicial incendiary comments. At the time, Thomas Bailey Aldrich was a well-respected American poet. One reference states, "To contemporary audiences, Aldrich's poem reeks of nationalism and white supremacy, a chilling portrayal of the xenophobic strains weaving through our country's history." Aldrich described "Unguarded Gates" as a "misanthropic poem" who has a general disdain for all humankind. He explained the intent of the poem "in which I mildly protest against America becoming a cesspool of Europe." Aldrich spoke of immigrants wanting anarchy, declaring his own "Americanism goes clean beyond yours. I believe in America for Americans." Or in essence his own proclamation as a White Nationalist.[159]

Boston and Social Darwinism

The "Italian-hating" Senator Lodge, born in a Boston suburb, was also acting in response to the overwhelming demographic change of his hometown. In a comparison, before 1880, less than 4,000 Italian immigrants in total entered the entire nation. Ten years later, over 4,700 settled just within in the city of Boston – exclusively within the old North End. By 1890, the North End neighborhood, home to the historic Paul Revere House of American Revolutionary fame, quickly became an enclave of thousands of Italians. According to Mandy Tuttle, an interpreter at the historic house in Boston, the "former home served as a tenement for Italian immigrants and housed various businesses from an Italian bank to a produce stand." The area became so dominant with an Italian presence, Tuttle added, "it is hard to imagine the surrounding North End neighborhood without its distinctive Italian flair."

---

[159] Thomas Bailey Aldrich, "Unguarded Gates, (1895)" American Studies University of Virginia.

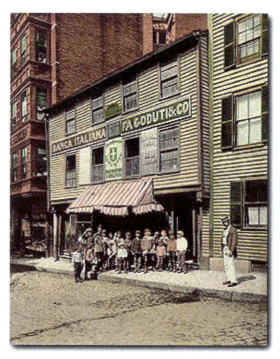

The Paul Revere House located in the North End neighborhood of Boston housed many different Italian businesses and immigrants during the late 19th century.
Courtesy: Paul Revere Memorial Association.

ESSAY: Italian Immigration to America and Boston's North End By: Mandy Tuttle

If you have ever visited Paul Revere's North Square home, it is hard to imagine the North End neighborhood without its distinctive Italian flair. In the late 19th and early 20th centuries, many Italians imagined a community in the North End of Boston; conversely, prominent Bostonians imagined a different American community without the immigrants. . . many of them settling in ethnic enclaves in eastern cities like Boston, Philadelphia, and New York. Each typifies the immigration struggle in America from 1880-1924, two competing forces existed simultaneously and in friction; many leading anti-immigration voices had connections to the city at the same time that many immigrants sought a better life in Boston.

In 1861, the disparate Italian states unified as the Kingdom of Italy. This political unification brought a period of long suffering for the people of southern Italy. Beginning in the 1870s, taxes on wheat and salt disproportionately affected farmers and merchants in places such as

CHAPTER 3

Naples and Sicily. Unfortunately, a series of natural disasters made life even worse . . . Blight ruined the grape crops in the 1880s, suppressing wine production, a cholera epidemic spread rapidly through the streets of Naples in 1882. A series of earthquakes and volcanic eruptions killed thousands of people. These events created a growing feeling of hopelessness, especially amongst the young men. Looking for a way to support their families, these young men, many of whom were illiterate, turned to America as a place to work and to send money back home. This process accelerated quickly. In 1877, 3,600 Italians immigrated to the U.S. In 1890, 4,700 Italians settled in Boston alone.[160]

Simultaneously, the Progressive movement was [at the] beginning in [America]. Based on social reform, they sought to address issues that arose with industrialization, urbanization, and immigration. Many arguments put forth by progressive reformers were rooted in Social Darwinism. While Social Darwinism has many facets, elite Americans frequently employed the inequality of races. Using newspapers, many prominent Americans imagined and promoted an America of "white Americans of native birth and parentage." Henry Cabot Lodge, a Harvard-educated Bostonian from Beacon Hill, was a disciple of Social Darwinism and believed that America's problems were "race problems." As a long [serving] United States senator from Massachusetts, Lodge championed immigration restriction as U.S. policy.[161]

When Italian immigrants arrived in Boston, many chose to settle in the North End. Previous waves of immigration to the neighborhood included the Irish, fleeing the potato famine in the late 1840s, followed by Eastern European Jews fleeing pogroms and persecution. The neighborhood provided access to work on the waterfront, ideal for many of the illiterate, unskilled laborers that were arriving. Paul Revere's former home served as a tenement for Italian immigrants, housing various business from an Italian bank to a produce stand. Italian Catholicism gained a foothold in the North End through Sacred Heart Church in North Square and St. Leonard's Church on Hanover Street in 1899. The people moving to the North End engaged in chain migration. Young men earned money to send to Italy so more family members could join them in America. This led to the formation of distinct ethnic enclaves within the neighborhood that preserved dialects and traditions from Italy. It also made cultural assimilation and Americanization less likely. Eager to preserve their heritage and identity, these individuals sometimes resisted the Progressive trend to become more American.

---

[160] Daniel Okrent, *The Guarded Gate*, pp. 40-43.
[161] Shelton Stromquist, *Re-Inventing "The People,"* p. 3. Benedict Anderson, *Imagined Communities.*

Several organizations were formed in Boston to help the new arrivals acclimate to their new environment. . . . A series of books were commissioned by The Daughters of the American Revolution entitled "How to be American" for those arriving from Italy, Ireland, and Eastern Europe. Not all leading figures took welcoming positions, however. President Teddy Roosevelt once said that Southern Italians were the "most fecund and least desirable population of Europe." In 1902, future President Woodrow Wilson wrote, "but now there came multitudes of men of the lowest class from the south of Italy ... having neither skill nor energy nor any initiative of quick intelligence." Between 1900-1919, 2 million Italians arrived in America; around 68% of them were illiterate. Bostonians such as Henry Cabot Lodge advocated for a literacy test that would ideally end immigration to America. By 1910, 74% of the Boston population was foreign born or had one parent who had immigrated. According to government-funded Dillingham Commission, 32% of Italian immigrants to the North End were general laborers, with no trained skills, leading the neighborhood to a "fundamental change for the worst."

World War I and the United States' entrance into the conflict in 1917 slowed immigration to the country. With the war's conclusion, in May 1921, Congress passed the Emergency Immigration Act. This act created a nation-by-nation quota, capping immigration for a country at a mere 3% of the individuals born in America by 1910. This act had devastating consequences for Italians wishing to settle in America, and specifically Boston. It cut Italian immigration by 82%, and imposed a 300-individual quota for Boston. On June 6, 1921, the SS Canopic, a steamship from Italy, docked at Boston Harbor with 1,040 individuals in third class alone. When authorities threatened not to let the passengers disembark, crowds gathered in protest.

Concurrently, Nicola Sacco and Bartolomeo Vanzetti, Italian immigrants, were arrested and tried for murder in Dedham, Massachusetts. The North End of Boston, according to police, was increasingly the headquarters for the leading Italian anarchists in America, advocating for violent overthrow of government. Such fears and tensions boiled over in front of the SS Canopic, requiring police presence to keep the protests under control. The passengers were allowed to disembark after being detained for days, but as a result "henceforth all excess-quota aliens would be denied admission and deported."

In 1924, Calvin Coolidge advocated, "America must be kept American," a permanent immigration act passed through Congress. Known as the Johnson-Reed Act, or National Origins Act, this legislation capped total immigration to America at 155,000 individuals per year. This act, while celebrated by men like Henry Cabot Lodge, had

CHAPTER 3   121

devastating effects in the coming decades for those attempting to flee the genocidal terror of Adolf Hitler.

While many prominent Americans, from Presidents to Senators, were imagining a country with little to no immigration, immigrants were busy making the best out of their circumstances upon their arrival to America. Many of these immigrants transformed cramped, tenement housing into single-family homes and developed businesses and community organizations that survive today, carving a place for themselves and their descendants in America. The cultural cachet of today's North End is heavily dependent on its rich Italian heritage, it is hard to imagine a time when this was not the case. That said, even the effort to save the Paul Revere House and open it as a museum was not without tension around how the home of an American hero could exist and function in a decidedly immigrant quarter. . . Today, the North End of Boston is a neighborhood rich in traditions. The colorful parades, festivals, food, and music connect people to the past and allow us to reflect on the transformation of one neighborhood in America.[162]

Mandy Tuttle is an Interpreter for the Paul Revere Memorial Association. The historical Paul Revere House is located at 19 North Square in Boston, Massachusetts.

Prompted by the ongoing crusade of Senator Lodge, a government-funded Boston survey known as the Dillingham Commission, claimed due to the large number of unskilled Italian immigrants, the North End neighborhood took a "change for the worst;" fears also echoed in the U.S. Senate.

Prof. Robert F. Foerster and
The Italian Emigration of Our Times

While many Americans and schools praised Christopher Columbus and of other Renaissance figures, historians overlooked the cultural contributions of southern Italians and Sicilians. Those studying the Italian Renaissance or Ancient Rome, dealing with Italians within America was a different story. Contemporary Harvard University historian Prof. Robert F. Foerster (1883-1941), provide disdain of Italian immigrants, stating,

"Even the most astute historian of the Italian immigration, Robert F. Foerster, wrote in 1919 of the brutalizing effects of the labor in which

---

[162] "Fundamental change for the worst," in Woodrow Wilson, *A History of the American People*, pp. 98-99. Okrent, *The Guarded Gate,* pp.83, 101, 291, 336.

the Italians engaged. He saw their spirits calloused by work, but attributed it to a lack of mental ability. . . . Foerster also wrote of Italians as being miserly, sober, tricky, lazy, docile, passionate, tireless workers, having a short-lived enthusiasm, secretive."[163]

A 1920 book review offered a brief summation of Foerster's popular publication *The Italian Emigration of Our Times* as,

"Italy has been, as Professor Foerster points out, one of the few great emigrating nations. In South Italy, an exodus, in depopulation; has been characteristically permanent.' The picture of the Italian peasant roused from an 'age-long lethargy' to flee from the profound economic disorders, the social maladjustments and the extremities of poverty of his native country is a thrilling story, and it is a story that must be studied by those who wish to understand the Italian peasant in his efforts to adapt himself to the complex social and economic life in [America]."[164]

Another review of *Italian Emigration of our Times* offered in *The Harvard Crimson* claimed "Prof. Foerster Believes Immigration Beneficial." A quick read of the headline offers a glimmer of possible compassionate Italian sentiment. However, Foerster states, "It is wholesome for the United States to admit a certain class of foreigners." The Harvard professor's "certain class" was described as "made up of more French, Belgians and Germans." The solution offered to prevent "the objectional class of aliens" [i.e. Italians] from entering the United States. Some critics might argue, within Foerster's 556-page publication only 90 pages were devoted to Italians who emigrated to America. However, he also provided data for the emigration of another 12 million Italians to other countries in Europe, South America, and Australia during the same time period.[165]

In a comparative statement written in July 2012, author Ed Falco posed the reflective question,

"We've forgotten the depth of prejudice and outright hatred faced by Italian immigrants in America. We've forgotten the degree to which we once feared and distrusted Catholics. If we remembered, I wonder how much it might change the way we think about today's immigrant populations, or our attitudes toward [other religions]"[166]

Editors in the far-away Hawaiian Islands did not understand why "the only exception is the Italian." In the situation of mob justice, as demonstrated in Louisiana, *The Pacific Commercial Advertiser* wrote of Italians "placed on terms

---

[163] Mangione and Morreale. *La Storia*, p. 201.
[164] Robert F. Foerster. *The Italian Emigration of our Times*, pp. xv, 556. See also: *American Political Science Review* Vol. 14 No. 3, August 1920, pp. 523-524.
[165] "Prof. Foerster Believes Immigration Beneficial." *The Harvard Crimson*, 1919. 2020.
[166] Ed Falco. "When Italian Immigrants Were 'the Other,'" *CNN*, July 10, 2012.

of equality with the negro." A lynching in 1899, for what history tells us only for the crime of being Italian, occurred in Tallulah, Louisiana, a small town in northeast Louisiana. The *New Orleans Daily Picayune* reported, "On July 20,1899, a fierce mob brutally lynched all five and forced two other Italians who lived in nearby Milliken's Bend to flee." The report claimed, the Italians "all had reputations of being bad and violent men, easily excited--thrown into a perfect furry [sic] at the least cause." The victims were Carlo Difatta, Francesco Difatta, Giuseppe Difatta, Rosario Fiducia, and Giovanni Cerami.[167]

"Five Italian Lynched" and "The Evil Eye"

On July 22, 1899 a story on page seven of *The New York Times* published a non-compassionate story of a lynching of the five Italains in Tallulah. The anti-immigrant editorial staff of *The New York Times,* said of the five lynched Italians, all belonged "of a class which has been troublesome for some time." One of the murdered lynch victims Frank De Fatta, a local merchant, owned goats which apparently over the course of many weeks "were found sleeping and running in the home and office of Dr. Hodge." The newspaper account said Hodge repeatedly asked De Fatta to contain the goats, with no acceptable response. Hodge decided to take matters into his own hands and shot one of the goats. An enraged De Fatta said, "You shoot my goat, now you better shoot me." The statement inferred, retribution on Defatta's guilt in a murder retaliation plot against Hodge.[168]

On July 22, 1899, *The New York Times* carried the lynching in Tallulah, Louisiana on page 7 as,

FIVE ITALIANS LYNCHED;
Shooting of a Louisiana Doctor
Avenged by Many Citizens.
HE WAS SHOT IN THE STREET.
Trouble Caused by the Physician Killing
a Goat Belonging to One of the Italians.
TALLULAH, La., July 21. -- Five Italians
were lynched here last night for the fatal
wounding of Dr. J. Ford Hedge. The dead
men are of a class which has been troublesome
for some time.

Goats were, and still are, an important part of an Italian peasant farmers profit and within the culture of Sicily. For a merchant such as De Fatta, and life among

---

[167] Edward F. Haas. "Guns, Goats, and Italian: The Tallulah Lynching of 1899." *North Louisiana Historical Association.* Vol. XIII, No: 2&3, 1982, p. 47.
[168] For a detailed account see: Edward F. Haas. "Guns, Goats, and Italian: The Tallulah Lynching of 1899." *North Louisiana Historical Association.* Vol. XIII, No: 2&3, 1982.

Italians, goats provided a continued source for cheese and even milk. As such, the incident would certainly be cause, among Sicilians, or southern Italians, to enact a "vendetta" against the perpetrator. (Media stereotyping conveyed "vendetta" would lead to retribution in the form of murder.)

Harper's Weekly August 5, 1899, "Recent Lynching of Italians at Tallulah, Louisiana – Three of the Victims." From left to right: "Frank De Fatta, with whom the Trouble began," Joe De Fatta, who shot Dr. Hodge; and Rosario Fiducia, A Cousin of the De Fattas. Courtesy of Jennifer Navarre, The Historic New Orleans Collection, Williams Research Center (No: 1989.91.3 i-iii_o2.jpg).

———————

In reality, retribution would be more likely achieved by placing the Sicilian "evil eye" (*malocchio*) - a curse - upon Dr. Hodge. As an old southern Italian and Sicilian myth believed the "evil eye," or a leering glance, upon an evildoer would bring them future pain and misery. In response, Italians believed defense from the "evil eye" could be thwarted by making the Catholic "sign of the cross." Others might also wear a crucifix or an amulet charm in the shape of a twisted red horn, known as a *cornicello* or *cornetto* – translated as "little horn."

The "little horn," is a common sight in both Italy and America, yet many do not know what it represents. As an "iconic symbol" of Naples, it is also quite common in other regions of Italy and Sicily; often seen among 21st century Italian-Americans. Writing in *L'Italo Americano*, Giulia Franceschini described the "Iconic Cornetto" as,

> "You are certainly familiar with it [the symbol], the *curnicello*, or*cornetto*, that red chili pepper Neapolitans use to attract good luck and be protected by evil forces, or *malocchio*, as they call it. Found often on market stalls, it has become a symbol of fortune a bit everywhere in Italy, even if, of course, its Neapolitan roots remain strong."

Part of the *cornetto* myth to ward off the "evil eye" is not to purchase one for yourself, rather it must be received as a gift. Many that are sold in novelty shops are usually inexpensive red plastic. Some more expensive, are made from gold, silver, sometimes bejeweled in expensive gems. Regardless, the shape is in the form of a chili pepper. Franceschini calls it "more than a symbol of Naples, it's a symbol of its history and of its people's ability to merge together the holy and the sacred, culture and lore, past and present, always perfectly, always seamlessly."[169]

The Italian "Evil Eye" or *cornetto*

As for the Tallulah incident, two days following the incident, *The Daily Picayune* described the lynch mob as "the crowd was orderly and quiet, but very determined." Describing the crowd as "orderly and quiet" presents an interesting twist to the story. In most eyewitness accounts and even biased newspaper accounts it is rare to find wording about lynch mobs such as rowdy, irate, angry. Editors of the newspaper offered justification for the mob lynching, claimed the incident was the "the third outrage of this kind committed by this class of people." Accusations added, "the people here believe the five men had planned to kill Dr. Hodge as he was going to supper." The lynching happened so quickly even though Dr. Hodge quickly recovered from his wounds.[170]

An almost word-for-word account appeared on the same day from *The Los Angeles Herald* of July 22, 1899 read,

A LOUISIANA LYNCHING
IN WHICH THE VICTIMS WERE
NOT NEGROES
FIVE SICILIANS ARE HANGED

The irony of the west coast headline of "the victims were not negroes" is revealing. Ongoing reports in America on lynching was such a common occurrence the assumption was the victims would be African American. In this case, the editors at *The Los Angeles Herald* felt the need to explain -- lynching of Italians was also becoming a regular occurrence.

---

[169] Franceschini. "Naples Luck and the Iconic Cornetto." *L'Italo Americano*, 2020.
[170] Edward F. Haas. "Guns, Goats, and Italian: The Tallulah Lynching of 1899," p. 51.

126 Italian Culture in America:
The Immigrants 1880 to 1930 From Discrimination to Assimilation

An often underlying reason was economic jealousy. Immigrants such as the De Fatta's owned a profitable business venture. The Tallulah lynching was similar to the 1891 New Orleans lynching. In 2012, Ken Scambray, writing "Corda e Sapone (Rope and Soap): How the Italians were lynched in the USA" for *L'Italo-Americano*, said of the incident,

> "By 1899 five Sicilians were doing a good business in Tallulah, with four small stores devoted to fruit, vegetables, and poultry. All but one of the men were relatives. Whites attacked the Sicilians [due to] economic competition. They had also been criticized for failing to comply with Jim Crow rules: if they had black customers waiting, they made new white customers wait their turn rather than giving the whites preference, as was the custom."

Lynching might have been common in America. In the Italian community, the lynching in Tallulah ignited outrage across the Atlantic to Italy. (A Consul for the Italian Government, named Signore Charles Papini, stationed in in New Orleans, reported the incident to the Italian government.) Sicilians, as immigrants, were not Naturalized Americans; therefore, still citizens of Italy; an issue undertaken by the Italian government in Rome. An important question of clarification was the citizenship status of the victims.[171]

The diplomatic Italian Charge d'Affaires in Washington D.C., Count Vinci petitioned for Secretary of State John Hay to authorize an investigation. An urgent request was made to provide legal protection for immigrants living in the United States against of future hateful attacks and mob retaliation. Response from Washington D.C. and the Louisiana governor was ambivalent. A different approach came from Europe,

> "In Italy, however, the *Fanfulla*, a newspaper, condemned the "indifference of the United States government, which has not the strength to vanquish fanatical prejudices . . . Another journal attacked "sham American civilization."[172]

From July 22 to December 7, 1899, a total of 51 correspondences of letters and telegrams transpired between Count Vinci of the Italian Embassy to John Hay Secretary of State in Washington D.C. adding Governor Murphy J. Foster. Count Vinci asked of Governor Foster to ascertain if the lynched were either Italian subjects or naturalized Americans. If American citizens, the Italian government should not question the events therefore, avoid a dispute. In a telegram on July

---

[171] Ken Scambray. "Corda e Sapone (Rope and Soap): How the Italians were lynched in the USA," *L'Italo-Americano*, December 13, 2012.

[172] Edward F. Haas. "Guns, Goats, and Italian: The Tallulah Lynching of 1899." *North Louisiana Historical Association*. Vol. XIII, No: 2&3, 1982, p. 48.

24th, Count Vinci was told "the governor of Louisiana is investigating the alleged lynching of persons born in Italy, and will take all legal steps to secure justice which the facts may warrant." Vinci declared "the incident was an atrocious act committed in the presence of many persons. It was not conceivable that the guilty parties can not be identified." The final audacious conclusion by Governor Foster reported, incorrectly, the De Ffatta's were naturalized American citizens, therefore, beyond the jurisdiction of the Italian government. Adding, "no further criminal proceedings are to be instituted against the lynchers."[173]

Among all but a few of the Italian-American community, a long-forgotten remembrance was provided by a drawing of the incident. The poster, printed in Italian, was not widely publicized; confined only to a small segment of the Italian community. The wording in Italian,

i cinque poveri italiani / Linoiati a Taluah in America
("The five poor Italians / flaxed [hung] in Tallulah in America.")

Italian Sons & Daughters of America cited the image as "Italian folk singer Antonio Corso (1858/59-1918) wrote a song in honor of the men and this image appeared above the printed transcription of the lyrics."[174]

An illustration of a lynching in Tallulah, Louisiana of
Five Italian Immigrants as victims. The translation from the Italian is,
"The five poor Italians / flaxed [hung] in Tallulah in America."

---

[173] Edward F. Haas. "Guns, Goats, and Italian, " p. 48.
[174] Will Crutchfield researching the origin of such a song wrote, "I don't see any signs of a song published in Torino, which is where Deaglio's book says it appeared. Two songs by Pini-Corsi published in Milano have titles that could belong to such a song: "Tristi pensieri" and "Senza speranza."

Two Centuries Later a Belated Catholic Burial

Over 120 years later, on March 19, 2021 the State of Mississippi and City of Vicksburg honored the five lynched Italians with an official Mississippi State Historical Marker. Located at the burial site of the victims in the Cedar Hill Cemetery in Vicksburg, Mississippi, the historical marker was sponsored by 21st century relatives of Giuseppe De Fatta. The ceremony attended by a small contingent of descendants of the victims, including the mayor of Tallulah and a few others. Prior to the dedication, the Mississippi governor wrote to the family stating, "This state historical marker will ensure that Mississippians will remember their names so that we will never repeat the tragedy of the past." It is difficult not to editorialize on a veiled hypocritical comment by the Mississippi governor, considering the long and continuous history of racial and immigrant discrimination lasted well into the 21st century.

A more somber and humanitarian response might best be understood as was written in response by Rosario Lapunzina, the Mayor of Cefalu in Sicily to the family, who said,

> "In today's world, there are too many signs that the terrible history of the nineteenth and twentieth centuries can be repeated, and that racism, prejudice and human stupidity are now a daily occurrence. For this reason, each of us has the duty to educate young people."

Beyond the important marker at the burial site was a correction to the supreme injustice for the five victims. Each was denied the sacrament of a Catholic burial. As part of the ceremony, the burial site was blessed by a priest from St. Paul's Catholic Church of Vicksburg.[175]

Harper's Weekly of September 1899 printed images of three of the victims. Left to Right: Frank Defatta, Joeph Defatta, and Rosario Fiducia. See also Edward F. Haas, "Guns Goats, and Italians. Public Domain.

---

[175] Linda Fatta Ott, "Italians Lynched in Tallulah, La., Honored with Historical Marker at Gravesite," March 31, 2021. National Italian American Foundation.

CHAPTER 3

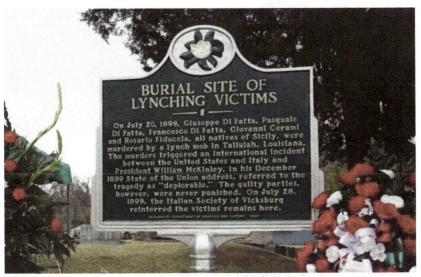

Mississippi State Historical Marker dedicated on March 21, 2021 at Cedar Hill Cemetery in Vicksburg, Mississippi, the gravesite of the five victims of the Tallulah Lynching. Photo courtesy of Charles Marsala and the National Italian America Foundation.

In September 1910, tensions flared during an ongoing labor strike in Tampa, Florida. A labor dispute resulted in a strike lasting over seven months culminating in a series of violent events. As described by historian Joe Scaglione, "One man was assassinated, two men were lynched, others were shot and assaulted." Others such as three union leaders were placed on trial and convicted "conspiring to prevent cigarmakers from working in Tampa's cigar factories." *The New York Times* page 1 headline of September 10, 1910, proclaimed,

> ITALIANS LYNCHED IN A TAMPA STREET;
> Accused of Shooting Employee of Cigarmakers,
> They Are Taken from Officers.

By 1910, *The New York Times* under new owner Adolph Ochs represented a changeover in the editorial staff. As such, the newspaper staff took a journalistic unbiased approach in reporting the news. Unlike the Tallulah lynching regulated to page 7, the Tampa lynching article was placed in the center of page one. Tampa's newspapers continued covering the strike for many months. *The Tampa Morning Tribune* later reported a bookkeeper for the cigar factory named J. Frank Easterling was the "the first American [attacked]." The obvious inference was as an "American" he was white; therefore, mob violence would not be tolerated

130

Italian Culture in America:
The Immigrants 1880 to 1930 From Discrimination to Assimilation

against the white race. Therefore "Easterling is and must be the very last American to be attacked in this bold, bloodthirsty manner."[176]

In 2008, Gene Burnett reminded Tampa residents of their dark past as "the appeal to them as Americans" meant "Anglo-Saxons."

> "The press began screaming in chorus at the "blood-lust possessed nationalities" who had 'the temerity to assault an American.' The union itself denounced the shooting and disclaimed any connection to it. The press had already spurred the organizing of a 'citizens committee' bankers, merchants, lawyers, etc. and began inflammatory appeals to them to 'do something.'"

One example of an editorial from *The Tampa Morning Tribune* adamantly agreed with the actions of Tampa's residents. Stating, "the verdict that the people of this city will not tolerate the business of assassination for hire." Tampa mayor Donald McKay (1868-1960) vowed to restore order and "protection of life and property."[177]

On September 20th, two Italians were arrested; one an unemployed 45-year-old former grocer named Castenge Ficarrotta, and a 25-year-old insurance salesman Angelo Albano. Although, neither was connected with the union; supposedly, both were seen in the crowd when Easterling was shot. As the two Sicilians were in transported in a horse drawn "hack," a mob (supposedly) overwhelmed sheriff's deputies at "gunpoint." The mob lynched the two men – hanging them "from a huge oak tree;" left for all to see; the bodies were photographed hung in a prominent location. On September 21, 1910, *The Tampa Morning Tribune*, page one headline reported on a "Dramatic Note is Pinned to Feet," read as,

BEWARE
Others take notice or go the same
Way. We know seven more. We are
Watching you. If any more citizens
Are molested look out. Justice.

The unnamed reporter revealed the "tragic note" clearly printed as, "Beware . . . was pinned to the trousers of Angelo Albano" helped spread the message to instill fear. Following the warning in livid detail, "through the reign of lynch law." The report described the bodies as,

---

[176] Gene Burnett. "Death and Terror Scar Tampa's Past," *Florida Trend,* June 1, 2008.Joe Scaglione. "City in Turmoil: Tampa and the Strike of 1910," pp. 55-57.
[177] Burnett. "Death and Terror Scar Tampa's Past," and Scaglione pp. 59-62.

CHAPTER 3

Swing in Moonlight

"Two human bodies the forms of the coatless men bathed in a wealth of light given from a full moon sending its days through the luxuriant foliage of a giant oak and full upon the lifeless beings, was a gruesome picture presented city and county authorities last night."

Reporting the title of "Back-to-Back" appears poem-like. In describing the bodies of Ficarrotta and Albano, the published account appeared as,

Back-to-Back

Back-to-Back the bodies of these
Italians depended from a limb branching
Westward from the giant tree a
Distance of twenty-five feet, the feet
of both being about seven feet from
the ground and the limb from which
they were hanged being about eighteen
Feet above the level of the ground

The reporter compared the "deportment" of the two linked victims, describing Albano as "much neater in his personal pride than Ficarrotta." Beyond a comparison of the victims shirts, shoes, trousers, suspenders, belts, the reporter went so far as to the type of rope used to hang the victims even taking note of the fact on how Ficarrotta's "feet were tied together but not in the same knot which fastened those of Albano."[178]

With technology of photography, added to the written description was a new aspect of lynching provided a gruesome attachment to the crime. As an unwarranted offshoot of late 19th and early 20th century photographs recorded lynch victims for wide dispersal. Obviously as what is known as "Gallows Humor," the mob sought further humiliation of the victims even in death. A *Tampa Morning Tribune* reporter rote, "The picture was the more realistic and interesting in that Ficarrotta wearing a beard of two days growth and heavy black mustache, still had his derby on his head and a small pipe in his mouth." In 2009, historian Stefano Luconi responded appropriately, "As a desecrating insult to the corpses."

Among the crowd, photographers took pictures and hurriedly printed copies for sale to the local residents. Sadly, the main reason for the photographic evidence, was to serve as a warning, just as the note pinned to Albano's trousers. The sale and distribution of photographs of lynched victims was quite common.

---

[178] "Dramatic Note is Pinned to Feet." *Tampa Morning Tribune*, Sep. 21, 1910, p. 1.

132 Italian Culture in America:
The Immigrants 1880 to 1930 From Discrimination to Assimilation

In many instances, whites proudly posed with the victims. The protection for whites under the "lynch law" knew no repercussions would happen. Tampa newspapers reported no "sympathy" for Ficarrotta, who had a "well-known" reputation. One account claimed he had previously murdered a family member who was his uncle.

The Tampa Morning Tribune claimed the mob was in its right to take actions, audaciously stated, "Albano is known to have fired the shot which struck Easterling convinced many that the summary treatment handed him was more effective than that usually given through the courts." In what could be considered a carbon copy response to just about any lynching throughout the history of the United States, no legal action was taken. On September 22, 1910. *The Tampa Morning Tribune* reported,

> "Judge Boyett declared last night that so far there is absolutely no clue as to the identity of the members of the mob, but that is will be the endeavor of the jury to ascertain this if possible. He admitted that hope of ascertaining the identities of the person was slim."

The Tampa Morning Tribune reiterated, "Castenge Ficarrotta and Angelo Albano, were lynched by a mob of unknown men, and there was hardly a ripple of disorder or uneasiness which indicated that anything unusual had happened." In a livid response, the Italian government, through the Italian consulate in America, lodged a formal protest to Florida Governor A.W. Gilchrist. In the same request as the Tallulah lynching, protection was sought for Italian citizens as immigrants in America. Reports noted that Governor Gilchrist made an inquiry; a terse response was, "Two Italians lynched last night were American citizens."[179]

On September 25, 1910, a sympathetic editorial in *Il Progresso Italo-Americano* revealed a little-known fact of lynching in America. The newspaper editors wrote,

> "Those who know statistics about lynching are aware that the victims are Black people. Europeans have not been lynched except for Italians only."

Historian Stefano Luconi researching Italian lynchings discovered "at least thirty-four people of Italian birth were lynched throughout the United States between the mid-1880s and the early 1910s." Those numbers, hidden through most pf history, are appalling.[180]

---

[179] Joe Scaglione. "City in Turmoil: Tampa and the Strike of 1910," p. 55.
[180] Stefano Luconi "Tampa's 1910 Lynching: The Italian-American Perspective and Its Implications" *The Florida Historical Quarterly*, Vol. 88 Summer 2009 No. 1., pp. 30-31.

Two lynched victims Castenge Ficarrotta and Angelo Albano. A reporter for *The Tampa Morning Tribune* wrote, "The picture was the more realistic and interesting in that Ficarrotta wearing a beard of two days growth and a heavy black mustache, still had his derby on his head and a small pipe in his mouth."

Prof. Luconi cited one Federico Villarosa in Vicksburg, Mississippi in 1886 as "the first official Italian victim of the "lynch law" in America." Villarosa awaiting trial was overtaken as a mob. As Luconi's research revealed a list of other incidents followed a similar trend,

> "Other lynchings of Italian Americans occurred including Mississippi and Arkansas, both in 1901. Italians were lynched in Louisville, Kentucky, in 1889; in Davis, West Virginia, in 1903; and in the state of Colorado, in Gunnison in 1890; in Denver in 1893; and in Walsenburg [Colorado] in 1895, including three victims at Hahnville, Louisiana in 1896 and five at Tallulah in 1899. In all these incidents, which had different motivations, it was the national origin of the victims that incited the anger of the crowd."[181]

In 2019, Frank Viviano, writing in an article, "Atrocities America Forgot" for *The New York Review*, commented, "Between the 1870s and 1900 the specters of immigration and race led to waves of extrajudicial killings. Most victims were

---

[181] Stefano Luconi. "Tampa's 1910 Lynching," pp. 32,

African-American. But there were at least fifty lynchings of Italians between 1890 and 1924." Lawlessness regarding Italians did not end. In 1915, Joseph Strando was lynched in Johnston City, Illinois. Other instances, such as the famed Sacco and Vanzetti trial during the 1920s, has often been framed as a legal political lynching has been attributed to "political railroading."[182]

Above: Lynching in Minneapolis, Minnesota of a person by the name of Frank MacManus, c. 1882. In the photo, a mob has turned and faced the camera witout any fear of retribuition. A close look at the assemblage appears defiant and sending a warning message. Reproduction Number: LC-USZ62-2462 Library of Congress Prints and Photographs Division.

---

[182] Frank Viviano. "Atrocities America Forgot." *The New York Review*, June 6, 2019.

CHAPTER 4A

AN INNOCENT, A DIPLOMAT, BOOKER T. WASHINGTON, AND A TRAVEL EXPERT IN ITALY

"Travel is fatal to prejudice, bigotry, and narrow-mindedness,
and many of our people need it sorely
on these accounts." Mark Twain, 1869

Thomas Jefferson in Italy

In the early years of America, probably the most famous person to visit Italy was Thomas Jefferson. In that same sense, he is also most likely the least known Italophile. From 1785 to 1789, Jefferson was living in Paris as an America Ambassador. Whenever possible, he took the time to travel throughout Europe. In April of 1787, a planned crossing of the Alps led to spending three weeks touring the northern regions of Italy. Along the way, Jefferson journeyed to the northern cities of Turin, Vercelli, Milan, Cassino, and Genoa. Along the way, the journey was interspersed with some forty other smaller towns and communes in Lombardy, Piedmont, and Liguria. During the journey, Jefferson continuously observed common everyday Italian life; such as making Parmesan cheese; or ferrying passengers across the Po River in a flat bottom boat. Included were a compilation of daily detailed notes in his travel diary.[183]

Thomas Jefferson's recollections of Italy are numerous, but can be summed up in a brief quote he wrote while in Albegna, Italy,

"If any person wished to retire from their acquaintance, to live absolutely unknown and yet in the midst of physical enjoyments, it should be in

---

[183] Ralph G. Giordano. *Italian Culture in America: How A Founding Father Introduced Italian Art, Architecture, Food, Wine, and Liberty To The American People* (Academica Press 2020), p. 335.

136 Italian Culture in America:
The Immigrants 1880 to 1930 From Discrimination to Assimilation

some of the little villages of this coast [of Italy], where the air, earth, and water concur to offer what each has most precious."[184]

The trip yielded a wealth of first-hand Italian experiences, further deepening his love of Italian culture and influence after return to America. Within Jefferson's world-changing events are many complex attributes attaining similar wide-ranging influence such as his affinity for Italian culture. Throughout his lifetime, Mr. Jefferson was a devout Italophile, influential in introducing many sustaining cultural aspects of Italian art, architecture, food, wine, and liberty to the American People. As historian Eric Martone in the compendium *Italian Americans, The History and Culture of a People*, revealed, "Virtually every aspect of American culture has been influenced by Italian immigrants and their descendants."[185]

Thomas Jefferson was not the first American to visit Italy. During his time, Americans who visited Italy were few and far between; those who did were usually prominent individuals on the Grand Tour studying art and cultural artifacts. Throughout the 220 years or so since Jefferson, visitation to Italy by Americans remained a trickle. It was not until the post-World War II period, Americans in growing numbers entertained thoughts of a cross-Atlantic journey. The idea was to see and experience cultural aspects of European countries such as Italy. By the 21st century Italy ranked as one of the worlds' top tourist destinations. (In 2017, Italy was the fifth most visited tourist destination with 58.3 million arrivals.) In the years between 1787 and 2017, a reverse flow of Italian immigration to America increased from a slow-trickle to a massive onslaught numbering in the millions during the peak years of 1880 to 1920.

***

Mark Twain an "Innoncent Abroad" in Italy

We should consider a simple fact -- many of the social critics who disdained Italian immigrants never visited Italy; nor made an attempt to visit, or intermingle within Italian neighborhoods on any type of fact-finding friendly mission. For those which might have traveled abroad, or even studied the history of Italy; it was to the northern cultural cities notable from the Renaissance. Criticism of immigrants by Senator Henry Cabot Lodge, or historians as Eugene E. Foerster; comparisons were often based on preconceived notions of hearsay, specific prejudices, or simply political fear mongering. For Lodge and his supporters, it was purely politically motivated; or in situations such as the New Orleans lynching, and other enacted forms of discrimination in cities and towns, to steal the economic thunder away from established immigrant entrepreneurs.

---

[184] Thomas Jefferson, "Notes of a Tour into the Southern Parts of France 3 March–10 June 1787," *Founders Online,* National Archives.
[185] Eric Martone, ed. *Italian Americans, The History and Culture of a People,* 2016.

CHAPTER 4A

In contrast, one social critic who did visit Italy was the famous American writer Mark Twain (1835-1910). Born in Missouri, Samuel Langhorne Clemens (took the pen name "Mark Twain") is one of the best known and beloved authors. Twain's indelible contribution to American literature, often intertwined with humorist and moralist themes seem to transcend time. Two of his more famous works provided American culture with lasting iconic images in *The Adventures of Tom Sawyer* (1876) and *Adventures of Huckleberry Finn* (1885). Both novels are still required reading in many schools and universities. Others continue to seek out the novels from bookstores and libraries. For well over a century, Twain's literature has been praised, scrutinized, criticized, and sometimes banned.

During his own lifetime, Mark Twain published a few other classical works. Each was based upon his own real-life experience as a Mississippi river boat captain and personal travels. A few example included *Roughing It* (1872) and *Life on the Mississippi* (1883). Unlike many other authors, Twain achieved national and international fame – while he was alive - both through his writing and in-person lectures. And of course, many of his publications were well-read and portrayed in movie versions long after his passing. Of his many classic writings, it was his first published work, a travel narrative titled *The Innocents Abroad* (1869) that sold the most copies during his lifetime. Over time, the tales of Twain's voyages are mostly forgotten; yet remain a valuable resource.[186]

The Innocents Abroad recounted an earlier voyage to Europe, including an almost three week stay in Italy. In June of 1867, Samuel Clemens sailed to Europe aboard the *Quaker City* a decommissioned Civil War era sidewheel steamship. The full title on the book cover read as,

INNOCENTS ABROAD
Or
THE NEW PILGRIMS' PROGRESS;

Being Some Account of the Steamship Quaker City's Pleasure Excursion to Europe and the Holy Land; with Descriptions of Countries, Nations, Incidents and Adventures, as they Appeared to The Author.

---

[186] See: "Innocents Abroad (1869)." *Mark Twain's Geography.* Accessed October 23, 2020. Note: Twain's adventures in Italy are presented in chapters 17 to 31.

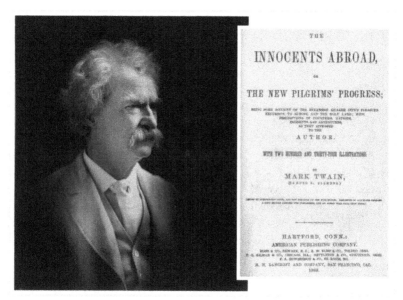

Above Left: Portrait of Mark Twain (nee: Samuel Langhorne Clemens 1835-1910) photograph by: A.F. Bradley. Library of Congress Prints and Photographs Division. Reproduction Number: LC-USZ62-28777. **Above Right:** Title page of Mark Twain's Innocents Abroad, from an 1869 First Edition (Public Domain).

The publication contained Two Hundred Thirty-Four Illustrations with credit of authorship under his new pen name of "Mark Twain" with the birth name of (Samuel L. Clemens) in parenthesis. (He used his pen name as early as 1863; adopting it officially around 1873.) Within *Innocents Abroad*, Twain chronicled a trans-Atlantic voyage aboard the *Quaker City* entering through the port city of Genoa, Italy. Later sailing into Livorno (known to Americans as "Leghorn"). An inland railroad journey took Twain and his travel companions to Milan, Lake Como, Venice, Florence, Pisa, and Rome. Unlike earlier travelers who took the Grand Tour of the Renaissance art and architecture, Twain and companions traveled among cities and towns observing Italian lifestyles and culture. After the required visitation of tourist sites, Twain and a small group often wandered among the sites and scenes of everyday Italian life. Among all the cities of Italy, a stark contrast was noticed by Twain between American cultural lifestyles as compared to those of Italians of all regions. Twain noted,

> "We walked up and down one of the most popular streets enjoying other people's comfort and wishing we could export some of it to our restless, vitality-consuming marts at home. Just in this one matter lies the main charm of life in Europe comfort. In America, we hurry which is well; but when the day's work is done, we go on thinking of losses and gains, we

CHAPTER 4A   139

plan for the morrow, we even carry our business cares to bed with us, and toss and worry over them when we ought to be restoring our racked bodies and brains with sleep. We burn up our energies with these excitements, and either die early or drop into a lean and mean old age at a time of life which they call a man's prime in Europe. What a robust people, what a nation of thinkers we might be, if we would only lay ourselves on the shelf occasionally and renew our edges!"[187]

This candid observational cultural aspect by Twain offers vivid insight as to why a prevalent misconceived notion of Italian immigrants were portrayed as "lazy" in America. This notion was gradually ingrained into the American cultural psyche beginning in the 1880s. That mythical notion was especially problematic among those Italian immigrants who had both a birth history from their home country, combined with their adopted new country of America. The unfortunate discrimination came despite working for long and physically demanding hours of labor. In America with work aside, Italian immigrants sought to enjoy the simple pleasures of family and friends through conversation and leisurely meals; a misunderstood experience to Americans. In an honest evaluation of his own familiar lifestyle of the American Midwest, Twain put aside any preconceived notion of nationalistic pride. Of the Italian people he wrote,

"I do envy these Europeans the comfort they take. . . They are always quiet, always orderly, always cheerful, comfortable, and appreciative of life and its manifold blessings. One never sees a drunken man among them. The change that has come over our little party is surprising. Day by day we lose some of our restlessness and absorb some of the spirit of quietude and ease that is in the tranquil atmosphere about us and in the demeanor of the people. We grow wise apace [quickly]. We begin to comprehend what life is for."[188]

Twain's overall assessment contrasted the litany of contemporary American critics, such as the fear-mongering Henry Cabot Lodge, and many prejudicial accounts published in newspapers and magazines. Another contrast to other first-hand accounts by earlier foreign travelers, Twain's journey included traveling south from Rome to Naples and Pompei. While their ship was in temporary quarantine due to a Cholera epidemic, the Twain group stayed in Naples and the local area for 10 days.

At 140 miles (226 km) south of Rome, Naples is along the western coast of the Italian peninsular. The coastal city is among some of the most beautiful geography in all of Europe; if not the world. Naples serves as a major seaport for

---

[187] Mark Twain. *The Innocents Abroad: or the New Pilgrims' Progress*. Project Guttenberg, August 16, 2006, p. 61.
[188] Mark Twain. *The Innocents Abroad: or the New Pilgrims' Progress*, p. 161.

Italy among the southern regions of Bari, Calabria, Foggia, and Sicily. A significant number of Italian immigrants to America from these regions left from the port of Naples aboard similar ships such as the *USS Quaker City*. Upon arriving in Naples, Mark Twain offered sparkling commentary on the stunning natural geography as,

> "See Naples and die. Well, I do not know that one would necessarily die after merely seeing it, but to attempt to live there might turn out a little differently. To see Naples as we saw it in the early dawn from far up on the side of Mt. Vesuvius, is to see a picture of wonderful beauty."

In a litany of poetic pose, Twain continued to praise the geographical beauty of the Neapolitan locale, as he added,

> "The frame of the picture was charming, itself. In front, the smooth sea--a vast mosaic of many colors; the lofty islands swimming in a dreamy haze in the distance; at our end of the city the stately double peak of Vesuvius, and its strong black ribs and seams of lava stretching down to the limitless level campagna--a green carpet that enchants the eye and leads it on and on, past clusters of trees, and isolated houses, and snowy villages, until it shreds out in a fringe of mist and general vagueness far away."

The natural Neapolitan geographical beauty, however, could not contain the visual existence of an ongoing devastating, not of regular volcanic eruption, rather a Cholera epidemic.

A sidewheel steamship, the *USS Quaker City* built in 1854 in Philadelphia was a decommissioned Civil War era warship converted for commercial use. In June of 1867, the *Quaker City* sailed to Europe with Samuel Clemens (aka "Mark Twain") aboard. Drawing by Clary Ray, c. 1900. Courtesy of the Navy Art Collection, Washington, DC. NH 57840 (Public Domain).

Late 19th century oil on canvas painting "A View of Naples and Vesuvius" about the same years of Mark Twain's visit. Unknown artist (U.S. Public Domain).

One of the basic functions to contain a Cholera epidemic is a routine of daily bathing and washing provided by a clean water supply. Twain made a critical observation on the cleanliness of the inhabitants of Naples, which, in all likelihood, contributed to a high death rate. In contrast to the awe-inspiring natural beauty, Twain cautioned,

> "But do not go within the walls and look at it in detail. That takes away some of the romance of the thing. The people are filthy in their habits, and this makes filthy streets and breeds disagreeable sights and smells. There never was a community so prejudiced against the cholera as these Neapolitans are. But they have good reason to be. The cholera generally vanquishes a Neapolitan when it seizes him, because, you understand, before the doctor can dig through the dirt and get at the disease the man dies."

When spoke in a colloquial sense, the term "to die for" is of a positive awe-inspiring response. In the sense of the opening line, "See Naples and die" might very well reflect Mr. Twain's gallows humor. The geography and lifestyles are certainly an "eye-opening" positive experience; as some in America would say "to see it is to die for." On the other hand, Twain's wry humor during a Cholera epidemic applies the fact that a visit to the beautiful location of Naples, could literally result in physical death.

Despite it all, the first-hand experience of spending time in Italy (and other parts of Europe) brought Mr. Twain to a thought-provoking affirmation. Offered as an antidote to the preconceived notions spewed by politicians and mimicked

142   Italian Culture in America:
The Immigrants 1880 to 1930 From Discrimination to Assimilation

by the hateful treatment of Italian immigrants by sheltered privileged Americans, Twain appropriately analyzed,

> "Travel is fatal to prejudice, bigotry, and narrow-mindedness, and many of our [American] people need it sorely on these accounts. Broad, wholesome, charitable views of men and things cannot be acquired by vegetating in one little corner of the earth all one's lifetime."[189]

Another who traveled extensively in Europe observing other cultures and lifestyles was an American diplomat named Eugene Schuyler.

Eugene Schuyler an American Diplomat in Italy

Amidst the furor for immigration restriction to the United States, one American diplomat offered a contradictory alternative response. An obituary once described Eugene Schuyler (1840-1890) as "an American diplomat who served in many countries including Bulgaria, Greece, Romania, Serbia, Turkey, and as American Consul General in Rome beginning in 1879." As a noted PhD "scholar, writer, explorer, and diplomat," Schuyler authored numerous books and often wrote of his unique travel experiences for *National Geographic*. In October 1889, Schuyler received an appointment as the U.S. Consular General in Cairo, Egypt serving under President Benjamin Harrison. By all accounts, the European posting was thoroughly enjoyed; taking time absorbing the history and travel experience. An unfortunate condition due to the harsh climate, the natural beauty of Egypt was often disrupted. As a result, Schuyler contracted malaria; as he explained at a time "when the Nile is overflowed . . . and the consequent flies, mosquitoes, etc., beggar all description." Requiring to convalesce in a welcoming climate, Schuyler opted for Venice, Italy; unfortunately, where he died in July of 1890. His legacy was praised in a posthumous review of his essays and memoirs published in 1901 in the *New York Times* describing Schuyler as "one of America's most brilliant scholars, patriots, and men of letters."[190]

---

[189] Mark Twain. *The Innocents Abroad: or the New Pilgrims' Progress*, p. 161.
[190] "Eugene Schuyler Obituary," *The New York Times*. July 19, 1890.

Photo of Eugene Schuyler taken while serving as American Consul-General in Constantinople, c. 1876 (Public Domain).

As an influential scholar, Eugene Schuyler often wrote of contemporary "immigrant problems." One year before his death, he published "Italian Immigration into the United States" in the *Political Science Quarterly*. Unlike, false political accusations against Italian immigrants in America, an "insider" view of the situation was offered. He agreed all Americans "should be, deeply concerned in the amount of this immigration when it is directed to our own shores." As a different approach, Schuyler tried to offer his readers to understand the reasons why any individual would leave their homeland. Research provided a slew of emigration statistics covering the years 1884 to 1886; from the larger population embarkation ports of such as Florence, Genoa, Milan, Naples, Palermo, Rome, and Turin. One comparative trend noticed less emigration from the larger cities, yet larger numbers from the smaller towns and rural countryside. Schuyler provided,

> "The small amount of emigration from the large cities of Italy is peculiarly noticeable. Naples is the largest town, and has a density of population superior to that of London, Paris, Berlin, or Vienna; yet its emigration is less than from many a good-sized village of the Basilicate or Calabria."

One common factor was observed not just from Italy, but similar to other European countries. The commonality was "bad harvests, low wages, want of

144 Italian Culture in America:
The Immigrants 1880 to 1930 From Discrimination to Assimilation

work, desire to get on in the world, and invitations of friends who have already emigrated." A summation, unlike the obvious, was one word "misery" - mainly prevalent in the southern regions and more so in Sicily, was a systematic "feudal type" arrangement still existed. Although not necessarily living as serfs, many Italians were indebted to working upon lands which they did not own; while forced to pay rent for cottages they could not afford to buy. The result was a continuing cycle of poverty "because their wages are not enough for their needs."[191]

Of most importance was Schuyler's study of "the general morality of the Italians." In direct contrast to the many unsubstantiated claims of American politicians and the prejudicial newspapers to the contrary, the former Consul General of Rome gave "a very favorable account." He did not perform an analysis of crime, since he explained,

> "Criminal statistics are in general worthless, except in comparisons with other countries - and even then, are worth little, unless there be a certain equality in civilization and a similarity in the modes of administering justice."[192]

Some might quickly dismiss the statement on the supposed criminality of Italians and Sicilians. Included was the American press and the likes of Senators and Mayors who routinely claimed Italians as a "criminal class." In contrast to the American slander, Schuyler offered from "personal experience" of living three years in Italy. He wrote,

> "I have travelled in almost every part of Italy at all times of day and night, and have never been in any way molested or had any suspicion of trouble. Theft here is rare, burglary unknown; so that we have slept for weeks with doors unlocked and even open - after the earthquake for instance and never think of locking them during the day. A murder has not been known for fifty years. Illegitimate children are very rare; crimes produced by lust are almost unknown. Taking everything together it would seem that the Italians, in spite of poverty and illiteracy, are if they will remain in the United States - a desirable element to fuse with our motley population. They bring to us the logical qualities of the Latin race, and they show in the long run the effect of an experience which no other people in Europe has had of over two thousand years of civilization."[193]

---

[191] Eugene Schuyler. "Italian Immigration into the United States." *Political Science Quarterly*, Vol. 4, No. 3 (Sep., 1889), p. 480.

[192] Schuyler. "Italian Immigration into the United States." p. 480.

[193] Eugene Schuyler. "Italian Immigration into the United States." *Political Science Quarterly*, Vol. 4, No. 3 (Sep., 1889), pp. 485-486.

CHAPTER 4A

Schuyler's observations affirms the 19th century observations of Mark Twain; who as with many others, fully understand "seeing is believing." Added to "seeing" is an opportunity to debunk "prejudice, bigotry, and narrow-mindedness." Added to the ongoing positive affirmations in the 21st century is the travel expert and historian Rick Steves

---

Rick Steves: *Travel as a Political Act* and *"Bell' Italia"*

In 2020, historian and travel expert Rick Steves (b. 1955) based a profitable travel business on a similar philosophy. (As a descendant of Norwegian immigrants, Steves said his family, "left their homeland to escape and came to America because they wanted to work hard and contribute in a land of opportunity and justice.")[194] Steves terms travel to foreign countries as a "political act" to eliminate preconceived prejudicial notions. A simple offering in his 2018 publication *Travel as a Political Act*, suggests,

> "It's good for you! Americans who approach travel thoughtfully — as a political act — can have the time of their lives and come home with a better understanding of the interconnectedness of today's world and just how our nation fits in."[195]

In fact, Mr. Steves espouses social responsibility as an integral part of "our company's mission." The mission extends well beyond the overlying capitalistic motives so much ingrained overtly in American culture. Expertise and tours offered by Steves travel company are almost exclusively European; directly connected to a significant number of American customers with ancestral roots to European immigrants. Mr. Steves strives to help Americans understand a study of our shared immigrant heritage can provide for a healthier compassionate environment at home. He explains,

> "Our mission at Rick Steves' Europe is to inspire, inform, and equip Americans to have European trips that are fun, affordable, and culturally broadening. We value travel as a powerful way to better understand and contribute to the world in which we live. . . . We strive to keep our own travel style, our world outlook, and our business practices consistent with these values."[196]

As it applies to Italian culture in America, Mr. Steves travel advice represents a reverse process for the Italian contribution to American culture. During the 1890s to 1930, most Americans did not have the financial opportunity to travel as was

---

[194] "Thoughts About My Immigrant Heritage," *RickSteves.com*, January 14, 2018.
[195] Rick Steves. *Travel as a Political Act*, 2nd Edition, 2018
[196] "Rick Steves Social Activism & Philanthropy." Accessed October 23, 2020.

afforded to authors such as Mark Twain or diplomats as Eugene Schuyler. Travel culture was mostly reserved to the upper rungs of the wealthier class. For Italian immigrants, their voyages to America was the first time most had ever ventured even beyond a few miles of the land of their birth.

The third-class accommodations of ocean travel at the time was nowhere near a leisurely "vacation." For many Italian immigrants the relocation in America afforded an opportunity for creativity and profitability. The idea of creating a product or business within the time frame of the 1890s, known as the Gilded Age, often came at the physical abuse of immigrant labor. The unbridled monopolistic pursuit, and acquisition, of conspicuous wealth was mainly confined to white American nativists. The path for incorporating cultural contributions is often paired with wealth; which in America is often the only defining value of the word "success." In America, as in Europe, the wealth was, and is, contained within a very small segment of society without concern for what it might provide for the overall population.[197]

Often overlooked, similar values prompted so many immigrants, especially Italians, who contributed to American society in fields such as architecture, art, education, film, culinary arts, labor unions, mutual aid societies, opera, music, technology, toys, and sports, among others. Each of these cultural contributions requiring the ingenuity, talent, creativity, innovation, and perseverance, offered monetary wealth to individuals, while offering a refreshing repose for enjoyment as a contribution to the overall fabric of American society. As such, travel experts such as Rick Steves recognize the beauty of places such as Italy. As Steves observed,

> "Bell' Italia! Italy has Europe's richest, craziest culture. After all, this nation is the cradle of European civilization established by the Roman Empire and carried on by the Roman Catholic Church. As you explore Italy, you'll stand face-to-face with some of the world's most iconic images from this 2,000-year history: Rome's ancient Colosseum and playful Trevi Fountain, Pisa's Leaning Tower, Florence's Renaissance masterpieces and the island city of elegant decay Venice. Beyond these famous sights, though, Italy offers Europe's richest culture. Traditions still live within a country that is vibrant and fully modern. Go with an eye open to both the Italy of the past and of the present. Sicily is a fertile mix of geology and culture. Eruptions from its volcano, a glowing sun, generations of hard work, and wave after wave of civilizations storming through over the centuries — they all come together here, giving visitors a full-bodied travel experience that engages all the senses."

---

[197] "Rick Steves Social Activism & Philanthropy." Accessed October 23, 2020.

Historian and Travel Expert Rick Steves overlooking "*Bell' Italia*" in Italy's Cinque Terre. Courtesy of Lisa Werner and Rick Steves. Photo by Zachary Scott.

As a further distinction between Sicily, and not just Italy, but also was a comparative statement regarding the multi-cultural "Italian island of Sicily is perhaps more than any corner of Europe a layer cake of civilizations European continent." Within the "layer cake" of Sicilian history was also a hidden horror of "child slaves" that observed by another American visitor during an earlier visit in 1910; and subsequently published in 1912.[198]

Booker T. Washington and The Horrors of *La Carusi* in Sicily

As a former American slave and leader of the Tuskegee Institute, Booker T. Washington (1856-1915) was uniquely qualified to recognize inhumane conditions in society. Born into slavery in Franklin County, Virginia, Washington later rose to prominence as an African American intellectual of the late 19th century. The Editors at History.com state, "His mother [a slave] was a cook for the plantation's owner. His father, a white man, was unknown to Washington." After the Civil War, Washington at nine years old and his family were freed; moving to Malden, West Virginia. Unlike others pursuing vocational skills, Washington pursued an educational path, although not an easy one. Each day he worked at least five hours prior to attending school. In 1872, Washington enrolled at Hampton Institute in Virginia founded in 1868 for formerly enslaved people.

---

[198] "Sicily." *Rick Steves Europe*, and "Discovering Layers of Culture." *Rick Steves Europe*, Accessed November 9, 2020.

At Hampton, "he was an excellent student and received high grades." In 1881, Washington was recommended to head a new school for African Americans at The Tuskegee Industrial Institute in Alabama (now Tuskegee University); a position held for 35 years.

The post-Civil War years in America were particularly dangerous for any non-white individuals living in the southern states. States such as Alabama were reeking with retaliatory violence against any perceived progressive advancements for African Americans or recent immigrants. A struggle continued to maintain advancement while avoiding possible physical destruction of Tuskegee, by the likes of discriminatory legislation or violence by the Ku Klux Klan. To avoid potential conflicts Washington assumed a position of a continuous advocation of social advancement. The basic premise to "dignify and glorify common labor." He disavowed political action assuming instead acceptance of segregation which stood in opposition to other contemporary African Americans.

 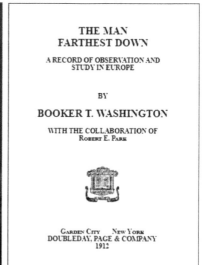

Above Left: Portrait of Booker T. Washington, c. 1905, by Harris & Ewing.
Above Right: Title page of *The Man Farthest Down*, c. 1912, containing accounts of Booker T. Washington's visit to Italy and Sicily. (Public Domain)

Washington's stance "as the most influential African American speaker of his time," earned distinction as the first African American invited to a dinner at the White House – as a guest and advisor rather than a servant or slave. (President Abraham Lincoln once invited a delegation of African Americans to the White House, but not to sit for dinner.) In October of 1901, President Theodore Roosevelt, a progressive reformer invited Washington to sit for dinner alongside

CHAPTER 4A

149

the Roosevelt family. To no surprise the invitation caused overt moral outrage from many in Congress, especially among Southern politicians, newspaper editors, and individuals across the nation.

The legacy of Booker T. Washington is readily available through many easily accessible sources; including an autobiography, publications, biography, and research. Among the lasting historical significance is an often over looked 1912 publication *The Man Farthest Down: A Record of Observation and Study in Europe*; a memoir of a six-week tour of Europe. During his exploration, Washington visited many of the European countries which served as an influx of immigrants to the United States. Included countries were the United Kingdom, Denmark, Hungary, Russia, Germany, Italy, and Sicily. The comparative study focused on a relationship to the contemporary status of the Negro in America. ("Negro" was commonly used for many years. From the 1960s to the 1980s, the term "Negro" was deemed socially unacceptable; replaced with either "African American" or "Black.")[199]

From August 28 to October 7th of 1910, Washington's Italian trek came with the full intention of observing Europe's poorest classes, common living conditions, and particular circumstances which might increase their social standing. Of particular interest and curiosity for Washington was an attempt to find out firsthand what the lives of Italians and Sicilians were like. Moreso, to answer the question why would they leave their home country to immigrate to America and often supplement the American Negro for lower wages in the agricultural fields, dangerous factories, and unsafe mines. A surprising sight confronted Washington in Sicily during visits to Palermo and Catania; witnessing extreme poverty and the inconceivable horror of young children working the Sulphur mines. As incredulous as it may seem, Washington found a social class in Sicily on a scale below African Americans. He wrote,

> "I have described at some length the condition of the farm labourers in Italy because it seems to me that it is important that those who are inclined to be discouraged about the Negro in the South should know that his case is by no means hopeless as that of some others. The Negro is not the man farthest down. The condition of the coloured [sic] farmer in the most backward parts of the Southern States in America. . . is incomparably better than the condition and opportunities of the agricultural population in Sicily."[200]

---

[199] "Booker T. Washington," History.com Editors. October 29, 2009.

[200] Original in: Booker T. Washington. *The Man Farthest Down*. New York: Doubleday, Page and Co., 1912, p. 144. See also: Jerre Mangione and Ben Morreale. *La Storia: Five Centuries of the Italian American Experience*, p. xv.

One observation examined the legal structure of land ownership in Sicily and Italy. In a shocking discovery, Washington discovered a higher level of social acceptance among former slaves in America than among those Sicilians and Italians in their own homeland. As Washington explained,

> "But there is great difference between the Negro farmer in the South and the Italian farmer in Sicily. In Sicily a few capitalists and descendants of the old feudal lords own practically all the soil and, under the crude and expensive system of agriculture. . . there is not enough land to employ the surplus population . . . Thus, between the upper and the nether millstone the farmer is crushed."

The application of the word "crushed" might be viewed as an applied metaphor. Yet, in the most severe case of irony, the word reveals the cruel horrific truth behind the literal meaning of the word; as Washington also discovered the existence of *La Carusi.*

The direct translation of *La Carusi* is "The Boys" – in Sicily the translation was known as "The Mine Boys." All were universally born of extreme poverty as many Sicilian families often "lent out" their young children (aged as young as 4 to 12) in the form of indentured servitude to owners of the Sulphur Mines. In exchange for a cash sum, the child was relinquished to a life of mandatory work in a factory or mine at the complete mercy of the overseer. In truth, the Sicilian family never earned enough money to release their child from the "loan" provided. Washington later explained the harsh reality to an American audience, as his memoir was published in the popular nationwide magazine *Outlook,*

> "The father who turns his child over to a miner receives in return a sum of money in the form of a loan. The sum usually amounts to from eight to thirty dollars, according to the age of the boy, his strength and general usefulness. With the payment of this sum the child is turned over absolutely to his master. From this Slavery there is no hope of freedom, because neither the parents nor the child will ever have sufficient money to repay the original loan."

Witnessing the situation of *La Carusi*, Washington expressed comparative dismay, saying, "The cruelties to which the child slaves of Sicily have been subjected are as bad as anything reported of the cruelties of Negro slavery." For those who held any possible disbelief of the "cruelties" inflicted upon *La Carusi*, in comparison to the cruelties inflicted upon African slaves, Washington reported,

> "These boy slaves were frequently beaten and pinched, in order to wring from their overburdened bodies, the last drop of strength they had in them. When beatings did not suffice, it was the custom to singe the calves of their legs with lanterns to put them again on their feet. If they sought

CHAPTER 4A

151

to escape from this slavery in flight, they were captured and beaten, sometimes even killed."

For an individual who experienced the horrors of American Slavery it is almost inconceivable to relate the plight of Italian and Sicilian boys of the *La Carusi* as vividly as Washington provided. For an individual so well aware of American slavery and segregation, a summation offered, "I am not prepared just now to say to what extent I believe in a physical hell in the next world, but a Sulphur mine in Sicily is about the nearest thing to hell that I expect to see in this life."[201]

As a startling revelation, prior to visiting Italy, Washington freely admitted, like so many other Americans he had believed the social "myth" placed against Italian immigrants. Myths such as published in so many erroneous reports in contemporary American newspapers often describing Italians as "murderous thieves." Or in 1880 as *The New York Times* described Italian immigrants as the "filthy, wretched, lazy, ignorant, and criminal dregs of the meanest section of Italy." While touring the Italian countryside and interaction with locals gave Washington an understanding of all the falsehoods labeled against Italian immigrants. Undertaking of such a situation of realization beyond America, he revealed,

> "I went to Italy with the notion that the Sicilians were a race of brigands, a sullen and irritable people who were disposed at any moment to be swept off their feet by violent and murderous passions. I came away with the feeling that, whatever might be the faults of the masses of the people, they were, at the very least, more sinned against than sinning, and that they deserve the sympathy rather than the condemnation of the world. The truth is that, as far as my personal experience goes, I was never treated more kindly in my whole life that I was the day when, coming as a stranger, without an introduction of any kind, I ventured to visit the region which has the reputation of being the most wicked, and is certainly the most unfortunate, in Europe. If anyone had told me before I went to Sicily that I would be willing to entrust my life to Sicilians away down in the darkness of a Sulphur mine. I had read and heard so much of murders, of the Mafia in Sicily, that for a long time I had had a horror of the name of Sicilians; but when I came in contact with them, before I knew it, I found myself trusting them absolutely."

Another myth dispelled was the constant nostalgic view of the beauty of the *Bel Paese* life in the southern areas of the Italian peninsula and the island of Sicily.[202]

---

[201] Booker T. Washington, *The Man Farthest Down*, p. 145; also published as "Child Labor and the Sulphur Mines," *Outlook*, 98 (June 17, 1911), pp. 342-349.
[202] *The Booker T. Washington Papers*, ed. Geraldine McTigue, Vol. 11: 1911-12, p. 214-215. Reprinted in "Child Labor and the Sulphur Mines," *Outlook*, 98 (June 17, 1911), pp. 342-349.

152 Italian Culture in America:
The Immigrants 1880 to 1930 From Discrimination to Assimilation

In no way is there any attempt to dissuade any notion against the absolute magnificent natural geography and stunning natural beauty of the Mediterranean region. Yet, as the country was in the midst of an Industrial Revolution, many of the areas experienced similar problems as the urban cities such as London, New York, and Chicago, to name a few. Booker T. Washington described many of the Italian regions an "abomination of desolation." Citing, as he saw, "many miles [of] poisonous smoke and vapors from the smelters [a factory process for removing iron from ore] the whole country has a blotched and scrofulous appearance."[203]

Washington's observations were not singular; rather he witnessed similar conditions in the regions of Catania, Campofanco, and Palermo. The horrid physical abuse was not confined solely to the Sulphur mines. Washington visited factories producing macaroni, musical instruments, and metalworking, among others. In all situations, he found many young boys and girls working in dangerous conditions, some as young as 7 and as old as 12. He recalled witnessing child labor as,

> "About nine o'clock Saturday night my attention was attracted to a man engaged in some delicate sort of metal tool-making. What particularly attracted my attention was a little girl, certainly not more than seven years of age, who was busily engaged at this late hour in polishing and sharpening the stamps the man used. I could but marvel at the patience and the skill the child showed at her work. It was the first time in my life that I had seen such a very little child at work, although I saw many others in the days that followed. I am certain that if I had not seen them with my own eyes, I would never have believed that such small children could carry such heavy loads, or that they could work so systematically and steadily."

When *The Man Farthest Down* was published, Booker T. Washington was well-known in America. The publication came after five previous works, including his classic 1901 autobiography *Up From Slavery*. Despite the acclaim, Washington was still a Black man in a strictly segregated society. Therefore, it was unlikely many whites read any of Washington's work; nor the revealing *The Man Farthest Down*. Considering the existing contempt for African Americans and Italian immigrants in America, it is hard to conceive how many would have any sympathy to the unforgiving truth as witnessed by Booker T. Washington.[204]

---

[203] *The Booker T. Washington Papers*, ed. Geraldine McTigue, Vol. 11: 1911-12, p. 232. Quoted from: Michel Huysseune. "This Country, Where Many Things Are Strange and Hard to Understand: Booker T. Washington in Sicily," RSA Journal, 25: 2014, pp. 173-190. Booker T. Washington. *The Man Farthest Down*, pp. 214-215.
[204] Booker T. Washington. *The Man Farthest Down*, p. 197.

Looking back on early travelers such as Booker T. Washington, Thomas Jefferson, Mark Twain, and Eugene Schuyler, and contemporary observations by Rick Steves, it is important to reflect on the reason for the mis-interpretation of Italian Culture through the ages. As posited by Italian Scholars, such as Anthony Tamburri of the John D. Calandra Italian American Institute in 2020, the suggestion states,

"We need to take Italian American culture more seriously. We cannot continue to engage in a series of reminiscences that lead primarily to nostalgic recall."[205]

Photograph outside a Sicilian Sulphur mine, c. 1899, by Eugenio Interguglielmi (1850-1911). (Public Domain)

---

[205] Quoted in: Tom Verso, "Child Slavery in Sicily 1910," *i-italy.org*, January 20, 2008.

CHAPTER 4B

CONSTANTINO BRUMIDI, GIUSEPPE GARIBALDI, AND ANTONIO MEUCCI

"Culture is by far the most important element of Italian foreign policy . . . Italy is a cultural superpower." Giulio Terzi di Sant'Agata, Italian foreign minister, 2013

"Even as our nation grew and our Capitol itself expanded; Italian influences remained." Nancy Pelosi, Speaker of the U.S. House of Representatives, 2007

In the years before the massive number of Italian immigrants began arriving in America, three Italians, namely, Constantino Brumidi, Giuseppe Garibaldi, and Antonio Meucci, all prior to 1880, established a lasting impact upon American culture. During a 50-year period dating from 1820 to 1870, Italian immigration numbered less than 25,000, mainly from northern Italy. The U.S. Library of Congress reports, "These early arrivals settled in communities all across the country, from the farm towns of New Jersey and the vineyards of California to the ports of San Francisco." Among them was an Italian artist Constantino Brumidi, who spent decades creating the paintings and frescoes that adorn the U.S. Capitol, including frescoes on the interior of majestic dome designed by architect Thomas Ustick Walter (1804-1887) and completed in 1863.[206]

Professor Francis V. O'Connor writing the journal article "The Murals by Constantino Brumidi" in *The Italian Presence in American Art 1860-1920*, said,

> "Though he was a naturalized citizen, Brumidi's foreign birth made him unpopular during his lifetime among envious American artists who could not paint a wall to save their lives. Their spleen has tainted the literature about him to this day, and the dismal condition of his rotunda and rooms

---

[206] "Italian Immigration." *The Library of Congress,* Accessed December 31, 2018.

until just recently, and the all too great visibility of his atelier's hybrid and now grossly overpainted corridor decorations, have prevented art historians from giving this great master of the mural his just due."[207]

Prof. O'Connor pulls no punches when speaking of the slight to Brumidi. Added was O'Connor's subtle phrase of "Brumidi's foreign birth." The reference to a sad indicative of the time as Italian immigrants of all talents were heavily discriminated against in America.

Giuseppe Garibaldi – "The Hero of Two Worlds"

A notable Italian listed in the *United States Senate Catalogue of Fine Art* honored with a marble bust is Giuseppe Garibaldi (1807-1882). The legendary name is often found in American high school history textbooks as leading an army of "Red Shirts" to achieve unification of Italy. Not often mentioned is a connection to the United States and Italian culture in America. Within the illustrated *United States Senate Catalogue of Fine Art*, an acknowledgement is stated as,

> "After Giuseppe Garibaldi's death in 1882, a group of Washington, D.C., residents of Italian descent formed the Society for a Monument to Garibaldi. They commissioned Giuseppe Martegana, an Italian artist living in Paris, to create a bust to commemorate the patriot. In a letter to the president of the Senate dated December 14, 1887, Dr. Tullio de Suzzara-Verdi offered the Garibaldi bust, executed in Italian marble, to the United States. He asked on behalf of the society that it be accepted "as a link in the chain of sympathy that all free men feel for the champions of liberty and popular government." The work also was presented as an expression of Italian achievement in sculpture. On August 23, 1888, the Senate approved the acquisition, resolving that "the Senate of the United States expresses its sense of the patriotism and liberality which prompted this noble gift from these adopted citizens of Italian birth, and extends to them, the countrymen of the great champion of Italian liberty, the assurance of the admiration of the people of this land for his noble life and distinguished deeds."[208]

A significant reason applied for commissioning a marble bust of Giuseppe Garibaldi in the halls of the United States Capitol coincided with his embodiment of the ideals of American liberty as a lifelong "a foe of tyranny." His crusade was to liberate and unite the Italian peninsular that for centuries existed as a series of regions under various leadership and often under control of foreign nations such as France and Austria.

---

[207] Irma B. Jaffe *The Italian Presence in American Art 1860-1920*, p. 81.
[208] Congressional Record (23 August 1888) vol. 19, pt. 8: 7863. Also: S. Doc. 107-111, United States Senate Catalogue of Fine Art, pp. 164-165.

Biography of Giuseppe Garibaldi

Giuseppe Garibaldi rose from modest beginnings to become one of Italy's foremost military heroes. Born in 1807 in Nice, Garibaldi was a sailor, a merchant captain, and an officer in the Piedmont-Sardinia navy. In 1834, after an unsuccessful mutiny, in part to spark a republican revolution in Piedmont-Sardinia, he fled to France. By 1836, Garibaldi was in South America, as a mercenary fighting in Brazil and Uruguay. As news of his victories in South America reached Italy, he was hailed as a hero. A return to Italy in 1848 was during the tumultuous revolutionary events occurring all throughout Europe prompted by as a rising tide of Nationalism sought to overthrow the renewed conservative monarchies.

In Italy, Garibaldi led an army of "Redshirts;" working in consort with Giuseppe Manzini (1805-1872) and Camilo Cavour (1810-1861), joined alongside the *Risorgimento*; a movement to unify the disparate Italian states. The goal included gaining Italian territory from foreign powers such as the French army sent by Louis Napoleon in control of Rome. A defense of Rome against the French army in 1849 and a heroic escape from Austrian forces increased Garibaldi's legendry fame. His wife Anita reportedly fought "alongside him." Unfortunately, he was not able to hold Rome; during the retreat his pregnant wife died. His continued republican sympathies did not endear him to the monarchs of the Italian states as Garibaldi found himself once again exiled. In 1850, prior to Italian unification while still in exile, Garibaldi sailed the Atlantic; for a brief time in South America. In July of that same year, he landed in New York, living for 18 months in a cottage on Staten Island with Antonio and Ester Meucci.

In 1854, Garibaldi returned once again to Italy. In 1859, he was victorious driving the Austrians out of northern Italy. In 1860, landing in Sicily, a military campaign defeated a French garrison at Calatafimi. And another victory followed at Palermo; eventually seizing control of the Kingdom of the Two Sicily's. Those victories "gained worldwide fame and respect of many Italians." He continued across the Strait of Messina toward Naples in September. In essence, he won the battles, therefore could have declared himself ruler. In October 1860, the leader of the Red Shirts essentially handed over "the newly unified nation of southern Italy" to Victor Emmanuel II; who would assume the title of "King" as the new Kingdom of Italy was proclaimed in 1861.

During the late 19th century, Otto von Bismarck instigated a series of three wars leading a Nationalistic cause for German unification. In 1866, Garibaldi led a force of over 40,000 into Venetia engaging in a series of battles with the Austrian army. Prussia prevailed in the war, leading to an Armistice which the Austrian-Hungary Empire ceded the Venetia region to Italy. In 1867, Garibaldi led a campaign to annex Rome, but did not succeed as his forces were repelled. A second opportunity to take Rome occurred in 1870; without Garibaldi. In 1870, Germany started another war, this time with France; once again Italy allied with Prussia. Garibaldi, however, travelled to France enlisting his services to fight against Prussia. The war resulted in French forces withdrawn from Rome allowing an Italian army to take control. In 1871, Rome became the capital city as all of the territory below the Alps became a united Italy. Giuseppe Garibaldi was hailed as a conquering "Hero of Two World's" and was offered an opportunity for a third.[209]

Above Left: Photograph Giuseppe Garibaldi in Naples, Italy, c. 1861. Library of Congress Reproduction No: LC-DIG-ppmsca-08351. **Above Right**: Marble Bust of Garibaldi by Giuseppe Martegana, Cat. No. 21.00007.000. U.S. Senate Collection. Courtesy of the Office of Senate Curator.

Civil War Italians and Luigi di Palma Cesnola

A few decades before the massive onslaught of Italian immigration to America, the U.S. Civil War indirectly involved Italy. In the official history of the United States, "The unification of the Italian states impacted the foreign policy of the United States in numerous ways." The northern U.S. American states engaged in a naval blockade of most of the coastal areas of the American continent and wary about the Confederates seeking foreign allies. As the *Office of the Historian* of the United States noted,

---

[209] "Who was General Giuseppe Garibaldi?" *Garibaldi-Meucci Museum*, 2019.

The Kingdom of Italy was proclaimed [1861] just as the U.S. Civil War began. U.S. President Abraham Lincoln wanted to ensure that the new Italian state did not recognize the U.S. Confederacy. [Lincoln] also worried that, with Italy's long coastline, Confederate ships might seek shelter in Italian waters. With this in mind, the Italian government gave "strong assurances that no Confederate ship would be admitted to Italian ports unless it was a question of adverse weather conditions or other [adverse situation]."

An assurance from Italy not to engage the Confederacy engaged Lincoln with other ideas for Garibaldi to return to America and fight for the North. Evan Andrews writing for the *History Channel* states,

"As a result of his contributions to Italian unification, the man known as the 'Hero of Two Worlds' became a military celebrity. Countless dime novels were written about him, and newspapers and magazines chronicled his every move. Garibaldi was particularly beloved in America."

The *New York Herald* newspaper supported Lincoln's choice; writing of Garibaldi, "Few men have achieved so much for the cause of freedom."

Historians suggest the reason for wanting Garibaldi was due to his record of successful strategy in military campaigns. Students of the American Civil War easily trace the early defeats of the Union Army suffered at the hands of the Confederate forces to somewhat incompetent Union generals. Garibaldi was one who had a proven war record. The timing appeared right during the *Anniversario dell' Unità d'Italia* (the official Italian unification of the Kingdom of Italy), was celebrated on March 17, 1861. One month later the American Civil War began. Lincoln thought enlisting the aid of Garibaldi "to lend the power of his name, his genius, and his sword to the Northern cause." In September 1861, an American envoy met with Garibaldi on the small island of Caprera near Sardinia. Garibaldi conveyed a message he would be "very happy to serve a country for which I have so much affection." His terms for serving were twofold; first he asked for total command of the entire Union Army; second, he wanted to fight a war when ended in victory would be the abolition of slavery. At the time, President Lincoln had not yet entertained ideas about linking the cause of the war to ending slavery. Garibaldi was offered a commission as a Major General with a singular command over a regiment; which he refused.[210]

Lincoln was not able to secure the services of Garibaldi, but inspiration of the Italian was conveyed through the formation the Northern 39th New York Infantry Regiment. Known as the "Garibaldi Guard," the regiment was made up of Italians

---

[210] Evan Andrews. "Why Lincoln Wanted an Italian Freedom Fighter to Lead His Army,"

and other European immigrants. In total, including the Garibaldi Guard, at least 7000 Italians took part in battles among all ranks in the American Civil War. (At the time, the total number of Italians in America numbered only about 25,000.) Immigrants were enticed to join the cause either as "paid replacements" or with promise of American citizenship. (At the time, a citizen who was drafted could opt out of service paying a substitute $300 to take their place, in some cases a recent immigrant.) Many of the Italian volunteers previously served with Garibaldi in Italy. Although Garibaldi never took part in the American Civil War, he was aware of its notable events. After Lincoln issued the Emancipation Proclamation, Garibaldi wrote to the President saying, "Posterity will call you the great emancipator a more enviable title than any crown could be, and greater than any merely mundane treasure."[211]

"Print shows uniformed men of the Garibaldi Guard Regiment, New York Volunteers marching past President Abraham Lincoln and General Winfield Scott during a parade of 20,000 troops in Washington, D.C. A large American flag waves above the reviewing stand, while a soldier walks with the Italian "Dio e Popolo" flag." Library of Congress LC-USZ62-6238. As it appeared in *The Illustrated London News* August 3, 1861, Vol. 39, p. 111.

---

[211] "Issues Relevant to U.S. Foreign Diplomacy: Unification of Italian States," *Office of the Historian*. See also: Evan Andrews. "Why Lincoln Wanted an Italian Freedom Fighter to Lead His Army," *History.com*, August 31, 2018.

CHAPTER 4B

Most Italians in the Union Army served with the Garibaldi Brigade. Some, such as William B. Taliaferro (1822-1898) was a Confederate General. In the Union Army Generals Edward Ferrero (1831-1899) and Francis B. Spinola (1821-1891) served. (Ferrero led a Dance Academy in New York catering to the wealthy elite. Spinola was the first Italian elected to the U.S. Congress representing New York for two terms beginning in 1887.) Both participation and engagement in the Civil War was not conciliatory; at least six Italians were awarded the U.S. Congressional Medal of Honor. One recipient was a recent immigrant Luigi Palma di Cesnola (1879-1904) as a member of the 11th New York Infantry. He was wounded and taken as a prisoner of war; after release was naturalized as an American citizen in 1865, later leaving in search of archeological excavations in Cyprus.[212]

The archeological excavations proved astounding leading to an appointment serving as the first Director of the Metropolitan Museum of Arts in New York. A brief description provided by the curators explain,

"Luigi Palma di Cesnola (1832–1904) can accurately be called a soldier of fortune. Born in Turin, Italy, he emigrated to the United States about 1858 after serving in the Crimean War. In 1862 he joined the Union army in the Civil War, ultimately rising to the rank of brigadier general. In 1865 he went to Cyprus as American consul and took up archaeological excavation as a productive way of spending his time. He returned to America with about 35,000 objects and, after much effort, he succeeded in selling a large selection to the Metropolitan Museum. In 1879, he became the Museum's first director. Consisting of six quarto volumes, the "Cesnola Atlas" was published to present the collection of Cypriot antiquities to the scholarly world."

The archaeological discoveries prompted nations such as France to house the collection at the Musée du Louvre in Paris. The collection was briefly displayed in London, creating much public attention aided by his 1878 publication *Cyprus: Its Ancient Cities, Tombs, And Temples.*[213]

---

[212] "Col. Luigi Palma di Cesnola," *Rantings of a Civil War Historian*, October 16, 2007.
[213] "Cesnola Collection at The Metropolitan Museum."

Above Left: Luigi Palma di Cesnola serving in the Union Army during the American Civil War, c. 1863. **Above Right**: Luigi Palma di Cesnola, c. 1900 from the publication *Deeds of valor; How America's Heroes won the Medal of Honor*, 1901, p. 212. (Public Domain)

The final destination for Cesnola's discoveries was the newly designed Neo-classical building of the Metropolitan Museum of Art in New York. Cesnola oversaw the collection "of Cypriot material" leading towards an appointment as the first director of the Metropolitan Museum in 1879. Nearby, the museum in Central Park is a statue dedicated to Giuseppe Mazzini; further south in Washington Square Park of Giuseppe Garibaldi.

Garibaldi's fame was kindled in countless ways and many tributes. Christine Webb in *Italy Magazine* said, "About 5,500 of the 8,100 [towns and regions] in Italy have a street, road, lane or piazza carrying the name Garibaldi." Statues of Garibaldi are all over the world, erected "in "Taganrog in Russia and Montevideo in Uruguay," and many cities in North and South America in in Buenos Aries, Venice, Palermo, Rome, Chicago, and dozens of others. And a statue in a prominent location of Washington Square Park in Manhattan.[214]

After Garibaldi's death, honor for the legendary figure was organized *Il Progresso Italo-Americano* for a monument in Central Park. Artist Giovanni

---

[214] Christine Webb. "Garibaldi - the first Italian." *Italy Magazine,* April 20, 2009.

Turini (1841-1899) an Italian immigrant who once served as "a volunteer member of Garibaldi's Fourth Regiment" was chosen. Turini created a full-figured bronze statue placed atop a pedestal depicting Garibaldi drawing his sword leading his troops into action. Located in New York's famed Central Park along the West Drive at 67th Street, south of the Metropolitan Museum of Art, is a statue of another hero of the *Risorgimento* -- Giuseppe Mazzini. The bronze bust dedicated in 1878 sits atop a granite pedestal created by the same artist Giovanni Turini.[215]

Above Left: Garibaldi Statue erected in 1888 at Washington Square in New York. Photo c. 1943. **Above Right**: Bust of Giuseppe Mazzini in Central Park in New York created c. 1878. Library of Congress.

Harkening back to June 1850, as news arrived of Garibaldi's sailing to New York during exile reports in the *New York Daily Tribune* said, "It caused a stir." Garibaldi was not seeking fanfare; within a few days of arrival, he found friendship with a recent Italian immigrant Antonio Meucci. Each sought relative obscurity provided by a cottage house located in a country-like atmosphere of Staten Island that would later be the home of the Garibaldi-Meucci Museum.[216]

---

[215] "Washington Square Park: Giuseppe Garibaldi." *New York City Department of Parks & Recreation*, April 14, 2018. Also "Giuseppe Mazzini." *NYC Dept. of Parks.*
[216] Michael J. Fressola. "Tracking Garibaldi on Staten Island." *SI Advance*, 2011.

Garibaldi-Meucci Museum in Rosebank, Staten Island. Yellow arrow indicates a tribute inscription for Giuseppe Garibaldi located over the entrance door of the Staten Island home of Antonio Meucci. A memorial of Meucci is on the front lawn. Photo by: Rolfmueller - Own work, CC BY-SA 3.0, Wiki Commons.[217]

Guest of the Garibaldi-Meucci Museum

A tribute on March 8, 1884, was placed over the entrance door of the Staten Island home of Antonio Meucci. The inscription reads,

Qui visse esule d' al 1851 al 1853
Giuseppe Garibaldi
l' Eroe dei Mondi
8 Marzo, 1884   *Aleuni amici posero*

Here he lived in Exile from 1851 to 1853
Giuseppe Garibaldi
The Hero of the World's
March 8, 1884   *Placed by some Friends*

---

[217] "The Story of the House." *Garibaldi-Meucci Museum.*

Center: Bust of Giuseppe Garibaldi in the Garibaldi-Meucci Museum Staten Island, New York. **Background Left**: Color portrait of Garibaldi wearing his distinctive "Red Shirt." Background Right: Reproduction of drawing of the "Garibaldi Guard" as it appeared in *The Illustrated London News* in 1861.

In 1907, the home was remembered for the "Hero of Two Worlds." On the 100th anniversary of Garibaldi's birth a planned celebration coincided with the American July 4th holiday. The "Garibaldi Memorial" completely encased the small cottage within a "Pantheon." The four-columned portico and pediment arch on all sides was reminiscent of Andrea Palladio's Villa Rotonda in Vicenza, Italy. As a Neo-classical structure equal to a popular architectural style of the day it was appropriately Italian in style. The house was owned by the estate of one Frederick Bachmann who bequeath the house "to the keeping of the local Italian patriotic societies." As explained by journalist Henry Tyrrell for *Frank Leslie's Illustrated*, "The gift of the house did not include the ground which the house originally stood, so the house was removed three years ago to its present and permanent site. The "Pantheon" built over and around it, was dedicated with picturesque pomp and circumstance two years ago the centennial anniversary of Garibaldi's birth it meant to protect as well as glorify the poor, ungarnished wooden shrine."[218]

---

[218] Henry Tyrrell. "A Patriots Neglected Home," *Frank Leslie's Illustrated*, 1901.

Photograph taken about 1937 shows the four-columned portico Neoclassical "Garibaldi Memorial" encasing the Antonio Meucci home. The Miriam and Ira D. Wallach Division of Art, Prints and Photographs: Photography Collection, The New York Public Library Digital Collections.

After Antonio Meucci died, the Italian community looked to preserve the house as a memorial and renamed it the "Garibaldi Homestead." Land was secured a few blocks from its original location and according to the curators of the Garibaldi-Meucci Museum, "In 1907 Meucci's house was moved to its present location at 420 Tompkins Avenue and Chestnut Avenue." The move crossed a neighborhood line from "Clifton" to "Rosebank."[219]

A commemorative postcard titled "Garibaldi Memorial, Rosebank, Staten Island, N.Y." Irma and Paul Milstein Division of United States History. The New York Public Library Digital Collections.

---

[219] "The Story of the House." *Garibaldi-Meucci Museum*. See also: "Garibaldi Meucci Museum Restoration." *Order Sons of Italy in America*, May 4, 2009.

CHAPTER 4B

Onlookers, who may have seen, as journalist Henry Tyrell estimated "ten thousand citizens of Italian descent met on July 4th at the structure erected to honor Giuseppe Garibaldi," might have confused the assembly with an American holiday celebration. Ironically, two important dates associated with Giuseppe Garibaldi coincide with dates of national celebration in America. March 17, 1861 is Italian Unification Day and July 4, 1807 is remembered as Garibaldi's date of birth.

In 1919, administration of the house was assumed by the Order Sons of Italy in America. A later restoration project proposed removing the protective "pantheon" (which was in place until at least 1950) and restore the house to its original condition; although not original location. In 1956, with unofficial recognition of Antonio Meucci as the "true inventor of the telephone," the house was opened to the public as the Garibaldi-Meucci Museum. Soon thereafter, the house was placed on the U.S. National Register of Historic Places. Artifacts were gathered worldwide for display "with the assistance of the cultural department of the Italian Embassy."[220]

The renamed Garibaldi-Meucci Museum has a long standing Italian American cultural tradition. The mission statement as *an Italian-American Cultural Heritage Center* reads as,

"To collect, hold, own, maintain, preserve, and exhibit historical objects and artifacts relating to the lives of Giuseppe Garibaldi and Antonio Meucci; promote an understanding of Italian-American heritage and a positive image of Italian-Americans; conduct educational, cultural, and artistic programming designed to eliminate ethnic and racial prejudice for a diverse and growing audience."

"Who was Antonio Meucci?"

Two mid-19th century Italians of cultural importance to America -- and to an extent the world – were Giuseppe Garibaldi and Antonio Meucci. When Garibaldi died in 1882, Antonio Meucci, was relatively unknown. Garibaldi, on the other hand was known internationally. Garibaldi still known as the "Hero of Two Worlds" is well documented throughout history. Meucci, after many years of obscurity, is recognized as the inventor of the telephone; as such creator of a device used by billions of people worldwide. For many years, a recurring question was, "Who was Antonio Meucci?" The curators of the Garibaldi-*Meucci Museum* answer,

"Antonio Meucci was a prolific Italian inventor, engineer, and practical chemist who is most known for developing a form of voice

---

[220] "The Story of the House." *Garibaldi-Meucci Museum*, 2020. See also: "Garibaldi Meucci Museum Restoration." *Order Sons of Italy in America*, May 4, 2009.

communication apparatus in 1857. He has long had champions arguing that he should be credited with the invention of the telephone."

Biographical information on the website *Famous Scientists* on the Italian inventor adds "Antonio Giuseppe Meucci was an Italian inventor. It can be argued that it was Meucci who was the first to invent the telephone rather than Alexander Graham Bell."[221]

Antonio Meucci (1808-1889) was born in the pre-unified San Frediano region of Florence under the 300-year reign of the Grand Duchy of Tuscany (1569 to 1859). In 1821, Meucci enrolled as the youngest student admitted to study engineering at the legendary Florence Academy of Fine Arts; studying chemical engineering, mechanical engineering, and electricity; subjects contributing to his later work as an inventor. By 1830, Meucci was employed at *Teatro della Pergola* opera house in Florence, built in 1656. (It remains as the oldest working theater and opera house in Florence.) In 1834, Meucci designed "an acoustic pipe telephone." Similar to onboard ship communication, the system provided a person behind the stage the ability to speak with someone in a control room in another part of the theater. Later that year, Meucci married costume designer Esterre (sometimes as "Esther" or "Ester") Mochi (1810-1884) in the Santa Maria Novella in Florence. In 1835, with concern of the ongoing political turmoil, the young couple immigrated to Cuba. The multi-talented engineer secured a position "as chief engineer at the *Gran Teatro de Tacón* in Havana;" Esterre was Director of Costumes.[222]

Above Left: Photograph of Antonio Meucci, c. 1878. **Above Right:** An 1856 design of Meucci's *Telettrofono* a telephone device to communicate with his ailing wife. (Wiki Commons)

---

[221] "Visit the Museum." *Garibaldi-Meucci Museum*, 2020.
[222] "Antonio Meucci." *Famous Scientists*, November 8, 2020, n.p.

CHAPTER 4B

During 15 years in Havana, Meucci invented a "water purification system" for the city residents and an electroplating factory for the Cuban military. Other employment and inventions proved successful; providing significant financial income. While working at the *Gran Teatro de Tacón*, he developed an automatic moving theater curtain. Around 1848, experimentation with "electricity to relieve pain;" possibly to relieve migraines, or to deal with the arthritic pain which later crippled Esterre. According to biographical information at *Famous Scientists*, while experimenting with electro-medicine, "Meucci accidently discovered the "electrophonic" effect using "oral electrodes." Continued adaptations with various incarnations of the device included a "talking telegraph."[223]

In early 1850, Meucci and Esterre moved to the United States. Entering America, via New York, the Meucci's were met by former acquaintances Lorenzo Salvi and Domenico Mariani. The pair arranged temporary housing in a Manhattan boarding house. Meucci later recalled,

> "For a few weeks I remained in Leonard Street, New York, and having met my friend, General Garibaldi, and Lorenzo Salvi, the General suggested to come and settle with me in some house in the country."

Therefore, Meucci and Garibaldi viewed some possible locations in New Jersey until, a "country place" was suggested by another "friend" in the Clifton area of Staten Island in Richmond County. (Staten Island did not become an official part of New York City until 1898.)[224]

The "friend" who suggested renting "Forest Cottage" on Staten Island was Max Maretzek (1821-1897). In 1848, as a Czechoslovakian immigrant arriving in New York, Maretzek founded the "Max Maretzek Italian Opera Company." The troupe continued in operation for fifty years producing Italian and German operas.

Meucci came to know Maretzek through their mutual association while working in the theater industry. The Gothic Revival style cottage house on Staten Island was owned by a New York newspaper publisher William Townsend, who previously rented the home to Maretzek who now wished to sub-let the cottage to Meucci. Upon hearing one of the new tenants would include the famous Giuseppe Garibaldi, Townsend and wife Susan were more than willing to accept the agreement.[225]

---

[223] "Antonio Meucci." *Famous Scientists*, November 8, 2020.
[224] "Visit the Museum." *Garibaldi-Meucci Museum*, 2020.
[225] Basilio Catania. *Antonio Meucci: The Inventor and his Time*, Rome: Seat Divisione, 1999, p. 82. Note: Townsend, a publisher, owned the *New York Evening Express*.

Original: "The Meucci-Garibaldi House at Clifton, Staten Island, As It Is Today." Drawn by Harry Fenn (1838-1911) from a photograph, c. 1900. New York Public Library Collection. The Miriam and Ira D. Wallach Division of Art, Prints and Photographs: Picture Collection. NYPL catalog ID (B-number): b17097102.

Once settled into the cottage, Meucci set up a laboratory experimenting with electronic voice communication devices. Within a few years, Esterre developed severe pain from arthritis requiring her "confined to an upstairs bedroom." In order to communicate with his wife, Meucci developed a "teletrofonic system;" so he could speak to her as needed. By 1850s, Meucci constructed other working models of the *teletrófono* (telephone); described as handheld, cup shaped devices. One 1857 entry described the *teletrófono* as, "A vibrating diaphragm and in a magnet electrified by a wire wounded around it. When the diaphragm vibrates the magnet modifies the wire current. These modifications, once they reach the other end of the wire, impresses similar vibrations to the receiving diaphragm, which reproduces the words." In 1860, description of the communication device was published in an Italian language newspaper.[226]

Continued development and experimentation created "more than 30 types of telephone devices based on his prototype." A dated notebook entry of August 17, 1870, noted "I have obtained a [transmission] distance of about one mile." In early December 1871, he formed a business partnership named as the "Telettrofono Company" and applied to the U.S. Patent Office. The application was difficult and led to complications. Filing for a temporary patent in December of 1871, was complicated by Meucci's own inability to fully understand the nuances of the

---

[226] "Antonio Meucci." *Secret Price of History*. November 16, 2020.

contractual language. As an added complication, funding of his invention was drawn from his life savings; eventually exhausting all to the point of not having sufficient funds to renew the application. As suggested by a lawyer, Meucci opted for a *caveat* a temporary one-year renewable notice of an impending patent to the US Patent Office. On December 28, 1871, Meucci secured the legal caveat No. 3335, Sound Telegraph, from the U.S. Patent Office. The patent came at the end of a tragic year, both physically and financially debilitating and a multi-faceted complication.[227]

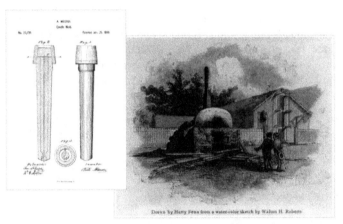

Above Left: Meucci's U.S. Patent No. 22,739-1859 – Candle Mold. **Above Right**: Ruins of the Meucci-Garibaldi candle-making furnace and caldron at Clifton, Staten Island, c.1884, image c. 1907. Library of Congress LC-USZ62-78111.

Earlier in 1851, friend in exile Giuseppe Garibaldi entered into a business partnership with Meucci which included a beer brewery and a factory producing smokeless candles. Unfortunately, many years after Garibaldi returned to Italy, the factory was destroyed by fire in 1871. Eventually the candle business went into bankruptcy; disallowing him the finances to pursue the patent on the talking device. During that same year, as he perfected a working telephone device, Meucci was "badly scalded in a fire." The "fire" was suffered during one of the worst nautical tragedies in the history of New York City.[228]

On Sunday afternoon July 30, 1871, Meucci was aboard *Westfield II* a Staten Island Ferry traveling from Manhattan to Staten Island. *The New York Times* reported "a boiler explosion almost totally wrecked the Staten Island ferry." Of an estimated 400 passengers the *Staten Island Advance* reported "more than 126 people died and at least 200 were seriously injured." Many of the dead drowned

---

[227] "Who Was Antonio Meucci?" *Garibaldi-Meucci Museum*, November 11, 2020.
[228] Jan Somma-Hammel. "Flashback," *The Staten Island Advance*, June 19, 2020.

in the boiling waters or were trampled. Others injured were "scalded by steam, burnt by flames or were maimed by flying debris." Meucci was one of those passengers badly burned. His injuries were severe enough to remain hospitalized for three months. The disaster was covered by all local New York newspapers and national publications including the widely circulated *Frank Leslie's Illustrated Newspaper* and *Harper's Weekly*.[229]

The ship disaster was later included as part of a deposition by Antonio Meucci for trial proceeding, as he recalled the incident,

> "I was on board the ferryboat "Westfield," of Staten Island, when her boiler exploded, killing more than one hundred persons. I was seriously wounded; remained in bed for about three months. I was burned nearly over my entire body, especially my face, head and hands. My life was despaired of; my friends thought I would die. I was confined to my house a few months."

The recollection was accurate; yet understated the severity of injuries. An account in *The New York Tribune* wrote Meucci was between life and death for almost three months.[230]

Above Left: A drawing of the *Westfield II* exploded, killing and maiming hundreds of passengers on July 30, 1871. **Above Right**: Staten Island Ferryboat *Westfield II* No. 26504 commissioned in 1862 built at Jeremiah & Simonson shipyard Greenpoint Brooklyn.

During the recovery, a despondent Esterre, sold most of the telephone devices and other laboratory paraphernalia; with Meucci unable to work the family lacked income. Of significance, Meucci did not have money to extend his U.S. Patent caveat beyond 1874. Two years later, Meucci read a newspaper account of a telephone invention by Alexander Graham Bell. During a long court trial, Meucci

---

[229] "Worst Ferry Disaster in City Was in 1871." *New York Times,* Nov. 8, 1978, B9.
[230] Basilio Catania. *Antonio Meucci: The Inventor and his Time*, p. 271.

could not provide physical evidence of his telephone invented before Bell. Some say Meucci was swindled, due to his status as an Italian immigrant. A significant item, not discussed during Meucci's legal fight, was the possible situation of discrimination as an Italian immigrant. As provided by the curators of the Garibaldi-Meucci Museum, "prejudices associated with his nationality prevented financiers from knowing of his developments." Adding,

> "In the summer of 1872, Meucci and his friend Angelo Bertolino went to Edward B. Grant, Vice President of Western Union Telegraph Company of New York, to ask for permission to test his telephone apparatus on the companies telegraph lines. He gave Grant a description of his prototype and a copy of his caveat, encouraged by Grant that he would be contacted for the test run."

Meucci and Bertolino were either too trustworthy or naïve. Both were most likely unaware of America's long history of individuals cheated out business ventures.

In American parlance, Meucci and Bertolino were stonewalled. Grant, did not reply to any of Meucci's many visits to the Western Union Telegraph Company. Meucci asked on many occasions for his documentation and working models be returned. After two years Grant sent a message claiming "all of Meucci's materials had been lost." Meucci engaged his patent attorney Thomas D. Stetson to take the legal matter to court. The trial proved "messy" as a contradicting court case arose in March of 1886. In *The U.S. Government vs. Alexander Graham Bell and the Bell Company*, the Scottish invented was accused of "fraud, collusion and deception in obtainment of the patent." As a result, two days later, Bell Company attorneys filed a countersuit against Meucci. The case dragged on for 10 years, eventually moot due to the duration.[231]

As with any ongoing protracted trail, Meucci was desperate for money. After discovery of Bell's patent, Meucci legally assigned his telephone invention to the Globe Telephone Company. In 1885, the Globe Company made a public advertisement for the purchase of a talking device. The Bell Company filed suit for patent infringement. In July 1887, Judge William Wallace ruled in favor of Bell. The judge (who historians cited as "anti-immigrant") said "Meucci was not able to provide adequate evidence [and] was deliberately involved in attempts to defraud investors." Historian Angelo Campanella writing, "Antonio Meucci, The Speaking Telegraph, and The First Telephone," summarized, "Thus, to all intents and purposes, Meucci's claim to priority in the invention of the telephone had been decided from the legal point of view and Meucci had lost."[232]

---

[231] "Who was Antonio Meucci," *Garibaldi-Meucci Museum* and Catania, pp. 270-271.
[232] Angelo Campanella. "Antonio Meucci, The Speaking Telegraph, and The First Telephone." *Acoustics Today*. March 10, 2007, pp. 276-278.

174 Italian Culture in America:
The Immigrants 1880 to 1930 From Discrimination to Assimilation

The Meucci family in financial ruin sought financial assistance. The owner of the Staten Island cottage allowed them to live rent free. Other living expenses were not covered and they often borrowed from friends. For the remainder of their years, they lived on a form on "public assistance." For the remaining few years of his life, the destitute Meucci maintained a stout confidence in his resolve as the original inventor of the telephone.[233]

Antonio Meucci died on October 18, 1889 without a resolution as the rightful inventor of the telephone. The day after his death, an editorial in the *New York Herald* noted, "Antonio Meucci died in the full belief of the priority of his claim as inventor or the telephone, which during the intervals of his sickness, he declared must be recognized sooner or later." In the years since Antonio Meucci's death, American history books credited Alexander Graham Bell as the "true" inventor of the telephone. Generations of American school children of all ages grew up believing the "myth" as fact. Meucci's legacy was not secured until well over 100 years since his passing. In June 2002, U. S. Congress House Resolution 269, introduced by Rep. Vito Fossella of Staten Island officially "recognized the life and achievements of Antonio Meucci" and made known his work resulted in the invention of the telephone.

Meucci may have died in somewhat obscurity, however, claim as the true inventor of the telephone was finally recognized over a century later by the United States Congressional Resolution. A more significant gesture which would certainly have satisfied Antonio Meucci was an "applause" by the Italian government hailing the 2002 resolution. As noted by journalist Rory Carroll in *The Guardian* newspaper,

> "Italy hailed the redress of a historic injustice yesterday after the US Congress recognized an impoverished Florentine immigrant as the inventor of the telephone rather than Alexander Graham Bell. Historians and Italian-Americans won their battle to persuade Washington to recognize a little-known mechanical genius, Antonio Meucci, as a father of modern communications, 113 years after his death."[234]

Sadly, "the battle" may have been won, but the mythical attachment of Alexander Graham Bell has become so ingrained in American popular culture myth well into the 21st century.

––––––––––––

[233] Kyle Lawson. "A Look Back: 1871 Staten Island Ferry Explosion Kills, Maims Hundreds." *Staten Island Advance*, July 30, 2019.
[234] Basilio Catania. "Antonio Meucci Revisited." See also: Rory Carroll. "US Finally Admits Italian Invented Telephone." *The Guardian,* June 16, 2002.

CHAPTER 5

WHERE DID THEY GO?
AND WHAT DID THEY DO?

"With all his conspicuous faults, the swarthy Italian immigrant has his redeeming traits. He is as honest as he is hot-headed. . . [he] toils peacefully with pickaxe and shovel on American ground." Jacob Riis, 1890

A misnomer often confuses the influence of Italian culture upon America. Most would think Italian cultural influence began with the overwhelming number of immigrants as the main impetus for change, influence, or even assimilation. Actually, it began much earlier with the 25,000 or so Italian immigrants, who were mostly refugees from northern Italy settling in the colonies prior to 1820. The earlier years of Italian immigration was dispersed widely throughout America. The *U.S. Library of Congress* states the scant number of Italian immigrants from 1820 to 1850, as "too small to constitute a significant presence." Within the following twenty years the numbers increased, but not significantly. By 1870, the nationwide number totaled about 25,000; a growing number from the southern *Mezzogiorno* region who were leaving due to unsettling conditions of Italian unification. Still the number was somewhat inconsequential; the largest numbers settled in California at 2,805 and New York claimed 1,862. Within a decade the number of Italian immigrants numbered over 300,000.[235]

"The Little Italian Organ Grinders and the "Orphan Train"

During the time period 1850 to 1890, Italians continued a steady increase in the number of immigrants to America. As a new class of "undesirables" entered America, discrimination added with stereotypes emerged. Despite the hardworking efforts of either unskilled laborers, garment workers, or business

---

[235] "Italian Immigration." *The Library of Congress,* Accessed December 31, 2018. See also: "Immigration Timeline" *The Statue of Liberty Ellis Island Foundation,* 2019.

owners, derogatory Italian stereotypes persisted such as the Organ Grinder and Rag Picker, among others. Before the large wave of new immigration, newspaper articles often made note of the unique trade of an "Organ Grinder" street musician dating to the 1850s on the Lower East Side of New York. An "Organ Grinder" was a street musician who played a barrel organ by turning a handle. Historian Tyler Anbinder claimed one in every twenty Italians living within the Lower East Side employed themselves in this trade. *The New York Times*, as one example, published numerous articles of the growing number of impoverished Italians living in the densely populated area of the lower East Side of New York; many who earned a meager living as an organ grinder.

Above Left: "Organ grinder on street, East Side, New York," Bain News Service. Library of Congress Prints and Photographs Division. Reproduction No: LC-DIG-ggbain-03238. George Grantham Bain Collection. **Above right**: Stereotyping of Italian Organ Grinders portrayed in popular culture through derogatory songs such as, "De Dago, de Org, and de Monk." Sheet Music, Publisher: Shapiro, Bernstein & Von Tilzer, c. 1901. Music Division, The New York Public Library Digital Collections. 1901.

One who shed light on the phenomena was Charles Loring Brace (1826-1890). As a Congregational minister, Brace was also a child welfare advocate, founder of the New York Children's Aid Society, and co-organizer of the Orphan Train movement. One aspect was spent as a journalist for a regular column for *The New York Times* titled, "Walks Among the New-York Poor." In many instances, he witnessed Italian organ-grinders with a monkey – sometimes outfitted in a costume. The monkey attracted attention and to "charm" the crowds; sometimes of only a few children. The monkey somewhat trained, yet leashed, sauntered towards onlookers to solicit coins. In 1853, Brace said, "It is very poor music, but it is the only music some of our neighbors can ever afford to hear." Anbinder added, "The organ grinder-monkey team playing carnival-like music was a popular street entertainment act for decades."[236]

---

[236] "Brace, Charles Loring." *VCU Libraries Social Welfare History Project*, 2020. See "Ephemeral New York." See also: Tyler Anbinder, "Five Points."

CHAPTER 5

Rev. Brace, true to his Protestant faith, sought help for the many homeless "Street Children" living among the squalid conditions. In an 1872 memoir, Brace wrote of the type of work engaged by the Italian children included "blackening boots, selling flowers, [and] sweeping walks" or begging for money. Brace obviously reacted, but was not so kind and a bit derogatory as he wrote of the southern Italians,

> "So degraded was their type, and probably so mingled in North Italy with ancient Celtic blood, that their faces could hardly be distinguished from those of Irish poor children an occasional dark eye only betraying their nationality."[237]

Comments written by Brace were somewhat typical of the time. Some Americans were aware of the historical achievements of Columbus and the Italian Renaissance, yet totally unaccustomed to the ways and culture of the poorer peasants from the *Mezzogiorno* of southern Italy and Sicily.

Completely misunderstood among individuals and religious leaders such as Brace and others, was the life Italian immigrants chose to leave behind from rural towns and small cramped cottages. Although Italian immigrants were accustomed to small enclosed living spaces; they embraced the beauty of the wide-open countryside of Italy. Once relocated to America, Italians often lived in tightly compacted tenement housing in cities such as New York, Boston, and Philadelphia, to name a few of the most populous. Not available was significant outdoor space.

One of the most common tenement situation was located in New York City – mainly Manhattan. The standard city block in Manhattan was zoned in a rigid grid pattern each about 260' by 900' feet (or roughly 80 m×274 m). Other cities contained areas about the same size. One tenement block usually housed more people than an entire town in Italy. The overcrowding led to unsanitary living conditions; coupled with poverty and orphan children. To Brace's credit he recognized the situation of orphans while offering compassion,

> "I felt convinced that something could be done for them. Owing to their ignorance of our language and their street-trades, they never attended school, and seldom any religious service . . . Some of the little ones suffered severely from being indentured by their parents in Italy to a "Bureau" in Paris, which sent them out over the world with their *"padrone,"* or master, usually a villainous-looking individual. The lad would be frequently sent forth by his *padrone,* late at night, to excite the compassion of our citizens, and play the harp. . . sometimes on winter-nights half-frozen and stiff with cold."[238]

---

[237] Charles Loring Brace, *The Dangerous Classes of New York*, p. 194.
[238] Charles Loring Brace, *The Dangerous Classes of New York,* p. 194.

In 1853, at a time when orphan asylums and almshouses were the only available resources for poor and homeless children, Rev. Brace joined with other ministers creating the Children's Aid Society. One portion offered was a program called the "Orphan Train Movement."[239]

Above left: Children pose as they ride the "Orphan Train." (Public Domain.) **Above Right**: "Charles Loring Brace," from The Miriam and Ira D. Wallach Division of Art, Prints and Photographs: Print Collection,
The New York Public Library Digital Collections.

As part of the "Orphan Train Movement," Brace and his organizers placed thousands of "homeless" children in an early form of "foster care" in far-away rural areas of the United States. The name "Orphan Train" was a literal description as children were placed on a railroad train transported to live in the care of "farm families" in distant parts of the United States. Brace explained the relocation thereby claiming "the cultivators of the soil are in America our most solid and intelligent class."

Relocating Italian orphans removed them from their own cultural heritage, including Catholicism. In 2001, journalist Stephen O'Connor of writing in "When Children Relied on Faith-Based Agencies," revealed, "Brace presented his organization as nondenominational, but he was strongly anti-Catholic and had few misgivings when many Catholic children he had sent away converted to Protestantism." In 1854, the first of many orphan tarins left in transit to the small rural town (about 5,800) of Dowagiac in Michigan.[240]

Historian Andrea Warren in *Orphan Train Rider: One Boy's True Story*, cited statistical evidence "between 1854 and 1929, an estimated 200,000 American children some orphaned, others abandoned, all in need of families traveled west by rail in search of new homes." During peak years of 1855 to 1875, a yearly average of 3,000 children "rode the trains." Prior to leaving New York, "each was dressed in new clothing, given a Bible in the care of Children's Aid Society agents

---

[239] Brace, C.L. (1872). *The Life of the Street Rats.*
[240] Stephen O'Connor. "When Children Relied on Faith-Based Agencies," p. A13.

who accompanied them west." Most of the children ranged from newborn to 13 years of age. Only a few were "claimed" prior to departure. For most, as they unboarded the train, they were met by a group of local townspeople. The "unclaimed" children were arranged for "viewing" by prospective adoptive parents. (Formal adoption was did not exist in America until the 1880s.)

Warren painstakingly researching available newspaper accounts of the time discovered the arrival was an "auction-like atmosphere." Each of the children was examined for a variety of reasons, the most common was physical condition for farmwork. Conditions included labeling children as a "light complexion" or a "dark complexion" as well as potential for future good behavior. The indignation of "viewing" the children in a line-up was no different than examination of African slaves. Warren described,

> "After children survived the viewing and found a new family, some faced other obstacles, ranging from prejudice of classmates because they were "train children" to feeling like outsiders in their families all their lives."[241]

By the year 2000, Warren estimated at least 500 of the original orphan train children were still alive; living in dispersed areas of America. To counter the attempt at Protestant conversion, Catholic mutual aid societies such as the New York Foundling Hospital applied a similar situation with the intent of placing orphans in Catholic homes. (Those relocations were termed "Mercy Trains.") In 1869, the Sisters of Charity of New York (a shelter mostly for abandoned infants) set up a system placing infants and toddler children in "prearranged Roman Catholic homes in the Midwest and south from 1875 to 1914."

In 2018, journalist Ron Grossman examined the historical legacy calling the process "a noble idea that went off the rails," Grossman added,

> "The movement was inspired by a lofty ideal . . . Many of New York's homeless children were the offspring of immigrants, and sending them into the heartland would expose them to the civilizing influences of American life."

The underlying purpose of the movement was to "speed their assimilation" towards a white native Protestant view of American society. The idea instituted by religious organizations, viewed the "alien" cultures required assimilation to the dominant American view.[242]

Not lost among the information available for the Orphan Train Movement revealed of the many "Street Children" some were discovered "earning" money

---

[241] Andrea Warren. "The Orphan Train." *The Washington Post*, November 1998.
[242] Ron Grossman. "The Orphan Train: A noble idea that went off the rails," *Capital Gazette*, July 19, 2018.

following organ grinders. In 1872, Brace described the situation in a chapter "The Little Italian Organ-Grinders," as,

> "Among the various rounds I was in the habit of making in the poorest quarters, was one through the Italian quarter of the 'Five Points.' In large tenement-houses, were packed hundreds of poor Italians, mostly engaged in carrying through the city and country the everlasting hand-organ. In the same room I would find monkeys, children, men and women, with organs and plaster-casts, all huddled together; but the women contriving still, in the crowded rooms, to roll their dirty macaroni, and all talking excitedly; a bedlam of sounds, and a combination of odors from garlic, monkeys, and most dirty human persons. They were, without exception, the dirtiest population I had met with."

In an unpublished thesis, Michael David Accinno referenced the "Organ Grinder" stereotype as a popular culture iconic from a *Merry Melodies* cartoon series. One 1933 example, titled "The Organ Grinder" caricatured "an overweight, jovial Italian organ grinder cranks his instrument as he navigates an urban streetscape with his monkey." In 1937, the popular *Popeye the Sailor Man* featured an episode "Organ Grinders Swing" with a similar stereotype. Added was the typical "fight" between the antagonist "Bluto" and Popeye fighting among a street tenement.[243]

Above Left: "The Organ Grinder," c. 1892 by Overspeck, Hamilton. Photograph. Retrieved from the Library of Congress, **Above Right:** "Organ Grinder and Monkey in New York City," Photograph by Samuel H, Gottscho, 1875-1971). Library of Congress, www.loc.gov/item/2018722365/.

---

[243] Brace, *The Dangerous Classes of New York*, p. 194. Michael David Accinno. "Organ Grinder's Swing: Representations of Street Music in New York City, 1850-1937," *University of Iowa,* July 2010.

CHAPTER 5   181

The practice of real-life organ grinders was outlawed in 1936 through a City
Ordnance enacted by New York Mayor Fiorella LaGuardia (1882-1947).
LaGuardia had recollections of growing up on an Army base in far-away Arizona.
He remembered being berated by other children making fun of his Italian heritage
often berating him by calling out "Where is your monkey?" In 2006, journalist
Michael Pollock noted,

> "By mayoral fiat he declared them public nuisances, ordered the police
> to roust them on sight and refused to relent, despite pleas from citizens.
> La Guardia may have had another reason for being so rankled by organ
> grinders: they became an Italian immigrant stereotype, which he
> personally resented."[244]

As a two-term Congressman and three-term Mayor of New York City from 1933
to 1945, Fiorello La Guardia was born in America soon after his parents
immigrated from Italy around 1880. From 1907 to 1910, he worked as a multi-
language interpreter at Ellis Island; witnessing thousands of wide-eyed Italian
immigrants.[245] A description by the *U.S. Library of Congress* states,

> "The Italian immigrants who passed the test of Ellis Island went about
> transforming the city that they found before them. Many previous
> immigrant groups, such as those from Germany and Scandinavia, had
> passed through New York City in decades past, but most had regarded
> the city merely as a way station, and had continued on to settle elsewhere
> in the country. This generation of Italian immigrants, however, stopped
> and made their homes there; one third never got past New York City."[246]

Settlement in New York was within the crowded confines of tightly nested streets
and tenements. Others traveled elsewhere. According to historians Jerre
Mangione and Ben Morreale writing in *La Storia: Five Centuries of the Italian
American Experience,*

> "By 1910, Italians could be found in almost every nook and cranny of
> America – working the textiles mills of New England, sharecropping in
> Bryan, Texas, onion farming in Canastota, New York, mining and union

---

[244] Michael David Accinno. "Organ Grinder's Swing: Representations of Street Music in
New York City, 1850-1937," *University of Iowa,* July 2010 (Summer 2010). Accinno
noted: "As was the custom with Warner Brothers shorts in the early 30s, the cartoon
featured a song "The Organ Grinder," with music by Sam Stept and lyrics by Herb
Magidson, published in 1932 by Warner subsidiary Whitmark."
[245] "Profiles in World War I Immigration History: Fiorello La Guardia," *U.S. Citizenship
and Immigration Services,* Department of Homeland Security. October 18, 2018.
[246] "Italian Immigration." *The Library of Congress,* "A City of Villages." *Immigration and
Relocation in U.S. History,* The Library of Congress.

organizing in Colorado, cow-poking in West Texas, and lumberjacking in Seattle, Washington."

A vast majority of Italian immigrants arriving during the high-demand labor years of 1880 to 1920 concentrated in urban areas. Italians, as with all other ethic immigrants, were often forced to live in slum areas. In many cases, Italians found themselves among other immigrants from the same town or region; neighborhoods that became known as "Little Italy."

LITTLE ITALY

As for the location of the immigrant population, The U.S. Library of Congress reports Italians "clustered heavily in cities in the Northeast region." About 90 percent of all Italian immigrants settled in only eleven states: New York, New Jersey, Pennsylvania, Massachusetts, California, Illinois, Connecticut, Ohio, Michigan, Missouri, and Louisiana. In New York, more specifically Manhattan, a large concentration of Italians settled into the Lower East Side near Mulberry Street. Thereafter, the area became known as the heart of Italian Culture as its own designation as "Little Italy." Although, Mulberry Street might remain as the most well-known, other neighborhoods of a designated "Little Italy" arose in other cities across America including Boston, Chicago, Cleveland, Philadelphia, San Diego, San Francisco, and St. Louis, to name just some. Beyond the New York City "Little Italy," a large Italian population in neighborhood enclaves arose in all of the five boroughs of Manhattan, Bronx, Brooklyn, Queens and Staten Island. Philadelphia had the second largest number.[247]

"Little Italy" as a neighborhood with a centric Italian-American presence existed among many cities in the continental United States. The most densely populated area was in Manhattan. From the earliest days of immigration, the destination was often the lower East Side near Mulberry Street. The area maintained a unique Italian flavor reminiscent of Old-World culture and *festas*.[248]

---

[247] "A City of Villages." *Library of Congress*, Immigration and Relocation in U.S.
[248] "The Great Arrival," *The Library of Congress*, Immigration and Relocation in U.S. History. September 24, 2020.

"Little Italy" at Mulberry Street, New York City, c. 1900. The crowded street of multi-story tenements is filled with push carts and street vendors. Detroit Publishing Company photograph collection. Library of Congress.

The distinctive feature was rows and rows of pushcarts and street vendors crowding the already overcrowded street. Behind the street vendors, many of the tenements had street level storefront shops, mostly owned by Italians such as bakeries, barber shops, grocery stores, shoe makers, and other household goods servicing the familiar needs for Italians. As such the area served as an "open-air market" to buy fresh fruits, vegetables, and other food sources reminiscent of Italy. (A feature which was distinct in other Italian areas such as Arthur Avenue in the Bronx or the Italian Market in Philadelphia.) The physical sight could often be conceived as confusing or a calamity; yet for Italians it served as one of the few opportunities to literally be outside. Many stories recall the sights and smells, not all were described as pleasant; however, the shopping did offer a temporary reprieve from the depressing tenements.[249]

---

[249] "The Great Arrival," *The Library of Congress*, Immigration and Relocation in U.S. History. September 24, 2020.

Italian push carts and street vendors on Mulberry Street, New York City, c. 1900-1910. Detroit Publishing Company photograph collection (Library of Congress Prints and Photographs Division Washington, D.C.)

By 1890, with immigrants pouring into the country, there were very few opportunities for places to live. By 1900, New York City was by far the most populous city in the United States. More than 3.4 million people lived in the recently incorporated New York City. More than half the total population lived in multi-story tenement buildings. (The number living in New York's tenements was about the same as the total number living in all of Chicago; the second most populous city.) For the most part tenement style buildings permeated in three New York City boroughs of Manhattan, Brooklyn, and Bronx, lesser extent in Queens and fewer on Staten Island.

Population of Top Three Cities in America c. 1900

Rank	Place	Population
1	New York City	3,437,202
2	Chicago	1,698,575
3	Philadelphia	1,293,697

CHAPTER 5

The need to satisfy the housing situation led to narrow and long building designs known as a "Tenement" trace to 1811. During that year, New York City was only the borough of Manhattan; contained mostly in the lower half in a land area of only 23 square miles. Population growth led to the need for multi-story buildings on narrow lots. In that year, the city adopted a unique zoning plan which laid out streets in a rigid grid pattern of back-to-back building lots 20 feet wide by 100 feet deep; some were 25 feet wide. Broadway bisected many streets creating some oddly shaped lots. North of 59th Street was a large area for Central Park.[250]

A "tenement building," is not necessarily, and was not always associated with a negative connotation. The basic definition is "a room or a set of rooms forming a separate residence within a house or block of apartments." By the early 1800s, the multistory buildings were often occupied by well-to-do families. Those families were often known as "Knickerbockers;" who traced their lineage to original Dutch settlers. The term "Knickerbockers" was derived from a male fashion style of baggy trousers known as "knickers." The trousers gathered just below the knee accompanied by long fashionable socks.

Typically, an entire floor, or even the entire tenement building, housed a single family. As the number of immigrants increased causing wealthier established families to relocate to the north end of Manhattan, landlords partitioned the tenement buildings housing many families per floor. (The density eventually reached over 250,000 within one square mile.) The growing profitability for rentable living spaces led to more and more landlords carving up the narrow floor plans into more and more apartments, sometimes only one room for an entire family. With profit as the only motive, sanitary conditions were ignored; as was ventilation and limited indoor plumbing. Garbage overflowed as all sorts of vermin, such as rats and mice, were common. The overcrowded buildings and neighborhoods led to outbreaks of many diseases of cholera, typhus, and tuberculosis. The squalid filthy condition of the tenements was chronicled in a September 1910 daily newspaper *The New York Call* that vividly described the conditions as,

> "Everything is thrown out of the windows; garbage is rolled up in newspapers and thrown into the streets where the toilets are in use by the many families, the mother allows the children to use paper as toilet receptacles and it too is thrown out the windows. And the vermin kitchens swarming with, not thousands but millions of roaches. Bed bugs are everywhere. Thousands of mothers leave their children in the care of the older boy and girl and go to work early in the morning in the factories or work shop to return at night to do the work of the family. In this

---

[250] The other boroughs are much larger with Bronx at 42.5 sq. mi.; Staten Island 59 sq. mi.; Brooklyn 69.5 sq. mi.; and Queens 108 sq. mi.

terrible existence day after day this worn out half famished mother continues her burden of life."[251]

Considered a "Socialist Newspaper," *The New York Call,* true to its name, regularly called for social reform in New York City. Many of the stories brought forward the plight of the ignored, or "other half," of American society living in poverty. For many years, the living conditions of on the interior of tenement housing was rarely seen by the American public. That soon changed as an investigative journalist employed new technological advances in photography; the name was Jacob Riis who revealed to the world "How the Other Half Lives."[252]

Jacob Riis and *How the Other Half Lives*

In 2016, the U.S. *Library of Congress* sponsored a retrospective exhibition on the life and work of Jacob Riis. The advance notice advertised,

"Today Jacob Riis is regarded as one of photography's great innovators. Riis was well aware of the power of photographs but did not consider himself a photographer. This exhibition repositions Riis as a multi-skilled communicator who devoted his life to writing articles and books and delivering lectures nationwide to spur social reform. It examines Riis as a writer, photographer, lecturer, advocate, and ally and provide visitors with an opportunity to understand the indelible mark Riis's brand of social reform left on the United States at the end of the nineteenth century and the beginning of the twentieth century."[253]

Jacob Riis started in America as just another poor immigrant. Arriving in 1870 on a steamship from Denmark, Riis traveled in the same type steerage accommodations as millions of others who would come after. Similar to millions of immigrants, Riis did not have any defined skill other than a desire to work. Employment was found in various labor jobs as "a farmhand, ironworker, brick-layer, carpenter, and salesman." Without steady employment, he experienced poverty, sickness, tenement living, and the squalor of immigrant life. This personal experience is most-likely which led Riis to seek a path as a social reformer.

In 1873, Riis was living a life among the lowest of the social class in New York. As with so many other recent immigrants, he was looking for employment. On a hunch he applied for, and received, an interview with a local New York newspaper. The job known as a "Police Reporter" involved covering crime within the Lower East Side of New York. As a densely populated overcrowded area with

---

[251] *The New York Call* September 3, 1910, quoted in Jean H. Baker *Margaret Sanger: A Life of Passion,* New York; Hill and Wang, 2011, p. 47.
[252] "Tenements and Toil." *Immigration and Relocation in U.S. History.*
[253] "Jacob Riis: Revealing How the Other Half Lives." Exhibition April-September 2016.

recent immigrants living in tenement buildings, Riis as part of his daily investigations, discovered more than physical crime. The squalid filthy conditions was cause for a very high infant mortality rate hovering at 10 percent (or 1 out of 10 babies died). In addition, Riis discovered many of the children were often undernourished and working at a very young age.[254]

In 1877, Riis secured a similar position reporting on crime with *The New York Tribune*. By 1888, employed by *The New York Evening Sun* in a similar capacity, his work proved transformational. A biographical retrospective by the *International Center for Photography*, cited "where he began making the photographs that would be reproduced as engravings and halftones in *How the Other Half Lives*, his celebrated work."

Above Left: Portrait Jacob Riis, c. 1900. Photo by Frances Benjamin Johnston (1864-1952). Library of Congress No. LC-USZ62-47078. **Above Right**: Cover of original *How the Other Half Lives*, c. 1890.

The title for the groundbreaking publication of *How the Other Half Lives: Studies Among the Tenements of New York* was explained within the first sentence of the Introduction. Riis wrote, "Long ago it was said that one half of the world does not know how the other half lives." The summation why one half did not know about the other half was a simple fact of life, "because it did not care." As an unfortunate aspect, Riis explained,

> "The half that was on top cared little for the struggles, and less for the fate of those who were underneath, so long as it was able to hold them

---

[254] Jimmy Stamp. "Pioneering Social Reformer Jacob Riis Revealed "How the Other Half Lives" in America." *Smithsonian Magazine,* May 27, 2014.

188 Italian Culture in America:
The Immigrants 1880 to 1930 From Discrimination to Assimilation

there and keep its own seat. There came a time when the discomfort and crowding below were so great, and the consequent upheavals so violent, that it was no longer an easy thing to do, and then the upper half fell to inquiring what was the matter and the whole world had its hands full answering for its old ignorance."[255]

Within *How the Other Half Lives* was twenty-five descriptive chapters, with the addition of a Preface, Introduction, Appendix and Explanatory notes supplemented with over 40 illustrations.

The journalistic work by Riis provided a groundbreaking exposé analyzing many different aspects of the Tenement starting with the earliest designs, aptly titled as the "Genesis." As an example, following is a sample of pertinent excerpts from Chapter One.

CHAPTER I. GENESIS OF THE TENEMENT

THE first tenement New York knew bore the mark of Cain from its birth, though a generation passed before the writing was deciphered. It was the "rear house," infamous ever after in our city's history. There had been tenant-houses before, but they were not built for the purpose. Nothing would have shocked their original owners more than the idea of their harboring a promiscuous crowd; for they were the decorous homes of the old Knickerbockers, the proud aristocracy of Manhattan in the early days. Their comfortable dwellings in the once fashionable streets along the East River front fell into the hands of real-estate agents and boarding-house keepers; and here, says the report to the Legislature of 1857, when the evils engendered had excited just alarm, in its beginning, the tenant-house became a real blessing to that class of industrious poor whose small earnings limited their expenses, and whose employment in workshops, stores, or the warehouses and thoroughfares, render a near residence of much importance."

Riis supplemented the drawings and observations with statistical data and illustrated floor plans, such as the following

Number of tenements in New York, December 1, 1888	32,390
Number built from June 1, 1888, to August 1, 1890	3,733
Rear tenements in existence, August 1, 1890	2,630
Total number of tenements, August 1, 1890	37,316
Estimated population of tenements, August 1, 1890	1,250,000
Estimated number of children under five years in tenements, 1890	163,712

Table from Appendix in: Jacob Riis, *How the Other Half Lives*, p. 304.

---

[255] Jacob Riis, *How the Other Half Lives*, 1890, p. 2.

CHAPTER 5 189

Above Left: "An Old Rear-Tenement in Roosevelt Street." From the original 1890 publication of *How the Other Half Lives* authored by Jacob Riis. **Above Right**: Front piece illustration titled "Gotham Court" from the same 1890 publication. (Public Domain).[256]

"TENEMENT OF 1863, FOR TWELVE FAMILIES ON EACH FLAT 2 D. dark L. light. H. halls." "D" label is a small dark room, some without windows. The "L" label denotes "Light."
(From 1890 edition of *How the Other Half Lives*, p. 12.)

---

[256] See: Project Gutenberg, *How the Other Half Lives: Studies Among the Tenements of New York*, April 26, 2014, pp. 7-8. Produced by KD Weeks, David Edwards and the Online Distributed Proofreading Team at www.gutenberg.org.

190   Italian Culture in America:

Chapter 1 cleverly titled "Genesis of the Tenement" referenced as the first chapter of the Bible, likening the American creation of a tenement slum neighborhood with the inhuman treatment of immigrants to the first sin of murder as Cain slew Abel. Riis likened the creation of tenements as not an accident; but premeditated conditions created by unscrupulous landlords responsible for the high death rate in the overcrowded neighborhoods. In a 1902 publication chapter titled "Dens of Death," Riis charted,

> "Twenty cases of typhoid fever from a single house in one year was the record that had gone unconsidered. Think of living babies in such hell-holes; and make a note of it, you in the young cities who can still head off the slum where we have to wrestle with it for our sins. Put a brand upon the murderer who would smother babies in dark holes."

Some of the apartments were "so small" Riis was "unable to get a photograph even by placing the camera outside the open door. At one he estimated the width as "three short steps across either way would have measured its full extent." Some single room apartments housing five families of "20 persons") only measured a scant 12' x 12' (144 sq. ft.).

Others lived in similar crowded spaces "with scarcely room enough to turn around." Despite the tight conditions, worse yet were the "thousands living in cellars." Riis counted at least "three hundred underground lodging-houses." Discovered among the tenements were the lower levels of all sorts of buildings and abandoned churches "had been converted into tenements." One particular reform group the Society for the Improvement of the Condition of the Poor summed up the tenement as,

> "Crazy old buildings, crowded rear tenements in filthy yards, dark, damp basements, leaking garrets, shops, outhouses, and stables converted into dwellings, though scarcely fit to shelter brutes, are habitations of thousands of our fellow-beings in this wealthy, Christian city."[257]

In a follow-up *The Battle with the Slum*, Riis found "bedrooms in tenements" were nothing more than interior "dark closets, utterly without ventilation." Due to lack of ventilation, beside the diseases, were moldy conditions due to "constant moisture."[258]

As an early pioneer in the use of flash attachment for his camera allowed Riis the ability for innovative nighttime photographs. He often went inside the dark interior of tenements; literally illuminating an entirely new world. In 2020, journalist Kelly Richman-Abdou explained, "the photographs presented a grim peek into life in poverty to an oblivious public." As such, the photographic images

---

[257] Jacob Riis, *How the Other Half Lives*, pp. 1-5, 21.
[258] Jacob Riis. *Battle with the Slum*, pp. 21, 152.

literally "lingered in the mind." The photographic documentation was supplemented with investigative journalism. (Many of the images in the first publication were hand-drawn illustrations from Riis photographs. Later editions contained photographs.) The work was a major impetus for legislation leading to improving social living conditions of many immigrants. Some early Riis photographs have been lost, however a significant amount survived. Regardless, those that have survived provide valuable visual reference to the squalid conditions endured by immigrants. (Many can be found at the United States Library of Congress and the New York Public Library.)[259]

Images in the 1890 publication *How the Other Half Lives* remain powerful. A biography written by the Editors of Encyclopedia Britannica explain,

> "Riis's revelations and writing style ensured a wide readership: his story, he wrote in the book's introduction, 'is dark enough, drawn from the plain public records, to send a chill to any heart.' Theodore Roosevelt, who would become U.S. president in 1901, responded personally to Riis: 'I have read your book, and I have come to help.' The book's success made Riis famous, and *How the Other Half Lives* stimulated the first significant New York legislation to curb tenement house evils."[260]

Original title: "Tenement, New York." This photograph by Jacob Riis, c. 1890, is most likely of Italian immigrants. It clearly illustrates the one-room apartment for seven members of the same family.
Library of Congress Prints and Photographs Division.

---

[259] Kelly Richman-Abdou. "Jacob Riis: The Photographer Who Showed "How the Other Half Lives" in 1890s NYC." *My Modern Met*, July 21, 2020.
[260] "Jacob Riis American journalist." The Editors of Encyclopedia Britannica.

The Italian in New York

Within *How the Other Half Lives*, Riis covered a multitude of living conditions and lifestyles of many immigrant groups including Chinese, German, Irish, Italians, Polish, and Jewish, among others. Some of the specific chapters devoted to Italians were,

Chapter 4: The Down Town Back-alleys
Chapter 5: The Italian in New York
Chapter 6: The Bend [as in "Mulberry Bend']
Chapter 7: A Raid on the Stale-Beer Dives

Riis began Chapter 5, with a vivid description of "The Italian in New York, as he wrote,

> "Certainly, a picturesque, if not very tidy, element has been added to the population in the 'assisted' Italian immigrant who claims so large a share of public attention, partly because he keeps coming at such a tremendous rate, but chiefly because he elects to stay in New York, or near enough for it to serve as his base of operations. . . . The Italian comes in at the bottom, and in the generation that came over the sea he stays there. In the slums he is welcomed as a tenant who 'makes less trouble' than the contentious Irishman or the order-loving German, that is to say: is content to live in a pig sty and submits to robbery at the hands of the rent-collector A really desirable tenant."[261]

The work of Jacob Riis caught the attention of future president Theodore Roosevelt, who at the time was head of the Board of Commissioners of the New York City Police Department; a post held from 1895-1897.[262]

As a commissioner, Roosevelt was intrigued over the night time work of Police officers and often accompanied Riis. Of his night time ventures into the slum areas such as "The Bend," Roosevelt wrote,

> "The countless evils which lurk in the dark corners of our civic institutions, which stalk abroad in the slums, and have their permanent abode in the crowded tenement houses, have met in Mr. Riis the most formidable opponent every encountered by them in New York City."[263]

Some of the most troubling heart wrenching discoveries were the large number of children living in impoverished conditions. Some worked in support of their families; others were orphans without any means of livable shelter. Part of the problem disappeared with the "Orphan Train."

---

[261] Jacob A. Riis. *How the Other Half Lives* Chapter V. The Italian in New York, p. 41.

[262] See also: Our Founder." *Jacob A. Riis Neighborhood Settlement.*

[263] Kelly Richman-Abdou. "Jacob Riis: The Photographer Who Showed "How the Other Half Lives" in 1890s NYC." *My Modern Met*, July 21, 2020.

CHAPTER 5 193

Riis exposé in *How the Other Half Lives* provided insight on the daily life of Italian immigrants. Throughout the week Italians worked long hours over the course of six days. For most, Sunday was for religious and family activities. (Some worked a half-day on Sunday.) Riis likened Italians to Chinese as "born gamblers;" insinuating the peaceful behavior of an Italian changes "when he settles down to a game of cards and lets loose all his bad passions." Riis' comment only added to a common stereotype of an Italian male having a knife ready to use in anger or retribution.

Adding to the so-called hot-headed stereotypical temper, Riis told his readers, "[The Italian] soul is in the game from the moment the cards are on the table, and very frequently his knife is in it too before the game is ended." Located specifically on "The Bend" (Mulberry Street in the heart of the Italian conclave of Little Italy), Riis claimed no Sunday was without some kind of "murderous affrays coming to the notice of the police." The regular occurrence into a crime ridden Sunday, he claimed, only started after the area "became a suburb of Naples." Riis spoke of criminal activity, including murder was not one which the people would engage the police; as "the wounded man can seldom be persuaded to betray him."[264]

Despite the negative association, Riis did provide redeeming qualities, he informing of a divided role of Italian males and females.

"With all his conspicuous faults, the swarthy Italian immigrant has his redeeming traits. He is as honest as he is hot-headed. There are no Italian burglars in the Rogues' Gallery; the ex-brigand toils peacefully with pickaxe and shovel on American ground. . . The women are faithful wives and devoted mothers. Their vivid and picturesque costumes lend a tinge of color to the otherwise dull monotony of the slums they inhabit. The Italian is [happy], light-hearted and, as inoffensive as a child."

Riis, took note of the ever-growing number of Italians required additional living areas. The Little Italy area of Mulberry Bend was so overcrowded an additional enclave of housing was found in northern Manhattan. Riis described it as, "The process can be observed in the Italian tenements in Harlem (Little Italy), which, since their occupation by these people, have been gradually sinking to the slum level."

Riis continued investigating, photographing, and lobbying for social change. In a follow up exposé, *Battle With The Slum*, he wrote,

"A model was shown of a typical East Side block, containing 2781 persons on two acres of land, nearly every bit of which was covered with buildings. There were 466 babies in the block, but not a bath-tub except

---

[264] Riis. *How the Other Half Lives,* Chapter V. The Italian in New York, pp. 42-43; 147.

one that hung in an air shaft. Of the 1588 rooms 441 were dark, with no ventilation to the outer air except through other rooms."

Despite many problems associated with overcrowding, such as extraordinary high numbers of diphtheria, tuberculous, and compounded poverty, Riis reported "the rent-roll was all right."[265]

A heartbreaking photograph of shoeless street children (possibly orphans) titled "Nomads of the Street," Photograph by Jacob Riis, c. 1900. (Possible location on Mulberry Street in Manhattan.)

Riis investigative work brought public attention to the unsanitary living conditions endured by immigrants. The onset of disease caused by the overcrowded conditions was totally unfamiliar to Italians in their home country. In a 1904 interview with Dr. Antonio Stella on the high incidence of tuberculosis amongst Italians, Riis explained,

> "Six months of life in the tenements are sufficient to turn the sturdy youth from Calabria, the brawny fisherman of Sicily, the robust women from Abruzzi and Basilicata, into the pale, flabby, undersized creatures we see dragging along the streets of New York and Chicago, such a painful contrast to the native population. Six months more of the gradual deterioration, and the soil for the bacillus tuberculosis is amply prepared."[266]

---

[265] Riis. *How the Other Half Lives,* Chapter V. The Italian in New York, pp. 42-43; 147.
[266] "Tenements and Toil." *Immigration and Relocation in U.S. History.*

By 1900, the "Little Italy" area of Mulberry Street was so densely populated with Italian immigrants, it sustained the publication of at least ten daily and weekly Italian language newspapers; focusing on the desperation of Italian immigrants; all were sentimental to their plight.[267]

The Battle With the Slum

Jacob Riis continued to write, lecture, publish, and work as a crusader for immigrants and their social conditions. As a follow-up to *How the Other Half Lives*, Riis chronicled the history of "slum living" in a 1902 publication *The Battle with the Slum*. A historical revelation claimed the slum was "as old as civilization." He did offer a contradiction as the reason for slums in New York "is our own we made it, but let us be glad we have no patent on the manufacture." In the Preface to *The Battle with the Slum*, termed a "sequel," Riis explained the reason for another publication as,

> Three years ago, I published a series of papers intended to account for the battle with the slum since I wrote "How the Other Half Lives." So many things have happened and has held public attention, that this seems the proper time to in review once more. That I have tried to do in this book, retaining all that still applied of the old volume and adding as much more; "stories." They are fact, not fiction. If the latter, they would have no place here."

Above Left: Typical tenement yard from *How the Other Half Lives*, c. 1890.
Above Right: Alley between tenement buildings "The Mott Street Barracks" in *The Battle With the Slum*, c. 1902. Photo by Jacob Riis.

---

[267] William E. Davenport. "The Italian Immigrant in America," p. 32.

Riis cited the advancements and legislation which came about by the tireless efforts of social reformers. In the "sequel," Riis added a photograph of President "Teddy" Roosevelt praised as an ally and "A valiant battler with the slum." Prior to the 1902 publication, Roosevelt as governor of New York State appointed a Tenement House Commission which eventually ended many abuses. Mandated changes included outdoor playground space with each new school construction. Natural light and ventilation became a mandatory requirement for all new buildings. A retroactive requirement by the New York City Department of Health had over 40,000 new windows cut into existing building walls for interior light and ventilation. Architectural competitions encouraged plans to solve the problems of old tenements. An overwhelming response of "more than 170 architects sent in plans in the competition for a humane tenement that should be commercially profitable." Included were line drawings of seven comparative floor plans tracing the history of the tenement from the single family "Knickerbocker" to the many various incarnations of overcrowded tenements.[268]

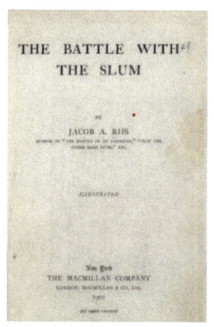 

Above Left: Title page Jacob A. Riis. *The Battle with the Slum*, c. 1902. **Above Right**: Photograph of President Teddy Roosevelt, p.1.

---

[268] Jacob Riis. *Battle with the Slum*, New York: The MacMillan Company, 1902.

1. Old Knickerbocker Dwelling.
2. The same made over into a tenement.
3. The rear tenement caves.
4. Packing-box tenement built for revenue only.
5. The limit; the air shaft – first concession to tenant.
6. Double-decker, where the civic conscience began to stir in 1879.
7. Evolution of double-decker up to date.

Above seven comparative floor plans tracing the history of the tenement. Jacob Riis, *The Battle with the Slum*, 1902, p. 150. (Public Domain).

A typical tenement building that survived into the year 2020, located at the corner of West 35th Street and 10th Avenue in Manhattan, New York City. (Photograph by Author).

"The Little Italian Slave in America" and The Padrone Act of 1874

For Italian immigrants, work was the main reason for entering America. Some with a prearranged work agreement, others took a chance convinced of the so-called "streets paved with gold." It was not uncommon after disembarking from an Ellis Island Ferry, they were solicited by a work boss who arranged for transport and employment. One historian described it as "a contract labor system utilized by many immigrant groups to find employment in the United States, most notably Italian, but also Greeks, Chinese, Japanese, and Mexican Americans."

The Italian word for the work boss was *Padrone*. Sometimes the *padrone* was a *paisan* from the same town, who met immigrants at the point of arrival. At times, meeting was prearranged; in other instances, the *padrone* solicited new arrivals. Historian Tyler Anbinder in *City of Dreams*, described *padrone* as "an Italian labor contractor." The *Padrone* was more than a work boss, more akin to a "master" controlling a system of employment requiring a percentage of the wage earnings. The *Library of Congress* claimed,

> "In practice, many *padroni* [plural of *padrone*] acted more like slave holders than managers. A padrone often controlled the wages, contracts, and food supply of the immigrants under his authority, and could keep workers on the job for weeks or months beyond their contracts. Some padroni built vast labor empires, keeping thousands of workers confined in locked camps, behind barbed wire fences patrolled by armed guards. Many thousands of Italian immigrants found themselves prisoners of the *padrone*, or patron, system of labor. The *padroni* were labor brokers, sometimes immigrants themselves, who recruited Italian immigrants for large employers and then acted as overseers on the work site."[269]

A half-century earlier, a Catholic Boston newspaper *The Pilot*, founded in 1858, carried a story of the Padrone System in New York, as,

THE LITTLE ITALIAN
SLAVES

A Diabolical Traffic

The Padrone System in New York

THE CROWDED DENS

A Shocking Institution[270]

---

[269] "The Great Arrival," *Library of Congress*.
[270] "The Little Italian Slaves," *The Pilot*, Vol. 36, No. 36, Sep. 6, 1873, p. 5.

CHAPTER 5   199

The September 6, 1873 article cited a recent court case of an Italian Vincenzo Motto the "King of the Padrones," for "the most brutal and inexcusable species of human slavery." The "slavery" in question was for young children. The Catholic appeal was "a determined effort" to enact a law preventing the practice of placing children in involuntary servitude. Justification for ending the child labor system stated such a practice should not occur in "the land of the free." An unknown number of non-orphan children were also brokered from parents in Italy, as explained,

> "Sometimes they make a bargain with a child's parents, agreeing to take the boy to America, to give him a thorough Christian and secular education, to teach him music, and to help him along in the world. A glowing picture of America are drawn to the ignorant back-country farmer told his son will rise to eminence and great wealth in a few years."

Sometimes, a *padrone*, or an agent would canvass the docks of port cities such as Naples or Marseilles looking for stray children. The agent would entice the children with all sorts of promises; yet in effect *The Pilot* inferred the child was "kidnapped . . . a cheaper and more common way . . . between this country and Italy for fresh supplies of slaves."[271]

The article revealed transporting children to the Lower East Side of New York; housed them in tightly compacted tenement houses. Back alleys were "peculiarly adapted to concealment, and unrivalled in cheapness." The ploy instructed the child in one or two musical tunes played on a harp or violin to send the child to the street playing music to collect money from sympathetic adults. Non-compliance was worthy of being "beaten horribly." *The Pilot* further revealed,

> "Should they venture back with the slightest fraction less than the stipulated sum . . . they are hung up by the thumbs, or some equally devilish punishment is their lot. At night they are compelled to sleep, huddled together spoon fashion, in a close, cramped room, swarming with fleas and other vermin, and in an atmosphere whose stench is absolutely indescribable."

The story was published in 1873 – only a few years after the America Civil War. Abolition of Slavery was a contentious issue throughout the United States with Emancipation during the Reconstruction period brought all sorts of new horrors and debauchery. In New York, institutions such as The Italian Society were formed to combat the social ills perpetrated upon immigrants and children. In New

---

[271] "The Little Italian Slaves," pp. 5-7.

200 Italian Culture in America:
The Immigrants 1880 to 1930 From Discrimination to Assimilation

York, some limited success was had; yet it was reported wealthier *padrones* simply "fled to other cities."[272]

In July of 2020, *The Italian Tribune* reminded 21st century Italian-Americans of the mostly forgotten Padrone system of their ancestors, stating, "While slavery ended in one form with Lincoln's Proclamation, the groundwork for another insidious form was created through. The abuse of southern Italians and Sicilians by the Act amounted to indentured servitude sanctioned by the United States Congress."[273]

The situation created by the *Padrones* was actually in violation of the 13th Amendment to the United States Constitution which reads as,

> "Neither slavery nor involuntary servitude, except as a punishment for crime whereof the party shall have been duly convicted, shall exist within the United States, or any place subject to their jurisdiction."

The "contractual agreement" by *Padrones* with Italian immigrants was viewed as an overt condition of indenture servitude. To eradicate the problem, the U.S. Congress passed the Padrone Act of 1874 as the first "Anti-Human Trafficking Law" in American history. The explicit purpose was to protect Italians, Sicilians, and children from further slavery in the United States. The text of the law read as follows,

> § 446. (Criminal Code, section 271.) Bringing Kidnaped Person into United States. "Whoever shall knowingly and willfully bring into the United States or any jurisdiction thereof, any person inveigled or forcibly kidnaped in any other country, with intent to hold such person kidnaped in confinement or to any involuntary servitude; or whoever shall knowingly and willfully sell or cause to be sold, into any condition of involuntary servitude, any other person for any term whatever; or whoever shall knowingly and willfully hold to involuntary servitude any person so brought or sold, shall be fined not more than $5,000 and imprisoned not more than five years. (March 4, 1909.)"[274]

The Italian Tribune stated, "it abolished Italian and Sicilian slavery, or the form of it known as the padrone system." Unfortunately, laws are only as good as compliance and enforcement. The system existed unfettered well into the 1920s and possibly the 1930s.[275]

---

[272] "The Little Italian Slaves," pp. 5-7.
[273] "The Truth About Italian Slaves in America – Padrone Act of 1874." *The Italian Tribune*, July 16, 2020.
[274] U.S. Code 1946 Edition, Title 18: Criminal Code and Criminal Procedure, Part I: Crimes, Chapter 10: Slave Trade and Peonage, Sections 421-446. "United States Code: Slave Trade and Peonage, 18 U.S.C. §§ 421-446 (1946). *Library of Congress.*
[275] "The Truth About Italian Slaves in America – Padrone Act of 1874."

CHAPTER 5   201

Despite the legislation the system continued. In 1890, Jacob Riis wrote of the *padrone*; describing the unscrupulous system as

> "The padrone having made his ten per cent. Receives him at the landing and turns him to double account as a wage-earner and a rent-payer. In each of these roles he is made to yield a profit to his unscrupulous countryman, whom he trusts implicitly with the instinct of utter helplessness. In the city he contracts for his lodging, subletting to him space in the vilest tenements at extortionate rents."[276]

A typical story of the *Padrone* was revealed in a first-hand biographical account from a real-life "pick and shovel" Italian immigrant day laborer turned literary poet.

Pascal D'Angelo the "Pick and Shovel Poet" and *Son of Italy*

On April 20, 1910, Pasquale "Pascal" D'Angelo (1894-1932) with his father Angelo and seven *paisans* from Abruzzo arrived in America. As a 16-year-old immigrant, with no knowledge of the English language and limited schooling, all were in search of work. After disembarking from an Ellis Island Ferry, they met a work boss (*padrone*) who arranged for transport and employment. Work was offered as day laborers for road building about 125 miles north of New York City. Over a period of two years the "D'Angelo work gang" were employed as day laborer "pick and shovel" men requiring hard physical labor not permanent in any one location. They traversed most of upper New York State venturing to the Catskills, Adirondacks and into Western Pennsylvania, West Virginia, and Maryland. D'Angelo later recalled, "Everywhere was toil, endless toil, in the flooding blaze of the sun, or in the slashing rain – toil."[277]

Describing the "pick and shovel," historian Nicola Colella cited a 1902 magazine publication *The World's Work* that described the Italian immigrant "pick and shovel" work as,

> "In an open ditch, red and raw under a broiling sun, sixty-five Italian immigrants, stripped to the necessities, toiled silently with shovel and pick. A hard-faced, red-necked man, their taskmaster, walked up and down the trench, and wherever he stopped the men worked with feverish speed. Temporarily at least, this will be the fate of thousands of the other immigrants who flowed through Ellis Island."

The statement was not sympathetic to Italian immigrants. The monthly magazine focused on national issues supporting big business. It did not champion immigration from non-English speaking nations – especially Italy. The editors at

---

[276] Jacob A. Riis. *How the Other Half Lives,* "V. The Italian in New York," p. 41.
[277] Quoted in: Tyler Anbinder, *City of Dreams*, p. 383.

The World's Work did not degrade all Italians; opinions segregated between high-cultured northern Italians and poor immigrants from southern Italy and Sicily. Colella quoted from another issue as the editorial staff claimed, "Italians from the southern portion of the peninsula make poor citizens; but those from the northern part of Italy rank with the Swiss and other desirable nations."[278]

Discrimination against southern Italian immigrants was quite common which did not provide any compassion for their plight. In the specific case the D'Angelo group worked as "pick and shovel men" involved digging for road building. Work was not permanent in any location, one consistent, the work was always dangerous. Among a gang of nine, two were killed as D'Angelo remembered "crushed to death by a falling derrick on a railroad construction site." No compensation was included for death or injury; the remedy was to hire more laborers.

Above Left: A typical pickaxe. **Above Right**: Typical Shovels of the type used by Pasquale D'Angelo. (Wikimedia Commons. Shovel by Angie from Sawara, Chiba-ken, Japan - Flickr, CC BY 2.0).

Weary of the two year trek of hard labor, D'Angelo and his father Angelo settled in lower Manhattan along in "Little Italy." D'Angelo's father, who could not save enough money to bring his wife and other children to America, returned to Italy. A significant but all too common occurrence; Pasquale decided to stay in New York. In 1921, Pasquale D'Angelo changed his first name to "Pascal" as a devoted full-time poet. D'Angelo's story is like so many optimistic Italian immigrants ending with a tragic consequence. Writing in *City of Dreams*, Tyler Anbinder said, "Pascal D'Angelo may not seem like the typical Italian immigrant, but in most ways, he really was. . . recognizing that he might never succeed." In a literary sense he did succeed; in the monetary sense he did not.[279]

---

[278] Nicola Colella, "Southern Italian Immigration." *Italia America*, 2020.
[279] Tyler Anbinder, *City of Dreams*, p. 129, 383-385

D'Angelo made a choice to leave the physical pain of hard labor behind only to encounter a meager existence as a poet of a different, yet same, circumstance. He learned English from an old worn dictionary and reading old newspapers. Without much in the way of writing implements, resorting to scrawling "on the moldy walls of a boxcar;" since that was where he was living. Once dedicated to writing poetry, he did not have financial resources, therefore he took advantage of the free use of the Brooklyn Public Library; perseverance kept him focused on poetry.

An estimated 200 poetry submissions were sent to magazines, journals, and newspapers – all rejected. In early 1922, he submitted three poems for a contest for *The Nation*, without any response. A frustrated D'Angelo wrote directly to editor Carl Van Doren (1885-1950). The noted literary Columbia professor was impressed by the poetic tone of the letter thereby recommending publication. Van Doren encouraged D'Angelo to write a full-length autobiography, published in 1924, titled *Son of Italy*. Within the preface, Van Doren later praised the work as "a precious document" of contemporary American literature. D'Angelo's as a true *Son of Italy* told of the unforgiving toil of hard labor and harsh working conditions revealing the previously invisible life of unskilled labor in the use of a pickaxe and shovel.[280]

Above Left: "The Pick and Shovel Poet," in *The Brooklyn Daily Eagle* on March 25, 1923, p. 4. **Above Right**: Photograph of Pasquale "Pascal" D'Angelo at work as a day laborer as it appeared in *The Literary Digest International Book Review* Vol. IV, No. 4, p. 232. The photo might be "posed" for publication.

---

[280] Anbinder, *City of Dreams*, pp. 129, 383-388. Mangione and Morreale, pp. 354-360.

Son of Italy created a mild sensation among the literary world, mostly in New York. A headline in *The New York Times Book Reviews* of January 4, 1925, proclaimed "Poet of the Pick and Shovel; Pascal d'Angelo, Has Learned the Great Lesson of America." D'Angelo's work received critical acclaim from many viable literary critics. One of the most important came from Elizabeth Stead Taber in the *Literary Digest International Book Review* praising D'Angelo.[281]

The "pick and shovel poet" might have been better titled the mystery writer. A few months after publication, D'Angelo "dropped off the [literary] map." For unknown reasons, he moved to an impoverished apartment near the less than desirable Gowanus Canal in Brooklyn; described by *The New York Herald Tribune* as an "incredibly bare and cold shanty." An obituary on March 20, 1932 in *The Brooklyn Daily Eagle* noted his death at Kings County Hospital of appendicitis.[282]

Gravesite of Pasquale "Pascal" D'Angelo at St. John's Cemetery, Queens, NY. (Photograph and permission granted by: B. G. Firmani, c. 2017.)

---

[281] Elizabeth Stead Taber. "Pascal d'Angelo, Son of Italy," *The Literary Digest International Book Review, 1926* Vol. IV, No. 4, pp. 219, 222-223.
[282] Anbinder, *City of Dreams*, pp. 388-389. Mangione and Morreale. 354-360.

CHAPTER 5

An internet blog *Forte E Gentile*, by B. G. Firmani cites Pascal D'Angelo as "largely forgotten today as a poet, or even as a writer of an immigrant narrative." Firmani provided a thoroughly researched account of the hard life and subsequent disappearance from public life of Pascal D'Angelo. The meticulous article was assembled from archival sources including the Brooklyn Public Library. Firmani traced D'Angelo's last known residence and burial site, personally visiting and laying flowers at his graveside at St. John's Cemetery in the borough of Queens in New York City.[283]

"The Mysterious Italian Genius" of Italian Culture

In 1989, art historian Irma B. Jaffe in *The Italian Presence in American Art 1760-1860* noted:

> "It would be impossible to overstate the debt of insight and inspiration that the Western world owes to Italian culture. Can we even begin to estimate how much our aesthetic and intellectual expectations have been nourished by the literature, the music, the painting, the sculpture, the architecture of Italy? The United States as much as any nation in the world, has been enriched by the mysterious Italian genius, and before we had achieved nationhood, we had already found our way into the fountain."

Jaffe's "mysterious Italian genius" is high praise. Therefore, questioning the discovery of genius of any culture is important. Carl Van Doren understood as he questioned, "No American after watching a gang of brown Italians in a ditch, can help asking himself whether there is not some Pascal D'Angelo among them."[284]

The story of Pascal D'Angelo might be viewed as a one in a million occurrence – a fluke – a happenstance. Of the almost 5 million immigrants of the Great Arrival we might say it was more of a "One in Five Million" chance of occurrence. Tracing the legacy of Italian American writers after 1880, the list of published authors is noticeably limited. After World War II, a credible compilation of two comprehensive bibliographies of Italian American writers appeared. In 1947 by Giovanni Schiavo (1903-1967) and a second in 1949 by Olga Peragallo (1910-1943) list of "just 59 writers, out of a population of nearly five million."[285]

It was not that southern Italian immigrants were devoid of artistic talent; rather no system existed in Italy nor in America to foster their artistic development. Recognizing genius portrayed through art is cited in *Sir Banister*

---

[283] B.G. Firmani, *"The Dreamlife of Pascal D'Angelo."* 2017. Firmani notes: St. John Cemetery is also the "final resting place" of many prominent Italian-Americans.
[284] Irma Jaffe, ed. *The Italian Presence in American Art 1760-1860*, p. vii.
[285] Francesco Mulas, Studies on Italian-American Literature, p. vii.

Fletcher's A History of Architecture. Specific reference focused on the great Renaissance architect Andrea Palladio (1508-1580) as a great artist of any genre. Fletcher states, "genius can produce works of art out of commonplace materials." Some might say the quote is simplified and void of complicity; the point here is to indicate genius as displayed by Pascal D'Angelo created from "commonplace materials." A similar concept of genius suggested a century earlier by American statesman Thomas Jefferson understood "genius was not by accident of birth," In 1787, Jefferson's *Notes on the State of Virginia*, made capturing of genius a crucial tenet for the benefit all of America as a whole. He explained,

> "By that part of our plan which prescribes the selection of the youths of genius from among the classes of the poor, we hope to avail the state of those talents which nature has sown as liberally among the poor as the rich, but which perish without use, if not sought for and cultivated. Genius and virtue, should be rendered by liberal education worthy to receive, and able to guard the sacred deposit of the rights and liberties of their fellow citizens, and that they should be called to that charge without regard to wealth, birth or accidental condition of circumstance."[286]

For Italian immigrants, placed below African Americans in social class, discovering artistic genius was virtually impossible. Among Italians during the Great Arrival, a few others emerged such as, Bernardino Ciambelli (1862-1931) known for writing *I Misteri di Mulberry Stritto* (The Mysteries of Mulberry Street, 1893); Arturo Giovannitti (1884-1959), a union leader and poet known as the "Bard of Freedom;" poet Emanuel Carnevali (1897-1942) published *A Hurried Man* (1925); and Constantine M. Panunzio (1884-1964) *The Soul of an Immigrant* (1922).

Panunzio (1884-1964) was born in Molfetta, from the Bari region of Italy. Unlike most other immigrants, Panunzio was not born poor; rather a family which stressed education. Against family objections, he left home to travel the seas as a sailor. In 1912, Panunzio "jumped ship" in Boston; yet found limited opportunities for Italians such as himself; struggling to find work. He described in *The Soul of an Immigrant* as, "We began to make inquiries about jobs and were promptly informed that there was plenty of work at "pick and shovel." We were also given to understand by our fellow-boarders that "pick and shovel" was practically the only work available to Italians." Not knowing any English, Panunzio practiced the only words he needed to obtain work – he wrote the words as the pronunciation in "broken English" the words "peek" and "shuvle."

By 1922, Panunzio was well-versed in English to understand the unscrupulous complexity and false promises of the work system for Italian immigrants. In an autobiography *The Soul of An Immigrant* he wrote, "The "padrone" came up to our group and began to wax eloquent and to gesticulate

---

[286] Thomas Jefferson, Query XIV, *Thomas Jefferson Writings*, p. 287.*Papers of Thomas Jefferson,* 2: 256-257. "A Bill for the More General Diffusion of Knowledge," (No. 79).

CHAPTER 5

about the advantages of a certain job." The *padrone* promised shelter to sleep and suggested a grocery store to buy food at a low cost. Panunzio described the padrone as a "brute" who required a percentage of their meager wages. They soon realized rent, groceries, and payment to the padrone left them with nothing and often in debt.[287]

Panunzio somehow managed to gain enrollment at Kent's Hill Academy in Maine. Adding an M.A. from Wesleyan University in 1912. Enrollment at the Boston University School of Theology. Social work was added to his life cause, overseeing the Social Service House in Boston. From 1917 to 1918, he "served as general organizer of the YMCA, and on the Italian front lines during World War I." After the war, Panunzio earned a Ph.D. and as a professor of sociology at UCLA, until retirement in 1951. At UCLA, the "Constantine Panunzio Distinguished Emeriti Award" remains honoring "outstanding scholarly work or educational service performed since retirement by a University of California emeritus or emerita in the humanities or social sciences," for any individual in the University of California system.[288]

---

[287] Constantine M. Panunzio. *The Soul of An Immigrant*, pp. 76-79.
[288] From Gordon H. Ball, et. al, "Constantine Maria Panunzio, Anthropology and Sociology: Los Angeles," in University of California: In Memoriam, April 1966.

CHAPTER 6

AMERICANS PLAY - ITALIANS WORK – HULL HOUSE – A FACTORY FIRE - MARGARET SANGER – AND ITALIAN LEISURE

"Few serious attempts were made to discuss how the Italian culture made the source of a man's pride his family and his honor, not his job. Despite the strong prejudices of this era, the Italian-American would face increasing prejudice in the years to come."

The period of the late 1890s, continuing until the United States entered into World War I, was a time in American history known as "The Progressive Era." The impetus was an attempt to limit the social problems caused by "industrialization, urbanization, immigration, and political corruption." The large influx of immigrants presented many changes to American society; mostly as a separate parallel development between the established mainstream apart from recent immigrants.

The decades did represent a struggle by progressive reformers promoting child labor laws, public education, safe housing, worker safety in factories, and breaking up corporate monopolies, among others. Those social changes were often in contrast to staunch politicians seeking to create an assimilated homogenous American, although strictly segregated, society. Prior to 1900, the issue was divided as black and white and as a divided country between White Protestants and immigrant religions such as Catholics and Jews. The 1896 U.S. Supreme Court decision *Plessy v. Ferguson*, legally allowed segregation of defined racial differences; however, legal discrimination also affected Italian immigrants.

The "neat and tidy" American view of law was quite complicated in many ways. As immigrants kept arriving, the United States suffered an economic

Depression from 1893 to 1898. With the onset of a depression, it was easy for Americans (especially Nativists) to blame immigrants for taking away jobs. The jobs immigrants "took" were menial involving digging tunnels, masonry, working in mines, or farms and plantations. The work was not guaranteed and often hazardous.

In stark contrast to the life of immigrants, the perpetuated media image of American lifestyles promoted leisure as an innocent time of family get togethers, picnics, Sunday strolls, bicycle rides, drives in a horse and carriage, or even the new automobile. A new age of American advertising of consumer goods offered Americans a wide array of leisure opportunities. Some opportunities were promoted in the public display by two American presidents of the time Teddy Roosevelt the 26th president from 1901 to 1909 and the 28th president Woodrow Wilson from 1913-1921. Roosevelt was known for promoting vigorous outdoor type of activities; often pictured encouraging lively play among his children, including wrestling and boxing. Wilson, quite opposite often seen playing golf with his wife; or evening time indoors with family, or reading.

Newspapers and popular magazines published stories and images of the Gilded Age "idle rich" enjoying leisurely activities such as boating, golf, tennis, and auto motoring. Although, it was only a small snapshot of the American population, those pursuits were costly and exclusive only to a select few. Those leisure pursuits publicized by the national media outlets were also in direct contrast to the daily life of immigrants. The average working immigrant family could not partake in the leisurely lifestyles as displayed by Roosevelt, Taft, Wilson, and Gilded Age rich.

"The Italian Immigrant in America"

In the overcrowded cities many Italians took unskilled labor jobs engaged in large scale public works projects. Those projects required physical labor such as digging trenches and foundations for building bridges, and "tunneling out the New York subway system." The Library of Congress, cited "nearly 90 percent of the laborers in New York's Department of Public Works were Italian immigrants." Among the remaining 10 percent, a significant number worked in "trades that have long been a haven for immigrants, such as shoemaking, masonry, bartending, and barbering."

In 1903, journalist William E. Davenport writing "The Italian Immigrant in America" for *The Outlook* magazine compiled a survey of the occupational trades of Italians living in New York City. He wrote, "In Manhattan some 2,300 Italians are devoted to the trade of St. Crispin (shoemaker); 1,300 who deal in cheese and groceries; 1,500 tailoring shops and 3,000 barbershops; a total of 500 butchers and bakers, and many who keep saloons; 200 tobacconists; and over 600 fruit stores."

Davenport was often asked a stereotypical question, "Why do all Italians deal in bananas?" The questioned was in response to the large number of push carts of fruits, vegetables, and conspicuous bananas, selling to workers in the lower Wall Street area. Davenport tried to clear up the misconception stating, "push-cart men are nearly all Greeks, most of the Italian fruit dealers have stands or stores of their own."[289]

Article: "The Italian Immigrant in America" by William E. Davenport as it appeared in The Outlook (weekly magazine) January 3, 1903, pp. 28-29. The caption under photograph by Arthur Hewitt reads: "A Sicilian Girl of Brooklyn."

Away from the long hours of work, Italians played simple games brought from their homeland, such as the card game *scopa*, (translated as "broom" or "sweep") or a simple street game termed *morra*. The game *scopa* was derived from a deck of cards played by two or more players. Each player placed down a card, whoever had the card of the higher number would "scoop" up the other cards. In *morra*, the players only used their hands as each quickly threw one hand forward extending from one to five fingers, simultaneously calling out a number, the player who guessed closest won.

American born children of Italian immigrants gravitated toward sports as

---

[289] William E. Davenport. "The Italian Immigrant in America," *The Outlook* Vol. 73, no. 1 (January 3, 1903): p. 34.

baseball and basketball, encouraged through the Americanization process of mandatory public education. Immigrants could not understand the undying American fascination of sports. For many Italians, the value of any activity was whether it was productive or harmful to the family. Although bocce was played for fun, it could be competitive with intensity, and sometimes gambled for money. Gambino explained "winning a competition that did not have direct bearing on the real life of family [was] regarded with disapproval."[290]

Cultural historian Kathy Peiss cited a study of immigrant leisure and recreation that immigrant men spent more leisure time with their families than American born men. Italians engaged in communal social gatherings such as feast day celebrations of patron saints. Almost all Italian recreational activities were usually close to home. Peiss told of one individual in New York's Lower East Side who described an impromptu event outside a tenement building as, "They would play dance music, and all the girls and boys would go in the yards and dance. How the people did enjoy that music! Everyone would be at their windows listening."[291]

A conflict existed between the "Old World" cultural habits of immigrants and the new Americanized leisure pursuits. (That conflict often existed between parents born in Italy and their children born in America.) Social reformer Jane Addams wrote on one such incidence in her recollections of *Twenty Years at Hull House*. "I recall a play written by an Italian playwright of our neighborhood, which depicted the insolent break between Americanized sons and old country parents, so touchingly that it moved to tears all the older Italians in the audience."[292]

Cindy Aron in *Working at Play* discovered, men found solace in saloons, fraternal lodges, social clubs, gambling, prizefighting, and bocce. Married Italian women often stayed indoors cooking and caring for the family. Any type of away time was usually spent on the front "stoop" of their building talking with neighbors. Outside was not always away from their family; it was also watching the children playing street games.

Barber was a common trade of Italian immigrants noted by Davenport providing an in-depth analysis of the trades, lifestyles, and entertainment. For Italian communities across the nation, he wrote,

> "Of the Italians of Chicago, we need not speak, for Miss Jane Addams, of Hull House, says: "There are women's clubs in Chicago which study Italian history, read Dante and go into the art of Italy, but fail to know that right at their doors is this very interesting colony of 10,000 South

---

[290] Richard Gambino. *Blood of My Blood*, pp. 137-138.
[291] Kathy Peiss. *Cheap Amusements: Working Women and Leisure*, pp. 15, 17, 179.
[292] Jane Addams, *Twenty Years at Hull House* (1910).

CHAPTER 6

Italians, reproducing their country's habits and manners carrying on their transplanted life with a great deal of charm and a great deal of beauty, and yet these women's clubs know nothing about them. . . yet here are these people who with their life would offer a genuine addition to our own life and social endeavor and stimulus."

In cities such as Chicago, settlements houses such as Hull House serviced Italian immigrants offering acclimation while providing cultural programs of the Italian homeland.[293]

HULL HOUSE AN "ITALIAN NEIGHBORHOOD"

In New York City, neighborhoods of the wealthy were separated by only a few city blocks from impoverished immigrants. In response to the plight of the urban poor, some middle-class reformers introduced the idea of Settlement Houses, such as Lillian Wald (1867-1940) at the New York Henry Street Settlement and Hull House in Chicago, by Jane Addams (1860-1935) and Ellen Gates Starr (1859-1940). Settlement houses offered a solution promoting neighborhood recreation with self-help courses in English language, sewing, crafts, social dancing, and a community center of safe refuge for immigrants, mainly women and children.

An earlier visit to Europe enlightened Addams and Starr. In 1888, a European tour included a trip to Rome and England. While in London, they visited a settlement at Toynbee Hall in the impoverished East End. At Toynbee Hall, the staff of students from Oxford and Cambridge Universities worked to ease conditions of the working poor. A need awoke for Addams and Starr to do the same in America. Arriving home, the two worked to provide a similar settlement for immigrants, mostly Italian, living in Chicago. They secured a location in the former home of a wealthy benefactor Charles Jerald Hull (1820–1889). Built in 1856, "Hull House" located at 800 South Halsted Street was granted to his niece Helen Culver (1832-1925), who in turn offered it for use as a Settlement house. In an autobiography, Addams described the area was woefully neglected with poor street lighting, inadequate schools, "foul" smells, unenforced sanitary conditions, and "families crowded into the same residence."[294]

---

[293] Davenport, "The Italian Immigrant in America," *The Outlook* 73:1, p. 37.p. 37.
[294] Linda J. Tomko. Dancing Class: Gender, Ethnicity, and Social Divides, pp. 83-84.Jane Addams, Twenty Years at Hull-House, p. 98.

Above Left: Ellen Gates Starr co-founder of Hull House in Chicago photograph as it appeared in the Chicago Daily Tribune, c. 1914. Public Domain American Memory Collection Library of Congress. **Above Right**: Jane Addams of Hull House, Library of Congress Prints and Photographs Division, No: LC-USZ61-144.

The *Italianate* Architectural Style

In 1856, Charles Hull commissioned building a home in the *au currant* architecture of "Italianate;" a distinct short-lived 19th-century style. The original style was derived from the Neo-Classical revival in Europe and America during the 19th century; derived from the 16th century Italian Renaissance architect Andrea Palladio (1508-1580). The defined Italianate characteristics as a building comprised of,

> "2 or 3 stories, rarely 1 story; low-pitched roof, widely overhanging eaves; large, decorative brackets under an ornamental cornice; tall, narrow windows (most often on commercial buildings), commonly arched or curved above; an occasional square cupola or tower (campanile), elaborate wrap-around porch (or smaller entry porch) with decorative Italianate double columns."

As for the distinctive architectural Italianate Style of the 1850s to 1880s," White listed seven "Identifying Features" as,
1. The style was derived from medieval Italian villas.
2. The growing popularity of pattern books in the 1840s created a consistent architectural template that spread across the country.
3. Many (but not all) will have a belvedere.
4. Overhanging eaves with brackets are a key feature.
5. Tall, narrow windows are an easy way to spot the Italianate style.
6. Most residential structures have one-story porticoes.
7. Many Italianate structures have cast iron decoration.

The number of Italianate styled buildings increased from the eastern states across the nation into the Midwest and other areas as people moved westward settling in cities and towns. Some likened the style resembling an Italian farmhouses.as it was widely adapted to a variety of American building types including train stations, barns, and rural homes.[295] The Italianate architectural style was popular, from about 1850 to 1880. (It is speculative if the style faded due to anti-Italian discrimination emerging after 1880; therefore, the wealthy elite avoided any negative association.) The Italianate homes, when left unattended easily fell into disarray. As was the former Hull residence and neighborhood, "when Addams was searching for a location for her experiment, it had descended into squalor. This was partly due to the rapid and overwhelming influx of immigrants into the Near West Side neighborhood."[296]

A typical Italianate styled residential home. The Albert L. Scott House, 29 South Market Street, Petersburg, Virginia, c. 1872-1873. Library of Congress Prints and Photographs Division Reproduction No: HABS VA,27-PET,25--1

---

[295] Meghan White. "What Is Italianate Architecture?"
[296] Franz Schulte and Kevin Harrington. *Chicago's Famous Buildings*, pp. 212–213.

Italians at Hull House

In *Twenty Years at Hull-House*, Jane Addams outlined the basic objective of their endeavors for Settlement Houses. "Life in the Settlement discovers above all what has been called 'the extraordinary pliability of human nature,' and it seems impossible to set any bounds to the moral capabilities which might unfold under ideal civic and educational conditions." The establishment of Hull House and the growing number of Italian immigrants entering into the city caught the attention of Nora Marks a journalist from the *Chicago Daily Tribune*. The daily newspaper founded in 1847 was still in print into the 21st century.[297]

Hull House was a complex of 13 buildings and the original Hull mansion. This Postcard image c. 1907 was published by V.O. Hammon (Public Domain).

Nora Marks (1863-1942) as an investigative journalist employed by the Chicago Daily Tribune. often went undercover or incognito. Marks often went unauthorized into work areas and establishments; such as children's work houses, prisons, charity houses, and the Salvation Army, among others. As a pen name "Nora Marks" (real name was Eleanor Atkinson, nee Stackhouse), her investigation encompassed both sides, posing as a wealthy employer; another time as a poor person seeking a job. Marks reporting of the disparages, was chronicled as a feature story in the Chicago Daily Tribune. In one two-year period from 1888 to 1890, no less than eighty feature stories appeared as "Nora Marks;" soon becoming a well-known name, but not recognized in person. In one specific

---

[297] Jane Addams. *Twenty Years at Hull-House*, pp. 453-454.

CHAPTER 6   217

instance Marks did not have to go "undercover" as an invited guest to observe an evening at Hull House.

The cordial invitation for Saturday evening of May 17, 1890 addressed to "*Mio Carissimo Amico*" (My Dearest Friend) offered "a visit with American and Italian friends." Marks willingly attended, providing one of the earliest primary sources of life within Hull House; writing her encounter, which was published in the *Chicago Daily Tribune* two days later, as a page 1 article, as,

"Two Women's Work: The Misses Addams and Starr
Astonish the West Siders,"
By: Nora Marks, Chicago Daily Tribune, 19 May 1890.

Nora Marks described a "unique invitation went on to say that the Misses Addams and Starr were of a distinguished family and that they had come to live among these children of Italy and desired their friendship." The host was Mastro-Valerio "a humble editor of *L'Italia,* but he is also the Chicago Garibaldi who is trying to lead the Italians out of the bondage of ignorance." Marks experienced a wealth of Italian culture of attendees "in peasant dress, the American costume being good enough for only ordinary occasions." A sense of joy was exhibited as, "the Italians seemed to feel among friends. They unburdened their simple thoughts and reveled in simple pleasures. The undisguised family affection among them was something beautiful [as] was singing in Italian." The Chicago community of the Hull House neighborhood contained large numbers of Italian immigrants; as revealed in Nora Marks 1890 story. On the evening Marks visited as a *"Mio Carissimo Amico"* of Hull House, completely enthralled with the presentation of Italian culture, which was called "memorable."[298]

"Nora Marks," journalism career was short-lived, but as a writer. Thereby publishing as Eleanor Atkinson achieved considerable fame. In 1890, with husband and journalist Francis Atkinson, they founded The Little Chronicle Publishing Company on education and children's titles. Atkinson authored numerous books, including a 1912 classic in children's literature, the popular novel *Greyfriars Bobby* (still published in the 21st century). In 1961, the Walt Disney Company made a movie based on the book titled, *Greyfriars Bobby: The True Story of a Dog.*[299]

---

[298] Nora Marks, "Two Women's Work," *Chicago Daily Tribune*, May 19, 1890, p. 1.
[299] Compiled from multiple sources. See also: Leonard, John William, ed. *Woman's Who's Who of America*, 1914, p. 59.

"Nora Marks" pictured as married name Eleanor Atkinson, listed as "Editors and Contributors" from a compilation volume *The New Student's Reference Work* c. 1914 a literary encyclopedia over 4,500 pages. Entry notes her as co-founder of The Little Chronicle Publishing Company and author of the 1912 children's **classic** *Greyfriars Bobby*. (Public Domain – Wiki Commons)

Through the 1890s, the Italian population in the Hull House neighborhood increased. One survey discovered the neighborhood was "overwhelmingly Italians." The Jane Addams Papers Project substantiated confirmation of the survey by Bethlehem-Howard Neighborhood Center Records as,

> "As early as the 1890s, 'The Hull House Neighborhood' was overwhelmingly Italians. Those demographics suggest virtually the entire community from the Chicago River on the east end out to the western ends known as "Little Italy" of the Hull House Neighborhood, was wall-to-wall Italian from the 1930s through the 1950s.[300]

By 1907, Hull House was a 13 building complex built around the original Charles Hull home. Included were a kindergarten, art rooms, auditorium, gymnasium, performance stage, and reading rooms, and other educational spaces. The entire complex became, as Addams called it, the "Hull House Neighborhood." The

---

[300] Quote is in many sources. See: "Addams, Jane (1860-1935)," Jane Addams Papers, 2020. Also: Vince Romano, ed. "Taylor Street Archives," December 23, 2015.

CHAPTER 6   219

space provided for a wide array of services and entertainment. A typical weekly schedule at Hull House was as follows,

- Monday:
  o Afternoon a club of young women meets and reads.
  o Lecture on Medici and Savonarola.
- Tuesday:
  o Schoolboys' Club meets reading aloud from books in the circulating library.
  o Girl's cooking class.
  o Evening: boys lecture on what to do in emergencies.
  o Class reading Shakespeare
  o Class beginners studying the three Rs.
- Wednesday:
  o Evening Workingmen's Discussion; "on strikes, labor unions, the eight-hour question."
  o Lecture on Child Labor conditions.
- Thursday:
  o Afternoon lecture for women "on physiology and hygiene and how to raise healthy children.
  o Cooking class.
  o Evening "social evening of reading, and music."
- Friday:
  o Afternoon Schoolgirls' Club "to sew, embroider, and cook."
  o Encouraged to "taking home a book from the library."
  o Evening "working girls come in to enjoy a lecture or concert."
  o Evening "social evening of reading, music, and cakes and ale."
- Saturday:
  o "Taking home a book from the library."
  o Schoolgirls' Club "to sew, embroider, and cook."
  o Evening "Typical Italian Entertainment."
- Sunday:
  o Reserved for to partake in religious offerings.

Programs and daily schedules appeared in newspapers such as *L'Italia* an Italian language newspaper. Editor A. Mastro-Valerio was a frequent visitor. Italian evenings with Mastro-Valerio were described as, "every Saturday evening the entire families of our Italian neighbors were our guests. Many educated Italians helped us, and the house became known as a place where Italians were welcome and national holidays observed."

Evidence is abounding with appreciation of Italian culture and national celebrations at Hull House. Addams and Starr had seen firsthand the splendor of

Rome and the beauty of the Italian countryside during a visit in 1888. In *Twenty Years at Hull House*, Addams writes of offering Italian immigrants a glimpse into their history, with affectionate admiration as,

> "To me personally the celebration of the hundredth anniversary of Mazzini's birth [1905] was a matter of great interest. Throughout the world that day Italians who believed in a United Italy came together. They recalled the hopes of this man who, with all his devotion to his country was still more devoted to humanity and who dedicated to the workingmen of Italy, an appeal so philosophical, so filled with a yearning for righteousness, that it transcended all national boundaries the Chicago branch of the Society of Young Italy marched into our largest hall and presented to Hull-House a heroic bust of Mazzini."

The *Chicago Daily Tribune*, the most widely circulated paper in Illinois, printed many stories, as Starr and Addams became local celebrities. Despite the impoverished status of Italian immigrants, Addams wrote of a cultural respect (*rispetto*) and remembrance of their Italian homeland.[301]

Denison House and Amelia Earhart
"The Flying Social Worker"

In Boston, Denison House founded in 1892, was modeled after Jane Addams's Hull House. As a woman-run endeavor, the focus on Boston's poor provided social services and education. In contrast to assimilation, local ethnic groups "were encouraged to celebrate their heritage through cultural festivals and craft exhibitions." One Italian-American group the *Circolo Italo-Americano* often sponsored cultural events. Professor Julie Garbus writing, "My Good Italian Friends" for *The New England Quarterly* described the *Circolo Italo-Americano* as, "A Progressive-era group of educated Italian immigrants and affluent Bostonians integrate Italians into American life . . . included Italian leadership and focused on immigrants' contributions, not on assimilation." One Columbus Day celebration on October 12, 1906 offered a musical program of Italian songs. One reason to avoid assimilation offered by Prof. Garbus, "These newcomers threatened the complacency of most assimilated Americans. Perhaps, some Americans worried, they were so different that they could never be absorbed into the country."

An interesting twist of fate, in a rather anonymous historical focus on Denison House involved the famous aviator Amelia Earhart (1897-1939). The aviatrix was anything but conventional gaining an interest in aviation eventually earning a pilot's license. As one of the most famous women in American history,

---

[301] Jane Addams. *Twenty Years at Hull-House*, pp. 231-232; 257-258.

little is often told of her social work with immigrants. In the years prior to becoming a world-famous aviator, Earhart was a social worker at Denison House. From 1925 through 1927, Earhart served as "a teacher, a counselor, and nurse driving sick children to the hospital." As described in a biographical sketch, "At the time Earhart began working at Denison House, settlement houses were designed to serve immigrants and the urban poor. Earhart caught this vision and quickly became immersed in her job."[302]

Whenever possible Amelia Earhart continued to fly. At one point in 1927 she piloted an airplane over the Boston dropping leaflets for an event at Denison House. Keith O'Brien writing in *Fly Girls*, said at the time newspapers called Earhart, "The best-known girl in America." Earhart's tenure ended soon after a historic flight aboard an airplane named *Friendship* in June 1928 as the first woman to cross the Atlantic Ocean in an airplane. Earhart's greatest fame lie ahead setting all sorts of aviation records as a female pilot – not as a passenger.[303]

Above Left: Italian language "Programma" of musical presentations at Denison House in celebration of Columbus Day October 12, 1906, sponsored by the Circolo Italo-Americano. **Above Right**: Illustration of Denison House at 93 Tyler Street, Boston, Massachusetts, c. 1913. (Wiki Commons - Public Domain)

---

[302] Julie Garbus. "My Good Italian Friends." *The New England Quarterly*, p. 531.J. Miller-Cribbs and J. Mains. (2011). "Amelia Earhart (1897-1937): Social worker, women's advocate," *Social Welfare History Project.* May 19, 2022.
[303] Keith O'Brien. *Fly Girls*," pp. 60-61; p. 69.

Urban Parks and Mulberry Bend

Within the crowded cities in immigrant areas, open space was not always available. In 1858, the idea of an urban park began with the design of the 840-acre Central Park in New York. The renowned landscape team of Frederick Law Olmstead (1822-1903) and Calvert Vaux (1824-1895) through planning of urban spaces, held democratic views that public parks should be open to all without regard to wealth status. For the working-class poor, Central Park was an inexpensive. It did not have an entry fee; to enjoy the amenities. Providing a brief repose for families to picnic, stroll, bike, sit, read, relax, or do whatever they pleased.

For Italians, Central Park may have rekindled images and recollections of their idyllic countryside left behind. All was not ideal as many of the Gilded Age rich, living in opulent mansions alongside the park, objected to the fraternization that the design of the park encouraged. The working class believed activities in the park should include fun and games to relive the daily drudgeries. Other cities and municipalities opted for smaller County Parks, playgrounds, and recreation centers. In 1895, Essex County in New Jersey developed the first county park. Parks and playgrounds sprout up in and around cities and towns from coast to coast to escape the drudgery. Added features included carousels, band shells, pavilions, fishing piers, boating, and other recreational facilities.[304]

In 1897, prompted in part by the investigative photojournalism of Jacob Riis, planners in Manhattan enacted an early form of "urban renewal" encompassing the Little Italy section of Mulberry Street. One portion known as "Mulberry Bend" (named due to the curvature of the street) was considered one of the worst criminal activity areas. An area named due to an oblique intersection of five New York City streets. The adjoining area was severely overcrowded with tall tenements and numerous backyard buildings accessed by narrow alleyways allowing easy prey for street robberies. Riis photographed many of these areas with nefarious nicknames such as the "Bandit's Roost."

By decree of City Commissioners, a number of tenements and storefronts over an area of a few city blocks was demolished. In its place was an urban park named "Mulberry Bend Park." In 1903, William E. Davenport observed the Italian game of *Pallone* played with "a large inflated leather ball beaten about very much a in our football [soccer] games." Another noted the musical activity in the park as,

> "The sons of Italy . . . are fond of music and outdoor life; and in New York they enjoy both of these luxuries when the band plays in Mulberry Bend Park from a hundred tenements listening to the strains of *Il Trovatore*."

---

[304] Spiro Kostof, *America by Design*, p. 222.

Il Trovatore (translated as "The Troubadour") is an Italian opera written by Giuseppe Verdi. Opera in America was a favorite of working-class Italians. During the length of a half-century or so, Opera moved within the American cultural hierarchy sphere from the poorer peasants to the wealthy echelon. "High Culture."[305]

In 1911, in honor of the dominant Italian community, Mulberry Bend Park was renamed "Columbus Park." New York City Department of Parks & Recreation explains, "after Christopher Columbus the Italian explorer credited with discovering America, or at least with awakening Europe to the opportunities there." Other types of entertainment were Italian theaters of "light comedies, heroic tragedies, and dialect plays."[306]

Above: "Mulberry Bend" in Little Italy, notorious for overcrowding and criminal activity. In 1897, the area was renovated for an urban neighborhood park. **Bottom**: The Renovated "Columbus Park," c. 1905 Detroit Publishing Company Library of Congress Reproduction No: LC-DIG-det-4a12691.

---

[305] Davenport, "The Italian Immigrant in America," p. 32.
[306] "Columbus Park." *NYCParks.org*.

ITALIAN HARLEM

The term "Little Italy" was applied to any city neighborhood enclave populated mainly by Italian immigrants. Cities nationwide isolated into ethnic immigrant neighborhoods, such as German, Irish, Jewish, Chinese, and of course Italians, among others. Each offered a refuge for shared culture, common language, and heritage. As famous as Mulberry Street became in the lexicon of American culture, a second more populated Little Italy existed in upper Manhattan in an equally famous neighborhood known as Harlem. Matthew Small, writing "Harlem's Hidden History," tells us the area of East Harlem in Manhattan from about the 1880s to after World War II was "the largest Italian American community in the United States" (three times the size of Little Italy in lower Manhattan). As such, it "was the first area in New York designated "Little Italy." Small adds,

> "Italian restaurants of all kinds opened up; barber shops, bakeries, and meat markets were established; churches were built by the Italian craftsmen that worshipped at them, emulating the architecture of their homeland."

With the growing Lower East Side neighborhood of Mulberry Street the upper Italian neighborhood was commonly known as "Italian Harlem." The area was home to over 100,000 Italians crowded into similar tenements as their downtown *paisans*.

A park similar to Mulberry Bend Park was located in "Italian Harlem." In response to the recreational needs of the Italian community, New York City authorized building the "Thomas Jefferson Park and Community Center." According to the official website of the New York City Department of Parks & Recreation,

> "This park was planned and named by the Board of Aldermen in 1894, though the land for it was not purchased until 1897. It opened on October 7, 1905 to provide organized play to the children of "Little Italy," as the crowded tenement district in East Harlem was then known."[307]

The park contained a "children's farm garden;" opened on May 20, 1911 provided 1,008 small plots "for children to grow flowers and vegetables." The park, as with Mulberry Bend, was "designed as a place of respite." Larger than Mulberry Bend, the park in Italian Harlem contained two playgrounds, public baths, gymnasiums, and comfort stations. A classical inspired pavilion stood until the 1970s; destroyed by vandals.[308]

---

[307] Thomas Jefferson's affinity as an Italophile can be found in: *Italian Culture in America* (Academica Press 2020).
[308] Matthew Small. "Harlem's Hidden History," *Harlem Focus*, July 17, 2016.

Photograph shows children in the farm garden of Thomas Jefferson Park, New York City, which opened on May 20, 1911. Published by Bain News Service, c. 1911-1915. Library of Congress Prints Reproduction No: LC-DIG-ggbain-09228.

IL Progresso and the Triangle Shirtwaist Factory Fire

For almost all immigrants, especially Italian, working days were long and did not allow much time for leisure. One working immigrant rarely could earn enough money to support a family, therefore all the children worked. Pre-teen males often worked in family trades, stocked shelves, hawked newspapers, shined shoes, or hazardous factory conditions. Unmarried daughters contributed to the family income as a seamstress or clerical. A situation representing over 40 percent of the total national labor force.[309]

---

[309] Davenport. "The Italian Immigrant in America," p. 32.

Above Left: "One of the many children under twelve working in the lint-laden air of cotton mills," c. 1909. New York Public Library. **Above Right:** Pre-teen Italians shining shoes known as a "Bowery Bootblack" in New York c. 1910. Photographs by Lewis W. Hine. Library of Congress.

One of the most notorious tragedies in the history of New York City was a fire at the Triangle Shirtwaist Factory on March 25, 1911. A historical account from the U.S. Library of Congress, summarized the incident as,

> "At approximately 4:40 p.m. on [Saturday] March 25, 1911, a savage fire breaks out at the Triangle Shirtwaist Factory in New York City. With doors to stairwells and exits locked, 146 garment workers perish, mostly young immigrant women, some of which leap from windows to their deaths. Though factory owners are acquitted of any responsibility, the tragedy leads to pivotal labor law reforms in New York."

Some may take note the fire occurred late on a *Saturday* afternoon. At the time, working hours were not regulated. Most employment, including unmarried women, was a six-day workweek of 10-12 hours each day. (A 5-day 48-hour workweek was not had until 1929.) For almost all unmarried working-class women, employment outside the home usually ended upon marriage.[310]

---

[310] Jane Addams. *Hull House Maps and Papers* (1895), cited in "Italians – The Great Arrival – Immigration," *U.S. Library of Congress*, Accessed December 5, 2020. See also: "Triangle Shirtwaist Factory Fire." Topics in Chronicling America, *U.S. Library of Congress*, 2020.

Upper Left: Front page *Il Progresso* newspaper of March 25, 1911 of the Triangle Shirtwaist Company fire, with a list of Italian American victims. Library of Congress Newspaper and Periodicals Reproduction No: LC-DIG-ppmsca-02924. **Lower Right**: *Il Progresso* line drawing as first published in *The New York Evening Journal* the day after the fire. "This is one of a Hundred Murdered, Is Anyone to be Punished for this? Placard sign satirical reads "Operators Wanted." Library of Congress, 1911.

The Triangle Shirtwaist Company employed over 500 people, all tightly jammed within the top three floors of a ten-story building at 23-29 Washington Place in Greenwich Village. Owned by Isaac Harris and Max Blanck, the factory was one of dozens the garment industry manufacturing clothing employing a large percentage of women. Garment factories, such as the Triangle Shirtwaist Company, were known as "sweatshops" due to the stifling overheated conditions and minimal, if any, air circulation. The term remained for decades.[311]

In 1911, factory conditions were not one that workers could complain, especially among unskilled with an abundance of competition. Social reformer Jane Addams made note of the impoverished situation as early as 1895 in *Hull House Maps and Papers*. She discovered,

---

[311] I can attest to the hot sweaty conditions created by machinery and steam pressing irons. My parents, children of Italian immigrants, owned and operated a garment factory in Brooklyn, New York from 1947 to 1985. As a child through my college years, I worked in the family business sorting and sewing large amounts of fabric. Dust was a constant time-consuming activity in keeping any potential hazards under control. Thankfully, we never suffered a tragic incident.

> "No trades are so overcrowded as the sewing-trades; for the [sewing] needle has ever been the refuge of the unskilled woman. The wages paid throughout the manufacture of clothing are less than those in any other trade. . . [We] have carefully investigated many cases, and are ready to assert that the Italian widow who finishes the cheapest goods, although she sews from six in the morning until eleven at night, can only get enough to keep her children clothed and fed; while for her rent and fuel she must always depend upon charity or the hospitality of her countrymen."

Clothing of all kinds hand-made from the "sewing-trades," were in high demand. One of the most popular garments was the women's shirtwaist.

One company, Harris and Blanck produced a specific type of garment known as a women's shirtwaist; a blouse loosely tailored after a man's shirt with a collar, buttons, and a seam at the waist. As described in the *Encyclopedia of Fashion*, the shirtwaist "took the place of the stiff tight, high-collared bodices of the nineteenth century." Josh Jones writing of the history of the shirtwaist said,

> "The garment proved so popular among hundreds of thousands of working women that its production became a hugely competitive industry. The push for sales drove the extreme "efficiency" measures responsible for the fire in the Triangle Shirtwaist Factory."[312]

The popularity was the result of new widespread advertising campaigns selling consumer products. By the early 1900s, newspapers and magazines were essential in carrying advertising to millions of readers. In 1900, America counted 1,600 daily newspapers; with an increase to 2,600 by the end of the decade. Daily circulation nationwide was over 24 million.

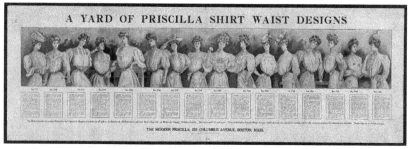

Advertisement for *The Modern Priscilla,* a needlework magazine, showing 16 different designs for shirtwaists. (Artist: Ethelyn J. Morris for the Priscilla Publishing Co. of Boston, c. 1906. Library of Congress.

---

[312] "Triangle Shirtwaist Factory Fire." Topics in Chronicling America, *U.S. Library of Congress*, 2020. Josh Jones. "Shirtwaist Fashion,"*Flashbak.com*, September 5, 2018.

CHAPTER 6

Above Left: *The New York Herald* gruesome photographs of dead bodies being tagged for identification and a photograph of the burning building. **Upper Right**: *The Boston Sunday Globe* descriptive headline: "Blazing Bodies Whirl to Street."

The Triangle Shirt Waist factory fire started on the eight-floor. Caused, most likely from a discarded lit item tossed into one of the many bins of cloth remnants strewn about the floors. The final tally of 146 victims was 129 women and 17 men died in an inferno lasting 18 minutes. Almost all who died were young girls aged 13 to 16 divided between Italians and Jewish immigrants, one was a Polish immigrant. The New York City Fire Department responded quickly. A tragic occurrence was compounded by the safety and rescue equipment ladders only capable of reaching a height of six stories. An external fire escape collapsed due to an overload of evacuees. Internal exit doors were locked preventing escape, leaving many to jump from the windows.

Typical of the day - a horse-drawn fire engine on the way to the burning factory fire. George Grantham Bain Collection Library of Congress.

A New York City Police Office and onlookers watch helplessly as young girls leapt to their death while the fire raged at the Triangle Shirtwaist Factory. At the feet of the officer are a few of the dead bodies who jumped. Photo c. 1911. Library of Congress (Public Domain).

Rescue personnel, Police Officers and onlookers watched helplessly. As the fire engulfed the building young girls leapt to their death. The dead were soon scattered along the concrete sidewalks as officers could only tag and identify the victims. Not all were identifiable, Amy Tikkanen, writing on the history of the fire said, "It took several days for family members to identify the victims, many of whom were burned beyond recognition. Six of the victims (five woman and one man) were not identified until 2011. On the 100th anniversary, Joseph Berger writing for *The New York Times* called the fire "a wrenching event in New York's history." Berger listed the names of the unidentified six victims.[313]

---

[313] Amy Tikkanen, "Triangle shirtwaist factory fire." *Encyclopedia Britannica*. See also: Joseph Berger. "A Century Later," *New York Times* February 21, 2011, p. A13.

Triangle Shirtwaist Factory building is still ablaze on March 25, 1911. Image was published on the front page of *The New York World*.

The publicity generated by the Triangle Shirtwaist fire brought other unsafe conditions into the focus of public attention. One concern was children in the workforce. In a 2016 retrospective exhibition, *Soulmaker: The Times of Lewis Hine* at Stanford University, the curators explained,

> In 1908, Lewis Hine felt so strongly about the devastating effects of child labor that he quit working as a New York school teacher to become an investigative photographer for the National Child Labor Committee. Hine spent the next 10 years traveling New England, the South and the Mid-West, photographing children at work in mills, coal mines and factories. proof to the public that child labor was thriving, helped change American labor laws."

In one 1909 instance, Hine traveled to Macon, Georgia observing "some boys were so small they had to climb up on the spinning frame to mend the broken threads and put back the empty bobbins."

Other reformers as Mary Harris Jones ("Mother Jones"), led a continuing crusade to alleviate abuse of children in the work force. In 1912, after years of diligent persistence, the U.S. Congress authorized a Children's Bureau for mandatory public education and minimum working age. The social progressive law resulted in a steep decline in the number of working children. The decrease went from a previous total of about 20 percent of the nationwide work force to less than 5 percent by 1920.

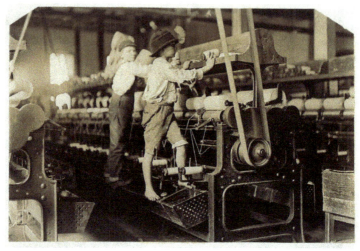

Young boys in a factory in Macon, Georgia dangling in a precarious dangerous position upon active machinery. Photograph by; Lewis Hines, c. January 19, 1909. Library of Congress, www.loc.gov/item/2018674998/.

A requirement for children regulated to schoolrooms provided a "captured audience" to assimilate and "Americanize." Ironically, the overt message focused on the value of morals and work while promoting a disdain for any idleness. The intent was outlined in a report issued by the *National Education Association* citing, "The unworthy use of leisure impairs health, disrupts home life, lessens vocational efficiency and destroys civic-mindedness." As a positive, many cities mandated open-air playgrounds for all new school construction. In rural areas some situations for mandatory education and recreation areas existed. The implementation of those mandates were often hash in the Americanization process.[314]

---

[314] Richard Krauss. *Recreation and Leisure in Modern Society*, p. 200.

CHAPTER 6

Italians Working Across America

A common perception exists of Italian immigrants all living in larger urban cities such as New York. Many images by photographers such as Lewis Wickes Hine (1874-1940) and Jacob Riis (1849-1914) documented the Italian immigrant urban experience, mostly in New York, adding to the perceived image. In comparison, the U.S. Library of Congress, states many Italians were "Working Across the Country," in non-urban areas,

> "In Appalachia and the mountain West, they went into the pits and mines, digging for coal and ore. Stonemasons who had learned their trade on the rocks and crags of southern Italy worked in the quarries of New England and Indiana. Meanwhile, Italians labored on farms and ranches in every corner of the country, from the cranberry bogs of the northeast to the strawberry beds of Louisiana to the bean fields of California."[315]

For both Riis and Hine, a series of well-documented photographs clearly illustrated the plight of Italian immigrants. Hine often ventured into rural areas. Dozens of photographs held in the National Child Labor Committee collection at the U.S. Library of Congress documented Italian migrant of "berry pickers" working on farms scattered throughout New Jersey and Delaware. During one venture, Hine and an investigative reporter Edward F. Brown, photographed the Arnao family from Philadelphia of husband, wife, and five children aged 3 to 13, all who worked hand-picking berries.

At the time of the photograph in September of 1910, the Arnao's were pictured Truitt's farm in Delaware to pick berries on nearby farms in central New Jersey. After the family completed its allotment of picking strawberries, they moved to "Carmel, N.J. From New Jersey, the family "followed the work" traveling south to Hitchen's Farm in Seaford, Delaware, where they were housed in a former chicken coop sharing space with another family; of 17 children (aged 3 to 13) and 5 elders occupied the same living space. Other Italian migrant families moved farther west.

---

[315] "Working Across the Country." *The Library of Congress.*

Top Left: A migrant Italian family (named Arnao) in New Jersey, c. 1910. **Above Right**: Interior of the living conditions endured by Italian immigrant families. This image of "Shanty # 2" in New Jersey housed the family of Rocco De Gruerio in a single room 6 ft. x 7 ft. wide and 7 ft. high. **Bottom Left**: A former chicken coop was the living quarters for the seven members of the Arnao family on Hitchen's Farm in Seaford, Delaware. A total of 17 children (aged 3 to 13) and 5 elders occupied the same space. (Photographs by Lewis Wickes Hine, September 1910. National Child Labor Committee collection, Library of Congress, Prints and Photographs Division.)

Mining in Washington State

As wine production in the agricultural fields increased in Washington State; the production was heavily dependent upon Italian immigrant labor so was the need for underground in mining. One prominent area was Black Diamond a small city in King County with a population in the year 2010 numbering less than 5,000. According to historian, Rita Cipalla,

> "When coal was king in Black Diamond, a small mining town in the Cascade foothills of southeastern King County, immigrants from Italy provided much of the muscle power that operated the coal mines. The work was hard and dangerous and those who could went on to other enterprises. The last mine near Black Diamond closed in 1974, but many descendants of the Italian coal miners still live in the community."

CHAPTER 6

As with all mining operations across America tragic accidents seemed inevitable. One explosion in April of 1907 resulted in the death of seven men. A newspaper report in *The Seattle Times* listed the names of the deceased including "three Italian miners: 23-year-old Joe Belmonti and 25-year-old Albert Domini, both unmarried, and Philip Domenico, married with one child." As many other unsafe mining and factory conditions across the nation, tragic accidents often led to attempts at forming unions calling for safer working conditions and equitable wages. The fledging United Mine Workers of America formed in 1890 organized a local chapter at Black Diamond, but denied facilities for meetings.[316]

The Colorado Ludlow Massacre

During the early 20th century labor actions and worker strikes, many led by Italian immigrants, occurred all over the nation; usually involving safety in mining operations or factories. Historian Jonathan H. Rees, cites one of the most notorious included a 1912 textile strike in Lawrence, Massachusetts organized by three Italians of the Industrial Workers of the World ("IWW" or by the nickname "Wobblies"). The IWW arose as a separate organized workers union due to discrimination by many of the nation's other labor unions who did not allow immigrant membership. The U.S. Library of Congress explained, the Italian immigrant experience as,

> "Italian immigrants fought against many unscrupulous management and unsafe conditions by taking organized action. Because several of the major U.S. unions barred foreign workers from membership for many years, immigrants formed their own unions, such as the Italian Workers union in Houston, or joined the International Workers of the World. Italian union organizers fanned out across the nation, often risking arrest or death for their efforts. Italian workers were active in most of the great labor struggles of the 20th century's early decades."[317]

Response to strikes by workers were usually met with harsh and violent retribution by corporate owners supported by the U.S. Government, state National Guard units, and local police. At Lawrence, as one example, "organizers Arturo Giovannitti and Joseph Ettor, along with striker Joseph Caruso, were imprisoned on false murder charges."[318]

In a series of events during 1910, accidental explosions in Colorado mines resulted in the deaths of large numbers of miners – including young boys. Early in the year an explosion in Primero Colorado caused injury and death to "77 men and adolescent boys." In October, an explosion in a Starkville mine killed at least

---

[316] Rita Cipalla. "Italian Immigrant Coal Miners in Black Diamond," April 14, 2018.
[317] "The Great Arrival," *The Library of Congress*.
[318] Stefano Luconi. "Tampa's 1910 Lynching," pp. 30–53.

56. The following month, another 79 workers died at the Delagua mine. The accumulated tragedies prompted one of the most violent and notorious retributions in Ludlow, Colorado located 186 miles due south of Denver.

Known as "The Ludlow Massacre of 1914," Colorado National Guardsmen attempted to end the miners' strike employing military action. Striking workers claimed the owners of the mining operation were not following the basic safety standards put into effect by legislation enacted by the State of Colorado. As described by Jonathan H. Rees writing of the history of the "Ludlow Massacre," for the *Colorado Encyclopedia,*

> "The Ludlow Massacre began on the morning of April 20, 1914, as a battle broke out between the Colorado National Guard and striking coal miners at their tent colony in Las Animas County. Nobody knows who fired the first shot, but the incident is remembered as a massacre because the miners and their families bore the brunt of the casualties. At least nineteen people died, including one guardsman, five miners, and thirteen women and children who suffocated as they hid from the gunfire in a pit. No matter how the casualties are counted, the Ludlow Massacre is one of the bloodiest events in American labor history."

The strike itself began during the early fall of 1913, lasting almost eight months through an unusually cold winter. The strike ended in a massacre during the spring of 1914 - including the death of two women and at least eleven children - all Italian immigrants.[319]

In ending the strike, Colorado National Guard employed military action including armored vehicles and machine guns. A tent city of about 1,200 migrants, and some buildings were all torched causing complete and utter destruction. Reports in the aftermath said the former migrant tent colony resembled a war zone. On April 21, 1914, Professor Andrew Gulliford provided a well-researched account as,

> "The Ludlow camp is a mass of charred debris, and buried beneath it is a story of horror unparalleled in the history of industrial warfare. In the holes which had been dug for their protection against the rifles' fire the women and children died like trapped rats when the flames swept over them. One pit, uncovered [the day after the massacre] disclosed the bodies of 10 children and two women."[320]

A few other publications reported on the harried plight of the immigrant and working classes in America. In an ironic twist of truth, journalist Ben Mauk

---

[319] Jonathan H. Rees. "Ludlow Massacre," *Colorado Encyclopedia,* July 6, 2021. See also: Ben Mauk. "Ludlow Massacre Still Matters." *The New Yorker,* April 18 far, 2014.
[320] Quoted in: "The Ludlow Massacre," *American Experience,* PBS.org. See also: Andrew Gulliford. "Blood and Struggle in Ludlow." *The Journal,* April 18, 2014.

writing a "look back" 2014 article "Ludlow Massacre Still Matters" for *The New Yorker* magazine. revealed the prevailing thought of the social status of Italian immigrants. The article with accompanying images and illustrated summarized,

> "At the turn of the 20th century, Colorado offered better protection for the donkeys and mules that worked in mines than for the miners themselves. Mules and donkeys were mandated by law to spend a month each year out of the mines so they would not go blind. Miners, however, had few safety provisions, could not easily join unions and saw their wages steadily decreased."

Migrant family, presumably Italian, outside a "tent home" in Ludlow, Colorado - site of a coal strike and massacre, c. January 1914. Courtesy of The Denver Library. (Public Domain - Wiki Commons).

One monthly magazine, *The Masses* sympathetic "to the interests of the working people" published the story accompanied by a full color front cover illustration. The 1914 image portrays a striking worker fighting against an onslaught of the Colorado National Guard. The solitary figure holds a dead child (presumably his own) while standing over a dead woman (presumably his wife). Leaving no interpretation to misconception, a summary by the U.S. Library of Congress clarified, the "Cover illustration shows a mine worker firing a gun after his wife and children were killed in a massacre at their tent camp by the Colorado National Guard and Colorado Fuel & Iron Company camp guards." A remembrance to "not forget" memorial was erected by the United Mine Workers of America at the Ludlow Massacre site. The marble statue depicts a mine worker alongside his wife holding and protecting a young child.[321]

Ruins of the Ludlow Colony in Colorado after the attack by the Colorado National Guard in April of 1914. From the George Grantham Bain Collection at the Library of Congress Prints and Photographs Division. (Public Domain)

---

[321] Ben Mauk. "Ludlow Massacre Still Matters." *The New Yorker*, April 18, 2014.

Above Left: Magazine cover of *The Masses*, titled "Massacre during Colorado Coal Strike at Ludlow, Colorado," c. 1914 by John Sloan (1871-1951). Library of Congress Prints and Photographs (Public Domain). **Above Right**: A Marble Statue erected by the United Mine Workers of America in 1918 to commemorate the site of the Ludlow Massacre portraying a mine worker alongside a wife protecting a young child. Photograph taken on April 28, 2005 by Mark Walker Creative Common License 2, CC BY 2.0

Margaret Sanger and "What Every Girl Should Know"

In the United States, one newspaper *The New York Call*, often lobbied for social reform. Articles revealed the multitude of immigrants in urban poverty; or the ignored "other half" as Jacob Riis wrote. A compounded problem was high birth rates. Social reformers such as Margaret Sanger (1879-1966) equated poverty to the large number of children borne into immigrant families. In contrast for voluntary restraint, Sanger offered a practical solution to provide information in various means of birth control - an immediately contentious issue among puritanical American society leading to forced closing of Sanger's clinics, and arrests on obscenity.[322]

In late 1912, Sanger wrote a twelve-part series of informational articles, "What Every Girl Should Know" published in *The New York Call* from November to March of 1913. Each explained sensitive topics such as various

---

[322] In Jean H. Baker *Margaret Sanger: A Life of Passion*, p. 47.

types of sexual conduct, means of reproduction, and sexually transmitted infections, among other socially taboo topics. In 1916, Max Maisel, a publisher and owner of a bookstore in New York City collected all of Sanger's articles in one publication titled, "What Every Girl Should Know." Sanger continued publishing pamphlets and books on immigrant health concerns; many directly in response to growing number of Italian immigrants in New York.[323]

In 1920, Margaret Sanger's publication *Woman and the New Race* promoted contraception as opposed to the Malthus suggestion of voluntary restraint. The preface to the publication was written by English physician Havelock Ellis (1859-1939); who "studied human sexual behavior and challenged Victorian taboos against public discussion of the subject." Ellis' *Studies in the Psychology of Sex* was a seven-volume set published from 1897 to 1928. *Encyclopedia Britannica* rates Ellis' publication as,

> "A comprehensive Encyclopedia of human sexual biology, behavior, and attitudes. In separate volumes he examined such topics as homosexuality, masturbation, and the physiology of sexual behavior. Ellis viewed sexual activity as the healthy and natural expression of love, and he sought to dissipate the fear and ignorance that characterized many people's attitudes toward human sexuality."

At the time, the mere thought of discussing human sexuality was not only taboo, but considered obscene; subject to criminal prosecution. Other volumes of Ellis work were published in the United States; yet up until 1935, the books were only legally available for purchase to the members of the medical profession.

Above Left: Havelock Ellis.
Above Right: *Studies in the Psychology of Sex Vol. 1*, c. 1900.

---

[323] Lakshmeeramya Malladi, "What Every Girl Should Know," December 12, 2017.

Margaret Sanger, seated behind desk, surrounded with other staff members and supporters. Photograph c. 1920. Library of Congress Prints and Photograph Reproduction No. LC-USZ62-105460.

Despite criticism to the contrary, both Havelock Ellis and Margaret Sanger understood the value of motherhood. The consistent claim was for a woman maintaining sole control of her own reproduction. In support, Ellis wrote for the opening preface of Sanger's *Woman and the New Race*,

> "Woman, by virtue of motherhood is the regulator of the birthrate, the sacred disposer of human production. It is in the deliberate restraint and measurement of human production that the fundamental problems of the family, the nation, the whole brotherhood of mankind find their solution. The health and longevity of the individual, the economic welfare of the workers, the general level of culture of the community, the possibility of abolishing from the world the desolating scourge of war—all these like great human needs, depend, primarily and fundamentally, on the wise limitation of the human output."

In contrast to Margaret Sanger and Havelock Ellis, among a few scant others, the view prevalent in America continually portrayed women as the "weaker sex" requiring regulatory oversight and coddling. As society, especially for immigrants, promoted a long six-day work week of a 12 to16-hour workday

242 Italian Culture in America:
The Immigrants 1880 to 1930 From Discrimination to Assimilation

(sometimes a half day on Sunday); health and safety concerns of the worker were mostly non-existent. Two landmark legal cases before the First World War affecting the legal length of a working day stand out for different reasons – gender. In one case it was *illegal* to regulate the *hours of labor* of males – in contrast – in another case it was *legal* to regulate the *hours of labor* for females.

Lochner v. Muller - **Contradicting Female Restraints**

Both Supreme Court cases of *Lochner v. New York* (1905) and *Muller v. Oregon* (1908) cited the same Section 1 of the 14th Amendment to the U.S. Constitution, commonly known as the "Due Process Clause." In sum, the 14th Amendment states,

> "All persons born or naturalized in the United States and subject to the jurisdiction thereof, are citizens of the United States and of the State wherein they reside. No State shall make or enforce any law which shall abridge the privileges or immunities of citizens of the United States; nor shall any State deprive any person of life, liberty, or property, without due process of law; nor deny to any person within its jurisdiction the equal protection of the laws."

The earlier U.S. Supreme Court Decisions of *Lochner v. New York* dealt with an attempt by the State of New York to limit the workday for male bakers a 5-4 decision invalidated the New York law; ruling on the basis of "difference between the sexes." In writing the majority opinion, Justice Rufus Peckham (1838-1909), cited the 14th Amendment prohibited any state from depriving "any person of life, liberty, or property, without due process of law." Justice Peckham wrote,

> "The general right to make a contract in relation to his business is part of the liberty protected by the Fourteenth Amendment, and this includes the right to purchase and sell labor, except as controlled by the State in the legitimate exercise of its police power. There is no reasonable ground, on the score of health, for interfering with the liberty of the person or the right of free contract, by determining the hours of labor, in the occupation of a baker. Nor can a law limiting such hours be justified as a health law to safeguard the public health, or the health of the individuals."[324]

Justices ruled the New York law unconstitutional. Outrage came from Progressives and Social Reformers over the disregard for regulation of working conditions. In retort to the decision, Margaret Sanger wrote,

> "Our industries have taken advantage of their [immigrants] ignorance of the country's ways to take their toil in mills and mines and factories at

---

[324] (Quoted in part from: U.S. Supreme Court Decision *Lochner v. New York*, 198 U.S. 45 (1905). See also: Margaret Sanger's *Woman and the New Race*, pp.10-11.

CHAPTER 6   243

starvation wages. We have herded them into slums to become diseased, to become social burdens or to die. We have huddled them together like rabbits to multiply their numbers and their misery. Instead of saying that we Americanize them, we should confess that we animalize them.[325]

In another hourly wage case arising in February 1903, the State of Oregon enacted a gender specific law limiting a woman's maximum workday in factories and laundries to no more than 10 hours in any 24-hour period. The legislation argued the state of Oregon had "a compelling interest in protecting the health of women." The stated protection of "health" was to protect the defined "weaker" gender in preservation of motherhood. The first section of the Oregon Legislation read, "That no female [shall] be employed in any mechanical establishment, or factory, or laundry in this State more than ten hours during any one day."

The U.S. Supreme Court in *Muller v. Oregon.* ruled the Oregon law was in legal according with the same 14th Amendment of the U.S. Constitution. Justice David J. Brewer, writing the unanimous 9-0 opinion. A summation by the official history of the U.S. Supreme court stated, "Its reasoning was based on somewhat anachronistic and paternalistic notions that the child-bearing role and physical frailty of women allowed the state to take measures to protect them." The Court further stated,

> "This Court takes judicial cognizance of all matters of general knowledge such as the fact that woman's physical structure and the performance of maternal functions place her at a disadvantage [and] justifies difference in legislation in regard to some of the burdens which rest upon her. As healthy mothers are essential to vigorous offspring, the physical wellbeing of woman is an object of public interest and the right to preserve the health of the women."[326]

In essence, the Supreme Court decision allowing freedom from "industry work" provided more time for females engaging in household work such as cooking, cleaning, and childbirth. In *The Story of American Freedom* historian Eric Foner said the decision "solidified the idea that women workers were weak, dependent, and incapable of enjoying the same economic freedom as men."[327]

In immediate opposition to the legal restrictions placed upon women, Margaret Sanger led a call for a radical change, writing,

> "We must set motherhood free. Motherhood, when free to choose the father, free to choose the time and the number of children who shall result

---

[325] Margaret Sanger's *Woman and the New Race*, pp.10-11.
[326] U.S. Supreme Court, *Muller v. Oregon*, 208 U.S. 412 (1908), No. 107. Argued January 15, 1908. Decided February 24, 1908. 208 U.S. 412.
[327] Foner, Eric. *The Story of American Freedom.* New York: Norton, 1998, p. 123.

from the union, automatically works in wondrous ways. . . it brings few children into homes where there is not sufficient to provide for them."

Sanger said preserving "potential motherhood" was a clandestine reason for providing a larger number of children available for the workforce. In *Women and the New Race*, she wrote, "Immigrants or their children constitute the majority of workers employed in many of our industries." Quoting *National Geographic Magazine* statistics, Sanger cited,

> "Seven out of ten of those who work in iron and steel industries are drawn from this class, seven out of ten of our bituminous coal miners belong to it. Three out of four who work in packing towns were born abroad or are children of those who were born abroad; four out of five of those who make our silk goods, seven out of eight of those employed in woolen mills, nine out of ten of those who refine our petroleum, nineteen of twenty of those who manufacture our sugar are immigrants or the children of immigrants."[328]

Sanger was aware children and immigrants working in the "clothing industries, railway and public works construction." All employed for low wages, long hours - while regulated to living in impoverished conditions. Overpopulation among poor immigrants led to living conditions of malnutrition and susceptible to disease. Poverty created other issues as the large number of school children "undernourished" with about 20 percent classified as "in immediate danger." Birth control was a taboo subject among puritanical American society; remaining into the 21st century.

Somewhat accepted was the "unmentionable" subject of men engaging with prostitutes; or for a married Italian man having a *gumma* ("mistress"). An obvious consequence of was contracting venereal disease; a condition easily spread among married couples. Information offered by Sanger included pamphlets such as "*The Venereal Diseases*" and other practical information on topics such as birth control. Within the absurdity of the time, any discussion of venereal disease or sexual fornication was condemned by religious denominations. Another was not to discuss or acknowledge any sexual activities of men and especially not to sully the reputation of any "fine young woman."

---

[328] Margaret Sanger. *Woman and the New Race*, pp.13-14.

The Sanger Clinic located at 46 Amboy Street Brooklyn, New York.
Library of Congress Prints and Photographs Division.

A common criticism from Sanger's day also continued well into the 21st century was connecting Birth Control with Abortion. In reality, as Sanger advertised – Birth Control is NOT Abortion. In October 1916, she organized with others to open the first Birth Control clinic in America, located in a Brooklyn neighborhood populated exclusively of poor Jewish and Italian immigrants. One poster for a Brooklyn clinic advertised in three languages of English, Yiddish, and Italian, delineates the fact as,

MOTHERS!
Can you afford to have a large family?
Do you want any more children?
If not, why do you have them?
DO NOT KILL, DO NOT TAKE LIFE, BUT PREVENT
Safe, Harmless Information can be obtained of trained Nurses.

Yet, establishing Planned Parenthood for disseminating information on birth control and contraception was considered a crime. Ten days after the clinic opened, New York City Police raided the premises and arrested Sanger. She refused a plea deal and served a 20-day sentence. In later years, Margaret Sanger was dismissed as an important social reformer. Sanger claimed it was ignorance of reproduction as the main cause of disease and overpopulation. A solution proposed by Sanger was disseminating information and products, citing,

"We must, therefore, not permit an increase in population that we are not prepared to care for to the best advantage—that we are not prepared to do justice to, educationally and economically. We must popularize birth control thinking."

Sanger exposed another unmentionable subject which was women of the wealthy social class were "privileged" to have access to medical care which in fact provided access to birth control methods and safe abortions. Despite it all, an ironic contrast to the U.S. Supreme Court as citing a "woman's physical structure and the performance of maternal functions place her at a disadvantage" was disavowed by a simple bicycle.

The "Weaker Sex." Bicycle Design, and Italian Leisure

American born children of Italian immigrants were more likely to be lured by advertising of fashion and bicycles as a means of assimilation. Prior to the 1890s, were unsafe; almost exclusively ridden by men. In 1885, British inventor John Kemp Stanley (1854-1901) developed the "safety bicycle" with a pair of foot pedals turning a sprocket connected by a chain to a rear sprocket, turning a wheel equal in size. Handlebars, foot brake, and hollow metal tube frame remained consistent into the 21st century.

A hinderance for bicycles were cultural misconceptions of females. Historian Ellen Gruber Garvey cited contemporary medical research claimed bicycle riding "would be dangerous for women to expend so much of their strength on physical activity." According to research by Karen Calvert, an accepted prevailing societal thought of the time, claimed "one of the cardinal rules of child-rearing in the 19th century forbade girls to sit straddling any object." Despite the fact bicycles were safe to ride, straddling of the upper cross bar and seat was considered taboo for females, especially the decorum required of Italian daughters and wives. To increase bicycle sales, advertising made a distinction between female and male bicycles. Promotion of specific gender designs such as the Victor and Victoria sold by the Overman Wheel Company; or ads claiming a bicycle ride "would end in married happiness." Others.

One difference, the "Victoria" model eliminated the upper cross bar so a female did not have to raise her leg over the cross bar. Eliminating the triangular shape of the upper cross bar weakened the overall structure. To compensate, heavier and thicker metal tubing was used to strengthen the frame. Ironically, the change added weight to the female bicycle, often as much as 10 pounds. Therefore, the so-called "weaker sex" pedaled harder to keep up with their male partners; a metaphor for generations. One ad noted, "A most desirable feature is the Victoria Tilting saddle, which simplifies mounting improprieties." By 1900, yearly production was over one million bicycles; appealing to many of the social classes. Italian immigrants did not overly engage bicycles for leisure, rather mainly as a means of practical transportation.[329]

Top Left: Illustration of the Overman Wheel Company factory and founder, A. H. Overman from *The New York World* of December 29, 1897, p. 9. **Bottom Left**: The male Victor "Flyer" bicycle of 1893. Illustration from *The Farmer's Vindicator,* 29 July 1893, p. 3. **Top Right**: Advertisement for the female "Victoria" bicycle from the same time period. (Wiki Commons Public Domain).

---

[329] Ellen Gruber Garvey. *The Adman in the Parlor* pp. 107-109, 114.

CHAPTER 7

BIRTH OF AMERICAN VAUDEVILLE AND SHOW BUSINESS

---

*"Farfariello's caricatures reveal the real problems and the
emotional issues of the immigrants of the first generation. We
see these poor people confronting the new circumstances of
their lives; often unable to understand what was going on
around them."*

Relaxation, Coney Island, and Jimmy Durante

A common relaxation time for Italians often occurred, sometimes on a hot summer day or in the early evening engaging in stoop gossip with neighbors; while children played sidewalk or street games. Neighborhood activity was sometimes filled with street amusements provided by organ grinders or by vendors peddling their wares in push carts. In New York City, as others, church function celebrations of saint's days such as *San Gennaro* along the Italian section of Mulberry Street, provided for weeklong festivities and socialization. The feast, a celebration of the patron saint of Naples St. Januarius (d. 305 AD) – in Italian "San Gennaro," was a carryover from a Neapolitan tradition of southern Italy. The *San Gennaro* festival, which began as a strictly Italian affair, attracted all ethnic and social classes from throughout the five boroughs of New York City and eventually beyond; continuing as a popular yearly festival into the 21st century. Throughout the nation, similar festivals in other cities with their own "Little Italy" was a yearly time for celebration of Italian tradition and culture.

In places as New York City, a vast mass transportation system of an underground subway (with tunnels dug by thousands of Italian immigrants) and above ground elevated rails connected neighborhoods with the famous beach and amusement parks at Coney Island. A one-day excursion to Coney Island was one of the very few affordable for the working class. The free access beaches allowed a brief time for relaxation from the sweltering summer heat; the only cost a nickel fare (5¢) for public transportation. By 1900, on any given summer weekend day or holiday estimates placed over 300,000 to 500,000 people attended. During one summer season in 1909, over 20 million visited the beaches.

The Coney Island Boardwalk with three amusement parks and dozens of entertainment venues were popular inexpensive attractions for the working-class. Moral critics and religious organizations, however, were dismayed by the vibrant rides and titillating attractions; viewed as promoting promiscuity and immoral behavior. Most critics never visited Coney Island, solely reacting to the attraction names such as *Barrel of Love*, *Wedding Ring*, and *Razzle Dazzle*. Each ride provided close contact and interaction among total strangers of different genders. Despite the critics, the public loved the inexpensive fun and could not get enough. A recollection by American stalwart entertainer Jimmy Durante recalled the diversity of the summertime crowd that attended Coney Island. He said,

> "They were young people – husky men and pretty girls in cheap finery; shipping clerks or truckmen or subway guards escorting their sweethearts [who] didn't have much to spend but [knew that at Coney Island one] could go a long way on a few dollars."[330]

Durante, was one of the earliest, if not first, to popularize "being distinctly Italian" in American popular culture.

Jimmy Durante (1893-1980) was born "James Francis Durante" on the Lower East Side of Manhattan to Italian immigrants from Salerno, Italy; a port city southeast of Naples. Father Bartolomeo was a barber, a trade dominated by Italians; mother Rosa (nee: Lentino) raised four children. With a career extending over 60 years, Durante became one of the most recognizable, prominent, likeable, and popular entertainers in America. Starting as a Ragtime pianist, Durante later appeared in vaudeville, Broadway revues, and radio variety shows. A facial feature of a distinctive large ruddy nose; was played up, led to the nickname "*The Great Schnozzola.*" A career included over 45 popular Hollywood films (comedy and musicals) in later years, a popular guest of major television shows with appearances beginning in 1930 to 1970 (he retired in 1972). His trademark performance closing was fondly remembered as he would say in a raspy New York accent, "Goodnight, Mrs. Calabash, wherever you are." (A mystery person whose identity was never revealed.)[331]

---

[330] Giordano, *Fun and Games*, p. 16.

[331] Peiss, p. 124; and Nasaw, p. 3. See also: "Jimmy Durante: Italian of the Week," *Sons of Italy Blog*, August 2015.

CHAPTER 7

Above Left: Promotional photograph of Jimmy Durante, c. 1964 (Public Domain).
Above Right: Jimmy Durante poses with the author (lower left) and author's brother Thomas Giordano at the Copacabana Nightclub in New York City, c. 1962.
(Giordano Family Archives).

Eduardo Migliaccio "King of Italian Vaudeville Entertainers"

Another "mystery" person of sorts is Eduardo Migliaccio. As an entry that might be viewed as best placed under the category of "Once Famous – Mostly Forgotten" in the next chapter, or even inclined for inclusion with the legendary legacy of Enrico Caruso; Eduardo Migliaccio rightfully belongs alongside the birth of American Vaudeville and Show Business. As noted in the 21st century by descendants,

> "In a career spanning 46 years, Eduardo Migliaccio left a body of work consisting of over 500 macchiette (comedic musical monologues), audio recordings, and several movie films. His characters were based on real people in the Italian American immigrant community."

Eduardo Migliaccio (1880-1946) was born in Cava de' Tirreni province of Salerno, Italy. Contrary to a large majority of Neapolitan's immigrating to America, Migliaccio's family was described as "well-to-do." Grandson Richard Migliaccio said, "The family home in Via Santi Quaranta rests in the hills overlooking the Gulf of Salerno." Eduardo's 1897 immigration was preceded by a grandfather who upon arrival in America invested in a Pennsylvania mine; and later "lost everything."[332]

---

[332] Eduardo Migliaccio 1880-1946. Farfariello.com "His Story."

An entertainment career began in small theaters in the Little Italy section of New York City. A half-century career, performing "live, on the radio, record albums, and in film" extended across the myriad of Vaudeville theaters throughout the United States; eventually to his native Italy. With a repertoire expanding to over 500 characters, "that mirrored the sociological and anthropological types of Italian immigrants," Migliaccio was billed simply as "Farfariello." As explained by grandson Richard the Italian term was translated as the "Little Butterfly."

Experimenting with the fledging recording industry, "Farfariello" recorded his on-stage performances. Between 1907 and 1935, 126 of his songs were recorded with the Victor Talking Machine Company. One 1924 recording for the Victor label (77478-A) was titled *L'Immigrazione* (The Immigration); described as a "comic song with orchestra; Italian (Neapolitan Dialect)." In 1932, Farfariello's performance was released as a film "Movie Actor." During his lifetime Eduardo Migliaccio, as the stage character "Farfariello," was billed and known as the "King of Italian Vaudeville Entertainers." A website launched in January of 2023, as "an evolving work in progress," has a treasure trove of archival information and photographs. Additional archival information from 1909 to 1958 were donated by the Migliaccio Family to the Immigration History Research Center Archives at the University of Minnesota.

Between 1907 and 1935 Eduardo Migliaccio recorded 126 songs from his stage performances. Pictured above are six on the Victor Record label. Discography of American Historical Recordings. (Courtesy of The Migliaccio Family)[333]

Italian American theater began as a trickle in the late 19th century rising into prominence by the early 20th century. Performances by both male and female live stage performers presenting drama, comedy, explained,

---

[333] See: Discography of American Historical Recordings.

CHAPTER 7

"Italian American Theater came to life in New York City shortly after waves of immigrants poured into the U.S. in the 1870s. This mass migration brought both the performers and audiences necessary for theatrical entertainment. Looking for recognition, support and a social setting outside the home, the men and women from Italy formed amateur theatrical clubs as a way of retaining what was familiar to them from their homelands. By 1900, the community had planted the seeds for the Italian American Theater of the years to come."

Conflicting factors among culturally proud Italians was an historical fact. As most of the world's civilizations, including a youthful American nation with barely a 200-year history, the Italian cultural heritage reached back centuries as a "great civilization." The major influences being Ancient Rome and the Renaissance - a complete opposite exited in America.[334]

The New York Press

Farfariello is the King of Italian Vaudeville in New York.

If Farfariello is "up to the minute" in his sketches from New York life there is something about the technique of his art that suggests centuries of tradition as its basis. It is mediaeval in its realistic satire and its essentially robust comedy. Rather than to characterize it as realistic, however, one should say that it is caricature based on a close observation of the actual.

A contemporary newspaper account acknowledging "Farfariello as the "King of Italian Vaudeville in New York."

Recognizable was Migliaccio's creation of the *Macchietta Coloniale* characters. The sketches combined "verse, prose, and song satirizing the immigrant experience of Italian-Americans in the United States." Therefore, one of the endearing, and possibly the most important factors, of Migliaccio's affection held by the audiences of Italian immigrants was described in a July 1962 article held in the Brooklyn College archives,

"Farfariello's caricatures reveal the real problems and the emotional issues of the immigrants of the first generation. We see these poor people confronting the new circumstances of their lives; often unable to understand what was going on around them and constantly penalized because they could not make sense of reality."[335]

---

[334] See: Emelise Aleandri, *The Italian-American Immigrant Theatre of New York City*, Arcadia Publishing, 1999. See also: Migliaccio, Eduardo. "His Story."
[335] "Caricatures and Characters from the World of the Transplanted." July 15, 1962.

Top: Eduardo Migliaccio starred in a 1932 film "Movie Actor." Pictured is title card and photo of Migliaccio from the movie (George Eastman Museum - https://www.eastman.org). **Middle**: Left - Poster advertising "Farfariello" at the Loew's 46th Street Theater in Brooklyn (Italian American Museum). Right - Farfariello character of an Italian immigrant recently drafted into the American Army (Immigration History Research Center Archives). **Bottom**: Four of hundreds of characters in costume and prosthetics portrayed by "Farfariello." From left is Mark Twain, Enrico Caruso, a Farmer, and immigrant. (Caruso and Farmer courtesy of Immigration History Research Center Archives, University of Minnesota Libraries. Bookend photos courtesy of Migliaccio Family Archives.)

One of Farfariello's endearing characters was of a friend and Neapolitan *paisan*. During one performance in support of the combined American and Italian cause of the First World War was Farfariello's character of an Italian immigrant recently drafted into the American Army. Another was of a recurring character of the world-famous opera singer – Enrico Caruso; who on one occasion was in

CHAPTER 7

prominent attendance in the audience. Of the event, biographer Esther Romeyn described,

> "In the front, Enrico Caruso was present as well. The stage was all adorned with Italian flags. Then Farfariello made his appearance. The thunderous and moving applause for a moment stopped him. Farfariello performed "The Italian at the Cooperative." Everyone's eyes filled up with tears when Caruso, who applauded feverously, could no longer restrain himself; abandoning his seat he dashed on the stage to press the artist, his admired son, to his heart."

The legendary opera singer Enrico Caruso and Eduardo "Farfariello" Migliaccio shared a common southern Neapolitan heritage as *paisans*, In a comparison between the two, historian Esther Romeyn observed, "Both performers, in different ways, appealed deeply to the sensibilities of this [Italian] immigrant community caught between two worlds, struggling to adjust to a new life and new cultural environment."[336]

Many of Migliaccio's characters contained a "clown." Inclusion of the Italian clown is traced to the *Commedia dell' Arte.* Another common trait is the Italian tradition of each region or town adopting its own patron saint, such as San Gennaro of Naples; each also had a similar "native Italian clown tradition." From this tradition Migliaccio adopted his forte as a *Pagliacci* (Italian for "clown). The "clown tradition" is also prevalent in Italian Opera; the most famous is *il Pagliacci* - famously portrayed by Enrico Caruso. A signature song was *Vesti la Giubba*, translated as "put on the costume" of a clown, was a shared entity of both entertainers; although perceived by lowbrow and highbrow audiences differently. Opera permeated among the poorer social classes. Eventually appropriated by the wealthier social classes into "highbrow." In contrast vaudeville remained "lowbrow," with roots drawn from the *Commedia dell' Arte.*[337]

The Italian *Commedia dell'arte*

The rise of American Vaudeville in the mid-19th century had its roots in the 16th century Italian *Commedia dell'arte* - literal translation is "Art Comedy." Adam Augustyn for *Encyclopædia Britannica* translated it as "comedy of the profession." As an Italian theatrical presentation, *Commedia dell'arte* was accepted throughout Europe well into the 18th century. Augustyn described this early form of Italian theater as,

> "The *commedia dell'arte* was a form of popular theatre that emphasized ensemble acting; its improvisations were set in a firm framework of

---

[336] Esther Romeyn, "Performing High, Performing Low," pp. 165-166.
[337] Caruso recorded the song on three occasions in 1902, 1904 and 1907.

masks and stock situations, and its plots were frequently borrowed from the classical literary drama. Professional players who specialized in one role developed an unmatched comic acting technique . . . of the itinerant commedia troupes throughout Europe. Despite contemporary depictions of scenarios and masks and descriptions of particular presentations, impressions today of what the commedia dell'arte was like are secondhand. The art is a lost one, its mood and style irrecoverable."[338]

Augustyn elaborated on the difficulty to connect the distinct Italian art form with "preclassical and classical mime and farce." Attempts at earlier connections before the 16th century remain "merely speculative."

The Italian *Commedia dell'arte* provided a variety of entertainment such as acrobats, comedy, drama, magicians, parody, musicians, and others. The Italian stage acts often relied on actors wit, spontaneity, and improvisation with "little scenery of costumes." Earliest performances date to 1545 by the Gelosi Company, as the most famous of all the *Commedia dell'arte* troupes. Formed in Milan in 1568, the Gelosi lasted over 35-years. One 1574 performance in Venice was for visiting King Henry III (r. 1574–89) of France led to a personal invitation. In 1577, King Henry asked the Gelosi Company to perform before his Royal Court at the city of Blois, France. The royal endorsement soon branched out to other local Italian performance companies, such as the Desiosi Company formed in 1595, each plying their trade throughout Europe.

"Actors from the *Commedia dell'Arte* on a Wagon in a Town Square," c. 1640. Painting by Jan Miel (1599-1663), of a group of Flemish painters in Rome knowns as "Bamboccianti" who often portrayed scenes of Italian peasant life.
(Public Domain – Wiki Commons).

---

[338] Adam Augustyn. "Commedia dell'arte: Italian theatre," *Encyclopædia Britannica*.

CHAPTER 7

American Vaudeville and "The Day Show Business was Born"

In America, from 1880 into the early 1900s, live performance on the vaudeville stage was the most popular form of entertainment. The standard vaudeville fare included a similar variety of stage acts. Included were comedy sketches, short plays, dancing, animal tricks, juggling, singing, music, burlesque, and minstrel numbers, among other performances. All cities across America, both big and small, had at least one Vaudeville theater offering at least two shows a day. Some were continuous through the day and into the evening. Audiences attended for one simple reason -- to be entertained. *The New York Times* on May 6, 1906, reported, "A chain of vaudeville houses from Boston to San Francisco [existed with] over a hundred first-class vaudeville houses where the higher-class acts are sure of continual and profitable booking, besides hundreds of smaller houses."

Although vaudeville performers included Black, Jewish, Italian, or Asians; segregated racial and stereotypical attitudes persisted -- none were immune from stereotype or slander. Some of the infamous performances came from white performers in "black face" presenting African Americans as backward feeble-minded buffoons. Another common stereotype was the Italian organ grinder "Mustache Pete" speaking in "broken English." Historian Norman Simms said of the performances, "Few serious attempts were made to discuss how the Italian culture made the source of a man's pride his family and his honor, not his job. Despite the strong prejudices of this era, the large number of Italian-American immigrants would continually face increasing prejudice in the years to come."[339]

By 1906, Vaudeville was closely monitored, not to eliminate prevalent discrimination or stereotyping. Instead, shows stayed within an acceptable moral code of societal behavior; intended to appeal to the widest audience. Wholesome Vaudeville performances, however, was championed years earlier before by a possible Italian named Tony Pastor, credited historically as the "Father / Dean of Vaudeville."

Vaudeville historian Donald Travis Stewart (b. 1965 known as Trav S.D.) claimed, "Two of the most important vaudeville impresarios Tony Pastor and Sylvester Poli, were Italian Americans." Antonio "Tony" Pastor (1833/37-1908) is cited an "American Impresario" as defined by *Merriam-Webster* as an English word borrowed "directly from Italian,"

> **impresario** • noun. 1: the promoter, manager, or conductor of an opera or concert company. 2: person who puts on or sponsors an entertainment (as a television show or sports event). 3: manager, director.

Pastor fits all the definition as an American Impresario. He did it all as a performer, producer, financier, and theater owner. Born in Manhattan, he is

---

[339] Norman Simms, p. 1.

possibly the first "Italian-American" contributing to popular American culture of entertainment – "possible" since his father might have been born in Italy; in contrast to unverified birth origins. Closer to historical significance, Vaudeville historian Trav S.D. cites Tony Pastor as the "Father of Vaudeville." Trav S.D. writes, "Within a few months, Pastor settled down to concentrate on his great contribution to American popular culture: straight, clean variety." Prior to Pastor, the theater variety stage shows were often bawdy affairs attracting mostly male audiences partaking in drinking and vulgarities.[340]

Pastor employed top names in entertainment; while toning down bawdier elements; advertising and delivering "The Great Family Resort of the City" without "the vulgarity." Audience numbers doubled attracting women and children enjoying clean wholesome family entertainment. The opening of "Tony Pastor's 14th Street Theater" from the 1880s and 1890s reigned as New York's most famous Vaudeville Theater.

Above Left: Illustration "Tony Pastor's Opera House," opened in 1865 at 201 Bowery. **Above Right**: Portrait titled "Vaudeville Showman Tony Pastor," c. 1880. (Wiki Commons – Public Domain).

Throughout Vaudeville history, many stage acts appeared courtesy of Tony Pastor. Many performers were Italian, or simply billed with Italian sounding names, or persona. One example was Leonard "Chico" Marx (1887-1961) of the legendary Marx Brothers, born on the Upper East Side of Manhattan of poor Jewish immigrants. Each of the four (originally five) brothers employed an alter

---

[340] David Monod. "Art with The Creation of Vaudeville," pp. 171-205.

ego on the Vaudeville stage; later Broadway and Hollywood. Chico, for his part took on the role of a stereotypical Italian speaking in broken English. Another was a mid-19th century Vaudeville act billed as "Prof. Bollini the Italian Magician." As Trav S.D. added, "Some were real. But the cache was so great, many artists would fake an Italian name."[341]

A disputed aspect of Pastor's Italian heritage is found in research by Victoria Moses for the American Vaudeville Museum at the University of Arizona. Moses claims the senior Pastor was born in Seville, Spain, adding the younger "Tony" was born in 1833, as opposed to a citation of 1837. Little else is known of Pastor's personal life. A first marriage to a woman named "Anna" ended as she died in 1866 from consumption."[342]

Vaudeville performer billed as "Prof. Bollini The Italian Magician."
Metropolitan Litho. Studio, c1879. From the Magic Poster Collection
Library of Congress Prints and Photographs Division.

Despite possible contradictions of Pastor's Italian birth, no ambiguity exists for Sylvester Z. Poli (1859-1937) as Italian. Born in the Piano di Coreglia region of Tuscany in Italy, Sylvester Zefferino Poli can also be described as an American

---

[341] See: Trav S.D. (Donald Travis Stewart) *No Applause, Just Throw Money*.
[342] Victoria Moses. "Tony Pastor: The Clean Vaudeville Entrepreneur."

impresario as "an Italian American theater magnate." While Piano di Coreglia was in the midst of the Franco-Prussian War (July 1870 – May 1871), Poli's family provided refuge to a French born sculptor named M. Dublex. Apparently the young Poli was intrigued to apprentice in Paris under Dublex. A few years later, in 1881, Poli, at the age of 21, immigrated to America, beginning a career at a museum sculpting wax figures. In 1885, he married Rosa (nee: Leverone), fathering five children. He soon gained some as he sculptured wax figures such as anarchists, European royalty, American presidents, and Jesus.

Poli's initial foray into American entertainment was a result of opening a series of wax figure museums in Toronto and New York. Historian Eric Martone tells us, in 1892, Poli moved his family to New Haven, Connecticut opening a wax museum called the "Poli Eden Musee" and "Poli's Wonderland Theater" to stage vaudeville shows. Similar to Tony Pastor, Poli promoted a new level of vaudeville. He was once quoted as saying, "Always, and at all times, I have been a strong believer in morality, I have insisted always on clean shows, and have never tolerated anything that could be fairly regarded as unfit for public presentation."

Above Left: Poli Theater in Washington D.C., c. 1920. (Gift: Herbert A. French; 1947). Library of Congress Prints and Photographs Division Washington, D.C. Reproduction Number: LC-DIG-npcc-29258. **Above Right**: Portrait of Sylvester Z. Poli published by "Poli Theatrical Enterprises." (National Vaudeville Association – Public Domain).

The New England Historical Society said, ownership expanded to a series of theaters in Connecticut, Massachusetts, New Jersey, Pennsylvania, and Washington D.C. The theaters were built by prominent architects as elaborate grandiose public "Palaces." By 1916, Poli was considered the largest individual theater owner in the world. Eventually ownership included 28 theaters, three

CHAPTER 7   261

hotels, and over five hundred office spaces. The focus of Poli's entrepreneurship satisfied the unfulfilled entertainment familiarity for Italian immigrants. Rafaele Fierro writing for *Connecticut History* said for most of the Italian immigrants in the New England area,

> "The region's many industrial factories attracted thousands of immigrants who found the hours long and the wages short. For many, the better life they had imagined had not panned out. Factory work proved long, difficult, and grinding. Conditions were sometimes deplorable."

Poli understood inexpensive entertainment was important to alleviate the daily, sometimes deadly, toil of immigrants. As an Italian, Poli certainly epitomized the ability of immigrant *paisans* adding to American cultural success from a financial standpoint. As an Italian personifications of the "American Dream;" Poli was a positive example to dissuade prejudice and stereotyping against Italians. As described by historian Eric Martone,

> "[Poli] never lost touch with his working-class roots, staying involved with the Italian community and helping the working poor. During World War I he helped organize a National Guard Company of Italian soldiers to demonstrate their patriotism to the United States."[343]

Despite amassing great wealth, the influential and wealthy native white residents of Connecticut, "found Poli's ethnicity reprehensible, but his connection to vaudeville a new form of marketable entertainment they derided made him even more contemptible." Prof. Rafaele Fierro, added the "old guard" New Englanders "perceived their culture as progressively diminishing, due in large part to the increasing numbers of immigrants who'd come to US shores since the 1870s."

Disregarding the New England prejudice, and his own Tuscany *paisans*, Poli remained a staunch supporter of his own heritage and the working-class Italian community. As an Italian born in the cultured north, Poli did not exhibit the all too common inherent prejudice against the peasants of the south. Professor Fierro explained the nuance as,

> "The theater magnate's popularity even overcame the Italian North-South cultural divide that existed on both sides of the Atlantic. While a solid majority of the state's Italians hailed from southern Italy, Poli himself came from Tuscany to the north. By the start of the 20th century, Connecticut's northern Italians had formed the Northern Italian League to distinguish themselves from southern Italians and to make sure that

---

[343] Eric Martone, ed. In *Italian Americans*, pp. 393-394. "S. Z. Poli, the Italian Immigrant Who Horrified the Yankees." *New England Historical Society,*

Yankees understood the vast cultural differences between the two groups."[344]

Poli retired in 1934, transferring ownership of some of his theaters to the Loew's Group. Others were demolished during the early years of the Great Depression, which wreaked havoc on all parts of the nation's economy. (By mid 1930s, Hollywood movies, screened in the grand theater palaces such as owned by Poli, served as escapist fare and regained profitability.)

A low resolution photo of a theater in Buffalo New York, c. 1900 advertising, "Continuous Vaudeville." (Public Domain – Wiki Commons).

Sylvester Poli and Tony Pastor are cited by many historians and cultural researchers, as either individually or combined, for creating the established American idea of "the variety show into vaudeville." Less well-known in the American tradition is Eduardo "Farfariello" Migliaccio. That so-called "American idea" of stage shows ingrained in American culture was based solely on the long Italian tradition which became the forerunner of the entire American entertainment industry.

It all dates back in recognition of its founding on February 25th in 1545 (sometimes cited as in Padua, Italy). With that date in history, each year extending

---

[344] Rafaele Fierro. "Sylvester Poli, Negotiating Cultural Politics in an Age of Immigration." *Connecticut History*, August 31, 2020. Accessed January 8, 2021.

CHAPTER 7

well into the 21st century many theater troupes celebrate International "Commedia dell'Arte Day." As Dr. Matthew R. Wilson writes, that day of February 25, 1545 exists as "the oldest extant record of modern actors thinking of their work as a legitimate business."[345]

Or as many others have noted, including Dr. Wilson, that date in Italy established by the *Commedia dell'arte* is - -

"The Day Show Business was Born"

---

[345] Rafaele Fierro. "Sylvester Poli, Negotiating Cultural Politics in an Age of Immigration." *Connecticut History*, August 31, 2020. Accessed January 8, 2021. A thorough explanation, accompanied by video reenactments, of February 25, 1545 as "Commedia Dell'Arte Day," see: Matthew R. Wilson, Dr., *"A History of Commedia dell'Arte," Fiction of Fools Theater Company*, 2010.

CHAPTER 7A

ITALIAN OPERA AND ENRICO CARUSO

---

*"Italy is the birthplace of opera, and numerous
are the Italian composers renowned the world over."*

---

*"Lorenzo Da Ponte was adamant in his defense of the culture,
language, and history of Italy."*

WHAT IS OPERA?

Italian Opera is most often termed "the quintessential Italian art form." Encyclopedia Britannica defined the cultural art form as,

> "A staged drama set to music in its entirety, made up of vocal pieces with instrumental accompaniment and usually with orchestral overtures and interludes. In some operas the music is continuous throughout an act; in others it is broken up into discrete pieces, or 'numbers,' separated either by recitative (a dramatic type of singing that approaches speech) or by spoken dialogue."[346]

Music historian Herbert Weinstock (1905-1971), author of some definitive opera histories, *The Opera; Music as an Art*, and co-author of *The World of Opera* and *The Opera: A History of Its Creation and Performance: 1600-1941*, offered a detailed explanation as,

> "The English word *opera* is an abbreviation of the Italian phrase *opera in musica* ("work in music"). It denotes a theatrical work consisting of a dramatic text, or *libretto* set to music staged with scenery, costumes, and movement. Aside from solo, ensemble, and choral singers onstage and a group of instrumentalists playing offstage, the performers of opera since its inception have often included dancers. Opera attracted both

---

[346] "Opera," *Britannica.com* Accessed May 15, 2021.

supporters and detractors throughout its history and has sometimes been the target of intense criticism. Its detractors have viewed it as an artificial and irrational art form that defies dramatic verisimilitude. Supporters have seen it as more than the sum of its parts, with the music supporting and intensifying the lyrics and action to create a genre of greater emotional impact than either music or drama could achieve on its own."

Other publications of important biographies of composers of the *Bel Canto* ("beautiful singing") style include Vincenzo Bellini (1801 - 1835), Gaetano Donizetti (1797-1848), and Gioachino Rossini (1792-1868). Despite the inconsistent cultural acceptance, Weinstock adds, "Music historians have continued to debate opera's ancestry." Some trace the beginning to plays staged by the Ancient Greeks. Others cite Biblical dramas during the Middle Ages.

Two Italian composers of the *Bel Canto* ("Beautiful Singing") style.
Above Left: Vincenzo Bellini.
Above Middle: A young Gioachino Rossini, c. 1810-1815.
Above Right: Photograph of Rosini later in life, c. 1865. (Public Domain)

Teatro San Carlo in Naples, c. 1830. Appears as it was rebuilt after an 1816 fire.
(Wiki Commons – Public Domain)

Brief Photographic Overview of Famous Italian Composers

Top Row Left to Right: Claudio Monteverdi (1567- 1643); Antonio Lucio Vivaldi (1678- 1741); Giuseppe Tartini (1692-1770); **Middle Row**: Antonio Salieri (1750-1825); Niccolò Paganini (1782 – 1840); Giuseppe Verdi (1813- 1901); **Bottom Row**: Giacomo Puccini (1858-1924); Pietro Mascagni (1863 - 1945); (Verdi Image: Engraved by H. Velton. Photograph. Retrieved from the Library of Congress, <www.loc.gov/item/2002710412/>).
(Public Domain).

"ITALY is the BIRTHPLACE of OPERA"

The history of stage performances from ancient times is not doubted. As for Opera, Weinstock states, "the earliest universally accepted direct ancestors of opera appeared in 16th-century Italy." As a cultural art form, very little debate exists in Europe and America for Opera tracing its roots directly to Italy. Tourism website *Discover Italy* adds a proclamation states, "Italy is the birthplace of opera."[347]

---

[347] "The Italy of Opera," *Discover Italy*, 2021. Weinstock. "Opera," *Britannica.com*.

268   Italian Culture in America:
The Immigrants 1880 to 1930 From Discrimination to Assimilation

Famous Italian Opera Houses arose in the northern regions of Milan and Venice. *Teatro San Bartolomeo* built in 1620 and *Teatro San Carlo* completed in 1737, both in Naples; and *Teatro dell' Opera di Roma* in Rome opened in 1880. During the 19th century in America, opera houses were in major cities as New Orleans, New York, Philadelphia, and San Francisco. At first, opera in America was considered a "lowbrow" art form ("not highly intellectual or cultured") catering to the large number of German and Italian immigrants. Over the course of a century from 1880 to 1980, opera in America was mostly a cultural appropriation by the wealthy in American society, viewed as "highbrow." Regardless, Opera has survived "in Western culture for more than 400 years."[348]

New Orleans: "The Opera Capital of North America"

Historian Jack Belsom in, "A History of Opera in New Orleans" cites the start of the musical art form in the city dating to 1796, with "Sylvain," as the city's first documented opera performance. In New Orleans the opera was performed at the *Theatre de la Rue Saint Pierre* a French theater in operation from 1792 to 1810. It might be semantics to claim any opera performance prior to April of 1812 was not a true American production, since Louisiana was not officially admitted to the United States until April 30, 1812. After statehood, the *Théâtre d'Orléans* was the predominant opera venue from 1819 to 1859. Belsom adds, "Opera has long been part of the musical culture of New Orleans since the early 19th century a resident company regularly performed opera in addition to traveling performers and companies." Those performances were not Italian, rather a "repertoire of French scores." There is no dispute as to New Orleans earning distinction for the first opera performance in America – however, it was French opera not Italian.

Belsom claims, "It wasn't long before New Orleans became, 'The Opera Capital of North America.'" A significant claim bolstered by the construction of a permanent opera house the *Théâtre de l'Opéra*. During its sixty-year run a wide array of operas were performed. Of particular note were the American premiers of Italian composers Vincenzo Bellini, Gioachino Rossini, and Giuseppe Verdi whose "Aida" played in 1880.

Lorenzo Da Ponte: "Mozart's American Librettist"

Lorenzo Da Ponte (1749-1838) is considered as famous as any other individual of his time, yet remains as another in the historical annals of the "mostly forgotten." The Italian born Da Ponte lived the last 33 years of his life in America from 1805 to the year of his death in 1838. Many in relative obscurity; eventual notoriety; and back to obscurity. In 2005, the 200th anniversary of Da Ponte's arrival in America. An exhibition titled, "Lorenzo Da Ponte, a Bridge from Italy to New

---

[348] Lawrence W. Levine. *From Lowbrow to Highbrow*, 1990.

CHAPTER 7A 269

York" was sponsored by Columbia University. The purpose was to rekindle the importance of Da Ponte's Italian contribution to American culture. Prof. David Freedberg, director of the Italian Academy at Columbia University announced,

> "Da Ponte was the first representative of cosmopolitan enlightened European culture in America, he was the bridge. There's something telling and very sad about the fact that he remains a completely unknown figure in the history of American cultural life."

As a cultural purveyor of many aspects of the arts, Da Ponte was the librettist for twenty-eight operas written for eleven different composers. As defined by the Oxford Standard Dictionary,

> **Librettist** /lə'bredəst/ *noun* -A person who writes the text of an opera or other long vocal work.

Of the many composers Da Ponte worked with as a librettist, the most famous collaborator was Wolfgang Amadeus Mozart (1756-1791).[349]

Mozart and Da Ponte met in 1783; collaborating on three operas from 1786 until 1790 (one year before Mozart's death at the age of 35). The three operas were, "The Marriage of Figaro" (1786); "Don Giovanni" (1787); and "Così fan tutte" (1790). Each have endured, cited by many as "the operas rank among the world's greatest - widely considered the most brilliant in the history of opera." Each remains prominent, yet as Mozart is revered, Da Ponte "is little remembered in America."

Lorenzo Da Ponte was born with the birth name of "Emanuele Conegliano" in Ceneda within the Republic of Venice; Italian by birth, Jewish by religion. In 1764, widowed father Geronimo converted the family to Roman Catholicism; changing the family name to "Da Ponte." Historian Dick Adler in *Smithsonian* magazine explained,

> "[Da Ponte] converted to Catholicism as a child when his father remarried, became first a priest, then an Abbé, then an infamous adulterer [fathering two children with a mistress], and then, like his good friend Giovanni Giacomo Casanova, a forced exile from his native Venice. He was subsequently appointed the official theater poet to Emperor Joseph II in Vienna and became the librettist for Mozart's three greatest Italian operas."[350]

The biography is only a brief summation of a varied cultural enriched lifetime - before embarking to America. In 1805, he sailed to America, to reunite with

---

[349] Jeremy Eichler. "A Long Life in America After Writing the Big Mozart Librettos," *The New York Times*, October 5, 2005.
[350] Dick Adler. "The Man Who Knew Mozart."

family. Landing in Philadelphia, he discovered his family had relocated to New York. He soon joined them. In his memoirs, he wrote, "with the hope of finding happiness in a country which I thought free."

Da Ponte lived in anonymity as a grocery store proprietor. Soon to embark on a trek of introducing Italian Culture to America. Biographer Rodney Bolt states, "to enrich American culture with the beauty of Dante and the Italian language-culture." At the time. . . Mozart and Italian opera were still largely unknown." Biographer Basilio Catania wrote of an opera connection between Antonio Meucci and Lorenzo Da Ponte,

> "Park Theater was famous because Italian opera was performed for the first time in the U.S., in 1825, thanks to the Venetian Lorenzo da Ponte and the opera company of Manuel García. Lorenzo Da Ponte was a distinguished personality of New York's first Italian colony. A writer of librettos and considered the founder of Italian culture in America. Up until his death in 1839, Da Ponte strove to promote Italian culture in the United States."[351]

By 1811 to 1818, he was well-established within the cultural circles of New York society. A chance occurrence led to an expanding Italian culture in America which brought Da Ponte out from obscurity in America.

Portrait (engraving) of Lorenzo Da Ponte (1749-1838), c. 1822.
Engraved by Michele Pekenino (19th century). Public Domain.

---

[351] Basilio Catania. *Antonio Meucci: The Inventor and his Time*, p. 82.

CHAPTER 7A

In 1807, Da Ponte entered the Riley & Co. in New York known as "a famous importer of European books and a pillar of culture." The intent hoped of brokering a deal to sell Italian language books. One customer Clement C. Moore overheard the conversation, supposedly saying "he could count the great Italian writers on one hand." Da Ponte responded, "I could spend a month naming eminent Italian writers and poets." The exchange highlights two important moments; one the lack of knowledge of Italian Culture by a prominent learned individual. Second, the meeting led to a lifelong friendship altering Da Ponte's future and began an introduction of Italian culture to a segment of prominent New Yorkers.[352]

Through lectures and frequent visits to Riley's bookstore, Da Ponte befriended and associated with such American literary cultural figures as Clement C. Moore (1779-1863), James Fenimore Cooper (1789-1851), and Washington Irving (1783-1859), among others. A cohesive respect and lifelong friendship with Moore, led to a teaching position at Columbia University. At the time, Moore a professor of Greek and Oriental Studies; obviously held some influence due to his father Reverend Benjamin Moore, (1748-1816) as past president of Columbia. The younger Clement Moore is best remembered in American popular culture as the author of "A Visit from St. Nicholas," written in 1823, commonly known as "The Night Before Christmas," a perennial Christmas classic.[353]

The appointment led to private tutoring of Italian language and Renaissance culture to children of New York's wealthy socialites. In 1819, lecture transcripts were published in leading literary magazines, promoting Italian cultural education. Biographer Rodney Bolt adds,

> "Da Ponte was adamant in his defense of the culture, language, and history of Italy, especially in the face of prejudices arising in the context of Italian immigration to New York City in 1820s. His biting debate with historian Prescott in 1824 in the *North American Review* was to defend the importance of the Italian influence in literature."

Prominent American historian, William H. Prescott (1796-1859) early in his career researched classic Italian poetry. In 1824, Prescott published two essays on Italian Narrative Poetry in the prestigious *North American Review*. A fifty-two page critical response by Lorenzo Da Ponte cited many inaccuracies. Thereafter, Prescott switched his focus to the Spanish influence upon America and Mexico.

In 1825, Columbia University established a new program in Italian literature with Da Ponte as its first professor. As part of the program, Da Ponte sold his personal collection of Italian literature of 264 volumes, to Columbia; 60 volumes went to the New York Public Library. Biographer Rodney Bolt notes, the books

---

[352] Paul Hond. "How Mozart's Librettist Became the Father of Italian Studies," p. 64.
[353] Columbia University was founded in 1754 as King's College.

"remain to this day the cores of their collections of Italian poetry and other literature."[354]

Da Ponte collaborated with Park Theater manager Stephen Price (1782-1840) staging a performance – in Italian – of "The Barber of Seville" on November 29, 1825. The lead performed by Spanish tenor Manuel García (1775-1832), might represent the first Italian opera in America. Another performance arranged by Da Ponte in 1826 at the Old St. Patrick's Cathedral in Little Italy changed America's cultural landscape with the introduction of Italian opera to New York City. In 1828, Da Ponte became a naturalized American citizen.[355]

During his many years in New York, Da Ponte realized his cultural contributions did not receive deserving media or academic recognition. He sadly wrote, "In more than twenty years not one charitable writer has been found so that the literary world, and in particular the Italians, may learn about it, what I have done in America!" In reality, Da Ponte might not have realized the growing discontent caused by the American Populist movement during the years before the American Civil War. Those years marked a time when the young American nation was trying to develop its own unique culture devoid of its European and African ancestry.[356]

Above Left: Wolfgang Amadeus Mozart (c. 1915-1925) created by the Detroit Publishing Co. Photograph Library of Congress, www.loc.gov/item/2016816928.
Above Right: Portrait Lorenzo Da Ponte, c. 1830 (Public Domain)

---

[354] Rodney Bolt. *The Librettist of Venice*, 2006.
[355] "Da Ponte's Oratorio: A Concert for New York," *PBS Thirteen*, October 22, 2021.
[356] Quoted in: Shelia Hodges, *Lorenzo Da Ponte*, p. 201.

A Befitting Monument in a Forgotten Grave

Lorenzo Da Ponte lived a long fruitful, yet, mostly forgotten life. Upon death reports did say "an enormous funeral ceremony was held in New York's old St. Patrick's Cathedral on Mulberry Street." A 21st century remembrance does exist at The Lorenzo Da Ponte Italian Library as,

> "An organic collection of Italian texts translated into English. Its role is to make available a series of one hundred works by Italian authors who have made significant literary, philosophical, juridical, and historical contributions to the world of international culture."[357]

Passing away shy of his 90th birthday, Da Ponte received the sacramental rites of a Catholic mass and consecrated burial on August 17, 1838, in a cemetery on East 11th Street in Manhattan. One half-century after Da Ponte's death a music enthusiast searched for the gravesite.

Headstone, dedicated 1987, in Calvary Cemetery in Queens, New York as a memorial marker for Lorenzo Da Ponte. The exact location of the burial site within the cemetery is unknown. Photograph by: Marcial, Queens, New York.

---

[357] Jeremy Eichler. "A Long Life in America After Writing the Big Mozart Librettos," *The New York Times*, October 5, 2005.

274 Italian Culture in America:
The Immigrants 1880 to 1930 From Discrimination to Assimilation

In 1887, Henry E. Krehbiel (1854-1923), considered "Dean" of an emerging new group of American music critics as editor at *The New York Tribune* could not find the grave. Working from information on the East 11th Street graveyard proved fruitless. Actually, the graveyard was earlier abandoned and built over. Scant information indicated the buried remains were removed and interred at Calvary Cemetery in the borough of Queens. In 1987, a permanent headstone was placed in Calvary Cemetery courtesy of a cooperative effort of the Italian Heritage and Culture Committee of New York, New York Historical Association, and a Queens Congressional Representative. (The headstone serves only as a memorial marker; the exact location of the burial site is unknown.) Inscription on the headstone dedicated in October 1987 during Italian Heritage and Cultural month cited Da Ponte as Mozart's librettist among other accomplishments.

The legacy of Lorenzo Da Ponte exists every time an Italian Opera is performed in America. It does not matter if the legends of Don Juan, Figaro, or Don Alfonso are presented in their original form or character referenced in the hundreds, if not thousands of American entertainment media creations; they are forever deeply entrenched in the American cultural psyche. A befitting epilogue to the totality of Italian Culture in America harkens back to another obscurity of a 16th century Italian Renaissance writer Giovanni Battista Gelli (1498-1563). The description may easily present us with an understanding as to why Lorenzo Da Ponte continued his quest. Gelli in *Ragionamento sulla lingua*, explained,

> "We have no empire, such as did the Romans, so powerful that subject cities spontaneously sought to emulate their rulers' speech. . . Nonetheless it can clearly be seen how, in our present times, many diverse people of intelligence and refinement, outside Italy no less than within Italy, devote much effort and study to learning and speaking our language for no other reason than love."[358]

In addition, Da Ponte's venture for a dedicated opera house foreshadowed the opening of opera houses of the New York Academy of Music in 1854 and the Metropolitan Opera House in 1883.

The Park Theater: Site of the First Italian Opera in America

Da Ponte's November 29, 1825 stage presentation of Italian Opera at the Park Theater in New York City in America was noted by Francis Rogers ninety years. He cited lead the tenor García as "our musical Columbus." Of extraordinary note, the opera was sung all in Italian, a language which García had learned. A significant aid to mastering the language included travel to Naples in 1812 "to

---

[358] The *Lorenzo Da Ponte Italian Library*, Accessed June 6, 2021. Note sometimes the name appears as "Giambattista Gelli"

CHAPTER 7A

study the art of singing and the theory of music under the best auspices." While in Naples, García met composer Gioachino Rossini and a change in artistic development after study in Italy. In 1817, García was proclaimed "the greatest tenor of the day."

Before García's 1825 performance at the Park Theater "New York had never heard an Italian opera." The performance signified a changeover as Italian opera was slowly gaining acceptance into high society. One newspaper reported the audience consisted of "an assemblage of ladies so fashionable, so numerous and so elegantly dressed [who] had probably never been in an American theater." García's in "The Barber of Seville" was repeated twice-a-week. Over ten months, seventy-nine performances including and other operas, were presented at the Park Theater.

In 1915, Francis Rogers recounted the transformational social acceptance of Italian Opera over the course of 90 years, stating,

> "Grand Opera in the United States is now so firmly established in our affection and interests that it is hard to realize that its full acceptance by us as a legitimate form of amusement dates back scarcely more than fifty years, and that its total history is less than a century old."

At the time, Rogers must have been aware of the full breadth of the accomplishments of the famed tenor Enrico Caruso (1873-1921). Yet, Rogers highly praised another tenor, proclaiming, "In all history there is no singer to match Manuel García in combined energy, intelligence and versatility." Rogers opinion of great singing talent is certainly warranted and allowable. Ignoring the great tenor Enrico Caruso, at the height of fame by 1915, might represent another slight against Italian immigrants. Commentary on the talents of the great tenors, however, did lead to any type of altercation or a riot as did a historical 1849 drama performance.[359]

---

[359] Francis Rogers, "America's First Grand Opera Season," *The Musical Quarterly*, pp. 94-97.

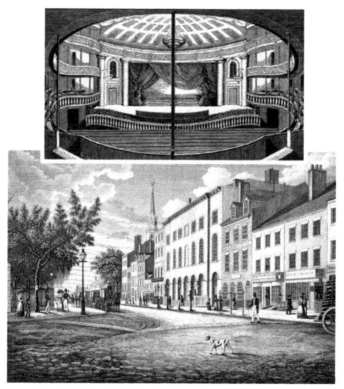

The Park Theater located at One Park Row in New York City; the location of the first presentation of Italian Opera in America. Illustration published in the *New York Mirror* of August 7, 1830.

Max Maretzek and the Academy of Music

In 1850, as Antonio Meucci (Italian inventor of the telephone) moved into America by way of New York City, he met the well-known Italian "Hero of the Two World's" Giuseppe Garibaldi. The famed Italian General was not seeking fame in New York; rather a life of a quiet solitude. Meucci and Garibaldi struck up a mutual friendship; each in search of a place to live without fanfare. Czechoslovakia immigrant Max Maretzek (1821-1897), an orchestra conductor and former impresario of the Astor Place Opera House, offered a proposal to rent a "Forest Cottage" which he owned located on Staten Island.

Meucci came to know Maretzek through their mutual association working in theater management. Maretzek, who had theater experience in Europe, only recently immigrated a few years before, choosing to pursue a career as an *impresario*. In 1849, the Max Maretzek Italian Opera Company was founded; a successful endeavor that continued from 1849 to 1878 producing Italian and German operas throughout America. Maretzek also some Italian operas at Castle Garden (the former immigration site).

Top Left: The Brooklyn Academy of Music, Brooklyn, NY, c. 1861. Illustration from Harper's Weekly February 2, 1861, p. 77. Middle Right: The New York Academy of Music, c. 1865. Bottom Left: American Academy of Music, Philadelphia, Pa., c. 1905. All photographs (slightly cropped from original) Library of Congress Prints and Photographs Division Washington, D.C.

One 1851 premier was *Marino Faliero* by Italian composer Gaetano Donizetti (1797-1848). In 1854, Maretzek featured an Italian production of Giuseppe Verdi's *Luisa Miller*. A featured performer was the Italian soprano and "prima donna" Teresa Parodi (1827 - 1878) born in Genoa. Maretzek arranged performances at similar named theaters in New York, Brooklyn, and Philadelphia, among others nationwide. The Academy of Music in Philadelphia, opened in 1857, with a seating capacity close to 3,000, remains as "the oldest opera house in the United States that is still used for its original purpose." The first Philadelphia performance was on February 25, 1857 with a Maretzek Italian Opera Company production of Giuseppe Verdi's *Il Trovatre*. With a traveling opera company, Maretzek needed to understand the "pulse" and possible prejudice of how the population of each city might respond to Italian Opera.[360]

---

[360] Basilio Catania. *Antonio Meucci: The Inventor and his Time.* Rome: Seat Divisione, 1999, p. 82. Note: The next year Castle Garden was converted into an immigration center lasting from 1855 to 1890 – see Chapter 2.

278   Italian Culture in America:
The Immigrants 1880 to 1930 From Discrimination to Assimilation

As a touring company, Maretzek did not present the same opera productions in every city. Preceding the large Italian immigration to Boston, the people of Boston showed a tendency to favor German musicians rather than Italian, leading Maretzek therefore to select German Operas. In contrast, Jacob Smith in an unpublished thesis described,

> "While Italian opera seemed to emerge victorious as the century progressed, Maretzek was still more conservative in the operas he chose to produce for this city. He relied on favorites such as Trovatore and Traviata, and there is no evidence of him ever producing Rigoletto in Philadelphia."

As for the so-called "riskier ventures such as Rigoletto," Smith tells us, some selections were easily accepted "for his home base of New York."[361]

One such New York venue was The Academy of Music seating 4,000 which had opened to welcomed fanfare on October 2, 1854. Almost immediately, the theater garnered the attention of many of New York's elite social classes. Within a short time, the theater hosted the American premiers of many Italian and German operas. By 1883, the upper ranks of New York society favored the new opulent Metropolitan Opera House. By 1886, reduced opera audiences at the Academy of Music caused a switch from opera to vaudeville. (The building was demolished in 1926.)[362]

In contrast, productions by later impresarios veered away from organizing traveling opera companies. In place of Maretzek's "Itinerant Opera" style, the opening of the Metropolitan Opera House, as one example, marked the beginning of a transition for Opera moving away from appealing to audiences of all social classes. In contrast, the posh theaters, such as the larger cities as New York, dedicated solely to Opera and Classical music composition into the realm of the wealthy.

Maretzek is often overlooked in cultural history, especially pertaining to Italian Culture in America. In contrast, research historian Jacob Smith credits Maretzek's "important role in establishing and promoting Italian opera in America, a tradition that we still enjoy today his contribution to opera in America was extraordinary."[363]

---

[361] Jacob Smith. "Maretzek, Verdi, and the Adoring Public: Reception History and Production of Italian Opera in America, 1849-1878," August 2016, p. 75.
[362] Jack Belsom. "A History of Opera in New Orleans." *Operalogg.com.*
[363] Jacob Smith. "Maretzek, Verdi, and the Adoring Public," p. 76.

Above Left: Max Maretzek, c. 1851. Photograph by: Matthew Brady Library of Congress Prints and Photographs Division Washington, D.C. <www.loc.gov/item/2004664206/>. **Above Right**: Lithograph portrait of Italian opera singer Teresa Parodi, c. 1851.

Giovanna Bianchi: "The Mother of Music in California."

Italian culture in California, notably San Francisco, was evident during the Gold Rush years of 1848 into the 1850s. With a growing population of all sorts of entrepreneurs, merchants, and fortune seekers, the area was in need of viable entertainment. Among Italian immigrant's opera was well-received. A review in the San Francisco *Evening Picayune* stated,

> "Opera's probable debut in San Francisco was in 1850, when Mathilda Korsinsky, a German-born singer, sang an aria from Verdi's *Ernani* during the intermission between a drama and a farce at the Jenny Lind Theatre."[364]

One Italian aria does not replicate an entire opera, but was a beginning. An early venue dedicated as an Italian theater opened in September of 1850. Maxine Seller writing a journal article for *Wiley Online Library* states,

> "Italians brought their love of music to California with them. As early as 1850 there was an attempt to establish an Italian theater in San Francisco. . . On September 13, 1850, a Signor Rossi opened an Italian theater on

---

[364] "Grand Opera in San Francisco," American Eras. *Encyclopedia*.com, June 1, 2021.

Kearney and Jackson streets. He offered a variety show including magic tricks and a ventriloquist act as well as music and dancing. The show got good reviews and ran for four nights before a fire closed down the theater. Rossi reopened the theater at a new location, only destroyed by fire again. . . after a third, then a fourth, and finally a fifth fire, Rossi and his theater disappeared permanently from the San Francisco scene."

Despite an unsettled performance schedule, an 1851 visit by the Pellegrini Opera Company staged a production of Vincenzo Bellini's two-act bel canto style *La Sonnambula*, considered "the first complete opera ever heard in the State." Visiting performances by the La Scala Ballet Company featuring dancer Marietta Bonfanti (1845-1921) arrived during the 1850s. In 1860, the visiting Bianchi Opera performed seven operas. The overwhelming response led to "a continuous run for fourteen years." A featured performer was an Italian Madame Giovanna Bianchi, singing Verdi arias; soon known as, "The Mother of Music in California."[365]

One source called it for a "brief moment San Francisco was at the forefront of opera in the United States." One contemporary San Francisco music critic in a publication *Alta* proclaimed, "the opera has become a regular institution among us." Opera was embraced as popular entertainment among impoverished Italian immigrants. A similar pattern of cultural transition was explained by Maxine Seller as, "Opera was Italian in language and cultural background, but opulent opera houses of 19th-century San Francisco remained the province of the wealthy Anglo-Saxons." Audiences did not necessarily become diversified beyond the "wealthy" white population. Yet, the virtuoso performers were Italian, such as a San Francisco favorite named Luisa Tetrazzini.[366]

Luisa Tetrazzini: *How to Sing*

Born in Florence, Luisa Tetrazzini (1871-1940) performed her Italian operatic debut in 1895 as a "dramatic soprano" in the role of "Inez" in the German opera *L'Africaine* by composer Giacomo Meyerbeer (1791-1864). Rave reviews prompted a tour across Italy and Europe; soon crossing the Atlantic performing in Mexico and South America. In 1905, Tetrazzini made an American appearance in San Francisco performing at the Tivoli Opera House (opened in 1879). Two years later, a London visit included performances of the Verdi opera *La Traviata* in the role of "Violetta." In 1908, a United States tour included the Manhattan Opera House which resulted in a contract dispute with Oscar Hammerstein. An

---

[365] Pontoniere, *From Italy to California Italian Immigration: 1850 to Today*, p. 4.
[366] Maxine Seller. "Antonietta Pisanelli and the Italian Theater of San Francisco," *Wiley Online Library*, January 1993, p. 161.

injunction issued at the legal bequest of Hammerstein, attempted to prevent Tetrazzini from singing professionally anywhere in the United States.

Above Left: Luisa Tetrazzini, full length portrait, c. 1911. **Above Right**: Photograph October 30, 1920, Tetrazzini holding Halloween jack-o'-lantern. Library of Congress Prints and Photographs Division Washington, D.C.

Ongoing legal entanglement with Hammerstein led to a return to San Francisco. Luisa was quoted in defiance, "I will sing in San Francisco if I have to sing there in the streets, for I know the streets of San Francisco are free." This defiant quote to "sing in the streets" has lived on in opera lore. In 1910, Christmas Eve, despite potential ramifications, Tetrazzini, sang an outdoor concert at the corner of Market Street and Kearny Street in the heart of the city, directly in front of the headquarters of the *San Francisco Chronicle*. All media accounts praised and applauded her daring singing adventure; yet accounts varied widely on the crowd size as thousands crowded along the city streets to hear the popular songstress.

The *San Francisco Chronicle* devoted the entire front page to Tetrazzini's Christmas Eve concert with a Christmas Day banner headline,

TWO HUNDRED AND FIFTY THOUSAND HEAR TETRAZZINI

SING IN THE OPEN AIR BEFORE THE CHRONICLE BUILDING

Below the headline, a half-page spread of Tetrazzini photographed upon a makeshift stage. Below, three articles praised her performance, titled,

- Queen of Song Sings From Her Heart to Worshipful Throng In San Francisco's Streets;
- Great Artist Reveals Her Very Soul to the People She Loves;
- One Little Woman, Prodigal with Talent, Charms Greatest Crowd that Ever Heard Singer.[367]

Newspaper accounts of the performance was not limited to the local area. News of the concert was covered across the content. *The New York Times* of March 6, 1911, quoted Luisa Tetrazzini, as saying, "Never, never in all my life have I had an experience like that of Christmas Eve when I sang for the people in the streets of San Francisco." Reports referenced the stage was outside the *San Francisco Chronicle* newspaper headquarters. The convenient location in the downtown area was popular among people of San Francisco known as "Lotta's Fountain."[368]

Lotta's Fountain

Lotta's Fountain was named after a popular San Francisco entertainer named Lotta Crabtree (1847-1924). The monument remains in the square; bestowed as a gift from Crabtree to the residents of San Francisco on September 9, 1875. A commemorative plaque at the base of the fountain cites two later historical events; one as a meeting place after the 1906 earthquake and second as the location of the "memorable performance" by Luisa Tetrazzini. (Lotta's Fountain is listed as a National Historic Place.)

Born as Charlotte Mignon "Lotta" Crabtree in New York City. At the age of six Crabtree, traveled to California. The young Lotta began performing around the age of eight – singing and dancing in the streets. A continued career of a "song-and-dance comedy routine" – led to becoming a darling "revered entertainer" of San Francisco. Popularity led to a nationwide tour; and across Europe. During her lifetime she accumulated a very large fortune in excess of $4 million dollars. A portion of that early fortune was used to erect the fountain. Lotta's Fountain gained legendary lore during her lifetime. In the aftermath, of the devasting 1906 San Francisco Earthquake, the fountain was one of the very few structures still standing. The intact fountain served as a rallying and meeting point for survivors. A few years later, in 1910, it was the site of Luisa's Tetrazzini's famous concert before a crowd estimated at 250,000 people. Crabtree remains part of San Francisco history as does Luisa Tetrazzini.[369]

---

[367] The *San Francisco Chronicle*, December 25, 1910, Vol. XCVII, No. 163, p. 1.
[368] *In Cerca di Una Nuova Vita: From Italy to California Italian Immigration: 1850 to Today*, Museo ItaloAmericano. Oct 16 2009 – January 17, 2010, p. 17.
[369] Weirde. "Lotta's Fountain," *Shaping San Francisco's Digital Archive*, 2021.

Above Left: Portrait of Lotta Crabtree (1847-1924), unknown date. **Above Right**: "Lotta's Fountain," c. 2012, site of Luisa Tetrazzini's 1910 Christmas Eve concert in San Francisco. Photographs in Carol M. Highsmith's America Project, Library of Congress, Prints and Photographs Division.

Luisa Tetrazzini's Later Life

During the 1913-1914 season, Luisa Tetrazzini was in demand in other parts of the nation as she sang with the Chicago Opera. Biographer John M. Cunningham described "Tetrazzini's voice was light in quality. . . Her vocal technique, however, was stunning and remained so until her death." As a professional opera singer Tetrazzini's career occurred before the devasting world conflict of the First World War in Europe. After the war, singing performances were only occasional. During the 1920s, she published two important books in connection with her opera career and singing style. The first was an autobiographical description of her career in *My Life of Song* (1921). The second was an informative and instructional *How to Sing* (1923); a discussion on the art of singing. She continued to teach singing in Milan until her death in 1940.[370]

As a quirky side note to the mostly forgotten life of Luisa Tetrazzini relates to the most common Italian cultural assimilation in America – food. A continuing popular food dish served in America is "Chicken Tetrazzini" named in her honor.

---

[370] John M. Cunningham, "Soprano," *Encyclopedia Britannica*, September 5, 2012.

Many sources cite this origination, as one example a blog *Good Life Eats* attributes,

> "The dish is named after the famous Italian-born opera star Luisa Tetrazzini. It is widely believed to have been invented ca. 1908-1910 by Ernest Arbogast, then chef at the Palace Hotel in San Francisco, California, where Tetrazzini was a long-time resident. However, other sources attribute the origin to at the Knickerbocker Hotel in New York City."

The recipe includes macaroni mixed with chicken pieces tossed in a creamy parmesan sauce. Other ingredients are often added, thereby having no exact recipe; a common trait among Italian dishes. The lasting legacy of a cultural food delicacy would have certainly brought a tinge of humble acceptance within the overall focus of assimilation of Italian culture in America. In 1914, Luisa Tetrazzini returned to San Francisco; this time not to accept any honors for herself, rather she traveled to pay honor to one of the greatest of all opera composers - Giuseppe Verdi.[371]

Photograph aboard a Trans-Atlantic ship crossing of popular opera singer Luisa Tetrazzini (1871-1940) "with photographers taking her picture." Bain News Service, publisher c. 1915-1920. Library of Congress <www.loc.gov/item/2014711735/>.

---

[371] "Chicken Tetrazzini," Attributed to Katie. *Good Life Eats,* January 23, 2020./

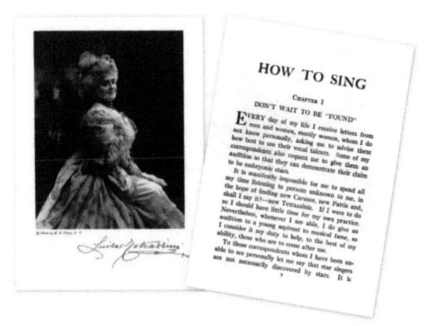

Above Left: Photograph insert of Luisa Tetrazzini in first edition of *How to Sing*, c. 1923. **Above Right**: Sample page from the publication *How to Sing*, Chapter 1 titled: "Don't Wait to be "Found."

Verdi Monuments from Coast to Coast

On March 23, 1914, a Giuseppe Verdi monument was dedicated in Golden Gate Park in San Francisco, California. (The park over an area of over 1,000 acres was dedicated on April 4, 1870; the famous bridge of the same name was dedicated in 1937.) The monument was presented as a gift representing accomplishments of the large Italian immigrant community in San Francisco. The idea to erect a monument to Verdi was headed by editor and publisher Ettore Patrizi (1869-1946) of the daily San Francisco Italian language newspaper *L'Italia*. The sculptor was an Italian artist from Milan named Orazio Grossoni (1867-1952) who chose to depict four Greek muses of mythology wrapped around the stone base. The symbolic muses represent the emotions of Love, Tragedy, Joy, and Sorrow, each individually and collectively represent the creative aspects of an artist.

Above Left: Verdi Monument in Golden Gate Park, San Francisco, California, c. 1914 by Orazio Grossoni. Photograph by: Daderot, c. 2015. **Above Right**: Giuseppe Verdi Monument in Verdi Square Park in New York City. By Pasquale Civiletti (1858-1952), depicts Verdi flanked by four of his most popular characters: Falstaff, Leonora of La forza del destino, Aida, and Otello. Photograph by: Paul Klenk, c. 2015.
(Wiki Creative Commons)

The highlight of the dedication ceremony was Luisa Tetrazzini singing a Verdi aria from "Aida" to an audience estimated over 20,000. Financial and media support by Ettore Patrizi arose from his Italian cultural appreciation of Verdi's art form. Information at Find-a-Grave tells us,

> "Mr. Patrizi, through his newspaper *L'Italia*, was a major promoter of the opera. The newspaper sponsored parties for Italian opera stars with receptions for visiting Italian opera stars and composers. He corresponded with opera composers such as Verdi and Mascagni. Enrico Caruso, was a shareholder in the newspaper."

A bronze plaque at the base reads, "Erected by the Italian Colony Through the Initiative of the Daily L'Italia and Donated to the City of San Francisco March 1914." The San Francisco Verdi monument remains meticulously preserved. In 2021, Mauro Battocchi, an Italian Ambassador in San Francisco wrote of his personal observations. In one essay, "At 200, Verdi Lives on in Golden Gate Park," Battocchi offered "one can find a remarkable bridge between the Italian and American communities of a century ago. In this place, about twenty feet tall,

CHAPTER 7A

stands a bust of a man, his head gilded all in gold and perched atop a stone pedestal." The reference is the 1914 Golden Gate Park monument of Giuseppe Verdi.[372]

Many other Verdi monuments were located throughout Italy in towns and cities such as Busseto, Cagliari, Milan, Palermo, and Trieste, among other locations. Back across the Atlantic Ocean a Verdi monument was erected in San Paolo, Brazil. An American monument honoring the composer Giuseppe Verdi was dedicated in Verdi Square Park across the continent in New York City at the intersection of West 72nd Street and Broadway in Manhattan. (an official naming of the park in honor of Verdi occurred in 1921.) The park is located directly adjacent to the New York City IRT-Broadway line 72nd Street subway station which opened in October of 1904. Much of the very same tunnel system dug by hundreds of un-named Italian immigrants. The existing station has been restored to the original condition as "one of the original 28 stations of the New York City Subway system." The towering New York monument by Pasquale Civiletti (1858-1952), depicts Verdi flanked by four of his most popular opera characters: "Falstaff" from the opera of the same name; "Leonora" from *La Forza del Destino*; and both "Aida;" and "Otello" based on the Shakespeare play.

As an Italian cultural artifact, the New York statue was dedicated to Verdi as an Italian born in Italy; sculpted by an artist born in Palermo, crafted from Carrara marble and Montechiaro limestone, quarried from the Tuscany region of northern Italy. Unveiling concurred with a celebration of Columbus Day. As noted by the official history of New York City,

> "The Verdi monument was unveiled on October 12, 1906, the 414th anniversary of Columbus's discovery of America. The day began with a march of Italian societies from Washington Square to the site at Broadway and West 72nd Street. Over 10,000 people attended the unveiling, uniting Italian-Americans in celebration of their cultural and artistic heritage."

Carlo Barsotti (1850-1927) editor of New York's Italian language newspaper *Il Progresso* led the monument committee. An inscription at the monument informs us, 'Barsotti, championed public recognition of pre-eminent Italians as a source of inspiration for New York's large Italian-American community." The Verdi monument remains under the care and maintenance of the New York City Department of Parks; only a short distance from the world-famous Metropolitan Opera.[373]

---

[372] Mauro Battocchi. "At 200, Verdi Lives on in Golden Gate Park," *San Francisco, Italy,*" June 12, 2021.

[373] Verdi Square." *New York City Department of Parks & Recreation.* June 26, 2021.

Above Left: Giuseppe Verdi Monument located in Verdi Square Park in Manhattan, New York City. **Top Right**: New York City Subway station entrance located adjacent to Verdi Square Park restored to an early 20th century condition as it would have looked during the dedication. **Bottom Right**: Verdi Square Park, the monument is slightly evident in the far left of the photograph, c. 2020. (Courtesy of the New City Department of Parks & Recreation.)

Giulio Gatti-Casazza: "The First Italian to Direct at the Metropolitan."

A significant example of a broader and long lasting legacy of Italian culture occurred as Giulio Gatti-Casazza (1869-1940) earned nationwide fame as managing director of the Metropolitan Opera House in New York City. Another prestigious honor in American culture was bestowed upon Gatti-Casazza when featured on the cover of the nationwide publication of *Time* magazine of November 5, 1923; reaching millions of readers. Gatti-Casazza earned the distinction as "the first Italian living in the United States" to achieve that honor by the magazine. (Another appearance was on November 1, 1926.) In the ensuing years between *Time* cover issues, another prominent publication of American popular culture *The New Yorker* published a profile on February 21, 1925, "Maestrissimo!"[374]

---

[374] Gilbert W. Gabriel, "Maestrissimo!" *New Yorker* (21 February 1925): pp. 9-10.

CHAPTER 7A

The direct "Maestrissimo!" Italian translation is "Masterful;" or loosely translated as "teacher." Among many references to the loose or even literal translation, as applied to "Gatti," A subtitle in Time magazine of 1923, confirms the impresario status as, "Gatti Dominates the Heights to Which He Has Brought His House." (The article referred to him simply as "Gatti," a term often used with affection.) The nationwide notoriety and cultural allocates lauded upon Gatti-Casazza recognized the complete financial and artistic quality of opera productions at the Met. In 1908, as Gatti started as managing director, the "Metropolitan and deficit had become synonymous words." The editors added and credited Gatti-Casazza with the fortitude of "subtle intelligence and masterful hand was needed to put the Metropolitan on its [financial] feet."

Gatti-Casazza was born in Udine, Italy about 75 miles (120 km) northeast of Venice; close to the Austrian border of the Alps. An early engineering career shifted to succeeding his father as director of the Municipal Theatre in Ferrara, followed as managing director at the historic *La Scala* opera house. In Milan from 1898 to 1908, he established a tradition of artistic quality while keeping the finances profitable. Gatti-Casazza proven years of financial success brought the same fortitude to the Metropolitan Opera House in New York. Within a few years in New York, Gatti-Casazza established "a sound financial base" while not sacrificing performance quality. The position earned him not only respect among many of the cultural elite; also from Italian immigrants. As such the position in New York earned Gatti-Casazza distinction as "the first Italian to direct at the Metropolitan."

As a hint at the prevailing images of Italians in America, *Time* added, many of the current Metropolitan "customers thought the opera staff should have patriotically selected an American." As an added note to cultural stereotypes, *Time* stated "the Germans were powerful and combative" leading an ongoing "New York opera feud between the Italians and the Germans." American music critics preferred the German born Andreas Dippel (1866-1932) as manager.[375]

---

[375] *Time* magazine November 5, 1923, Vol. 11 No. 10.

Above Left: *Time* magazine November 5, 1923 featuring Giulio Gatti-Casazza. (Wiki Commons cites "Public Domain" published before January 1, 1926.) **Above Right**: "Photograph of Giulio Gatti-Casazza (1869-1940), an Italian opera manager who directed the Metropolitan Opera in New York City from 1908-1935." Reproduction No. LC-DIG-ggbain-33214 from George Grantham Bain Collection. Library of Congress Prints and Photographs Division.

Native critics expressed concern over the selection of opera productions would only consist of Italian operas. Other critics worried "the rule of an Italian would mean the ruin of Wagnerian opera at the Metropolitan." The controversy was cited in his *New York Times* obituary of 1940, recalling,

> "At the beginning of his tenure as manager, Gatti-Casazza had to fight against the many stereotypes that circulated about Italians. For example, as long as Italians fell into the above categories (singers, directors, set designers) the American press's comments were mostly inclined to benevolence; on the contrary, when Gatti-Casazza was offered the opportunity to become general manager of the most important opera house in the United States, the reactions were negative. Many American music critics would have preferred to have a German manager."[376]

That concern was waylaid as the recent Italian immigrant was offered a conditional one-year contract with a stipulation of "co-partnership with Andreas Dippel, who directed the German operas." The situation was resolved at the end

---

[376] "Gatti-Casazza Dies at 71," Obituary *The New York Times.* September 3, 1940.

CHAPTER 7A 291

of the first season as "Gatti" was offered a contract as the sole managing director; lasting from 1908 to 1935. Under "Gatti-Casazza's guidance the German operas grew better." Lost in the brouhaha was the fact Gatti was not wedded to only Italian opera, he favored any quality Italian, French, or German opera. While at *La Scala* in Milan he was known to have "made a specialty of Wagner."

A contributing factor to Gatti's success was not focusing on a "star system" to attract and audience. A pattern began with 1908 productions; all focused upon "orchestra, chorus, ballet, and production." During Gatti-Casazza's first year as manager, the backing chorus reached a "high standard" of excellence under the direction of a newly hired Italian immigrant Giulio Setti (1869-1938); a position that continued for twenty-seven years until retiring to Italy. In the ensuing years, a tradition arose earning distinction as "the Metropolitan had always enjoyed a fine orchestra." Musical stability for maintaining the quality orchestra was insured by one caveat. Prior to accepting the position as managing director, Gatti-Casazza insisted upon a stipulation written into the contract to hire the Italian orchestra conductor Arturo Toscanini. An additional irony to the ongoing German-Italian debate did not reveal the Italian Toscanini was world renowned as a Wagnerian conductor. (The orchestra conductor was not limited to Toscanini, Gatti also retained other "first-rate" conductors of Italian, French, and German origin.) Diversity added to the ongoing success and was maintained throughout Gatti's long tenure. Announcing the first week schedule for the Metropolitan opera season, as an example, offered a mix of Italian, French, and German opera. A commentary noted in the *Time* magazine article announced, "It is the 16th year of Mr. Gatti-Casazza's directorship. Deficits, the bane of opera, are not heard of." After 27 year of successful presentation of quality opera at the Metropolitan Opera in New York, Gatti-Casazza, retired to the land of his birth. Cited as a world-class *impresario*, he died in the city of Ferrara, Italy at the age of 71. A posthumous autobiography *Memories of the Opera* was published in 1941. A major legacy of *impresario* Giulio Gatti-Casazza's success included the long tenure of Arturo Toscanini.[377]

Conductor: Arturo Toscanini

Arturo Toscanini (1867-1957), as "one of the most acclaimed musicians of the late 19th and of the 20th century," was born in Parma in northern Italy midway between Milan and Cremona. Toscanini studied in various musical conservatories. Early studies mastered the cello. Among a travelling orchestra group of Italian musicians performing in Rio de Janeiro, some unforeseen circumstances enlisted a young Toscanini into service as temporary conductor for Giuseppe Verdi's "Aida." Somewhere between legend and fact, the 19-year-old

---

[377] *Time* magazine November 5, 1923, Vol. 11 No. 10 .

Toscanini conducted "from memory." A succinct summation of Arturo Toscanini provided by Will Crutchfield, Director of the Historical Teatro Nuovo, states,

> "More than fifty years after his final performance, Toscanini – known for his photographic memory, strong beliefs in music interpretation, and demand for perfection – reigns supreme as one of the world's greatest conductors. From 1908 to 1915, he conducted at the Metropolitan Opera House. In 1926, he began conducting with the New York Philharmonic Orchestra and led a European tour of the company in 1930. Seven years later, with plans to make radio educational and cultural, the NBC Symphony Orchestra was created for Toscanini. Many credit him today for bringing classical music to the masses."

Toscanini's talent was evident; quickly rising in prominence. In 1898, he earned an appointment as musical director in Milan at *La Scala*. In Milan, he paired with director Giulio Gatti-Casazza which led to Toscanini's tenure at the Metropolitan Opera House in New York from 1908 to 1915. After a return to Italy, he was back in America conducting the New York Philharmonic Symphony Orchestra (which lasted from 1928 to 1936). Toscanini's widespread fame was aided by the development of radio.[378]

Top Left: Photograph of Italian conductor Arturo Toscanini, c. 1900. **Top Right**: Dinner in honor of Giulio Gatti Casazza and Arturo Toscanini, at the Hotel St. Regis in New York City on November 22, 1908. U.S. Library of Congress.

Guglielmo Marconi and Radio

A major factor for presenting opera to a wider audience was radio; owing its creation to an Italian born in Bologna Italy named Guglielmo Marconi (1874-

---

[378] Virginia Gorlinski. "Arturo Toscanini." *Encyclopedia Britannica*, March 21, 2021.

1937). An initial patent in 1896, known as a "wireless telegraph," was obtained after demonstrating wireless transmission and receiving. The U.S. Library of Congress traces the first transmission of signals across the Atlantic to 1901; soon leading to a 1909 Nobel Prize Award for Marconi. In 1920, the first commercial wireless broadcast by radio station KDKA in Pittsburgh allowed for inexpensive in-home entertainment.

Radio became the main proponent as a cultural influence among the American people. By the mid-1920s, wide-spread installation of telephone lines made it possible for simultaneous live radio broadcasting known as "networking." Radio was an inexpensive entertainment; requiring only the initial purchase of the device and a few cents for electricity. All social classes, rural and urban, had a wide array of programs to choose, including adventure shows, drama programs, newscasts, comedy, sporting events, musical concerts, comedy, and religious sermons, among others. Those who could not visit a ballpark, or vaudeville theater, or an opera, all shared in the same experience. By 1929, over 600 radio stations regularly broadcast commercial programs to over 12 million households.[379]

Above Left: Guglielmo Marconi photographed by Pach Brothers, c. 1908. Library of Congress. Reproduction No: LC-USZ62-39702.
Above Right: First radio transmitter built by Marconi in August 1895. (From "Looking Back over Thirty Years of Radio," *Radio Broadcast* magazine.
Vol. 10, No. 1, November 1926, p. 31. (Public Domain)

---

[379] Giordano, *Fun and Games in Twentieth Century America*, pp. 59-60.

294　　　　　　　　　　Italian Culture in America:
The Immigrants 1880 to 1930 From Discrimination to Assimilation

Popularity of radio could be attributed to the fact it allowed an escape into a fantasy world of entertainment, thereby forgetting the hardship of daily life; all with little or no cost. The freedom of turning a dial for alternative programing allowed a family to experience new forms of entertainment without an added expense of a ticket purchase for a live event. Radio broadcast "live events" such as the NBC Symphony Orchestra conducted by Arturo Toscanini. In order to accommodate the large "NBC Symphony Orchestra" a broadcast studio was built in Rockefeller Center housing Radio City Music Hall and the NBC Radio Studios.

Radio broadcasts increased Toscanini's fame among a growing number of the American people who did not have the means to attend an opera or classical performance; such as impoverished Italian immigrants. For Toscanini, as director of the NBC Symphony Orchestra, Virginia Gorlinski adds, "this led to his becoming a household name through his radio and television broadcasts and many recordings of the operatic and symphonic repertoire." The Radio Corporation of America (RCA) sponsored a symphony orchestra airing weekly musical broadcasts - many conducted by Arturo Toscanini. The program aired through World War II into the post war period. Around 1950, "Studio 8H" was converted to a TV studio, with the symphony relocated to the equally famous Carnegie Hall. In 1975, Studio 8H became the location for a new late-night weekly television show *Saturday Night Live*; for over 45 years.[380]

The Metropolitan Opera House vs.
The Manhattan Opera House

Arturo Toscanini and Giulio Gatti-Casazza had a prestigious building in the Metropolitan Opera House New York. The U.S. Library of Congress states the significance as, "The Metropolitan Opera House was the home of the Metropolitan Opera Company from 1883 until 1966 and during these eighty-three years played an important role in operatic tradition."

Successful opera performances in New York City, was evidenced by many productions staged at the Metropolitan Opera House, prompting other venues to compete. In 1906, a new theater opened at 311 West 34th Street under the auspices of famed musical lyricist and theater producer Oscar Hammerstein (1895-1960), known simply as "The Manhattan Opera House." The venue offered quality opera performances. For a few years, the two Manhattan theaters engaged in a heated competition for sole recognition as the leading opera house in New York. Newspapers and magazines often chronicled the competition between Giulio Gatti-Casazza of the Metropolitan Opera House and Oscar Hammerstein's Manhattan Opera House. Some publications such as the sarcastic *Puck Magazine* parodied the dispute in a November 11, 1908 cover illustration "Grand Opera

---

[380] Virginia Gorlinski. "Arturo Toscanini." March 21, 2021.

Opens." The illustration portrayed Gatti-Casazza and Hammerstein throwing puppets of opera performers at each other. Fortunately, the feud did not turn violent; nor did it simmer for a long time.

The Metropolitan Opera House, c. 1905, at 1423 Broadway between West 39th and West 40th Streets in New York City. Detroit Photographic Company. Library of Congress Reproduction No. LC-D401-18310.

The Manhattan Opera House at 311 West 34th Street in New York City, c. 1900-1910, by: Detroit Publishing Co Library of Congress.

A sarcastic "Illustration shows Giulio Gatti-Casazza and Oscar Hammerstein throwing puppets labeled Tenor, Second Tenor, Contralto, Baritone, Basso, Mezzo Soprano, [and] High Soprano at each other. "Grand Opera Opens," *Puck Magazine*, November 11, 1908, Vol. LXIV No. 1654. Reproduction No. LC-DIG-ppmsca-26320. Library of Congress Prints and Photographs Division Washington, D.C.

CHAPTER 7A

ENRICO CARUSO: "The World's Greatest Tenor"

Of the many opera stars rising to prominence in America many are forgotten to history – one however is not. Any opera aficionado or music historian would be hard-pressed to dispute the lasting legendary fame of tenor Enrico Caruso (1873-1921). It could also be safely assumed, even among non-opera fans, name recognition exists. Without any dispute, Caruso *was* the greatest tenor of his time; and possibly remains to the present day *as* the greatest tenor of all-time. To understand the vocal range of a "Tenor," the Oxford Standard Dictionary describes,

> **ten·or** /ˈtenər/ *noun* singing voice between baritone and alto or countertenor, the highest of any adult male range.[381]

The vocal range of tenor applied to Enrico Caruso, was described by culture editor at *Encyclopaedia Britannica*, Gloria Lotha as,

> "Sensuous, lyrical, and vigorous in dramatic outbursts and became progressively darker in timbre in his later years. Its appealing tenor qualities were unusually rich in lower registers abounded in warmth, vitality, and smoothness."

Henricus "Enrico" Caruso (1873-1921) was born into a poor Italian family in Naples of seven children. (Baptismal records list birth name as "Henricus" which is a Neapolitan version of "Enrico.") Caruso did not receive any formal vocal training until he was 18 years of age. At that time, he studied with a local voice teacher named Guglielmo Vergine. Many sources cite Vergine suggesting a name change to "Enrico." Similar information cites Vergine as teaching the young Caruso without payment; the caveat was a promise of twenty-five percent of Caruso earnings for the first five years of a professional career.[382]

Caruso's opera debut came in March of 1885, at the age of 22, in *L'Amico Francesco* at the Teatro Nuovo in Naples which dates to 1724. By 1900, Caruso achieved acclaim in a prominent debut at *Teatro alla La Scala* in Milan. The debut was part of a musical tribute organized by Arturo Toscanini, at the time musical director of *La Scala*. The following year, Caruso sang in his hometown of Naples, however a bad review led to a lifetime vow "never again to sing in Naples." By that time, Caruso's fame was known in many parts of the world, garnering singing international engagements. In November 1903, Caruso sailed to America; with an opening night debut in *Rigoletto* at the Metropolitan Opera in New York; a pairing for 18 seasons, with 607 performances ending on Christmas Eve of 1920, singing in the role of "Eléazar" in *La Juive* ("The Jewess"). a five-act opera by

---

[381] Oxford Standard Dictionary. Accessed April 25, 2022.
[382] "Enrico Caruso." *Encyclopedia Britannica*, February 21, 2021.

French composer Fromental Halévy (1799-1862). At the time of his New York debut, historian Amy Tikkanen, said "Caruso became the most celebrated and highest paid of his contemporaries worldwide. He made recordings of about 200 operatic excerpts and songs; many of them are still being published."

Original Caption: "Caruso with phonograph," Library of Congress Prints and Photographs Division. Reproduction No. LC-DIG-ggbain-29835.

Historian Giuliana Muscio, writing on "The Long Tradition of Italian Immigrant Performers," reflects upon Enrico Caruso as,

"An unmatched ambassador of Italian high culture. . . [who] established the primacy of Italian opera among the American upper and middle classes, while at the same time generating public awareness of his links to Italian immigrant communities and performers."

Caruso did not limit to only opera; he often sang and recorded traditional Neapolitan songs of poor southern Italians. A facet of his singing style known as *verismo*, (direct translation "realism") described by Muscio as, "a modern naturalism to his performances, an expressiveness and clarity to his recordings." As defined by the Oxford Standard Dictionary,

ve·ris·mo – *noun* realism in the arts, especially late 19th-century Italian opera. verismo as a genre of opera, as composed by Puccini, Mascagni, and Leoncavallo.

Opera was previously a cultural art form appreciated among poor and working-class immigrants; it was not an "elitist" culture; yet it was Caruso who is considered the popular culture impetus who "introduced Italian opera to the living rooms of the upper and middle [social] classes;" while at the same time not dismissing the working class.[383]

Fame added to Caruso's ability to add his celebrity name promoting a wide-range of commercial products, such as musical instruments, food, and tobacco products. With an interest in an expanding technical and media advancing society, Caruso contracted with Famous Players-Lasky Corporation to film two movies, the first *My Cousin* released in 1918 in America and the second in 1919, *The Splendid Romance*; both by Belgian film director Edward José (1865-1930). The irony of these two movies – they were Silent Films; therefore, without Caruso's voice the movies did not do well financially. Actually, after the initial financial failure at the box office of *My Cousin*, the second feature *The Splendid Romance* was not released in America.

Three Images of Enrico Caruso. **Above Left**: In costume, c. 1908. Reproduction No. LC-USZ62-61497. **Center**: Half-length portrait photograph, c. November 1910, Reproduction No. LC-USZ62-61510. **Above Right**: In character costume dressed as a clown for *I Pagliacci*, circa 1908. Reproduction Number LC-USZ62-61515. Retrieved from the Library of Congress, Public Domain.

---

[383] Giuliana Muscio. "East Coast/West Coast: The Long Tradition of Italian Immigrant Performers," *eScholarship.org*. Accessed February 16, 2021.

A very unusual ironic twist of fate, Caruso died in a Naples hospital after undergoing an operation "for removal of an abscess between the liver and diaphragm, causing acute peritonitis." An obituary in the *Colorado Loveland Reporter* of August 2, 1921, "Enrico Caruso Famous Singer Dies in Naples," called him the "Man with the Golden Voice." A brief excerpt recounted events leading to untimely demise.

> "He was apparently recovering from his illness that began last winter [1920] when he burst a blood vessel in his throat and was compelled to retire from the stage during one of his entertainments. Caruso, after this, sometimes had trouble with his throat, which he usually overcame with a little rest and care and at certain intervals, rumors that "Caruso will never sing again," were frequently printed."

The unfortunate affliction occurred during a singing performance at the Brooklyn Academy of Music. Reports indicated in a short time Caruso "was stricken with pleurisy." The cause was due to many years of "strenuous opera seasons."[384]

His allocates on the opera stage spread far beyond his native Naples in Italy, across Europe, into America, and worldwide. Well-remembered over 100 years since his passing; least mentioned in the current day was his impact on the recording industry. *Encyclopedia Britannica* praises Caruso as, "the most admired Italian operatic tenor of the early 20th century and one of the first musicians to document his voice on recordings." Very few, if any, recording artists can claim having their original recordings released so many years after their death. Author, educator, and researcher Janice Therese Mancuso explains,

> "Recognized by many as the world's most acclaimed tenor, Caruso's recordings launched the phonograph industry and prompted other singers to start recording their music for sale. His recordings have been researched and studied more than any other singer."

Caruso's recording of *Vesti La Giubba* from Act I of *I Pagliacci* was the first to sell over one million copies.

During the early 1900s, a thriving commercial market existed in the United States for Italian American vocal music. Author Mark Rotella, in *Amore: The Story of Italian American Song,* cites Caruso's recording "would determine the course of how music was recorded, and, through the purchasing power of its millions of listeners, how records were bought." In 1987, more than a half-century after the death of the world famous tenor, the National Academy of Recording Arts & Sciences ("Grammy Award") posthumously conferred a Lifetime

---

[384] "Enrico Caruso Famous Singer Dies in Naples," *Colorado Loveland Reporter.*

CHAPTER 7A

Achievement Award upon Enrico Caruso for artistic contributions to the recording industry.[385]

A living tribute to the great Neapolitan exists in the 21st century at the Enrico Caruso Museum of America. Located in a private home in the Homecrest / Sheepshead Bay neighborhood of Brooklyn, Aldo Mancusi maintains a vast collection of original memorabilia. Founded in 1989, Mancusi states the mission of the museum as,

> "Built in tribute to the first and the most famous operatic tenor in the world. Our museum proudly displays several rare items: records, heirlooms, and we also provide a theater where you can view rare films of Enrico Caruso."

In December of 2014, as a result of his dedication to preserving the legacy of Caruso as a distinct form of Italian culture, Mancusi was bestowed the honor "Commendatore" (equivalent to the title of "Knighthood") by the Italian government in recognition of his personal "contribution to the arts community, both in America and in Italy."[386]

Mancusi may curate a museum, however many of Caruso's recordings are not extinct, as they are readily available and continue to sell into the 21st century. In addition, the U.S. Library of Congress maintains a large collection of digitized songs and sheet music readily available to the public. The curators of the Library of Congress state,

> "The rich musical heritage that the Italian immigrants brought with them has had a major impact on shaping United States culture as a whole; Italian Americans and Italian nationals who have spent significant amounts of time in the United States have played an important role in both classical and popular music in the United States."

Enrico Caruso was the first paving the way for Italian immigrant singers. The path of assimilation and cultural acceptance, for many, came through the popular music and songs by Italians and children of Italian immigrants. As an additional point of information, the Library of Congress adds,

> "By 1940, more music and language recordings had been made by Italian Americans than by any other non-English-speaking group. In the 1940s and 1950s, Italian American vocal music entered mainstream [American] culture."

---

[385] Mark Rotella. *Amore*, p 12. "Italian American Song." *The Library of Congress,* January 9, 2021.
[386] See: Aldo Mancusi. "The Enrico Caruso Museum of America," c. 2020. Accessed May 5, 2021.

During the formative years of World War II and after, a significant number of singers of Italian heritage became endeared in American popular culture. Some included were Frankie Avalon, Tony Bennett, Perry Como, Vic Damone, Bobby Darin, Dion DiMucci, Fabian Forte, Annette Funicello, Dean Martin, Louis Prima, Bobby Rydell, and Frank Sinatra, among countless others. Each were household names in America. In prior years, many of the well-publicized opera stars were forgotten including, Lina Cavalieri, Antonio Pini-Corsi, Josephine Lucchese, Gaetano Merola, and Rosa Ponselle, to name just a few.[387]

Above Left: An array of the vast memorabilia in "The Enrico Caruso Museum of America" in Brooklyn, New York. **Above Right**: *Commendatore* Aldo Mancusi, founder and curator, poses alongside a bust of Enrico Caruso, c. 2020. (Photographs courtesy of Aldo Mancusi and TJ Borriello.)

ONCE FAMOUS BUT MOSTLY FORGOTTEN

The French Can-Can Dance and the "Great Morlacchi"

The Can-Can Dance is as French as any cultural phenomenon; as Italian as any immigrant adding to American culture is Giuseppina Morlacchi. The connection of the two very diverse cultural norms is credited to Morlacchi introducing the

---

[387] "Italian American Song." *The Library of Congress*, Accessed January 9, 2021.

enduring Can-Can dance to America. Giuseppina Antonia "Josephine" Morlacchi (1836/46-1886) born in Milan was educated as a ballerina at La Scala. In 1856, debut came at the Teatro Carlo Felice opera house in Genoa, Italy. Described as a "prima ballerina" Morlacchi was "one of the most refined and well-regarded women of her profession." Part of a well-known touring company throughout Europe, the young dancer was persuaded by manager Don Juan "John" DePol to travel to America." An 1867 debut in New York City was performed under the Americanized name of "Josephine." Morlacchi set upon a nationwide tour billed as the Morlacchi Ballet Troupe in first-rate venues from 1867 to 1872.

Within a few months, Morlacchi was the most sought-after dancer in the nation. Biographer Chris Enss writing "Wild Women of the West: Giuseppina Morlacchi," for *Cowgirl Magazine*, cited an 1867 article in *The New York Evening Transcript* proclaiming,

> "The Great Morlacchi whose power of thoughtful, fanciful dancing – music addressed to the eye – has never been equaled by any artist who has visited the country. She has sparked an excitement among the most cultivated classes of our citizens and everyone wants to see her perform."[388]

One January 1868, newspaper reports cited Morlacchi and a few others, performed the high-energy Can-Can dance in Boston. Descendant Rick Omohundro said, "The sheer enthusiasm of the dance and Giuseppina's interpretation left them breathless." Omohundro described an "onstage persona was vibrant and unreserved; off-stage she was quiet and shy. The dichotomy that made her public adore her." As a result, Morlacchi's fame grew even more widespread.[389] The popular dance still prevalent in the 21st century, is defined by Merriam-Webster dictionary as,

> ***Cancan*** / **noun** can·can | \ 'kan-ˌkan \ : a woman's dance of French origin characterized by high kicking usually while holding up the front of a full ruffled skirt.

The Can-Can is most often performed in a chorus line with high kicks (and sometimes cartwheels) revealing the petticoat underneath a woman's dress. Despite credited to the French, the origin of the dance is unknown; most trace it to the 1840s music halls of France, such as the world-famous Moulin Rouge in Paris. Of the Can-Can, biographer Matthew Kerns writing on "Morlacchi's American Debut" said,

---

[388] Chris Enss. "Wild Women of the West: Giuseppina Morlacchi," *Cowgirl Magazine*.
[389] Rick Omohundro. "Giuseppina Antonia 'Josephine' Morlacchi Omohundro." *Find-A-Grave*, April 14, 2013.

"The dance was a sensation, and the night after it was introduced proved to the theater's highest grossing night ever. Morlacchi, already regarded as the best dancer in America, became one of its biggest stars. Using her new fame, Morlacchi started her own ballet troupe . . . to tour across America, with long stands in New York, Boston, Chicago, San Francisco, and many major cities."[390]

On the cusp and overlapping "The Great Arrival" of Italians to America, Giuseppina Morlacchi was one of the most famous dancers in America. As such, Morlacchi was sought after by many promoters.

"Giuseppina Morlacchi" The New York Public Library Digital Collections. From a book published by Henry Atwell Thomas, c. 1860-1869. Jerome Robbins Dance Division, The New York Public Library Digital Collection 1860 - 1869. (Public Domain)

One of the most famous of the time contracted with Morlacchi was Ned Buntline (1821-1886), a publisher, author, and promoter. Buntline created idealized fictious versions of the American West, Cowboys, Cowgirls, and Indians through "Dime Novels," newspaper articles, and stage shows. Buntline's lore permeated

---

[390] Matthew Kerns. "Morlacchi's American Debut." *The Dime Library*, January 19, 2021.

into a "compendium of cliches" of the Old West deeply imbedded into American culture. Buntline's fiction gave rise to American cultural legends such as Buffalo Bill, Texas Jack, and Annie Oakley. Two legends of American culture William "Buffalo Bill" Cody (1846-1917) and John Baker "Texas Jack" Omohundro (1846-1880), both served as real-life Frontier Scouts. From a dose of reality of the frontier scouts, Buntline added all sorts of fictional images such as the nicknames of "Buffalo Bill" and "Texas Jack." In 2021, biographer Matthew Kerns called Texas Jack Omohundro "America's First Cowboy Star [and] the genesis of the American cowboy in popular culture."[391]

Souvenir postcard for "The Scouts of the Prairie," c. 1872/3. **Left to Right**: Ned Buntline, William "Buffalo Bill" Cody, Giuseppina Morlacchi, and John Baker "Texas Jack" Omohundro. Photograph attributed to Italian American Carlo Gentile. (Public Domain)

Annie Oakley (1860-1926), born Phoebe Ann Moses, was billed as a "sharpshooter" and memorialized in American Culture with the 19th century Wild West Shows and years later in a very popular 1946 Broadway musical "Annie Get Your Gun." The fictious legacy spurred a successful Hollywood movie (dir.

---

[391] Matthew Kerns. "The Scouts of the Prairie." *The Dime Library*, December 16, 2019.

George Sydney, 1950), a series of made for television movies, revivals on Broadway, local theater productions, and countless High School productions across the nation. Annie Oakley was not the first female in the Wild West Shows of either Ned Buntline or Buffalo Bill Cody; that honor belongs to Giuseppina Morlacchi.

By December 1872, Morlacchi in the role of an American Indian princess named "Dove Eye" was billed "as a feature attraction" in Ned Buntline's production of the western drama *The Scouts of the Prairie*. Professor Andrea Harris explained, Buntline's production "marked the beginning of a performance genre that would have significant impact on the American national imagination." As the character of the Indian Princess Dove Eye, Prof. Harris cited a *New York Evening Transcript* at the time proclaiming, "[Morlacchi] has sparked an excitement among the most cultivated of our citizens and everyone wants to see her perform." A Boston newspaper review concurred, "Many of the refined and cultivated people . . . whose knowledge of art has been perfected by European experiences have been the first in America to detect the genius of this danseuse." Another Boston reviewer said of Morlacchi, "In the opening piece . . . she danced exquisitely and with all her accustomed grace and skill, and the audience recognized her merit and called her before the curtain accordingly."[392]

The "Western Duo" of Morlacchi and Omohundro settled in Lowell, Massachusetts with "an additional home in Leadville, Colorado." Between performance tours, of Buntline and Cody productions, Morlacchi often danced solo and with her own Morlacchi Ballet Troupe in "opera house for productions of *Ahmed* and her own production of *La Bayadère*." Two other La Scala trained Italian ballerina's Rita Sangalli (1849-1909) and Marie Bonfanti (1845-1921) were contemporaries. In 1901, a report in *The New York Times* for "Revival of the Ballet," reported Sangalli and Bonfanti performed together at the Metropolitan Opera House, "during the inaugural season of ballet." By then, Morlacchi was deceased. In 1880, upon the death of "Texas Jack" Omohundro the Italian ballerina retired from performing. During the final years of her life, she lived "quietly with her sister [and] teaching ballet lessons in Lowell, Massachusetts."[393]

---

[392] Andrea Harris. "*Sur la Pointe* on the Prairie: Giuseppina Morlacchi and the Urban Problem in the Frontier Melodrama." *The Journal of American Drama and Theatre (JADT)*, Vol. 27 No. 1. Harris cites the quote from: Barbara Barker. *Ballet or Ballyhoo*, p. 121.

[393] "Revival of the Ballet." *The New York Times*, September 1, 1901, p. SM3.

Staged promotional scene from *The Scouts of the Prairie* of Texas Jack Omohundro and Giuseppina Morlacchi, c. 1875. The photograph listed as "unknown author" may also be attributed to Italian American photographer was Carlo Gentile. (Public Domain)

Carlo Gentile: An Italian Photographer

As part of the popular promotion Italian photographer Carlo "Charles" Gentile (1835–1893) was hired by Ned Buntline to photograph, for sale, promotional photographs of *The Scouts of the Prairie*. Born in Naples, Italy, Gentile inherited a significant sum of money upon his father's death in 1856. Subsequently, Gentile embarked as a world traveler. Along the way, he developed an interest in photography. One early type included small postcard like images such as those created for *The Scouts of the Prairie*. In 1867, Gentile's perked an interest leading him to the "Gold Fields" of California. Biographer Cesare Marino in *The Remarkable Carlo Gentile* tells of frequent moves between California and Arizona. In 1871, an interesting account tells of Gentile "purchasing" a young boy named Wassaja, who became his adopted son. The pair "participated" in some of the Western productions along with Buffalo Bill and Ned Buntline.

Above Left: Carlo "Charles" Gentile produced promotional photographs of *The Scouts of the Prairie*. Date unknown. **Above Right**: Gentile's adopted son Wassaja known as "Carlos Montezuma" c. 1890. (U.S. National Archives and Records Administration).

Gentile's continued as a photographer moving to Chicago, and involved in publishing Italian language newspapers. He founded the Photographer's Association of America; later lobbying for a photography exhibit at the 1893 Chicago World's Columbian Exposition. Gentile also recognized his "son" needed an advantage. Wassaja was renamed Carlos Montezuma and was the first Native American Indian graduate of the University of Illinois. Wassaja continued to the Chicago Medical College, becoming the first Native American male to earn a medical degree.[394]

---

[394] Cesare Marino. *The Remarkable Carlo Gentile*, 1998.

Rosa Ponselle:
"One of the greatest sopranos of the 20th Century"

Lesser-known, yet famous was Rosa Ponselle (nee: Ponzillo, 1897-1981) born in Meriden, Connecticut, "populated by immigrants from the south of Italy." Italian parents immigrated from Caiazzo, about 30 miles (50km) north of Naples. As a teen, she often played piano for silent movies; sometimes singing between movie reels. At age 16, Ponselle appeared in Vaudeville singing with sister Carmela billed as "The Ponzillo Sisters;" Followed by a long stint at the *San Carlino* theater in New Haven Carmela, a mezzo-soprano later sang opera at the Metropolitan Opera House. A name change to "Ponselle" came during Rosa's opera debut.

Above Left: Rosa Ponselle about 18 years old. **Above Right**: Publicity photo of Rosa Ponselle as "Lenora" falling into the arms of Enrico Caruso in *La forza del destino*, by Giuseppe Verdi, during her opera debut in 1918 at the Metropolitan Opera.

Soprano Rosa Ponselle, at the age of 21, garnered an operatic coup, debuting in her first ever role as "Leonora" in Giuseppe Verdi's *La Forza del Destino* ("The Force of Destiny") on the stage of the Metropolitan Opera. The role was secured at the bequest of Enrico Caruso, who "was deeply impressed" by Ponselle's voice; leading to a personal recommendation to appear opposite Caruso. The ever amorous and notoriously unfaithful Caruso may have been captivated by Ponselle's beauty. Without formal training, Ponselle's vocal talent proved worthy

310

Italian Culture in America:
The Immigrants 1880 to 1930 From Discrimination to Assimilation

of the difficult role of "Leonora." Biographer Mary Jane Phillips-Matz described the role was "a dramatic soprano part usually reserved for experienced singers whose voices have grown gradually over the years to requisite richness and size." On the Metropolitan Opera stage, Ponselle's voice captivated the audience. A career at the Metropolitan for nineteen seasons included twenty-two different roles. Ponselle traveled the Atlantic performing in London and Florence, Italy. A final performance at the Metropolitan in February 1937 was in the title role of Bizet's "Carmen."

Ponselle may have ended live performances, yet stayed close to both singing and opera for many years thereafter. Absent from the stage, she married and lived in an estate near Baltimore. Ponselle assumed the role as "artistic director of the Baltimore Opera." In doing so, serving as a teacher and mentor to "many aspiring singers." She continued to record into the mid-1950s, and often appeared on radio broadcasts. One biographer claimed, "Those later recordings are of a voice that was still rich, though darker and of a more limited range than it had been."[395]

Mainly forgotten by the general public, in later years after a series of strokes, Ponselle was confined to a wheelchair. Journalist Allen Hughes writing her obituary for *The New York Times*, cited Rosa Ponselle, as "indisputably one of the greatest operatic talents this country has ever produced." Despite her fading from public view, she is often considered "one of the greatest sopranos of the 20th Century." In 1981, almost 45 years after Ponselle stopped performing, Hughes wrote in praise,

> "An operatic career that lasted less than 20 years, Miss Ponselle made an indelible impression through the impact of her phenomenal voice. It was a dramatic soprano that seemed to move seamlessly from low notes of a contralto to a dazzling high C. She had coloratura flexibility, a splendid trill, powerful fortes, delicate pianissimos and precise intonation."

In celebration of Ponselle's 75th birthday, music critic Harold Schonberg (1915-2003) wrote, "That big, pure colorful golden voice would rise effortlessly, hitting the stunned listener in the face, rolling over the body making one wiggle with sheer physiological pleasure."[396]

Lina Cavalieri: "The Most Beautiful Woman in the World"

In 2018, the Salvatore Ferragamo Museum in Florence, Italy, display of "Italy in Hollywood," showcased various exhibits "each highlighting a distinctive theme of Italian-American culture. The focus, according to cultural historian Samantha Vaughn, "tackles all manner of questions surrounding mass Italian immigration

---

[395] Mary Jane Phillips-Matz. *Rosa Ponselle: American Diva*, p. 119.
[396] Allen Hughes, "Rosa Ponselle, Dramatic Soprano Dies," p. C24.

at the turn of the 20th century, from stereotypes to inspiration." One exhibit praised four of the biggest Italian stars of the era, actress/photographer Tina Modotti, actor Rudolph Valentino; Opera singers Enrico Caruso and Lina Cavalieri.

Above Left: Lina Cavalieri, promotional photograph, c. 1900. **Above Right**: "Lina Cavalieri, full-length portrait, standing, facing front wearing gown and long beaded necklace," c. 1914. Photograph. Retrieved from the Library of Congress,

---

The fame, legacy, and influence of Caruso and Valentino lived on well beyond their untimely deaths. Unfortunately, the fame of Tina Modotti and Lina Cavalieri did not; each remains to a lesser degree and partial obscurity, other than devotees of similar professions. Across the Ocean in Italy, the curators at the *Museo Salvatore Museum* "understand the great love Americans had for these figures; [and] the impact Lina Cavalieri had on aesthetics long after her death."

Natalina "Lina" Cavalieri (1874-1944) was born in Viterbo, Lazio region of Italy about 60 miles (100km) northwest of Rome. Biographical information on her formative years is sketchy; many agree she was born into a poor family. Both parents may have died when she was a teenager; providing credence for living in a Catholic orphanage managed by nuns. At a young age, working at odd jobs and singing in and around Rome, a voice teacher was enthralled and arranged professional training.[397]

---

[397] Samantha Vaughn. "Italy in Hollywood Exhibition," *The Florentine.net*, Also: Ashot Arakelyan. "Lina Cavalieri (Soprano)," *Forgotten Opera Singers* Blog April 29, 2012.

312   Italian Culture in America:
The Immigrants 1880 to 1930 From Discrimination to Assimilation

An opera debut in 1900 moved forward; including a performance at the *Opéra de Monte-Carlo* in 1904. An article in *Italian Ways* stated,

> "Although her vocal range was not extraordinary, presence on stage helped her stand out on the most important opera theaters in the world, from the San Carlo in Naples to the Imperial Theater in Warsaw, from the Massimo in Palermo to the São Carlos in Lisbon, from London's Covent Garden to Genoa's Carlo Felice, from the Sarah Bernhardt in Paris to the Metropolitan in New York."

Critics might overlook Cavalieri, as "forgotten," due to a short singing career of less than two decades. It is hard to discount her performance as the female lead appearing opposite the great Enrico Caruso more than once. In 1905, in *I Fedora* composed by Umberto Giordano (1867-1948) with a libretto by Arturo Colautti (1851-1914) in Paris.[398]

In 1906, the production company sailed to America to perform *I Fedora* at the New York Metropolitan Opera House – once again with the leads of Enrico Caruso and Lina Cavalieri. In January of 1907, the duo performed Puccini's adaptation of *Manon Lescaut.* Of the performance the Director of Archives for the Metropolitan Opera Peter Clark states,

> "Enrico Caruso, already idolized by audiences, assured a public success . . . while the title role was taken by Lina Cavalieri, an Italian soprano reputed to be the "world's most beautiful woman." While Caruso's talents were undeniably vocal, Cavalieri's laurels were, by most critical observers, due in large part to her physical appearance.

Operas by Umberto Giordano were some of the many featuring Lina Cavalieri. An opera website *Italian Ways* recalls a December 1906 occurrence, which may or not have been spontaneous. During one special performance, "Lina Cavalieri gave tenor Enrico Caruso a passionate kiss in front of an astounded audience, caught completely by surprise by the opera singer's intense gesture." The "kiss" brought Cavalieri great publicity; soon becoming "one of the most photographed stars of her time." The moniker of "the world's most beautiful woman," was adopted and turned into a profitable celebrity career.[399]

Cavalieri's opera career was bracketed with appearances in movies and vocal recordings. One Columbia Records advertisement described, "The world-famous dramatic Soprano sings exclusively for the Columbia. Heard on Columbia Records her voice is the living voice of Cavalieri – rich, clear, sweet and unmistakable."

---

[398] "Lina Cavalieri and the Most Beautiful Kiss in the World," *Italian Ways*, 2017.
[399] "Lina Cavalieri and the Most Beautiful Kiss in the World," *Italian Ways*, 2017.

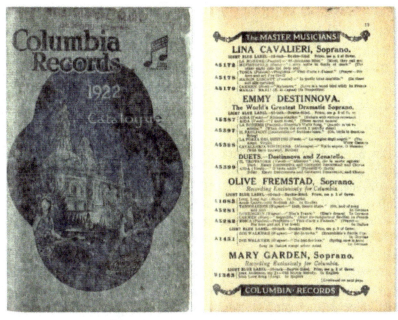

Above Left: Columbia Records 1922 Catalogue Cover. **Above Right**: Page 13 of the Columbia Records Catalogue listing three recordings for "Lina Cavalieri, Soprano." Public Domain.

Lina Cavalieri may not have been the greatest Soprano, if compared to the Italian Faustina Bordoni (1697-1781) who debuted in Venice in 1716. Bordoni is credited as the standard for the "diva stereotype." Nor was Cavalieri on the same range as her contemporary Rosa Ponselle (1897-1981); or as later day Maria Callas (1923-1977); or modern-day Renée Fleming (b. 1959) considered by many the greatest of all sopranos. Unlike the others, Cavalieri holds a special place both within opera history and beyond in American culture. Cavalieri understood the allure of celebrity status as influential among the public. Despite a limited vocal range, or what some might attribute as "luck in her career" due to her beauty, biographer John Haag explained the importance of Cavalieri prominently listed among Women in World History as, "A master at self-promotion, Cavalieri developed a great persona that attracted a wide public. Her voice was small scale but she made the most of all of her assets, particularly her great beauty."[400]

Foreshadowing a common 20th century advertising concept known as "Celebrity Branding," or 21st century "Influencer," Cavalieri's notoriety led to a significant number of beauty product endorsements such as Palmolive Soap and

---

[400] John Haag. "Lina Cavalieri: 1874-1944," 2021.

the Gellé Frères line of perfumes and body lotions. In 1909, Lina Cavalieri authored a series of beauty articles; "My Secrets of Beauty" was promoted by the *New York Herald* newspaper as,

> "MME. LINA CAVALIERI the famous beauty and the well-known grand opera soprano, who has made a life-long study of beauty culture, and has, indeed, herself worked out many recipes whose secrets are her own, has arranged to write for this newspaper a series of extremely interesting and valuable articles on the Secrets of Beauty."[401]

The newspaper column led a similar feature in 1911 on beauty advice for a French magazine *Femina*. A compilation of the articles was published in book-length as, "Lina Cavalieri: *My Secrets of Beauty*." Her column was published nationwide by the influential Hearst news corporation as "My Secrets of Beauty." The additional fame led to a successful opening of beauty shops in two prestigious locations; one located on Fifth Avenue in Manhattan, another on the famed Champs Élysées, in Paris.

Financial success led to opening other beauty salons in France and Italy. Her forte was a continuing to introduce new perfumes and beauty cosmetics such as lotions, lipsticks, rouge, mascara, and eye shadow, among "essentials." Cavalieri's opera performances may have been long over, yet her popularity carried on well after her stage career. Cavalieri relocated permanently to Europe, at first living in Paris managing her beauty shops; soon settling back in her birth country living in a villa near Florence in Italy. In 1936, she published an autobiography *Le mie veritá* ("My Truths").[402]

Life in Italy was somewhat unsettled by the events of World War II, subsequent Fascist rule, and German occupation. As a result of the war, Cavalieri suffered tragic fate in 1944, as she was killed in an Allied bombing raid. At the time, she was not soon forgotten. In October 1955, a film *La donna più bella del mondo* (dir. Robert Z. Leonard), translated as "The Most Beautiful Woman in the World," was released in Italy starring Gina Lollobrigida (1927-2023), in the lead role as "Lina Cavalieri."[403]

Antonio Pini-Corsi: *Baritono Brillante*

Many of the early Italian opera singers in America, such as Antonio Pini-Corsi (1858/59-1918), an internationally acclaimed *baritono brillante*, are mostly forgotten. Pini-Corsi lists at least 75 issues on Columbia Recording and Pathé

---

[401] James Bennett. "Lina Cavalieri: Cosmetics and Skin." *Cosmetics and Skin*. Also: Armstrong, "Lina Cavalieri, the famous beauty of the operatic stage," pp. 77- 78.
[402] See: Grace Hummel. "Parfumerie Lina Cavalieri," March 18, 2015.
[403] "Lina Cavalieri Biography," IMDb.com, 2021. Cavalieri and Paolo D'Arvanni. *Le mie veritá*, and *My Secrets of Beauty*, New York: The Circulation Syndicate, 1914.

Records from 1905 to 1909; that still exist. As researched by Will Crutchfield of General Director of *Teatro Nuovo*,

> "Antonio Pini-Corsi is remembered, if at all, for being the first Ford in *Falstaff* and the first Schaunard in *La Bohème*. And he was part of a lively, busy operatic sector that is even more forgotten than he is. How many Italian comic operas can you name between *Don Pasquale* and *Falstaff*? For most opera lovers the answer is zero. Pini-Corsi sang in twenty-seven."

Pini-Corsi, as one example, upon his death he took with him an "old-fashioned Italian opera style." Will Crutchfield described, "His style was derived from 19th-century Italian traditions of the *buffo caricato* (literally a "caricature comedian"), and in this he had no successors at all - so his 75 recordings are a fascinating glimpse of a vanished manner." Between bass and tenor is "Baritono Brillante . . . as the range and vocal equipment to sing a classic Verdi baritone part."

Antonio Pini-Corsi was born to Italian parents in Zara (later Zadar) a province of the Kingdom of Italy (now modern-day Croatia). Elizabeth Forbes in an extract for *Grove Music Online* cites an 1878 Italian debut in the Italian city of Cremona appearing as "Dandini" in the Rossini opera *La Cenerentola*. Performing professionally throughout Italy for about 15 years, Pini-Corsi achieved wide-acclaimed for many comedic opera roles, including "Alfonso" in *Favorita*; "Enrico" in *Lucia*; and "Alfredo Germont" in *La Traviata,* and others including some non-comedic roles.

Antonio Pini-Corsi (1858/59-1918) photo portrait c. 1914.
(Public Domain)

From a period from about 1892 to 1909, Pini-Corsi was well known, achieving the "height of his fame." Performances occurred in London, Buenos Aires, and New York. Information, some sketchy, is available from various sources as the U.S. *Library of Congress* list three sources as,

- Covent Garden on record, p1991: v. 1, container insert (Antonio Pini-Corsi; 1858-1918; Italian baritone);

- Baker, 7th ed. (Pini-Corsi, Antonio; b. June 1858, Zara, Italy; d. Apr. 22, 1918, Milan; Italian baritone);

- Grove music online, January 23, 2020 (Pini-Corsi, Antonio; born June 1858, Zara (now Zadar), Dalmatia; died April 22, 1918, Milan; Italian baritone).[404]

The *Discography of American Historical Recordings* at the University of California Santa Barbara Library, lists twenty-seven recordings, as,

"An Italian operatic baritone of international renown. He possessed a ripe-toned voice of great flexibility and displayed tremendous skill at patter singing. Pini-Corsi participated in numerous operatic premieres, creating such roles on stage as Ford in Giuseppe Verdi's *Falstaff* and Schaunard in Giacomo Puccini's *La Bohème*. Part of the first generation of recorded musicians, Pini-Corsi was one of the finest buffo singers of his era."[405]

Beyond the stage, Pini-Corsi may have been acutely aware of the severe Italian discrimination in America, such as the lynching of Italians in New Orleans 1891 and Tallulah, Louisiana in 1899. An online article posted by *Italian Sons & Daughters of America* "Italian folk singer by the name of Antonio Corso (1858/59-1918) wrote a song in honor" of the five Italians lynched in in Tallulah Louisiana. The information cannot be confirmed if the reference is an incorrect spelling, since the dates of birth and death do coincide with Antonio Pini-Corsi.[406]

Antonietta Pisanelli: "The Italian Colony's First *Impresario*"

Throughout the history of opera, female singers have certainly earned fame equal to male counterparts. Beyond the stage, it is rare to find a female *impresario*. One woman *impresario* was Antonietta Pisanelli (1869-?). In addition to singing and acting skills, the Bancroft Library at tells us, "The first major figure in Italian theater [in San Francisco] was Antonietta Pisanelli, who was the first established professional entertainer in the Italian community." Born in Naples, immigrating

---

[404]Will Crutchfield. "Brillante: Antonio Pini-Corsi." Elisabeth Forbes. "Pini-Corsi, Antonio (Opera)." *Grove Music Online.*

[405] "Pini-Corsi, Antonio, Discography." UC Santa Barbara Library, 7 June 2021.

[406] Elisabeth Forbes. "Pini-Corsi, Antonio (Opera)." *Grove Music Online.*

CHAPTER 7A 317

to New York sometime after 1900, Pisanelli began "singing, dancing, and acting" on various theater stages in cities such as New York, New Haven, and Philadelphia; continuing to the Midwest in Chicago and others.

Historian Maxine Seller explains, "In essence anywhere a significant Italian population settled, Pisanelli often found her way to the appeal of Italian immigrants by engaging performances of Neapolitan folk songs." As a *paisan* to the people of Naples, she was among thousands from the same region. The journey led to San Francisco, settling into the North Beach Italian community. Pisanelli's was were well received as she organized many performances catering to the local San Francisco Italian community. Eventually leasing other theaters, historian Maxine Seller tells us, Pisanelli continued "her career as manager, producer, director and star in San Francisco's first successful professional Italian theater." Accounts of the day indicate Pisanelli delivered professional performances.[407]

Historian Deanna Paoli Gumina cited, "The exciting performance marked the debut of the Italian colony's first impresario." Pisanelli monitored the creation of "the professional *Teatro Italiano* that became a central social institution in the half-century-old San Francisco Italian community." Gumina added,

> "Until Signora Pisanelli's presentation, Italian theater-goers had been entertained by amateur drama groups, composed of more and less talented volunteers from social clubs in the Italian colony. Despite the less than stellar quality, their performances were well-received by Italian audiences anxious to hear their favorite operatic arias and folk songs."

Maxine Seller confirmed the praise as Antonietta Pisanelli "went on to create singlehandedly, the Italian-American theatre of San Francisco."[408]

Pisanelli's career encompassed many talents as theater manager, producer, director, and sometimes star performer. From 1909 to 1914, she opened and operated the Washington Square Theater equal to any theater in the nation. Rather than extended runs of one opera, Pisanelli sought a wide array of performances, offering a different opera performance each night. In 1900, a vagabond journalist J.M. Scanland (1843-1935), known as an infamous writer of western lore on Wyatt Earp and others of the Old West, described a typical opera performance as, "Italians look upon opera as a necessity and also as an amusement, and they want it strong and good, artistically and musically. They care little for scenery-they want the acting, and upon this and the music everything depends." Operas chosen by Pisanelli were not obscure; rather famous productions such as *La Traviata* and *Rigoletto*; even a Shakespeare drama such as *Othello*. Sometimes a performance

---

[407] "Room Five: Italian Theater," 2007. Maxine Seller, pp 162-164.
[408] Deanna Paoli Gumina. *"Connazionali, Stenterello,* and *Farfariello*, p. 27.

318 Italian Culture in America:
The Immigrants 1880 to 1930 From Discrimination to Assimilation

included the popular Italian *Commedia dell'arte*. Pisanelli understood her California audience was not among the wealthy elite such as in New York, rather the North Beach community was comprised of southern Italian immigrants of limited means. As the 1920s progressed, so did a slow decline for demand of Italian theater. The reason was twofold; one the previous years coincided with the rising number of immigrants entering into America from 1880 through the 1920s. The secondary reason attributes a growing attempt to assimilate into American culture, mostly by the American born children of Italians; thereby rejecting traditional Old-world ways.[409]

Josephine Lucchese: "The American Nightingale" and Virginia Colombati

Opera soprano Josephine Lucchese (1893–1974) was born in San Antonio, Texas as one of seven children to Italian immigrant parents. (Father Salvatore Lucchese was a famous bootmaker. Unlike contemporary opera singers, Lucchese received all her musical training in America. Biographer Judith N. McArthur for the Texas State Historical Association, revealed, "Lucchese was an operatic success at a time when it was considered impossible to achieve an international reputation without having first studied in Italy. She took up the study of the mandolin at age six and the piano at age ten; at fifteen she began voice lessons with Virginia Colombati." Lucchese did have Italian parents encouraging education in cultural arts of their native homeland.[410]

For a future Operatic career, Lucchese was fortunate to study under the accomplished Italian soprano Virginia Colombati (1863-1956). Born in Pergola, Italy, Colombati is another of the "forgotten" Opera stars. A debut for Colombati came in 1891 as "Rosina" in the legendary Rossini Opera *The Barber of Seville*. Colombati's performance at the *Teatro Comunale* in Ravenna was the first of many rave reviews. From 1891 to 1906, she performed throughout Italy, and other areas of Europe. In 1893, in America performing in New York at the Metropolitan Opera and at the Philadelphia Opera House. The following year, Colombati appeared at the *Teatro Quirino* in Rome in the Giuseppe Verdi opera *La Traviata*. Giovanni Martinelli added, "Virginia Colombati was unsurpassed in the air of skill and passionate singing." In 1906, Colombati, immigrated to America; performing until 1910, marriage ended her career.[411]

In so-called retirement in San Antonio, Texas, a career began as a music and voice teacher. One student was future soprano star Josephine Lucchese. A few

---

[409] Maxine Seller. "Antonietta Pisanelli Alessandro and the Italian Theater of San Francisco," pp 162-164.
[410] Judith N. McArthur, "Lucchese, Josephine," Handbook of Texas Online, 2010.
[411] Giovanni Martinelli. "Virginia Colombati: A star for the blues of triumphal art."

CHAPTER 7A

years later, Colombati went to teach in New York; encouraging Lucchese to join. Colombati secured a prestigious debut for Lucchese as "Olympia" in *The Tales of Hoffmann* on September 22, 1920. A New York performance at the Manhattan Opera House came as a cast member of the San Carlo Opera Company a touring group organized by the Italian born *impresario* Fortune Gallo (1878-1970). In 1923, Lucchese was featured at the *Teatro Nacional* in Havana, Cuba. Tours throughout America and Europe continued through into the 1930s billed as the "American Nightingale." Other international performances with various opera companies were in Berlin, Hamburg, Prague, New York, Chicago, and San Francisco. For a time, Lucchese was billed as a "resident artist with the Dutch National Opera and appeared as a guest artist at several opera houses in the Netherlands." One six-month stretch in 1930 produced 150 concerts in North America. After that strenuous tour, she settled into the Philadelphia Grand Opera as the leading soprano from 1929-1932.[412]

Lucchese married twice, her first marriage to Major Adolfo Caruso (1885-1941) born in Rome, who managed Lucchese's career, ended upon his death by a cerebral hemorrhage. She remarried in 1949 to American-born Florentine Donato (1896-1980) in Philadelphia. As she ended her Opera career, she harkened back to the inspiration of Virginia Colombati. Settled back in San Antonio, Lucchese taught voice at the University of Texas from 1956 until another "retirement" in 1968. Never to forego love of singing, Lucchese continued teaching private voice lessons until her death in September 1974.[413]

Gaetano Merola: "Opera Conductor"

Conductor Gaetano Merola (1881–1953), born in Naples immigrated into America in 1899, soon as assistant conductor at the Metropolitan Opera to another Italian immigrant Luigi Mancinelli (1848-1921). A similar position in Boston followed traveling with the San Carlo Opera Company; the same performance company as Josephine Lucchese. Travels as a conductor took him back to The Manhattan Opera Company. In 1922, aided by a growing San Francisco Italian community, Merola founded a resident opera company; a position he maintained for 30 years.

The first Merola performance was held at the Stanford University football stadium with over 30,000 in attendance for *Carmen*, and *I Pagliacci*. In 1953, during an outdoor performance, he collapsed and died. Forgotten by current generations, yet his death in 1953 was a front page headline of the *San Francisco Chronicler*. One year later, a report in *The New York Times* announced Giuseppe Verdi's "Requiem Mass" was scheduled at The War Memorial Opera House in

---

[412] Ashot Arakelyan. "Virginia Colombati" Forgotten Opera Singers Blog May 23, 2016.
[413] McArthur, "Lucchese, Josephine (1893-1974)," Also: *FindaGrave.com*.

San Francisco." Built in 1932, the Opera House listed on the National Register of Historic Places by architect Arthur Brown Jr. (1874-1957) bears a striking resemblance to the UNESCO World Heritage Site by Renaissance architect Andrea Palladio's *Basilica* in Vicenza, Italy built c. 1549-1614.[414]

Above Left: Photo enlargement of "Mme. Josephine Lucchese," from a *Music Trades* advertisement "The Stars of the San Carlo Opera Co." **Above Right**: Promotional photograph as "Gilda" in *Rigoletto*, c. 1922. Caption reads, "Josephine Lucchese beautiful star of San Carlo Opera Company.

Palladio (1508-1580) is cited by Architectural historians, and often recognized as the greatest – if not the most influential - of all the Renaissance architects. His work was almost exclusively in the northern Italian region in and around the city of Venice. Palladio's work illustrated in *I quattro libri dell'architettura* (*The Four Books of Architecture*) was the major influence upon Thomas Jefferson (and generations of later architects) when applying the Italian style of architecture based on Ancient Rome and the 16th century Renaissance upon the classical styles at the capital city of Washington DC and eventually throughout America.

---

[414] John Dizikes. *Opera in America: A Cultural History*, pp. 467-468, 487. See also: *In Cerca di Una Nuova Vita*, p. 16.

Top: San Francisco's War Memorial Opera House, c. 2005 by: Leonard G. **Bottom**: *Basilica Palladiana* façade on *Piazza dei Signori* in Vicenza by Andrea Palladio c. 2016 by: Didier Descouens (Wiki Creative Commons.)

Ferruccio Giannini: "Opera Recording Pioneer"

Ferruccio Giannini (1868-1948) did not have success as a singer, yet holds a distinct place in music history. (Ferruccio should not be confused with another opera singer of the same last name. Will Crutchfield explained, "an unrelated Francesco Giannini, was prominent in Italy around the same time, came to America for a few seasons with the legendary Mapleson touring company.") Ferruccio, born in Ponte all'Ania, Barga, Province of Lucca in Tuscany, Italy, was among the earliest of over 4 million Italian immigrants arriving after 1880;

322
Italian Culture in America:
The Immigrants 1880 to 1930 From Discrimination to Assimilation

himself emigrating around 1885. Giannini's legacy was not as a performer; rather as an early proponent of music recording; making opera accessible to a wider portion of the general public. Ferruccio Giannini holds an historical first dating to January 21 1896. With only piano accompaniment, Giannini made a 90 second commercial recoding of the song "La donna è mobile" from the 1851 Giuseppe Verdi opera "Rigoletto." Opera historian Will Crutchfield cites this innocuous occurrence as,

> "It was almost certainly the first commercial operatic recording in history. Caruso's studio debut and the exponential growth of the market for such records lay almost seven years in the future."

A stupendous achievement, yet mostly forgotten, other than some opera aficionados. Crutchfield adds praise for Giannini as "an enterprising musician who had joined early in a project destined to change the world." The next year, recording discs could capture 2 ½ minutes; allowing for longer recordings: which became an industry standard for most of the 20th century. One of the main reasons, radio wanted as much revenue as possible through offering on-air advertising space, therefore longer recordings impeded upon the airing a commercial advertisement.[415]

---

[415] Will Crutchfield. "Pioneer: Ferruccio Giannini." *Teatro Nuovo*,

CHAPTER 7B

JAZZ AND ITALIAN ORIGINS

"For centuries, Italian has been the language of music."

"But what accounted for the rapid spread of Jazz — or "jass" — was the mesmerizing synthesis of its myriad musical characteristics by musicians of various ethnicities, not least of them Italian."

In January 2018, Wendi Maloney of the U.S. Library of Congress offered "Some historians characterize [Jazz] as America's greatest cultural gift to the globe." A true statement that is hard to negate the dominant influence of Jazz as an original American cultural creation; especially its subsequent impact upon both the nation and the world. Looking back from the present day it is hard to even imagine Jazz as controversial, or possibly detrimental to American society. Music and rhythm have existed as long as life on Earth. Despite ever-growing newer and creative innovations in music, an equal resentment towards any deviation from established contemporary styles has also prevailed. An easy bracket to a discussion of Jazz would place it between harsh moral reaction against Rock 'n' Roll in 1950s America, or the scandalous Waltz of 17th and 18th century Europe. The historical discussion of continued puritanical reaction against music and dance styles in America and Europe have filled volumes.[416]

Ragtime to Jazz

The birthplace of Jazz is well-known as in and around New Orleans drawing from the vast diversity of its inhabitants, settlers, and immigrants over the years. The regional influences derived from Creole, Spanish, and African American rhythms joining with musical influences brought by New World immigrants including

---

[416] Wendi Maloney. "World War I: American Jazz Delights the World," *Library of Congress Blog*, January 24, 2018.

French and Italians, among others. Very few dispute Jazz as an original American cultural art; which has traversed the world. Sometimes termed as "The Great American Art Form" or "America's Gift to the World," a description is noted by National Museum of American History Behring Center as,

> "Jazz developed in the United States in the very early part of the 20th century. New Orleans, near the mouth of the Mississippi River, played a key role in this development. The city's population was more diverse than anywhere else in the South, and people of African, French, Caribbean, Italian, German, Mexican, and American Indian, as well as English, descent interacted with one another. African-American musical traditions mixed with others and gradually jazz emerged from a blend of ragtime, marches, blues, and other kinds of music. "

Some dispute exists in naming the first Jazz musician in New Orleans. Credit is often given to Benny Bolden (1877-1931) an African American cornet player; described as a "jass" style from earlier Ragtime music.[417]

A consensus among many music historians for the New Orleans origins by Georgetown University Music Professor Anna Celenza adds,

> "As genres go, New Orleans-style jazz is the quintessential musical hybrid, mixing everything from brass band marches and French quadrilles to beguine, ragtime and blues. There's no disputing that the cross-fertilization was carried out under an innovative performance style that first took root in New Orleans in the hands of African-American musicians. But what accounted for the rapid spread of jazz — or "jass" — was the mesmerizing synthesis of its myriad musical characteristics by musicians of various ethnicities, not least of them Italian."[418]

No argument has risen to the lineage preceding Jazz in New Orleans such as Blues and the syncopation provided by Ragtime. Ragtime was a piano driven style embraced by many of the younger generations responding with an accompanying nationwide dance craze. The music provided a faster dance beat with a "uniquely American syncopation." Music choreographer Agnes de Mille (1905-1993) in *America Dances* described syncopation as distinctly American, espousing,

> "A new kind of 'rhythm' took over in the nation's songs and dances; the accent was placed, not on the downbeat as in European, *one*-two, but on the upbeat, or offbeat, one-*two*. This was African, but it became American."

---

[417] "What is Jazz," *National Museum of American History Behring Center*, Smithsonian. Accessed January 17, 2021.
[418] Anna Celenza. "Our Jazz is Culturally Black, but its Global Dissemination owes a lot to Italians," The Lens, May 1, 2017.

Ragtime (sometimes slang as "Rag") originated in America during the 1890s straddling across racial, ethnic, social, and economic barriers.[419]

As with other new American music, which reached popular acceptance, at first Ragtime was not well received. In 1901, as one example, at the annual convention of the American Federation of Musicians adopted a resolution calling Ragtime "unmusical rot" and pledged a resolution to "make every effort to suppress and to discourage the playing and the publishing of such musical trash." The convention was held in the far west city of Denver, Colorado, yet the story was carried as a page one headline in the *Brooklyn Eagle* in New York City.

Regardless of attempted suppression, Ragtime swept the nation, especially among the youth and as the dominant (and profitable) style of dance music from the late 1890s until World War I. As the desire to dance increased, so did the foreseeable profitability of specific dance music. It was Ragtime that first sought to accompany specific dances with syncopated rhythms which prompted the development of new dance steps during a pre-World War I dance craze.[420]

Vernon and Irene Castle and James Reese Europe

As a dance craze emerged across America during the 1910s, so did the rise in the number of bands catering to dancers. As with any attempts to determine "who was first?" finding an answer can be difficult. Regardless of who was "first;" we do know the first prominent dance band of the early 20th century was led by James Reese Europe (1881-1919). Larger than five-piece Ragtime or Jazz Bands, Europe fronted an eighteen-piece all-black band; more so than a band it was an orchestra. By the time James Reese Europe's Society Orchestra was hired to accompany the celebrity dance team of Vernon and Irene Castle in 1914, he was a well-known performer of Ragtime music.[421]

By the second decade of the 20th century a series of playful couple dances responding to Ragtime, known collectively as "Animal Dances," were embraced by the younger generation. To no surprise the older generation and moral reformers called them "vulgar." The well-known and socially influential dancer Irene Castle (1893-1969) remembered,

> "By the fall of 1913 America had gone absolutely dance mad. The whole nation seemed to be divided into two equal forces, those who were for it and those who were against it. The battle of the newspapers began. Half of them condemned the new dances as not only unsightly, but downright immoral."[422]

---

[419] Agnes de Mille *America Dances*, p. 13. Albert McCarthy, *The Dance Band Era*, p. 9.
[420] "Oppose 'Ragtime' *Brooklyn Eagle*, May 14, 1901, p.1.
[421] Albert J. McCarthy. *The Dance Band Era*, p. 9.
[422] Irene Foote Castle. *Castles in the Air:* DaCapo Press, 1980, p. 85.

326 Italian Culture in America:
The Immigrants 1880 to 1930 From Discrimination to Assimilation

More so than any other performers of the 20th century, Vernon and Irene Castle were responsible for making couple dancing acceptable for all classes of American society at dance halls, cabarets, and restaurants; accompanied by the Ragtime music of James Reese Europe.

The ITALIAN LANGUAGE of MUSIC

Alongside Ragtime, arose Jazz as a significant number of composers focused on forming orchestras specifically geared for the dancing public. Composing music for dancing corresponds to the "tempo;" or pace (speed) of which music is played. Often described in one of three ways: 1. Beats Per Minute (BPM); 2. In Modern Language; or 3. commonly as "Italian Terminology." Film composer Hans Zimmer teaching an online *Master Class* describes Italian terminology as,

> "For centuries, Italian has been the language of music. On a musical score, particularly in classical music, musicians are given instructions in Italian. When it comes to tempo, certain Italian words convey tempo change through specific information about the speed of the music. Some Italian tempos are used more than others (particularly popular are *largo*, *andante*, *allegro*, and *presto*), classical musicians are typically familiar with at least a dozen Italian tempo indications."[423]

For any individuals responding to the music through the expression of dancing – consistent tempo is essential.

Italian musical terminology involves numerous "tempo markings," including slow tempos of *Largo*, *Lento*, *Larghetto Adagio*, and *Adagietto*, (progressively ranging from 40 bpm to 80 bpm). An easy danceable popular tempo is *Andante* "at a walking pace" (76 to 108 bpm). Moderate paced tempos include *Moderato* and *Allegretto* (108 to 124 bpm). Quicker Jazz tempos and lively dancing responded to the "heart rate tempo" of *Allegro* (120 to 168 bpm); very fast invigorating tempos are *Vivace* (168-176 bpm). Others even faster include *Vivacissimo* and *Allegrissimo*. The faster and danceable only for the most energetic are *Presto* and *Prestissimo* (168 to 200 bpm). All music, however, is not played in a consistent tempo. As such, another Italian term known as *rubato*, indicates no set tempo.

ITALIAN MUSIC by ANOTHER NAME – JAZZ

A significant number of music historians (both academic scholars and amateur sleuths) credit the Original Dixieland Jazz Band (ODJB) as the first to apply the word "Jazz" namely in their title. In early 2020, Matthew Burgos writing the cleverly titled "All that Italian Jazz," said,

---

[423] Hans Zimmer. "Tempo." *Master Class 101*, January 28, 2021.

"Although jazz music poses as the brainchild of the African-American clan, its evolution has nodded well to the Italian descent, fringing its sound with the mix of two cultures that blend well."[424]

With all due credit to the unparallel documentarian Ken Burns, it is also conceivable the ten-part 2001 documentary *Jazz* also placed some undue criticism upon one of the pioneers of an Italian American named Nick LaRocca and the Original Dixieland Jazz Band.

Nick LaRocca and
The "ORIGINAL DIXIELAND JAZZ BAND"

Dominic James "Nick" LaRocca (1889-1961) was born in New Orleans of Italian immigrant parents. In 1876, father Girolamo LaRocca (b. 1854) from Salaparuta and wife Vittoria DiNino, (sometimes as: Vita De Nina") of Poggioreale both in Sicily, sailed for Louisiana. The trek for many Sicilians was directly to New Orleans, rather than Ellis Island. The immigrant path to New Orleans followed an established shipping route with Palermo; trading in cotton and citrus fruits. Those cargo ships also transported Sicilian immigrants, sometimes over 1,000 on each voyage. Once settled in New Orleans during the early 1880s, Girolamo LaRocca continued his trade as a shoemaker. Biographer Claudio Lo Cascio writes,

"Girolamo LaRocca, who had been at Salaparuta [Sicily] a shoemaker and cornet player in the band of the small town, and having served in the Army as a corporal-bugler for the Sharpshooters of General LaMarmora, opened at the ground floor [at 2022 Magazine Street in New Orleans] his shop of shoemaker, while living with his family on the upper floor."[425]

Nick LaRocca, who lived at 2022 Magazine Street from birth until 1915, was discouraged from playing the cornet by his musician father. Nonetheless, the younger LaRocca persisted to pursue music. As with so many musicians of the time (and throughout popular music history), could not read music therefore "learning by ear." As early as 1908, he started his own band. In 1916, he travelled to Chicago as a member of "Stein's Band from Dixie;" with drummer Johnny Stein (1891/95-1962) as its organizer and leader. Stein followed the path of another New Orleans musician Tom Brown (1888-1958) to play *jass* in Chicago laid opened just the previous year. Brown was recognized as "leader of the first New Orleans jazz band to go north and was the first known to advertise his band as a "jass" band." (Clarinetist Larry Shields was a member on Brown's band later

---

[424] Matthew Burgos. "All that Italian Jazz," *Italics Magazine*, May 12, 2020.
[425] Claudio Lo Cascio. "Sicilians in New Orleans, Nick La Rocca Story," *Tiscali.it.*

328 Italian Culture in America:
The Immigrants 1880 to 1930 From Discrimination to Assimilation

joining LaRocca in the Original Dixieland Jazz Band.) After Stein, decided to leave his own band, LaRocca formed the Original Dixieland *Jass* Band.[426]

As to the ***first*** commercial Jazz music recording and ***first*** to popularize Jazz across a wide audience; credible written research credits Nick LaRocca and the Original Dixieland Jazz Band. Superlatives have been placed upon the date of February 26, 1917. It is that specific date as the undeniable fact when the first recording of Jazz music was made by Nick LaRocca and the Original Dixieland Jazz Orchestra in the New York City studios of the Victor Talking Machine Company. The *New Orleans Jazz National Historical Park* provides,

> "Dominic LaRocca ultimately became leader of the Original Dixieland Jazz Band (ODJB). Initially named Stein's Dixie Band, LaRocca apparently wrestled leadership of the group from drummer Johnny Stein, and after a couple of personnel changes, he led the band into the New York studios of Columbia and Victor records successively in early 1917. Under their new name, the ODJB recorded the first commercially issued jazz recordings ever made."

The historical site acknowledges LaRocca's predecessors and contemporaries including Tom Brown and Charles "Buddy" Bolden (1877-1931) "recognized by many to be the first actual 'jazzman.'" Other notables include John Robichaux (1866-1939) "one of the earliest jazz band leaders," and Joseph "King" Oliver (1881-1938) "an early jazz cornetist and band leader." As for the February 1917 recording session, the Victor Recording Company saw the opportunity to capitalize on a new musical sensation. Rather, they literally "saw," the eagerness of young dancers responding to the band with the "strange name, playing the strange music, would be a good seller."[427]

---

[426] "New Orleans Jazz: Early Band Leaders in New Orleans," National Historical Park Louisiana, NPS.
[427] See: "New Orleans Jazz: Early Band Leaders in New Orleans," n.p. See also: Bryan Cornell, "The First Jazz Recording: One Hundred Years Later," *U.S. Library of Congress*, March 3, 2017.

Above Left: "Nick LaRocca, New Orleans jazz cornetist." Source: Hogan Jazz Archives. National Park Service. **Above Right**: A 1918 promotional card of the renamed "Original Dixieland Jazz Band. Left to right: Tony Sbarbaro (drums), Eddie Edwards (trombone), Nick LaRocca (cornet), sitting Larry Shields (clarinet), and Henry Ragas (piano). (Wiki Commons - Public Domain).

Jazz on the "Talking Box"

Based in Camden, New Jersey, the Victor Talking Machine Company founded in 1898, was an early innovator in recording live music. By the mid-1920s, Victor mass-manufactured record-player furniture cabinets advertised simply as the "Victrola." The brand name "Victrola" was so widespread Americans adopted the word as a generic term to describe record players of all kinds for the next half-century. The company also created an iconic logo image of a loyal dog, with its head slightly tilted, attentively looking into the gramophone listening to "His Masters Voice."

By 1920, the "Victor Record catalog" provided over 500 pages listing more than 5,000 selections by the "best dance orchestras." Included in the catalog was the first Jazz recording by the Original Dixieland Jazz Band - "Livery Stable Blues" (No. 18255). The 1920 catalog listed a separate category "Jazz Band Records" (with a cross reference for "Original Dixieland Jazz Band). The list of eighteen is misleading. Jazz aficionado Jeff Crompton notes a duplicity, "If it looks like more than nine records were listed, look again - each side is listed separately."

Above Left: "A' Side Label of Victor Recording No. 18255-A "Dixie Jass Band One-Step." **Above Right**: "B' Side Label of Victor Recording No. 18255-B "Livery Stable Blues – Fox Trot." The two-sided disc sold over one and a half million copies. (Image: Library of Congress).

Interspersed within ODJB recordings were some by Earl Fuller's Famous Jazz Band. Historian Bryan Cornell writing for the U.S. Library of Congress said of bands such as the Earl Fuller recordings, *"Victor followed up, not only with further ODJB recordings, but by a number of the impostors."* A few months after the Original Dixieland Band caused a sensation in New York, Earl Fuller's Famous Jazz Band was hired to perform Jazz as a regular engagement at Rector's Restaurant on Broadway.[428]

As for Nick LaRocca and the Original Dixieland Jazz Band, there are many stories as to how the band was hired for both a premier New York performance and for a recording Victor Records. Bryan Cornell documenting the history on the centennial of the recording date for the U.S. Library of Congress credits singer Al Jolson (1886-1950), a Lithuanian Jewish immigrant, as seeing the ODJB band in Chicago and recommending them to appear at Reisenweber's Café. By the 1920s, Jolson was probably America's best-known entertainer; at the very least he was the highest paid.

---

[428] Bryan Cornell, "The First Jazz Recording: One Hundred Years Later," *U.S. Library of Congress*, March 3, 2017.

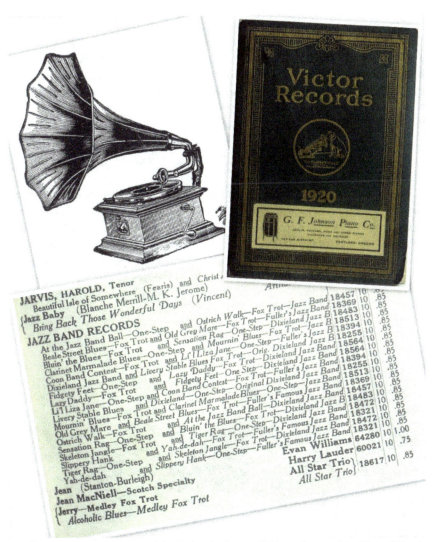

Top Left: An inexpensive model of Victrola from a 1911 catalogue of the United Watch & Jewelry Company. (Public Domain – Wiki Commons.) **Top Right**: The 503-page "Victor Record catalog" provided more than 5,000 musical selections, c. 1920. **Bottom**: Alphabetical listing page of "Jazz Band Records," including multiple listings for the Original Dixieland Jazz Band and "Livery Stable Blues," the very first Jazz recording (Public Domain).[429]

---

[429] Acknowledgement to Jeff Crompton. "1920 Victor Catalog," *Jeff's 78 RPM Blog*, May 23, 2014.

On January 26, 1917 the Original Dixieland Jazz Band introduced the new style of music to New York City at Reisenweber's located at the southwest corner of W58th Street and Eight Avenue near Columbus Circle in Manhattan. Opened in 1856, Reisenweber's was a three-story building offering entertainment on each levels; dancing on the third floor to the Emil Coleman Band, the lower street level presented a stage revue, and the ODJB was booked to play for a dance crowd at the second-floor 400 Club. (The building was demolished in 1922.) Music historian Arnold Shaw in *The Jazz Age: Popular Music in the 1920s*, cited the appearance by ODJB "is generally recognized as initiating the Jazz Age in New York."[430]

Jazz music played by the ODJB in New York City was considered "unorthodox." Speaking in 2017, son Jimmy LaRocca spoke of his father's influence and style. He described the "unorthodox syncopation" as, "Dixieland jazz is the original form. It differs from other styles; in that it is based on the opera. Three horns, with clarinet corresponding to soprano, trumpet to tenor, trombone to bass, calling and responding to each other, plus drums and piano, playing in the jazz idiom."[431]

West side of Columbus Circle – Building housing Reisenweber's Café – which was demolished in the early 20th century would have been located on the far lower left and out of the photograph. Library of Congress Prints and Photographs Division.

---

[430] Shaw, *The Jazz Age: Popular Music in the 1920s*, Oxford University Press, pp. 14-16.
[431] Valerio Viale. "First Recording in Jazz History has strong Sicilian roots." 2017.

Top: Street level entry to Reisenweber's (Courtesy: Museum of the City of New York.) Bottom: Advertisement from the 1917 Victor Records catalog of The Original Dixieland "Jass" Band. Left to right: Tony Sbarbaro (drums), Eddie Edwards (trombone), Nick LaRocca (cornet), Larry Shields (clarinet), and Henry Ragas (piano). (Public Domain).

334 Italian Culture in America:
The Immigrants 1880 to 1930 From Discrimination to Assimilation

Historians continually research, speculate, document, and at times, even revise subject matter. In such a vast territory as the global exchange of Jazz, Prof. Anna Celenza explained, "rarely can the advent of a musical revolution so huge be traced as precisely to a single moment: February 26, 1917." On that date, a combo from New Orleans called the Original Dixieland Jazz Band, featuring Nick LaRocca on cornet, walked into a Victor recording studio in New York and cut the first commercial jazz recording. Side A featured a tune called "Dixieland Jass Band One-Step;" the B side was "Livery Stable Blues." Of the two, "Livery Stable Blues" was the first recorded; thereby earning the distinction. The Victor Record catalog for 1917 provided a photo of the ODJB band claiming "The Jass Band is the very latest thing in the development in music."[432]

LaRocca and the Original Dixieland Jazz Band were known for upbeat, jaunty, and wild antics during their performances. At the time the ODJB performances were often compatible to a contemporary positive description as "crazy." Not to underestimate or miss a promotional opportunity the Victor Record Company advertised them in a comparable manner by distributing flyers with the description as,

"A Brass Band Gone Crazy!"

That's the way a wag [female] describes the original Dixieland "Jass" Band.

Beyond that description we can't tell you what a "Jass" Band is because We don't know ourselves.

As for what it does – it makes dancers want to dance more – and more and yes more! Just have another look at the picture above – you can almost *hear* the hilarious music of the "Jass" Band in your ears.

You'll want to hear the first Victor Record by this original Disorganization – it's a "winner." "Livery Stable Blues," a fox trot, and "Dixieland Jass Band One-Step" are played with charming ferocity and penetration.

[Note: spelling a in original Victor advertisement.]

News of the band reached across the Atlantic and were invited to perform in London. Prior to sailing, an unexpected change in personnel occurred. Pianist Henry Ragas (1891-1919) died due to the worldwide Flu Pandemic which had killed over 650,000 Americans and possibly 20 to 50 million worldwide. Eddie Edwards (1891-1963) was drafted into the U.S. Army. They were replaced with Emile Christian (1895-1973) on trombone and J. Russel Robinson (1892-1963) on piano.

---

[432] Anna Celenza, "Our Jazz is Culturally Black, but . . . a lot to Italians," 2017.

CHAPTER 7B

By all accounts the first Jazz performance on April 7, 1919 at the London Hippodrome, was well-received. For 15-months the band secured a regular gig at the recently opened *Hammersmith Palais de Danse* (an entertainment venue and dance hall holding in excess of 5,000). They also performed at other venues as Rector's Club and the London Palladium. One performance was before British royalty in the presence of the Prince of Wales, future King Edward VIII with a Command Performance for King George V at Buckingham Palace. During their stay in England, LaRocca arranged to record 20 songs for the English division of Columbia Records. The recordings were released in the U.S., and notably Italy. The band returned to America and toured for another four years.[433]

A Dispute Arises

As Prof. Lewis Porter corrected documentarian Ken Burns for an incorrect reference on the origin of the word "Jazz," an unfortunate negativity from the same PBS series arose against Nick LaRocca. The image and historical significance of The Original Dixieland Jazz Band was tainted by a quote from the 10-part PBS documentary "Jazz" (Ken Burns, 2001). In episode 1, titled "Gumbo: Beginnings to 1917" a quote attributed to Nick LaRocca was perceived as racist, thereby causing a stir as to his historical contribution. LaRocca said,

> "My contention is that the negroes learned to play this rhythm and music from the whites. The negro did not play any kind of music equal to white men at any time."

The 21st century brought vicious attacks which "eclipsed LaRocca's musical legacy." One film reviewer from the National History Education Clearinghouse, Prof. Frank Tirro added,

> "After Nick LaRocca's claim that jazz was invented by the white musicians of New Orleans, the ever-ebullient Wynton Marsalis's stunned silence and loss for words is drama at its best. Burns's camera captures every subtle inflection of eye movement, smile, shock, and grimace."[434]

Another factor since "eclipsed" was the fact Italians, namely Sicilians in New Orleans, were grouped in a social class lower than "Negroes." Music historian Dave Radlauer reminds of the historical circumstances. "It's very easy to forget that LaRocca grew up and lived during a time of considerable prejudice against his particular ethnicity: Sicilian-Americans

---

[433] King Edward VIII, crowned in January 1936, later abdicated that same year in December. Note: The offering of popular music by British Royalty easily compares to 1963 as The Beatles were part of a 17-act for a Royal Performance at Prince Albert Hall.
[434] Frank Tirro, "Film Review: Ken Burns's Jazz."

who took plenty of ethnic abuse of their own."[435]

In 2017, writing for *The Irish Times*, David Norris defended LaRocca and the Original Dixieland Jazz Band for their originality and for their place in Jazz history. Norris wrote,

> "The ODJB were the first band in the world to use the word jazz and despite the subsequent claims of Jelly Roll Morton, they were the real "inventors of jazz." . . . They became the victims of an inverse racism, and were accused of pirating and vulgarizing black music."[436]

Historian Bryan Cornell while compiling information for the U.S. Library of Congress on the 100-year centennial of the first Jazz music recording session, offered,

> "In the ensuing years their initial forays into the recording studio have been criticized; their genuineness brought into question. What stands out, however, is their music is not only recognizable as jazz, but boldly shines in comparison to that of their contemporaries. . . whereas the ODJB did not invent jazz, nor were they the first to introduce it up north, they did create it for the first time ever on a phonograph record, one-hundred years ago."[437]

It is almost universally agreed LaRocca did not invent Jazz in the same way Elvis Presley did not invent Rock 'n' Roll. Cultural historian Anna Harwell Celenza writing in *Jazz Italian Style* explained it as,

> "Nick LaRocca didn't invent jazz, but he was the first to capitalize on the fact that it was a financially profitable, popular art from that could cross various ethnic and national borders with relative ease."[438]

Nick LaRocca has not survived as iconic in American culture. In contrast, the name Elvis Presly has more than 50 years after his death. Re-reading of Celenza's quote replacing LaRocca's name with Presley's and "Jazz" with "Rock 'n' Roll" the debate might be fully understood.

> "[Elvis Presley] didn't invent [Rock 'n' Roll], but he was the first to capitalize on the fact that it was a financially profitable, popular art from that could cross various ethnic and national borders with relative ease."

Undisputable is the worldwide spread of Jazz due to LaRocca's direct influence with the European tour of the Original Dixieland Jazz Band, exposing the other side of the Atlantic to an original American culture.

---

[435] Michael Patrick Welch. "Jazz's Great White Hype." *Narratively.com*, 2014.
[436] David Norris. "Remembering the real 'inventors of jazz,'" The Irish Times 2017.
[437] Cornell, "The First Jazz Recording," *U.S. Library of Congress*, March 3, 2017.
[438] Anna Harwell Celenza. *Jazz Italian Style*, p. 4.

CHAPTER 7B   337

TO ITALY with JAZZ

It was LaRocca's nationality as a child of Italian immigrants which provided acceptance among Italians in Europe. Prof. Celenza explains,

> "When jazz arrived on Italian shores it was embraced, as a native" art form. . . praised its 'virile energy' . . . described it as 'the voice of Italian youth,' and musicians memorized its 'progressive' sounds, left the conservatories and flocked to dance halls and nightclubs."[439]

The transposition of American Jazz across the Atlantic to Italy is not fully credited to Nick LaRocca and the Original Dixieland Jazz Band. Matthew Burgos, Anna Harwell Celenza, and others, credit an Italian diplomat stationed in New Orleans named Chevalier Bruno Zuculin (1856-1929). In August 1919, Signor Zuculin, serving as Consulate General, wrote an article for his Italian compatriots describing the flourishing styles of Jazz music in New Orleans. An excerpt was published in Italy's widely read newspaper *Corriere della Sera.* Zuculin described two types as,

> "There are two categories of jazz bands: those that are mostly black, which perform in the hotels, restaurants, dance halls and social clubs; and those, often Italian, that play in the cinemas, in variety shows and in those numerous theaters where the most genuine theatrical product of North America flourishes."

The Italian Consulate General had only arrived in New Orleans the previous year, noticed the pivotal role of Italians in Jazz. Therefore, Signor Zuculin sent back to the cultural land of the birth of humanity a transposed version of the lineage from the Renaissance. As Celenza offers,

> "[Zuculin] was the first to state, quite emphatically, that Italian immigrants played a role in the genesis of jazz in the United States, and it was this belief, perhaps more than anything else, that later drove many Italians to embrace the music as a "native" art form."[440]

Looking back, Zuculin's delineation between Jazz bands identified as either "Black" or "Italian" combined the availability of acceptable venues divided as either "white" or "black." Herein lies a typical historical problem regarding racial distinctions; distinguished the Jazz music not always by racial segregation, rather by different application of "styles." Over time, assimilation of Italians lessened the inherent view of racism due to their skin color, yet persisted through discriminatory portrayal in American culture. The Prohibition Amendment, ratified by the states, took affect January 1, 1920. The subsequent Volstead Act,

---

[439] Anna Harwell Celenza. *Jazz Italian Style*, p. 4.
[440] Anna Celenza, "Our jazz is culturally black, but . . .owes a lot to Italians," 2017.

338　Italian Culture in America:
The Immigrants 1880 to 1930 From Discrimination to Assimilation

thereby allowed Federal enforcement of the law. Simply called "Prohibition," the era is widely remembered in history books and countless Hollywood movies as a dominant focus of media attention during the 1920s -- as did Jazz.[441]

In a 1954 autobiography *Satchmo: My Life in New Orleans*, Louis Armstrong (1901-1971) claims he purchased copies of the Original Dixieland Jazz Band recordings including in his own words "the first *Tiger Rag* to be recorded - it's still the best." Of note was Armstrong's personal take on Nick LaRocca and the ODJB, as he wrote,

> "In 1909, the first great jazz orchestra was formed in New Orleans by a cornet player named Dominick James LaRocca. They called him 'Nick' LaRocca. His orchestra had only five pieces, but they were the hottest five pieces that had ever been known before. LaRocca named this band 'The Old Dixieland Jass Band.' He had an instrumentation different from anything before, an instrumentation that made the old songs sound new."[442]

Arguably, as America's best known Jazz musician, Louis Armstrong in later years served as an international "Ambassador of Good Will" bringing his music throughout the world.

Italian Instruments: PIANO, BASS, and VIOLIN

Brass, reed, and horn instruments as the Cornet, Oboe, Saxophone, and Trombone, among others were developed in various parts of Europe, such as France and Germany; with the guitar of Spanish origin. The Banjo, often used in early Jazz has African slave origins. Some other Jazz instruments (including Classical, Folk, Opera) such as the Piano, Cello, Viola, Violin (fiddle), Upright or "Double" Bass are distinctly Italian. Although not a part of the Original Dixieland Jazz Band, the upright Bass was an integral part of Jazz, Swing, Blues, and early Rock 'n' Roll. The Bass was often paired with drums, to "lock in the beat." Bass instruments in classical compositions applied a bow across the strings. In 1542, the "bass viola da gamba" was invented in Venice by an Italian Silvestro Ganassi (1492-1565). Sometimes called a "Violone" (Italian: *violone da gamba* - translated as played between the legs) is part of the "Viol" family of musical instruments.[443]

---

[441] Brent Staples. "How Italians Became White." *New York Times,* October 12, 2019.
[442] Quoted in foreword for the 1993 Da Capo Press reprint of *Swing That Music*, p. ix.
[443] Denis Midgley Arnold. "Claudio Monteverdi: Italian Composer and Musician," *Encyclopedia Britannica*, November 25, 2020.

Above Left: A Baroque era painting by Sir Peter Lely, c. 1640, depicting a "Violone" of a *great bass viol*. (Wiki Commons – Public Domain). **Above Right**: An 18th century Italian Double Bass, by Bartolomeo Cristofori (1655–1731). Metropolitan Museum of Art. The Crosby Brown Collection of Musical Instruments, Gifts of Dr. and Mrs. Guido S. Corriero and Andrea Manley, 1980. Accession Number: 1980.112. (Public Domain).

Discarding the bow and "plucking" the strings, thereby producing a percussive sound, known as *pizzicato* (translated as "plucked") is not just an Italian word; rather developed by the Italian composer Claudio Monteverdi (1567-1643) born in Cremona, Italy. Music when played *pizzicato*, is markedly different than played with a bow. The technique was first applied in a 1624 "operatic scena" titled *Combattimento di Tancredi e Clorida* composed by Monteverdi. As explained by music professor Denis Midgley Arnold at the University of Oxford, "Monteverdi was the most important developer of the then new genre, the Opera. He also did much to bring a 'modern' secular spirit into church music." Monteverdi's *pizzicato* was adapted by many Jazz musicians with the similar plucking finger style rather than a bow.

A legendary creator of iconic musical instruments was Bartolomeo Cristofori (1655-1731). Not as well-known was crafting of a Double Bass in his workshop. Around 1700, his most famous music invention was the *forte piano*; the formal name for a piano. According to curators at the Metropolitan Museum of Art, "Cristofori was the first person to create a successful hammer-action keyboard instrument and deserves to be credited as the inventor of the piano." (Adaptation of an upright piano used by the early Jazz bands was developed in England around 1800.) Cristofori, born in Padua in the Venice Republic, later moved to Florence.

He might have collaborated and/or studied with the Amati family of violin makers. Music historian Stewart Pollens in *The Early Pianoforte* cites Cristofori as introducing the "pianoforte in Florence around 1700." The oldest pianoforte is a 1720 Cristofori model at the Metropolitan Museum of Art in New York. A 1722 model is in Rome at the Museo Nazionale degli Strumenti Musicali.[444]

Above Left: Piano Forte c. 1720 by Bartolomeo Cristofori (1655-1731). The example on display at the Metropolitan Museum of Art "is the oldest of the three extant pianos by Cristofori." The Crosby Brown Collection of Musical Instruments, 1889 Accession Number:89.4.1219a–c – Public Domain. **Above Right**: Amati Violin c. 1669 by Nicolò Amati (1596–1684). Metropolitan Museum of Art Gallery (684). Gift of: Evelyn Stark. Accession Number: 1974.229a-d – Public Domain.

Another string instrument known as a Violin or Fiddle, are basically the same. The main difference is the type of music played. The "Fiddle" is often played in the style of traditional Irish and Scottish folk music. The Violin often for European Classical compositions and Opera; at the time mostly Italian. The standard violin, in its "modern form" to the present day, was first crafted in Italy around 1550 by Andrea Amati (1505-1577). The curators of the Metropolitan Museum of Art cite Amati "violins "were known for their elegant design, responsiveness, and sweet sound." Wendy Powers an independent scholar for the Metropolitan Museum of Art tells us, "Violins are judged by their tone, responsiveness, elegance of design, visual appeal, and precision of their craft." Amati, who also invented the Cello, was born in the same Italian region of Brescia and Cremona, about 60 years earlier than Claudio Monteverdi. Another of the earliest violin makers was Gasparo di Bertolotti, sometimes as Gasparo da Salò (1542-1609), born in Salò in the northern province of Brescia, Italy. The tradition of finely crafted Violins continued with the Amati family, namely grandson Nicolò.[445]

---

[444] "Grand Piano: Bartolomeo Cristofori," *Metropolitan Museum of Art*,
[445] Wendy Powers, "Violin Makers: Nicolò Amati (1596–1684) and Antonio Stradivari (1644–1737)." In *Heilbrunn Timeline of Art History*. New York: The Metropolitan Museum of Art, October 2003.

A Violin and Double Bass in the Museo della Musica in in the San Maurizio Church in Venice Italy (Courtesy Museo della Musica)

Violins from Cremona, Italy crafted in the workshop of Nicolò Amati (1596–1684) are often as the finest of the long line of Amati family violins. Some original instruments have survived to the present day. One example by Nicolò dating from 1669 is on public view at the Metropolitan Museum of Art in New York City. The curators of the Met state,

> "The violins of Nicolò Amati (1596–1684), the preeminent violin maker of the Amati family of instrument builders, were known for their elegant design, responsiveness, and sweet sound, although they lacked the strength of violins by Stradivari and Guarneri 'del Gesù.' Nicolò Amati single-handedly carried on the Cremonese tradition of fine violin making after famine and disease in the years around 1630 had wiped out virtually all of the top violin makers; not surprisingly, violins from this period are very rare."[446]

The Amati family workshop produced, possibly, the finest tonal violins. The workshop spawned a training base for many future violin makers, possibly even Antonio Stradivari (1644–1737).

Located within the *Museo della Musica* in Venice Italy are a collection of musical instruments over a time span of over 300 years. The collection houses a significant number of Violins, Cellos, Mandolins, Lutes, and Double Bass, among others. The collection housed within the San Maurizio Church provides information on the museum website as,

---

[446] "Violin, Nicolò Amati (Cremona 1596–1684)." *Heilbrunn Timeline of Art History*, Metropolitan Museum of Art.

"The instruments form the core collection of masterpieces that belong to the past three centuries. The classical era of Italian violin making has given us the most celebrated, admired, preserved, and therefore imitated, production in the history of manufacturing musical instruments. . . . it is equally significant and no less fascinating to also document and preserve the production of these masters' students. The collection housed in this museum of 300 years of Italian violin making and includes splendid examples of the different regional schools."[447]

"The American Violin: From Jefferson to Jazz"

Incorporating Italian music and musicians as the founding nucleus of American culture was promoted by none other than Thomas Jefferson (1743-1826). Of the musical interests Jefferson favored, it was Italian style admired above all others. In 1778, a request for Italian musicians to emigrate to America was in letter to Italian naturalist Giovanni Fabbroni (1752-1822). Jefferson wrote to Fabbroni, "In a country like Italy, music is cultivated and practiced by every class of men."[448]

As an accomplished violinist and music enthusiast Jefferson owned a small collection of musical instruments including a "Cremona more than a hundred years old." Historians have speculated the violin was most likely crafted by Nicolò Amati in Italy.[449]

Posited as a forerunner to the historical development of Jazz, Library of Congress curators placed Mr. Jefferson as the "Founding Father" of introducing the Violin to America in an exhibit aptly titled "The American Violin: From Jefferson to Jazz." Denise Gallo of the Library of Congress Music Division said, Jazz, begin with Thomas Jefferson." Gallo added, "When thinking about the history and development of the violin, the names of great Italian makers such as Andrea Amati (1515-1580), Antonio Stradivari (1644-1737) and Andrea Guarneri (1626-1698) come to mind." Library of Congress Jazz specialist Larry Appelbaum linked the path of the Italian violin to "America's unique Jazz culture." Prof. Appelbaum rightfully acknowledged American Jazz as derived from a combination of many cultural art forms including Italian."[450]

---

[447] "Instruments," *Museo della Musica*, San Maurizio Church. Accessed May 13, 2021.
[448] "Thomas Jefferson to Giovanni Fabbroni, 8 June 1778," *Founders Online,*
[449] Helen Cripe, *Thomas Jefferson and Music*, p. 47.
[450] Denise Gallo. "The American Violin: From Jefferson to Jazz," *Library of Congress Information Bulletin*, May 2006 - Vol. 65, No. 5. The symposium was held April 6th-20th at the Library of Congress in Washington D.C.

CHAPTER 7C

CALIFORNIA (AND TEXAS)
HERE THEY COME

"The most important bank in America is Italian."

"The Italian contributions to Walla Walla's wine industry were huge and their impact felt for generations. The early Italians not only planted vines from their home country but they also planted their passion for growing and raising grapes."

California provided a unique opportunity for the vast and fast assimilation of Italian culture in America. Marianna Gatto writing for The Italian American Museum of Los Angles explains,

> "The Southern California Italian American experience differs in many respects from Italian American culture in other parts of the nation, and therefore represents a unique chapter of the diaspora. Southern California's Italian American community bears the imprint of the region's physical and cultural geography, which provided greater opportunities for self-expression and inclusivity than elsewhere in the country."[451]

Before the Great Migration, significant Italian immigration to the west, such as California, began in the early nineteenth century. Many, seeking a quick fortune, were encouraged by stories of the California Gold Rush starting in 1848. The Gold Rush prompted all sorts of individuals heading into California hoping to strike it rich panning for gold. Some traversed the continent others arrived by sailing ship. Within a few years, a massive influx of prospectors, settlers, fishermen, immigrants, migrant workers, and entrepreneurs, among others, initiated

---

[451] Marianna Gatto, "Culture: Part I," *Italian Museum of Los Angeles*, 2021.

statehood for California in 1850. The Gold Rush attracted settlers to areas such as San Francisco as a major port of entry; which soon developed a distinct Italian presence. Not all who ventured to California "struck in rich." Many millions of Italians remained poor; barely earning a meager existence. For individuals such as Andrea Sbarbaro and A.P. Giannini, California proved lucrative, as a gold mine of a different sort.[452]

Bel Paese and California

A "Hollywood in Italy" exhibit sponsored by the Museo Ferragamo in Florence recognized the connection of Italians and the lure of California. The curators stated "the exhibition explores Italian migration to California and the influence that the bel paese's myths and culture had on the state." California is similar to Italy with a long narrow geographical diverse area with a coastline almost 1,200 miles (1,900 km); when including bays and inlets the number increases to over 3,000 miles (4,800 km) of coastline. California land area is slightly larger (about 1.3 times) than Italy. High mountains and fertile lands, the allure of California might be the comparison of the natural countryside to the *Bel Paese* of Italy. Directly translated as "of the beautiful country;" a basic definition is,

> *Bel Paese* (bɛl paˈeːse, -eːze) [sometimes *Belpaese*] "is the classical poetical appellative for Italy, meaning the "beautiful country" in Italian, due to its mild weather, cultural heritage and natural endowment [geography]."

The term has come to distinctly represent Italy. It its truest sense, it is hard to discount Italy as one of the most beautiful countries not just in Europe, but also the world. As possibly the most distinctive geographic "boot" shape of any nation on earth, Italy is characterized by a significant number of mountains and hills throughout most of the peninsular. The most prominent mountain ranges include the northern canopy of the Alps and the Apennines extending 750 miles (1,200 km) along the full length of the peninsular; natural geography Italians would have compared to California.

Another similarity is the pleasant climatic conditions conducive for quality wine production. A Booklist review of Simone Cinotto's *Soft Soil, Black Grapes: The Birth of Italian Winemaking in California*, explained the development in America as,

> "Gallo's, Rossi's, Guasti's, and other North Italians founded and grew businesses along family, ethnic, and racial lines and had possessed little winemaking experience in their native Piedmont. They held onto the

---

[452] Marianna Gatto, "Culture: Part I," *Italian Museum of Los Angeles.*

strong bonds of extended family, encouraging whole clan lines to depart Italy for America's promise."[453]

The original Italian wine making in California occurred during the mid- to late 19th century. Yet, the Italian tradition of wine making in America coincides with the birth of the nation.

Philip Mazzei and California Wine

Italian wine making in America dates to early 1773 in Virginia. At that time, Thomas Jefferson (1743-1826), a lifelong wine aficionado engaged Philip Mazzei (1730-1816) born in Tuscany, to replicate an Italian vineyard adjacent to Monticello.

In America, the oldest winery is the Brotherhood Winery in Washingtonville, New York, established in 1839. Wine making on the continent dates to 1769 at the Spanish Mission San Diego de Alcala in California; at the time considered part of Mexico. Imported vines were in Los Angeles by 1833 by a French immigrant Jean-Louis Vignes (1780-1862); considered the first commercial wine maker in the region before official statehood in 1850.

These wineries were not founded by Italians, yet records of Italian immigrants tending to the agricultural aspects as farm laborers and aiding in wine making are numerous. According to an exhibition sponsored by The Bancroft Library at the University of California Berkeley,

"As early as 1840, settlers from Genoa began to arrive in the valleys of California after hearing their relatives talk about how ideal the valleys were for vinting. the wine industry in California was mostly built by Genoese."[454]

Others, such as The Bernardo Winery was established in 1889 on a land grant in the San Diego area. During the 1920s, ownership transferred to an Italian immigrant named Vincent Rizzo. The history of the winery state,

"Family owned and operated since 1927 by the Rizzo family, is the oldest family owned and operated winery in Southern California. Since 1927 the Rizzo family has been growing and producing wine in the same Italian tradition for three generations."[455]

Prior to 1880, many northern Italy Italian immigrants in California were working in agriculture. In 1869, Italian immigrants from Genoa arranged a Columbus Day celebration in San Francisco; as a *paisan* from Genoa.

---

[453] Simone Cinotto. Soft Soil, Black Grapes: The Birth of Italian Winemaking."
[454] "Italian Americans in California: The Gold Rush," *The Bancroft Library*, University of California Berkley, 2021.
[455] See: History," *Bernardo Winery* website. Accessed April 23, 2019.

The Bernardo Winery, established in 1889 in San Diego. In the 1920s, an Italian immigrant Vincent Rizzo assumed ownership.
(Photograph by Thelma Olsen, c. 2019.)

San Francisco developed a thriving Italian community; historical records cite a growing number of both northern and southern Italians migrating to California during the Gold Rush of 1848-1850. Some worked the mines, others in all types of service industries. Research by the University of California Berkeley claimed, "By 1860, the largest number of Italian immigrants in the United States lived in California, and, as late as 1890, there were more Italian immigrants in the Pacific coast states than in New England." Not necessarily geographically distinct as the localized "Little Italy" established in cities such as New York, nonetheless, Italians built local communities in California. One example in San Francisco was the publication of an Italian language newspaper beginning in 1859. Cultural aspects included Italian Opera productions dating from 1851 (see Chapter 7A). Similar to other cities in later years, Mutual Aid societies for Italians, were patterned on a French immigrant community in San Francisco.[456]

In the years after the Gold Rush other skilled northern Italians such as marble cutters and stone craftsman were in demand due to the newfound wealth. The "newly rich" had the money to build large opulent mansions in Italian influenced Romanesque, Neo-Classical, and Italianate architectural styles. The warm waterfront climates such as Fisherman's Wharf in San Francisco Bay provided fertile ground for Sicilian fishermen. Wine was and still is a major agricultural product of California. The climate produced fertile soil in many valleys allowing the agricultural skills of Italians contributing to the added cultivation of grapes and other citrus fruits.

---

[456] "Italian Americans in California," *The Bancroft Library*, UC Berkley.

SIMI WINERY:
"The Oldest Continuously Operating Winery in California"

In 1859, the California Gold Rush enticed two Italian brothers named Giuseppe and Pietro Simi to leave their homeland in the northern region of Montepulciano in Tuscany. The Simi brothers failed in their quest as prospectors. Falling back on a common trade among Italians, the Simi's grew produce in Pescadero, California. Information provided by Kathleen Thompson Hill, tells us, the brothers "found their real gold mine: grapes." A few years later, the Simi brothers relocated a winery in the North Beach area of San Francisco.[457]

The Simi family held a connection with Italian banker A.P. Giannini (see later this chapter) as Giuseppe's wife Isabelle nursed the Giannini children. Apparently, mother Isabelle never learned English, yet typical of the children of immigrants, daughter Isabelle (1886-1981) assimilated to America graduating from Santa Rosa Business College. At age 18, Isabell was crowned "Queen of the Healdsburg Flower Festival" and concurrently served as supervisor of the Simi Winery. Isabelle continued overseeing winery operations until retirement at age 84 in 1973. The Simi Winery, in the 21st century holds the distinction "as the oldest continuously operating winery in California."[458]

Above Left: Isabelle Simi, at age 18, crowned "Queen of the Healdsburg Flower Festival" and supervisor of the Simi Winery. **Above Right**: Simi Winery, c. 1904. (Courtesy of Simi Winery – Public Domain).

Secondo Guasti: "The "Wine King"

A few legendary Italian California wine makers ventured into the age-old craft. Some notable Italian winemakers included Giovanni Santino Pedroncelli (1885-1980), Robert Mondavi (1913-2008), and brothers Ernest Gallo (1909-2007) and

---

[457] Kathleen Thompson Hill. "Simi Winery: History in a Wine Glass," 2012.
[458] Kathleen Thompson Hill. "Simi Winery: History in a Wine Glass," 2012.

348   Italian Culture in America:

Julio Gallo (1910-1993). Before those icons of American culture began wine production, the tradition was born by an earlier Italian immigrant. In an article, "From Penniless Immigrant to Wine King," Marianna Gatto tells us, "Long before Napa became California's wine center, Secondo Guasti, an immigrant from Piedmont, Italy, established himself as the state's wine king."[459]

Secondo Guasti (1859-1927) left Italy at age 21, settling first in Panama, South America. Without any commercial enterprises rising to fruition, Guasti ventured to other areas of Central America, the Southwest of America, and San Francisco; eventually relocating in 1883 to Los Angeles. He soon enticed investors to establish a vineyard in the Cucamonga Desert about "40 miles east of Los Angeles." In 1865, the region became accessible with the construction of the Southern Pacific Railroad a railway depot station. In 1910, Secondo Guasti bought the entire town, renaming it Guasti, California forming a mostly self-sufficient community. Guasti "organized the immigration of a large Italian community" of skilled in working vineyards. Added were artisans and craftsman needed to build a community accommodating over 250 families. In founding a cooperative as the Italian Vineyard Company comprised of over 5,000 cultivated acres formed into the "globe's largest vineyard;" he imported vines from Italy that thrived in the similar California climate.[460]

Italian-Swiss Colony Wine

Italian immigrants Pietro Carlo Rossi (1857-1911) and Andrea Sbarbaro (1839-1923) founded the Italian-Swiss Agricultural Colony in the Sonoma Valley. Around 1881, Rossi trained as a chemist at the University of Turin, became "chief wine-maker of the Italian-Swiss Agricultural Colony in Asti, California." Sbarbaro previously established as a shopkeeper, landowner, and banker; later partnered into the Italian-Swiss Colony Wine Company. Historians Jerre Mangione and Ben Morreale, explained,

> "If Sbarboro saved the Colony, it was Pietro Carlo Rossi who made it prosper. Rossi a wine master from Asti, Piedmont, improved the quality of the wine attracted world attention by winning the Grand Prix for his wineries at an international congress held in Turin [Italy]."[461]

A caveat for workers in the vineyards of Italian-Swiss Colony, allowed, when able financially, to buy shares into the cooperative.

Unfortunately, within a few short years of the partnership abruptly ended as Rossi was killed in an accident at the age of 54. On October 10, 1911, the *Santa*

---

[459] Marianna Gatto. "From Penniless Immigrant to Wine King," 2021.
[460] "Guasti Plaza | City of Ontario, California." Prospectus, June 20, 2011.
[461] Mangione and Morreale, *La Storia*, p. 198.

Rosa Press Democrat reported "the tragic death of the wealthy vineyardist." The story added, "The community and state at large were profoundly shocked on Sunday afternoon when the news spread that President P.C. Rossi of the Italian Swiss Colony, had met a sudden and most unexpected death at the Asti Vineyards in this county."

As a result of the Italian contribution California outdistanced all the other U.S. States in wine production – at 84% of all wine in America. By the 21st century, wine became a favored consumption item among Americans as well as a profitable venture.[462]

TOP 10 - NUMBER of WINERIES per U.S. STATE 2017		
Rank	**State**	**Wineries**
1	California	4,391
2	Oregon	793
3	Washington	792
4	New York	403
5	Texas	352
6	Virginia	291
7	Pennsylvania	285
8	Ohio	254
9	Michigan	191
10	North Carolina	171

- Top Ten wineries - $142 billion economic impact.
- Over 900,000,000 gallons of wine produced annually.
- California makes 85 percent of all U.S. wine.
- U.S. accounts for 12 percent of the world's wine production.
- The U.S. leads the world in wine consumption.
- 10,043 wineries in the America.

———

Statistics: The National Association of American Wineries.

---

[462] See: "Rossi, Pietro Carlo," *Islapedia*, August 12, 2020.

350   Italian Culture in America:
The Immigrants 1880 to 1930 From Discrimination to Assimilation

DEL-MONTE BRAND

An outgrowth of the Italian Swiss Colony wine making cooperative came from an associate named Marco Fontana (1849-1922). Fontana, an immigrant from northern Italy near Genoa, speculated in other business ventures as a fruit vendor, produce shipper, and owner of a cannery company - all failed. Obtaining new financing in 1891, another cannery was known as M.J. Fontana and Company in San Francisco. By the end of the decade the company merged as the California Fruit Canners Association. Canning of produce would allow shipment to prosperous East Coast markets without spoilage.

Fontana and associate Antonia Cerruti an immigrant from Genoa, formed the now famous "Del Monte" brand. In 1907, a factory was built which came to be known simply as "The Cannery." As noted on the history of the company "to cultivate the best wholesome vegetables, fruits, and tomatoes." Within a few years, the Del Monte plant was the largest food-processor was hailed as "the largest fruit and vegetable cannery in the world." The building, although not in use, remains in the 21st century as "one of San Francisco's treasured landmarks." The can label bearing a "tomato-like" shield of white letters on a red background trimmed in gold stating "Del-Monte Brand Quality" appeared in 1909. It has been a common sight in grocery food stores nationwide into the 21st century.[463]

Joseph Maggio "Carrot King" and Swiss-Italians

Many other food items became so common in food marts into the current day that the original source of their Italian heritage is usually all but forgotten. Joseph Maggio (1906-1990), serves as an excellent example from among many Italian immigrants who became produce farmers in America. He was known as the "Carrot King," a moniker that transferred over as the company name. After his death, the company, run by his son registered "Carrot King" as a U.S. Trademark for fresh vegetables.

Others such as Swiss-Italians, from the northern regions near the Switzerland border, were known for growing food products such as grapes, olives, and oranges. By the first decade of the 20th century, Italians introduced bell peppers, artichokes, eggplants, and broccoli to the California farms. Many other types of food produce, not necessarily foreign to California, yet heavily dependent upon farmers and agricultural experts of Italians, provided local markets with large quantities of fresh fruit, dried fruit, cereals, potatoes, and beans, to name just a few items.

Other well-established food companies in America founded by Italian Americans include *Chef Boyardee*, *Contadina*, *Progresso*, *Pastene* and *Prince*

---

[463] See: "Our Passion for Quality goes back Generations," History of Del Monte.

Pasta. Each have grown into well-established profitable business serving all walks of life in America. *Prince Pasta* as one example was begun in 1912 in Boston by three Sicilian immigrants Gaetano La Marca (1878-1955) in administration; Giuseppe Seminara (1884-1961) sales; and Michele Cantella (1872-1935) "pasta maker;" in Boston's heavily Italian populated North End. In similar fashion *Pastene* was formed in 1874 by Sicilian immigrant Luigi Pastene and son Pietro.

Walla Walla Washington and Italian Wine

California was not the only state producing wine in the Italian tradition. Walla Walla, located in the southeastern area of Washington state has a geography of fertile soil combined with climatic conditions similar to the California wine regions. During the 1980s, Washington state recorded a major expansion in the wine industry, placing it third among the Top-Ten number of Wineries in America. Since that time "more than 100 wineries and nearly 2,000 acres of vineyards" arose in the immediate area of Walla Walla. The flourishing wine industry matched a common trend in the rise of wine consumption of the general public across America; as historian Rita Cipalla writing on winemakers in Walla Walla explains,

> "The roots of Walla Walla winemaking stretch back more than a century before that, to when the first Italian immigrants settled in the valley and began growing grapes, along with other crops, and making wine."[464]

Agricultural workers are often forgotten. Cipalla adds, "together, they forged an industry whose imprint would be felt 150 years later."

Frank Orselli (b. 1833-1894), born in Lucca, Italy a commune town in the Tuscany region, was "believed to be the first Italian to arrive in the Walla Walla Valley." Around 1857, sources indicate he was an army veteran serving in the Walla Walla valley before the American Civil War; and stayed after discharge. Information at *Find a Grave*, reveals,

> "Frank Orselli from Lucca, Italy, arrived in Walla Walla as an infantryman at Fort Walla Walla in 1857 and settled here. He planted 180 acres of wine grapes, orchards and a vegetable garden. . . . Orselli started the California Bakery, selling wines, liquor, tobacco, groceries, fruits, vegetables and wine grapes. In 1876, he reported he made 2,500 gallons of wine and sold it at the bakery."

A local newspaper indicated, "Mr. Orselli has the largest winery in the valley and in a few years, expects to manufacture wine upon a large scale." It is not known

---

[464] Rita Cipalla. "Italian Immigrants," 2018.

352
Italian Culture in America:
The Immigrants 1880 to 1930 From Discrimination to Assimilation

how much wine was produced, nor if Orselli met his goal. His legacy however, certainly exceeded his wildest dreams.

Orselli was not alone as other Italian immigrants settled in the region engaging in similar agricultural endeavors. Noted wine expert and educator Regina "Reggie" Daigneault based in Seattle, Washington wrote,

> "The Italian contributions to Walla Walla's wine industry were huge and their impact felt for generations. The early Italians not only planted vines from their home country but they also planted their passion for growing and raising grapes in Walla Walla and throughout Eastern Washington. Whether they planted Tuscan, Piemonte, or southern Italian varieties, they had the foresight to see that Eastern Washington could one day produce amazing wines."[465]

Overlooked by many, by the year 2020, Washington state ranked second to only California as a leading wine producer in America.

Wine making was not the only employment for Italian immigrants in Washington state. Historian Rita Cipalla writes,

> "When coal was king in Black Diamond, [Washington State] a small mining town in the Cascade foothills of southeastern King County, immigrants from Italy provided much of the muscle power that operated the coal mines. The work was hard and dangerous and those who could went on to other enterprises. The last mine near Black Diamond closed in 1974, but many descendants of the Italian coal miners still live in the community."

Within a western state with a long tradition of descendants of Italian immigrants is California, specifically the city of San Francisco.[466]

San Francisco

By 1920, Italians in San Francisco numbered over twenty percent of the foreign-born population; second only to New York City. San Francisco, in particular, had a distinct attraction for Italian immigrants. As described,

> "The pattern of immigration into San Francisco during the latter half of the 19th century was significantly different from that of anywhere else in the United States. The demography of the gold-rush city was summed up concisely by a real-estate firm that advertised it could 'transact business in the English, French, German, Spanish and Italian languages. San

---

[465] Quoted in: Rita Cipalla. "Italian Immigrants: How They Helped Define the Wine Industry of Walla Walla," History Link.org, July 19, 2018. Accessed February 13, 2021.
[466] Rita Cipalla. "Italian Immigrant Coal Miners in Black Diamond," 2018.

CHAPTER 7C   353

Francisco remains one of the most Mediterranean of American cities and Italians are still the dominant European minority."[467]

Most accounts, relate the cause of population increase in San Francisco as the "premier city of the West" was the mid-19th century Gold Rush.[468]

By 1890, with a new immigration station in Astoria, Oregon, the West Coast maintained three other immigration ports of entry at Port Townsend in Washington; including two in California in San Diego, and Angel Island in San Francisco. Of Angel Island, one historian said "was the same process as at Ellis Island in New York harbor, but without the inspiring statue of Lady Liberty."[469]

In 1849, among Gold Rush hysteria, two Roman Catholic priests, Father Giovanni Pietro Antonio "John" Nobili (1812-1856) and Father Michele Accolti (1807-1878), worked among the Native Indian tribes in Oregon. The Italian born priests looked for "missionary and educational opportunities." Nobili was appointed pastor at the Mission Santa Clara de Asís. The Jesuit priests obtained sole use of the mission site with a plan for educational use. The two priests established, "the first college for the education of young Americans in the west."

In 1851, with limited funds and no faculty, Nobili and Accolti, founded Santa Clara College (later Santa Clara University). Other faculty were also Italian Jesuit priests with previous experience at American universities. An expansion in San Francisco led to the founding of Saint Ignatius College, later morphing into the University of San Francisco. The *Museo ItaloAmericano* cites, "both schools were focal points for Italians providing an education based on the classical Italian curriculum for their American born children."[470]

Beyond the spiritual and educational, to satisfy the need of the overabundance of miners and prospectors, all sorts of business ventures arose. Among the millions of Italian immigrants, three entrepreneurs in California, Domenico Ghirardelli (1817-1894), A.P. Giannini (1870-1949), and Salvatore Ferragamo (1898-1962), created individual legacies still looming large over American Culture well into the 21st century. The commonality was certainly Italian heritage; however, their products were as diverse as banking, confectionary chocolate, and shoemaking.

---

[467] Barnaby Conrad, et. al., "San Francisco." *Encyclopedia Britannica*, 2020.
[468] Mangione and Morreale. *La Storia*, p. 193.
[469] "Pacific Coast Port of Entry for Immigrants Puts History on Display," *Voice of America*, October 27, 2009.
[470] See: *In Cerca di Una Nuova Vita: From Italy to California Italian Immigration: 1850 to Today*, Museo ItaloAmericano, Paolo Pontoniere, pp. 6, 21.

Domenico "Domingo" Ghirardelli and Chocolate

Born in 1817 in Rapallo, located along the western coast of Italy about 20 miles (30 km) south of Genoa, Domenico Ghirardelli (1817-1894) was the child of a family of food importers. As an apprentice youth "with a local candy maker," he became familiar with "the chocolate and confectionary trade." Around 1837, Ghirardelli left Italy sailing to Uruguay in South America; a common destination for Italian emigration. Argentina, as one example, cites over 60 percent of its 21st century population with some, or all, Italian ancestry; 30 million from a total population of over 40 million.

In 1847, in South America, Ghirardelli with partner James Lick (sometimes "Link") the pair established a confectionary merchant business, processing chocolate. The next year, with a significant amount of chocolate to sell, Lick sailed to San Francisco as the Gold Rush boom began. With an enlarging market of prospectors with ready money to spend, business was booming, prompting Ghirardelli's immigration in 1849 to San Francisco. The partners opened a store in Stockton, California dealing in confectionaries and wares for miners. The shop prospered, coupled with a discovery of the "Broma Process" producing "a more intense chocolate flavor than other techniques." The development of a unique and distinct flavor set Ghirardelli's chocolate apart from others.[471]

Above Left: Domingo" Ghirardelli, c. 1860. **Above Right**: Portrait Domingo Ghirardelli later in life. National Portrait Gallery, Smithsonian Institution.

By the mid-1880s, chocolate products were shipped throughout the United States. The geographic location along the Pacific Ocean aided shipments to Mexico, Japan, and China. Founder, Domingo retired in 1892, and died two years later during a trip to Italy. The company with three grown Ghirardelli sons as business

---

[471] History.com Editors. "History of Chocolate," *History.com*, 2018.

CHAPTER 7C

partners of a rapidly growing business, purchased a manufacturing building on the northern area of San Francisco's waterfront site of the now famous "Ghirardelli Square."[472]

Ghirardelli Square on San Francisco's famous Pier 39 rates as "one of the busiest and well-known tourist attractions in the United States." Fisherman's Wharf at Pier 39 is an active destination "watching fishermen prepare the crab catch and mend their nets" most are unaware of its distinct Italian origin. As noted in the "History of Pier 39,"

> "San Francisco's Fisherman's Wharf gets its name and neighborhood characteristics from the city's early days of the mid to later 1800s when Italian immigrant fishermen came to the city to take advantage of the influx of population due to the gold rush. Most of the Italian immigrant fishermen settled in the North Beach area close to the wharf and fished for the local delicacies."

The tradition of fishing was a skill learned in Italy, which due to the natural fishing opportunities of San Francisco's waterfront offered Italian immigrants a livelihood other than speculation and prospecting for gold.

"The Most Important Bank in America is Italian"

The lure to immigrate to America for Domingo Ghirardelli was a direct result of the California Gold Rush. Another indelible part of American culture connected with the Gold Rush – but more specifically Italian – is the modern banking system. Italian might not be the first image which comes to mind when discussing the American banking system. Yet the foundation for banking in western civilization traces directly to northern Italy during the early 15th century. The first European bank, more so as a "financial institution," was the *Banco dei Medici* in Florence; founded in 1397 in existence until 1494. In contrast to later banks, the Medici's did not lend to common people. As with other aspects of the Renaissance, Italian banking soon spread to other parts of Europe. In 1407, the *Banco di San Giorgio* (Bank of St. George) in Genoa, Italy created the foundation for the modern banking practices. Not necessarily as the "first" type of financial institution as in Genoa, the oldest bank in continuous operation since 1472 is the *Banca Monte dei Paschi di Siena*, in the Tuscan city of Sienna; followed by the Banco di Napoli in Naples since 1539.[473]

As for the modern banking system in Europe and North America, it is distinctly Italian. As Enza Ferreri writes in "Italy Invented Banks,"

---

[472] "About Ghirardelli." *Ghirardelli Chocolate*, 2021.
[473] George Macesich. *Central Banking: The Early Years: Other Early Banks.* Series: *Issues in Money and Banking*, p. 42.,

356 Italian Culture in America:
The Immigrants 1880 to 1930 From Discrimination to Assimilation

"The English word "bank" derives from the Italian term "banco," stemming from the Frankish word "bank." In Italian, "banco" originally referred to a bench with a back, then a bench's wooden seat, in the 1300s a shop counter, in the 1500s a craftsman workbench. Finally, the counter where money was exchanged, collected and lent."

Ferreri adds, "Other than this mainly formal recognition, banking was an Italian invention." As Ferreri explains, "bankers accepted to be the guarantors of payments, by signing a letter (called "of credit") which committed as a 'promissory note' to pay sums of money to the holder of the letter of credit, who was a seller of goods or services." The Italian banks, therefore, offered a collateral guarantee to pay the bill of fare, if any of the merchants failed to pay.[474]

In America, Alexander Hamilton is credited with the idea of a national bank of the United States in 1791. At the time bank institutions operated as singular units. In contrast, the idea of "satellite," or branches of the same banking institution was first devised in San Francisco, California, by an Italian. The editorial staff at *NonèRadio*, an Italian language news site proudly states, "The Most Important Bank in America is Italian." The "claim" is true as the referenced financial institution is the Bank of America. Existing in modern day as not only the largest bank in the United States, but also one of the largest in the world. First known as the Bank of Italy; founded in 1904 by A.P. Giannini; it was later renamed "Bank of America." The editorial staff at *NonèRadio* added, with a tremendous sense of ethnic pride, as the son of Italian immigrants, A.P. Giannini "revolutionized the world of banks in America." (In 2022, Bank of America was rated as the second largest asset holder of all American bank with $2.16 trillion. The leader was Chase Bank at $2.87 trillion.)[475]

A.P. Giannini and The Bank of America

Amadeo Peter "A.P." Giannini (1870-1949) was born in San José, California to Italian parents Luigi Giannini (1840–1877) and Virginia Demartini (1854–1920). In 1849, hearing of the Gold Rush in California, Luigi emigrated from the northern region of Liguria in the Kingdom of Sardinia of a pre-unified Italy. Similar to many Italian immigrants, Luigi retuned to Italy a few years later. Unlike the many millions of later Italian immigrants, the elder Giannini traveled to Italy only to marry and quickly return to America. A few years after son Amadeo was born, Luigi was killed in a monetary dispute. The widow Virginia, managing a family produce business founded by Luigi, remarried. Step-father Lorenzo

---

[474] Enza Ferreri. "Italy Invented Banks," *Italy Travel Ideas*, Accessed March 1, 2021.
[475] Macesich. *Central Banking*, p. 42. See also: Enza Ferreri. "Italy Invented Banks," *Italy Travel Ideas*, March 1, 2021.

Scatena (1859–1930) took over management of the produce company. At the age of fourteen, A.P. Giannini left school joining the family business. By age of 31, Giannini, as a partner, earned enough money from the family produce business to, in effect, "retire."

An early retirement did not last; the following year Giannini was named a board member to the Columbus Savings and Loan Society located in an Italian neighborhood of San Francisco. Working at the bank led to a resignation after six months as he objected to a banking system which only "lent the money to the rich, with the conviction that the rich would have no difficulty in returning it with interest." In deference to the financial plight of recent immigrants Giannini said, "in a country where you die for a dollar, the money should be lent to the poor."[476]

In support, Giannini opened the "Bank of Italy" on October 17, 1904 in a converted storefront in San Francisco. Possibly in defiance, the Bank of Italy was located, directly across the street from Columbus Savings and Loan Society. Within the predominantly Italian section of North Beach, the Bank of Italy began issuing loans to working class individuals. In 1906, a significant event was the San Francisco earthquake causing unimaginable destruction. After the earthquake Giannini authorized "granting loans to residents to rebuild." The earthquake severely damaged his own storefront bank; nonetheless "Giannini, took all the contents of his vault, including 3 gold bars, and moved the business, on a bench made of an axle and two barrels, to the port area, where the earthquake victims were gathered."[477]

A Series 1902 $5 United States National Bank Note issued in 1927 by the Bank of Italy of San Francisco. (The Bureau of Engraving and Printing - Public Domain – Wiki Commons.)

The Bank of Italy continued to prosper, eventually applying a name change in 1928 as the "Bank of America." Giannini aware of a name associated with only

---

[476] "A.P. Giannini." *Encyclopedia Britannica*, 2020.
[477] "The Most Important Bank in America is Italian," *NonèRadio*, July 8, 2019.

Italians, affected a merger with Orra E. Monnette (1873-1936) of the "Bank of America, Los Angeles." Giannini eventually assumed total control; merging Bank of Italy into a financial powerhouse. As a pioneer; he soon opened a series of 400 "branches" throughout California – the concept known as "branch banking" – the first of its kind.

Giannini's amazing success involved financing early productions of the Hollywood film industry and the California Wine industry. Many in the wine industry were operated by Italians, or winery's which hired mainly Italian migrant workers. (The Hollywood film industry was also permeated by immigrants of varying nationalities.) In 1923, Giannini offered financing to the fledging United Artists.[478]

A.P. Giannini and the Golden Gate Bridge

On April 2, 1928, the nationally prominent *Time* magazine recognized Giannini's achievements featuring him on the cover of its publication. Despite the recognition, bigger achievements still were ahead as the nation faced financial ruin. As the Great Depression placed all portions of the country in financial ruins, some large-scale projects were promoted to stimulate the economy. One such project proposed the world's longest suspension bridge in San Francisco. By 1932, engineer Joseph Strauss was on a 14-year crusade to fund the project. At the time, the wealth of Bank of America was solvent and so large, Giannini was in position to offer financing. Funds as "bonds" for the construction were issued for the longest suspension bridge in the world – the Golden Gate Bridge.[479]

Above Right: Amadeo "A.P." Giannini, c. March 1927. **Above Left**: The Golden Gate Bridge in San Francisco, California. The editors of PBS *American Experience* stated, "Without Giannini's assistance, it is doubtful that the Golden Gate Bridge would ever have been built." (Public Domain).

---

[478] See: Paolo Pontoniere. *In Cerca di Una Nuova Vita*, p. 19.
[479] *Time* magazine, April 2, 1928. Vol XI No 14.

CHAPTER 7C   359

Giannini did not need much convincing as he said, "We'll take the bonds, we need the bridge." The Bank of America purchased $6 million worth of bonds. A quirk to the financing came with a caveat of "no interest." In return Giannini stipulated "all the workers engaged in the realization, were residents of San Francisco and in particular, all people to whom the Bank of Italy had issued a loan." As a double-edged innovation, Giannini assured work for many of the Italian working class; thereby, with the growing depression, the workers' salaries would in effect allow solubility to repay any outstanding loans to the Bank of America. The editors of PBS *American Experience* cited, "without Giannini's assistance, it is doubtful that the Golden Gate Bridge would ever have been built."[480]

Giannini's added significance in American popular was financing an additional $2 million for the overbudgeted Walt Disney Classic *Snow White and the Seven Dwarfs* (1937). The Disney film was "the first full-length animated motion picture to be made in the U.S." In financial terms it was a tremendous blockbuster as *Snow White* became the top-grossing movie of 1937. By 1945, Bank of America was the world's largest commercial bank; California had almost 500 branches (483 to be exact) with additional branches opening across the United States.

Giannini's legacy extended to adding to the desperately needed cash funding American war engagement in World War II. The bank served as an early funding agency for many fledging companies; such as Hewlett-Packard and Transamerica Corporation, among many others. By the 21st century, over 4,300 branches of the Bank of America existed throughout the United States; as the second largest bank in the United States. In all summation, A.P. Giannini, son of Italian immigrants, was often called "The People's Banker." In 1973, Giannini was honored with his image placed upon a U.S. Postal Stamp.

Levi Strauss and Denim Jeans - (An Italian Fabric)

The California Gold Rush also ignited one of the most ubiquitous items of American Culture. The laboring speculators almost universally adapted a rugged clothing item which achieved its own iconic cultural status with a quirky Italian connection. As such, any individual might be hard-pressed to find a more popular clothing item spanning all cultural social classes, in America and internationally, as a pair of basic denim Blue Jeans. The first of the iconic brand simply known as "Levi's" was named after a Jewish Bavarian immigrant named Loeb "Levi" Strauss (1829-1902).

In 1847, Strauss immigrated to New York joining the family Dry Goods business. Drawn to San Francisco around 1853 by news of the Gold Rush was an opportunity to open a Dry Goods business. Strauss offered an established

---

[480] "Amadeo Giannini: Golden Gate Bridge," *American Experience*, PBS Thirteen.

360   Italian Culture in America:
       The Immigrants 1880 to 1930 From Discrimination to Assimilation

reputation selling quality products, including "waist overalls." Overalls were the early precursor to denim jeans which combined copper rivets on pants, such as the pockets, creating sturdy work pants and overalls. In 1873, in partnership with a tailor named Jacob Davis (1831-1908), Levi Strauss & Co. sold denim jeans as durable work pants to miners and prospectors.

The patented process of "waist overalls" was the forerunner of "Levi's 501 Jeans®." (The designation of "501" might denote the number placed upon fabric shipments by customs inspectors.) Levi Strauss "did not invent the cut or fit of the waist overalls; what [the company] did was take traditional men's work pants and rivet them, creating the new category of workwear which we today call blue jeans." The strong sturdy fabric and rivet process was favored as a product worn exclusively by laborers. At first it was related as a clothing item worn by a working-class individual usually poor. Over time, Blue Jeans became a fashionable item among all walks of society, from inexpensive to extremely pricey.[481]

Denim fabric is derived from the word *de-nîmes* meaning "from Nîmes;" a city in southern France dating to ancient Roman origin. The immigrant path to California was part of a trade route between Italy, Sicily, and New Orleans. For most cargo shipments, no direct route existed, rather it was Palermo in Sicily, to Genoa in northern Italy, to New Orleans. Those cargo ships transported immigrants, sometimes over 1,000 on each voyage. Returning ships to Italy were often ladened with cotton which was employed in clothing. Denim is a cotton fabric as an Italian / Roman / French creation from the city of Nîmes; one of the largest populated Roman cities (outside of Rome) in excess of 50,000 people. Its geographic location offered a strategic crossroads for dispersing Roman Legions west to Spain, north to Gaul, and Brittany. In the 21st century, Nîmes has more well-preserved Roman antiquities than any city outside of Rome. The most prominent is the Arena of Nîmes, an oval double-tiered Amphitheater (70 AD). A 4 to 5-minute walking distance from the amphitheater is the Maison Carrée (2 AD); a perfectly preserved ancient Roman temple which served as inspiration for many Neo-classical buildings in America.[482]

Many other ancient Roman remnants are scattered near and throughout the city of Nîmes. The most majestic is the engineering marvel the Pont du Gard aqueduct (1st c. AD), 14 miles (23 km) northeast of the city. As the largest of all arches built by the Romans, it brought fresh water into the city of Nîmes. An ingenious aqueduct system the Pont du Gard moved water by gravity, filling wide canals and lakes in the city center of Nîmes. Large amounts of fresh water provided a growing population with a safe drinking and cooking supply. It also

---

[481] History of Levi's 501 Jeans®." *Levi-Strauss Company*, Accessed March 11, 2021.
[482] Giordano, *The Architectural Ideology of Thomas Jefferson*, pp. 92-105.

provided high volumes of water required for producing a durable twilled fabric called *Serge de Nimes*. The fabric commonly known in America as "Denim" was transported out from the Italian port city of Genoa. The French word for Genoa is "Gênes," therefore denim fabric made into pants became known as Denim Jeans.

Above Left: The Pont du Gard, most famous of all Roman Aqueducts, provided a steady stream of water into the city of Nîmes critical to the production of Denim. **Above Right**: One of the many canals in Nîmes with water supplied by the Pont du Gard. **Lower Left**: The Roman Arena of Nîmes, an oval shaped double-tiered Amphitheater. **Lower Right**: The Maison Carrée; a perfectly preserved ancient Roman temple, served as the inspiration for many Neo-classical buildings in America. (Photograph by Thelma Olsen, c. 2018)

The Italians of Texas are Upon You

Italian immigration from 1880 onward was not limited to major cities. A significant number of immigrants worked in mines and farms dispersed throughout the nation including the Midwest and South. By the 1880s, southern states such as Texas witnessed a significant influx of Italian immigrants. The Institute of Texan Cultures notes,

> "Not until the 1880s, however, did Italian immigrants begin to arrive in Texas in large groups. These were mostly farmers who settled in three areas the Brazos Valley, mainland Galveston County, and Montague County."

In 1870, census records listed only 186 Italians within the entire state of Texas.

By 1920, Texas counted over 8,000. Similar to populated areas of Little Italy in Boston, Chicago, New York, San Francisco, or St. Louis, Italians in Texas congregated in geographic areas settled by other Italians. For example, according to The Institute of Texan Cultures,

> "Piedmontese settled in Montague County. Individuals from Venice and Modena joined Piedmontese in the coal mines of Thurber. And Sicilians settled in Galveston County and up the Brazos river valley. Urban communities followed in Galveston, Houston, and San Antonio."

The small number might pale in comparison to the millions of Italian immigrants dispersed in other areas of the country, however the cultural impact upon Texas and America is astounding. Typical of Italians in Texas was Frank Qualia (? - 1936), who in 1880 or so immigrated from Milan in northern Italy. Most likely arriving in Galveston, eventually finding his way to Del Rio Texas in 1881, hearing of the promise of fertile land. With new wife Mary Franke, vines were planted to make homemade wine for family use – an age-old tradition among Italians. Two years later, the pair began commercial operations forming the Val Verde Winery in 1883.[483]

Italian Wine in Texas

The Simi Winery claim the "oldest continuous" winery in California; whereas Val Verde claims the "oldest established" winery in Texas. The terminology can be explained due to historical circumstances. In the 1920s, during Prohibition almost all production of legal alcohol ceased breaking a continuous run of wine production – a technicality. Throughout the 1920s, the Simi Winery in California continued production of wine with alcohol content only for sacramental wines, which was legal under the Constitutional Amendment. In contrast, Val Verde Winery remained in operation throughout Prohibition, not through wine production, rather "by selling table grapes from the Qualia family vineyards."[484]

Val Verde remained in "single-family-ownership" over 140 years, solidifying claim as the "oldest winery" in Texas. The Italian winery is not unique. In the vast state known for cattle production, the Texas beef industry created an economic impact over $12 billion in 2015. Not necessarily known for wine production – in 2005 the total economic impact hovered around $1 billion; a significant number, but not by Texas standards. Buoyed by the Val Verde Italian winery, by the 21st century over 350 Texas wineries were in operation. A number placing Texas as the fifth-largest for wine production in America. Similar reports estimated a rapidly advancing wine industry with a possible total economic impact over $13

---

[483] "The Italian Texans," The Institute of Texan Cultures, 2018, pp 1-2.
[484] "History of Winery," *Val Verde Winery*. Kathy Weiser, "Del Rio, Texas."

billion in 2017. The financial dollars was one aspect; another factor indicated at least 60,700 individuals were directly employed in the wine industry, extending to supporting over 104,000 jobs.[485]

Jessica Dupuy, providing a descriptive illustrative article "Texas: A Wine Drive Through Hill Country," for *Food & Wine* magazine cites travelling along U.S. Highway 290 traversing due west form Austin Texas is a series of wineries as "the central corridor for Hill Country wineries." One city along that corridor, Fredericksburg (pop. 11,200) located 78 miles (125 km) due east of Austin, boasts over 50 wineries. Dupuy offered high praise for the region, "If Napa Valley is California's quintessential wine county, then Hill Country plays that role for Texas."[486]

Salvatore Lucchese: Bootmaker

The 19th century wine industry does not conjure images of Texas and the legend of the American West. A distinctive American cultural iconic Texas image are Cowboy Boots. Often associated with Texas, yet indicative of many midwestern states, is a long-standing American fashion staple of cowboy and rodeo attire. As a "uniform style" combined with denim jeans as Levi's or Wranglers are "Cowboy Boots."

Many popular brands of Cowboy Boots exist; apart from an inexhaustible number of boot manufactures are two "gold standard" standouts -- The Tony Lama Boot Company® and Lucchese Bootmaker™ -- both founded by Italian immigrants. Albert Muzquiz states,

> "Surprisingly, the cowboy boot - that symbol of American conservatism and cowboy machismo - would be perfected by the Lucchese brothers, not blue-blooded Americans, but two Italian immigrants who arrived in Texas in 1882."

In November of 1882, Salvatore "Sam" Lucchese (1868-1929) left Palermo, Sicily sailing to Galveston Texas. Two other brothers Michael (1865-1912) and Antonio (1873-1897) soon followed as the brothers started the Lucchese Boot Factory at Fort Sam Houston, a U.S. Cavalry School in San Antonio. The brothers arrived with a skill indicative of a "meticulous Italian craftsman" learned from their Sicilian cobbler father Gaetano Lucchese (1825-1919). Upon relocation of from Sicily to Texas, the Lucchese's "applied their old-world cobbling skills in the military town of San Antonio." The fort and cavalry school kept up demand and the Lucchese brothers sought to hand-make the supply."[487]

---

[485] "The Wine Industry Boosts the Texas Economy," 2021.

[486] Jessica Dupuy, "Texas: A Wine Drive Through Hill Country," *Food & Wine*, p. 62.

[487] Albert Muzquiz. "Sicily to San Antonio: The Story of Lucchese Boots," Education / History *Heddels.com*, September 20, 2018.

Both father Gaetano and mother Josephine Lucchese (1837-1914) immigrated joining their sons in San Antonio. The Lucchese company website also cites father Gaetano for instilling "a strong appreciation for Italian culture, opera, and fine craftsmanship." The cultural fostering is likely the reason Salvatore Lucchese purchased a Mexican-American theater named the *Teatro Zaragoza* in San Antonio as well as providing a path for daughter Josephine Lucchese (1893-1974) to pursue what became an internationally known Operatic career. (See Chapter 7A).[488]

Above Left: A postcard illustration of Bexar County Court House, c.1896-1907. (Public Domain). **Above Right**: The earliest known photo of Salvatore Lucchese, founder of Lucchese Bootmakers, c. 1893.
(Public Domain)

Salvatore Lucchese remained in America, becoming a citizen on September 26, 1906 in a ceremony at the Bexar County Courthouse in Texas. Built from 1891 to 1896, the courthouse was designed in the Romanesque architectural style derived from classical forms of Ancient Rome, popular in America between 1870 and 1900. (The Bexar County Courthouse building remains in the current day added to the National Register of Historic Places in 1977.) A tragic occurrence on January 15, 1929, as recorded in Lucchese history said, "While playing dominoes at home with his family, Salvatore died in San Antonio." Management of the company passed to son Cosimo (1900-1961), which continued to thrive.

Lucchese boots are available for everyday wear. Many are often "displayed in store cases like rare jewels." The Lucchese brand offered affordable everyday boots to "high-end, exotic collections as python, calf, goat, snake, ostrich, buffalo, lizard, alligator, stingray, boar skin and crocodile." In 2008, Lucchese produced

---

[488] See: Albert Muzquiz. "Sicily to San Antonio: The Story of Lucchese Boots."

CHAPTER 7C

125 pairs of its 125th Anniversary Boot, Hollywood movie star and former Governor of California Arnold Schwarzenegger purchased a pair at the $12,500 golden price tag.[489]

The Tony Lama Boot Company®

Another "gold standard" in Texas is from Tony Lama Boot Company, advertised as "The World's Most Recognized Western Boot Brand Since 1911." Named for founder, Anthony "Tony" Lama (1887-1974) born in Syracuse New York, a mere six months after his Italian parents immigrated to America. An unfortunate illness to parents caused the young Lama as an orphan at age eleven. Left in the care of an uncle, Lama apprenticed with a local shoemaker "and quickly learned the ways of boot making and the leather trade industry." At age 16, the young apprentice "lied about his age in order to join the US Cavalry stationed in Fort Bliss, in El Paso, Texas." He was assigned as a "cobbler handcrafting boots for the soldiers." After discharge in 1911/12 he started a boot company located on East Overland Street in El Paso. Not far from Fort Bliss.[490]

In 1917, Lama married Esther Hernandez, a pianist and music teacher. The couple had six children all of whom "continued to learn the many ways of the industry and eventually all became active participants in the company." Business continued to prosper, only slowing down during World War II as raw material of all kind, including leather, was strictly rationed in favor of the war effort. After, Lama's death, the company continued under family ownership. In 1990, the company was sold to a conglomerate of Justin Industries a division of Berkshire-Hathaway, continuing to produce boots under the Tony Lama Boot Company® brand name. As such, it might be easy to compare Tony Lama Boots as the "Ferragamo's" of the boot world. Prices range from very affordable to extremely pricey custom-made boots such as the commemorative 100th anniversary Diamond and Gold studded design priced at $50,000.[491]

Salvatore Ferragamo: "Shoemaker for the Stars"

Many Italian immigrants to America carried over skills learned in the "old country;" one of the most common was shoe making. Neighborhoods in cities throughout the nation featured many a shoe repair business owned by an Italian immigrant. Work hours were long, income often low, yet all plying a noble necessary trade learned in the old country. Thousands toiled in obscurity, some such as Tony Lama and Salvatore Lucchese reached iconic status in American

---

[489] "The Legend of Lucchese," *Lucchese.com* (Company Website).
[490] Amy Richmond. "Texas Roots for Italian Boots," *Frisco Style*, Feb. 1, 2018. William Manns, "How the Cowboy Got the Boot," *American Cowboy*, March–April 2000, p. 52.
[491] "The Story of Tony Lama" *Tony Lama* Company Website. Accessed May 4, 2021.

culture. One earned distinction as a "shoemaker for the stars" named Salvatore Ferragamo.

Born in Bonito, Italy a commune village about 60 miles (97 km) inland east from Naples, Salvatore Ferragamo (1898-1962) was the 11th of 14 children born of Antonio and Mariantonia Ferragamo. As the Ferragamo story is told, Salvatore, at the age of nine, crafted a pair of shoes for himself and a pair of high heels for two of his sisters to wear for the important Catholic rite of Confirmation. It is hard to imagine, the poverty existing among southern Italians especially one with such a large number of children. Added to the poverty was the death of father Antonio when Salvatore was only ten years old. With or without a father, it was not unusual for children to work at a young age. In addition, purchasing products was rarely an option, therefore, just about all clothing and other items of necessity were fabricated in the home. As a pre-teen, Ferragamo apprenticed to a shoemaker in Naples; opening his own shop in his hometown of Bonito at the young age of around 13 or 15.[492]

The Ferragamo path to America was traced to an older brother who recently immigrated to America working in a shoemaking company in Boston, Massachusetts. (Some sources say the factory produced Cowboy boots.) The younger Ferragamo decided to join his older brother in America arriving in 1915. Prior to World War I, production, such as the shoe factory in Boston were highly industrialized. In Boston, Ferragamo witnessed large-scale production, while also discovering the limitations to his creative inclinations. A few years later, he was encouraged to join another older brother in Santa Barbara, California. Living within the small West Coast city, Salvatore opened a small shoe repair shop. While still in Santa Barbara, Ferragamo began designing and crafting specialty shoes for use in film work. In quick succession, many in the film industry including two famous Hollywood directors D. W. Griffith (1875-1948) and Cecil B. DeMille (1881-1959), purchased from Ferragamo.

About 90 miles (145 km) south of Santa Barbara was the neighborhood called Hollywood located within the growing city of Los Angeles. Nearly seventy years after the Gold Rush, Los Angeles as the center of the Hollywood Film Industry was just beginning to flourish. In contrast to the East Coast film production, Southern California offered two important aspects. One was consistent good weather conducive to year-round production. The second was far removed from the monopolistic control of the Motion Picture Patents Company, which basically controlled all aspects of film production on the East Coast. In less than a decade, Los Angeles was transformed from a backwater region into a major film

---

[492] "Salvatore Ferragamo," *Fondazione Ferragamo*, 2016. Accessed March 4, 2021.

CHAPTER 7C

production area. Due to the Hollywood film industry, the population grew to 1.25 million; among then was Salvatore Ferragamo.[493]

In 1923, Ferragamo purchased the Hollywood Boot Shop located at 6687 Hollywood Blvd. The simple name of the "Hollywood Boot Shop" might not conjure up images of affluence; yet the store location was on the prestigious Hollywood Boulevard. (A glimpse of the store was in a 1928 silent film *Show People* (dir. King Vidor) Clients regularly visiting to purchase specialty footwear included top movie stars of the day including Charlie Chaplin, Lillian Gish, Pola Negri, and Mary Pickford, to name a few. Utilizing creative talents fabricating shoes for film and world-famous movie stars, Ferragamo once said, "I seem to see a parallel between the film industry and my own. Just as the motion picture industry has grown and developed from those fledgling days, so too, I hope, has mine."[494]

One of the regular clients visiting the Hollywood Boot Shop was actress Joan Crawford (1904-1977). Crawford's early career began as an accomplished dancer winning many Charleston contests; garnering attention from Hollywood producers. (Crawford appeared in over 100 films from 1923 to 1972; winning an Oscar for Best Actress for the 1946 film *Mildred Pierce*.) A promotional photograph of Crawford during the time of *Our Dancing Daughters* featured Ferragamo sizing a pair of shoes in his Hollywood Boot Shop.

Ferragamo's curiosity to make a specialty shoe, not only stylish, but comfortable, led to enrolling in classes studying in Human Anatomy, Chemical Engineering, and Mathematics. The educational knowledge combined with old-world skills "created custom wooden lasts (models) in the shape of the foot of many of his regular clients." The result was a specialty hand-made custom shoe "to achieve the perfect fit for the individual foot." Ferragamo explained the connecting of design, anatomy, biomechanics, style, and comfort with quality craftmanship as,

> "I discovered that the weight of the bodies when we are standing erect drops straight down on the arch of the foot. I constructed my revolutionary lasts, which supporting the arch, make the foot act like an inverted pendulum."[495]

Demand for Ferragamo shoes was so plentiful, he could not fill all outstanding orders. One problem was lack of skilled workers capable of producing individual products. At the time, mass-production in America was astonishing, but current American labor was not capable of producing the quality as hand-produced by

---

[493] In 2020, Santa Barbara population was 92,000. Los Angeles population 12.5 million.
[494] "Salvatore Ferragamo," *Fondazione Ferragamo*, 2016. Accessed March 4, 2021.
[495] "Salvatore Ferragamo - Designer Biography," FineClothing.com.

Ferragamo. He returned to Italy, settling in Florence, a city renowned for quality workers in leather goods.

In Italy he was able to employ skilled craftsman to export shoes to America, namely Hollywood. Many shoe manufacturers have existed for years – Ferragamo is no exception. The legacy of the Ferragamo designs differentiate by the iconic museum quality designs. In Florence the *Museo Salvatore Ferragamo* maintains a collection of over 10,000 designs. As his company museum states,

> "Salvatore Ferragamo is a designer who left a legacy. He started small and grew to be one of the most well-known women's shoe designers in the world. He designed shoes for the Hollywood elite, and is credited as being one of the first designers to truly consider the anatomy of the foot in their designs. His philosophy of comfort and artistic value is greatly admirable, and continues to set his brand apart from the crowd. Today, his shoes continue to be design with quality, comfort, art and history in mind."[496]

The Ferragamo legacy is worthy for inclusion in notable museums. As one example, the prestigious Metropolitan Museum of Art in New York, boasts 50 pairs of Ferragamo shoes in their fashion collection. One of the most famous pair in the collection is known as "Rainbow (1938)." The shoes were personally created for actress Judy Garland (1922-1969) for her signature song "Over the Rainbow" from the classic movie *The Wizard of Oz* (dir. Victor Fleming, 1939).

Salvatore Ferragamo's time living in California lasted only a few years from 1915 to 1927. The impact upon American and International culture is stupendous. After relocation to Italy in 1927, until his demise in 1960, an exclusive business blossomed. Top movie icons continued as clients, including Greta Garbo, Judy Garland, Audrey Hepburn, Sophia Loren, and Marilyn Monroe. Into the 21st century, the shoes (and other accessories) are sold in 660 single-brand stores in 90 countries on three continents of Europe, Asia, and America. Ferragamo's shoes were crafted not only for women, but also men. One of his earliest and iconic clients was a *paisan* – an Italian immigrant named Rudolph Valentino.[497]

---

[496] "Salvatore Ferragamo - Designer Biography," FineClothing.com, November 19, 2014.
[497] "Salvatore Ferragamo," *Fondazione Ferragamo*, 2016. See also: "Italy in Hollywood Exhibition," *Salvatore Ferragamo Group*, May 24, 2018. Note: The exhibit curated by Giuliana Muscio and Stefania Ricci at Palazzo Spini Feroni; Florence ran from May 24, 2018 to March 10, 2019. See: "Italy in Hollywood Exhibition," *Salvatore Ferragamo Group*, May 24, 2018.

Hollywood publicity photo of Salvatore Ferragamo presenting a pair of custom-made shoes to movie actress Joan Crawford in the Hollywood Boot Shop, c. 1928. (Public Domain).

CHAPTER 7D

ITALIANS IN HOLLYWOOD AND RUDOLPH VALENTINO

"No star better symbolizes the emergence of the cult of celebrity in America than Rudolph Valentino, who became the first pop icon."

Vaudeville to Broadway to Hollywood to the "It Girl"

At the 20th century dawned, the most popular form of inexpensive stage entertainment was Vaudeville. Performances were limited to a singular place, on a singular day; repeated day after day in town after town. After 1910, vaudeville experienced a slow attendance decline; losing appeal to the pricier Broadway productions and inexpensive Hollywood movies. One different factor for Broadway (limited mostly to New York City) was an American art form favored as a leisure pursuit of the wealthy and some middle class. Broadway also led the way in fashion trends, fads, and dance steps. At the same time, motion pictures started as a major form of entertainment, pushing Vaudeville into oblivion. Sound accompaniment to movies with spoken dialogue or a music soundtrack did not begin until 1927. Movie houses often employed a piano player or limited contingent of musicians playing prearranged music partnered with the film.[498]

Advancement of Motion Pictures created a sociological sensation of some of the most popular American cultural icons. Images of dashing actors and beautiful actresses graced the large silver screens productions. The adaption of the word "Silver Screen" was twofold; first as a description of the color tint, second as a symbolic metaphor. Movie screens were coated with a reflective metallic silvery paint enhancing the projected picture quality of black & white images. As newer technological projection screens were created; such as glass bead, the term morphed into a different usage. By the 1920s, "Silver Screen" was the name

---

[498] See: *This Fabulous Century 1910-1920*, p. 260.

applied to just about any projected motion picture. In some usages, a performer might be referenced as star of the "Silver Screen;" soon it became a reference to the Motion Picture industry as a whole. In 1930, a monthly magazine titled *Silver Screen* premiered focusing on the Hollywood film industry and celebrities. The publication lasted well into the 1970s.

Throughout film history, thousands of actors and actresses have appeared on the "Silver Screen." Very few have conveyed the magical movie glow often explained as "It." As a sociological phenomenon trying to describe "It" is an intangible. For sometimes unexplainable reasons, the camera delivers a magical appeal, which permeates into the psyche of adoring fans. As a product, many Hollywood producers have tried to copy or create the mythical appeal or tragic "rags to riches" back story of many of an aspiring star; an approach difficult to obtain. The all-important screen test for the "Silver Screen" often captures an indescribable feature or appeal only translated as she or he simply has -- "It!"

Cabiria **and Italian Influence on Hollywood**

In the history of American cinema, the 1915 release of D. W. Griffith's *The Birth of a Nation* is cited as the birth of the movie "Blockbuster." As true as that may be, *The Birth of a Nation* is the first "American" made blockbuster. In the definition of both box office success, widescale distribution, and influential legacy, the distinction as the first Blockbuster film belongs to an Italian film *Cabiria* (dir. Giovanni Pastrone, 1914). Some cite *The Birth of a Nation* as the first feature length movie screened by a sitting president *inside* the White House. A true statement; however, the first movie viewed *at* the White House was *Cabiria.* Griffith's film was shown in the East Room on February 18, 1915; while the previous year *Cabiria* was viewed by President Woodrow Wilson and his family on June 26, 1914 *outside* on the White House lawn.[499]

Both movies relate the historical past of each nation; yet a cultural contradiction exists between the American release of *The Birth of a Nation* and the Italian release of *Cabiria* that celebrated the birth of the ancient Roman Republic. With a screenplay written by Gabriele D'Annunzio (1863-1938), the movie was based on a book of the history of Ancient Rome titled *Ab Urbe Condita* from 25 B.C. by Titus "Livy" (b. 59 B.C.). *Internet Movie Database* (IMDb.com) described the plot summary as,

> "*Cabiria* is a Roman child when her home is destroyed by a volcano.
> Sold in Carthage to be sacrificed in a temple, is saved by Fulvio, a Roman

---

[499] Note: The term "Blockbuster" did not come into widespread use until the 1940s.

CHAPTER 7D

spy. But danger lurks, and hatred between Rome and Carthage can only lead to war."[500]

In 2006, legendary film maker Martin Scorsese introduced a restored version of *Cabiria* - viewed on at the world-wide famous Cannes Film Festival. Scorsese said "it all began with *Cabiria*." In response to the presentation, American film critic, Roger Ebert, said of the film,

> "Giovanni Pastrone's 'Cabiria' was famous in its day, a global box-office success, but has fallen into neglect. . . now here was the original film. . . restored to within three minutes of its original running time. . . The Cannes screening was prefaced by videotaped remarks from Martin Scorsese, the most passionate film historian among active directors. What he said, essentially, was that Pastrone invented the epic and deserves credit for many of the innovations often credited to D. W. Griffith and Cecil B. DeMille. Pastrone helped free movies from static gaze."[501]

Any film historians credit *Cabiria* and early Italian cinema as a major influence upon movies made in Hollywood. From an artistic and technical points of view Pastrone is noted "for the invention of dollies and special effects, among many other innovations for the film industry." More than a few sources cite *Cabiria* as a Tuscany film; a correct statement as to the production center. Before major movie productions in Hollywood around 1915; Turin in Piedmont, as part of the Tuscany region of Italy, was considered "the most important cinema production center in the world." (Turin is nestled in northwest Italy below the Alps near the borders of France and Switzerland; about 100 miles (160km) west of Genoa and Milan.) It was within Turin that film production of *Cabiria* began.[502]

Giovanni Pastrone (1883-1959) is historically recognized as a "pioneer Italian motion picture director and producer." Entering upon a creative and artistic endeavor in the early days of movie production, Pastrone was accomplished in the musical study of the cello. He was known for continuing an age-old Italian tradition of hand crafting his own musical instruments. As noted by the Editors of Encyclopedia Britannica,

> "He constructed several musical instruments by hand, and, though his passion for music eventually waned, his experience in making instruments honed within him a perfectionist streak characterized his later work in film."

---

[500] *Internet* "Cabiria," Plot Summary, *IMDb.com*.
[501] Roger Ebert, *"The Stuff of Dreams,"* RogertEbert.com July 2, 2006.
[502] "Giovanni Pastrone," *Encyclopedia Britannica*, 2020.

Around 1909, Pastrone maintained a position as lead producer status in a newly formed motion picture group the *Italia Film Company*.[503]

Above Left: Photo still from director Giovanni Pastrone's groundbreaking film *Cabiria*, c. 1914. **Above Right**: Poster Print for *Cabiria*, c. 1914. Reproduction Number: LC-USZC4-13505 (color film transparency). Library of Congress Prints and Photographs Division Washington, D.C. (Public Domain)

In the field of movie production, Pastrone created many innovations which became standard in the industry. In 1912, he patented the *carrello*; a "carriage;" which was a "mobile camera stand" allowing easy movement of the camera to follow action. Other technical innovations developed during the filming of *Cabiria* included "diffused light, parallel sequences, panoramas, grandiose sets, and miniature models." At the time of release, credit for the film was given to Gabriele D'Annunzio a prominent Italian poet and writer. Credit as director for *Cabiria* did not arise until 1931, when Pastrone contributed sound to a restored version of the film. Of the wide array of the filming sites, noted film historian Roger Ebert wrote,

> "The film was made with limitless scope and ambition, with towering sets and thousands of extras, with stunts that (because they were actually performed by stuntmen) have an impact lost in these days of visual effects. Hannibal's elephants actually cross the Alps in this movie. But there is room for the tiny detail."[504]

---

[503] Translated as: *Il conte Ugolino*, "The Count Ugolino;" *Agneses Visconti*, "Agneses Visconti;" and *La caduta di Troia*, "The Fall of Troy."
[504] Roger Ebert, "*The Stuff of Dreams*," RogertEbert.com July 2, 2006.

Included within the feature length movie, with a running time of 2 hours 28 minutes, was an epic historical recreation of the Second Punic War between Rome and Carthage. As a long-running film, *Cabiria*, as did others of the Silent Era applied Title Cards withing the film sequences. In Silent Films, title cards were interspersed as a movie frame to convey dialogue, storytelling, or information to set a scene or convey action.[505]

One epic extravagant scene incorporated hundreds of extras to film Carthaginian general Hannibal (? – d. 81/83 B.C.) crossing the Alps replete with hundreds of movie extras, including real-life horses, and elephants.[506] To convey the event, the Title Card reads, "With extraordinary persistence and strength, Hannibal crosses the Alps. The thrust of his advance threatens Rome." As an early "Blockbuster," *Cabiria* was released to worldwide success. In cities such as New York and Paris, the movie remained in theaters for over one year. The film remains into the 21st century as influential among film students and movie historians, especially for study of the technological advancements and adaptations in film making. Granted the Italian immigrant of soon-to-be assimilated culture was rarely if ever depicted in the movies, despite the omission, the future Hollywood production of the film industry was heavily influenced by Italians.

Two Individuals responsible for the production of *Cabiria*. **Above Left**: Director Giovanni Pastrone. **Above Right**: Screenwriter Gabriele D'Annunzio.

---

[505] The formal name for "Title Cards" is "Intertitles;" were first applied around 1903.
[506] The entire feature is available from various online sources including YouTube. See: "Giovanni Pastrone: Cabiria (1914)," *YouTube*, posted June 5, 2013.

Screenshots from Giovanni Pastrone's epic movie *Cabiria* c. 1914.
Top Left: Title card reads: "With extraordinary persistence and strength, Hannibal crosses the Alps. The thrust of his advance threatens Rome." **Top Right**: Hannibal (actor Emilio Vardannes) atop the Alps eyeing the Italian Peninsular. **Middle Left and Right**: Hundreds of extras portraying Hannibal's troops marching through a mountain pass. (Evident are dozens of animals including horses and elephants.) **Bottom Left and Right**: Hundreds of movie extras marching across the real-life snow-covered Alps.
(Public Domain)

CHAPTER 7D

Italian Contributions to the Hollywood Film Industry

Pastrone's work remained in Italy, yet many Italian immigrants became integral to American film production in Hollywood. Despite the influence of individuals such as Pastrone, negative stereotypes of Italians in Hollywood movies were prevalent. Norman Simms article "The Italian-American Image During the Twentieth Century," in the journal *The Histories* provides an aspect of Italian culture in America, as portrayed by the Hollywood film industry, which persisted for many years to come. Simms reminds us,

> "Films like *The Italian* (1914) and *The Organ Grinder* (1909) showed [Italian] immigrants struggling to assimilate into the American culture. The movies combined both comical and serious elements to show how these various groups became Americanized. In many films, the various immigrant groups were stereotyped. . . and Italians would go weeks without a shower."[507]

Historian and documentarian Rosanne De Luca Braun provides a succinct summary in the 2008 documentary "Made in Hollywood: Italian Stereotypes in the Movies." Braun states,

> Behind the camera, the early Italian immigrants helped launch Hollywood's film industry while on-screen they were typecast in roles still recognizable today. Among the Italians who immigrated to America . . . were men and women whose talents were useful to the brand-new American movie business. Their training in stonecutting and sculpture, church decoration and garment-making made them natural resources as costume designers, set decorators, painters, masons, and the all-purpose artisans desperately needed on the movie set.[508]

Despite the valued behind-the-scenes work, the American public only saw the on-screen images portrayed by actors and actresses. During the prominent development of Hollywood as the sole arbiter of movie imagery, DeLuca Braun categorized the on-screen Italian stereotypes included, "urban brute, Latin lover, sensual earth mother, musical clown, [and] gluttonous outsider." Most of the American public remained unaware of the skilled Italians responsible for the actual film production.

One well-known name totally ingrained into the American cultural fabric is the cartoonist and animator Joseph Roland Barbera (1911-2006). Born in New

---

[507] Norman Simms, "The Italian-American Image During the Twentieth Century," The Histories: Vol. 5: Issue 1, Article 4, p. 20. La Salle University Digital Commons. Accessed January 8, 2021.
[508] Rosanne De Luca Braun. "Made in Hollywood: Italian Stereotypes in the Movies," October 30, 2015.

York City to Italian immigrant parents, Barbera began work as a movie animator in Hollywood during the late 1920s. In 1930, he partnered in Hollywood with William Hanna (1910-2001) forming the soon-to-be famous cartoon team of Hanna-Barbera. The pair created legendary movie and television characters such as, *The Flintstones*, *Huckleberry Hound*, *Yogi Bear*, and *The Smurfs*, among dozens of others.

Another was legendary film director Frank Capra (1897-1991); born Francesco Rosario Capra from Palermo, Sicily, who achieved legendary fame during the 1930s. Yet, he developed his filmmaking craft during the Silent Era. During the changeover to talking pictures, Capra was one of, if not the most prominent movie director to make the transition. Throughout a long career Capra was nominated six times for an Academy Award for Best Director; awarded the top prize three times, all in the 1930s, the three films are *It Happened One Night* (1935); *Mr. Deeds Goes to Town* (1937); and *You Can't Take It With You* (1939

TINA MODOTTI
One of "Four of the Biggest Stars of the Era"

Mostly forgotten in American popular culture is Tina Modotti (1896-1942) a Silent film actress, photographer, and political activist; born "Assunta Adelaide Luigia Modotti Mondini" in Udine, Friuli in Italy about 80 miles (130 km) northeast of Venice. Although not necessarily a well-known name in America popular culture, Modotti's work was significant to be classified by the "Italy in Hollywood" exhibit in the Museo Ferragamo as one of "Four of the Biggest Stars of the Era" alongside Hollywood movie idol Rudolph Valentino and Opera singers Enrico Caruso and Lina Cavalieri. Nevertheless, many of her photographs are in the permanent collection at the Metropolitan Museum of Art in New York City. Curatorial Assistant Kelly Sidley at the museum described Modotti's photographs "blend formal rigor with social awareness."

At a young age Modotti worked in a textile factory. In 1913, she traveled to the United States, at the age of 16, joining her father and sister in San Francisco. She soon entered into the entertainment profession quickly becoming "a popular actress on the Italian-language stage." A few years later, encouraged by an artist companion, she moved to Los Angeles for work in films. She garnered a few acting roles in silent films and sometimes posed as a model. In 1923, she moved to Mexico with photographer Edward Weston (1886-1958); learning the craft. Modotti became an accomplished photographer of "meticulously composed and finely detailed images of decontextualized objects, places, and people."[509]

---

[509] Samantha Vaughn, "Italy in Hollywood Exhibition." n.p.

Portrait of Tina Modotti, actress, photographer, and political activist, c. 1920. (Public Domain)

During the 1920s, Modotti was involved supporting "class solidarity among Mexican workers." Her photography of critical photojournalism "captured Mexico's sights and people." Modotti became ensnarled in all sorts of other political turmoil in Mexico and later Europe, eventually travelling to Spain during the Spanish Civil War acting as a humanitarian. In the ensuing years attachment to political causes and Communist sympathy alienated interest in her professional work. Modotti accepted the political rational associated with the plight of Spain and Europe returning to Mexico, suffering an untimely, some say suspicious, death in 1942.[510]

First Male Sex Symbol of the Silver Screen: RUDOLPH VALENTINO

"Shoemaker to the Stars" Salvatore Ferragamo provided service for many screen stars of the emerging Hollywood film industry. Some passed into obscurity; others became screen legends such as *paisan* Rudolph Valentino, who visited Ferragamo

---

[510] See: Kelly Sidley. Curatorial Assistant, Department of Photography, "Tina Modotti: Italian, 1896–1942," 2016. See also: Patricia Albers. "Tina Modotti," 2021

on a regular basis. Visits were not just to procure shoes; rather the two developed a friendship of a shared Italian immigrant experience of culture, language, and rising Hollywood success.

Looking back at 100 years of American culture and movie history, it might be hard to grasp the nationwide exposure and public excitement caused by just one film star – and of an Italian immigrant. A simple explanation is provided by film historian Robert Sklar. In *Movie-Made America: A Cultural History of American Movies*, Sklar states, "Valentino was a presence the silver screen had never seen before."[511]

Above Left: Promotional movie poster for Rudolph Valentino's *The Son of the Sheik*, c. 1926; illustrates the "female fantasy" of being swept up and carried away into Valentino's bedroom. **Above Right**: Publicity portrait of Rudolph Valentino in character as "Julio Desnoyers" in the 1921 Metro Pictures production *The Four Horsemen of the Apocalypse*.
(Public Domain - Wiki Commons).

Rudolph Valentino (1895-1926), birth name of "Rodolfo Alfonso Raffaello Pierre Filibert Guglielmi di Valentina d'Antonguolla," was born in Castellaneta, Italy. A small commune bordering on the Ionian Sea, Castellaneta is located about 25 miles (40 km) north of Taranto in the Apulia region of southern Italy. Biography notes indicate he was the son of an Army officer and veterinarian. His Italian father died when Valentino was young leaving his upbring to his French mother. Military-type schooling did not go well, leaving to study agriculture.

---

[511] Robert Sklar. *Movie-Made America*, New York: Vintage Books, 1994, p. 99.

CHAPTER 7D 381

Around 1912, he traveled in search of work to Paris, France. Unable to find employment he resorted to "begging on the streets." He returned to for a brief time to Castellaneta, soon departing the following year for New York City.[512]

Immigration archives cite the future icon arrived in America on December 23, 1913. His passage may, or may not, have been arranged as did millions of other Italian immigrants – by a *padrone* Francesco "Frank" Mennillo (1882-1936), born in Naples, Italy, known as the "Olive King." Some sources list him as an "unsavory" character; doubting his role acting on Valentino's behalf as a padrone. Despite some conflicting reports, in 1926, biographer and manger S. George Ullman cited, "Frank Mennillo, one of Rudy's dearest Italian friends."[513]

In New York, Valentino's life was "somewhat erratic," without listing a permanent address, working at odd jobs including dishwasher and waiter. Other work was as a gardener, a skill learned in Italy. In New York, Valentino frequented Maxim's, an upscale New York dance palace offering himself as a male dance partner for single women. For male dance hosts, such as the young Valentino, the disparaging title was often "Tango Pirate," or more so, a "Dance Gigolo."

As "Rudolph Valentino," a different persona emerged as many closeups revealed his handsome facial features that literally glowed on the huge Silver Screen. Valentino's roles were not so much as the lone male action hero, or lovable humble comedic actor; rather presented as an artful display of exuberant emanation of human sexuality. Historian Rosanne De Luca Braun described the Valentino screen image as,

> "Darkly handsome, muscular yet lithe and graceful, Valentino's on-screen persona represented long-forbidden eroticism to American women, and on his slender shoulders his fans hung the mantles of passionate lover, sex icon, and exotic liberator of sexual mores."[514]

Valentino's appeal was to women in stark contrast to the likes of demure wholesome female portrayals or swashbuckling male heroes.

---

[512] Biography.com. "Rudolph Valentino Biography," *Biography.com*, April 2, 2014, n.p.
[513] George S. Ullman. *Valentino as I Knew Him*, pp. 26, 216.
[514] Rosanne De Luca Braun. "Made in Hollywood: Italian Stereotypes in the Movies," October 30, 2015. *The Seattle Star* (Seattle, WA), Dec. 10, 1921, p. 3, Image 3, col. 2-4.

A promotional photograph of Heavyweight Boxing Champion Jack Dempsey (left) and Rudolph Valentino (right). Prominently pictured on Valentino's left foot is a Salvatore Ferragamo two-tone Oxford shoe. (The actual shoes are in the collection of the Museo Ferragamo in Florence featured in an exhibition, "Italy in Hollywood.")

As with all of the on-screen Hollywood images, Prof. Braun adds, "Ironically, his real life bore no resemblance to his screen persona." A statement concurred by manager and friend S. George Ullman (1893-1976), in a 1926 biography *Valentino as I Knew Him*. Ullman explained,

> "In attempting to construct such a story, I am confronted by the problem of separating colorful stories in newspapers and magazines from the real Valentino. I gather my material from stories he told me here and there, some related in his Hollywood home, some on our long railway journeys between California and the East."[515]

Looking back over a century from Ullman's sensitive portrayal, Braun notes, "Valentino helped Americans redefine the boundaries of acceptable romantic behavior; ambiguous foreignness and sexuality (envious men were certain he was homosexual) enabled movie audiences to explore their own repressed emotions at

---

[515] George S. Ullman. *Valentino as I Knew Him*, p. 13.

a safe distance." Valentino did portray a "stereotype" of a foreign Latin Lover; yet, from the 1930s onward, the typical Italian stereotype was more often as a gangster or criminal.[516]

In 1919, the Valentino legend provides claim to possibly the shortest celebrity marriage in Hollywood history – a mere six hours. Early in his acting career, Valentino met an actress named Jean Acker (1893-1978). After a very brief acquaintance, the two married. Apparently, the marriage was not consummated as Acker locked Valentino out of her bedroom – divorce quickly. (After divorce they remained on friendly terms. In 1926, Jean Acker was one of the few allowed to visit him while in the hospital; although not on the final day.)

Soon after the Acker affair, Valentino was cast as Julio Desnoyers in *The Four Horsemen of the Apocalypse* (dir. Rex Ingram, 1921) produced by Metro Pictures. Valentino's first appearance in the movie involves him "cutting-in" on a dance couple. Some male stares are exchanged; Valentino's gaze enraptures the female as he takes the woman in his arms leading her through a seductive Tango dance. The mania was almost instantaneous as female fans swooned over their new idol. During that same year, Valentino was cast as the lead in *The Sheik* (dir. George Melford, 1921). In the lead role as Ahmed Ben Hassan. Internet Movie Database described the plot of *The Sheik* as, "A charming Arabian sheik becomes infatuated with an adventurous, modern-thinking Englishwoman and abducts her to his home in the Saharan desert." One typical review for the nationwide sensation proclaimed "The Sheik is Monumental Achievement."

The Scandalous Tango dance scene from *The Four Horsemen of the Apocalypse*. Valentino dancing with actress Beatrice Dominguez. (Wiki Commons – Public Domain)

---

[516] Rosanne De Luca Braun. "Made in Hollywood: Italian Stereotypes in the Movies."

A series of publicity photos of Rudolph Valentino: **Upper Left**: Billed as "Rodolfo Di Valentina" in an early film role, c. 1918. **Upper Right**: The "gaze" which captivated a legion of adoring female fans, c. 1919. **Lower Left**: Promotional photograph in character from *The Sheik*, c. 1921; the movie which made him a major movie star. Photograph by: Donald Biddle Keyes (1894-1974) National Portrait Gallery, Smithsonian Institution. Object number: NPG.95.81. **Lower Right**: Rudolph Valentino, c. 1925. Photograph by Russell Ball (1891-1942) National Portrait Gallery, Smithsonian Institution Object number: NPG.78.4 (Public Domain).

"Blood and Sand," Natacha Rambova, and Mrs. Rudolph Valentino

Another of the top-grossing Valentino films of the year was *Blood and Sand* (dir. Fred Niblo, 1922). In *Blood and Sand*, Valentino was cast as the Spanish matador bullfighter Juan Gallardo. The plot involved the romantic image of the dashing Gallardo torn from his wife and "falls under the spell of a charming seductress" played by actress Nita Naldi (1894-1961). As Valentino's stereotype was a "Latin Lover," Naldi was often cast in another stereotypical role as a "vamp." A "vamp" was considered a female sexual seductress often preying upon married men.[517]

Above Left: Promotional photograph of Natacha Rambova and Rudolph Valentino, c. 1924. **Top Right**: Natacha Rambova, c. 1925. **Lower Right**: Possibly the last photograph of Rambova and Valentino together before she filed for divorce, c. January 1926. (Public Domain)

Natacha Rambova (1897-1966), born Winifred Shaughnessy to a Catholic father and Mormon mother in Salt Lake City was raised in San Francisco. She was educated in England, summer vacationed in France, and trained as a ballerina in Theodore Kosloff's Russian Ballet School in New York City – all before the age

---

[517] The four movies were: *Blood and Sand* (1922), *A Sainted Devil* (dir. by Joseph Henabery, 1924), an unfinished *The Hooded Falcon* (dir. Joseph Henabery, 1924), and *Cobra* (dir. Joseph Henabery 1925).

of 19. (During ballerina training she adopted the name "Natacha Rambova.") By her twentieth birthday, Rambova entered the movie business as a set and costume designer working for famed movie director Cecil B. DeMille in New York. When DeMille relocated to Los Angeles, Rambova went along as costume designer.[518]

Rudolph Valentino and Natacha Rambova in stage costume worn during their 1922-1923 nationwide dance tour sponsored by Minervala Beauty Clay Products.

Biographer S. George Ullman recalled, Rambova first met "Rudy" in 1921 "during production of *Uncharted Seas* (dir. Wesley Rogers)." During the production of another Valentino movie *Camille* (dir. Ray C. Smallwood, 1921), the two became romantically involved as Rambova "helped Rudy with his costumes [and] with the arrangement of his hair." The romance blossomed, leading to marriage and scandal. As filming for *Camille* completed, Valentino and Rambova headed to Mexico to marry on May 13, 1922. Upon return, Valentino was arrested for bigamy. At that time, although divorced from Acker, current law required a full one-year waiting period before entering into another marriage. A brief jail stay for a few days by local authorities was heavily publicized. Since Valentino and Rambova were not married outside of the one-year time frame, they were required to divorce to avoid further legal entanglements. During a later nationwide dance tour, the pair remarried "officially" on March 14, 1923. The dance tour was a success, both financially and promotionally; however, the famous duo later divorced "again" in January 1926.[519]

---

[518] The Bolero-style jacket known as "Suit of Lights" worn by Valentino is on permanent display in the Collection of Motion Picture Costume Design in Los Angeles.
[519] Hala Pickford. "Rudolph Valentino Biography," IMDb Mini Biography, Accessed March 22, 2021.

Johnny *Blood* and Ralph *Sand*

The movie *Blood and Sand* is part of the mythical lore of the National Football League (NFL). As the story is told, John Victor McNally (1903-1985) and a friend Ralph Hanson responded to a call for a tryout with a semi-pro football team. Both had played some college football and did not want to jeopardize their amateur standing. It was not unusual in the early days of professional football to play in somewhat anonymity or false names. Therefore, not to forfeit their amateur status, they assumed the nicknames "Johnny Blood" and "Ralph Sand." In a 1984 article for *Sports Illustrated,* McNally recalled how he adapted the nickname.

> "On the way [to the football tryout], we passed a theater on Hennepin Avenue [in Minneapolis], and up on the marquee I saw the name of the movie that was playing, *Blood and Sand* with Rudolph Valentino. Ralph was behind me on the motorcycle, and I turned my head and shouted, 'That's it. I'll be Blood and you be Sand.'"[520]

McNally made the team, Hanson did not. McNally, eventually played professional football in the fledging NFL for 14 years, mainly with the Green Bay Packers. He was part of the inaugural 1963 class enshrined in the National Football League Hall of Fame in 1963; forever known as John "Blood" McNally.

Above Left: Valentino as matador "Juan Gallardo" wearing the Bolero-style suit designed by Natacha Rambova. **Above Right**: Movie poster for the Paramount Studios production of *Blood and Sand* c. 1922. (Wiki Commons – Public Domain)

---

[520] See: Jeremiah Tax, "A Passel of Pro Football Immortal Recall the Early Days of the Game," *Sports Illustrated*, December 17, 1984. Note: Professional football as entrenched in the psyche of American culture did not blossom as a major American sports attraction until the 1950s.

A promotional story for the soon-to-be released *The Son of the Sheik* which appeared in *Picture-Play Magazine*, March-August, 1926, p. 78. (U.S. Library of Congress, Motion Picture, Broadcasting and Recorded Sound Division.)

The Sheik made Valentino a major star, Hollywood icon, and fantasy desire for countless numbers of adoring female fans. Yet, the mythical movie screen image haunted Valentino for years. At first, he was reluctant to appear in the 1926 sequel *The Son of the Sheik*. As Donna Hill writes "Although Valentino enjoyed making the 1921 film and the fame it brought him, he loathed being characterized as a "Sheik" in off-screen life and had trouble understanding why his fans could

CHAPTER 7D

not separate the man from the image." Hill quoted an explanation provided by Valentino of the contrast between the dashing fantasy screen image and real life. Valentino said, "Women are not in love with me but with the picture of me on the screen. I am merely the canvas on which women paint their dreams." Nevertheless, the image of the real-life Rudolph Valentino and Hollywood sexual fantasy did not easily separate from American culture.[521]

"Pink Powder Puffs" and Effeminacy

In 1915, years before international fame, still known as Rodolpho Guglielmi, he was arrested and jailed on a "charge of effeminacy." A term applied "for a non-masculine homosexual." A significant reason for the accusation was Valentino's known prowess as an accomplished ballroom dancer. Part of the reason, he left New York; eventually to Hollywood and unparalleled stardom. Within a decade, Hollywood's male sex symbol, was once-again faced with the claims of "effeminacy;" causing much consternation for Valentino. Film historian Robert Sklar, provided a similar analysis, saying, "Valentino always projected himself in a way that [Douglas] Fairbanks, the smiling, clean-cut, genteel American hero, rarely did, if ever – as a sexual being." Journalist Gilbert King, writing for *Smithsonian Magazine* in 2012, added, Valentino "single-handedly change the way generations of men and women thought about sex and seduction." Therein lies the cause of the attacks on Valentino's masculinity. Sklar, writing in *Movie-Made America: A Cultural History of American Movies*, explained, "[Valentino] had passion; he loved, openly and fully; his love was strong but could be tragic weakness too." The "tragic weakness," was one of not conforming to the prevalent dominant view of masculinity as prescribed within contemporary American culture.[522]

Missing in the equation is the culture shattering and reversal of the predefined roles of male and female in American society which can be attributed to Rudolph Valentino. The word attachment as a "lover" was easily understood as sexual intercourse, which aroused the sexual fantasies of millions of female fans and of course envy among American males. A reaction that was strictly taboo as a subject of public discussion. 1920s society was two-pronged as one facet slowly accepting change; another severely chastising any notion of a woman freely engaging in unmarried sexual relationships purely for pleasure rather than procreation. The verbal assault and cultural criticism against Rudolph Valentino was not isolated to just the film star, nor Hollywood.

Within the fast-paced rapidly changing decade questions of morality continued to haunt Valentino. In 1922, Dick Dorgan writing for *Photoplay* offered

---

[521] Donna Hill. "Film Essay for "The Son of the Sheik," *Library of Congress*.
[522] Robert Sklar. *Movie-Made America*, p. 99.

a twofold verbal discriminatory accusation against Valentino; one as an Italian immigrant, the second as effeminate. Of the many insults, Dorgan called Valentino's "mother was a *wop*" - an unforgiveable insult to any Italian son; despite Dorgan's ignorance to the fact Valentino's mother was actually French born. The other criticism claimed the actor was a "guy who danced too well;" a direct hint as an effeminate homosexual. Valentino responded, "You slur my Italian ancestry; you ridicule upon my name; cast doubt upon my manhood."[523]

A follow-up in *Photoplay* by a writer named Herbert Howe, pushed the issue further. In a critique of Valentino's influence upon other leading men in Hollywood, Howe claimed, "The movie boys haven't been the same. They're all racing around wearing spit curls, bobbed hair and silk panties. . . This can't keep up. The public can stand just so many ruffles and no more." Added to effeminacy insults, Valentino also suffered from commonly held prejudices that denied acting roles to Italian immigrants for being "too foreign." In fact, only one month before his untimely tragic death, the slurs continued. Gilbert King added, "he spent his final weeks engaged in an indecorous feud with an anonymous editorialist who had questioned his masculinity and blamed him for America's degeneration into effeminacy."[524]

The slurs in question appeared on July 18, 1926 as an unsigned newspaper editorial in the widely circulated *Chicago Tribune*. Published under the audacious title "Pink Powder Puffs," the editorial viciously attacked the Latin Lover,

"A powder vending machine! In a men's washroom! Homo Americanus! Why didn't someone quietly drown Rudolph Guglielmo, alias Valentino, years ago? Do women like the type of "man" who pats pink powder on his face in a public washroom and arranges his coiffure?"

The retort insisted, "Hollywood is the national school of masculinity" that should not promote the image of "Rudy, the beautiful gardener's boy, as the [new] prototype of the American male."

Prototypical machoism is an undeniable facet of American culture. As film historian Robert Sklar, explained,

"Valentino seemed to fulfill the fantasies of millions of American women . . . also the tangled resentment and emulation he aroused in American men. His grace, his ease with his body, his skill as a dancer, all clearly attractive to women, seemed to cause some men considerable unease. For a man to make himself appealing to women they consider a certain sign of effeminacy,"

---

[523] Hala Pickford. "Rudolph Valentino Biography," IMDb Mini Biography, 2021.
[524] Gilbert King. "The Latin Lover and his Enemies," *Smithsonian Magazine*, 2012.

CHAPTER 7D 391

Among the swirl of agony by effeminacy accusations and nationwide publicity for the release of *The Son of the Sheik*, Valentino suffered a tragedy ending his life.[525]

Rudolph Valentino Dies

On August 15, 1926, during a promotional tour for the soon to be nationwide release of *The Son of the Sheik*, Rudolph Valentino collapsed at the Hotel Ambassador in New York City. Valentino was hospitalized in Manhattan for emergency surgery of appendicitis and gastric ulcers. The surgery went well and deemed on the way to full recovery. An infection led to peritonitis; optimistic recovery quickly diminished. Thousands of fans formed a vigil outside the hospital while others swamped telephone lines seeking information of their idol. Valentino's health carried as a major news nationwide updated his condition with front-page headlines, such as *The Baltimore News* boldly reporting,

VALENTINO Dead in a Week if he Fails to Pass CRISIS TONIGHT.

As the eight-day media vigil continued, *The Boston Globe* published an updated headline only a few hours before his death

"Sheik of the Movies, Wearing Hospital Nightshirt,
Besieged by Worshipping Fans and Press Agents,
Even in Grave Illness,"[526]

At the hospital, manager and friend S. George Ullman limited visitors to the star's bedside; other than Ullman, only actress Jean Acker and friend Frank Mennillo were present. Mennillo conversed with the star in Italian, whereas Valentino replied in English. Ullman said the screen idol was heard to reply, "Thank you, Frank. I'm going to be well soon." In a short time, knowing the end was near, a Catholic priest was summoned to administer the Last Rites. Rudolph Valentino smiled weakly and died; with a crucifix pressed to his lips.[527]

The shocking news of the Valentino's death captured the media attention of newspapers and magazines nationwide. Typical examples of front-page bold capitalized headlines included,

VALENTINO DEAD
RUDOLPH VALENTINO DIES
NATION MOURNS VALENTINO
RUDOLPH VALENTINO IS DEAD

---

[525] Joshi, *H. L. Mencken on Religion*, p. 11. See also: H.L. Mencken, "The Library," *American Mercury* 2, no. 5 (May 1924): pp. 120-21.
[526] "Sheik of the Movies, Wearing Hospital Nightshirt," *Boston Globe,* Aug. 22, 1926.
[527] See: Ullman, *Valentino As I Knew Him*, p. 216.

Newspapers continuously updated the public with details of Valentino's funeral services arranged in New York by Frank E. Campbell. One reporter likened Campbell as "the world's foremost mortician, as big a man in the funeral game as Rudolph Valentino was in the movies."

Frank E. Campbell (1872-1934), within his profession, was instrumental in changing the way Americans had funerals. Before his establishment, a viewing for a person's death was held within the home of the deceased, usually located in the parlor. In 1898, the Frank E. Campbell Burial and Cremation Company is credited as one who "basically invented the idea of the funeral chapel all by himself." At the time of Valentino's death, the convenience of a viewing in a Funeral Parlor such as provided by Frank Campbell became a common and profitable. The glamor created by Campbell was focused upon "everybody who was anybody" was laid to rest in the extravagant Gold Room on the second floor.

Thousands of fans assemble outside Campbell Funeral Home located on Broadway and 66th Street in New York City waiting to view the body of film star Rudolph Valentino. (Public Domain)

In August 1926, Valentino was Campbell's most famous client to date. The extravagant viewing set up in the Gold Room centered on a draped silver coffin valued at $10,000; encompassed by hundreds of flowers.

The Valentino funeral became a combination of Hollywood publicity stunt and real-life grief. An ingenious addition as part of the "stunt," included, as

Campbell told reporters, two "Black Shirted" guards would maintain a constant vigil and security adjacent to the coffin. Campbell said the guards were sent by Italian dictator Benito Mussolini ordered to stand in watch over a famous Son of Italy. In fact, none of it was true as the "thugs" were hired by the funeral homes. Despite a rainy day, the publicity encouraged mourners and fans jamming the streets of Broadway, soon estimated at over 10,000 people.

This photo on page one of *The Warren Tribune* newspaper of August 26, 1926, shows a knelling mourner at Frank E. Campbell Funeral Chapel named as "Eva Miller, a fan of Valentino's." The extravagant viewing set up in the Gold Room centered on a draped silver coffin valued at $10,000; the coffin was encompassed by hundreds of flowers valued at over $50,000. (Public Domain)

The following day, an estimated 50,000 people lined up waiting patiently to walk by the open casket to catch a glimpse of their idol. In a short time, possibly due to jostling and anxiousness, or on purpose, a riot ensued. Fifty or sixty New York City Police were soon at work swinging their nightsticks in an attempt to quell the riot among the "shrieking hordes of bereaved." A Catholic Funeral mass was held on West 49th Street; outside a huge crowd, estimated over 100,000, filled the streets. Valentino's burial would not occur in New York, as the casket was soon placed on a train for a cross-country trip to his final resting place in California. During the media frenzy, the movie production company for *The Son of the Sheik* seeking to capitalize on the free publicity quickly ordered another 200 distribution copies. Within the days of an avalanche of publicity, the movie played to rousing and mournful audiences across the nation.[528]

As incredulous as it sounds, despite the obvious financial rewards reaped by the media and Hollywood producers, no money was offered to properly bury the famous screen idol. A solution was provided by friend and screen writer June Mathis (1887-1927); the first female executive for Metro/MGM pictures. Mathis provided a burial crypt at Hollywood Memorial Park Cemetery (later renamed: Hollywood Forever Cemetery).

Possibly as a continuing publicity stunt, each year on the anniversary of the screen idol's death, a "mysterious "Lady in Black" appeared at his tomb and left a single red rose."[529]

Above Left: Promotional photograph of Rudolph Valentino and screen writer June Mathis on the movie set of *Blood and Sand*, c. 1922. The "Bolero-style" matador jacket was designed by Natacha Rambova, who would become his twice-married wife. **Above Right**: Rudolph Valentino Burial Crypt at Hollywood Forever Cemetery, provided by friend and screenwriter June Mathis. Photograph by Arthur Dark, June 2, 2015. (Published Domain under Wiki Creative Commons License).

Russ Columbo: "Radio's Valentino"

One of the earliest Italian popular music idols was Russ Columbo (1908-1934), born Ruggiero Eugenio di Rodolfo Columbo as the 12th child to Italian immigrant

---

[528] Jay Maeder. "When thousands swarmed . . . for Rudolph Valentino's funeral."
[529] History.com Editors. "Valentino Dies," *History A&E Television Networks*, February 9, 2010.

parents Nicola and Giulia Columbo. As a singer, actor, musician, and songwriter, Columbo achieved mild fame as a film actor, but much greater fame as a singer and host of a radio show in New York. Dashing good looks played well with female fans, publicized as "Radio's Valentino." Russ Columbo's vocal style arose from the singing style known as "crooning;" as a tantalizing low and slow tempo ballad. Crooning was made popular by superstars such as Bing Crosby (1903-1977) and possibly the greatest popular singer of all-time Italian American Frank Sinatra (1915-1998). Sinatra born to Italian immigrant parents in Hoboken, New Jersey (in sight of Ellis Island).[530]

Above Left: Promotional photograph of Russ Columbo, capturing a similar allure recalling an imagery of Rudolph Valentino. **Above Right**: Front page of a December 1931 trade publication *Radio Guide* promoting singer Russ Columbo as "Radio's Valentino." (Public Domain)

Colombo's mythical legacy also lived on after suffering a double heavily publicized tragic occurrence. While living in New York, he was involved in a well-publicized relationship with an actress named Dorothy Dell, who was later killed in an auto accident in June 1934. Only a few months later, in September, Columbo met an untimely accidental death at the age 26 caused by a ricochet of a bullet fired from an antique dueling pistol held by a friend. Hollywood publicists also linked Colombo in a romantic affair with other popular actresses of the time.

---

[530] "Radio's Valentino," *Radio Guide* Vol. 1. No. 6, December 1931, p. 1.

The Valentino Legacy: "The Cult of Celebrity"

Rudolph Valentino's rise to stardom in 1921 coincided with a nationwide crusade for censorship of Jazz music and restricting solicitous dancing, such as The Charleston and Tango. The attacks over his masculinity and effeminacy occurred as Federal Legislation severely limited immigration, especially Italians. As the ultimate coincidence, Valentino's untimely death coincided with the end of the Silent Film Era. Despite it all, his legacy continued. Numerous biographies, documentaries, and films on the screen legend abound. One example listed on Internet Movie Database of a 1961 documentary *The Legend of Rudolph Valentino*, described as, "A documentary of Hollywood's first great Latin Lover [as] a new ideal in romantic leading men." A feature length 1977 Hollywood film simply titled *Valentino* (dir. Ken Russell) with famous dancer Rudolf Nureyev (1938-1993) in the lead role. That same year a comedic parody of Rudolph Valentino titled *The World's Greatest Lover* starred and directed by Gene Wilder (1933-2016) was released to decent box office success. Dozens of another examples abound in American culture. In 1983, the ultimate tribute in American popular culture occurred as the ever-popular and world-renowned Muppet Kermit the Frog star of the *Muppet Show* was portrayed on a coffee mug wearing a Sheik costume with the added phrase, "World's Greatest Lover."

CHAPTER 8

THE 20TH CENTURY: HEROES, VILLAINS, AND CULTURAL NOTABLES

"With the arrival of the Piccirillis, it became unnecessary for American sculptors to go to Italy to have their sculpture translated into marble."

"I have been an American for so long – fifty years – that I often forget I was born in Italy. When anyone refers to me as a foreigner, or as an Italian, I pretend that I haven't heard and I don't usually answer.
Of course, I am an American."

History has obscured the abundance of contributions of Italians in all aspects of cultural development in America. A continued disparaging image has often buried the positive attainment under the negative. The "negative" is obviously a criminal association placed upon all Italians. An association of totally false summations by mythical Hollywood portrayals and media misrepresentations. Unfortunately, the negative association is one almost impossible to erase. Sources cite the 1891 lynching of Italian immigrants in New Orleans as the first use of the word "Mafia" to describe a criminal element associated with "all" Italians in America. One thesis by Maria Laurino explains,

> "Myths about Italian-American culture run deep into the fabric of American life, obscuring the complicated, nuanced, centuries-long story of the Italian-American experience that demands to be told."

One of the most egregious glaring examples of myth overlapping reality involves the trial and execution of two Italian immigrants named Nicola Sacco and Bartolomeo Vanzetti.[531]

---

[531] Maria Laurino, *Italian Americans: A History*, p. 1.

Sacco and Vanzetti: Guilty, Innocent, or "Legal Lynching"

An almost impossibility is to perform any type of individual search for either Sacco or Vanzetti without finding the biographical entry of one linked to the other. The search also leads directly to one of the most famous murder trials in the history of the United States.

Nicola Sacco (1891-1927) was born in the southern Italian town of Torremaggiore, 125 miles (200 km) northeast of Naples. At age 17, Sacco immigrated into the United States to Boston. He found work in a shoe factory in Stoughton, Massachusetts. In 1912, he married Rosina Zambelli and fathered son Dante (1913-1971) and daughter Ines (1920-2014).

Bartolomeo Vanzetti (1888-1927) was born in the Italian town of Villafalletto about 35 miles (60 km) south of Turin. In 1908, Vanzetti left the family farm entering through New York. The unmarried Vanzetti worked "as a fish peddler." Some state Vanzetti as "not interested in women," was a damaging reference to homosexuality, but not true.[532]

Above Left: Nicola Sacco **Above Right**: Bartolomeo Vanzetti from a Boston Police file photo on the date of their arresst of May 5, 1920.

---

[532] John Simkin. "Bartolomeo Vanzetti." *Spartacus Educational*, 1997-2020.

A commonly reproduced photograph of Bartolomeo Vanzetti (left) and Nicola Sacco (right), c. 1923; are physically linked in handcuffs as they are symbolically linked forever in history. (Courtesy Boston Public Library Public Domain).

Regionally and culturally as Italians, one born in the north and one born in the south, the pair could not have been so different. Once in America, however, the two joined in a common political cause. For each, daily work and personal observations produced experiences to the way working class immigrants were regularly mistreated in America. Each became involved in political groups advocating for fairer treatment of workers. Vanzetti often embracing "left-wing politics" attended anarchist meetings in and around the Boston area. While attending those meetings an association developed with Sacco. Sometime in 1917, the two men became friends and often attended the same political meetings together. Research historian John Simkin writing a combined biographical sketch said,

> "Like many left-wing radicals, Sacco and Vanzetti were opposed to the First World War. They took part in protest meetings and in 1917, when the United States entered the war, they fled together to Mexico in order to avoid being conscripted into the United States Army. When the war was over the two men returned to the United States."

In the aftermath of the horrific First World War, a "Red Scare" claiming Bolsheviks and Anarchist were rampant throughout the country rallying immigrants to violent action. The growing Nativism reaction against labor unrest routinely placed blame on the overwhelming "horde of foreigners invading American shores." As the 1920s began another incident causing public outcry involved Italian immigrants. On April 15, 1920, Frederick Parmenter (1874-1920) a paymaster for Slater and Morrill a shoe factory and a security guard Alessandro Berardelli (?- 1920) were shot and killed during a payroll robbery in South Braintree, Massachusetts. A few weeks later Nicola Sacco and Bartolomeo Vanzetti were arrested as perpetrators to the crime. A trial began on May 21, 1921.

The sensationalized murder was part of the paranoia and fear of internal anarchy – sweeping Sacco and Vanzetti into the frenzied whirlpool.[533]

In analyzing the court proceedings, many historians agree that Sacco and Vanzetti were subjected to a mishandled trial, as judge, jury, and prosecution were biased because of their anarchist political views and Italian immigrant status. Harvard Law School professor and future U.S. Supreme Court Justice Felix Frankfurter (1882-1965) chronicled the trial for *The Atlantic Monthly* magazine. Prof. Frankfurter focused on the injustice suffered by Sacco and Vanzetti. Frankfurter wrote,

> "Exploitation of their alien blood, imperfect knowledge of English, their unpopular social views, and their opposition to the war, the District Attorney invoked against them a riot of political passion and patriotic sentiment; and the trial judge cooperated in the process."

In a series of articles, Frankfurter provided a detailed account of the trial with quotes worthy of an official court transcript. Frankfurter's article provided by the editors of *The Atlantic Monthly* stated, despite the fact of "arguments brought against them were mostly disproven in court" Sacco and Vanzetti were convicted of the robbery and murder. The sentence came with a death penalty by the Electric Chair.[534]

Norfolk County Courthouse in Dedham, Massachusetts, c. 2008 on the National Register of Historic Places. Design influenced by the Italian architect Andrea Palladio.
(Photo by: Biruitorul released into Public Domain – Wiki Commons)

---

[533] Susan Tejada. *In Search of Sacco and Vanzetti: Double Lives*, 2012.
[534] Felix Frankfurter. "The Case of Sacco and Vanzetti." *Atlantic Monthly*, 1927.

CHAPTER 8

Discussion on the trial, verdict, and subsequent historical legacy is not necessarily a question of guilt or innocence. Rather according to the University of Virginia Law archives "their conviction became a symbol for jury bias and erroneous verdicts." 50 years after their execution, Massachusetts Governor Michael Dukakis issued a proclamation Sacco and Vanzetti were unfairly tried and convicted. Journalist Fred Hanson correctly explained the reason no pardon was issued "because that would imply, they were guilty." A question for the entire trial and execution might be, was it just a sham to allow a "legal lynching"?[535]

Al Smith: The Irish Catholic "Italian" Governor

On February 17, 1919, as the 369th Infantry Regiment of the famous "Harlem Hellfighters," proudly marched in a World War I victory parade in New York City. *The New York Herald Tribune* reported, upon passing a reviewing stand, a host of dignitaries included "New York's popular Irish Catholic governor Alfred E. Smith." Gov. Smith publicly identified with the prominent and politically influential New York Irish American community. However, his ethnicity was not fully Irish. Four grandparents of different ethnic backgrounds were Irish, German, Anglo, and *Italian*. Paternal grandfather, Alfredo Emanuel Ferraro born in Genoa, Italy, changed the family name upon immigration to America due to anti-immigrant discrimination. As journalist Mark Phelan writing for *The Irish Times*, explained in a 2016 article, "Despite his neutral patronym, Smith's paternal roots were actually Italian. Faced with anti-immigrant hysteria, his grandfather, Alfredo Ferraro, had adopted an English version of his birth-name *"ferraro"* being the Italian for blacksmith." The last name *Ferraro* translates closely as "blacksmith." in Italian.[536]

Alfred Emanuel Smith (1873-1944) entered politics at age of 29; elected in 1903 to the New York state assembly; in 1918 elected Governor of New York - reelected four times. In 1924, Smith's national prominence made him a presidential candidate, securing the nomination in 1928. As a child born of immigrants, Smith represented what any American could achieve in the United States. Although he did not drink, he supported the repeal of Prohibition. As a non-drinking Catholic in full support of repealing Prohibition, Smith's 1928 candidacy was shaped as a contest of "Wets" (favoring repeal) versus "Dry's" (favoring Prohibition). In essence Protestant dominance versus the Roman Catholic Church. As a national candidate, Smith's Italian ancestry was hardly ever

---

[535] Fred Hanson. "Braintree dedicates memorial to 2 men killed in famous 1920 murder-robbery." *The Patriot Ledger,* April 16, 2010. See also: "Dengrove Recreates the 1921 Sacco and Vanzetti Trial." University of Virginia Law Archives. March 26, 2022.

[536] *The New York Tribune*, February 18, 1919. See: Henry Louis Gates. "Who Were the Harlem Hellfighters?" *PBS.org*, February 4, 2021.

mentioned. Organized Protestant religious leaders as the New York based Rev. John Roach Straton staunchly opposed to New York Governor Al Smith's campaign for president of the United States. The main reason for united opposition was Smith's Catholicism.[537]

Historical accounts of the 1928 election focus, as *Time* magazine stated, "Prohibition has been made an issue in a Presidential campaign." Any credible research of the time reveals the obvious reason was a non-Protestant candidate was running for president of the United States. On October 1, 1928, one month before the national election, reports surfaced of a leaflet labeling and therefore attacking "Roman Catholic Al Smith" was distributed in over 30,000 Protestant Churches nationwide. The national Protestant newsletter *The American Issue,* derided Smith stating,

"If you believe in Anglo-Saxon Protestant domination you will vote for Hoover rather than Smith. The Anglo-Saxon Protestants, working through both parties, have dominated America, and made it what it is today a world leader."[538]

Portrait of Alfred E. Smith, c. 1920-1930 from the Harris & Ewing Collection at the U.S. Library of Congress. (Public Domain)

Contrary to the Protestant falsehoods, Stanley Walker city editor of the *New York Herald Tribune* stated the obvious, "Of all the many counts against Smith, one was that he was a New Yorker. As such, he was to be taken as the high and menacing symbol of evil and his name held up before the country as the man who represented all that was abhorrent about the great city from pronunciation to liquor-drinking."

---

[537] Mark Phelan. "An Irishman's Diary: Al Smith," *The Irish Times* October 25, 2016.
[538] "30,000 Churches," *Time* October 1, 1928. Walker, *The Night Club Era*, p. 65.

Earlier in April 1927, Charles C. Marshall, an Episcopal New York lawyer said "Smith was continually badgered by the Protestant suspicion of Catholics connection with the Pope in Rome." As the Ku Klux Klan was entrenched with Protestant Fundamentalists, it was easy to apply trigger words accusing Smith as "the candidate of Rum, Romanism and Rebellion." Historical instances of anti-Catholic bigotry by the Ku Klux Klan are many. One horrid example existed in the Zarephath community in Somerset County, New Jersey. An Evangelical preacher Branford Clarke (1885-1947), who openly supported the Ku Klux Klan, personally illustrated many anti-Catholic political cartoons. One 1926 example, "The Subtle Conspirator" in the newsletter *Klansmen Guardians of Liberty* was published by Clarke's Pillar of Fire Church in Zarephath. The illustration portrays an individual representing the Catholic Church sent from Rome camped under an American flag tent outside a public school building. The "perpetrator" is preparing Catholic propaganda for the young children.[539]

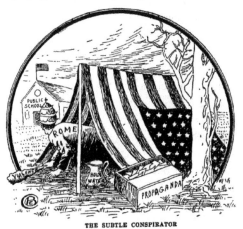

"The Subtle Conspirator," a 1926 anti-Catholic political cartoon in the newsletter "*Klansmen: Guardians of Liberty*" published by the Pillar of Fire Church in Zarephath by Branford Clarke an Evangelical preacher who openly supported the Ku Klux Klan.

A barrage continued associating Smith as "servant" of the Catholic religion. Fear was continually spread throughout America with cartoons, newspaper stories, and pulpit preaching often illustrated by caricatures of Smith extending the New York / New Jersey Holland Tunnel all the way to the Vatican in Rome. The Ku Klux Klan newsletter *Fellowship Forum* parodied a "President Smith

---

[539] "30,000 Churches," *Time* October 1, 1928.

Cabinet" held with the Pope surrounded by Catholic Priests with an obliging Smith "serving them liquor."

Representation of Smith as the servant of the Catholic hierarchy appeared in *The Fellowship Forum*, November 3, 1928, a widely circulated nationwide publication of the Ku Klux Klan. It is typical of the extreme anti-Catholic KKK propaganda. (New York State Library, Albany)

Another illustration showed a victorious Klan member holding an American flag and a Bible seated over a defeated Smith, with remnants of Catholic paraphernalia strewn about. The crusade by "Dry" Protestants resulted in a lopsided electoral return of only 87 for Smith against 444 by Herbert Hoover. Smith lost four key southern states Virginia, North Carolina, Florida, and Texas that had consistently voted Democratic since 1876; but were overwhelmingly Protestant and "Dry." Smith said the defeat was based "on anti-Catholic bigotry."[540]

Illustration of a Klan member holding an American flag and a victorious Bible seated over a defeated Al Smith; remnants of Catholic paraphernalia are strewn about.

---

[540] "Deadliest Foe." *TIME.com*, 20 August 1928.

Aviation History - *Storia dell'aviazione* and Charles Lindbergh

When brothers Orville Wright (1871-1948) and Wilbur Wright (1867- 1912) launched a "flying machine" from the grounds of Kitty Hawk in North Carolina on December 17, 1903, the event lasting about 12 seconds garnered little attention. Motorized flight in an airplane was considered a novelty and in many parts of the nation virtually unknown. By the second decade, airplanes were a permanent presence within America and Europe; playing a formidable role during World War I. Speeds reached over 100 mph at altitudes of 15 to 20,000 feet with an endurance of about 2 to 3 hours. Through the next decade, air flight turned its attention away from warfare towards commercial capabilities.

In 1927, aviation interest reached a frenzy as Charles Lindbergh (1902-1974) completed the first solo trans-Atlantic crossing. The feat was covered by national newspapers, magazines, and radio broadcasts; all hailed him as a hero. Upon return to America, Lindbergh was honored with a massive ticker-tape parade along Broadway known as "The Canyon of Heroes" in New York City. The airplane, a custom built Ryan parasol-wing monoplane, christened the *Spirit of St. Louis*" became as famous as Lindbergh. The original, hangs above the entryway at the Smithsonian National Air and Space Museum in Washington, D.C. Other replica's exist such as on display at the San Diego Air & Space Museum; a flying version is located at Old Rhinebeck Aerodrome in upstate New York.

A replica of Charles Lindbergh's *Spirit of St. Louis* on display at the San Diego Air & Space Museum, c. 2019. (Photograph by Author).

Lindbergh's accomplishment was recognized by an official proclamation of the U.S. Congress. One year after the event, Congress appropriated funding for a 50-

foot high bronze statue immortalizing the aviator's historic flight. The work awarded to Italian artist Frank Vittor imagined "a winged youth spanning the Statue of Liberty and the Eiffel Tower."

Frank Vittor (1888-1968) was born "Francesco Fabio Vittori" in Mozzate outside of Milan in northern Italy. A significant amount of Vittor's work is located in and near the city of Pittsburgh, Pennsylvania. One work, a statue of Pittsburgh Pirate baseball player Honus Wagner (1874-1955), is outside the stadium. Near the end of Vittor's life a commission was awarded for a statue of Christopher Columbus located in Pittsburgh's municipal Schenley Park. A 2008 article in the *Pittsburgh Tribune-Review* credits Vittor with "more than 50 statues and fountains, as well as numerous other works, including a dozen historical panels."

"Statue of Christopher Columbus" by artist Frank Vittor. In the foreground is a National historical marker placed by Pennsylvania Historical and Museum Commission in 2008. Photo by: Staticshakedown, August 17, 2014 released "under the Creative Commons Attribution Share Alike 4.0 International license."

Lindbergh's astounding accomplishment earned distinction by *Time* magazine (founded in 1923) to proclaim Charles Lindbergh "Man of the Year" for 1927; but not on the cover. One aeronautical individual who did earn an honor on the *Time* cover for July 4, 1927, was Giuseppe Mario Bellanca, an Italian immigrant whose airplane was the first choice Lindbergh wanted to purchase for the soon-to-be historic flight.[541]

Fiorello La Guardia and Giuseppe Bellanca – Italian Pioneers

Upon entry into the grand entrance hall of the Cradle of Aviation Museum in Long Island, New York, a glance upwards allows a clear view of a parasol airplane

---

[541] *Time* magazine July 4, 1927, Vol. X No. 1.

CHAPTER 8

N1911G, designed and built by Italian Giuseppe Bellanca. The museum text titled "Giuseppe Bellanca: Son of Italy Long Island Aviation Pioneer" describes,

> "In 1911 [Bellanca] built his first airplane in America in the back of the family bakery in Brooklyn, a high wing monoplane of his own design. After construction was completed, he took the small craft to the Mineola Flying Field [Long Island] and proceeded to teach himself to fly. By early 1912, having successfully taught himself to fly, Bellanca then set about teaching others. Between 1912 and 1916 he operated the Bellanca Flying School on the Hempstead Plains Airfield, now the site of the Roosevelt Field Mall. His first student was Fiorello La Guardia, the future Mayor of New York City.

Fiorello Henry La Guardia (1882-1947), son of immigrant parents of Italian-Jewish heritage served as a bomber pilot during World War I. After the war La Guardia was elected to the U.S. Congress; and later elected as 99th Mayor of New York City serving from 1934 to 1945.[542]

Prior to the war, La Guardia worked as an interpreter (of many languages) at the Ellis Island Immigration Station. The biography leading towards election to the U.S. Congress and as a World War I aviator would be significant for anyone in history. A unique situation volunteering for military service during the war came while serving as a member of Congress. The Official Website for the Department of Homeland Security cites, "becoming the first sitting member of Congress to serve in the U.S. Army." After the war, La Guardia returned to America "and accepted a position as an interpreter at Ellis Island."

As an interpreter, most would assume it was translating Italian to English, however a "mastery" of many languages proved invaluable assistance to many immigrants of various nationalities. As an added caveat, his time at Ellis Island allowed him to learn "Yiddish" – a talent which proved valuable during his campaigns for Congress and New York City Mayor. As a member of Congress, he was outspoken in his staunch opposition to the Immigration Act of 1924. Throughout his long career he was a strong defender of immigrant rights, especially for Italians and their descendants in America. As a stout patriotic American, he was noted for "his long-standing connections with Italian immigrant communities in New York and the anti-fascist Italians in Italy – thereby making him a persuasive and popular voice." Little is often said about La Guardia's association with the Italian aviation pioneer Giuseppe Bellanca.[543]

---

[542] Sometimes cited as: "LaGuardia." Museum Text – Cradle of Aviation Museum, Garden City, Long Island, NY.

[543] "Profiles in World War I Immigration History: Fiorello La Guardia," *U.S. Citizenship and Immigration Services*, Department of Homeland Security. October 18, 2018.

Giuseppe Mario Bellanca (1886-1960) born in Sciacca, Sicily, attended the Technical Institute in Milan, graduating with a teaching degree in mathematics in 1908. He became enamoured of aviation; setting out to design and build his own airplane. In 1909, in Italy, Bellanca, with partners Enea Bossi and Paolo Invernizzi, "built his first airplane which became the first Italian designed aircraft to fly." A follow-up design was built, but did not fly due to lack of money for an engine. Seeking a better opportunity, Bellanca left Italy to join his brother Carlo in America.

In 1911, Bellanca built a parasol type airplane (his third design in the backyard of a family bakery in Brooklyn, New York.) The aircraft, powered by a 3-cylinder 30hp Italian built Anzani engine, was transported to a flying field in Mineola on Long Island, where Bellanca "proceeded to teach himself to fly." Almost immediately thereafter, Bellanca organized and operated a flying school at the site. Instruction was offered from 1912 to 1916, while continuing advancing aircraft design.[544]

Bellanca continued to design and build aircraft with other partners and manufactures. In the 1920s, with the Wright Aeronautical Corporation of New Jersey, Bellanca was tasked to design an airplane powered by a new Wright Whirlwind engine. The design, as the Wright-Bellanca WB-1, achieved some mild success. In 1925, the design was improved as the WB-2, recognized as the first enclosed cabin aircraft design in American aviation history. The prototype Bellanca WB-2 designated "Bellanca C.F." is on display at the Smithsonian Air and Space Museum in Washington DC. The curators described the historical design as, "Italian immigrant Giuseppe Bellanca, embraced a completely new vision and design in the early 1920s, offering four passengers comfort and cover in a cabin while keeping the traditional open cockpit for the pilot."

In June 1922, at a midwestern air competition, the Bellanca C.F. "won all four events of speed, time to climb, and gliding endurance." Over the next two years aviation "wins" included the 1923 National Air Races. Despite success, the Wright Aeronautical Company decided to concentrate on only aircraft engines and did not put the WB-2 into production. Bellanca purchased the rights to the WB-2, parted with Wright, forming the Columbia Aircraft Company in partnership with Charles Levine (1897-1991). The WB-2 continued to set speed and altitude records; adding an endurance record of over 50 hours without refueling.[545]

---

[544] See also: "Giuseppe M. Bellanca" *Bellanca Airfield Museum,* Accessed July 24, 2021.
[545] See: "Bellanca C.F. *Smithsonian Air and Space Museum.* (Levine, who was not a pilot, was destined to become the "first trans-Atlantic passenger.")

The third aircraft design, and first for Bellanca in America, flew on May 12, 1912 at a flying field in Mineola, Long Island. Pictured above, the parasol-type aircraft, powered by a 30hp Anzani engine, hangs in the entrance hall of the Cradle of Aviation Museum Hall in Garden City Long Island, NY. (Photograph by Author, c. 2017. By Permission of Cradle of Aviation Museum).

Restored Bellanca CF - held in the National Air and Space Museum Collection, Boeing Aviation Hangar, Steven F. Udvar-Hazy Center in Chantilly, VA. Gift of August T. Bellanca Record No. A19620015000 (CCO – No Known Restrictions on Publication).

The endurance record caught the attention of aviation pioneer Charles Lindbergh (1902-1974) who wanted to purchase the plane for a solo tarns-Atlantic flight. Financially out of reach, Lindbergh settled on a custom built Ryan monoplane *Spirit of St. Louis* crossing the Atlantic on May 20-21 in 1927. Less than one-month later pilot Clarence Chamberlin (1893-1976), with Levine as a "passenger," flew the Bellanca WB-2 non-stop - New York to Germany - exceeding Lindbergh's record.[546]

The original Bellanca C.F. passed through many owners. For a time, the C.F. was at the Roosevelt Field Air Museum on Long Island. Later returned to the Bellanca family in Maryland. After Giuseppe Bellanca died in 1960, the family donated the C.F. airplane to the Smithsonian Air and Space facility at Silver Hill in Maryland. It was restored with many rebuilt parts with a major addition of an original 110 hp Anzani engine.[547]

The Bellanca WB-2 "Columbia," upon completion of a transatlantic flight in June 1927 from New York to Eisleben in Germany. Less than one month after Charles Lindbergh. (RAF Museum - Public Domain)

The Engines of Alessandro Anzani

The engine on two of Giuseppe Bellanca's famous airplanes was designed by Italian Alessandro Anzani (1877-1956), born in Gorla near Milan. With little formal education, Anzani had a strong interest in all things mechanical; possibly encouraged by his father who repaired sewing machines. As an apprentice to an uncle, Anzani took to bicycle racing, a popular sport of the time. In 1902, building motorcycles, led to a new development. As an offshoot of motorcycle engines Anzani built a lighter two cylinder engine. In 1905, the Anzani engine set a world motorcycle speed record; the prize money was used to establish his own factory.

---

[546] See: "Bellanca C.F. *Smithsonian Air and Space Museum*. See also: Derek O'Connor. "An Outstanding American Citizen," *HistoryNet.com*.
[547] Paul Freeman. "Abandoned & Little-Known Airfields: New York City, Staten Island," January 17, 2021. Ed Drury. "Staten Island: The Other Cradle of Aviation Paperback."

As noted in a blog "The First Air Races," Anzani "realized that his lightweight air-cooled engines would be suitable for the emerging airplane industry. Further development of a lightweight three-cylinder engine was later used by Louis Blériot [1872-1936] for the first airplane crossing of the English Channel." (The 1909 channel crossing by Blériot rates among one of the most famous feats in early aviation history ranked with the Wright Brothers invention and Charles Lindbergh's solo Atlantic flight in 1927.) The astounding feat and media coverage, of Blériot's flight created a large demand for Anzani airplane engines. In 1912, *paisan* Giuseppe Bellanca applied a three-cylinder Anzani engine on his first American built parasol monoplane.[548]

Top Left: Anzani Military Model Fan type 3-cylinder aircraft engine.
Top Right: Anzani Y-type 3-cylinder 30hp engine in the Shuttleworth Collection in England. **Bottom Left**: Ten-cylinder 110 hp Anzani engine in the National Museum of the U.S. Air Force. (Wiki Creative Commons).

Enea Bossi – Aviation Pioneer

Among Giuseppe Bellanca's future business partners was Italian Enea Bossi (1888-1963). An aeronautical engineer and aviation pioneer, Bossi born in Milan, earned a degree in physics and mathematics at the *Instituto Tecnico*. With an interest sparked by news of the Wright Brothers, he was "fascinated with flight." Considered only the second Italian to earn a pilot's license (most likely taught by Bellanca) Bossi began designing aircraft. He soon developed various aircraft systems including landing-gear braking system, fuel systems, and seaplanes.

---

[548] "Alessandro Anzani 1877-1956," *The First Air Races*, Accessed July 23, 2021.

During World War I, Bossi was a bomber pilot. After the war, Bossi immigrated to America receiving naturalized citizenship in 1925. In the 1930s, Bossi designed "the first [all] stainless steel aircraft" the Budd BB-1 Pioneer on permanent display since 1935 outside the Franklin Institute Museum in Philadelphia.[549]

Above Left: Portrait of aviation pioneer Enea Bossi c. 1920s." **Above Right**: Enea Bossi in a typical Italian family portrait with wife Flora nee: Kehrer (1898-1991) and children Charles (1922-1989) (left) and Enea Jr. (1924-1999) (right).

The Budd BB-1 *Pioneer* airplane designed by Enea Bossi was the first aircraft made of stainless steel. It has been on display in front of Franklin Institute in Philadelphia, since 1935. Photograph by Andrew Bossi, c. 2018. (Published under Wiki Creative Commons

Jacuzzi, Airplanes, Toothpick Propeller, and the Hot Tub

Airplanes require quality engines and propellers. An unlikely 21st century recognition of the word "Jacuzzi" conjures up images of a hot tub spa. In

---

[549] "Enea Bossi: Aviation Pioneer," 2017.: Jessica Rodriguez, "Enea Bossi."

American culture the word "Jacuzzi" recalls images of blissful relaxation and feelings described in words such as "oohs" and "aahs." The device owes its origins to an Italian immigrant family. What should come as a surprise was the Jacuzzi family contributions to the aviation industry.

The family industry began with Giovanni (1855-1929) and Teresa Jacuzzi (1864-1943) from Casarsa in northeastern Italy. From 1907 to 1921, father, mother, and 13 children immigrated to America specifically southern California. In 1911, Rachele Jacuzzi (1886-1937) "designed and built a successful wooden propeller" nicknamed as "The Toothpick." It is on display in the Smithsonian Air and Space Museum. Rachele did not receive much formal education beyond the 3rd grade; often described as having "a passion and genius for aviation." The "narrower, longer, and lower pitched" design allowed the engine to run at increased RPM's with greater power output The propeller also earns the distinction as the first in a long line of Jacuzzi inventions and product designs.

Located in Berkeley, California, the Jacuzzi Brothers family business operated out of a large factory-type building. Within that building "Rachele Jacuzzi built a prototype of a small monoplane." Another was a larger monoplane; proposed to fly as a commercial airplane along a "ninety-mile route to connect San Francisco, Oakland, Richmond, and Sacramento." Early organizational flights led to tragedy with a crash killing four, including a younger Jacuzzi brother prompting the family out of the aviation business. The tragedy may have ended many a business venture, however as noted by *Museo Italo America* the situation encouraged "Rachele and his brothers to develop the Jet Pump, which revolutionized the way water is extracted from wells, thus helping California's agricultural industry." A significant financial gain accrued by the Jet Pump allowed for greater flexibility in creative design – the most famous arising from caring for another family member. One of the brothers Candido (1903-1986) sought an effective way to ease the pain upon his two-year-old son inflicted with juvenile rheumatoid arthritis. The subsequent design was a device easily adaptable within a home the "Hot Tub;" known simply as a "Jacuzzi."[550]

---

[550] Paolo Pontoniere, "In Cerca di Una Nuova," *Museo ItaloAmericano*, p. 10.

Photo of the Jacuzzi J-7 Monoplane, c. 1921 (Public Domain).

Giulio Douhet and *Rules for the Use of Airplanes in War*

One Italian General who specialized in aviation never immigrated to America, but his military treatise did. **Giulio Douhet** (1869-1930), born in Caserta in Campania Italy, was an early "proponent of strategic bombing in aerial warfare." Douhet's theories were first implemented in a 1911 war engaging Italy against Libya. In 1912, the lessons learned were published in *Rules for the Use of Airplanes in War*. Douhet's treatise was highly influential among early air power strategist throughout Europe, beginning in the First World War. Upon the United States entering the First World War an early "disciple" was American General Billy Mitchell (1879-1936). Mitchell, a pilot, implemented Douhet's strategies in the final year of the war. The premise discouraged the heroic lone hero prevailing in legendary dogfights; rather assigning large formations of aircraft bombing strategic areas accompanied by protective fighter aircraft.

Douhet's 1921 *Il Dominio dell'aria* (translated as *The Command of the Air* in 1942) was applied during the Second World War. During the Second World War, Douhet's "disciples" included Britain's Hugh M. Trenchard (1873-1956), known as the "father of the Royal Air Force." In Germany, proponent General Walther Wever (1887-1936) was an early organizer of the pre-war German Luftwaffe. During the 1930s, Mitchell's insistence for the U.S. to prepare for air power over the "ship of the line" battleships was met by many skeptics in the armed services; leading to an unwarranted and highly publicized court-martial. The history of the Second World War proved Mitchell, Trenchard, and Wever correct in learning from Douhet. In 1939, a realization was the German Luftwaffe in full support of the ground army unleashed its "Blitzkrieg" war machine across Europe. In 1940, an attempt to subjugate England by the Luftwaffe during the Battle of Britain was thwarted by the RAF. In 1941, the "surprise" air attack by

CHAPTER 8   415

the Japanese neutralized the American Navy at Pearl Harbor in Hawaii. A quick
learning curve, (although costly in human destruction), led to combined actions
in the overall Allied success by the American Air Force and RAF in both Europe
and Pacific as the decisive factors in thwarting the German and Japanese
enemies.[551]

During the Second World War when Douhet's influence was also
championed by General Curtis E. LeMay (1906-1990) for the American Air Force
in the European conflict from 1942 to 1944; partnering with the British allies. In
1944, a transfer to the Pacific Theater was necessitated. Historians cite LeMay for
"a controversial strategic bombing campaign." In fact, the campaign was not
necessarily an original plan; rather it "summed up Douhet's theories in the Pacific
War." As noted by historian Francis P. Sempa in "Giulio Douhet and the End of
the Pacific War," of LeMay's decision "the horrors of the strategic bombing of
Japan in WWII followed the advice of [an] Italian author." The book that
influenced General LeMay was *Command of the Air*, of which Douhet explained
aerial warfare "means to be in a position to wield offensive power so great it defies
human imagination." History recalls both World Wars in great detail yet very
often overlook Douhet. A similar occurrence for Italians in America such as the
Piccirilli brothers.[552]

The Piccirilli Brothers
Laboring in Obscurity Set our National Narrative in Stone

An obituary of the last surviving of the six Piccirilli Brothers provides a
summation of understanding of Italian Culture in America. A *Washington
Evening Star* report on the 1954 death of Orazio Piccirilli stated "people who
perhaps never heard their name have reason to be grateful for their labors." It was
quite rare, if ever, to find the Piccirilli name on any work, yet their "labors" are
located in prominent public spaces across the United States. Rescue from
obscurity in the 21st century resulted from exhaustive tireless research of Mary
Shelley and Bill Carroll.

---

[551] See also: Thomas Hippler. *Bombing the People: Giulio Douhet and the Foundations of
Air-Power Strategy, 1884-1939*, 2013.
[552] Francis P. Sempa. "Giulio Douhet and the End of the Pacific War," 2015.

Top: "Sitting Abraham Lincoln" designed by Daniel Chester French carved by Italian immigrants the Piccirilli Brothers c. 1911-1921
Bottom: The Lincoln Memorial in Washington D.C. designed by architect Henry Bacon in the prevalent Neo-classical style to emulate an image of the capital city as the "New Rome." (Courtesy National Parks Service).

Shelley and Carroll first learned of the Piccirilli's "while taking sculpting courses at the Art Students League in Manhattan." In 2015, research historian Peter A. Balaskas tells us, "Carroll's interest was piqued when he discovered they were known for carving the Lincoln Memorial statue in Washington, D.C. [starting] on a journey to learn about the family of master carvers." At first, researching the historical accomplishment of the Piccirilli's difficult since the names were not listed nor carved into the work. Research led though numerous New York City archival records, particularly the Metropolitan Museum and the Bronx County Historical Society. Painstaking research revealed a multitude of some of the most iconic statues in America.

Above Left: The Piccirilli Brothers at work assembling the "Sitting Lincoln." (National Archives). **Above Right:** Putting the finishing touches on the Abraham Lincoln sculpture. [Between 1921 and 1922] Retrieved from the Library of Congress:

Among hundreds of works by the Piccirilli brothers is the world famous "Sitting Abraham Lincoln." Designed by Daniel Chester French (1850–1931) the sculpture proved an arduous task translating French's model into a monumental version. Work began in the Bronx studio in 1911 as the Piccirilli brothers carved 28 separate pieces of marble blocks obtained from a Georgia quarry. French often visited to inspect the work and from time to time aiding in the labor. In late 1920, the finished blocks of marble were transported to Washington D.C. for assembly within the open air portico of the Lincoln Memorial. The building as designed by architect Henry Bacon (1866-1924) reflects a comprehensive overall effort of the nation's capital city at Washington D.C. of monuments and temples each designed as an edifice to reflect a "New Rome."[553]

Prior to the Piccirilli's immigration to America, skilled sculptor work from Carrara marble was basically non-existent among an American born stone carvers. One recalled, "If American sculptors were working on a figure that was going to be in marble, they would have to send their model to Italy to be carved." Albert Ten Eyck Gardner (1909-1967), Curator of American Sculpture at the Metropolitan Museum of Art added,

> "With the arrival of the Piccirillis, it became unnecessary for American sculptors to go to Italy to have their sculpture translated into marble.

---

[553] Peter A. Balaskas. "Meet the Brothers Behind the Construction of NYC Landmarks,"

418   Italian Culture in America:
             The Immigrants 1880 to 1930 From Discrimination to Assimilation

> Some were quite content to model in clay, and have all their stonework
> done by the Piccirillis."

As an Italian irony, in a 1967 press release of Gardner's untimely death at age 58, noted the curator was educated "at a Montessori kindergarten."[554]

All six Piccirilli brothers – Ferrucio (1864-1945), Attilio (1866-1945), Furio (1868-1949), Masaniello "Thomas" (1870-1951), Orazio "Horace" (1872-1954), and Getulio (1874-1945) were born in the town of Massa in the Tuscany region of Italy near the renowned marble quarries of Carrara. Father Giuseppe (1844-1910), a master stone carver, taught the trade to all six sons. (The elder Piccirilli once served with Giuseppe Garibaldi.) Two of the sons, Attilio and Furio, continued studies at the Accademia di Belle Arti in Rome. Around 1887/8 the family immigrated to America. Work was found at Adler's Monument and Granite Works on East 57th Street in Manhattan. Prosperity led to purchasing vacant land in the Mott Haven Section of the South Bronx. In an area populated by German, Irish, and Italian immigrants; the Piccirilli family built two large studios and a family residence at 467 East 142nd Street.[555]

The stonework by the Piccirilli's embodies a watershed moment of American cultural history. Although born in Italy, the Piccirilli brothers fully embraced their new country and American citizenship, each acclimating to America. In a 1938 interview Attilio Piccirilli recalled,

> "I have been an American for so long – fifty years – that I often forget I
> was born in Italy. When anyone refers to me as a foreigner, or as an
> Italian, I pretend that I haven't heard and I don't usually answer. Of
> course, I am an American. Once I went back to my native city and
> planned to stay there for a year or more. I locked the door of my studio
> in New York, said goodbye to all my friends and went to the homeland
> where I had been born. What did I find? I was a foreigner in Italy. I could
> speak the language of course, but I couldn't think Italian. I had planned
> to be away for a year, but in four months I was on my return trip to the
> Bronx. I first *knew* that I was a real American when I brought my
> mother's body back from Italy where she died on a visit. We buried her
> here [in America] and I made a statue of motherhood for her grave. I had
> worked here and taken an oath of allegiance. But it is when you bury one
> you love in a country's soil that you realize that you belong to that soil
> forever."[556]

---

[554] Balaskas. "Meet the Brothers." See also: Mary Shelley and Bill Carroll. "History: Piccirilli Brothers." *Leman.edu*, "Albert Ten Eyck Gardner, Metropolitan Museum of Art Associate Curator, dies suddenly at 58." Metropolitan Museum press release, 1967.
[555] Donald Martin Reynolds. "*Monuments and Masterpieces*," p. 352.
[556] Quoted in: Mangione and Morreale *La Storia*, p. 23.

The six Piccirilli brothers outside their Bronx studio at 467 East 142nd Street flanking their mother Barbara Piccirilli nee: Geirgi (1844-1911). Manuscripts and Archives Division, The New York Public Library Digital Collections.

Comparable to the "Sitting Lincoln" are many other public monuments such as the Washington Square Arch and a pair of lions adorning the 42nd Street entrance to the New York Public Library both in New York City. Each of those New York landmarks have served as backdrops in hundreds of Hollywood movies and American television shows. An Internet Movie Database (IMDb) search lists over 100 prominent Hollywood movies featuring the Washington Square Arch and dozens more at the New York Public Library. As described by historian Lucie Levine,

> "The Piccirillis not only helped set our national narrative in stone they also left an indelible mark on New York City. They carved hundreds of commissions including the 11 figures in the pediment of the New York Stock exchange, the 'four continents' adorning the Customs House at Bowling Green, the two stately lions that guard the New York Public Library, statues of George Washington for the Washington Square Arch, and 500 individual carvings at Riverside Church."[557]

The Washington Square Arch designed in 1871 by architect Stanford White (1853-1906) was dedicated in 1891 on the centennial of George Washington's

---

[557] Lucie Levine. "How six Italian immigrants from the South Bronx." July 31, 2018

presidency. On either side of the arch are two Piccirilli works representing two phases of Washington's legacy are,

George Washington as Commander-in-Chief,
Accompanied by Fame and Valor, c. 1916;

George Washington as President,
Accompanied by Wisdom and Justice, c. 1918.

The triumphal arch design at the southern terminus end of New York's Fifth Avenue is wholly inspired by the ancient Roman triumphal arch. The ancient Romans are credited with inventing the arch; if not, the forebearers of the Italian peninsular certainly perfected applying the arch in dramatic ways. A similar monumental achievement might be the most famous work to come out of the Piccirilli studio The prime example was Stanford White's arch honoring the dual achievement of the victorious General Washington and peacetime president. Millions of Americans and visitors from all over the world have stood awestruck in wonderment at the arch.

During the late 19th and early 20th century, skilled stone work by the Piccirilli's was nowhere else to be found on the American continent. As a result, they were in high demand with the most productive sculpture studio in America of an entire city block. A 1935 article in *Art Digest* described the collective non-usurping atmosphere within the Piccirilli Bronx workshop. Regardless of the project, none of the brothers took singular credit for the work, whether an original design or the finely tuned finished product by another artist. Response was always "we" as "close and effective teamwork." The report conveyed a collegial camaraderie during all aspects of the work task. Maria Castro reported, "the brothers were known to break into song as they carved, and Attilio often cooked lunch for the entire workshop." The "joviality" conveyed from their "old world" Italian workshop perked the interest of another *paisan,* New York City Mayor Fiorello La Guardia. The mayor and Attilio had developed a close friendship and known to frequent the workshop; often to share a meal cooked by Attilio.[558]

Mayor Fiorello La Guardia was a frequent visitor, as were hundreds of others welcomed in the workshop. (As devout Italian sons their mother was always welcome.) Among the throngs throughout the years included three Presidents of the United States - Teddy Roosevelt, William Howard Taft, and Woodrow Wilson. Another frequent guest was the famous Italian opera singer Enrico Caruso. As Attilio cooked or worked, Caruso was known to sing "while the brothers worked." It is not known, if Attilio ever accompanied the great Caruso.[559]

---

[558] Maria Castro. "The Piccirilli Brothers." *The Bronx Journal* April 2001, p. A2. Adeline Adams. "A Family of Sculptors." *American Magazine of Art,* Vol. 12, No. 7, p. 223.
[559] Peter A. Balaskas. "Meet the Brothers," *Bespoke Concierge Magazine,* July 20, 2015.

The Piccirilli's were most comfortable within the friendly confines of their studio and Bronx neighborhood of the Bronx. Unfortunately, reports indicate the talented brothers were often subject to the prevailing anti-Italian prejudice in America. Research by Lucie Levine revealed,

> "The brothers faced some anti-immigrant sentiment even as they worked to realize some of the United States' most patriotic sculptures. The Art Commission of Virginia rejected Attilio's sketches for a bust of Thomas Jefferson, noting that the name Piccirilli would not be welcome in Virginia. Similarly, The Lincoln Memorial Commission rejected French's suggestion to have "Piccirilli" inscribed on the pedestal of the Lincoln Memorial."

Washington Square Arch by architect Stanford White, c. 1891 for the Centennial of George Washington as First President of the United States. Adjacent piers are figures carved by the Piccirilli brothers **Top Left**: East pier *Washington in War*, c. 1916. **Top Right**: West pier *Washington in Peace*, c. 1918. (Photographs by: Beyond My Ken, c. 2011. Wiki Creative Commons)

Obscurity of the Piccirilli Brothers has continued into the present day. As discovered by Levine, prejudice from the Art Commission of Virginia is a logical answer why Piccirilli work went unsigned, un-attributed, and regulated to anonymity. All six Piccirilli brothers are long ago deceased and their home and workshop have been physically demolished and built over. Yet as the research historian Lucie Levine succinctly reminded us,

"Their art remains an integral part of the American cultural fabric reflecting research, education, emancipation, honor, remembrance – most importantly a reminder of the humanity of their art in the pursuit of social justice."

An "integral part" as an example of the Piccirilli's lifetime achievements involves *Patience* and *Fortitude*. Each word is a noun defined as,

pa·tience /ˈpāSHəns/ *noun* the capacity to accept or tolerate delay, trouble, or suffering without getting angry.

for·ti·tude /ˈfôrdəˌt(y)o͞od/ *noun* courage in adversity.

Each word applied separately or collectively reflects different aspects of human life and artistic endeavors. *Patience* and *Fortitude* are the names of not only two works of art by the Piccirilli brothers, but also representative of their own life with the contemporary life of immigrants.[560]

Patience and *Fortitude*

The definition of patience and fortitude was certainly demonstrated during the Piccirilli's lifetime, especially dealing with prejudice displayed against Italian immigrants. Their cultural legacy is fully evident in two lion statues at the entrance to the Main Branch of the New York Public Library in the heart of New York City. The New York Public Library explains,

"*Patience* and *Fortitude*, the world-renowned pair of marble lions that stand proudly before the majestic Beaux-Arts building at Fifth Avenue and 42nd Street in Manhattan, have captured the imagination and affection of New Yorkers and visitors from all over the world since they were placed on their pedestals days before the building was dedicated on May 23, 1911."[561]

The Beaux Arts style of the New York Public Library building is located within one of the busiest tourist centers in the world between. The architectural style, named after the *École des Beaux-Arts* school in Paris, was derived from the Italian Renaissance and the classical styles derived from Ancient Rome and Greece. The style, popular from the mid-1880s to 1920s, coincided with the Great New Wave of Immigration. Beaux Arts is more decorative than the prominent Neoclassical style of the same period. (Actually, Beaux Arts is often described as a "subset" of Neoclassical.)

---

[560] Lucie Levine. "How six Italian immigrants from the South Bronx," 2018. Levine founded a tour company taking New York's history out of archives and into the streets.
[561] "The Library of Lions." *New York Public Library*. Accessed March 10, 2022.

New York Public Library "Opening Day" photograph, c. 1911. The famous stone lions, carved by the Piccirilli Brothers nicknamed "Patience and Fortitude" flanking the grand entrance have remained in place for over 100 years.
(Library of Congress)

Architecture critic Paul Goldberger called the Piccirilli lions "New York's most lovable public sculpture." Photograph by Carol M. Highsmith, c. 2006. Retrieved from the Library of Congress, <www.loc.gov/2010646310/>.

The lion sculptures were originally named after two wealthy donors, during the Great Depression each of the lions were given their lasting nicknames. Archives of the New York Public Library say, "Mayor Fiorello La Guardia dubbed them 'Patience' and 'Fortitude,' after the qualities he felt New Yorkers needed. As the world has changed, our lions have been there remaining a steadfast symbol for what the Library represents: a source of inspiration and strength for all." Architecture critic Paul Goldberger (b. 1950) called them "New York's most lovable public sculpture." A long-standing New York City tradition during each Christmas Holiday season has wreaths placed on the necks of each lion. During the worldwide Covid-19 Pandemic of 2020-2022 *Patience* and *Fortitude* served as a social example. Each fitted with a face mask, recalled the Great Depression idea promoting solidarity for the American public. Despite fame and notoriety of *Patience* and *Fortitude*, very few know the work was carved by the Piccirilli Brothers.[562]

An abundance of Piccirilli Brothers work are in public view throughout the United States. A significant number of public projects are listed on the National Register of Historic Places and individual state Historical sites. Some smaller works are within museums. A select list of notable public works by the Piccirilli Brothers include,

- *USS Maine National Monument*, c. 1913, Columbus Circle.
- *Firemen's Memorial*, c. 1913, Riverside Park, New York City.
- California Building in San Diego's Balboa Park, c. 1915.
- Stonework at the Panama-California Exposition, c. 1915.
- Stonework outside Riverside Church, c. 1930, New York City.
- *Tomb of the Unknown Soldier*, c. 1931, Arlington National Cemetery.
- Pedimental Sculpture: at the Brooklyn Museum, c. 1913.
- *Apotheosis of Democracy* (1916), United States Capitol, c. 1916.
- *The Arts* and *History*, New York Public Library, c. 1917.
- *Joy of Life*, Governor's Mansion, Richmond, Virginia, c. 1931.
- *Joy of Life*, frieze Rockefeller Plaza, New York City, c. 1937.
- *Guglielmo Marconi Memorial*, Washington D.C. c. 1941.

---

[562] "Patience and Fortitude: NYPL's Lions Through the Years." *New York Public Library*, 2022.

Collage of prominent work by the Piccirilli brothers. **Top Left**: Detail of pediment sculpture *Apotheosis of Democracy* located over the east entrance to the U.S. House of Representatives at the U.S. Capitol building in Washington D.C. (Photo: Andreas Praefcke, 2007). **Top Right**: *Tomb of the Unknown Soldier* in Arlington National Cemetery, Virginia, c. 2005. **Middle Left**: *USS Maine National Monument* in New York City. *Memorial* (Photo: Einar Einarsson Kvaran, 2005). **Middle Right**: Tympanum California State building in Balboa Park San Diego. (Photo: Andreas Praefcke, 2007). **Bottom**: Pediment Sculpture and Cornice at the Brooklyn Museum (Photo: Jim Henderson, 2008). Wiki Creative Commons / GNU Free Documentation License)

The Piccirilli's opened a pathway followed by many others. A legion of unnamed Italian laborers constructed many buildings in America of stone, marble, and intricate carvings. One example was Union Station in Washington D.C. (built 1905-1908). Six façade statues on the progress of railroading by artist Louis Saint-

Gaudens (1854-1913) were sculpted by an Italian named Andrew Bernasconi (b. – d.?). Another is the massive Gothic styled Washington National Cathedral, began 1905/1907 built over 80 years. During the early decades of construction Italian American stone carvers Roger Morigi (1907-1995) and Vincent Palumbo (1936 -2000) "spent decades creating the sculptural works."

Equally famous to "Sitting Lincoln" is the Mount Rushmore Monument in South Dakota. On August 10, 1927, a dedication ceremony by President Calvin Coolidge signaled the beginning of carving the monument. As a touch of irony, as one Italian stone carver responsible for completion of the monument was unknown to the world, one of the most publicized trials in American history culminated 13 days later on August 23, 1927 as two Italian immigrants Sacco and Vanzetti were electrocuted.

Luigi Del Bianco Fulfills the "American Dream"

During the 1930s, another Italian provided a significant contribution to an iconic American monument at Mt. Rushmore in South Dakota. History recorded Gutzon Borglum (1867-1941) and son James Lincoln Borglum (1912-1986) as "designer and chief engineer." The Borglum's managed hundreds of workers at the monument in the Black Hills containing faces of four American Presidents, George Washington, Thomas Jefferson, Theodore Roosevelt, and Abraham Lincoln. Almost 75 year later, it was an Italian stone sculptor Luigi Del Bianco as "chief carver" was added to the historical narrative. A dedication properly credited Luigi Del Bianco (1892-1969) occurred on September 16, 2017. A recap was televised on "CBS Sunday Morning." Grandson Lou Del Bianco explained,

> "As chief carver, [Luigi Del Bianco's] priority was refining the facial expressions on the presidents' 60-foot-high heads. He fixed a foot-deep crack in Jefferson's lip with a patch and he sculpted Lincoln's eyes, highlighting the pupils with wedge-shaped granite stones to reflect the light."

A 25-year quest began in the 1980s by son Caesar Del Bianco (1931-2009) and grandson Lou Del Bianco in the U.S. Library of Congress discovering Borglum's diary of the Mt. Rushmore project. Of Luigi Del Bianco, Borglum wrote "He is the only intelligent, efficient stone carver on the work who understands the language of the sculptor." The reason for the omission of credit for Del Bianco might be the result of inherent anti Italian discrimination. According to many sources "Sculptor Gutzon Borglum was deeply involved with the Ku Klux Klan."[563]

---

[563] "The Creator of Mount Rushmore's Forgotten Ties to White Supremacy," *The Washington Post*, July 2, 2020. https://www.washingtonpost.com › history › 2020/07/03.

Mount Rushmore, South Dakota (left to right) Presidents George Washington, Thomas Jefferson, Theodore Roosevelt, and Abraham Lincoln. Photograph by Carol M Highsmith -Library of Congress.

Luigi Del Bianco (1892-1969) was actually born "aboard a ship" as his parents were sailing home to Italy. The younger Del Bianco wrote of his grandfather, "Raised in Meduno, northeast of Venice, he studied stone carving in Vienna and Venice starting when he was 11." Immigration to Vermont at age 17 was prompted by a cousin who wrote "skilled carvers were in demand." As World War I began, Luigi Del Bianco returned to his homeland to enlist in the Italian army. After the war, Del Bianco settled in Port Chester, New York; where he met Gutzon Borglum and the two soon worked together in a North Stamford, Connecticut studio.[564]

Above Left: Rare color photograph of Luigi Del Bianco refining Washington's left eye on Mount Rushmore. **Above Right**: Del Bianco (center on scaffold) refining Jefferson's lip. (Courtesy of Lou Del Bianco).

---

[564] Lou Del Bianco. *Out of Rushmore's Shadow*. See also: Jim Axelrod. "Mount Rushmore's Chief Carver Gets his Due," *CBS Sunday Morning*, September 17, 2017.

Many would say the rest is history, however it took 75 years, before Luigi Del Bianco was given his rightful pace in American history by the U.S. National Parks Service. The succinct biography posted by the U.S. National Park Service states, "Artist Luigi Del Bianco came to work at Mount Rushmore at the request of Gutzon Borglum, the designer and engineer of the stone sculpture. Del Bianco worked for Mr. Borglum during the seasons of 1933, 1935, 1936 and 1940."[565]

In June 2014, a memorial bronze plaque was dedicated across from 68 North Regent Street in Port Chester, New York. During that same year, biographer Douglas Gladstone in *Carving a Niche for Himself: The Untold Story of Luigi Del Bianco* offered, "If being the chief carver at Mount Rushmore is not the American dream for an immigrant to these lands, what is?" Comments well-deserved, yet does not tell the complete story. The definitive biography *Out of Rushmore's Shadow: The Luigi Del Bianco Story* is a well-written and thoroughly researched book by Lou Del Bianco. Of the biography, noted American historian Douglas Brinkley said Del Bianco's book "turns orthodox history on its head."[566]

Bronze plaque unveiled September 16, 2017 dedicated at Mount Rushmore properly crediting Luigi Del Bianco. (Courtesy of Lou Del Bianco)

Luigi Del Bianco
Chief Carver on Mount Rushmore
*"He will have complete charge of the
Practical ways and means of dealing with
the finesse of carving and instructing the
Other carvers . . ."* Gutzon Borglum

---

[565] Sam Roberts. "An Immigrant's Contribution to Mount Rushmore Is Recognized, 75 Years Later," *The New York Times*, June 29, 2016, p. A20.
[566] Douglas Gladstone. *Carving a Niche for Himself: The Untold Story of Luigi Del Bianco.* Bordighera Press, 2014. Conversations and Email correspondence with Lou Del Bianco.

CHAPTER 9

BIOGRAPHIES OF ITALIANS SHAPING AMERICAN CULTURE

"For the first time, I believe, the interest of the whole country has been aroused, the history of educational thought, and not only in the work of Dr. Montessori in Italy, a new movement has come to the present state of education in this front through the medium of a country." Ellen Yale Stevens

"The Italian immigrants inherited this anti-Catholic hostility upon arrival; they generally did not bring with them priests and other religious individuals who could help ease their transition into American life."
Victor Cangiano

Thousands of cities, towns, roads, parks, and organizations, among others are named in honor of Christopher Columbus. Similarly, the formal nomenclature of many everyday conveniences and devices with an Italian connection is uniquely prevalent in American culture. The list is quite extensive, yet some of the most common examples of representative words of a system, product, or machine with an Italian origination include Zamboni, Jacuzzi, Caesar Salad, and a Montessori school, to name just a few. Most Americans are likely unaware of the original source; yet each represents the name of an Italian person responsible for its creation. "Montessori," for example, is associated with an educational system prevalent in America. As a pure representative of an educational method, one might wonder if anyone realizes it all began with an Italian woman.

Maria Montessori: "A Wonder Worker in Education"

Maria Tecla Artemisia Montessori, MD (1870-1952) was born in the town of Chiaravalle in the Italian Province of Ancona situated near the coast of the

Adriatic Sea about 150 miles (250 km) due east of Florence. Father Alessandro Montessori (1832-1915) served in the military during the unification of Italy, later as a civil service accountant. Mother Renilde Montessori nee: Stoppani (1840-1912) was a school teacher. Soon after Maria's birth the family moved to Rome enrolling her in a "local state school." An official biography states, "As her education progressed, she began to break through the barriers which constrained women's careers."

Above Left: Title page of *The Montessori Method*, c. 1912. **Above Right**: Portrait of Maria Montessori. Public Domain image from the *Nationaal Archief* of the Dutch National Archives, donated in the context of a partnership program.

Maria Tecla Artemisia Montessori, MD (1870-1952) was born in the town of Chiaravalle in the Italian Province of Ancona situated near the Adriatic Sea 150 miles (250 km) east of Florence. Rejecting the wishes of her parents to pursue an acceptable societal career as a teacher, the young Maria chose a technical career studying at the Regio Istituto Tecnico Leonardo da Vinci. Maria gained entry into the male exclusive medical profession at the University of Rome. Overcoming many prejudicial experiences, in 1896, Montessori "became one of the first female doctors in Italy." Which became the foundational training for a revolutionary new way of teaching young children. Dr. Montessori's early medical career was dedicated to nurturing and care the poor and their children.[567]

---

[567] See: Janice Therese Mancuso. "Thirty-One Days of Italians," 2020.

CHAPTER 9

This social awakening led to continued study and analysis on "the subject of children with learning differences." An innovative discovery led to an appointment as co-director, with Giuseppe Montesano (1868-1961), at an experimental institution. A professional relationship with Montesano evolved into a romantic entanglement; resulting in a child out of wedlock. To avoid the child was sent away, since Montesano married another woman. Montessori left the medical profession; most likely suffering the personal emotional pain prompted Maria's dedication to the development and educational nurturing of children. As noted in an official biography,

> "In this moment of absolute defeat, she did something remarkable. Instead of crumbling under the strain, she went into the seclusion of a convent to meditate. As a woman of her time, and as an Italian, she was of course a Roman Catholic. But her faith was the faith of a scientist and a scholar, skeptical and refined . . . she emerged from this period of self-examination with a set of goals which seem unbelievable to the modern observer. She moved forward with a resolution that is at once baffling and inspiring."[568]

In 1899, Dr. Montessori visited Bicêtre Hospital in Paris to study the innovative work of Édouard Séguin (1812-1880) in sensorial education for children with disabilities. Dr. Montessori began a transition of "her professional identity from physician to educator." In 1904, Montessori accepted a post at the Pedagogic School of the University of Rome, which she held until 1908. In one lecture she told her students,

> "The subject of our study is humanity; our purpose is to become teachers. What really makes a teacher is love for the human child; for it is love that transforms the social duty of the educator into higher consciousness of mission."

In 1906, Montessori was asked to create a childcare center in San Lorenzo, a poor, inner-city district of Rome. The school, named *Casa dei Bambini* opened in January of 1907. Two more schools were opened that same year. Students comprised of young children deemed "unable to learn" were introduced to "engaging in hands-on learning experiences."

By 1909, a compendium of notes from observations at the *Casa dei Bambini* schools were published in Italy as *Il Metodo della Pedagogia Scientifica applicato all'educazione infantile nelle Case dei Bambini*. The following year a significant number of European schools began applying Montessori's pedagogy. By 1912, Dr. Montessori's book was translated in ten different languages; including an English version published in the United States succinctly titled as *The Montessori*

---

[568] Robert Gardner. "The Maria Montessori No One Knows," *OurKids.Net*, 2022.

Method. Within a brief period of time, a rapid expansion of schools applying the "Montessori Method" appeared around the world.

With the growing Progressive Movement in America advocating for mandatory public education for children, interest on Montessori among American educators was rising. It was not until a popular mainstream magazine began praising the accomplishments of Dr. Maria Montessori that led to prominence in America. The first visit to the United States in December of 1913 was preceded by a large amount of media anticipation throughout the nation. (A diary of the 2-week trans-Atlantic crossing was translated and published in 2013 by great granddaughter Carolina Montessori as *Maria Montessori Sails to America*.) The most prominent appeared in *McClure's* magazine; advertised as "one of the most popular, innovative, and influential American magazines during the period."[569]

In 1911, the progressive *McClure's Magazine* presented the first in a series of articles aptly titled "A Wonder Worker in Education: The Marvels of Maria Montessori," with a photographic essay by: Josephine Tozier of May 1911, preceded Maria Montessori's visit to America. *McClure's* as a literary format; remained influential in progressive issues, including a series on Maria Montessori and education.

The first in a series of articles appearing in *McClure's* magazine, "A Wonder Worker in Education: The Marvels of Maria Montessori, c. May 1911.

---

[569] "Biography of Maria Montessori." *Association Montessori Internazionale*. January 20, 2022. Quoted in: Rita Kramer. *Maria Montessori: A Biography*. Chicago: 1976, p. 52.

CHAPTER 9

From 1911 into 1913, *McClure's* magazine, billed as "The Marketplace of the World," with over 500,000 home subscriptions offered strong support for the Montessori movement in America. The History of Montessori Education explained, *"McClure's* Magazine was clearly a driving force in bringing Montessori into the mind of everyday culture, rather than simply the academic world." Five in-depth illustrated articles were published from December 1911 to July 1913.

Two articles written by Ellen Yale Stevens (1855-1927) Montessori Method and American Kindergarten," (Nov.1912); and "The Montessori Movement," (July 1913), were formulated from a first-hand account of a personal visit to Italy. Stevens, a grammar school principal at the Brooklyn Heights Seminary School, studied Educational Psychology at the University of Chicago under the famous educator John Dewey (1859-1952). In 1911, Stevens spent in her own words, "a three months trip to Italy where I had the advantages of personal conferences with Dr. Montessori and the best exponents of her 'method,' and also extended visits to all the schools in Rome where her methods have been introduced."[570]

Stevens began with an analysis of the changing attitudes towards public education for American children, claiming,

> "For the first time, I believe, the interest of the whole country has been aroused, the history of educational thought, and not only in the work of Dr. Montessori in Italy, a new movement has come to the present state of education in this front through the medium of a country."

The July article recapped the desire for information on the educational success. Stevens wrote an introduction for a new monthly feature titled as "A McClure Department."

> "Two years ago, McClure's published on the work of the great Italian educator Dr. Maria Montessori. At that time Dr. Montessori was scarcely known outside of a limited circle in her own country. In a few weeks, however, her name had reached practically every part of the world."

One 1913 request to *McClure's* for a "Montessori Bibliography" listed over 50 articles from prominent nationwide American magazines and newspapers. By 1914, that number was over 180 articles and books written about Montessori education. One reason for the perked curiosity was the fanfare provided for Dr. Maria Montessori's visit to America.[571]

---

[570] Ellen Yale Stevens. *A Guide to the Montessori Method.* New York: Frederick A. Stokes Company, 1913, p. viii.
[571] Ellen Yale Stephens, *McClure's,* Vol. 41: July 1913, p. 182.

Above Left: Article: "The Montessori Schools in Rome," by: Josephine Tozier (December, 1911). **Above Right**: Article: "The Montessori Movement: A McClure Department," by Ellen Yale Stevens (July 1913) as each appeared in *McClure's* monthly magazine.

In December of 1913, Montessori's arrival in America was greeted with much fanfare. Widespread interest in the now famous progressive educator was honored with a dinner with over 400 people in Washington DC. In attendance was the daughter of President Woodrow Wilson, and an array of "foreign ministers and dignitaries." Part of a 3-week sold-out lecture tour, a New York Carnegie Hall appearance turned away over 1,000 people – prompting a second lecture. Dr. Montessori wrote, "I did not invent a method of education, I simply gave some little children a chance to live." A demonstration of giving "little children a chance to live" was put on full display during a second American visit in 1915; accompanied by son Mario (1898-1982), reacquainted with after 15 years. The visit was an invitation to demonstrate the Montessori Method in San Francisco at the Panama–Pacific International Exposition.[572]

---

[572] See: "History of Montessori," *American Montessori Society*® February 21, 2022.

A Guide to the Montessori Method by Ellen Yale Stevens published in 1913 was a first-hand account of Stevens three-month visit to Italy to personally confer with Maria Montessori and observe classroom methods. The photo is of "Dr. Maria Montessori."

Critics, Decline, Fascism, and a Return

Dr. Montessori was not without critics. After an astounding initial acceptance and growth in America, by the 1920s the Montessori Method "almost completely faded away." According to the Official History of Montessori, the cause was attributed to the changing cultural climate in America. Reasons for the decline included "Language barriers, World War I travel limitations, anti-immigrant sentiment, and the disdain of a few influential educators." A significant factor of "influential educators" was not criticism of any specific portion of the system, rather in opposition to the entire Montessori Method.[573]

One prominent progressive educator William Kilpatrick (1871-1965), also a former student of John Dewey, was highly critical in his 1914 publication, *The Montessori System Examined*. As explained by the Association Montessori Internazionale,

---

[573] "The Glass Classroom: Montessori on Display." *American Montessori Society*, 2022. See also: Sam Whiting. "Class Act of the 1915 Fair: A 104 year Old Remembers." *The San Francisco Chronicle* February 25, 2015.

"Kilpatrick criticized Dr. Montessori's credentials, perspectives, and overall philosophy. He dismissed her beliefs of the role of the teacher, ideal classroom size, and classroom materials. Kilpatrick's negative assessment of Montessori quickly became widely known and accepted throughout the U.S."

The decline did not represent the end of Maria Montessori and her influence upon the education of children. In an unpublished thesis, "The Great Italian Educator: The Montessori Method and American Nativism in the 1910s," Elise M. Klaske reminds us, "The Montessori Method has experienced three waves of popularity in the United States." Three distinct periods were: 1911 to 1917; 1956 to 1979; and 1995 to the present. As for the decline after 1917, Klaske claims, "Protestant Nativism did not overtly contribute to the decline of the Montessori Method."

As quickly as Montessori appeared to continually fascinate and captivate the American public, her fame was overtaken by distractions of the First World War and the catastrophic Flu Pandemic of late 1918 through 1919. Almost as quickly as the sudden media attention gave rise to Dr. Montessori's fame in America, so did the complete absence of significant media attention after 1917. In Europe, decline of the Montessori educational system during the early 1920s was due to the rise of Fascism mainly in Spain, Italy, and Germany. As explained,

"By 1933 all Montessori schools in Germany had been closed and an effigy of her was burned above a bonfire of her books in Berlin. In 1936, two years after Montessori refused to cooperate with Mussolini's plans to incorporate Italian Montessori schools into the fascist youth movement, all Montessori schools in Italy were closed."[574]

Dr. Montessori's concept "promoting independence and fostering growth at an individual pace" was in contradiction of Fascism. Added to the growing decree of Fascism across Europe was the de-emphasis of knowledge accessible through books and libraries. A brief description of the reason for book burnings was provided by the Nazi Propaganda minister Joseph Goebbels (1924-1945) as,

The Book Burnings of May 10, 1933: "*[Any book or work of art] which acts subversively on our future or strikes at the root of German thought, the German home and the driving forces of our people [should be destroyed].*"— Joseph Goebbels

By the late 1920s into the early part of the 1930s, Maria Montessori and son Mario were placed under political surveillance as ordered by Mussolini. On two occasions they were forced to flee for safety of their own lives. With help from the British, the Montessori's escaped to India. In 1946, a return to Europe, specifically the Netherlands, to reunite with grandchildren. Circumstances of

---

[574] "Biography of Maria Montessori." *Association Montessori Internazionale*. 2022.

CHAPTER 9

world survival contributed to a long gap in educational publications. In 1949, with a long historical record of successful endeavors in education, Maria Montessori received the attention as a cherished Humanitarian from the Nobel Peace Prize committee – yet never recognized with the prize. Montessori passed away in the Netherlands in May of 1952, her educational legacy continued. A "third wave" from the 1990s into the 21st Century counted many public schools in America adopting the Montessori Method. By the 21st century, about 20,000 Montessori schools existed, with 3,000 in America.[575]

Mother Cabrini and the Missionaries of St. Charles Borromeo

Among millions of Italian immigrants passing through Ellis Island, one of the most influential in the cause of human compassion was Mother Cabrini (1850-1917). Born in Italy in the mid-century year of 1850, Frances Xavier Cabrini arrived in New York City on March 31, 1889; passing through the immigration station at Ellis Island at the not so young age of 43 years old. The incongruous arrival was just one among the thousands of other anonymous immigrants disembarking on that same day. The reason for the ocean crossing was actually part of an assigned religious journey. Sent from her birthplace of Sant'Angelo Lodigiano in the Lodi Province; located about 26 miles (24 km) southeast of Milan to New York by Pope Leo XIII (1810-1903), Cabrini's "mission" was to offer aid to poor Italian immigrants in America.

The daunting task was an astounding success story – one cherished as a cultural aspect of any immigrant seeking the path of hard-work leading to achieving the "American Dream." Although the Catholic religion held a prominent presence in New York City, it was under strict accord of established Irish hierarchy – one that shunned Italians from partaking in religious rites such as communal mass among the Irish. An explanation was provided on the official website of Our Lady of Pompeii Church in the Greenwich Village neighborhood since 1892,

> "Italian immigrants inherited anti-Catholic hostility upon arrival; unlike some of other Catholic immigrant groups, they generally did not bring with them priests and other religious individuals who could help ease their transition into American life. [Cabrini] helped to establish hundreds of parishes to serve the needs of the Italian communities, such as Our Lady of Pompeii in New York City."[576]

---

[575]"History of Montessori." *Association Montessori Internazionale* See also: Matt Bronsil. "McClure's Magazine and Montessori." 2021, and Klaske, pp. 4, 7.

[576] "History - Our Lady of Pompeii NYC." *Our Lady of Pompeii Church.* April 17, 2016. See also: Victor Cangiano. "Congregation of Missionaries of St. Charles Borromeo." *Catholic Encyclopedia.* Vol. 10, p. 60.

The foundation of a "Parish for Italians" arose with support of the Saint Raphael Society for the Protection of Italian Immigrants. The social organization was "founded to care for the many Italian immigrants of the day, who, it was feared, would fall prey to those who would exploit their labor or overcharge them in the course of their travels."

One pivotal example occurred during the days immediately after the tragic 1911 Triangle Shirtwaist Factory Fire. Located only a few walking blocks from the church, an Italian parish priest Father Antonio Demo (1870-1936) "comforted grief-stricken families." Information from the church cited Our Lady of Pompeii played a pivotal role in the History of Italian-American immigration in New York City, as well as throughout the United States of helping [Italian] immigrants to assimilate in America.

Above Left: Prayer card issued by Columbus Hospital honoring the beatification titled, "Blessed Frances Xavier Cabrini," c. 1939. Library of Congress Prints and Photographs Division, Reproduction No: LC-USZ62-35110. **Above Right**: Statue of St. Frances Xavier Cabrini outside the Holy Ghost Roman Catholic Church in Little Italy of the Federal Hill neighborhood in Providence, Rhode Island," c. 2018. Photograph by Carol M. Highsmith. Library of Congress Prints and Photographs Division. Reproduction No. LC-DIG-highsm-52544. (Public Domain)

The first task charged to Cabrini and the Missionaries of St. Charles Borromeo centered upon the Little Italy section of the Mulberry Street

CHAPTER 9   439

neighborhood in lower Manhattan. The focus expanded to literally build churches, schools, and missionary homes "in the various Italian colonies in North and South America, and to train youths for the priesthood." The first Catholic Church to be built was the Church of the Resurrection on Mulberry Street in lower Manhattan in the "Little Italy" neighborhood.

Another specific need focused on continued anti-Italian discrimination. As such, few social agencies in America were available, or willing, to offer help. In a limited access environment for social services, Cabrini arrived literally at the doorstep of Italian immigrants who quickly welcomed her as a "saint" – (a term often applied to a person who provides unexpected free aid and services to the poor). Cabrini was a "saint" in all definitions of the word.

In 1946, *Time* magazine, upon an announced canonization, described Mother Cabrini as "a tiny, frail nun, daughter of a Lombard farmer, arrived in New York with six members of the order she had formed, the Missionary Sisters of the Sacred Heart of Jesus." This "tiny, frail, nun" was a dynamo of energy and commitment, another generation might have termed her as a "go-getter" or even "feisty" -- *Time* called her "witty, forceful, and canny." At the time of beatification, a *Time* wrote,

> "Pope Leo XIII had sent her to work among the Italian immigrants who were finding neither a welcome nor prosperity in the New World, and worse, in the eyes of the Church, were losing their faith and piety. Mother Cabrini and her six set to work in the New York slums. . . . Cabrini's masterful will again & again overcame obstacles that seemed insuperable."[577]

For 28 years, Cabrini "traveled indefatigably" across the nation to cities with large numbers of Italian immigrants in Chicago, Philadelphia, New Orleans, Los Angeles, Seattle, and Denver. News of her accomplishments garnered requests for Cabrini's help in Europe, Central and South America. A busy pilgrimage included 23 trans-Atlantic crossings establishing "67 institutions: schools, hospitals, and orphanages."

In each stop, Cabrini's task was not singular. Personal involvement included organizing social programs, spiritual catechism, educational guidance, establishing and building schools. The task added administering healthcare in hospitals in Italian neighborhoods – with an Italian speaking staff. Another aspect developed a program for orphanages (possibly to counteract the "Orphan Train" system. The first was established as the Sacred Heart Orphanage in Ulster County in upstate New York (later renamed the "Saint Cabrini Home). A significant

---

[577] Lily Rothman. "How Mother Cabrini Became the First American Saint." *Time*, July 6, 2016. "First U.S. Saint." *Time* magazine. July 15, 1946, No. 3, pp. 74-75.

addition involved the complicated process of opening the Columbus Hospital located on the Lower East Side of Manhattan. The hospital eventually expanded in size and increased offerings in many social services (later renamed the "Cabrini Medical Center;" the hospital closed in 2008.).

Cabrini's dedication to Italian immigrants in America transpired as a commitment to stay permanently in America. In 1909, Cabrini gained American citizenship. In 1946, *Time* magazine cited Mother Cabrini as "an American after America's heart, and in her 59th year, she became a U.S. citizen." Adding, "though she had been born in Italy, that citizenship would earn her the title of the first American saint." Lily Rothman explained in *Time* magazine, "It takes a long time to become a saint — unless you're Frances Cabrini." Catholic sainthood was not a routine occurrence. Unlike others considered for sainthood the process was usually a long and tiresome event. Rothman added, "The process of investigating miracles performed by the candidate became so involved that the church was less willing to undertake it without strong pre-existing support for the person, and the candidate also had to have been dead for at least 50 years." Unlike thousands of Catholic saints through history, the Blessed Frances Xavier Cabrini, was not regulated to obscurity – hundreds of remembrances exist nationwide[578]

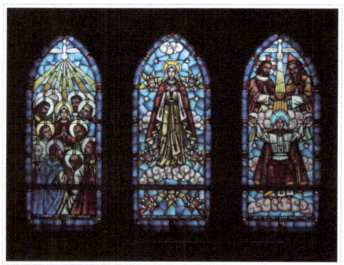

"Stained-glass windows inside the chapel at the Mother Cabrini Shrine in Golden, Colorado." Gates Frontiers Fund Colorado Collection within the Carol M. Highsmith Archive, Library of Congress, Prints and Photographs Division. <www.loc.gov/iyem/2017687508/>.

---

[578] "The Saint Entombed in Washington Heights." *Ephemeral New York*, Jan. 17, 2022.

Mother Cabrini Tomb and Statue

In the history of Catholicism many achieved sainthood; yet few attain acclaim in the public sphere within American culture. Mother Cabrini, was so beloved, shrines and statues arose all across the nation in locations such as in Chesapeake, Virginia; Chicago, Illinois; Golden, Colorado; New York (both city and state); coupled with the naming of many churches, schools, orphanages, and hospitals throughout the nation. And a place not often remembered for Italian immigrants in America a small city in Colorado named Golden. The city of Golden has a Mother Cabrini Shrine containing an assemblage of quality stained-glass windows honoring the saint. Another honor was naming a Catholic New York City High School and adjoining shrine located in a neighborhood where Cabrini spent a part of her life. The all-girls high school, founded in 1899, was almost exclusively from "the children of Irish and Italian immigrants."

The high school neighborhood is where Mother Cabrini's body is entombed in death. According to information provided by the *Missionary Sisters of the Sacred Heart of Jesus*, "Cabrini's remains rest at the altar of the St. Frances Cabrini Shrine in upper Manhattan." In its present location, without delving into macabre details, it is sufficed to say the skeletal remains are encased in a mostly wax replica body lying in repose in a glass coffin-like encasement in full view at the altar. The shrine is open in the 21st century serving as a Catholic pilgrimage site and for adventurous tourists; in other words, not heavily trafficked. In contrast, Mother Cabrini is honored into the 21st century with a statue placed in one of the most heavily trafficked tourist destinations in New York City in sight of the Statue of Liberty and Ellis Island.[579]

Over 130 years after the once anonymous Italian immigrant Sister Frances Xavier Cabrini stepped off the boat at Ellis Island, her figure literally stands in a boat sailing back towards Ellis Island. The statue, however, was not an attempt to "return home" or even satisfy the nasty creed so prevalent among late 19th and early 20th century American Nativists to send the "dirty Italian immigrants" back to Europe (see Chapter 2). Rather, the memorial honors the Patron Saint of *all* immigrants to America, regardless of ethnicity, religion, or social preference.

---

[579] See: "The Body of a Saint is Displayed at a Church in Manhattan." *Strange Remains*, April 22, 2014. See also: "The Saint Entombed in Washington Heights." *Ephemeral New York*, Accessed January 17, 2022.

Top: Mother Cabrini in repose in a glass coffin-like encasement in full view at the altar in the St. Frances Cabrini Shrine, c. 2022. Photo Courtesy of Julia Attaway St. Francis Cabrini Shrine NYC. **Bottom**: St. Frances Cabrini Shrine built in 1959 in the Washington Heights neighborhood of Upper Manhattan. Photograph c. 2010, by Jim Henderson.

Declared as the Patron Saint of Immigrants by Pope Pius XII in 1950, an accompanying honor unveiled in 2020. Located at the southern tip of Manhattan at the site of the first immigration station at Castle Clinton, the site attracts millions of visitors each year to purchase ferry tickets for a trip to visit the historic Ellis Island and Statue of Liberty. The memorial was unveiled on a day celebrating Italian culture - Columbus Day October 12, 2020 in Battery Park City. The Associated Press reported,

> "The statue depicts Mother Cabrini, patron saint of immigrants, in a boat with two children, looking forward. The girl is grasping a book as a symbol of Mother Cabrini's commitment to educating children, and the boy is holding luggage and ocarina, a wind instrument, representing music and culture immigrants have brought to America."[580]

---

[580] "Mother Cabrini Statue Unveiled in NYC on Columbus Day." *AP News*, October 12, 2020. See also: "New York Unveils Mother Cabrini Statue in Manhattan," *Cabrini University,* October, 15, 2020.

The unveiling ceremony was presided over by two 21st century prominent politicians of Italian-American heritage New York Governor Andrew Cuomo (b. 1957) and New York City Mayor Bill de Blasio (b. 1961). Governor Cuomo's office described Cabrini as "an Italian-American Roman Catholic nun - founded the Missionary Sisters of the Sacred Heart of Jesus, a Catholic religious institute that was a major support to fellow Italian immigrants to the United States."

Mother Cabrini statue located at Battery Park City.
Photo Courtesy of Kevin McCabe - Battery Park City Authority.

Upon closer examination of the statue, for an individual who had a lifelong "fear of water," Mother Cabrini is shown symbolically standing in a "paper boat." Cabrini's biography revealed, "As a young girl, Mother Cabrini made paper boats, filled them with violets, and set them off in a stream as her 'missionaries.'" The symbolism of "The Paper Boat" at the memorial is described by the curators of the *Battery Park Authority* as,

The Paper Boat

"The paper boat is a symbolic representation of Mother Cabrini's journey to America, her steadfastness in the face of adversity, and her unflinching commitment to helping her fellow immigrants. Although fragile and delicate, it can hold against the water's currents and stay afloat— symbolizing how she always maintained a perfect balance with resolution and the trust of never being defeated in her beliefs of faith, charity, and strength."

About the Memorial

"The cloak represents a sail against the adverse winds that Mother Cabrini faced throughout her life. The three figures are all facing the

Statue of Liberty, a beacon of hope for immigrants as they entered New York Harbor to begin their new lives in America. The young girl, a reflection of Mother Cabrini's youth, is holding a book, a symbol of Mother Cabrini's commitment to educating children. As music has been important to the heritage of immigrants, the young boy is holding luggage and an ocarina, an instrument invented near Francesca's birthplace, representing the music and culture immigrants have brought to America."

A set of carved stone panels by the husband and wife team of American artist Jill Biagi (nee: Burkee, b. 1953) and Italian born artist Giancarlo Biagi (b. 1949) encircle the sculpture. Each studied art in Italy and maintained both a New York studio and in Pietrasanta, Italy. The panels, tells the illustrated life story of Mother Frances Cabrini from birth to Sainthood. The Biagi's art is not isolated to Cabrini, their work is found in major museums around the world. The talented duo have "created sculptures for several public commissions with the goal of capturing the life story and preserving the legacy of revered individuals."[581]

Italian Joseph Stella: "American Artist"

At a time during the 1920s as staunch conservatives and religious zealots created a morality furor against Modernism, an Italian immigrant rose to prominence among the New York art world scene "for his depictions of Modernist icons." Giuseppe Michele "Joseph" Stella (1877-1946) was from the southern region of Potenza in Lucano a village about 100 miles (160 km) east of Naples. Stella's work is displayed and categorized among "American Art" and is continually referenced as an "American Artist."

Joseph Stella was born into a somewhat financially secure middle class Italian family of an older brother as a doctor and a grandfather and father as attorneys. In 1896, Stella followed the family professional tradition traveling to America intending to study medicine. The pursuit of the medical field did not come to fruition as Stella was smitten by prominent art schools such as the Art Students League of New York. Once settled in the crowded metropolis, he became aware of the overwhelming display of wealthy industrial development in stark contrast to a multitude of impoverished *paisans* living in squalor in the overcrowded New York City tenements. With a pedigree described as an excellent draftsman, biographer Irma B. Jaffe in *The Italian Presence in American Art 1860-1920* described the living experience reflected Stella's early work, stating,

"His first paintings were depictions of city slum life with a particular interest in immigrant and ethnic life. From 1905, he worked as an illustrator, publishing his realist drawings in magazines. He prowled the

---

[581] "Mother Cabrini Memorial." *Hugh L. Carey Battery Park Authority*. May 16, 2022.

CHAPTER 9

streets, sketch pad and pencil in hand, alert to catch the pose of the moment, the detail of costume or manner that told the story of a life."[582]

As part of a Progressive Era initiative, the problems of overcrowding in the urban communities by recent immigrants was seen firsthand.

Conditions in America were not conducive to Stella's sensibility as an overall unhappy dissatisfaction resulting in a return to Italy in 1909. As a desire to be in his native land of Italy, Stella described living in America as, "an enforced stay among enemies, in a black funeral land over which weighed the curse of a merciless climate." Return to Europe introduced him to the growing movement of Modernism.; but lasted only a few years. As biographer Robert Hughes added, "by 1911, he had departed Italy, where the omnipresence of the Renaissance presented its own kind of obstacle for contemporary painters, and relocated to Paris." Among Impressionists in France, Stella expanded his Modernist style which some historians have called him a "Futurist Painter."[583]

The New York Armory Show

In 1912, as the International Exhibition of Modern Art was preparing exhibits, Stella returned to New York submitting two entries for display. As explained by the *Smithsonian Institution Archives of American Art*, "The Armory Show, as it came to be known, had a profound effect on American art – it marked the dawn of Modernism in America. A succinct accurate statement, yet for the time period the Armory Show sent shockwaves through a stoic American society. Unlike the classical nudes of antiquity or even the possibility of applying realism to a contemporary female nude, Duchamp's *Nude Descending a Staircase* was a complete abstract jarring the pre-condition senses of American audiences.

In fact, the word "nudity" in itself was quite shocking. Most importantly, standing on its own ground as the legends of French art, as noted by *Smithsonian* "two-thirds of the paintings on view were by American artists." Included among the American Gallery E were two still life's by the Italian born Joseph Stella. The art on display at the Armory Show provided a glimpse of the cultural shift in the following decade. The introduction of Modernism caused a backlash (more like a whiplash) by conservative American Populists and Nativist supporters. Modernism caused a tidal wave of shock resulting in all sorts of cultural changes and legal restrictions as the 1920s began. During the 1920s, Joseph Stella produced some of his most famous work as he emerged a superstar of the art world and truly defined as an American artist.

---

[582] Irma B Jaffe, ed. *The Italian Presence in American Art 1860-1920*, 1992.
[583] Quoted in: Robert Hughes, *The Epic History of Art in America*. New York: Alfred A. Knopf, 1999, p. 374.

After the Armory Show: An American Legacy

After the Armory Show, Stella painted *Battle of Lights, Coney Island* (1913-1914) – the first in a series of paintings depicting the world famous Brooklyn beach. Stella's interpretation is also considered among the earliest American Futurist works. Another *Coney Island* (1914) by Stella on view at The Metropolitan Museum of Art is described by the curators as, "A kaleidoscope of dazzling color and fragmented form, Stella's abstract painting evokes the electric lights and energetic crowds of Brooklyn's Coney Island amusement park and boardwalk. According to art historian Sam Hunter (1923-2014), the success and prominence of the Armory Show vaulted Joseph Stella into "a much-talked-about figure in the New York art world, [and] an object of virulent attacks from conservative critics who found Modernism threatening."[584]

Battle of Lights, Coney Island, Mardi Gras (1913–14) by Joseph Stella. (Oil on canvas 77 × 84 3/4 in.) Gift of Collection Société Anonyme No. 1941.689. Photo credit: Yale University Art Gallery (Listed as Public Domain)

In 2015, a Brooklyn Museum exhibition, *Coney Island: Visions of an American Dreamland, 1861–2008*, was a compendium of art (painting, photographs, poems,

---

[584] See: *Coney Island* (1914) on view Gallery 910 at the Metropolitan Museum of Art.

song, odes, and personal narratives) in five different sections over a 150-year period. The exhibit first opened at the Wadsworth Atheneum Museum of Art in Hartford Connecticut curated by Robin Jaffee Frank. Coney Island, called "The World's Greatest Playground" was a welcome haven for immigrants seeking an inexpensive relief in the waters off Brooklyn for little or no cost.

Since its inception, Coney Island has been memorialized in American Culture through countless Hollywood movies, television, works of literature, poems, popular song, and art, among others. Brooklyn Museum Curator of Art Connie Choi offered an explanation describing the attraction, "Coney Island has always attracted artists because it has always been accepting. Immigrant artists were attracted to Coney Island because it was the melting pot, it was what they expected America to be."[585]

Brooklyn Bridge (1919-1920) by Joseph Stella
Oil on Canvas (84 in. by 76 in.) at the Yale University Art Gallery Gift of Collection Société Anonyme No. 1941.690.f Art. (Public Domain)

---

[585] Stav Ziv. "An Offsite Tour of Coney Island." *Newsweek*, Nov. 28, 2015.

448
Italian Culture in America:
The Immigrants 1880 to 1930 From Discrimination to Assimilation

The 1920s was a tumultuous decade of cultural change highlighted by the constant struggle between Old World 19th century conservative morality versus the cultural values of New World Modernism. Stella's Modernism delved into geometric shapes evident in the public industrial achievements in full view throughout Lower Manhattan. One of the best examples, and Stella's most famous work, is *Brooklyn Bridge* (1920), described as,

> "*Brooklyn Bridge* is Joseph Stella's best-known and most moving testimonial to the power and majesty of America's modern industrial landscape. Fascination with the bridge began with his first sight of it shortly after his arrival in America in 1896 from native Italy. . . as the shrine containing all efforts of the new civilization of America.

The Brooklyn Bridge was a fascination as Stella returned to the subject "of the bridge many times." In his own words Stella described,

> "Many nights I stood on the bridge - a defenseless prey to the surrounding swarming darkness crushed by the mountainous black impenetrability of the skyscrapers here and there lights resembling suspended falls of astral bodies or fantastic splendors of remote rites - shaken by the underground tumult of the trains in perpetual motion, like blood in the arteries—at times, ringing as alarm in a tempest, the shrill sulphurous voice of the trolley wires—now and then strange moaning's of appeal from tugboats, guessed more than seen, through the infernal recesses below—I felt deeply moved, as if on the threshold of a new religion or in the presence of a new Divinity."[586]

As an artist of influential renown, Stella's work remains into the 21st century on public view at internationally known prominent museums all across the United States. Stella died in 1946, buried in Woodlawn Cemetery in Bronx of New York City; a cemetery with an Italian legacy.

"The Italian Influence at the Woodlawn Cemetery"

Internment for Joseph Stella at Woodlawn Cemetery holds two legacies. One - buried in American soil. Second Woodlawn Cemetery had an Italian connection; especially for Italian artists. A 21st century essay on the official website, "The Italian Influence at the Woodlawn Cemetery" references a multitude of Italian sculpture, of particular interest, "Among the most photographed is the Gerould Memorial, a replica of the famous Monteverde Angel in the Staglieno cemetery in Genoa, Northern Italy."

Prior to the 1880s, some the local American monument dealers were known to travel to Genoa, an Italian port city close to the location of the much-desired

---

[586] *Coney Island* (1914) on view Gallery 910 at the Metropolitan Museum of Art.

CHAPTER 9 449

Carrara marble. Over a period of time some skilled stone carvers such as the Piccirilli brothers made their home in America. Some of their work was placed within Woodlawn; also the final resting place for at least four of the brothers, parents, spouses, and children, within their family burial plot. Woodlawn cemetery, however, is not just the sole realm of the Piccirilli family. Many famous Italian Americans reside in Woodlawn including Fiorello LaGuardia, among many others.[587]

Skilled Italian immigrant stone carvers who produced sculptured monuments at Woodlawn Cemetery included John Grignola (1859-1912). Grignola's more prominent artistic endeavors are located beyond the cemetery. The curators at Woodlawn note, "One of his best known works, the "Bronx River Soldier," guards the entrance to the Valentine Varian House, headquarters of the Bronx County Historical Society." One of the most prominent pieces by Grignola are capitals for the Rotunda at the University of Virginia. Grignola is buried at Woodlawn)

The Italian inspired architectural design of the Library Rotunda at the University of Virginia by Thomas Jefferson, incorporated column capitals. In 1895, a fire destroyed much of the Rotunda requiring intensive restoration. Matt Kelly of the University of Virginia, confirmed the Rotunda capitals for the renovation was commissioned to "the firm of Pompeo Coppini (1870-1957) and John Grignola of New York City." The firm received the commission, yet sources often cite Grignola as the main stone carver of the UVA Rotunda capitals. Coppini, an Italian immigrant was born in Moglia. Noted in his biography, Coppini's work is found throughout America and abroad in Mexico.[588]

The work was overseen by architect Stanford White (1853-1906), of the New York City firm of McKim, Mead & White. (White was well-versed in Italian architecture as evidenced by his arch at Washington Square Park and Gould Memorial Library for New York University, to name just a few. The Gould Memorial Library was greatly influenced by the ancient Roman Pantheon c. 120-124 A.D. and Jefferson's Rotunda.)[589]

A significant amount of work was produced by Pompeo Coppini in the state of Texas – including in Austin on the grounds of the Texas State Capitol building and University of Texas. Famous, at least to Texans, is Coppini's massive "Alamo Cenotaph" at the historical site of The Alamo in San Antonio. Buried at Sunset Memorial in San Antonio, information from *FindAGrave.com* cites, "Nationally known sculptor who sculpted the Alamo Cenotaph, busts of many famous Texans,

---

[587] "The Italian Influence at the Woodlawn Cemetery." April 12, 2022.
[588] Matt Kelly. "A Year in, Rotunda Renovation Reveals Clues." *UVAToday*, 2015.
[589] See: *Italian Culture in America* (2020), pp. 463-494.

and other Americans. In all, by thirty-six public monuments, sixteen portrait statues, and about seventy-five portrait busts."[590]

The Gould Memorial Library designed in 1899 by architect Stanford White for New York University. Library of Congress.

During the 1870s, Casoni & Isola is listed as the first company to provide commissioned monuments for Woodlawn Cemetery. Partners Vincenzo Casoni (1821-1875) and Pietro T. Isola (?) carved *The Farragut Memorial* at Woodlawn Cemetery, listed in 2012 as a National Historic Landmark. Little information on the pair is available. Research by Jeff Richman discovered an obituary of April 10, 1875 in the *New York Daily Tribune*. The Obituary cited Vincenzo Casoni as follows, "born in Carrara, Italy in 1821." Immigrated to America around 1855, partnered with Isola.[591]

Richman adds, "Some of the Italians setting up shop in New York established businesses outside the cemetery gates." One included the firm of Setz and Bianchi (d. ?) makers of the *Herman Melville* memorial; another was Peter Celi (d. ?). Other stone companies were known to have "employed many carvers from Italy."

---

[590] Matt Kelly. "A Year in, Rotunda Renovation Reveals Clues." *UVAToday*, May 8, 2015. See also: "Alamo Cenotaph." *Handbook of Texas Online*. Texas State Historical Association. September 17, 2011.
[591] "Obituary Vincenzo Casoni." *New York Herald Tribune*, April 10, 1875.

Without a multitude of readily available biographical information, Susan Olsen Director of Historical Research at the Woodlawn Cemetery claims,

> "In addition to establishing a cultural community of Italian artists surrounding the cemetery, the contributions of these talented sculptors provided Woodlawn with the "largest and finest collection of funerary art in the nation."[592]

Auto Racing, Baseball, Boxing, and Professional Sports

Raffaele "Ralph" De Palma (1882-1956) born in Baccari; Italy was an Italian-American racecar driver who won almost 2,000 races in his career. A biography from the International Motorsports Hall of Fame, cited one victory included the 1915 Indianapolis 500. Nephew Pete DePaolo (1898-1980) followed into motorsports with a win at the 1925 Indianapolis 500. During the 1925 Indy 500, DePaolo averaged over 100 mph becoming the first driver to complete 500 miles in under five hours. In a two-year period from 1925 to 1927, DePaolo won ten national racing championships. In later years one of the most popular and successful motor sport drivers of all-time was Italian-American Mario Andretti (b. 1940).[593]

Italian-American race car driver Raffaele "Ralph" De Palma (1882-1956), in race car #4, at the Harkness Auto Handicap, Sheepshead Bay Race Track, New York, June 1, 1918. Bain News Service, Library of Congress (Public Domain).

---

[592] Jeff Richman. "Master Carvers: Casoni & Isola." *Greenwood.com*, April 5, 2011. The Italian Influence at the Woodlawn Cemetery." *Woodlawn Cemetery*.
[593] "Peter DePaolo," *Indianapolis Motor Speedway*.

Baseball "America's National Pastime," Ping Bodie, "The Great Bambino," and Ed Abbaticchio

Baseball as a professional sport, dates to 1883 with the National League. The American League was founded in 1900. In 1903, both leagues agreed to play the first World Series championship; as a "best of nine game" outcome, between the top team in each league. Over 100,000 spectators attended the eight games of the series won by the Boston Americans 5 games to 3 over the Pittsburgh Pirates. Between 1903 and 1908, attendance doubled at major league baseball stadiums. Attendance, was not based upon low prices; as tickets averaged $1 per ticket (expensive for that time). The notorious "cheap seats" in the bleachers (25 cents) were occupied by working class immigrants mainly Irish and German. Blacks, when allowed in at all, were regulated to undesirable segregated sections. The rise in spectators was aided in part by the construction of new stadiums close to intersecting trolley lines in densely populated cities such as Philadelphia, Pittsburgh, Boston, Chicago, Manhattan, and Brooklyn.

Above Left: Ping Bodie c. 1918 with the New York Yankees. **Above Right**: Ed Abbaticchio (1877-1957) c. 1903. Chicago Daily News, Inc. (Public Domain)

Some cite the first Italian-American to play professional baseball as Ping Bodie. Born Francesco Stephano Pezzolo (1887-1961) in San Francisco of Italian immigrant parents. Most claim the first name "Ping" came "for the way the ball sounded when it came off his 52-ounce bat." However, that may be disputed in the late 20th century metal, or aluminum bats, made a distinctive "ping" sound upon the bat striking a ball. The name of "Bodie" came from a former California

CHAPTER 9   453

Gold Rush town where he once lived. Some family members say the name change came because as an Italian "he felt he would be ridiculed."[594]

Bodie's professional career began in 1911 with the Chicago White Sox. In four years with Chicago, Bodie compiled hitting statistics of four consecutive yearly averages of .289 (with 97 RBI); .294, .265, and .229. In 1915, he was assigned to the minor leagues. In 1918, he was traded to the New York Yankees, later rooming with Babe Ruth. (Some sources cite the nickname of "The Great Bambino" for Babe Ruth came from Ping Bodie.) In three full seasons with the Yankees, Bodie registered respectable batting averages of .256, .278, and .295. Bodie was considered as "the first of the San Francisco Italians to join the Yankees." Other players of Italian heritage joining the Yankees included Tony Lazzeri (1903-1946); Frank Crosetti (1910-2002); and Joe DiMaggio (1914-1999). Baseball historian Paul Glader said, San Francisco "was something of a hotbed of Italian-American talent on the baseball field during the 1920s and 1930s."

All four players were later inducted into the National Italian American Sports Hall of Fame. On the other hand, Ed Abbaticchio (1877-1957) born in Latrobe, Pennsylvania is often considered as the first Italian-American Major League Baseball player. In 1897, he appeared in only a few games with the Philadelphia Phillies. In the ensuing years he played in various other types of professional baseball leagues. He returned to Major League Baseball with the Pittsburgh Pirates from 1907 to 1910. Abbaticchio was known to play football in semi-professional leagues about 20 years before the National Football League formed. It is not known how many other Italians were in professional baseball. As evident by Ping Bodie, a name change may have avoided discrimination.

Pugilist – a Latin term for "Boxer" – and Ralph Giordano

One sport with a significant legacy of Italians, and aliases – was boxing. Legalized boxing (also known as prizefighting) was scattered during the late 19th and early 20th century. Boxing, had conflicting appeal among the public and moralists due to the brutal nature of the contest, often fought "bareknuckle." Rules and regulations varied from state to state - some states outlawed the sport completely. Bare-knuckle fighting was still popular, some cities such as New Orleans, added safety requirement of the contestants for the boxers to wear padded gloves, while limiting rounds to 3-minutes. In contrast, many of the Ivy League colleges stressed boxing as a gentlemanly sport worthy of athletic-scholarly competition. President Theodore Roosevelt, who practiced the sport while attending Harvard,

---

[594] Ping's brother Dave wrote to the editor of *Sporting Life* on February 17, 1912, citing Ping's name in Italian was "Franceto Sanguenitta Pizzola." See: Ralph Berger. "Ping Bodie." *Society for American Baseball Research.*

often promoted the fisticuffs of boxing as an activity worthy for young males on a national level. Roosevelt wrote in his autobiography, "I did a good deal of boxing and wrestling in Harvard," A parody of Teddy Roosevelt's acumen for boxing was portrayed on the June 1, 1904 cover issue of the national *Puck* magazine.[595]

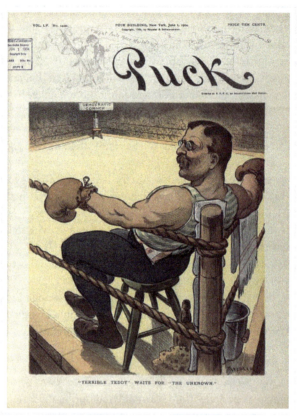

Cover illustration of *Puck* magazine, June 1, 1904 shows President Theodore Roosevelt as a boxer sitting on a stool with his arms resting on the ropes in the near corner of a boxing ring, waiting for a challenger to enter the ring. Titled: "Terrible Teddy" waits for the "unknown." Artist: Udo J. Keppler. Photograph Retrieved from the Library of Congress. <www.loc.gov/item/2011645537/>. (Public Domain)

Americans were astutely aware of the flamboyant Teddy Roosevelt and the sport of boxing. It was not until 1920, when the New York State Athletic Commission

---

[595] David Nasaw. *Going Out: The Rise and Fall of Public Amusements*. pp. 97-100. Victor Bondi, American Decades: 1900-1909, p. 492.

CHAPTER 9 455

passed the "Walker Law," professional boxing became a legal entity as a regulatory agency. California enacted similar legislation in 1924, in quick succession over one dozen states followed with establishment of the National Boxing Association; as the sport gained widespread public acceptance. A significant factor for boxing to become one of the most popular spectator sports in America, was being readily accessible to the public in any number of the thousands of neighborhood gyms and arenas across the nation.

Boxer / fighter Jack Dempsey (1895-1983), was one of America's most popular celebrities; while also garnering huge paydays. In July 1919, Dempsey nicknamed "The Manassa Mauler" after his hometown in Colorado, won the World Heavyweight boxing title beating Jess Willard of Kansas. Throughout the 1920s, Dempsey made personal appearances movies, his fights received major media attention with crowds regularly numbering 60,000 to 90,000 and millions of radio listeners. The crowd at Dempsey's 1926 Heavyweight championship fight against Gene Tunney (1897-1978) was numbered at over 120,000 as the largest to witness any live sporting event in America. The following year, a rematch in Chicago, exceeded all attendance records with over 145,000 spectators.

Dempsey reigned supreme as both Heavyweight Champion and financial lucrative sports celebrity, far outdistancing even the legendary Babe Ruth of the New York Yankees. Dempsey's career was formidable, yet as Fausto Batella, writing for *We the Italians*, tells us the only loss Dempsey ever suffered by a knockout during his career occurred on February 14, 1918 at the hands of "Fireman Jim Flynn" real name was of an American born of Italian immigrants named Andrew Chiariglione (1869-1935). An essay "Boxers of the Golden Age" for *American Experience*, related the popularity of the sport of boxing as, "Americans loved boxing in the 1920s and '30s. Every immigrant neighborhood had its champion, and boxing was a flag of racial or ethnic pride." A significant number of boxers at the time were comprised of American born children of recent immigrants from Ireland, Poland, Lithuania, Albania, Mexico, Panama, and Italy, to name a few. From the late 19th century, continuing well into the 21st century, boxing has continued as a major spectator sport. Despite neighborhood "acceptance" of ethnic and immigrant boxers, overt prejudice and discrimination continued. For boxing, some of the appeal to outsiders may obviously have included the distorted enjoyment of watching any number of "undesirables" literally receive a physical beating within a boxing ring. Unfortunately, the situation existed in that same manner for Italians. Some such as boxer Young Corbett III who changed his name from Ralph Giordano to hide his Italian birth.[596]

---

[596] Not known to be related to the author. "Boxers of the Golden Age." *American Experience*, 1996–2022 WGBH Educational Foundation.

Raffaele Capabianca "Ralph" Giordano (1905- 1993), one boxing magazine listed his birthplace as Naples, Italy; another as Rionero in the Basilicata region of Italy. An obituary in 1993 cited Giordano's birth on May 27, 1905 in Potenza, Italy. Regardless of the birth discrepancy, all agreed he was born in Italy. Immigration to America was as a child with parents settling in Fresno, California. Known professionally as Young Corbett III, the Italian-born American boxer fought major bouts through the 1920s; gaining the World Welterweight Championship in 1933. (In 1938, he added the Middleweight title.)

One account for the alias professional name from the *Fresno News* reported, a ring announcer would not say the name of the fighter as "Ralph Giordano" (possibly due to prejudice); instead introduced the young boxer as "Young Corbett III." Giordano as "Young Corbett III" is still considered as one of the greatest southpaws (dominant left hand) of all time. The International Boxing Hall of Fame, lauded Giordano as "a tough southpaw, he did not have strong punching power but was known for his great speed and determination."

Above Left: Italian American Boxer Young Corbett III (Ralph Giordano) posing for a publicity photo during training for an upcoming fight, c. 1931.
Above Right: Young Corbett III (facing camera) won the World Welterweight title in his 131st professional fight at Seals Stadium in San Francisco on February 22, 1933. (Public Domain)

The professional name of Young Corbett III remained. Giordano's 21-year career amounted to record 126 wins, 10 loses, and 16 draws (with a scant 33 knockouts). 110 of those fights occurred during his first ten years of the 1920s. A 1983, UPI obituary claimed,

"Corbett, who went undefeated in 22 fights in 1926, was invited to box in San Francisco in 1927. San Francisco had a large Italian population and Giordano became the biggest draw in the city's boxing history."

CHAPTER 9   457

On Feb. 22, 1933, in his 131st fight, Young Corbett III finally gained an opportunity to fight for a title before 16,000 fans at San Francisco's Seals Stadium, Giordano winning a 10 Round decision. After winning the World Welterweight title, a return to his hometown of Fresno California was greeted by "a parade and riotous welcome" by the local residents. He moved up in weight class later winning the vacant Middleweight title in March of 1938. Later that year, in a fight at the famous Madison Square Garden in New York on November 18, 1938, he lost the opportunity to unify the title. He ended his career with a win on August 20, 1940 fittingly in the Italian Entertainment Park in Fresno, California.

On April 30, 1983, the United Press International (UPI) released a story carried in many major newspapers across the country. Under a banner headline, the story recalled, "Young Corbett III was welterweight champion of the world, lionized by an adoring Italian community in San Francisco and a beloved hometown hero in Fresno." An obituary by the Associated Press (AP) on July 23, 1993 appeared in many newspapers nationwide including *The New York Times*. The obituary indicated Giordano was mostly forgotten by the public, but not the Boxing world. Prior to his death, in 1959, as Young Corbett III he was inducted into the Fresno Athletic Hall of Fame and the Italian-American Sports Hall of Fame in 1982. In 2004, a posthumous honor came with induction into the International Boxing Hall of Fame.[597]

Giordano was only one in a long list of famous boxers of Italian heritage. The list could even include fictional portrayals such as "Rocky Balboa" in the *Rocky* movie series starring Italian American actor Sylvester Stallone (b. 1946). In 2020, boxing historian Brittany Andrews writing, "Ranked: The Five Greatest Italian-American Boxers" revealed,

> "There can be little doubt that the story of working-class Italian-Americans making the big time in boxing is a truly loved and time-tested one; especially with an abundance of such heroes hailing from New York."

A reason for the abundance of Italian American boxers originating from New York was due to Ellis Island serving as a major point of entry for Italian immigrants. (Boston, New Orleans, and Philadelphia also served as major immigration ports of entry for immigrants.) Andrews added,

---

[597] "Young Corbett III, Boxer, 88." *The New York Times,* July 3, 1993, p. A20See: "Young Corbett III - Boxing Encyclopaedia." *Boxrec.com.* Note: *BoxRec* listed as "Boxing's Official Record Keeper" cites 122 wins, 12 loses, and 20 draws. Wikipedia 123 wins, 12 loses, and 20 draws. Another as 123 wins 11 loses, 17 draws and 33 knockouts. Yet another lists: a possible record of 129 wins, 10 loses, and 16 draws.

"From the "*Rocky*" [movie] franchise to "Raging Bull," popular culture has also played its part in incubating the relationship between American citizens of Italian descent and the noble sport, and how the world embraces that relationship."

Three of the greatest fighters of all-time (regardless of nationality) were Italian American: Rocky Graziano, Brooklyn born as "Thomas Rocco Barbella" (1919-1990); Giacobbe "Jake" LaMotta, born in Manhattan (1922-2017); and Rocky Marciano, born "Rocco Francis Marchegiano" in Brockton, Massachusetts (1923-1969). Each born of Italian parents; all World Champions. Marciano is the only Heavyweight Champion to retire undefeated; a large majority of those wins were by a knockout.[598]

Although Rocky Graziano, Jake LaMotta, and Rocky Marciano boxed under changed names, their "refined" names and public persona did not hide their Italian cultural heritage. In contrast, many Italian immigrants during the 1920s did fight under Americanized names.

- o **Johnny Dundee** (1893-1965) born "Giuseppe Curreri" in Sciacca, Sicily. From 1910 to 1932, 334 fights. In his 261st fight, won the Junior Welterweight title. Inducted into Ring Magazine Hall of Fame in 1957 and International Boxing Hall of Fame. induction in 1991.
- o **Johnny Wilson (1893-1985)** "Giovanni Francesco Panica" Italian Harlem in New York City. From 1911 to 1926, at least 100 bouts. In 71st fight, the first of Italian heritage to win World Middleweight title.
- o **Pete Herman** (1896-1973) born "Peter Gulotta" New Orleans; Bantamweight World Title from 1917 to 1920. Inducted International Boxing Hall of Fame in 1997.
- o **Frankie Genaro** (1901-1966) born "Frank DiGennaro" New York City. Gold Medal at 1920 Olympic Games. World Flyweight title in 1928. Posthumous induction into International Boxing Hall of Fame came in 1998.
- o **Sammy Mandell** (1904-1967) "Salvatore Mandala" Palermo, Sicily; Known as the "Rockford Sheik" so named due to resemblance to popular Hollywood idol *The Sheik* Rudolph Valentino. World Lightweight title in 1926. International Boxing Hall of Fame in 1998.
- o **Primo Carnera** (1906-1967) born Friuli-Venezia in Italy. Heaviest of all Heavyweight World Champions (about 275 lbs. – 124.7 kg.) In 21st century still holds the record of "winning more

---

[598] Brittany Andrews. "Ranked: The Five Greatest Italian-American Boxers. *NYFights*, November 22, 2020.

CHAPTER 9   459

fights by knockout (72) than any other Heavyweight Champion."
Unlike the other Italians of the time, Carnera did not change his
name since he fought as an Italian citizen.

o   **Battling "Bat" Battalino** (1908-1977) born Hartford, CT as
"Christopher Battaglia" World Featherweight 1929. International
Boxing Hall of Fame in 2003.

o   **Tony Canzoneri** (1908-1959) born New Orleans, in 176 fights -
titles in three different weight classes; Featherweight, Lightweight,
Light Welterweight. Ring Magazine Hall of Fame, International
Boxing Hall of Fame in 1990.

o   **Tommy Paul** (1909-1991) born "Gaetano Alfonso Papa" to Italian
immigrant parents in Buffalo, New York. World Featherweight title
holder in 1932.

o   **Willie Pep** (1922-2006) the World Featherweight Champion born
"Guglielmo Papaleo" Middletown, CT. 134 fights with only one
loss after 63rd bout. Career of 229 wins, 11 loses and 1 draw. After
first loss Pep went a string of 72 wins, no losses, and 1 draw. No
fighter in the history of the sport has matched or exceeded Pep's
accomplishment. No. 1 ranked Featherweight of the 20th century,
International Boxing Hall of Fame.

The list is not complete for all the boxers of Italian heritage who fought during
this era. The list highlights the most distinguished champions.[599]

An Italian Immigrant
Medical Doctor and Grandson of Immigrants

Medical doctors of Italian heritage number in the thousands. One early Italian
immigrant was **Dr. Vincenzo Sellaro** (1868-1932). Born in Sicily with a degree
from the University of Naples, Sellaro immigrated to the United States around
1897. In America he earned a degree from Cornell Medical School. Dr. Sellaro
was instrumental in the founding of Columbus Italian Hospital in New York
offering immigrants service in both Italian and English. In 1905, he began the
fraternal Order of the Sons of Italy in America. In 1922, both accomplishments
were recognized by the Italian government bestowing Sellaro with the title of
Knighthood.[600]

Listing the accomplishments of a wide array of medical doctors of Italian
ancestry is worthy of its own publication. As applied to not only to America, but
also the world; is one of the most famous medical doctors during two horrendous

---

[599] Fausto Batella. "The Italian American stars in US sports: Boxing." And compiled from
various Boxing sites and the valuable *FindAGrave.com.*
[600] See: OSIA Blogger. "Vincenzo Sellaro: Italian of the Week," January 24. 2015.

pandemics in American history is **Dr. Anthony Fauci** (b. 1940). As Director of the National Institute of Allergy and Infectious Disease (NIAID) and associated with the National Institutes of Health (NIH), Dr. Fauci became a well-respected national celebrity during two worldwide pandemics of HIV/Aids during the 1980s and Covid-19 during the 2020s. His influence and advisement reached well beyond America, becoming well respected internationally. Born in Brooklyn, New York, three of Fauci's grandparents immigrated from southern Italy, with the fourth from Switzerland. Individuals such as Fauci are a continuation of a long line of medical professionals of Italian heritage.

A Smooth Ice Surface

Frank Joseph Zamboni, Jr. (1901 –1988) bears the iconic statue in American culture with his namesake of the modern ice resurfacer. Zamboni represents another of the thousands of the emerging group of children born of Italian immigrant parents who became ensconced in the litany of American culture. Born in Utah, the family moved to an Idaho farm. In 1920, Frank Jr. and brother Lawrence (1901-1985) relocated to Los Angeles as older brother George (1890-1926) managed an auto repair shop. Frank Jr. and Lawrence opened an ice-making business. Before the abundance of affordable home refrigerators, households contained an "ice box" requiring a delivery of ice blocks. In 1939, the Zamboni brothers invested in an ice skating rink aided by their ice making equipment. Ice rinks regularly required maintenance of resurfacing (smoothing the surface); a work task performed by a small group of workers. In 1949, Frank Jr. invented an ice resurfacer for skating rinks requiring operation by only one person, hence the birth of the "Zamboni."

Attending a professional hockey game is not solely watching the teams. Fan anticipation of witnessing a Zamboni as "the official ice resurfacer of the NHL" is a unique thrill. The Zamboni is not limited to professional hockey. Just about any ice rink surface either professional or amateur requires a smooth surface; imperative for amateur, professional sports, or international competition such as the Olympics. Surface preparation is usually by a "Zamboni" a proprietary reference to a machine invented by Italian-American inventor Frank Zamboni. In American culture the word "Zamboni" is basically a large tractor-like device driven over a surface smoothing and polishing the ice.[601]

---

[601] See: "The Zamboni Story," Zamboni.com. "The Italians Who Built America: Frank Joseph Zamboni, Jr." The National Italian American Foundation (NIAF), 2021.

An Italian Founder of the F.B.I. and an Italian NYPD Police Officer

Among sensational and numerous accusations against Italians with crime and a "Mafia" organization arose two major figures in enforcing the law. Charles Joseph Bonaparte (1851-1921), born in Baltimore, Maryland traced an Italian ancestry to the island of Corsica as grandson of Jérôme Bonaparte (1784-1860) youngest brother of Emperor Napoleon Bonaparte (1769-1821) of France. After graduating Harvard Law School in 1872, Bonaparte entered a law career as an attorney. He was chosen by President Teddy Roosevelt as a member of the U.S. Cabinet, later as U.S. Attorney General from 1906 to 1909. As Attorney General, Bonaparte created the "Bureau of Investigation" transformed during the 1920s; renamed in 1935 as the Federal Bureau of Investigation (F.B.I.) under legendary Director J. Edgar Hoover (1895-1972). An ironic twist to the foundation of the F.B.I. by an American of Italian heritage was a long-standing distinction during when it was termed the "F.B.I. so-named as "Forever Bothering Italians."

Portrait of Charles Bonaparte. U.S. Library of Congress Digital ID No. cph.3c02547. Reproduction Number: LC-USZ62-102547.
(Public Domain)

Another was Joseph Petrosino (1860 – 1909) born Giuseppe Petrosino in Padula, Sicily. As a New York City police officer, he was an early proponent in the fight against those of Italians involved in organized crime. Some "crime fighting techniques" employed by Petrosino are standard within most police agencies into the 21st century. In a police department heavily employing generations of Irish descendants, Petrosino was the first NYPD officer who spoke the Italian language; and the first Italian to achieve the rank of Lieutenant. In 1909, while traveling to Sicily investigating a crime connection, Petrosino who had earned a reputation as an "honest cop" was assassinated. To the current day his memory is kept alive at his birth house in Padua, Italy which contains his New York City Police Department (NYPD) uniform, badge, and other memorabilia in the Casa-Museo Joe Petrosino di Padua.

Above Left: Official NYPD photograph of Lt. Joseph Petrosino, c. 1909. **Above Right**: Petrosino's uniform. Photo from Joe Petrosino's House & Museum in Padula, c. 2018 by Luciano Coda. Released under Wiki Creative Commons Attribution Share Alike 4.0 International license. (Public Domain)

Planters Peanuts Company and "Mr. Peanut"

Amadeo Obici (1877-1947): born in Veneto, Italy turned an Italian stereotype into an iconic American brand. As a teen he sailed to America living with an uncle in Scranton, Pennsylvania. He later purchased a pushcart selling shelled peanuts alongside city streets. Inquisitiveness led to roasting peanuts in a different fashion, as well as removing the peanuts from the shells making them easily snackable. In 1906, in partnership with Italian immigrant Mario Peruzzi, (1875-1955), the pair founded Planters Peanuts Company. The advertising logo of "Mr. Peanut" as a shelled peanut dapperly dashed out in formal attire with gloves, top hat, cane, and monocle of a dignified gentleman is an American icon.

The Little Red Wagon and Radio Flyer

As iconic as Mr. Peanut became in American culture firmly planted within American culture, so is a little red wagon. Antonio Pasin (1896-1990), born near Venice, Italy, immigrated in 1914. Within a few years Pasin founded the Radio Flyer Company and the iconic "Little Red Wagon." Author, educator, and

CHAPTER 9   463

researcher Janice Therese Mancuso explains, classic Radio Flyer wagon was an immigrant from Venice "who learned his woodworking skills from his father and grandfather in Italy and began making wagons from wood in America. He later produced metal wagons and named the company Radio Flyer after Marconi's invention of the radio and Pasin's [own] interest in flight."[602]

During the early 1920s, Pasin started the Liberty Coaster Company (so-named in representation of the Statue of Liberty). The appeal of the red wagon received wide recognition at the 1933 Chicago World's Fair, where he arranged an exhibit of "a 45-foot-tall structure of a boy atop a wagon." Sales continued throughout the Great Depression allowing the company to operate "at full capacity." Radio Flyer later expanded into all sorts of children's toy products including various wagon shapes, tricycles, and bicycles. The distinctive trademark red color remained well into the 21st century. Notably, "as one of the oldest toy companies in America, it is still family owned." The subliminal ideal of the Radio Flyer Red Wagon is so ingrained within American culture it has frequently been portrayed as part of the "American Dream." One family descendant and CEO explained, "It can be anything the child imagines it to be—it can be a spaceship, a train, a race car, [or] a submarine."[603]

The Italian Business of "Fireworks by Grucci"

A memorable event of American culture is a celebratory fireworks display on Independence Day of July 4th. Befitting that event in the formation of the American nation is coupled with fireworks displays at all sorts of celebratory events including college graduations to U.S. Presidential Inaugurations and just about any other significant event. One of the oldest fireworks companies in America and well-known throughout the world was founded in 1850 by an Italian family is "Fireworks by Grucci."

American born Felix James Grucci, Sr. (1905-1993) was the son of Italian immigrants James Grucci (1878-1938) a grocer and Maria Lanzetta (1888-1973). An obituary cited Felix Grucci as "patriarch of America's first family of fireworks." The first two "generations" were maternal uncle Anthony Lanzetta (1851-1927) and uncle Angelo Lanzetta (?). In the mid-19th century, Angelo started a fireworks business in the Adriatic port of Bari in Italy. In 1870, Lanzetta, preceding the new wave of immigration, with son Anthony emigrated to America.

Leaving Bari, in southern Italy, the Lanzetta's passed through Ellis Island, settling on Long Island, New York, continuing as pyrotechnicians learned in Italy. In 1923, the skill was passed on to nephew Felix Grucci serving as an apprentice

---

[602] Janice Therese Mancuso. "Thirty-One Days of Italians," 2020.
[603] See: Maya Wei-Haas. "How an Italian Immigrant Rolled Out the Radio Flyer Wagon Across America," *Smithsonian Magazine*, June 3, 2016.

to "Uncle Anthony." In 1929, Felix Grucci led the business renaming it "Grucci Fireworks Company." Well into the 21st century "Fireworks by Grucci," counts six family generations staging large-scale events nationally and internationally; including the Olympic Games; U.S. Presidential Inaugurations; Centennial celebrations of the Brooklyn Bridge and the Statue of Liberty. One source cited a September 2008 event as the company planned the opening of the Atlantis Palm Hotel in Dubai; possibly the largest fireworks show up until that time.[604]

Lesser known, but just as influential is "Zambelli Fireworks" founded by Antonio Zambelli (1877 -1957) born in Teano, Italy about 38 miles (60 km.) north of Naples. In 1893, Zambelli sailed to America journeying to New Castle, Pennsylvania, about 55 miles (88 km) north of Pittsburgh. After a few years at a steel making company, Antonio joined the Fazzoni Brothers Fireworks Manufacturing Company; founded by an Italian immigrant named Leopoldo "Paul" Fazzoni (1868-1940) in 1886. An official biography notes, it was with Fazzoni that Antonio Zambelli "learned how to make and shoot-off fireworks." Over the years, Antonio purchased the Fazzoni company. In 1957, son George Zambelli (1924-2003) assumed management of Zambelli Fireworks (in 1960 renamed "Zambelli Fireworks Manufacturing Company).

As the second largest fireworks company in the U.S. (after Grucci) the official company website lists major exhibitions of fireworks displays at the famous New Year's Eve Ball Drop at Times Square in New York, Mt. Rushmore in South Dakota, the Statue of Liberty, all sorts of Las Vegas Hotel extravaganzas, including Presidential inaugurations and international displays. Closer to home, Zambelli produced a multi-location fireworks display for the 250th anniversary celebration of the birth of the city of Pittsburgh. Writing on the "Business of Fireworks," research historian Steve Wood reminds us,

> "What gets lost in the immigration rhetoric is how many of our American businesses got started by immigrants. So, as you watch beautiful fireworks, remember it was two immigrants to this country, Angelo Lanzetta and Antonio Zambelli, who created the two largest fireworks companies in the United States today – Fireworks by Grucci and Zambelli Fireworks."[605]

A contributing factor for both our added knowledge of Italian Culture in America, yet also lacking in full scholarly acceptance is Italian American Studies as an academic discipline. One such mostly forgotten individual is the groundbreaking academic work of Giovanni E. Schiavo.

---

[604] Wolfgang Saxon. "Felix James Grucci Sr., 87, Dies; Staged Fireworks Extravaganzas," *The New York Times*, January 12, 1993, Section A, Page 19.

[605] Steve Wood. "Business of Fireworks." *Steve on Leadership*, 2022.

CHAPTER 9   465

Italian American Studies and Myth Busting the Italian Mafia

Giovanni Ermenegildo Schiavo (1898-1983), an Italian American author and avid researcher was born in the Castellamare Del Golfo region of Sicily. Immigration to America in 1916 was prompted by mother Giuseppina relocating son and daughter Domenica to reunite the family with father Salvatore Schiavo in Baltimore, Maryland. (A report by the Center for Migration Studies said, "another son Gaspare, had to remain in Italy to serve in the military during the First World War.")

An earlier education at the Regio Liceo Vittorio Emanuele in Palermo springboarded Giovanni to enroll at two prestigious American universities; Johns Hopkins in Maryland and thereafter studied law at Columbia University in New York. Throughout a distinguished career he served as a regular contributor to Encyclopedia Britannica, the editorial staff of *The Baltimore Sun* and *New York Herald Tribune* newspapers, and an editor of *Atlantic Magazine*. A summary of Schiavo's publications was cited by the National Italian American Foundation (NIAF) as "influential in implementing Italian American studies." The NIAF added, "Schiavo's principal interest throughout his lifetime was the welfare of the Italian people in the United States. and this is reflected in all his papers." Listed among Schiavo's many published works on Italian-American studies and cultural influences are listed as,

- o   *Italian-American Who's Who*. Vigo Press, 1943.
- o   *Italian-American History*. Vigo Press, 1947.
- o   *Italian-American History: Book 1. Italian Music and Musicians in America. Book 2. Dictionary of Musical Biography. Book 3*. University of Michigan, 1947.
- o   *Four Centuries of Italian-American History*. University of Minnesota, 1951.
- o   *The Italian Contribution to the Catholic Church*. Vigo Press, 1947.
- o   *Antonio Meucci: Inventor of the Telephone*. Vigo Press, 1958.
- o   *Four Centuries of Italian American History*. Center Migration Studies, 1958.
- o   *The Truth about the Mafia and Organized Crime in America*. Vigo Press, 1962.
- o   *Italian-American History: Volume 2*. Arno Press, 1975.
- o   *The Italians in Missouri*. Arno Press, 1975.
- o   *The Italians in Chicago: A Study in Americanization*. Ayer Co. Publishing, 1975.
- o   *The Italians in America Before the Revolution*. Center for Migration Studies, 1976.

Schiavo was influential in implementing Italian American studies leading to recognition for an Italian Heritage Month. In 2022, the Italian American Studies

466   Italian Culture in America:
The Immigrants 1880 to 1930 From Discrimination to Assimilation

Association celebrated fifty-three years of academic inquiry into all things Italian and Italian American.[606]

A very important, and often overlooked work in Italian American Studies is Giovanni Schiavo's numerous publications on Italian-American history. One seminal work is *Four Centuries of Italian-American History* first published in 1952; republished in 1992 by the Center for Migration Studies. The Center for Migration Studies, founded in 1964, is an invaluable resource not only for Italian immigration, but a vast majority of "human migration movements" throughout history. A significant portion of Schiavo's work focused on Italian American organized crime and the mafia. A myth busting fact published in 1962, *The Truth About the Mafia and Organized Crime in America*, Schiavo demonstrated that crime was the domain of all ethnic groups. An undeniable fact of Schiavo's work on debunking the "mafia myth" was explained by the Center for Migration Studies as, "Two important points emerge: he argues that prejudice rather than facts support the American notion of mafia; mafia is an attitude and that is associated with some of the characteristics in Sicilian culture."

In a letter to the editor of *The New York Review* in December 1969, Schiavo applauded an article citing "the mythical mafia" calling it "the most sensible and logical piece of literature on the subject." In contrast, Schiavo took offense to a counter claim made by one Luigi Barzini one month earlier in October of 1969. Schiavo stated,

> "I am afraid that like other non-Sicilians and even some Sicilians who were not even born when the Mafia was crushed in 1927 (Barzini) confuses the Mafia attitude with the mythical mafia as a criminal organization. As an attitude, Mafia means "he-man," "red-blooded," also bully What Barzini calls Mafia is just plain gangsterism, or racketeering, American style. The modern Mafia [in Italy], or what some Italians call *mafia*, is just plain gangsterism, imported from America, and applies to all forms of crime and criminals, regardless of regional or national origins."

Criticism of Barzini centered on an essay promoting a recent "best-seller *The Italians*," which was similar to many negative Hollywood and media portrayals focused on a formula to "show the sensational side of a story, exaggerate, [and] doctor up." Schiavo related his own knowledge of Sicilians and family life, "I could assure him that the people my family used to associate with in Palermo were not the kind described by him."[607]

Schiavo's *The Truth About the Mafia and Organized Crime in America* was

---

[606] See: "Giovanni E. Schiavo Papers (CMS 085)." New York: Center for Immigration Studies. July 14, 2016. See also: "Guide to the Giovanni E. Schiavo Papers CMS.085 Finding aid prepared by Richard Del Giudice." New York: Center for Immigration Studies. February 20, 2015.

[607] Giovanni Schiavo. "Sicilians and Others – Giovanni Schiavo, reply by Luigi Barzini." *The New York Review* December 4, 1969.

CHAPTER 9 467

reviewed by Prof. Marvin E. Wolfgang in the *American Journal of Sociology*. Prof. Wolfgang termed Schiavo's publication as "interesting, well-documented, occasionally journalistic, but usually convincing book; describes its decline, the many misconceptions of the term, and the development and present status of organized crime in the United States." An analysis added naming of a litany of non-Italian historians as "false prophets or were deluded into believing there was an American Mafia; and they were irresponsible proponents of their ideas." Or simply placing them among those "who do not know the facts." An important comment added by Prof. Wolfgang stated Schiavo is "obviously a well-informed student of Italy and Italians in America." For those who do not know the facts, a significant focus was reminding the reader "The footnotes are very informative and should not be missed. The bibliography on the history and allegations about the Mafia is excellent."[608]

Added to the discourse, yet added to the discrimination was the attachment of the word "mafia" to non-Italian musical entertainers. Two cases include the musical entourage of Elvis Presley's so-called "Memphis Mafia." Another is Hip Hop or Rap of the late 20th and early 21st century. A good case in point is within an article "The Homage: Mafia Culture's Influence on Rap Music" by journalist David Drake which related the sensationalism of "gangsterism." The influence of course came from stereotypical Hollywood movies adding the double-sided negativity of similar defamation against African Americans. Drake summarized,

> "In the late 1980s and early 1990s, several New York rappers inspired by the long legacy of films like *The Godfather*, *GoodFellas*, and *Casino* introduced the world to hip-hop's cinematic equivalent. The Mafia's influence on hip-hop takes on different forms: idealizing the lives of mythic gangsters past and present. Celebrating the many rewards of the fast life, the sudden popularity of suits and wide-brimmed fedoras, or simply emulating the epic scope of the fictionalized, dramatized versions seen in film and on television the intertwining hip-hop obsessions of realism and flights of kingpin fancy are the absorbing tension at the heart of the Mafioso rap subgenre."[609]

Despite the testaments of many historians and research such as Giovanni Schiavo, providing relevant facts, the "mafia myth" remains stronger and continues in 21st century revisionist defamation of two gigantic notables contributing to the development of Italian Culture in America notably Christopher Columbus and Thomas Jefferson.

---

[608] Marvin E. Wolfgang. "The Truth About the Mafia. Giovanni Schiavo." *American Journal of Sociology*, Volume 69, Number 3, p. 309.
[609] David Drake. "The Homage: Mafia Culture's Influence on Rap Music," 2015.

CHAPTER 10

THE 1920S: THE DOOR CLOSES

"The time has arrived when we should shut the door."

"Strange as it may seem, the greater tractability of the urban
problem resides in the very condition to which people are
wont to attribute most of the city's ills –
I mean the density of the population."

Italian-American Heroes of World War I

As the First World War began in August 1914, the United States was not involved in sending troops into the conflict.[610] In April 1917, the United States declared war on Germany joining the horrific world war raging throughout Europe and other parts of the world. During the conflict a significant number of American ships traversed the Atlantic Ocean, some carrying supplies and military aid to its British allies. The most notorious U-boat attack occurred in May 1915 with the unprovoked sinking of the *RMS Lusitania*. Although the *Lusitania* was a non-military British ocean liner, of which almost 1,200 civilians lost their lives, over 120 who died onboard were American. Public opinion of the time viewed any attack by a German *Unterseeboot* (translated as "Undersea Boat;" more commonly known as a "U-Boat,") especially without warning was tantamount to a terrorist attack upon unknowing civilians. Death of American passengers created an outcry of resentment by the general public, yet was not enough to engage involvement by the United States in what was seen as a European war.

The main prompt for United States entry into the war was in response to a pre-conceived attempt via a secret telegram by German envoys to encourage

---

[610] At the time the conflict was often known as, "The War to End All Wars;" or commonly during the 1920s and 1930s as "The Great War." With the onset of another world war from the late 1930s to 1945, each was known as either "World War I" and World War II."

Mexico to launch a military strike into the United States. In response, the United States entered the European conflict. Within a short time, the war drastically changed American society as Congress enacted a military draft of over four million young men destined to go "Over There." Additional Congressional actions quickly passed the Espionage Act of 1917 and the Sedition Act of 1918 significantly altering American lifestyle choices on the home front.

The war also interceded on halting immigration from Europe, previously averaging one million per year from 1890 to 1914. Unlike the Second World War with Fascist Italy allied with Nazi Germany, during the First World War, Italy allied with Great Britain, France, and later the United States in the European war against Germany and the Axis powers. As a result of the war, immigration from Europe was severely limited, but Italian immigrants living in the United States played an active role in the U.S. military. According to an article by David Laskin, "Italian Americans and the Great War," posted by the *Order of the Sons of Italy*,

> "When Congress authorized a draft in June, 1917, immigrants were deemed eligible for service so long as they had taken out their "first papers" declaring their intention to become U.S. citizens. Tens of thousands of Italians from all over the country were swept into the armed forces and shipped out to the trenches of France."[611]

Laskin traced one path from Italian immigrant to American citizenship in *The Long Way Home*, recalling "how Italian immigrants and men from other groups became Americans by fighting in the Great War." A circuitous route proved ironic as the path of immigrants leaving Italy crossed the Atlantic Ocean entering. On American soil enlistment in the U.S. Army required basic training which then led to transport back across the Atlantic to Europe joining the fight with the U.S. armed forces.[612]

Immigrant Italians, who felt compelled to their nation of birth could have chosen to travel back to Italy. War was not the reason Italians left in the first place. For those choosing (or were coerced, or drafted) joining the U.S. Army provided a better opportunity than any of the other strenuous labor activities in their new nation. For those deciding to put down their "pick and shovel" to join the American Army; it was viewed as a possible quick path to citizenship. David Laskin in *The Long Way Home: An American Journey from Ellis Island to the Great War* provided painstaking researched to chronicle the tales of Italian immigrants entering through Ellis Island and soon enlisted for service. As for the Italian experience within the U.S. military, one individual who achieved the highest honor bestowed upon a member of the U.S. armed forces was recalled.

---

[611] David Laskin, "Italian Americans and the Great War," *Order Sons and Daughters of Italians in America.*
[612] Laskin, The Long Way Home.

CHAPTER 10

Laskin tells us, "Michael Valente, [was] the only Italian-American to win the Congressional Medal of Honor in World War I."

The well-deserved recognition might be a bit of nomenclature citing Michael A. Valente (1895-1976) as "Italian American" is a not fully accurate. His "Story of Service," posted by grandson Ralph J. Madalena cited Valente as, "An exemplary American citizen, heroic soldier, good neighbor and brotherly friend to all of the residents of Long Beach [NY], no matter what ethnic origin, faith, or race. He was loved honored and respected by all who knew him."[613]

Valente was born in the village of Sant'Apollinare in Italy. His immigration to America in 1913 placed him among the millions of other unknown Italians making their way across the Atlantic. Valente settled in Ogdensburg, in upstate New York later moving to Long Beach also in New York. A short time after immigration he enlisted in the New York National Guard and joined the U.S. Army in 1916/17. As a recipient of the U.S. Congressional Medal of Honor, conferred by President Herbert Hoover on September 27, 1929, the citation read:

> "The President of the United States of America, in the name of Congress, takes pleasure in presenting the Medal of Honor to Private Michael Valente, United States Army, for conspicuous gallantry and intrepidity above and beyond the call of duty in action with the enemy during the operations against the Hindenburg line, east of Ronssoy, France, 29 September 1918, while serving with Company D, 107th Infantry, 27th Division. Finding the advance of his organization held up by a withering enemy machinegun fire, Private Valente volunteered to go forward. With utter disregard of his own personal danger, accompanied by another soldier, Private Valente rushed forward through an intense machinegun fire directly upon the enemy nest, killing two and capturing five of the enemy and silencing the gun. Discovering another machinegun nest close by which was pouring a deadly fire on the American forces, preventing their advance, Private Valente and his companion charged upon this strong point, killing the gunner and putting this machinegun out of action. Without hesitation they jumped into the enemy's trench, killed two and captured 16 German soldiers. Private Valente was later wounded and sent to the rear."[614]

Valente may have received recognition with the highest military honor conferred by the United States, however many thousands of others served with distinction; at least 3,000 Italians died in service to America. Part of Laskin's research

---

[613] See: Michael. Valente, Sr. *The United States World War I Centennial Commission*, Accessed September 28, 2021.

[614] "Medal of Honor Recipients - World War I." Medal of Honor Citations. United States Army Center of Military History. August 3, 2009. Retrieved December 2, 2010. See also: The Wall of Honor Project.

uncovered a 1929 published account of the medal ceremony from an "Italian language newspaper," thereby quoting Valente stating,

> "I did not forget, while the president was conferring the award, that he had decorated an American of Italian origin – and that through him honor can come to all Italians who emigrated here."[615]

Laskin researched many of the other, mainly nameless, Italians who also served in World War I. One interview in 2006 was with "the last [living] Italian-American to have fought in the Great War," Antonio Pierro (1896-2007); who lived to the age of 110. Laskin remembered,

> "I sat down with a 110-year-old veteran of the All-American Division named Antonio Pierro and chatted with him about his childhood in Italy and his experience in the Great War. Born in Basilicata in 1896, Tony emigrated with a cousin in 1913, was drafted in October, 1917, and shipped out to France the following spring. Nearly a century later, he still remembered the snakes in his family's orchard in Italy, his anger at being called a "wop" [derogatory term] in boot camp, the shell that nearly killed him in the Argonne Forest, and the French girl he fell in love with."

President Herbert Hoover confers the Congressional Medal of Honor upon Private Michael Valente outside the White House. Photograph by: Harris & Ewing, September 27, 1929. Library of Congress Prints and Photographs Division, Public Domain.

---

[615] See: David Laskin, "Italian Americans and the Great War."

CHAPTER 10   473

Prohibition and Chicago Gangsters

A moral restriction was enacted in America when Prohibition became law with overwhelming support from religious evangelicals and some business groups as the U.S. Congress overrode President Woodrow Wilson's veto thereby ratifying the 18th Amendment, known as the *Volstead Act*.

Volstead Act: Section 1 of the law read:
Amendment XVIII (18th)

After one year from ratification of this article the manufacture, sale, or transportation of intoxicating liquors within, the importation thereof into, or the exportation thereof from the United States and all territory subject to the jurisdiction thereof for beverage purposes is hereby prohibited.

On January 16, 1920, Prohibition took effect as the required number of states ratified the Amendment. The Constitutional Amendment made it illegal for the manufacture, sale, or transportation of alcohol. Consumption was not theoretically prohibited; but it did not have to be as "Prohibition" became the law of the land. As such, the 18th Amendment became the only Constitutional Amendment enacted on the basis of morality.

Prohibition extended as an ongoing crusade of the Temperance Movement in America dating from the early days of colonization. During the 19th century, the formation of the Women's Christian Temperance Movement (WCTM) gained traction nationwide. Many added their disdain with alcohol consumption associated with the onslaught of immigrants such as Italians who were noted for wine consumption. In essence though, Prohibition was finally passed under the guise as a war aim. With America involved in World War I; Germany was the enemy. Many of breweries were operated by German immigrants or descendants; therefore, the beer breweries were ordered closed by government sanction to not provide aid to an enemy of the United States. With a government sanctioned order setting a precedent the next step to a Constitutional Amendment took full flight. With the 18th Amendment was passage of the 19th Amendment with strong support of a quid-pro-quo with the WCTM for women gaining a right-to-vote.

With war as a major distraction, Congress passed the Espionage Act of 1917 and Sedition Act of 1918 altering American freedoms on the home front. Those two acts were to stop supposed "enemy aliens" secretly living among recent immigrants. As a counter-measure, immigration from Europe, averaging one million each year from since 1890, was halted and all attention was turned towards the war effort. Once-again the precedent was set for widespread suppression of immigration during the 1920s.[616]

---

[616] Nathan Miller, *New World Coming*, pp. 12-13; 24-26.

Volstead Act enforcement, however, was very difficult and many individuals simply scoffed at the law and continued to drink. The illegal alcohol manufacture and smuggling gave way to the formation of gangland warfare and bootlegging. A replacement for the saloons, called "Speakeasies," broadened on a large urban scale, some becoming fashionable nightspots not only for drinking but also Jazz music, entertainment, and dancing. The small town equivalent of the "Speakeasy" was the "Roadhouse" or "Honky Tonk" usually on the outskirts of town or outside official city limits.

According to many historians, Prohibition was also responsible for the rise of organized crime in America. Before that time period, ethnic criminal activity was present; usually confined to ethnic neighborhoods. In Italian neighborhoods across America, loosely organized "Black Hand" criminals resorted to extortion enforced by violence. Italian criminals were often carryovers from Sicily and Naples mainly confined locally in a "Little Italy" and not a nationwide syndicate. Unlike, modern portrayals of organized crime associated with Italians, the fact of city life was routinely controlled by corrupt "Big City Bosses" of dubious elected political officials working in conjunction with corrupt local police.[617]

Throughout the 1920s, sensational newspaper and radio media outlets fueled the hysteria chronicling real-life gangsters that overran the city of Chicago. In fact, it was mostly American gangsters "battling over the profitable beer and alcohol supply for thousands of illegal saloons, pubs, roadhouses, and Speakeasies." National newspapers made celebrities of Chicago gangsters such as Dion O'Banion (1892-1924), Hymie Weiss (1898-1926), Johnny Torrio (1882-1957), and Al Capone (1899-1947), to name a few of the most notorious.

In 1924, O'Banion's murder in his flower shop and assassination attempt on Torrio garnered newspaper headlines. From 1924 to 1929, rivals Hymie Weiss and Al Capone held open warfare on the streets of Chicago as over five hundred were killed. A climax occurred on February 14, 1929 as seven of Weiss's henchmen were viciously murdered, supposedly planned by Capone. During a media frenzy decade of tabloid sensationalism, the press called it the "St. Valentine's Day Massacre." Many other cities located close to the Canadian border such as Buffalo, Cleveland, Detroit, and New York experienced similar gangland violence, but not on the scale and notoriety as Chicago. Gangland violence aside, many politicians and police officers did not wish to enforce Prohibition, therefore, "looked the other way" – many enjoyed an alcoholic drink and did not agree with Prohibition. One summation revealed many politicians and

---

[617] See: Elizabeth Kolbert, "The Big Sleazy: How Huey Long Took Louisiana, "The *New Yorker*, June 12, 2006.

CHAPTER 10

local police were "on the take" – meaning they accepted cash bribes allowing gangsters to operate an illegal alcohol trade with impunity.[618]

Illegal "bootlegging" did offer a financial opportunity in cities and rural towns. Entrepreneurial bootleggers were equally comprised of Irish, Jews, Poles, Italians, and others; many American born. Many of the new criminals were American born children of immigrants. One of the most nefarious was Al Capone. Reading the names of those who supposedly controlled illegal alcohol distribution during Prohibition, some of the more notorious included Jack "Legs" Diamond, Frank and Peter Gusenberg, Meyer Lansky, Owney Madden, George "Bugs" Moran, Dion O'Banion, Arnold Rothstein, Dutch Schultz, and Hymie Weiss, to name a few who were *not* Italian; unlike the mythical portrayal in later years. The "Italian" stigma grew mainly in fictionalized Hollywood movies. There is no denying Italians such as Charles "Lucky" Luciano, Johnny Torrio, and Al Capone were involved. It was sensational media attention that turned Capone into one of the most famous celebrities of the time, while aiding the negative stereotype of Italians.

One journal article in "Fontamara" published by the *American Association of Teachers of Italian* by a trio of Italian historians, analyzed the prevailing stereotypes arising during the years of Prohibition from 1920 to 1933. Obvious deference was noted of the existence of "Anti-Italian sentiment" existing before the Prohibition law. The stereotyping was greatly aided by the rise in popularity of the Hollywood film industry, especially with the advent of sound. In the article "Fontamara," Ignazio Silone, Cecilia Bartoli Perrault, and Mirella J. Affron, concurred,

> "The rise in popularity of feature films led to an increase in the exposure of Italian stereotypes. The image of the Italian gangster was promoted by such films as *Little Caesar* and *Scarface*. These films were associated with bootlegging and organized crime that was on the rise during Prohibition. Many academics believe that the portrayal of Italian Americans in media and film has damaged their image in the public eye. Stereotypes surrounding the love of food, family honor, possessing certain political opinions, and propensity to commit crime were portrayed often in film, newspapers, and other forms of media. According to scholars, these stereotypes continue to be associated with Italian Americans, due in part to the coverage of these stereotypes during the Prohibition Era."[619]

Overlooked due to the sensationalism, the Prohibition Act of 1920 dealt a big blow to California's wineries, forcing many out of business.

---

[618] Jon C. Teaford, *The Twentieth-Century American City*, p. 46.
[619] Ignazio, Perrault, and Affron, "Fontamara," *Italica*, Vol. 48, No. 2, pp. 277-278.

An exception to the law allowed sacramental and religious wine; which many California grape growers embraced, thereby marketed their products as "sacramental wines" or medicinal elixirs. An exception was added regarding winemaking in the home. A clause added, "the head of a family who has properly registered may make 200 gallons exclusively for family use." Immigrant Giuseppe "Joe" Gallo (1883-1933) grew grapes during Prohibition and sold them to home winemakers. Sons, Ernest and Julio, grew up helping their father in the vineyards. In 1933, a few months after Prohibition was repealed, Ernest and Julio opened Gallo Winery in a rented warehouse in Modesto.[620]

Sensationalism, Fads, Flappers, and "The Lost Generation"

In the 1920's College campuses became synonymous with freedom of the new youth as pledging fraternities and sororities became a rage. Inspired by the Valentino movie, college men called themselves "Sheiks" and females "Sheba's." Young men sought to fashion their image from the likes of Rudolph Valentino. In defiance of Prohibition, young men sported hip-flasks to hold their "hooch" (alcohol) and young women dressed in the image of the "Flapper." Jazz music was embraced by the youth responding with legendary dances such as The Shimmy, Black Bottom, Varsity Drag, and the defining dance of the era - The Charleston.

Above Left: "Flapper" displays a hip flask holding "hooch" in her garter, c. 1926.
Above Right: "Flapper" Louise Brooks, c. 1925. Library of Congress.

Criticism from the arbiters of popular culture was everywhere. In May 1920, one editor of the mass-market *Atlantic Monthly* mocked Jazz music for encouraging

---

[620] See: "Winemakers," in *In Cerca di Una Nuova Vita: From Italy to California Italian Immigration: 1850 to Today*, Museo ItaloAmericano, Paolo Pontoniere, p. 9.

CHAPTER 10

dancers to "trot like foxes, limp like lame ducks, one-step like cripples, and all to the barbaric yawp of strange instruments." Another came from the influential *Ladies' Home Journal* reaching over six million American households. Editor John R. McMahon (1875-1956) continually criticized the changing morality. Severest attacks were levied against the simple fun pleasure of dancing to Jazz music. In one especially harsh editorial McMahon wrote, "Jazz dancing is degrading. It lowers all moral standards." An Oregon minister echoed similar sentiment, claiming, "dancing is the first step and easiest step toward hell." A significant cause for the hysterics was in response to Jazz music and dancing encroaching into white culture from the likes of African Americans and Italian immigrants. The obvious result objected to the mixing of "the races" causing concern over improper morals of females.[621]

None of this obviously was fully embraced by Italian immigrants; yet it did appeal to some of their American born children assimilating to the American culture. Much of the appeal was learned and adapted from popular Hollywood movies of the time such as *The Sheik* portrayed by Rudolph Valentino, among many others. Looking back on the decade, F. Scott Fitzgerald writing in *Echoes of the Jazz Age* (1931) declared "It was an age of miracles, it was an age of art, it was an age of excess, it was an age of satire." The after effects of the war, flu, prohibition, and other moral restrictions left a new nation of youth "disenchanted." Novelist Gertrude Stein called them the "Lost Generation;" a term later adopted by famous novelist Ernest Hemingway in *The Sun Also Rises* (1926).

Wholesome Recreation, Luther H. Gulick, and Henry Ford

In contrast to the xenophobic preachers, was Luther Halsey Gulick (1865-1918). As a son of a missionary physician, prominent leader of the Playground Association, and one of the early founders of the Y.M.C.A., Gulick disagreed with the Evangelical preachers and morality critics such as editor John R. McMahon, and others. In 1909, Gulick suggested the proper "morality" of the type of recreation engaged by urban dwellers for the influential journal *Playground*. Gulick did not blame the people; rather agreed with reformers such as Jacob Riis, placed blame on overcrowded conditions. Gulick explained,

> "We are fast becoming a city people. Strange as it may seem, the greater tractability of the urban problem resides in the very condition to which people are wont to attribute most of the city's ills – I mean the density of the population."

Therefore, instituting public recreation was offered in both schoolyards and city

---

[621] Judith S. Baughman, *American Decades: 1920–1929*, p. 269.

parks promoted to cure any of the ills of society. Gulick, was a strong supporter of the city. Unlike, comments made by some clergy outside of New York City, often accusing it as a Modern Babylon, Gulick quoted the Bible saying - "Heaven is a city."[622]

Gulick's proposals were fully embraced by institutions such as the New York City Public School System; attended by many children born in America of Italian immigrants; as providing a path towards assimilation. Recreation activities in urban areas was promoted as respectable; giving rise to amusement parks and shoreline beaches. One of the most famous entertainment meccas was Coney Island in Brooklyn and Steeplechase Amusement Park along the boardwalk. Each was marketed towards inexpensive entertainment for the working class and immigrant population of New York City; an advantage taken by many Italian immigrants and their American-born children. On any given weekend or holiday over 300,000 to 500,000, attended. The cost was usually nothing more than an inexpensive subway ride. With so many distractions happening during the 1920s, it was somewhat easy to overlook the wide-open opportunity for politicians to finally enact immigration restrictions coupled with internal segregation laws. Auto pioneer Henry Ford (1863-1947) was widely publicized for his success; yet was most often quoted for outspoken beliefs of 100 percent Americanization, segregation, limits on immigration, anti-Semitism, and support of the emerging Eugenics movement.[623]

Eugenics, Madison Grant, and Immigration Quotas

During the peak years of immigration, a massive onslaught of "virulent prejudice and nativist hostility" arose. The historical significance is explained by the *U.S. Library of Congress* as,

> "Labor struggles were not the only conflicts Italian immigrants faced. During the years of the great Italian immigration, they also had to confront a wave of virulent prejudice and nativist hostility. As immigration from Europe and Asia neared its crest in the late 19th century, anti-immigrant sentiment soared along with it. The U.S. was in the grips of an economic depression, and immigrants were blamed for taking American jobs. At the same time, racialist theories circulated in the press, advancing pseudo-scientific theories that alleged that "Mediterranean" types were inherently inferior to people of northern European heritage. Drawings and songs caricaturing the new immigrants as childlike, criminal, or subhuman became sadly commonplace."[624]

---

[622] Luther H. Gulick, "Popular Recreation and Public Morality," pp. 33-36.

[623] Gulick, pp. 6, 38, 42. See also: Kathy Peiss, *Cheap Amusements*, p. 124.

[624] "The Great Arrival," *The Library of Congress*.

CHAPTER 10   479

Anti-immigrant furor continued into the 1920s, and severe restrictions on immigration were put into place by the U.S. Congress; which eventually ended the great era of Italian immigration.

Congressional Legislation regarding immigration was not new. The earliest is the Naturalization Act of 1790 as the United States Congress outlined basic requirements of citizenship. Stipulations applied only to "free white persons of good character." Thereby eliminating Native American Indians, African slaves, and other non-whites. Another restrictive legislation against national origin is the Chinese Exclusion Act of 1882. Although in 1855, legislation requiring health inspection of immigrants applied to the large wave of Irish Catholics, was in effect.

Commonplace was prejudicial U.S. Legislation of restrictive quotas upon immigrants. Passage of the Immigrant Quota Act of 1921 and the National Origins Act of 1924, limited the number of immigrants into the United States, effectively ended the era of mass immigration. The legislation can easily be explained as an effective way of "legalizing" the fears and lies placed upon the southern European immigrants, especially Italians. As an added caveat, the Congressional Legislation of immigration restrictions was not a spontaneous reaction while serving as a means to effectively counteract any form of legalized integration. Harkening back to 1880, as typical of the growing nationwide sentiment was echoed in just one of many negative editorials such as in *The New York Times* which often denigrated Italians as "the filthy, wretched, lazy, ignorant, and criminal dregs." Vicious attacks on Italians were not limited to the printed page. From the late 1880s onward, anti-immigrant societies sprang up around the country. The Ku Klux Klan, as one example, gained a legal spike in membership. As a result, Catholic churches and immigrant aid societies were often severely vandalized. Numerous instances of violence against Italians increased.

Attached to the new restrictive immigration legislation was a revised processing system for entry. Immigrants were processed onboard arriving ships docked in close proximity to ports such as Ellis Island. Accepted immigrants disembarked for transport to Ellis Island - serving primarily as a temporary detainment center. From 1925 to the closing of Ellis Island in 1954, only 2.3 million immigrants legally passed through the New York City port of a nationwide total of about 4 million from other entry points. Comparing the years from 1880 to 1920 numbering over 20 million immigrants entered America; of those 4.5 million were Italians. In essence, prior to 1920 the door was open – after 1920 the door was *slammed shut*, secured, and locked.

Unlike earlier years, the growing furor against immigrants was aided by so-called scientific evidence fostered by a growing Eugenics movement throughout the United States. In 1922, the American Eugenics Society was founded to counter the ever-growing number of "foreign" immigrants entering upon the shores of

America. The society promoted the false idea blaming immigrants as a rising threat of continued violence and subverting American culture with a "foreign influence." In 1926, the American Eugenics Society was officially founded and active until 1972, represented a unique widespread social movement in the United States. The society promoted high-profile "experts" such as Madison Grant (1865-1937); the intellectual chair of the New York Zoological Society and trustee of New York's American Museum of Natural History.

At its core Eugenics promoted superiority of the white races with the intent to preserve the "integrity" of the white race. As a mean of preservation, Eugenics favored the legalized "sterilization" of the "feeble minded" from among the incoming southern European immigrants and African Americans, thereby preventing "the perpetuation of worthless types." Grant outlined the basic Eugenic belief in *The Passing of the Great Race, or the Racial Basis of European History* first published in 1916. Within the publication, Grant provided so-called "scientific evidence" that offered credible "proof" of African Americans, Native American Indians, and especially the "Mediterranean" type of immigrants such as Italians as being inferior to the "white" race. Although published before American entry into World War I, the book received noticeable credibility during the 1920s. Grant was concerned the U. S. immigration policy routinely allowed in the "the weak, the broken and the mentally crippled from the lower stratum of the Mediterranean Basin and the Balkans [and] the hordes of the wretched, submerged population of the Polish ghettos." In summation, Grant, citing his own scientific credentials, claimed the current immigration policy was inherently detrimental to America.[625]

According to historian David Goldberg, "Few people had even heard of the Nordic race until Grant wrote his book." Thereafter, the term was widely adopted since it incorporated more of the so-called "white" nationalities; rather than newly defined "non-white" nationalities such as Asians and southern Europeans, such as Jews and Italians. Major support for those racist ideas was fostered among the rural American states; ironically heavily populated by immigrants - but not southern Europeans. By the 1920s, more than half of the population of eleven western states were immigrants of the acceptable "white" northern European ancestry such as Danish, Finnish, German, Norwegian, and Swedish descent. In states such as Minnesota and North Dakota northern European immigrants numbered over 74 percent of the population; in South Dakota the number was 60 percent; Montana, California, Utah, and Nevada all numbered well over 50 percent of the existing population. By definition as applied by the likes of Grant, those white "Nordic" immigrants were not included as part of the nationwide anti-immigrant hatred; nor under restrictive legislation.

---

[625] See: "American Eugenics Society," *Wikipedia, the Free Encyclopedia*, n.p.

Above Left: Title page of Madison Grant's 1916 publication *The Passing of the Great Race*. **Above Right**: Madison Grant, c. 1913.

During the 1920s, other publications with racial themes promoting white superiority included two by PhD Harvard professor Lothrop Stoddard (1883-1950). Stoddard's publication of *The Rising Tide of Color Against White World-Supremacy* (1920) included an introduction written by Madison Grant. Stoddard followed with *Revolt Against Civilization: The Menace of the Under Man* (1923). Others included a publication by Kenneth Roberts (1885-1957) in *Why Europe Leaves Home* (1922) and *The Jews in America* (1923) by Burton J. Hendrick (1870-1949). Roberts' book was a culmination of recent articles that appeared in the mass-market *Saturday Evening Post*, which at the time boasted the largest circulation of any magazine in America at well over six million copies. (The magazine was not isolated to just six million as it was often passed around within a family and among the public in many waiting rooms such as barbershops, bus terminals, and medical offices.) Industrialist Henry Ford provided the notorious *The International Jew: The World's Foremost Problem* (1920-1922) a rambling four-volume set of pamphlets which was translated into 12 languages and favored by the likes of the emerging Nazi Party in Germany under Adolph Hitler (1889-1945). Hitler was also inspired by Madison Grant's writings and theories.[626]

Paul A. Offit writing *The Loathsome American Book That Inspired Hitler*, described Madison Grant's book as it "may be the most dangerous scientific tract ever written." Upon publication, Adolph Hitler sent a letter to Grant praising *The Passing of the Great Race*, saying "This book is my Bible." A few years later, Hitler published *Mein Kampf*, often considered an "autobiographical manifesto" of his political

---

[626] David J. Goldberg, *Discontented America*, pp. 154-155.

ideology. In comparison, Offit, basically said *Mein Kampf* was a complete plagiarism of Grant's book; as Hitler "included whole sections of Grant's book in his own book." As Grant labeled the pure racial class the "Nordic Race," Hitler changed the term to the "Aryan Race." As Offit reminds us, "*The Passing of the Great Race* was reprinted in 1922, 1923, 1924, 1926, 1930, 1932, and 1936, selling more than a million copies—arguably, one of the most popular scientific tracts in history." By 1936, as Hitler was firmly in control of all political and social aspects, "the Nazi party in Germany listed *The Passing of the Great Race* (translated into German as early as 1926) as essential reading."[627]

To place American Eugenics influence into proper perspective, it is important to understand Adolf Hitler and the Nazi party in Germany were often described as "one of the world's most notorious eugenicists." As reminded by the Editors at History.com,

> "Adolf Hitler, drew inspiration from California's forced sterilizations of the "feeble-minded" in designing Nazi Germany's racially based policies. Hitler began reading about eugenics and social Darwinism while he was imprisoned following a failed 1924 coup attempt known as the Beer Hall Putsch. Hitler adopted the social Darwinist take on survival of the fittest. He believed the German master race had grown weak due to the influence of non-Aryans in Germany. To Hitler, survival of the German "Aryan" race depended on its ability to maintain the purity of its gene pool."[628]

When Adolf Hitler and the Nazis established complete power in the 1930s, they showed the world the horrors of Eugenics. The Nazis targeted certain groups or races considered biologically inferior for extermination; including Jews, Roma (gypsies), Poles, Soviets, people with disabilities, and homosexuals. It would take a Second World War in the 1940s to stop them, even as the U.S. quota system prevented many refugees from escaping the Nazis. By the end of World War II, Social Darwinism and Eugenic theories had fallen out of favor in the United States and much of Europe - partly due to their associations with Nazi programs and propaganda, and because the theories were scientifically unfounded.

Not until the Immigration Act of 1965 that American ethnicity-based quotas would disappear and the United States would adopt a more ethnically neutral way of controlling immigration. With references back to the 1920s in America, the idea of "Nordic" supremacy gained popular public support, eventually aided by legal action enacted by the U.S. Congress passing The Immigration Act of 1924

---

[627] Paul A. Offit. "The Loathsome American Book That Inspired Hitler," *The Daily Beast*, August 26, 2017.

[628] History.com Editors. "Social Darwinism," 2018. Note: History.com works with a wide range of writers and editors to create accurate and informative content.

CHAPTER 10

(Johnson-Reed Act), sometimes known as the "Johnson Quota Act of 1924" or the "National Origins Act of 1924." Once in effect, the Congressional laws severely restricted immigration from the areas of Southern Europe, Eastern Europe, and Asia. Historian David Goldberg described it as "a law that favored so-called Nordic immigrants and that stood out as one of the most significant pieces of legislation enacted during the entire decade."[629]

The immigration quota prejudicially based only upon ethnicity eventually adopted by the U.S. Congress was established by a previously selected group of anti-immigrant professors and eugenic supporters. The idea established a quota, not based on the first two decades of the 20th century, but a time before the massive onslaught of southern European immigration. As described by the Office of the Historian of the United States Department of State,

> "The Immigration Act of 1924 limited the number of immigrants allowed entry into the United States through a national origins quota. The quota provided immigration visas to two percent of the total number of people of each nationality in the United States as of the 1890 national census. It completely excluded immigrants from Asia."[630]

In order to tip the balance towards the white Nordic races, an established base point of American demographics for the year 1890 was chosen. (A significant immigration increase did begin in 1880, at least for Italians, but nowhere near the numbers occurring after 1890.) The steady flow of one million immigrants per year from southern and eastern Europe occurred between the years 1890 and 1914. Therefore, by eliminating any of the ethnic demographic calculations after 1890, it overwhelmingly favored the "Nordic" peoples; heavily populated by white Protestants. Among the 4.1 million immigrants entering America between 1919 and 1929, most were white northern Europeans from the British Isles and Scandinavia. In 1927, as one typical example, only 150,000 immigrants were allowed entry - of those 65,700 were Irish and only 5,000 were Italian.

During those early years of the 1920s, the American Eugenics movement continued to gain widespread acceptance - so did enactment of stronger racial segregation laws. History often describes these events, if at all, individually, conveniently omitting information that each was not an isolated occurrence, rather all were acting in legal tandem with the immigration quotas, yet the desire was simmering for many decades. The supporters of Eugenics often applied so-called "scientific evidence" claiming validation of *racial superiority* versus *racial*

---

[629] Goldberg, *Discontented America*, pp. 154-155.
[630] "The Immigration Act of 1924 (Johnson-Reed Act)," Office of the Historian, Foreign Service Institute United States Department of State. Almost all Asians, were prevented entry by virtue of the Congressional Chinese Exclusion Act of 1882; formally extended in 1902 and continued through 1943.

inferiority; thereby promoting and legalizing a social class system in America. In the year 2020, Prof. Henry Louis Gates, Jr. (b. 1950) referenced a 1981 publication quoting the validity of the social class system. In *The Mismeasure of Man*, author Stephen Jay Gould recalled intelligence tests administered by the U.S. Army for induction during World War I, stating,

> "European immigrants graded by their country of origin, with fair Nordic populations planted firmly at the top of the scale and darker-complexion Italians near the bottom." [just above "the Negro [who] lies at the bottom of the scale."

A sarcastic attribute for the statistical evidence of a time period of three decades after the racial classification in areas such as New Orleans, the Italians who were once placed in the lowest social class below "Negroes" moved past the "undesirables" into an assimilated social class.[631]

Immigration among Italians and other Europeans may have been severely limited, but very few actual deportations occurred. As a point of information, the 1930 Statistical Abstract of the United States ("U.S. Census") counted 1,623,000 Italian-born residents who had previously immigrated into and were living in the United States. That number of native born Italians remains as the highest number ever counted in the history of immigration to America. As a result, in the succeeding years, the number of Italian born immigrants slowed to a trickle. During those years, Italian immigration may have decreased; the total number of Americans of Italian ancestry increased as children of immigrants were born on American soil as U.S. citizens. By the year 2000, over 15.7 million claimed Italian ancestry. By mid-decade in 2015, the total number was placed at over 18 million Americans (six percent of the population) openly identified as "Italian-American."

Virginia and Racial Integrity Laws

Promoting a social class system of levels of racial superiority was just another means of continuing legal racial segregation in America. During the early colonial United States, the class system was mostly divided by colonists of northern "white" Europeans overseeing a legal slavey system comprised almost exclusively of Africans; while at the same time completely subjugating and attempting to eradicate all the Native American Indian tribes. Areas of the southwest, which in essence was Mexico, existed with a legal social class system, known as the *encomienda* system; placing native born Spaniards at the top and

---

[631] Henry Louis Gates, Jr. *Stony Road: Reconstruction, White Supremacy, and the Rise of Jim Crow*, p. 78. See also: Stephen Jay Gould, *The Mismeasure of Man*, pp. 226-227. Also: Museum Text Ellis Island.

CHAPTER 10

indigenous Indians at the bottom. Various social class levels existed between top and bottom.

Literacy Tests and "Uncle Sam"

The growing popular anti-immigrant disdain was also bolstered by the recent World War in Europe. In 1917, as part of American involvement in World War I, the U.S. Congress enacted immigration laws combined with an internal Sedition Act. The 1917 laws implemented a literacy test requiring all immigrants over the age of 16 to demonstrate basic reading comprehension in any language. Legislation also increased the required tax paid by new immigrants upon arrival; an added item provided for immigration officials to exercise more discretion in making independent decisions over whom to exclude. Other important provisions paved the way for the additional 1924 immigration restrictions.

Literacy tests alone were not enough to prevent immigrants from entering. To "safeguard" the new system, Congress added ways to restrict immigration. Republican Vermont Senator William P. Dillingham (1843-1923), known as an "immigration expert," introduced a measure to create immigration quotas set at three percent of the total population (later reduced) of the foreign-born of each nationality in the United States as recorded in the 1910 census (later pre-dated to 1880). This put the total number of visas available each year to new immigrants at 350,000. In opposition, President Woodrow Wilson who preferred a more liberal immigration policy, used the *pocket veto* to prevent its passage.

In early 1921, a reversal by the newly inaugurated Republican President Warren G. Harding (1865-1923), in support of immigration quotas, called Congress to a special session to pass the restrictive law. Appropriately labeled as "historic legislation," the Emergency Quota Act of 1921 quickly established strict limits on the number of immigrants who could enter the United States. In 1922, the act was renewed for an additional two years; and signed into federal law by succeeding President Calvin Coolidge (1872-1933).

One of many examples expressing the American popular opinion response to stem the flow of immigration were political cartoons. One political cartoon in *The Literary Digest* of May 1921, accompanied an article for "An Alien Anti-Dumping Bill" titled, "The Only Way to Handle It." The illustration depicted a funnel in Europe bridging the Atlantic Ocean with the larger open end crowded with European immigrants. At the entry point into the United States a narrow outlet, monitored by Uncle Sam, permitted only a small number to "trickle through." The "3%" tag held by Uncle Sam at the funnel "gate" was indicative of the proposal championed by Senator Dillingham (that was later reduced).

As the U.S. Congressional immigration debate began in 1924, the quota system was so well-established, no one questioned a consideration whether to maintain or eliminate it; rather discussion focused on how to adjust the requirements. Some in Congress advocated allowing a slightly higher percentage of immigrants, however, the supporters of even more restrictions triumphed. A plan was created thereby lowering the existing quota from 3% to 2% of the foreign-born population. The restrictions also pushed back the year on which quota calculations were based from 1910 to 1890. Another change altered the calculations. The current established quota was based on the number born outside of the United States. The new law traced the origins of the whole of the U.S. population, including natural-born citizens. Therefore, the new calculations added large numbers of British descent whose families had long resided in the United States. As a result, the percentage of visas available to individuals from the British Isles and Western Europe increased greatly; in contrast immigration from Southern and Eastern Europe, including Italy was further limited.

The 1924 Immigration Act added a provision excluding entry to any "alien" who by virtue of race or nationality might be ineligible for obtaining future U.S. citizenship. The added provision was an extension of existing nationality laws dating from 1790 and 1870 that expressively refused any people of Asian lineage from naturalization. The 1924 Act meant that even Asians not previously prevented from immigrating – Japanese in particular – would no longer be able to enter the United States. Japanese officials were offended by the new law, that in effect violated a 1907 "Gentlemen's Agreement" between the countries brokered by former president Theodore Roosevelt.

The illustration titled The Only Way to Handle It," in an article titled, "An Alien Anti-Dumping Bill" In *The Literary Digest*, May 7, 1921, p. 13. Library of Congress.

CHAPTER 10

487

In reality, the anti-immigrant furor of the 1920s was an extension of the long-standing Nativist and Populist movements of years past. Such as the forced removal of Native American Indians, combined with so many other historical acts of hatred and discrimination, the official U.S. reaction against the Great Immigration by Italians and others during the years 1880 to 1920 was nothing new. The response by the U.S. Congress was only a continuation of age-old policies. Any analysis might simply realize, it was the same old prevalent hysteria with different nomenclature; often validated by dubious scientific studies. A historical trip reveals legalized African slavery, to Jim Crow Laws hindering American citizens descended from slaves; to legal segregation supported by a U.S. Supreme Court decision of *Plessy v. Ferguson*, to the American Eugenics Society. Therefore, legislation against foreign immigration should not be a shocking revelation.

Not surprisingly, significant support for the Eugenics movement and Immigration Quotas was promoted by the likes of Senator Henry Cabot Lodge. In 2021, journalist Brent Staples charting the path of "How Italians Became White," wrote,

> "Facts aside, [Senator] Lodge argued beliefs about immigrants were in themselves sufficient to warrant higher barriers to immigration. Congress ratified that notion during the 1920s, curtailing Italian immigration on racial grounds, even though Italians were legally white, with all of the rights whiteness entailed."

The idea of criminalizing humans of a "mixed blood" relationship existed for years and by definition was not new. However, the legal definition did not become the official law of the land until after 1910. Precedent began with the 1896 Supreme Court decision of *Plessy v. Ferguson* legalizing racial segregation throughout America. Discontent among mainstream white America was wary of immigrants and fearful of race intermingling of marriage, known as "miscegenation," producing "mongrel" children.[632]

Within a few years, biased state lawmakers in Alabama, Georgia, Florida, Indiana, Kentucky, Maryland, Missouri, Nebraska, North Dakota, Oklahoma, and Utah joined the cause against Miscegenation. Sadly, by the 1950s, every state in America had some kind of similar legislation. Yet, the definition of who was "White" and who was "Colored" was strictly subjective. In fact, in a letter dated August 9, 1940, noted Virginia appointed enforcement agent Dr. Plecker admitted, "there is no test to determine the race of an individual."

---

[632] Brent Staples. "How Italians Became White." *The New York Times,* October 12, 2019. See also: Nancy D. Egloff, "Just One Drop: Virginia's 1924 Racial Integrity Act," April 16, 2021, *Jamestown-Yorktown Foundation.*

The restrictive principles of the immigration laws and segregation policies could have resulted in strained relations with some European countries as well. Potential problems did not appear for several reasons as the soon-to-be world-wide Great Depression of the 1930s and World War II dealing with emergency provisions resettlement of displaced persons helped the United States avoid conflict over its new immigration laws. It was not until the Immigration Act of 1965 that America's ethnicity-based quotas disappeared and the United States would adopt a more ethnically neutral way of controlling immigration; yet the "door" was still closed.

Immigration: The Door Closes

As the decade of the "Roaring 20s" literally "roared" in the textbooks as it was nostalgically remembered for musical flamboyancy and flaunting social conventions, it is hard to conceive a morality issue was the impetus to define the entire decade as did Prohibition. Many Americans, in cities as Chicago and New York, never imagined Prohibition would become a reality, nevertheless it was the law of the land. Therefore, any moral or social restriction was possible; including immigration among Italians and Jews from southern and eastern Europe, was severely curtailed.

In April 1924, U.S. Congress passed H.R. 7995 as "an Act to limit the immigration of aliens into the United States, and for other purposes." The legislation carried to the U.S. Senate as the Immigration Act of 1924, (Pub. L. 68–139, 43 Stat. 153). Often known as the Johnson Quota Act, included a "National Origins Act" and an updated "Asian Exclusion Act." The official revised language stated, "An act to regulate the immigration of aliens into the United States." The law read in part as protecting all American citizens from any "lunatics, idiot, or any person unable to take care of him or herself without becoming a public charge." In reality, the law was prejudicial and discriminatory as many others through American history. A significant effect was the reduction of Italian immigrants.

In 2017, Professor Maddalena Marinari for an article with the self-descriptive title, "Another time in history that the US created travel bans against Italians," recalled the virulent hatred against Italians – especially from Protestant clergy. Marinari wrote of a prominent Protestant Episcopal Church Bishop Charles Henry Brent (1862-1929) who garnered a fair share of American sentiment. In one 1914 instance Brent decried,

> "The United States is in far greater danger from the quality of immigration that comes from Southern Europe than from any peril that

CHAPTER 10   489

could come by Japanese ownership of lands in California, or from Asiatic immigration."[633]

By 1917, the lunacy of Rev. Brent's statement was not so far-fetched as the U.S. immigration laws required categorizing all immigrants by their "socioeconomic status, literacy, criminality, political beliefs, diplomatic standing, physical and mental health and sexuality." More so, the decision to evaluate immigrants for entry into the United States was transferred to the specific country of origin from which an immigrant resided.

One of just many examples of the virulent prejudice was in an April 17, 1921 article in *The New York Times*, boldly titled: "ITALIANS COMING in GREAT NUMBERS." The report in full support of the pending immigration quota announced, "The Number of Immigrants Will Be Limited Only By Capacity of Liners." In a direct nod to *The Literary Digest* article of May 7, 1921 illustrated as "The Only Way to Handle It," claimed Italians "were thronging the quays in the cities of Genoa and Naples." Reference was the new limitations on the number of immigrants allowed entry and long waiting time for processing of visas in Italy.

68TH CONGRESS }
1ST SESSION }

H. R. 7995

AN ACT

To limit the immigration of aliens into the United States, and for other purposes.

APRIL 10 (calendar day, APRIL 14), 1924
Ordered to lie on the table

Another of the common derogatory stereotypical statements was in association with the supposed criminality of Italians. An added caveat by *The New York Times* explanation described a way to prevent any illegal processing of Italians who might cheat the system; all medical inspection of potential immigrants would be

---

[633] Maddalena Marinari. "Another time in history that the US created travel bans — against Italians," n.p.

overseen by "American doctors on Italian soil." As explained by Prof. Maddalena Marinari,

> "The US demanded a uniform passport system, that Italy allow for medical inspections, and that Italian officials collaborate with US embassies and consulates to issue new types of documents to Italians who wanted US visas. The Italian government saw these demands as an infringement on its sovereignty, but it collaborated anyway because it hoped that the US would not pass more stringent immigration laws. They had a stagnant economy, while work was plentiful in the Americas, and the remittances Italians sent home were significant. Ironically, the more Italy tried to make sure that only "desirable" immigrants went to the US and the more they tried to protect Italians in the US, more American legislators called for restriction."

The desired result by U.S. politicians was achieved. Marinari added, "many aspiring Italian immigrants never left for the [United States]." Of the many false accusations, one was to locate American doctors in Italy. As falsely reported in *The New York Times*, the Italian government did not wish to "weed out undesirable Italians" adding "the Italian government could do more but didn't because it wanted to get rid of them."[634]

The "them" was a reference to "undesirables" among the "criminal element." As a result, the Quota Act remained in effect for many years; somewhat aided by convenient distractions such as the Great Depression and World War II. The 1920s immigration law was not officially repealed until many years later. On October 3, 1965 President Lyndon B. Johnson signed the "Immigration and Nationality Act of 1965" in a symbolic location on Liberty Island in New York Harbor a very short distance from historic Ellis Island. The bill abolished the national origins quota system adding language that all who wish to immigrate to America be "admitted on the basis of their skills and their close relationships to those already there." The Immigration and Nationality Act of 1965 might have repealed the decades old law, but it did not alleviate any of the derogatory criminal stereotype of Italians as criminals. An American cultural myth, which only increased during the mid-1950s, persisting into the current day.

Shut the Door and An "Un-American Bill"

At a time when the U.S. Congress rejected the Treaty of Versailles while also refusing to join the new League of Nations, Senator William Julius Harris (1868-1932) of Georgia introduced in the Senate "an amendment to shut the door" a

---

[634] Maddalena Marinari. "Another time in history that the US created travel bans against Italians," *The World*, October 2, 2017. See also: "Italians Coming in Great Numbers," *The New York Times*, April 17, 1921.

CHAPTER 10 491

legislative bill effectively seeking to not just reduce, but stop *all* immigration into America. The proposed 1924 Act was brought to the Senate floor for debate with a large majority in support of complete legislative restrictions. One telling justification came from Senator Ellison DuRant Smith (1864-1944) of South Carolina in full support of the Senate bill. The language revealed virulent anti-immigrant and racist beliefs of an overwhelming majority of elected officials. In regards to the United States immigration policy, Smith boldly said, "the time has arrived when we should shut the door." One of the basic tenets of the legislation "sought to promote a unique American cultural identity."

Reiterating a litany of dubious facts, Senator Smith echoed, for positive support, "the racist theories of Madison Grant." Within his 1500 plus worded document Smith suggested,

> "I would like for the Members of the Senate to read that book just recently published by Madison Grant, *The Passing of a Great Race.* Thank God we have in America perhaps the largest percentage of any country in the world of the pure, unadulterated Anglo-Saxon stock; certainly, the greatest of any nation in the Nordic breed. It is for the preservation of that splendid stock that has characterized us that I would make this not an asylum for the oppressed of all countries, but a country to assimilate and perfect that splendid type of manhood that has made America the foremost Nation in her progress and in her power, and yet the youngest of all the nations."

An unusual reference point, Smith justified immigration restriction as a means of avoiding another world war. As a unique argument Senator Smith claimed new "immigration restriction was the only way to preserve existing American resources." Within the wording was a nod to the Social Darwinism theory of natural selectivity. Smith continued,

> "I think that we have sufficient stock in America now for us to shut the door, Americanize what we have, and save the resources of America for the natural increase of our population. We all know that one of the most prolific causes of war is the desire for increased land ownership for the overflow of a congested population."

Granted students studying the history of the causes of World War II often cite Hitler's pre-war aims of promoting *Lebensraum* (translated as "living space"); the belief that lands adjoining Germany was necessary for food supply of the future development of the nation.[635]

Part of the process of annexing land of foreign nations by any means necessary also meant eradicating the native people from those same lands. The

---

[635] Ellison DuRant Smith, "A Senator Intends to 'Shut the Door' on Immigration."

492
Italian Culture in America:
The Immigrants 1880 to 1930 From Discrimination to Assimilation

added land contained valuable natural resources, necessary as history later confirms, for Hitler to aid in the increased production capabilities of his war machine. Historian Jeremy Noakes, writing for the BBC in England described the *Lebensraum* idea ,

> "was that after most of the indigenous population had been cleared, German farmers would settle the land. The settlers were to consist mainly of war veterans and urban workers, who were meant to be the key to ensuring the 'physical and ethical health' of the German nation."[636]

Comparisons can easily be made to Senator Smith referencing the ratio of an availability of "resources" to the overall population. Ironically the Senator spoke of a "pure breed" of American, an analogy to a dog, yet also the Nazi idea of white supremacy. (A common analogy by Evangelical preachers warned that racial integration would lead to a "marbelization" of American society or an "un-pure breed.") As Senator Smith asserted,

> "I think we now have sufficient population in our country for us to shut the door and to breed up a pure, unadulterated American citizenship. I recognize that there is a dangerous lack of distinction between people of a certain nationality and the breed of the dog. Who is an American? Is he an immigrant from Italy? Is he an immigrant from Germany? If you were to go abroad and someone were to meet you and say, "I met a typical American," what would flash into your mind as a typical American, the typical representative of that new Nation? Would it be the son of an Italian immigrant, the son of a German immigrant, the son of any of the breeds from the Orient, the son of the denizens of Africa? We must not get our ethnological distinctions mixed up without anthropological distinctions. It is the breed of the dog in which I am interested."

In summation, Senator Smith boldly suggested to the U.S. Senate, "The time has come when we should shut the door and keep what we have for what we hope our own people to be."[637]

In complete contrast to the rants of Smith, Congressman Robert H. Clancy (1882-1962), a Democrat representing Detroit, was one of the very few dissenting voices. (Clancy's district represented a significant number of immigrants of ethnic diversity including Italian, Jewish, and Polish.) Within the context of a speech made on April 8, 1924 on the floor of the U.S. Congress, Rep. Clancy provided a stunning corollary between the attacks on the current crop of immigrants – namely

---

[636] Jeremy Noakes, "Hitler and *Lebensraum* in the East," *BBC.co.uk*, March 30, 2011.
[637] Ellison DuRant Smith, April 9, 1924, *Congressional Record,* 68th Congress, 1st Session (Washington DC: Government Printing Office, 1924, vol. 65, 5961–5962.)

Italian – as compared to the immigration ancestry of the members of Congress who were seeking restrictions on European immigration.

Clancy reminded his fellow elected representatives of the history of America since the early days of Colonial settlement. Clancy stated, "complaint and more or less bitter persecution have been aimed at newcomers to our shores." Supporting the factual claim, Clancy provided a brief recap of the 300-year history "of abuse of English, Scotch, Welsh immigrants described as: paupers [and] criminals." Added to Clancy's description were later immigrants from Ireland and Germany. He read into the record how the descendants of those once discriminated group now called themselves American; yet forgot the past with similar derogatory epithets and derogatory accusations against the current immigration wave.

Above Left: Senator Ellison D. Smith, c. 1937, proposed to "Shut the Door" on immigration. **Above Right**: Congressman Robert H. Clancy, c. 1923, opposed the restrictive immigration policy. (Library of Congress Public Domain).

Discrimination imposed by the politicians, self-described as the "Know-Nothings," which Clancy described as the "lineal ancestors of the Ku-Klux Klan." Clancy said the past was saddled with accusations such as,

> "All are riff-raff, unassimilables, "foreign devils," swine not fit to associate with the great chosen people—a form of national pride and hallucination as old as the division of races and nations. But to-day [the 1920s] it is the Italians, Spanish, Poles, Jews, Greeks, Russians, Balkanians, and so forth, who are the racial lepers. And it is eminently fitting and proper that so many Members of this House with names as

494   Italian Culture in America:
The Immigrants 1880 to 1930 From Discrimination to Assimilation

Irish are taking the floor these days to attack once more as their kind was attacked for seven bloody centuries the fearful fallacy of chosen peoples and inferior peoples. One made to rule and the other to be abominated."[638]

Clancy also spoke of Italians living within his own Detroit Congressional district. Serving as a microcosm for all Italian immigrants who entered from the years 1880 to the 1920s, Clancy explained,

"Forty or fifty thousand Italian-Americans live in my district in Detroit. They are found in all walks and classes of life—common hard labor, the trades, business, law, medicine, dentistry, art, literature, banking, and so forth.

They rapidly become Americanized, build homes, and make themselves into good citizens. They brought hardihood, physique, hope, and good humor with them from their outdoor life in Sunny Italy, and they bear up under the terrific strain of life and work in busy Detroit.

One finds them by thousands digging streets, sewers, and building foundations, and in the automobile and iron and steel fabric factories of various sorts. They do the hard work that the native-born American dislikes. Rapidly they rise in life and join the so-called middle and upper classes.

The Italian-Americans of Detroit played a glorious part in the Great War. They showed themselves as patriotic as the native born in offering the supreme sacrifice. I am informed, over 300,000 Italian-speaking soldiers enlisted in the American Army, almost 10 percent of our total fighting force. Italians formed about 4 percent of the population of the United States and they formed 10 percent of the American military force. Casualties were 12 percent."

Clancy described the bill as "racial discrimination at its worst." Based on the long history of colonial settlement in America, he called out the fallacy of his Congressional representatives on the justification and xenophobia of an immigration quota or a "Shut the Door Policy." In summation, Clancy called the proposed bill "Un-American." Despite the "Un-American" analogy, the Senate overwhelmingly passed the restrictive immigration policy of the Johnson-Reed bill; only six senators dissented.[639]

---

[638] Speech by Robert H. Clancy, April 8, 1924, *Congressional Record,* 68th Congress, 1st Session (Washington DC: Government Printing Office, 1924), vol. 65, 5929–5932.
[639] Robert H. Clancy, April 8, 1924, *Congressional Record,* 68th Congress, 1st Session, 1924, vol. 65, 5929–5932.

CHAPTER 10

Changing Concepts of Education towards Americanization

The immigration restrictions centered on an Americanization process coincided with a call by Progressives to eliminate Child Labor in America. A contemporary influential educator, Ellwood P. Cubberley (1868-1941), as a pioneer in "educational administration," advocated mandatory public education for all children, especially immigrants. Mandatory universal education was considered indispensable to Democracy; therefore, fully justified as an appropriate exercise of state power. Cubberley's efforts refocused school policy to include teaching children, while advancing public welfare and strengthening American democratic institutions. In *Changing Concepts of Education* (1909), Cubberley laid the foundation for universal public schooling in America. A contingent of textbooks authored by Cubberley, emphasized the rise of American education as a powerful force for literacy, democracy, and equal opportunity, while justifying a for future higher education and advanced research institutions.

The continuing theme advocated enlightenment and modernization over ignorance, cost-cutting, and traditionalism in which parents tried to block their child's intellectual access to the wider world. For educational policy to improve, Cubberley proposed freeing all of the educational administration from technical ignorance and unyielding external political pressures. A solution advocated transferring all authoritative power to technically trained educators and urged for improved teacher training. Education, as exemplified by Cubberley, was the dominant path of schooling in America for much of the 20th century. Therefore, most biographies rightfully praise Ellwood P. Cubberley in establishing the study of "Education" as a degree bearing university-level subject.

Missing from Cubberley's biography was his staunch position for the total Americanization of immigrant children combined with written documentation in support of Eugenic theories. In 1909, the same year of *Changing Conceptions of Education*, Cubberley wrote,

> "These Southern and Eastern Europeans are of a very different type from Northern Europeans who precede them. Illiterate, docile, lacking in self-reliance and initiative, and not possessing the Anglo-Teutonic conceptions of law, order, and government, their coming has corrupted our civic life. Our task is to break up these groups of settlements, to assimilate and amalgamate these people as part of our American race, and as to implant in their children as far as can be done, the Anglo-Saxon conception of righteousness, law, order, and popular government, and to waken in them a reverence for our democratic institutions and/or those things in our national life which we people hold to be of abiding worth."

496 Italian Culture in America:
The Immigrants 1880 to 1930 From Discrimination to Assimilation

In researching cultural educational concepts promoted by Cubberley, historians Jerre Mangione and Ben Morreale writing a history on the Italian American experience in *La Storia* stated,

> "Most immigrant parents knew little of the Italian culture admired by genteel America. Those who went on to discover this culture felt deceived and cheated for having been taught little of it in the American schools."[640]

"Italian culture as admired by genteel America" was of the cultural northern Renaissance artists such as Michelangelo, DaVinci, Raphael, among many others. Even after the unification of Italy, cultural differences between the north and south Italian peninsular were vast.

By 1920 in New York City, grade school education was mandatory for all school-age children, recent immigrant or not. In New York, and the entire country classrooms allowed municipal reformers to "Americanize" (to assimilate) immigrants; thereby also instill so-called "proper morals" in all schoolchildren. In a structure similar to contemporary society, African Americans were segregated in all southern schools and also in many northern and western schools. On the West Coast, segregation of schoolchildren of Asian and Mexican descent began around 1905. In a system of federally mandated "Normal Schools," Native American Indians were forced to give up their culture and accept American standards.

A major part of the mandatory school system and Americanization process was conveyed through standard issue textbooks. As publications by the likes of Madison Grant and others was aimed at an adult audience, another series of books focused on school age children. In order to institute proper "American" ideals and morals, most Progressive school reformers provided public school students with reading aids such as *M'Guffey's Reader*. Within those early readers, information abounded proclaiming the superiority of the "White Race." The stories promoted and reinforced Victorian era American cultural values while stressing the idea that idleness and play were bad. Much was made that Henry Ford was raised on *M'Guffey's Reader*. Ford was also an outspoken proponent of "hard work" and support of 100% Americanization.[641]

The nationwide spread of cultural misinformation became ingrained within the standard educational curriculum. Surprisingly, it was one of the largest school districts on the forefront of mandatory public education as one of the main culprits. Child Labor Laws eliminated the pseudo child/slave labor in factories

---

[640] Mangione and Morreale. *La Storia*, p. 222.
[641] Spelling of "M'Guffey's" varies. Sometimes as "McGuffey's." A reprinted original edition in *American Studies*, 42:1 Spring 2001: 1, as "M'Guffey's Second Reader."

CHAPTER 10   497

and other business. Progressive Reformers welcomed the restrictions placed upon child labor. Overall promoting the best place for a child was in a schoolroom rather than in a hazardous factory or mine was a major leap forward. On the flip side, a 1926 textbook, mandated by the New York City Department of Education, and also throughout much of America, perpetrated stereotypical differences under the distinction of the "Five Great Races in America."

It's in the Textbooks and the "Five Great Races"[642]

The 1920s was an anomaly in American history. The era might have started with the hard fought Constitutional Amendment earning the right for women to vote; concurrent with an Amendment known as Prohibition founded on morality subsequently restricting consumption of alcohol. Nostalgic portrayals of the "Roaring 20s" flaunting prohibition while rebellious flappers danced the Charleston to Jazz music is often ingrained in selective historical memory. This is not to say those experiences did not occur – they did. The flamboyancy and rebellious fun nature was not an overtly accepted aspect of American culture. For the most part, the decade was a morally restrictive period for society, culture, and politics. The racial divide was evident in all political, social, and economic aspects of society; as power held firmly with total control of white male Protestants.

Very few exceptions existed as the reinforcement of negative stereotypes appeared in so many places. Similar to the other aspects of cultural misinformation was provided by "medical experts." Throughout the decade, continued false accusations made by the clergy and medical experts simply grasped at straws while making wild audacious claims about non-whites. One of many examples appeared in a 1924 editorial in the *Literary Digest* offered up a report by the *Medical Review of Reviews* supporting claims of social dancing associated with "primitives" and "promiscuity." The totally misguided view was quoted as follows,

> "[In] the dance among primitive peoples both parties rise to a passionate excitement; become intoxicated by the tones and movements, the enthusiasm rises higher and higher and swells finally into a real madness, which breaks out in violence. There can scarcely be any doubt that dancing came about as an adjunct to sexual stimulation. As such it still exists, undisguised among primitive peoples."

Editors of the *Literary Digest* reminded readers that "Medical men are not noted as ethical extremists." Therefore, it was important to reiterate any endorsement was "all the more significant" in condemnation of "degenerate" social dancing.

---

[642] Francis Trevelyan Miller and John W. Davis. *Geography by Grades, Grade 4B: The Earth, The Continents* (New York: Hinds, Hayden & Eldredge, Inc., 1926).

The new energetic dance styles embraced by the young such as the Charleston, Black Bottom, and Shimmy to Jazz music were described "as relics of jungle days, still employed by primitive peoples for immoral purposes." Furthermore, the continued use of phrases as "jungle days" and "primitive peoples" in opposition and harmful to "civilized peoples" reinforced the supposed superiority of Anglo-Americans over all the other immigrant ethnic groups.[643]

Some immigrant groups, such as Italians could appear to be white and would eventually overcome the "color," language, or religion discrimination by assimilation. The path to achieve assimilation involved clothing styles, religion, and language, among other cultural aspects not of the home country; rather adapting the prevailing pre-immigrant culture of America. The process, promoted as "Americanization," expected all newcomers to assimilate to the existing "dominant culture." A term sometimes applied to the assimilation process was "Melting Pot." The term had earlier origins dating to the 1700s, however, came into wider use after 1908 as a stage play "The Melting Pot" premiered in Washington, D.C., with President Theodore Roosevelt, in attendance. One year later, the play was featured in New York showcasing over 130 performances.

One of the many aspects of Americanization was applied in the public school system. By the 1920s, mandatory public education for grade school children was commonplace throughout the nation. As school children were a captive audience, it was easy to provide misinformation when it came justifying racial segregation. At home it was not uncommon to hear derogatory references to a particular race or nationally; therefore, continue to permeate into children's lifestyles and in turn maintain those similar beliefs as they grew older. Information on racial differences was available and disseminated as "factual;" regardless of the region.[644]

Reinforcement of the inferiority of the non-white races was often justified in schools by standard issue textbooks. One example adopted by the New York City Department of Education, and also in many schools in America, was the 1926 edition of *Geography by Grades, Grade 4B: The Earth, The Continents* by Francis Trevelyan Miller and John W. Davis. One chapter "The People Of The Earth And How They Live," provided a general description of "race" as,

> "Most persons whom we see about us have a very light color – a pinkish white. These people are said to belong to the **white race** [emphasis as published]. There are also many persons whose skin is of a very dark color. They are called Negroes and belong to the **black race.** There are

---

[643] Quoted in Editorial, *The Literary Digest* 80 (22 March 1924), p. 80.
[644] James Loewen. *Teaching What Really Happened*, p. 73. Note: Assimilation is defined as "the process by which minorities gradually adopt patterns of the dominant culture." Guy Szuberla, "Zangwill's The Melting Pot Plays Chicago," pp. 3-20.

CHAPTER 10

people who have skin of a yellowish color. They belong to the **yellow race.** Then there are the **brown race** and the **red race.**" [Note: Bold emphasis in original]

Throughout the textbook, a continued reference for each of the red, brown, yellow, black, and white races was described as generalized stereotypical attributes that could only be described as prejudicial, and stereotypical. The "White Race" was defined as native born Americans of northern European ancestry. Other racial distinctions were categorized as the "Five Great Races" of White, Red, Brown, Yellow, and Black. In contrast to positive attributes of the White race, the "lesser four" were listed with a litany of generalized false negative attributes.

The subtly worded text offered continued negative stereotypes constantly reinforcing inferiority of the Red, Brown, Yellow, and Black races. At the time, few if any Native American Indians or Middle Eastern people actually lived in New York City; however, dark-skinned Italians did. If the stereotypical generalizations were not enough, two poignant questions asked of the students were quite revealing. One was, "To which race do you belong?" and the second, "Which race has reached the highest state of civilization?" For any student required to look back in the text, the answers were quite obvious. The generalizations were not confined to textbooks. Many of the same stereotypes and fears placed upon immigrants in the 21st century remain contentious. Until the 1950s, racial inferiority was an openly acceptable and mistakenly understood as the "truth" among the mainstream in American public.[645]

Prevalent messages, in all areas of American culture, remained the status quo well into the 1950s. During the 1960s and 1970s the stereotypes experienced a slow reversal continuing towards the end of the 20th century. Sadly, by the second decade of the 21st century, the racial and immigrant negativity once-again reared its ugly machinations with a renewed xenophobic dedication to Populism, voter suppression, domestic terrorism, conspiracy theorists, and anti-immigrant legislation.

The American Mercury and Cultural Critics

Despite progressive views, some popular New York Broadway shows such as Eugene O'Neill's *All God's Chillun Got Wings* (1924) and *Showboat* (1925) by Jerome Kern, Oscar Hammerstein, and Edna Ferber, came under fierce criticism. Unlike other Broadway offerings, each show presented the stark reality of contemporary American society reflected on the theatrical stage. Each explored issues of race and miscegenation in America. *Showboat*, revealed issues of the 1920s masked in the South during the Civil War. The plot focused on a secret

---

[645] Miller and Davis, *Geography by Grades*, pp. 45-51.

interracial marriage of a mulatto woman and a white man with contemporary references to segregation and the "one drop of nonwhite blood" law.

Established nationwide laws, both written and un-written, prevented intermingling or socializing of the races; and in most cases included recent immigrants, such as Italians and Jews. Unwritten law, especially in the South, fiercely protected the purity of white females. The mere thought of a black man engaging in sexual relations with a white woman was among the worst imaginable fear, especially for the clergy; and unfortunately, a "crime" often punished by lynching. By the 1920s, that mindset was firmly entrenched and was often a subject of Sunday sermons. One specific scene in *All God's Chillun Got Wings* particularly angered clergy and moralists involved a white woman simply kissing the hand of a black man. A typical response was quoted in 1924 by the *Winston-Salem Journal*, a southern newspaper. The Rev. C. A. Owens of the First Baptist Church in North Carolina, told his congregation,

> "There is the greatest possible danger of the mingling of the races, so that in the future it may come to pass that you will send your daughter to the North for culture and she will come back with a little Negro."

Rev. Owens was just one of many thousands who continually spread the fear under the guise of misappropriation from the Gospel. Not always quoted in newspapers, but connected to the same condemnation was intermarriage of "whites" with the likes of Italians or Jews.

As for the direct criticism of cultural productions, none of the morality critics admitted to actually seeing any of the Broadway productions; usually working from hearsay. Despite it all, the morality critics were ruthless in their condemnations. A basic sampling of the morality critics included the nationwide chain of Hearst newspapers, Church leaders of all denominations, the Ku Klux Klan, moralists, and many patriotic groups. The American Legion, for example, a bastion of solid midwestern Protestant beliefs, said the Broadway shows were "subversive to 100 percent American Patriotism." With the First World War well within recent memory, added to the fear from the American Legion was a contemporary claim insinuating, "There may be German propaganda within the text of the play." In a review of *All God's Chillun Got Wings*, George Jean Nathan (1882-1958), coeditor of the popular literary monthly journal *The American Mercury*, termed all of the critics, clergy, and the American Legion, as "moral morons." Adding, the "Methodist-Baptist *bloc* of so-called churches" made that moronic justification very clear.

Above Left: *The American Mercury* a popular monthly literary magazine during the 1920s. **Above Right**: H.L. Mencken and George Jean Nathan editors of *The American Mercury*. Photograph by: Ben Pinchot originally published in *Theatre Magazine* August 1928, p. 37.

Nathan's co-editor of *The American Mercury* cultural critic H. L. Mencken (1880-1956) was one of the few who consistently spoke out against Americanization and the anti-immigrant furor. Mencken routinely dismissed the negative association of African Americans, Italians, Native Americans, Asians, immigrants, and others; calling the morality critics "local morons" and "native morons." The editor of the progressive literary magazine astutely asked the thought-provoking question,

> "If 100 per cent Americanism means absolute and dog-like subservience to the State, as is now taught in every schoolhouse, then obviously no Catholic can ever be 100 percent American [nor] the Methodist-Baptist *bloc* of so-called churches"

Mencken offered an interesting corollary between the Ku Klux Klan and church membership,

> "The Klan is simply the secular arm of these churches [and] flourished wherever the peasants and town workmen were mainly Methodists and Baptists – in brief, wherever the dominant local clergy whooped it up."[646]

The Ku Klux Klan was not overtly prominent in New York City, yet many of H.L. Mencken's and George Jean Nathan's "local moron" critics were ever present. Mencken suggested the reason the Ku Klux Klan never gained prominence in

---

[646] H. L. Mencken, "The Library," *American Mercury* 2, no. 5 (May 1924): pp. 120-121.

areas such as New York or New England, was due mainly to the fact that "most of the local morons are Catholics."

Anti-Catholic and Anti-Italian

Anti-Catholicism traces back hundreds of years to 1517 as Martin Luther posted his 95 Theses critical of the Catholic Church prompting the formation of the Protestant Reformation in Europe. (Granted evidence of severe anti-Catholicism dates to Ancient Rome.) In the ensuing years after Luther's proclamation, "Wars of Religion" and brutal persecution by Protestants upon Catholics and Catholics upon Protestants embroiled the European continent for decades as violent wars occurred between a mainly Protestant England and Catholic France. Into the mix were also other Europeans such as Spain and Germany, to name the most dominant. Religious conflict was not confined to Europe.

The history books are filled with stories within the North American colonies being settled and forming among Europeans who sought relief and religious freedom. Sadly, once firmly in the Americas both Catholics and Protestants forced unwanted religion, often with violent suppression, upon the native indigenous peoples. Religious dominance among the colonies was vastly separated geographically as Spanish Catholics dominated the Southwestern portion of North America whereas, Northern European Protestants dominated along the eastern portion of the continent. Despite an affiliation such as Catholicism – prejudicial differences existed within Catholics of different European regions.

A 1995 Columbia University publication listed under the somewhat religious title of *All the Nations Under Heaven* by emeritus historians Prof. Frederick M. Binder and Prof. David Reimers provided a differentiation between Italian Catholicism and Irish Catholicism. Professors Binder and Reimers stated,

> "Italian immigrants were Catholics, even if just nominally. However, their brand of Catholicism back at Italy had more to do with guidance for everyday life rather than following doctrine. Most Italians were, therefore, distrustful of the churches both in Italy and the U.S. because there were not of any help to these commoners. The men considered church going women's work and attended church only on special occasions like Christmas mass and weddings and funerals. In the city, the distrustful feelings went both ways. The churches in the city were Irish run who let Italian priests serve the Italian population in basements of the parishes. The Irish clergy thought that the Italians were inadequately trained in religion. They thought of Italians as a whole as an inferior group."

In New York City, Catholic parishes were usually dominated by Irish priests. Slowly, the hierarchy changed with more Italian priests in areas populated by Italian immigrants. By the first decade of the 20th century about 50 churches were

CHAPTER 10   503

staffed by 80 Italian priests. One aspect of this congeniality was a growing concern of "losing" Italians converting to the Protestant religion. Many of those same churches served, as Binder and Reimers added, as a "support center for immigrants." Services extended well beyond inner spiritual salvation to "help with finding jobs, dealing with the law, money, and even finding potential suitors."[647]

As one example, The Saint Raphael Society for Italian Immigrants founded in New York in 1890 maintained operations for over 30 years offering services for local Italian immigrants. As described by research historians at the Center for Migration Studies of New York,

> "Throughout its 32 years, the St. Raphael Society assisted newly arrived Italian immigrants in a variety of ways: finding jobs, adjusting irregularities in immigration papers, finding and contacting relatives, visiting sick Italian immigrants in hospitals. Its primary service consisted in offering food and shelter to those Italian immigrants, among them minors, who for a variety of reasons found themselves destitute, unable to gain a livelihood, or unable to proceed to their place of destination."

Beginning in the late 1880s, anti-ethnic sentiment increased, and Catholic churches were often vandalized and burned as Italians were often attacked by mobs. Italian neighborhoods were depicted as violent and controlled by criminal networks. All sorts of perpetuated myths continued to fervor, many fueled by age-old differences between the Protestants and Catholics; easily traced to the European years of the Protestant Reformation.[648]

The Catholic religion in America was not the same as Europe, or Italy. Professor Julie Byrne of Duke University, specializing in the religious history during the "Gilded Age" in America, provides a corollary between America and the Catholic religion. Prof. Byrne explained,

> "Many people of the upper classes didn't particularly pay attention to the Catholic religion, but assumed that because the immigrants were poor, foreign, and different, that meant they were also dirty, dangerous, and lazy. Many people of the lower classes assumed the immigrant's represented competition for jobs, homes, and social prestige that rightly belonged to them. On the other hand, the anti-Catholic prejudice was about religion. [In time], Catholics did become good American citizens [soon] winning political races, organizing labor unions, opening businesses, and founding schools and hospitals. But no matter how hard Catholics strived to prove they were good, upstanding, patriotic

---

[647] Frederick M. Binder and David Reimers. *All the Nations Under Heaven*, pp. 145-147.
[648] Center for Migration Studies of New York; St. Raphael Society for Italian Immigrants, New York, (CMS 005).

American citizens, Protestants would never accept them, simply because they were Catholic."[649]

The centuries old fraction between the ongoing Catholic Ritual and Protestant Christianity was, as this historian would describe as, "finite and minimal." To devout practitioners of Catholicism and Christianity they remain as irreconcilable differences.

Catholic vs. Protestant

An abridged summary lesson prepared by Prof. Byrne of the two religions was "much more continuity than difference." The basic tenet of each is,

Catholic:
1. Highly organized hierarchy.
2. Pope as sole source of spiritual nurture, divine authority, and final salvation.
3. Sacraments as means of human contact with the divine.
4. Pray to Saints "intercede" with God the Father and Jesus the Son.

Protestant:
1. Rejected Catholic emphasis.
2. Less hierarchy in church structure,
3. The Bible as the source of revelation from God,
4. Jesus, not the Saints as the only necessary intercessor with God the Father.

The list is concise, nothing really omitted other than a possible minor difference on Catholic belief of receiving the Communion Eucharist as having the body of Christ physically "within" their own body (termed "transubstantiation"). Whereas Protestant Communion believes only the Eucharist as a symbolic nature "representing" Christ's death on the cross. Despite the intriguing similarities the divide remains tumultuous.[650]

Italians, Grapes, and
the Ku Klux Klan in Vineland, New Jersey

A fallacy exists due to lack of discussion on the long-history of anti-Catholicism from the first settlements in the "original" 13 colonies of the U.S. – into and extending beyond the Great Migration years of 1880 to 1930. During that latter part of the 19th and early 20th century, anti-Italianism was a part of the anti-immigrant, anti-Catholic ideology of the revived Ku Klux Klan. In 2017, Prof. Linda Gordon writing of *The Second Coming of the KKK: The Ku Klux Klan of the 1920s* provided an analysis of stark differences of the virulent Ku Klux Klan

---

[649] Julie Byrne. "Roman Catholics and Immigration in Nineteenth-Century America."
[650] Julie Byrne, "Roman Catholics and Immigration in Nineteenth-Century America."

CHAPTER 10

to their transformative acceptance in mainstream society during the 1920s. A summary view of Gordon's work by *The NY Review of Books* described,

> "The Ku Klux Klan of the 1920s spread largely in cities above the Mason-Dixon line, enrolling millions of members by stroking xenophobic fears over the flood of "immigrant hordes" landing in America. . . an analysis of "chilling comparisons to the present day."[651]

White supremacist groups seeking to preserve the supposed dominance of White Anglo-Saxon Protestants often targeted Italian Catholics, not always reported was the Klan's influence upon the immigration quotas.

History easily provides information on the Congressional response to the Immigration reform of the 1920s. Not always reported was the influential role infused by the Ku Klux Klan throughout the process in achieving Federal legislation for the Immigration Act of 1924. In a 2017 article in *Time* magazine journalist Olivia B. Waxman revealed,

> "The Klan's biggest victory was its successful lobbying for immigration quotas, made law in 1924. The group got 16 members elected to the U.S. Senate, claimed it elected 75 to the U.S. House of Representatives and at least 11 Democratic and Republican governors to state houses."[652]

Linda Gordon added, "no one has been able to count all of the Klan candidates elected to state and local offices, as many non-members may have shared some points of Klan ideology." Unlike some urban myths, the Klan membership was not limited to the former Confederate southern states. Peak membership was reached around 1925 - at least 4 million – with almost half of the total number of members located in Ohio, Indiana, and Illinois; yet active throughout the entire nation with a particular ironic situation in the small town of Vineland in southern New Jersey.[653]

In 1861, before enactment of Prohibition, a small town in southern New Jersey was established by a Philadelphia lawyer named Charles K. Landis (1833-1900) "to create an alcohol-free utopian society based on agriculture and progressive thinking." Settling in the area of the proposed "Temperance Town," Landis quickly discovered the fertile soil in the region was "well-suited for growing grapes." With an understanding of the superior agricultural skill of Italian immigrants, Landis offered land grants of 20 acres to any Italian willing to clear the land to plant vines to "grow grapes." A significant number of Italians took the

---

[651] Linda Gordon *The Second Coming of the KKK: The Ku Klux Klan of the 1920s and the American Political Tradition*, (New York: W.W. Norton, 2017).
[652] Oliva B. Waxman, "How the KKK's Influence Spread in Northern States, *Time* magazine. October 24, 2017.
[653] Linda Gordon, *The Second Coming of the KKK*.

offer planting enough vines to grow and produce quality grapes leading to the eventual nickname which became the official name of the town as Vineland, New Jersey.

A few years later, in 1869, Thomas Bramwell Welch (1825-1903), a Methodist minister, created a process to make "unfermented wine." As an ardent supporter of temperance, the process was conceived for other ministers to supplement grape juice for sacramental wine. With son Charles Edgar Welch (1852-1926) they founded the Welch Grape Juice Company in Vineland, thereby purchasing the Italian grown grapes for sole production of grape juice. The fertile ground also proved conducive to growing quality tomatoes, attracting the Progresso Company, founded by Italians, to open a processing plant in Vineland for canning tomato soup. In the years of World War II, the town was remembered as a "peaceful wartime community that welcomed European Jewish refugees with open arms and the aroma of tomatoes could waft throughout the city streets."

Journalist Rob Spahr, writing on the 150th Anniversary for *The Press of Atlantic City*, said lost among the celebration, or more likely conveniently forgotten, or purposely omitted, was the fact Vineland was a hotbed of anti-Italian KKK activity that developed in Southern New Jersey in the mid-1920s. Despite the fact Italians in Vineland, pre-dated to the founding years of the town, a mass protest against the Italians living in the town was organized in 1933 by the Ku Klux Klan. At the time, Italians made up 20 percent of the total population. Tossed aside was the fact, Italians were instrumental in the financial success of Vineland.[654]

As the "truth" evolved, information revealed the Ku Klux Klan was not limited to only southern New Jersey, but also other areas of the state; soon spreading into Pennsylvania and upper New York state, and beyond. In 1924, rallies held in Washington D.C. occurred with over 40,000 proud KKK members marching (see Chapter 1). On July 4th of that same year, a Ku Klux Klan rally in Long Branch, New Jersey attracted over 15,000. An overwhelmingly large presence of the Klan was located in central New Jersey. Journalist Rob Spahr reported, "At its peak in the 1920s, an estimated 7,000 residents of Monmouth and Ocean counties – about 5.5 percent of the total population – were members of the Ku Klux Klan, the largest concentration of Klansmen anywhere in New Jersey." As a way of "righting history" of the tainted nostalgic portrayals of its 150 year history, the Vineland Historical and Antiquarian Society announced in September 2020 of the existence of the Ku Klux Klan, As an addition to their museum display the society stated,

---

[654] Rob Spahr. "Vineland Celebrates its 150th Anniversary," *The Press of Atlantic City*, August 8, 2011.

"It seems that the museum archives are home to a collection of Ku Klux Klan material from the 1920s that is related to Vineland and Cumberland County. . . It looks like that despite what we've been told over the years, the KKK had a home here in Vineland with a membership that included some very prominent citizens. At a time when our nation is in such chaos, some might question why we feel it's necessary to air such "dirty laundry." Our response to that would be that the truth of history is rarely pretty and it is always important to know the truth."[655]

---

[655] Erik Larsen, "The Ku Klux Klan was Welcomed at the Jersey Shore," *The Asbury Park Press, August* 22, 2017.

CHAPTER 11

ITALIAN FOOD SHAPING AMERICAN CULINARY CULTURE

Luckily, the other thing people think about when it comes to Italian-Americans is food.

For the first time, Italian food was being introduced to a mass market outside of the communities of Italian immigrants that had been enjoying it for generations, and Chef Boiardi is one of the reasons it soared in popularity.

As an unfortunate discriminatory occurrence in American Culture the first image that usually comes to mind about Italians in America is organized crime. Images of Italian gangsters has continually perpetrated through fictious Hollywood movies and sensationalized media stories. Fortunately, as historian Maria Laurino writes on the first page of *Italian Americans: A History*, "But luckily, the other thing people think about when it comes to Italian-Americans is food." In a wider common cultural contribution, the Italian born **Cesare Cardini** (1896-1956) known as "Caesar" was an Italian restaurateur, chef, and hotel owner. With his brother **Alex Cardini** (1899 – 1974) they originated the Caesar Salad at their restaurant named "Caesar's."[656]

Historian Janice Therese Mancuso tells us of some of the most common food items in the cities of New Orleans, Philadelphia, and San Francisco have Italian origins. Mancuso states,

"A visit to New Orleans is not fulfilled without a taste of a "*Muffuletta Sandwich*. A direct influence of the Sicilian population created in 1906 for Sicilian workers. The ever-popular *Philly Cheese Steak* was invented by an Italian, and the fish stew of San Francisco, *Cioppino*, originated

---

[656] Maria Laurino, *Italian Americans: A History*, p. 1.

510 Italian Culture in America:
The Immigrants 1880 to 1930 From Discrimination to Assimilation

from the Italian fish stew ciuppin, made by the Genoese fishermen who settled there."[657]

Not all cultural aspects are tangible such as religion or ideology. Others are tangible such as architecture. Food as cultural attributes can be both tangible and intangible. Gene P. Veronesi writing a history of Italian Americans reminds us, "Well-known is the significance of food in Italian culture and the family meal." That family dinner tradition has permeated American homes and restaurants in cities and towns. One of the oldest Italian Restaurants in America "Ralph's" is located in Philadelphia dating to the early 1900s. In 2015, the National Restaurant Association noted, "no other cuisine within America is as popular as Italian food." One survey revealed,

> "Sixty-one percent of people said they eat Italian food at least once a month; 26 percent said they eat it a few times a year. By comparison, the other two of the "big three" ethnic cuisines . . . Mexican and Chinese, were eaten at least once a month by 50 percent and 36 percent of those surveyed, respectively, and a few times a year by 31 percent and 42 percent of respondents, respectively."

The statistics are within "sit-down" restaurants serving a complete dinner – a fact most likely tied to the ethnic heritage of a family-style dinner.

The survey revealed, the highest percentage of diners eating at Italian restaurants is in the Northeast portion of the United States. This might not be a coincidence since almost 45 percent of all Italian Americans live within that region. Ironically during the late 19th century and into the early 20th century the idea of any American eating Italian food was considered "slumming." The restaurants, mostly located in Little Italy neighborhoods, were usually family owned within small urban storefronts (with owners living on the upper floors). The interior décor was minimal with requisite murals of their native home town and red and white checkerboard table cloth.[658]

---

[657] Janice Therese Mancuso. "A Brief History of Italian Food in America,"
[658] Bret Thorn. "Survey: Italian Remains Most Popular Ethnic Cuisine." *Nation's Restaurant News*, August 28, 2015.

The stereotypical Red and White Checkerboard tablecloth and mural in an Italian restaurant. A style prevalent among many of the Italian restaurants serving cuisine of the southern portion of Italy. This photograph is of an "Italian Restaurant" in the city of Oslo in Norway, c. 2014. (Author's Archives)

However, the reported population numbers of Americans with a distinct Italian heritage might be under estimated. As reported by the National Italian American Foundation (NIAF) in 2022,

> "As of the 2010 U.S. Census, the United States Federal Government removed "Italian American" from the question inquiring about ethnicity. Therefore, it was up to the individual to specify their Italian American heritage in the free space provided. As a result, 17,253,941 Italian Americans self-identified and wrote-in "Italian." However, experts predict that the community is actually larger with figures closer to 26 million."[659]

Food remains as the most prominent cultural connection in America. In 2014, a U.S. Census Bureau report cited 239,299 formal restaurants in America (not including quick-serve). About 12 percent (28,525) of the full-service restaurants served Italian food. (Full-service restaurants "comprises establishments primarily engaged in providing food services to patrons who order and are served while seated with waiter/waitress service and pay after eating.") Another 71,215 of the food establishments served Neapolitan style pizza; totaling over 99,700; a large percentage of all restaurants in America. (Of all the pizzerias, 53 percent were independently owned; as were 84 percent of restaurants.) Not included in the

---

[659] "Italian American Statistics." *National Italian American Foundation* (NIAF), 2022.

512

Italian Culture in America:
The Immigrants 1880 to 1930 From Discrimination to Assimilation

"Italian" total, 6,000 restaurants had limited-service Italian food on the menu. Very few restaurants of other ethnicities often served at least some type of Italian cultural food item such as cappuccino, espresso, garlic sticks, gnocchi, cannoli, calzones, or the ever-present American cultural mainstays of pizza and macaroni. Those two most common foods provided by Italian immigrants was not limited to restaurants or pizzeria's. One of the oldest Italian Bakery and Pastry shop is "Veniero" opened in 1894 in New York City by Antonio Veniero born in 1870 near Sorrento, Italy. Another famous bakery of Italian specialties and pastry "Ferrara" in New York's Little Italy dates its origins to 1892.[660]

Americans have come to associate "Italian Culture" with the Sunday afternoon dinner of macaroni and tomato sauce. For many Italians in America the Sunday afternoon dinner was held around 1:00 to 3:00 pm. The concept of a daily "afternoon dinner" was foreign to many Americans; yet for descendants of Italian immigrants it was the traditional meal time in Italy, as was a macaroni tradition. The macaroni path to America has been traced by historians from Italy via China from the travels of the famous Venetian explorer Marco Polo (1254-1324). Thomas Jefferson, who is usually credited with the introduction to America, universally applied the word "macaroni" to pasta as did many Italians. A large number of Italians who assimilated to America overwhelmingly applied the term "macaroni" to the many different shapes made from pasta ingredients, such as spaghetti, linguini, and ziti, to name a few. (By the late 20th century, the word "pasta" was a "trendy" word choice.)Considerably, Americans who "eat Italian" are usually not aware of the differences between northern and southern Italian cuisine. The southern difference is best known mainly due to Neapolitan pizza and the vast array of pasta shapes covered in a tomato sauce. With the availability of wheat and tomatoes, which are easy to grow in the Mediterranean climate, Finzi and other sources reveal that the poorer peasants in the city of Naples began combining tomatoes upon a flat bread (an early precursor to the Neapolitan pizza). Northern Italian food such as Polenta dates to the 16th century "common to Verona, Padua, and Venice." Polenta was often combined with fish such as the Italian version of salted Cod known as "Baccalà." Another of the common foods of the northern provinces is Risotto as a rice variant. Often it is mixed with other food ingredients even other varieties of rice. Yet, it is the "pasta dish" or macaroni, that has become a staple among Italians and Americans of various ethnic backgrounds.[661]Marco Polo is credited with "discovering" macaroni in China and introducing it to the Italian peninsular; however, some dispute the claim. As stated by independent historian Gene P. Veronesi, evidence exists of pasta/macaroni "being eaten in Italy during Etruscan times." Veronesi claims it was on the island

---

[660] "American Fact Finder." *United States Census Bureau.*
[661] Gene P. Veronesi. *Italian-Americans & Their Communities of Cleveland.* p. 285.

CHAPTER 11   513

of Sicily that "strands of dough" resembling a form of spaghetti existed at the time "of the Arab invasions, about 800 A.D." Veronesi adds the presumption that, "ravioli and fettuccini were known during the early Middle Ages."

In America, some of the other common food staples of southern Italians such as anchovy, eel, mussels, seabass, scallop, shrimp, squid, and octopus, to name a few, were not readily available near the urban American as cities as was common off the coast of Italy and Sicily. The cuisine of Southern Italian peasants, who often lacked meats on a regular basis, developed a protein diet of seafood combined with vegetarian dishes with tomatoes, eggplant, olives, spices, and other vegetables were often paired with bread. Eggplant might also have been introduced by the travels of Marco Polo (written records of the eggplant date to 544 in China).[662]

Il Pomodoro and Macaroni

Most Americans, know the common Italian cultural distinction is pairing a tomato – as "sauce" - with pasta as "macaroni." The earliest known pairing of tomato sauce with macaroni/pasta was in the city of Naples during the early 19th century. The first recorded recipe in Naples for *pasta al pomodoro* (translated as "pasta with tomato sauce") might be the first of its kind, at least in Italy. That recipe was kept in the family tradition by Italian immigrants in America. The soon to be world-famous delicacy known as a "pizza" also traces its roots to Naples. (Note: The patron saint of Naples is San Gennaro which a festival of food and culture is celebrated in America, notably in New York City.) Finzi tells us that the most common of all pizza's the "margherita" was named in 1899 shortly after Italian unification in honor of the then Queen Margherita. The margherita pizza has three ingredients of tomato sauce, mozzarella, and basil leaves placed upon pizza dough – three colors of the Italian flag.

It is not unusual for Americans to simply associate "Italian Culture" with the Sunday afternoon macaroni dinner. For many Americans of Italian heritage, that is a fact holding true for many subsequent generations. Yet, the tale of how the "dinner" combination arrived in America is often murky. The tomato as the prime ingredient of the Italian cultural staple of "Tomato Sauce" is most often associated with a macaroni dish or a Neapolitan style pizza. In Italian cooking, the tomato is a major ingredient beyond just sauce. Yet, "tomato sauce" is mostly found as a cultural staple of Italians only from the southern portion of Italy. Yet, Finzi traced the first mention of tomatoes (the *pomi d'oro*) in Italy to 1548 in the Tuscany region. Cookbooks published in Naples as early as 1692 made use of the tomato as a basic ingredient of various dishes (possibly copied from Spanish sources).

---

[662] Veronesi, p. 285.

The tomato in Italy took a circuitous route from South America via the discoveries of Christopher Columbus in the New World across the Atlantic Ocean to Europe and thus back across the Atlantic to North America. Jerry Finzi writing "How the Tomato Became Part of Italian Culture" reminds us, "The tomato was first 'discovered' by the Spanish Conquistadors while exploring and then conquering the Americas." Sources place the indigenous tomato to the Andes Mountains of Peru in South America. Therefore, as part of the Columbian Exchange the tomato was introduced to Europe and eventually in return to North America.[663]

Pizza an "Intangible Cultural Heritage of Humanity"

Another combination was tomato sauce on a flatten pasta dough creating the original Neapolitan Pizza. Naples is the birthplace of the modern pizza. (Ancestry of the pizza dates back a thousand years to ancient Rome with earlier combinations by the Etruscans and Greek colonists.) Naples as a 21st century city of about 960,000 people, boasts over 8,200 pizzerias. The world's oldest pizza establishment is Antica Pizzeria Port'Alba in Naples. Opened in 1783, in operation well into the 21st century.

The basic simple Neapolitan Pizza has morphed into all sorts of delicacies combining all sorts of shapes, ingredients, and toppings. Yet, the most famous, and the most common, pizza remains the *Margherita*. In 1889, the Margherita Pizza was created in honor of the visiting Queen Margherita of Savoy. The queen was heralded throughout the peninsular as wife of King Umberto I, the first King of the recently unified Italy. As the story is told, a Neapolitan *pizzaiolo* chef named Raffaele Esposito made three different pizzas for the reigning Queen. She favored the one representing the new flag of Italy comprised of *red* tomato sauce, *white* mozzarella, and *green* basil. As a reciprocal honor, Esposito therefore named the pizza style as "Margherita."[664]

In 2017, UNESCO (United Nations Educational, Scientific, and Cultural Organization) recognized and accepted the Neapolitan *pizzaiolo* chef as an "art" thereby placing the pizza pie on the world body's list of the Intangible Cultural Heritage of Humanity. Not as debatable as the Italian question of "Is it sauce or gravy?' nor "Is it Macaroni or Pasta?" - the question does remain is pizza really a Pie?

Looking to the basic definition as defined by Merriam-Webster the standard dictionary of the English language, defines "pie" as,

---

[663] Jerry Finzi. "How the Tomato Became Part of Italian Culture." *Grand Voyage Italy*, May 3, 2016. Finzi added: "The word *tomato* is derived from the Aztec word *xitomatl*, in Europe shortened to *tomatl*. In French, *pomme d'amour* later calling it simply *la tomate*.
[664] Franz Lidz. "Pie is a Constant: In Naples, the formula calls for Pizza." *Smithsonian* magazine, March 2021, p. 44.

CHAPTER 11   515

Pie: \ 'pī \ *noun*: a dessert consisting of a filling (as of fruit or custard) in a pastry shell or topped with pastry or both.

Merriam-Webster added to the definition,

Pizza: Neapolitan *pies* which are baked in a wood-fired oven imported from Italy.

We might also add another definition,

Macaroni: noun mac·a·ro·ni | \ ˌma-kə-ˈrō-nē \

1: pasta made from semolina and shaped in the form of slender tubes.[665]

Macaroni in America

By 1809, macaroni was available for sale in America from select merchants such as the Italian born Giovanni Baptiste "John" Sartori (1765- 1854) of Trenton, New Jersey. (Sartori's brother was famed neoclassical Italian sculptor Antonio Canova). Information from *The Thomas Jefferson Papers* cite "Sartori served as United States consul at Rome, 1797–1801, before opening a business in Trenton."[666]

Sartori owned a "well-stocked warehouse" in Civitavecchia, a port city near Rome. A 1792 emigration to Philadelphia, as a secular diplomatic envoy as consul of the Vatican coincided "as an importer of rare Italian goods." Included were marble statues, chandeliers, Italian chocolate, and Roman violin strings. In 1798, Sartori's Rome warehouse was ransacked by Napoleon's invading French army, disrupting his Philadelphia business. A return to Italy to rectify the situation failed. Returning to America a decision was made to settle permanently in Lamberton, New Jersey (sometimes listed as "Lemberton," later a part of Trenton). Information exists that Sartori may have been the first Italian resident to the area, as no record exists of any other Italians residing before 1800.[667]

Trenton was one of a few American cities attracting Italian immigrants before 1880. Tom Frascella writing for the *San Felese Society of New Jersey*, tells us,

"In the late 18th and early 19th century the town of Trenton saw a steady stream of notable individuals whose origin was the Italian peninsula passing through. Artists, scientists, poets, opera singers, classical musicians, and the like often stopped in Trenton on the way to the larger

---

[665] "Macaroni. *Merriam Webster Dictionary.*

[666] Thomas Jefferson Memorandum Book, 2:1235. See also: Editorial note by J. Jefferson Looney at: "Thomas Jefferson to Gordon, Trokes & Company, 30 December 1809," *Founders Online,* National Archives. See also: "Bishop Giovanni Battista (Giambattista) Sartori." *Geni.com,* Accessed April 17, 2019.

[667] "John Baptist Sartori: Where and When." *Square Space*, 2019. *Square Space* website was created on the history of the Sartori family and Rosey Hill Mansion in Trenton.

516   Italian Culture in America:
The Immigrants 1880 to 1930 From Discrimination to Assimilation

cities of Philadelphia and New York. Often, these individuals gave lectures, scientific demonstrations, and concerts for the entertainment of the local folk."[668]

In the New Jersey capital city of Trenton, the soon to be Americanized John Sartori developed a new business venture as a merchant. From 1802 to 1825 or possibly as late as 1832, he "owned and operated a factory making vermicelli and selling macaroni;" the first such factory of its kind in America. Sartori's "macaroni" clientele included "the upper echelons of American society" including Thomas Jefferson. For unknown reasons, in 1832 Sartori left New Jersey, moving back to Italy settling in Livorno (also known as "Leghorn"); residing in Italy until his death in 1854.

One of Sartori's first American clients was Thomas Jefferson (1743-1826). Jefferson's own "discovery of macaroni" (most likely a version of the proverbial "macaroni and cheese") occurred while in Paris from 1784 to 1789. During a personal tour of northern Italy in 1787 (see Chapter 4A), he experienced the Italian noodle, which he wanted to import upon return home to Virginia. In hopes of securing proper production of macaroni in America, he copied a recipe and drew the requirements for a macaroni machine found while in Italy. In praise, Jefferson wrote,

"The best maccaroni [sic] in Italy is made with a particular sort of flour called Semola [sic], in Naples: but in almost every shop a different sort of flour is commonly used; for, provided the flour be of a good quality, & not ground extremely fine, it will always do very well."

The recipe is similar to modern day methods for making pasta semolina dough into macaroni shapes. (My own recollection from my grandmother Anna Dattilo was basically the same.) The Library of Congress provides credible evidence stating, "Jefferson probably helped to popularize [macaroni] by serving it to dinner guests during his presidency."[669]

By the end of the century, macaroni and cheese was common in America. With the onset of the Industrial Revolution, American factory production eliminated importing macaroni from Italy, lowering the cost significantly. Factory production in America did require a large number of laborers, creating a U.S. policy of massive immigration of cheap labor; millions of those were Italians entering from 1880 to 1920. Despite losing its appeal to the wealthy, "macaroni" became common in the American lexicon and part of a patriotic tradition through song.

---

[668] See: Tom Frascella. "Giovanni Battiste Sartori." *San Felese Society of New Jersey,* June 2012.
[669] "Thomas Jefferson's Drawing of a Macaroni Machine," c. 1787. See also: Stacy Conradt. "5 Foods Thomas Jefferson Introduced or Made Popular in America."

CHAPTER 11

517

Stuck a Feather in his Cap and Called it Macaroni

A familiar American song lasting through the ages of popular culture is "Yankee Doodle Dandy." The original lyrics from the time of the American Revolution begin as,

Yankee Doodle went to town
A-riding on a pony.
Stuck a feather in his cap
and called it macaroni.

The original may have been in 1755; later as a derogatory reference during the American Revolution towards American colonists. "Maccaroni" was a British term for an 18th century "dandy;" a person known for "fastidious eating" and fashionable clothing. Some sources claim the term "dandy" referenced a derogatory non-masculine affinity. It is said British Army regulars often sang the song to mock their supposed inferior compatriots. During the American Revolution, the colonists sang the song in defiance to their British overlords. By the end of the Revolution, the song became a symbol of American pride; with lyrics to mock the British.[670]

Harkening back to the Italian connection, Thomas Jefferson "visited" Italy many times throughout his lifetime (see Chapter 4A). Only once in the physical sense; yet lifelong visits continued through research, books, correspondence, and personal interaction with Italians in America. As a confirmed "Italophile," Jefferson was well-versed in the language, music, art, law, wine, and culture. Much of Jefferson's personal appreciation for Italian culture was assimilated into the fledging nation – which permeated the culture and assimilated well into the 21st century.

In 1934, an article published by Vassar College located in Poughkeepsie, New York reviewed a lecture by Theodore Fred Kuper, who at the time served as director of the Thomas Jefferson Foundation. As an introduction, Kuper summed up American culture as one that has "taken from the best all other nations have to offer." In his talk Mr. Kuper stressed Jefferson "was a strong force in bringing to America, Italians, Italian art, and Italian literature, which have been molded into the make-up of American life." Another inclusion was ice cream.[671]

---

[670] "Yankee Doodle." *Online Etymology Dictionary*. Accessed October 5, 2018.
[671] "Italian Influence Great in Life of Thomas Jefferson: Title of Estate is Evidence." *Vassar Miscellany News*, Vol. XVIII, N0. 29, February 17, 1933 February 1934, pp. 1, 4.

We All Love Ice Cream in America
As derived from Italian Gelato

Those same merchant excursions by the famous Venetian explorer Marco Polo to China also was one to introduce ice cream to Italy. Not surprisingly, Ice Cream in America has a similar direct connection to Thomas Jefferson and a long-standing Italian legacy. Jefferson was not the first to bring ice cream to America, some reports claim the treat was in the American colonies around 1744; he was, however, the first to write down an ice cream recipe, often serving it to guests. Jefferson's first sampling of ice cream was during his years living in France (1784-1789).[672]

Ice Cream may have originated in China around 200 BCE as a mixture of milk and rice immersed in snow. Some reports of an "ice-cream-like food" made from "buffalo milk, flour, and camphor" date around 618 to 697 CE. In Ancient Rome, some accounts claim emperors desired a treat of flavored fresh snow. Roman Emperors supposedly sent slaves to mountain tops carrying back fresh snow adding flavoring. After Marco Polo somewhat officially established the delicacy of ice cream as a "treat" in Italy, it made its way to France via the marriage of the Italian Catherine de Medici (1519-1589) to French King Henry II (1519-1599). Subsequently, ice cream existed in England, known at least during the time of King Charles I (r. 1625 – 1649).

Historian Martina Zito, writing "The History of Ice Cream," tells us the modern form of ice cream was "Gelato" invented around the 1660s in Sicily. In 1668, a Sicilian fisherman named Francesco Procopio dei Coltelli invented the "first ice cream machine" and soon spread the tasty treat "all over Europe and then the world." In 1868, Coltelli's grandson of the same name opened *Le Procope* serving a revised ice cream recipe. *Le Procope* "soon became the most famous cafe in France, frequented by celebrities, intellectuals, philosophers and writers."[673]

Monticello research historian Anna Berkes reveals "There are no less than six references to ice cream being served at the President's House [during Jefferson's tenure] between 1801 and 1809." The ice cream treat was served in a bowl. It was not until the late 19th century; the treat went from a bowl to the traditional ice cream cone. Although some sources cite the introduction of the first ice cream cone in America occurred at the 1904 World's Fair in St. Louis; the first ice cream cone was invented and produced in 1896 in New York by the Italian born Italo Marchiony who was granted a patent in December 1903.[674]

---

[672] Anna Berkes. "Ice Cream." Monticello.org, June 28, 2013.
[673] "The Origin of Ice Cream." *BBC NewsRound,* Accessed April 13, 2019.Martina Zito. "The History of Ice Cream," *Italian Traditions,* June 5, 2016.
[674] Anna Berkes. "Ice Cream." Monticello.org, June 28, 2013.

CHAPTER 11   519

San Gennaro **Festival and Philadelphia's "Italian Market"**

In New York City, and "Little Italy's" across the nation, church functions and celebrations of the annual Saint's days such as *San Gennaro*, (a carryover from the Neapolitan tradition in southern Italy) provided weeklong festivities and cultural socialization. Both the underlying and overlying of all the prominent commonalty of the festivals was and is – ITALIAN FOOD.[675]

Similar situations and festivities occurred in other major cities such as in Philadelphia. Research historian Barbara Klaczynska writing for *The Encyclopedia of Greater Philadelphia* chronicled the quick growth of Italians into Philadelphia during the Great Wave of Immigration,

> "The number of Italians in Philadelphia skyrocketed from only 516 in the 1870 census to 18,000 by 1900. The surge continued with 77,000 Italian immigrants and their children living in Philadelphia in 1910, 137,000 in 1920, and 182,368 by 1930–making Italians the second-largest ethnic group in Philadelphia."

Many of the new Italian immigrants settled into an enclave neighborhood of South Philadelphia; establishing their mark soon acquiring the name of the area as "The Italian Market." Klaczynska added, "Philadelphia's Little Italy was the second largest in the country–surpassed only by New York." As an "Italian Market" the main product were food products such as fruits, vegetables, and meats. Added to the food distinction was establishing "the first Italian parish" in America - Saint Mary Magdalen de Pazzi.[676]

Not often stated is the overt discrimination suffered by Italians in Philadelphia. Barbara Klaczynska reminds us,

> "The Ku Klux Klan in Philadelphia boasted the third-largest number of initiations in any American city in the interwar years (35,000) [targeting] Italian immigrants because they were Catholic, foreign born, and former or current subjects of a totalitarian regime. While upper class Nativists such as Henry Cabot Lodge drew distinctions between Northern and Southern Italians, the Klan attacked all Italians without discernment."[677]

The self-protective Italian ethnic enclave within Philadelphia was described by Helen Tangires for *The Encyclopedia of Greater Philadelphia*, as,

> "The Italian Market . . . is the popular name for the food shops and curbside stands on Ninth Street between Fitzwater and Wharton Streets, where merchants sell fresh produce, prepared foods, imported products, goods, and equipment for both household and commercial consumption.

---

[675] David Nasaw. *Going Out: The Rise and Fall of Public Amusements*, p. 15.

[676] Barbara Klaczynska, "Immigration," *Encyclopedia of Greater Philadelphia*.

[677] Barbara Klaczynska, "Immigration (1870-1930)."

... The majority of [the] food establishments specialize in the sale of fruits and vegetables, cheese, meat, poultry, seafood, pasta, spices, and baked goods. Complementing the array of shops are restaurants, delicatessens, and cafes that offer dining and refreshment."

Many Italian vendors with storefront businesses lived above the shops. Tangires added, "Existing row houses on Ninth Street of contiguous structures were easily modified for family businesses, with stores at ground level and living spaces . . . on the upper floors."

The business area, "with ancestral roots in central and southern Italy and eastern Sicily," firmly established an "official curb market" within Philadelphia. As a "curb market" the area was reminiscent of the early days of Italian immigration as the streets of the Little Italy enclaves were crowded with "vendors selling from pushcarts, wagons, trucks, or sidewalk stands arranged in a linear fashion along a designated street." In 2007, the neighborhood area was designated an historical district by the Pennsylvania Historical and Museums Commission.[678]

Title: "Part of the 9th Street Italian Market, the Nation's oldest working outdoor market, Philadelphia, Pennsylvania. Between 1980 and 2006. Photograph by Carol Highsmith. Retrieved from the Library of Congress, <www.loc.gov/item/2011633564/>.

---

[678] Helen Tangires, "Italian Market," *The Encyclopedia of Greater Philadelphia*, 2011.

CHAPTER 11 521

By the 20th century, street vendors and local business were no longer exclusively Italian; of the remaining Italian vendors, many traced ancestral roots to the 19th century. Not known as to who, what, or when – the where is known as it pertains to the famous "Philly Cheesesteak" created during the 1930s by Italians morphing into the 21st century as a "nationally recognized street food." With just about every well-established district in American cities, by the end of the 20th century the area was scheduled for "redevelopment." Unlike other cities, the area was saved from demolition. The revitalization of capturing the original essence, creating an "historic" market worthy of a "must stop" tourist destination within one of the most historic of American cities. Within a short (1mi. 1.6km) walking distance from American cultural historic sites such as Independence Hall, the Declaration House, and Constitution Hall, among others, the Italian Market has literally become a "must stop" tourist destination.

Hand-Crank Macaroni Machine, Chef Boyardee, and "Elegant Italian" Dining

Most Italian immigrants made their own macaroni by kneading semolina ingredients into pasta dough, often on a kitchen table in the home; then rolled, flattened, and cut into shapes. In 1906, an easier way to produce macaroni was introduced. An Italian immigrant named **Angelo Vitantonio** (1848-1917) invented the first hand-crank pasta machine; thereby eliminating "the need to flatten and cut it by hand." Vitantonio was born in the commune of Ripalimosani in the Province of Campobasso, Italy about 120 miles (190 km) northeast of Naples. The family first immigrated to New York, later relocating to the Little Italy section of Cleveland, Ohio. A patent for the machine to make "Flat Macaroni" was applied by son Luigi on May 20, 1919 and granted on March 2, 1920. (The younger Vitantonio changed his name to "Louis De Vito.") The macaroni machine allowed the Vitantonio's to expand their business in Cleveland. After Angelo died, son Luigi (1887-1967) continued the family business adding an invention of another machine to make *Cavatelli* (small pasta shells made from semolina). The family business "Villaware" expanded into making small kitchen appliances as "one of the leaders within the home appliance industry" well into the 21st century.

Another means of mass-production distribution of Italian macaroni was available directly off a supermarket shelf in a canned product of "Chef Boyardee." Most Americans would assume **Chef Boyardee** was a fictionalized character created by a New York advertising company. The face of Chef Boyardee on canned macaroni food products that became so ubiquitous to legions of American families after 1945 was in fact a real person. Born **Ettore Boiardi** (1897-1985) in the town of Piacenza, in northern Italy about 42 miles (68 km) southeast of Milan, the "Chef," was known by the Americanized name of Hector Boyardee. In 1914,

Boiardi immigrated to America passing through Ellis Island, at the suggestion of his brother, who at the time was a waiter at the New York Plaza Hotel. As his culinary talents were discovered Boiardi was promoted as a chef. While working at the Plaza, according to biographer Matt Blitz,

> "Boiardi so impressed customers that he was hired away to be the head chef at Barbetta [Restaurant] on 46th Street (where it is still located to this day). He also garnered a summer job cooking at the historic and ritzy Greenbrier Resort in White Sulphur Springs, West Virginia. While in this job, he took on the immense responsibility of catering the 1915 wedding reception of President Woodrow Wilson to Edith Bolling Galt. So impressed with Boiardi's cooking, Wilson chose him to supervise the homecoming meal of 2,000 returning World War I soldiers in late 1918. Soon after, he was offered a job he couldn't turn down - to be head of the kitchen at Cleveland's famed and very popular Hotel Winton."

By early 1920, Boiardi "was one of the most famous chefs in America" as proprietor of his own restaurant in Cleveland *Il Giardino d'Italia*. By the end of the 1920s, Boiardi ventured into factory production in Cleveland. The idea was to replicate the Italian dining experience by letting customers "take out" food to prepare and serve within their own homes. Biographer Matt Blitz explained, "the product was specifically sold under the name "Boy-Ar-Dee" so that Americans would correctly pronounce his last name." By 1940, "the Chef Boyardee brand introduced Italian food to millions of Americans." As described by the company, for the first time,

> "Italian food was being introduced to a mass market outside of the communities of Italian immigrants that had been enjoying it for generations, and Chef Boiardi is one of the reasons it soared in popularity."[679]

Ettore Boiardi was known mostly for macaroni products. The patent for the first hand-crank pasta machine to make "Flat Macaroni" invented by Angelo Vitantonio was submitted on May 20, 1919 and granted on March 2, 1920. The product noted the elimination of "the need to flatten and cut it by hand;" was on the patent application submitted in Cleveland, Ohio by son Luigi (who changed his name to "Louis De Vito").

---

[679] Matt Blitz. "Chef Boyardee Was a Real Person Who Brought Italian Food to America." *Food & Wine*, September 30, 2016. "The Untold Truth of Chef Boyardee." *Mashed.com*, March 21, 2022.

CHAPTER 11

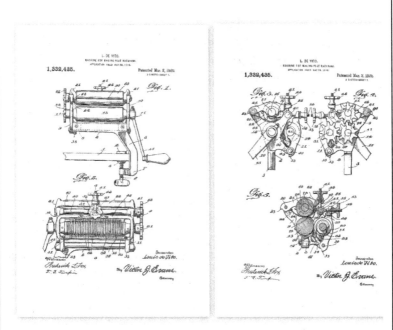

Copy of U.S. Patent issued March 2, 1920 for
"Making Flat Macaroni"
granted to Louis De Vito. (Public Domain)

"UNITED STATES PATENT OFFICE. LOUIS DE VITO, OF CLEVELAND, OHIO. MACHINE FOR MAKING FLAT MACARON I. 1,882,435.
Specification of Letters Patent, Patented War, 2, 1920.
Application filed May 20, 1919. Serial No. 298,353.
Be it known that, Louis De VITO, a citizen of the United States, residing at Cleveland, in the county of Cuyahoga and State of Ohio, have invented new and useful improvements in Machines for Making Flat Macaroni, of which the following is a specification.
"The object of my present invention is the provision of an efficient machine for making flat or ribbon-like macaroni."

Italian Food as "Cultural Cuisine"

Barbetta Restaurant (that once employed Boiardi) transformed the idea and the presentation of Italian "food" into "Cultural Cuisine" in America. Unlike the common attraction of southern Italian food choices, Barbetta offered the cuisine of Piedmont from the northwestern-most region. The "official history" on Barbetta's website cites,

> "Having celebrated its 100th Anniversary in 2006, [it] is the oldest restaurant in New York still owned by the family that founded it. A landmark among New York restaurants. . . . has been recognized by the prestigious and highly selective *Locali Storici d'Italia*, which has designated Barbetta a *Locale Storico* (Historic Establishment) the only restaurant in America to have been so named."

Originally "Maioglio Brothers" located on Manhattan's West 39th Street in 1906 by Vincenzo (b.?) and Sebastiano Maioglio (1880-2018), daughter Laura Maioglio took over in 1962. The official website notes, "The original restaurant was near the old Metropolitan Opera House and luminaries who dined there included Enrico Caruso, Giacomo Puccini and Arturo Toscanini" (see Chapter 7A). A stark departure from the southern Italian food, Barbetta Restaurant introduced some "firsts" into American culture under founder, Sebastiano Maioglio opening in 1906:

First Piemontese restaurant in New York
First to serve wild Porcini mushrooms
First to serve Risotto and Polenta
First Espresso machine in a restaurant (added in 1911)

Maioglio eliminated stereotypical décor of red and white checkerboard tablecloths providing an elegant interior décor. For over 100 years, Barbetta Restaurant was a stark departure from any previous association of eating Italian food. From its earliest days and well into the 21st century, Barbetta remains New York's "Most Elegant Italian Restaurant."[680]

---

[680] "History of Barbetta." *Barbetta Restaurant*, Accessed March 21, 2022.

CONCLUSION

A SCENARIO FOR A FINALE

---

*"Macaroni, Spaghetti, Pasta, Pizza, Pepperoni, Lasagna,
Gelato, Broccoli, Scampi, Minestrone, Panini, Cappuccino,
Espresso, Latte, Salami, Mozzarella, Opera, Diva, Ballerina,
Soprano, Solo, Stanza, Piccolo,* and *Extravaganza."*
(Some Italian Words in the American Vernacular)

They Came, They Saw, They Are Everywhere

The 2017 U.S. Census listed over 16.7 million people claiming Italian American heritage as permanently residing in the United States; almost six percent of the United States population of 325 million. Italian Americans were listed as the 7th largest ethnic group in America, but remain the most dominant culturally. The highest percentage of Italian Americans living within any one county was Richmond County in New York City at 38 percent. Followed by Suffolk County, also in New York with 28 percent; and Ocean County, New Jersey at 25 percent. The city of New Haven, Connecticut claims "the highest percentage of Italian Americans, making up 21.2 percent of the metro's population." Journalist Clare Trapasso claimed, a large number trace their ancestral roots to Naples, Italy resulting in a distinct "Pizza Culture" within New Haven.[681]

To dispel some myths, demographic surveys compiled by the Order Sons and Daughters of Italy in America (OSIA) reveals in *"A Profile of Today's Italian Americans,"*

> "Italian Americans are above average in their levels of education, income and occupation. The vast majority (88%) live in or near a big city, have small families (one child), low divorce rates (8%), and white-collar jobs (66%)."

The OSIA is "a support system for all Italian immigrants that would assist them

---

[681] Clare Trapasso. "CT city has the most Italian Americans in the U.S." *CTPost*, 2019.

with becoming U.S. citizens, provide health benefits and educational opportunities and offer assistance with assimilation in America."

Despite a long agricultural history of immigrants from small poor towns in southern Italy, many Italians took labor jobs in factories or as road crews. Many Italians arriving in America during the high-demand labor years of 1880 to 1920 were concentrated in urban "Metro Areas" (a shorten version of "Metropolitan Area" of the immediate region in the densely populated outlying areas closely situation near a major city).

The TEN METRO AREAS with The MOST ITALIAN AMERICANS

Rank	City	Italian Americans	Total Population
1.	New York	3,400,000	21,200,000
2.	Philadelphia	886,000	6,189,000
3.	Boston	801,000	5,800,000
4.	Chicago	637,000	9,158,000
5.	Los Angeles	568,000	16,373,000
6.	San Francisco	423,000	7,039,000
7.	Baltimore	378,000	7,600,000
8.	Pittsburgh	358,000	2,359,000
9.	Detroit	321,000	5,456,000
10.	Cleveland	78,000	2,946,000

Italians, as other ethic immigrant groups, often lived in slum areas. In many cases, Italians found themselves among other immigrants from the same town or region; neighborhoods became known as a "Little Italy."

The term "Little Italy" was applied to any neighborhood populated with a large majority of Italian immigrants who arrived within the cities after 1880. Most, if not all, American cities were comprised of various ethnic neighborhoods offering a refuge for shared culture, common language, and heritage. New York's Little Italy is the most famous; yet only one of many that include Baltimore, Boston, Chicago, Cleveland, Los Angeles, Omaha, Philadelphia, Providence, San Francisco, San Diego, and St. Louis, to name some of the most prominent. In Connecticut, Little Italy's are in the cities of Bridgeport, New Haven, and Waterbury. In New York State, in Rochester, Schenectady, and Syracuse. In the 21st century, San Diego in California boasts the largest Little Italy. Unlike others, the earliest Little Italy traces to Philadelphia settled during the 1700s. By mid-18th century at least 100 Italians settled in the City of Brotherly Love. In 1753, Benjamin Franklin recognizing the growing population proposed an Italian language course at Philadelphia College. The transition was often difficult, as

CONCLUSION

immigrants often maintained European customs which in turn became part of American culture; the most common was food.[682]

By 2017, Italy was the fifth most visited tourist destination with 58.3 million arrivals; as the flow of immigration of Italians to America has become almost non-existence. Many Italian Americans visit their ancestral homeland as tourists; a growing number apply for dual citizenship of America and Italy. A quirky aspects of tourism to New York City occurs as Italy represents the largest number of runners from any country, outside of the U.S. who compete and finish the New York City Marathon (3,125 out of 52,813 total runners in 2018 and 2,815 out of 53,640 in 2019). For runners, and tourists, the top destination is the Statue of Liberty. At the very least, to glimpse a view from a ride on the Staten Island Ferry, which many of those same runners see on marathon morning as they head to the start at the base of the Verrazzano Narrows Bridge; the famous bridge named after the Italian explorer. The lady in the harbor was a view that almost every Italian immigrant saw upon entry via the Ellis Island immigration center during the peak years of 1880 to 1920.

As reported in a 2019 statistical survey, journalist Clare Trapasso for the *Connecticut Post*, cited other metro areas with a high percentage of "Italian Americans in the U.S." include, Scranton, Pennsylvania and Ocean City, New Jersey both at 18.8 percent; nearby Atlantic City in New Jersey was at 17.9 percent; Central New York State of Kingston listed at 18.6 percent with an area to the north in the state capital city of Albany reported 17 percent. In nearby Connecticut the area of Bridgeport and Pittsfield, Massachusetts each at 16.5 percent. The Midwest area of Pittsburgh, Pennsylvania was 16.1 percent; nearby Youngstown, Ohio at 15 percent. Metro areas as Pittsburgh and Youngstown represent areas which once had large factory production centers such as steel making and mining, requiring a large immigrant labor force.[683]

The attraction for Italians settling in any area was simply "available work." For example, New Jersey urban centers within the New York Metropolitan region such as Newark, Patterson, and Jersey City, "all housed major industries and factories." According to the New Jersey Italian American Heritage Commission issued in 2010,

> "Italians make up the largest single ethnic group in New Jersey. The name New Jersey itself derives from the Latin *Nova Caesarea*. Nova is Latin for "new" and Caesarea comes from the Roman name given to the Jersey Islands off of England, in honor of Julius Caesar."

In the areas of southern and central New Jersey such as Ocean City, Atlantic City,

---

[682] Nile Cappello. "The Best Little Italy's to Visit Across the U.S." January 19, 2016.
[683] Trapasso. "CT city has the most Italian Americans in the U.S." *CTPost*, 2019.

528   Italian Culture in America:
        The Immigrants 1880 to 1930 From Discrimination to Assimilation

and Vineland "there were jobs on the area farms." An overview by the Italian American Heritage Commission explained,

> "[Italians] came to America in search to work in the burgeoning factories of the American Industrial Revolution. These factories included silk and cotton mills. Some Italians were skilled masons, stonecutters, and sculptors. Many men found work building new Catholic churches in New Jersey; women were seamstresses in the garment factories. Many settled in large urban centers such as Trenton, Newark, Paterson, and Jersey City. By the 1930s, Italian agrarian colonies were present in Vineland, Hammonton, and Woolwich, where Italians worked on farms as seasonal workers."

Statistics as applied to New Jersey mirrors the reason for the Italian immigrant migration throughout all the other areas of the United States.[684]

For many Italian-American descendants (such as this author) a familiar migratory pattern included Italian immigrants traveling through Ellis Island; some settling in New York City. For this author born in Brooklyn descended from four Italian immigrant grandparents, a migratory pattern during my teens took our family to the borough of Staten Island. An older adult life followed our own children into the suburban rural areas of Central New Jersey – fully assimilated in our American heritage yet ever mindful and thankful, of our Italian heritage.

Only Some of the Italian Words in the American Vernacular

Within American culture are words which are not always spoken on a daily basis. One example, such as "Impresario" is cited by *Merriam-Webster* dictionary as an English usage word borrowed "directly from Italian." As such dozens, if not hundreds, of words have found their way into everyday American vernacular tracing their origins directly from the Italian language.

The most prominent words might be *Macaroni*, *Spaghetti*, *Pasta*, and of course *Pizza*, possibly with *Pepperoni* as a topping. Is anyone unfamiliar with easily ordering *Lasagna*, *Gelato*, *Broccoli*, or *Scampi*. Or possibly *Minestrone* soup, or more recently a *Panini* easily accompanied by a *Cappuccino*, *Espresso*, *Latte*, and *Biscotti*. Americans regularly purchase "Italian Bread" or ask for "Tomato Sauce." A routine Deli order of *Salami* or *Mozzarella* occurs without a blink of the eye, nor with any credit to the Italian contribution.

Geography terms prevail including *Volcano* and *Lava*, some as the destructive Italian eruption at Pompei in southern Italy. Our world is haunted by the existence of unfortunate lethal maladies such as *Influenza* and *Malaria*. To alleviate the negative aspects of human existence some of the most respected

---

[684] "New Jersey Italian and Italian American Heritage Commission," 2010.

cultural elements of music include *Opera, Diva, Ballerina, Soprano*, and a *Solo*. Most are familiar with a musical *Stanza*, sometimes played on a *Piccolo*, presented as a *Scenario* for a *Finale* as an *Extravaganza*, which hopefully would not be a *Fiasco*.

Some film buffs, such as this author might associate *Magenta* as a character from the movie *Rocky Horror Picture Show*, others easily recognize it as a popular color representing "universal love at its highest level." The high heels worn by Frank N Furter (actor Tim Curry) in the aforementioned movie might be considered as *Stilettos*, or sometimes an association of the knife applied in a derogatory sense of the early Italian immigrants. Millions of Americans are familiar with gambling in a *Casino*; or the movie of the same name directed by the great Italian American director Martin Scorsese, also known for many movies portraying Italian mobsters.[685]

The wanton use of the word *Mafia* first gained nationwide derogatory association with Italians during the 1891 New Orleans lynching. More recently it is a term for a group aligned with a celebrity such as the "Memphis Mafia" for the Elvis Presley entourage, or its application among African Americans in the Rap music community. *Propaganda* as a word applied more so in the negative use by Nazi Germany as Europeans were forced into a *Ghetto*; which was also one placing Italians into tenements in American ghettos. A lively discussion can be held on the merits of *Graffiti* as an art form; or the *Paparazzi* as an intrusion upon the public life of a celebrity; a word associated with "celebration" which is not always complete without *Confetti*.

Despite the fact "Gonzo" takes on a very inappropriate connotation in pornography, or the exaggerated, bizarre, or crazy journalistic writing style (maybe even as illustrated by these paragraphs), I rather am enthralled by the lovable *Gonzo* of "Sesame Street" fame. And of course, I would not hold a personal *Vendetta* against anyone not realizing the word derivative of naming the nation as *America* in honor of the Italian explorer Amerigo Vespucci.[686]

---

[685] See: "The Color Magenta," *Empowered by Color*, Accessed January 13, 2021.
[686] See: Heather Broster. "50 Common Italian Words Used in the English Language," November 2, 2019. Accessed January 13, 2021. https://dailyitalianwords.com/50-common-italian-words-used-in-the-english-language/

CONCLUSION - *"CONCLUSIONE"*

With so many Italian immigrants achieving fame within America and influencing American culture, the immigrant parents and grandparents remain virtually anonymous. As a common factor in the Italian American experience, historian Janice Therese Mancuso created an honor role of "Thirty-One Days" each October to celebrate Italian History month. On each day of the month one notable Italian-American is "lauded for their contribution to this American country which adopted their immigrant ancestors." In 2020, Ms. Mancuso broke from the singular traditional honorific by acknowledging, not just the famous; rather all who immigrated during the "Great Arrival;" thereby proclaiming,

Day 1: The Italian Immigrant for Italian American Heritage Month

"This day is for the parents, grandparents, great-grandparents, and beyond – every Italian who journeyed to America from Italy, regardless of the route. It's to honor those who sought to make a better life for themselves and their families, to remember them for the sacrifices they endured, and to thank them for the opportunities they provided us and for their contributions to America."[687]

No better befitting conclusion is necessary since there is no ending to the Italian American cultural experience. A continued legacy of cultural influence continues to grow and become even more dominant in America through the years after the Second World War, and continuing into the 21st century.

Grazie a tutti

---

[687] See: Janice Therese Mancuso. "Thirty-One Days," October 1, 2020.

APPENDIX

Historical Italian Immigration Documents

Top: Cover page and page 8 of an Italian passport for Annina "Anna" Colocino (authors grandmother). **Bottom**: pages 6 and 7 of author's Great Grandmother Maria Paone. Note: The combined passport booklet contained 20 pages of documents for both Anna and Maria, c. 1920.

Naturalization Document declaring Antonio Dattilo (author's grandfather) "Naturalized" in 1929 and Citizenship granted in 1939.

Travel Visa and Immigration Document issued by "General of Italian Navigation – The Emigration Office of Naples for a Boarding Ticket – 3rd Class for Antonio Dattilo (author's grandfather) on the ship "Cristoforo Colombo" to depart with "eventual objective for New York from the Port of Naples, this date 7 September 1922." (Translation by Nicholas Pellegrino).

SELECT BIBLIOGRAPHY

Accinno, Michael David. "Organ Grinder's Swing: Representations of Street Music in New York City, 1850-1937." *University of Iowa,* July 2010.

Addams, Jane. Twenty Years at Hull-House with Autobiographical Notes. New York: The MacMillan Company, 1912.

Aleandri, Emelise. *The Italian-American Immigrant Theatre of New York City,* Mount Pleasant, South Carolina: Arcadia Publishing, 1999.

Allen, Frederick Lewis. *Only Yesterday: An Informal History of the 1920s.* New York: Harper Collins Perennial Classics, reprint 2000.

Anbinder, Tyler. *City of Dreams.* New York: Houghton Mifflin, 2016.

Andrews, Thomas G. *Killing for Coal: America's Deadliest Labor War.* Cambridge: Harvard University Press, 2008.

Armstrong, Louis. *Swing That Music. Cambridge, Massachusetts: Da Capo Press, 1993, (First printing 1936).*

Baker, Jean H. *Margaret Sanger: A Life of Passion.* New York: Hill and Wang, 2011.

Baughman, Judith S., ed. *American Decades: 1920–1929.* Detroit, Mich.: Gale Research, 1996.

Belfiglio, Valentine. *The Italian Experience in Texas.* Austin, Texas: Eakin Press, 1983.

Billington, Ray A. *The Protestant Crusade, 1800–1860: A Study of the Origins of American Nativism.* Chicago: Quadrangle Books, 1964.

Binder, Frederick M. and David M. Reimers. *All Nations Under Heaven.* New York: Columbia University Press: Revised Edition, 1996.

Block, Alex Ben and Lucy Autrey Wilson, eds. *George Lucas's Blockbusting.* New York: Harper Collins, 2010.

Bolt, Rodney. *The Librettist of Venice; The Remarkable Life of Lorenzo Da Ponte; Mozart's Poet, Casanova's Friend, and Italian Opera's Impresario in America.* Edinburgh, U.K.: Bloomsbury, 2006.

Brace, Charles Loring. *The Dangerous Classes of New York.* New York: Wynkoop & Hallenbeck Publishers, 1872.

Braden, Donna R. *Leisure and Entertainment in America.* Dearborn, Michigan: Henry Ford Museum & Greenfield Village, 1988.

Brockway, Wallace and Herbert Weinstock. *The World of Opera.* New York: Modern Library Giant, 1966.

Bruccoli, Matthew J., and Richard Layman, eds. *American Decades: 1900-1909.* and *1910-1919.* Detroit: Gale Research, 1996.

Brunn, H. O. *The Story of the Original Dixieland Jazz Band.* Literary Licensing LLC, 2011.

Cangiano, Victor. "Congregation of Missionaries of St. Borromeo." *The Catholic Encyclopedia.* New York: Appleton Company, 1913.

Catania, Basilio. *Antonio Meucci: The Inventor and his Time. New York 1850-1871.* Rome: Seat Divisione, 1999.

Carroll, Linda L. *Thomas Jefferson's Italian and Italian-Related Books. in* New York: Bordighera Press, 2019.

Cavalieri, Lina. *My Secrets of Beauty.* New York, 1914.

Celenza, Anna Harwell. *Jazz Italian Style from its Origins in New Orleans to Fascist Italy and Sinatra.* Cambridge University Press, 2017.

Ciotola, Nicholas P. "Ellis Island," in *Italian Americans*, Eric Martone, editor. Santa Barbara, California: ABC-Clio, 2017.

Corsi, Edward. *In the Shadow of Liberty: The Chronicles of Ellis Island.* New York: Macmillan, 1935.

D'Angelo, Pasquale. *Son of Italy: The Autobiography of Pascal d'Angelo, the Pick and Shovel Poet.* New York: Macmillan Company, 1924.

Davis, Ronald L. *The Social and Cultural Life of the 1920s.* New York: Holt Rinehart and Winston, 1972.

Delaney, Carol. *Columbus and the Quest for Jerusalem.* New York: Free Press, 2011.

Del Bianco, Lou. *Out of Rushmore's Shadow: The Luigi Del Bianco Story.* Niche Content Press, 2017.

Dizikes, John. *Opera in America: A Cultural History.* New Haven: Yale University Press, 1993.

Durante, Francesco, ed. *Italoamericana: The Literature of the Great Migration, 1880-1943.* New York: Fordham Univ. Press, 2014.

Ellenberger, Allan R. *The Valentino Mystique: The Death and Afterlife of the Silent Film Idol. North Carolina.* McFarland & Co. Inc., 2005.

Ellis, Richard J. *To the Flag: The Unlikely History of the Pledge of Allegiance.* Lawrence, Kansas: University Press of Kansas, 2005.

Faedda, Barbara. *From Da Ponte to the Casa Italiana: A Brief History of Italian Studies.* New York: Columbia University Press, 2017.

SELECT BIBLIOGRAPHY

Fields, Armond. *Tony Pastor, Father of Vaudeville*. Jefferson, North Carolina: McFarland, 2007.

Foerster, Robert E. *The Italian Emigration of Our Times*. Cambridge: Harvard University Press, 1919.

Foner, Eric. *The Story of American Freedom*. New York: Norton, 1998.

Gambino, Richard. Vendetta: The True Story of the Largest Lynching in *U.S. History*. Toronto, Canada: Guernica Editions Inc., 1998.

Gatti-Casazza, Giulio. Memories of the Opera [Autobiography]. New York, Scribner's 1941.

Garibaldi, Giuseppe. *Autobiography*. New York: Howard Fertig, 1971.

Gates, Jr., Henry Louis. *Stony Road: Reconstruction, White Supremacy, and the Rise of Jim Crow*. New York: Penguin Books, 2020.

Giordano, Ralph G. *The Architectural Ideology of Thomas Jefferson*. Jefferson, North Carolina: McFarland & Company, 2012.

Giordano, Ralph G. *Fun and Games in 20th Century America*. Westport, Connecticut: Greenwood Press, 2003.

Giordano, Ralph G. *Italian Culture in America: How a Founding Father Introduced Italian Art, Architecture, Food, Wine, and Liberty to the American People*. Academica Press, 2020.

Giordano, Ralph G. *Satan in the Dance Hall: Rev. John Roach Straton, Social Dancing, and Morality in 1920s New York City*. Lanham, Maryland: Scarecrow Press 2008.

Gladstone, Douglas. *Carving a Niche for Himself: The Untold Story of Luigi Del Bianco*. New York: Bordighera Press, 2014.

Gordon, Linda. *The Second Coming of the KKK: The Ku Klux Klan of the 1920s*. New York: W.W. Norton, 2017.

Gracyk, Tim. *Popular American Recording Pioneers 1895 -1925*. New York: Routledge, 2000.

Guglielmo, Jennifer and Salvatore Salerno. *Are Italians White? How Race is Made in America*. New York: Routledge 2003.

Higham, John. *Strangers in the Land: Patterns of American Nativism, 1860-1925*. New Jersey: Rutgers University Press, 2000.

Hodges, Shelia. *Lorenzo Da Ponte: The Life and Times of Mozart's Librettist*. Madison, Wisconsin: University of Wisconsin, 2002.

Iorizzo, Luciano J. and Salvatore Mondello. *The Italian Americans*. Youngstown, New York: Cambria Press, 2006.

Irving, Washington. *A History of the Life and Voyages of Christopher Columbus*. G&C Carvill, Broadway, New York, 1828.

Jaffe, Irma B., ed. *The Italian Presence in American Art 1860-1920*. New York: Fordham University Press, 1992.

Juliani, Richard N. *Building Little Italy: Philadelphia's Italians Before Mass Migration*. University Park: Penn State University, 1998.

Kilpatrick, William. *The Montessori System Examined*. New York; Houghton Mifflin, 1914.

Kline, Christina Baker. *Orphan Train*. New York: Harper Collins, 2013.

Kline, David. "Rudolph Valentino," in Block and Wilson, eds. *George Lucas's Blockbusting*. New York: Harper Collins, 2010.

Kramer, Rita. *Maria Montessori: A Biography*. Chicago: 1976.

Kraut, Alan. *The Huddled Masses: The Immigrant in American Society, 1880-1921*. Open Library: Harlan Davidson, Inc., 1982, 2001.

LaGumina, Salvatore, ed. *The Italian American Experience: An Encyclopedia*. New York: Garland, 2000.

Laskin, David. *The Long Way Home: An American Journey from Ellis Island to the Great War*. New York: Harper Perennial, 2011.

Laurino, Maria. *Italian Americans: A History*. New York: W. W. Norton & Company, 2015.

Loewen, James W. *Lies My Teacher Told Me: Everything Your American History Textbook Got Wrong*. New York: The New Press, 1995.

Macesich, George. *Central Banking: The Early Years* Westport, CT. Praeger Publishers, 2000.

Mangione, Jerre and Ben Morreale. *La Storia: Five Centuries of the Italian American Experience*. New York: Harper Collins, 1992.

Marchione, Sister Margherita. *Peter and Sally Sammartino: Biographical Notes*, Cornwall Books, 1994.

Marchione, Margherita. *The Religious Teachers Filippini in America*.

Mahwah: New Jersey, Paulist Press, 2010.

Marino, Cesare. *The Remarkable Carlo Gentile: Pioneer Italian Photographer*. Nevada City: Carl Mautz Publishing, 1998.

Martelle, Scott. *Blood Passion: The Ludlow Massacre and Class War in the American West*. New Brunswick: Rutgers Univ. Press, 2007.

Martone, Eric, editor. *Italian Americans: The History and Culture of a People*. Santa Barbara, California: ABC-Clio, 2017.

McGoldrick, Jane ed. *United States Senate Catalog of Fine Art*. U.S. Government Printing Office, 2003.

Miler-Cribbs, J. and J. Mains. (2011). "Amelia Earhart: Social worker," *Social Welfare History Project*. May 19, 2022.

SELECT BIBLIOGRAPHY

Miller, Francis Trevelyan and John W. Davis. *Geography by Grades, Grade 4B.* New York: Hinds, Hayden & Eldredge, 1926.

Miller, Nathan. *New World Coming: The 1920s and the Making of Modern America.* New York: Da Capo Press, Reprint edition 2004.

Molinari, Luca and Andrea Canepari, eds. *The Italian Legacy in Washington, D.C. Architecture, Design, Art and Culture.* Milan, Italy: Skira Editore, 2007.

Monod, David. "Art with the Effervescence of Ginger Beer: The Creation of Vaudeville," in *The Soul of Pleasure.* New York: Cornell University Press, 2016.

Montessori, Carolina. *Maria Montessori Sails to America: A Private Diary, 1913.* Association Montessori International, 2013.

Montessori, Maria. *The Montessori Method.* New York: Frederick A. Stokes Company, in English, 1912.

Mulas, Francesco. *Studies on Italian-American Literature,* Staten Island, New York: Center for Migration Studies, 1995.

Nasaw, David. *Going Out: The Rise and Fall of Public Amusements.* New York: Basic Books, 1993.

O'Brien, Keith. *Fly Girls: How Five Daring Women Defied All Odds and Made Aviation History.* New York: Mariner Books, 2018.

Okrent, Daniel. *The Guarded Gate: Bigotry, Eugenics and the Law That Kept Two Generations of Jews, Italians, and Other European Immigrants Out of America.* New York: Scribner; 2019.

Palmes, J.C. editor, *Sir Banister Fletcher's A History of Architecture,* New York: Charles Scribner's Sons; 18th edition, 1975.

Panunzio, Constantine M. *The Soul of An Immigrant,* New York: The Macmillan Company, 1922.

Pastor, Tony. *Tony Pastor's Great Sensation Songbook.* New York: Dick and Fitzgerald, 1863.

Peiss, Kathy. *Cheap Amusements.* Philadelphia: Temple University, 1986.

Peragallo, Olga. *Italian-American Authors and Their Contribution to American Literature.* New York: S. F. Vanni, 1949.

Phillips-Matz, Mary Jane. *Rosa Ponselle: American Diva.* Boston: Northeastern University Press, 1997.

Pitkin, Thomas. *Keepers of the Gate: A History of Ellis Island.* New York University Press, 1975.

Pucci, Idanna. *The Lady of Sing Sing.* New York: Tiller Press-Simon & Schuster, 2020.

Puzo, Mario. *The Fortunate Pilgrim.* New York: Ballentine Books, 1997.

Reynolds, Donald Martin. *Monuments and Masterpieces*. New York: MacMillan, 1988.

Riis, Jacob. *Battle with the Slum*. New York: The Macmillan Company, 1902. *Project Gutenberg E-Book*, November 20, 2020.

Riis, Jacob. *How the Other Half Lives: Studies Among the Tenements of New York.* New York: Charles Scribner's Sons, 1890.

Rolle, Andrew F. *The American Italians: Their History and Culture*. University of California Press, 1972.

Rolle, Andrew F. *Westward the Immigrants: Italian Adventurers and Colonists in an Expanding America.* Norman, Oklahoma: University of Oklahoma Press, 1999.

Rotella, Mark. *Amore: The Story of Italian American Song*. New York: Farrar, Straus and Giroux, 2010.

Sanger, Margaret. *Woman and the New Race*. Middletown, Delaware: Odin's Library Classics 2020.

Schiavo, Giovanni E. *Antonio Meucci: Inventor of the Telephone*. New York: Vigo Press, 1958.

Schiavo, Giovanni. *Four Centuries of Italian-American History*. New York: Center for Migration Studies, 1992.

Schiavo, Giovanni E. *The Italian Contribution to the Catholic Church*. New York: Vigo Press, 1947.

Schiavo, Giovanni E. *The Truth about the Mafia and Organized Crime in America.* New York: Vigo Press, 1962.

Schlup, Leonard and James G. Ryan. *Historical Dictionary of the Gilded Age*. New York: M.E. Sharpe, 2003.

Severini, Gino. *The Life of a Painter*, Princeton University Press, 1995.

Sklar, Robert. *Movie-Made America: A Cultural History of American Movies*. New York: Vintage Books, 1994.

Standing, E.M. *Maria Montessori: Her Life and Work*. New York, 1984.

Stephens, Ellen Yale. *A Guide to the Montessori Method*. Toronto: Bell and Cockburn, 1913.

Stutesman, Drake. "Natacha Rambova," in: Jane Gaines, Radha Vatsal, Monica Dall'Asta, eds. Women Film Pioneers Project. New York: Columbia University Libraries, 2013.

Tejada, Susan. *In Search of Sacco and Vanzetti*. Boston: Northeastern University Press, 2012.

Todd, Anne M. Italian Immigrants: 1880-1920 (Coming to America). Capstone Press

Tracy Terhune, *Valentino: The Unforgotten*. Bloomington Indiana: Author House, 2007

Tetrazzini, Luisa. *How to Sing*. New York: George H. Doran Co., 1923.

SELECT BIBLIOGRAPHY

Tetrazzini, Luisa. *My Life of Song*. London: Cassell & Company 1921.

Time-Life Books. *This Fabulous Century: 1900-1910, Vol. I.* New York: Time-Life Books, 1988.

Time-Life Books. *This Fabulous Century: 1910-1920, Vol. II.* New York: Time-Life Books, 1988.

Time-Life Books. *This Fabulous Century: 1920-1930, Vol. III.* New York: Time-Life Books, 1988.

Trav S.D. (Donald Travis Stewart). *No Applause, Just Throw Money: The Book That Made Vaudeville Famous.,* New York: Farrar, Straus, and Giroux, 2005.

Ullman, S. George. *Valentino as I Knew Him.* New York: A.L. Burt Company, 1927.

Vecoli, Rudolph J. "The Search for Italian American Identity: Continuity and Change," in *Italian Americans: New Perspectives in Italian Immigration and Ethnicity,* edited by Lydio Tomasi. Staten Island: Center for Migration Studies, 1985.

Venturi, Franco. *Italy and the Enlightenment.* New York: New York University Press, 1972.

Veronesi, Gene P. *Italian-Americans & Their Communities of Cleveland.* Online Digital of 1977 Print Edition updated March 2003. Cleveland State University Library Cleveland Memory Project.

Warren, Andrea. *Orphan Train Rider: One Boy's True Story.* New York: Houghton Mifflin, 1996.

Washington, Booker T. *The Man Farthest Down.* New York: Doubleday, Page & Co. 1912.

Zellers, Parker. *Tony Pastor: Dean of the Vaudeville Stage.* Ypsilanti: Eastern Michigan University Press, 1971.

SELECTED PERIODICALS

____ About Ghirardelli." *Ghirardelli Chocolate.* Accessed March 3, 2021. https://www.ghirardelli.com/about-ghirardelli.

____ "Abraham Lincoln." *Foundation of the Union League of Philadelphia,* October 2, 2020.

Adams, Adeline. "A Family of Sculptors." *The American Magazine of Art,* Vol. 12, No. 7 (July, 1921), pp. 223-230.

Adegeest, Don-Alvin. "Salvatore Ferragamo to launch 'Italy in Hollywood' exhibition." *Fashion United,* March 28, 2018.

Adler, Dick. "The Man Who Knew Mozart." *American Heritage* magazine April/May 1986, Vol. 37 No. 3.

Aiuti, Simona. "The Statue of Liberty is Born from an Italian Intuition." *Italiani l'Italia nel cuore,* April 7, 2019.

____ "Amadeo Giannini: Golden Gate Bridge." *American Experience,* PBS Thirteen, Accessed February 27, 2021.

___ "America's First City of Opera: New Orleans has long reigned as America's First City of Opera." *NewOrleans.com*.

Andersson, Mogens H. "American history of Opera from 18th Century." *Operalogg*, December 8, 2015.

Andrews, Brittany. "Ranked: The Five Greatest Italian-American Boxers." *NYFights,com*. November 22, 2020.

Andrews, Evan. "Why Lincoln Wanted an Italian Freedom Fighter to Lead His Army." *History.com*, August 31, 2018.

Angelini, Andrea. "How Many Italians Were on the Titanic?" *Italics Magazine*, May 16, 2020.

Antonucci, Pia. "Italo Marchiony, Inventor of the Ice Cream Cone." *Mt. Carmel Christian Society*, 2013.

Arakelyan, Ashot. "Ferruccio Giannini (Tenor)." *Forgotten Opera Singers*, August 21, 2011.

Armstrong, A. "Lina Cavalieri, the Famous Beauty of the Operatic Stage." *Munsey's Magazine*, 39 (1), April, 1908.

Augustyn, Adam. "Commedia dell'arte: Italian theatre." *Encyclopædia Britannica*, November 18, 2019.

Axelrod, Jim. "Mount Rushmore's Chief Carver Gets his Due." *CBS Sunday Morning*, September 17, 2017. *YouTube*, 5:00 min.

Balaskas, Peter A. "Meet the Brothers Behind the Construction of NYC Landmarks." *Bespoke Concierge Magazine*, July 20, 2015.

Batella, Fausto. "The Italian American stars in US sports: Boxing." *We The Italians* magazine, June 16, 2017.

Battocchi, Mario. "At 200, Verdi Lives on in Golden Gate Park." *San Francisco, Italy*.

Belsom, Jack. "A History of Opera in New Orleans." *Operalogg.com*.

Berger, Joseph. "A Century Later, the Roll of the Dead in a Factory Fire Now Has All 146 Names." *New York Times* 2/21/2011, A13.

Berger, Ralph. "Ping Bodie." *Society for American Baseball Research*. Accessed April 27, 2022.

Berkes, Anna. "Ice Cream." *Monticello.org*, June 28, 2013.

Blitz, Matt. "Chef Boyardee Was a Real Person Who Brought Italian Food to America." *Food & Wine*, September 30, 2016.

___ "Biography of Maria Montessori." *Association Montessori Internazionale*. Accessed January 20, 2022.

___ "Blaming Columbus for Every Evil since 1492 is Easy but Wrong." *The Times Herald*, October 9, 2017.

Botein, Barbara. "The Hennessy Case: An Episode in Anti-Italian Nativism." Louisiana History: *The Journal of the Louisiana Historical Association*, Vol. 20 No. 3 (Summer, 1979).

Bowen, Susan W. "Lorenzo Da Ponte: Mozart's American Librettist." *The Schiller Institute,* 2006.

Broster, Heather. "50 Common Italian Words Used in the English Language." November 2, 2019.

SELECT BIBLIOGRAPHY 541

Burgos, Matthew. "All that Italian Jazz." *Italics Magazine*, May 12, 2020.

Campanella, Angelo. "Antonio Meucci, The Speaking Telegraph, and The First Telephone." *Acoustics Today*. July 4, 2008.

Cannato, Vincent J., "How America Became Italian." *The Washington Post* October 9, 2015.

Carroll, Rory. "US Finally Admits Italian Invented Telephone." *The Guardian,* June 16, 2002.

Castro, Maria. "The Piccirilli Brothers." *Bronx Journal,* 2001, p. A2.

Celenza, Anna. "Our Jazz is Culturally Black, but its Global Dissemination owes a lot to Italians." *The Lens*, May 1, 2017.

Cipalla, Rita. "Italian Immigrant Coal Miners in Black Diamond." *History Link.org*, April 14, 2018.

Cipalla, Rita. "Italian Immigrants: How They Helped Define the Wine Industry of Walla Walla." *History Link.org*, July 19, 2018.

____ "Columbus Day started in Colorado." *The Denver Post*, September 23, 2010.

Cornell, Bryan. "The First Jazz Recording: One Hundred Years Later." *U.S. Library of Congress*, March 3, 2017.

____ Creative Commons License. *Wikipedia.org.* Accessed March 9, 2022. https://en.wikipedia.org/wiki/Creative_Commons_license

Crutchfield, Will. "Brillante: Antonio Pini-Corsi." *Teatro Nuovo*, 2020.

Davenport, William E. "The Italian Immigrant in America." (Illustrated with Photographs by Arthur Hewitt) *The Outlook* Vol. 73, no. 1.

Di Ionno, Mark. "PBS film on Italian-Americans Shows Forgotten, Painful History." *NJ Advance Media for NJ.com*, March 29, 2019.

Drake, David. "The Homage: Mafia Culture's Influence on Rap Music," *Complex*, June 15, 2015.

Editorial Staff. "The Most Important Bank in America is Italian." *NonèRadio*, July 8, 2019

____ "Enea Bossi: Aviation Pioneer." *Italy on this Day*, March 29, 2017. Accessed August 7, 2021.

____ "Enrico Caruso Famous Singer Dies in Naples." *Colorado Loveland Reporter* of August 2, 1921, No. 298.

Enss, Chris. "Wild Women of the West: Giuseppina Morlacchi." *Cowgirl Magazine*, April 16, 2019.

Falco, Ed. "When Italian Immigrants Were 'the Other." *CNN*, 2012.

Farrell, Helen Farrell and Anna McGee. "Santa Croce and the Statue of Liberty to Become Partners." *The Florentine,* July 8, 2016.

Femminella, Francis X. "The Impact of Italian Migration and American Catholicism." *American Catholic Sociological Review*, Vol. 22, no. 3, 1961, pp. 233–241.

Fierro, Rafaele. "Sylvester Poli, Negotiating Cultural Politics in an Age of Immigration." *Connecticut History*, August 31, 2020.

Firmani, B.G. "The Dreamlife of Pascal D'Angelo." February 25, 2017. *Forte E Gentile.*

Frankfurter, Felix. "The Case of Sacco and Vanzetti." *The Atlantic Monthly* (March 1, 1927).

Fressola, Michael J. "Tracking Garibaldi on Staten Island." *Staten Island Advance*, March 13, 2011.

Friswold, Paul. "The Forgotten History of Racism at the 1904 World's Fair in St. Louis." *Riverfront Times*, May 2, 2018.

Foerster, Robert F. "Italian Emigration of our Times." (Cambridge: Harvard University Press. 1919, Vol. 14 No. 3, August 1920.

Gallo, Denise. "The American Violin: From Jefferson to Jazz." *Library of Congress Information Bulletin*, May 2006 - Vol. 65, No. 5.

Gandhi, Lakshmi. "How Columbus Sailed into U.S. History, Thanks To Italians." October 14, 2013. *NPR.org,*

____ "Garibaldi Meucci Museum Restoration." *Order Sons of Italy in America*, May 4, 2009.

____ "Giuseppe M. Bellanca." *Bellanca Airfield Museum, 2021.*

____ "Giuseppe Garibaldi." *U.S. States Senate Catalogue of Fine Art.*

____ "The Great Arrival." *The Library of Congress*, Immigration and Relocation in U.S. History.

Gumina, Deanna Paoli. "*Connazionali, Stenterello*, and *Farfariello*: Italian Variety Theater in San Francisco." California Historical Quarterly (1975) 54 (1): pp. 27–36.

Haas, Edward F. "Guns, Goats, and Italian: The Tallulah Lynching of 1899." *North Louisiana Historical Association.* Vol. XIII, 1982.

Harlan, Jennifer. "Overlooked No More: Emma Stebbins, Who Sculpted an Angel of New York." *The New York Times*, May 29, 2015.

Harris, Andrea. "*Sur la Pointe* on the Prairie: Giuseppina Morlacchi and the Urban Problem in the Frontier Melodrama." *The Journal of American Drama and* Theatre, Vol. 27 No. 1.

Higham, John. "Origins of Immigration Restriction, 1882-1897: A Social Analysis." *The Mississippi Valley Historical Review*, Vol. 39.

____ "The Immigration Act of 1924 (Johnson-Reed Act)." Office of the Historian, Foreign Service Institute United States Dept. of State.

____ "Italian American Statistics." *National Italian American Foundation* (NIAF), 2022.

King, Gilbert. "The Latin Lover and his Enemies." *Smithsonian Magazine*, June 13, 2012.

Larsen, Erik. "The Ku Klux Klan was Welcomed at the Jersey Shore." *The Asbury Park Press*, August 22, 2017.

Latson, Jennifer. "Why Birth Control Pioneer Margaret Sanger Kept Getting Arrested." *Time* magazine, October 16, 2015.

Laurino, Maria. "The Italian Journey, Though Two Men." *The New York Daily News*, February 14, 2015.

Lederer II, Francis L. "Nora Marks, Investigative Reporter." *Journal of the Illinois State Historical Society* pp. 306-318.

SELECT BIBLIOGRAPHY

Librettist Became the Father of Italian Studies at Columbia." *Columbia Magazine* Winter 2020-21.

Lidz, Franz. "Pie is a Constant: In Naples, the formula calls for Pizza." *Smithsonian* magazine, March 2021, pp. 38-51; 78-81.

___ "Lina Cavalieri Biography," IMDb.com. May 19, 2021.

___ "Lina Cavalieri and the Most Beautiful Kiss in the World." *Italian Ways*, March 8, 2017.

Little, Becky. "U.S. Immigration History." *History.com,* 2020 A&E Television Networks, LLC.

Lodge, Henry Cabot. "Lynch Law and Unrestricted Immigration." *North American Review*, Univ. of Northern Iowa, Vol. 152, No. 414 (May, 1891), pp. 602- 612.

Luconi, Stefano. "Italians and Italy." *The Encyclopedia of Greater Philadelphia*, 2017, Rutgers University, July 5, 2021.

Maeder, Jay. "When thousands swarmed NYC's streets for 'Latin Lover Rudolph Valentino's funeral," *New York Daily News*, 9/17/ 2017.

Marinari, Maddalena. "Another time in history that the US created travel bans against Italians," *The World,* October 2, 2017.

Martegana, Giuseppe. "Giuseppe Garibaldi." *United States Senate*, Reprinted Courtesy of Office of the Senate Curator.

Mason, Patrick. "Blaming Columbus Misses, the Lessons of History," *Catholic News Agency*, October 9, 2017.

McMillan, Tracie. "How Italian Cuisine Became as American as Apple Pie." *National Geographic*, May 4, 2016.

Midgette, Anne. "Coming to the U.S.: 'The Year of Italian Culture 2013." *The Washington Post.* October 17, 2012.

Napp, Abigail. "Ellis Island: Finally, Lady Liberty Meets her Italian Twin 'Libertà della Poesia.'" *VNY La Voce di New York.* Oct. 20, 2019.

Norris, David. "Remembering the real 'Inventors of Jazz,'" *The Irish Times*, July 8, 2017.

Offit, Paul A. "The Loathsome American Book That Inspired Hitler," *The Daily Beast*, August 26, 2017.

Omohundro, Rick. "Giuseppina Antonia 'Josephine' Morlacchi Omohundro." *Find-A-Grave*, April 14, 2013.

Pantano, Kayla. "The Italy of Thomas Jefferson." *I-Italy.org* "All things Italian in America." April 18, 2017.

Pozzetta, George E., "From Immigrants to Ethnics: The Italian American Experience," *Journal of American Ethnic History,* pp. 67-95.

___ "Radio's Valentino." *Radio Guide* Vol. 1. No. 6, Dec. 1931.

Roberts, Sam. "An Immigrant's Contribution to Mount Rushmore Is Recognized, 75 Years Later." *New York Times,* 6/29/2016, A20.

Rodriguez, Jessica. "Enea Bossi: Father of the Stainless Steel Aircraft." *USAonRace*, May 26, 2010.

Romeyn, Esther (1994) "Performing High, Performing Low: Enrico Caruso and Eduardo Migliaccio," *Differentia: Review of Italian Thought*: Vol. 6, Article 15, pp. 165-175.

____ "Rudolph Valentino: Topics in Chronicling America." *The Library of Congress*.

Schuyler, Eugene. "Italian Immigration into the United States." *Political Science Quarterly*, Vol. 4, No. 3 (Sep., 1889), pp. 480-495.

Shelley, Mary and Bill Carroll. "History: Piccirilli Brothers." *Leman.edu*, March 13, 2022.

Sketch, Margherita. "Italy in Hollywood." *Controradio*, June 10, 2018.

Small, Matthew. "Harlem's Hidden History: The Real Little Italy Was Uptown." *Harlem Focus*, July 17, 2016.

Spahr, Rob. "Vineland Celebrates its 150th Anniversary with Parade, Fireworks, and Cake." *The Press of Atlantic City*, August 8, 2011.

Staples, Brent. "How Italians Became White." *The New York Times,* October 12, 2019.

Stevens, Ellen Yale. "The Montessori Movement: A McClure Department," *McClure's* magazine (July 1913).

Steves, Rick. "Italy." *Rick Steves Europe*, Accessed November 9, 2020.

Taber, Elisabeth Stead. "Pascal d'Angelo, Son of Italy." *The Literary Digest International Book Review* Vol. IV, No. 4, p. 232.

Thorn, Bret. "Survey: Italian Remains Most Popular Ethnic Cuisine." *Nation's Restaurant News*, August 28, 2015.

Trapasso, Clare. "CT city has the most Italian Americans in the U.S." *CTPost*, October 14, 2019.

____ "The Truth About Italian Slaves in America – Padrone Act of 1874." *The Italian Tribune*, July 16, 2020.

____ "U.S. Congress: Palladio, the Father of American Architecture." *Marcadoc Turismo Informazione Cultuanella Provincia Treviso.*

Vaughn, Samantha. "Italy in Hollywood exhibition, Salvatore Ferragamo Museum." *The Florentine.net*, July 10, 2018.

Viale, Valerio. "First Recording in Jazz History has strong Sicilian Roots." *Italoamericano.org* March 10. 2017.

Vivolo, Angelo. "Victory in Brooklyn: The Christopher Columbus Memorial Stays in Place in Front of Borough Hall," *Primo Magazine* 2023.

Waxman, Olivia B. "How the KKK's Influence Spread in Northern States," *Time* magazine. October 24, 2017.

Wei-Haas, Maya. "How an Italian Immigrant Rolled Out the Radio Flyer Wagon Across America." *Smithsonian Magazine*, June 3, 2016.

Welch, Michael Patrick. "Jazz's Great White Hype." *Narratively.com,* August 25, 2014.

____ "What is Jazz." *National Museum of American History Behring Center*, Smithsonian. 2021.

____ "Who Was Antonio Meucci?" *Garibaldi-Meucci Museum*, 2019.

____ "Who was General Giuseppe Garibaldi?" *Garibaldi-Meucci Museum*, 2019.

SELECT BIBLIOGRAPHY

Wigler, Stephen. "Valentino returns in Argento opera about a lost soul." *The Baltimore Sun*, January 9, 1994.

Wilson, Caryn A. and Patrick Boehler. "Italy's History of Deadly Earthquakes." *The New York Times, August* 24, 2016.

Wilson, Dr. Matthew R. "A History of Commedia dell'Arte," *Fiction of Fools Theater Company*, 2010.

____ "The Wine Industry Boosts the Texas Economy by $13.1 billion in 2017." *The National Association of American Wineries.*

Wolfgang, Marvin E. "The Truth About the Mafia. Giovanni Schiavo." *American Journal of Sociology*, Volume 69, Number 3, p. 309.

____ "World's Columbian Exposition of 1893." *Chicago Architecture Center*, Accessed September 21, 2020.

Zimmermann. Kim Ann. "Italian Culture: Facts, Customs, & Traditions." *Live Science* September 13, 2017.

INDEX

100 per cent Americanism, 496, 501, 502; *see also* Americanization

11th New York Infantry *see* U.S. Civil War and Luigi di Palma Cesnola

14th Amendment, 242-243; and "Due Process Clause," 242-243

1876 Centennial Exposition in Philadelphia, 55-56; *see also* Statue of Liberty

1893 Chicago World's Columbian Exposition, 308

18th Amendment (Prohibition), 473-476

18th Amendment, *see also* Prohibition

1904 St. Louis World's Fair, 109-111

1924 Immigration Act, 485-486

1928 Election; 401-404; *see also* Al Smith.

1930 Statistical Abstract of the United States, 484

1936 Olympic Games in Berlin, Germany, 47-48; *48*

21st Century Political Motives, 33-34,

39th New York Infantry Regiment, *see* "Garibaldi Guard,"

400th Anniversary Columbus Day Celebration, 45, 105-106

95 Theses critical of the Catholic Church, 502

A:

Abbaticchio, Ed (baseball player), 452-453; *452*

Abortion, Sanger opposed, 245,

Abortion, *see also* Margaret Sanger opposed

Abraham Lincoln Foundation of the Union League of Philadelphia, 62; *see also* Pio Fedi

Abruzzo Earthquake, 76-78

Academy Award for Best Director, 25

Academy Award for Best Director, 25

Academy Award, 25, 378

Academy of Music in Philadelphia, 277

Academy of Music, in New York, Brooklyn, and Philadelphia, 277

Academy of Music, New York City, 278

Accolti, Michele (priest), founding of Santa Clara College, 353

Acker, Jean (actress), 383, 391; *see also* Rudolph Valentino

Adagietto, see Italian Terminology of Music

Addams, Jane (reformer), 213-220; describes Italian evenings at Hull House, 219-220; visits Italy, 219-220; recalls "play written by an Italian playwright," 213; describes "sewing trades," 227-228, *214*; *see also* Ellen Gates Starr; Hull House

Adler, Dick (historian), 269; *see also* Lorenzo Da Ponte

Adriatic Sea, 429-430; *see also* Maria Montessori

Adventures of Huckleberry Finn (book), 137; *see also* Mark Twain

Advertising, 210

African American musicians, 4, 40, 96, 101, 150, 257, 324, 325, 336, 467, 496-497, 498

Age of Exploration, *see* Christopher Columbus

Agriculture, *photo 234*

Aida (opera), 268, 286; *see also* Giuseppe Verdi

Aiuti, Simona (research historian), 63-63; *see also* Statue of Liberty

Alamo Cenotaph, 450-451

Albano, Angelo (lynch victim), 130-133; *133*

Alberti, Peter Caesar (immigrant), 9; as first Italian to New York City, 21-22; *22*

Alcoholism and Crime, 86

Aldrich, Thomas Bailey (white nationalist), 116-117

All God's Chillun Got Wings (Broadway Play), 500

All the Nations Under Heaven (newsletter), 502

Allegretto, see Italian Terminology of Music

Allegrissimo, see Italian Terminology of Music

Allegro, see Italian Terminology of Music

Alps (mountain range), 376

Amati Violin, described, 341; *340*

Amati, Andrea (violin maker), 340-341, 342; *see also* "Italian Instruments"

Amati, Nicolò (violin maker), 339-340

America Dances (book), describes syncopation, 324

American Academy of Music, Philadelphia, *image 277*

American Association of Teachers of Italian (scholarly journal), 475

American celebration of Columbus Day, 37-39; *see also* Columbus Day

American Civil War and *The Birth of a Nation*, 23-24

American Civil War, 1, 21, 3-24, 351

American Committee for the Statue of Liberty, 57, 58; *see also* Statue of Liberty

American cowboy in popular culture, 303-307

American cultural "sugar-coating" of legal atrocities, 94-95

American Culture, 509-524

American Dream, 72-73, 431, 463; in *L'America*, 72-73; and Italian Immigrants, 260-261

American Eugenics movement, 482-484; *see* Eugenics

American Experience, The, and survivors of Messina earthquake, 72-73

American Federation of Musicians, call Ragtime "unmusical rot," 325

American Film Institute (AFI), 4

American flag salute and Ccontroversy, 47-48,

American Impresario, 257-259; *see also* Tony Pastor; Sylvester Poli; Vaudeville

American Industrialization, 25-27

American League, *see* Baseball

American Legion, 501

American lifestyles promote leisure, 210

American Mercury (literary magazine), 500-502; *501*

American Museum of Natural History, 480; *see also* Madison Grant; Eugenics

American Nativist Movement, 22-24,

American Political Science Review, 122; *see also* Robert F. Foerster

INDEX

American Vaudeville Museum at the University of Arizona, 259

American Vaudeville *see* Vaudeville

American Vaudeville, 251-255, 257-263

American Violin: From Jefferson to Jazz (exhibition), 342; *see also* Thomas Jefferson; *see also* "Italian Instruments"

American West of Cowboys, Cowgirls, and Indians, 303-306; *305*;

Americanization, 119-120, 212, 232, 377, 436, 458-459, 495-499, 501, 502

Americans of Italian Heritage (book), *see* Sister Margherita Marchione

Amore: The Story of Italian American Song (Biography), 300; *see also* Enrico Caruso

An Alien Anti-Dumping Bill (political Cartoon), *illustration 486*

Anbinder, Tyler (historian), 175-182; describes Pascal D'Angelo, 202-203

Ancient Roman Architecture, 364

Ancient Rome, 320, 364

Ancient Rome, 42, 44, 47-48, 320, 361, 364, 518; *361*

Andante, see Italian Terminology of Music

Andolini, Vito (fictional character), 4-5, *see also The Godfather, Part II*

Andretti, Mario (race car driver), 451

Andrews, Brittany (historian), ranks "Five Greatest Italian-American Boxers," 457-458

Andrews, Eva (historian), 159; *see also* Giuseppe Garibaldi

Angel Island, San Francisco, 353

Angel of the Waters (sculpture), 43-44; *44, see also* Emma Stebbins

Angelini, Andrea (journalist), describes "tragedy within tragedy" on *Titanic*, 74-75

Anglo-Saxon Protestants, 505

Animal Dances, 325; *see also* Ragtime; Vernon and Irene Castle

Annie Get Your Gun (Broadway musical), 305-306; *see also* Annie Oakley

Annie Oakley (performer), 305-306; *see also* Ned Buntline

Anti-Catholic bigotry by the Ku Klux Klan, 402-404; *403, 404,*

Anti-Catholic, 401-404, 502-507, 437; *403, 404*; *see also* Mother Cabrini; *see also* Ku Klux Klan

Anti-immigrant, 91-134, 94-95, 111-117, 278, 478-488, 504-507; and "Dagoes," 94-95; "virulent prejudice and nativist hostility," 478; *see also* Henry Cabot Lodge; and Lynching, 91-134

Anti-Italian hatred, in New Orleans, 101-111

Anti-Italian sentiment, 30, 117-121, 34-35, 36-37, 389-390, 473-474, 479, 502-507

Antonia Cerruti, Antonia (entrepreneur), 350; *see also* Del Monte Brand

Antonietta Pisanelli Alessandro, *see* Antonietta Pisanelli

Antonio Meucci: The Inventor and his Time (biography), 270

Anzani Engine, 410-411; *411*; *see also* Giuseppe Bellanca

Anzani, Alessandro (airplane engineer), 410-411; *see also* Giuseppe Bellanca

Appelbaum, Larry (jazz historian), 342; *see also* "Italian Instruments"

Architecture, 12; *see also* Thomas Jefferson; Andrea Palladio

Architecture, 214-216, 320, 321, 364, 450, *295, 321*

Are Italians White? How Race is Made in America (article), 98

Arena of Nîmes (amphitheater), 360; *361*; *see also* Ancient Rome

Arizona, 307

Armory Show *see* New York Armory Show

Armstrong, Louis (musician), 338; as "Ambassador of Good Will," 338; dedicates biography to the "Dixieland Five," 338; view on Nick LaRocca and Original Dixieland Jazz Band, 338;

Arnao, Italian Migrant Family, *234*

Aron, Cindy (cultural historian), gender leisure among Italian immigrants, 213

Arona, Italy, 63-64; *see also* Colossus of San Carlo Borromeo

Art Commission of Virginia, 421; discrimination against Piccirilli Brothers, 421

Art Students League in Manhattan, 416, 444; *see also* Piccirilli Brothers

Asian Exclusion Act, 488

Assassination of local New Orleans Police Chief, 102-105

Assimilation and Cultural Acceptance, 10, 13, 302, 220-221, 232, 284, 377, 436, 496-497

Assunta Adelaide Luigia Modotti Mondini, *see* Tina Modotti

Atkinson, Eleanor (author) *see* Nora Marks

Atlantic Monthly (magazine), 400, 465, 476-477

Atlantic Ocean, 469

Atrocities America Forgot, 101, *see also* New Orleans Lynching

Augustyn, Adam (historian), 256

Auto Racing, 451; ***photo 451***

Avalon, Frankie (Italian American singer), 302

Aviation, 404-415

B:

Baccalà (salted cod), 512

Baccari, Italy, 451

Bachmann, Frederick, "bequeaths" Meucci house," 165

Back-to-Back, poem-like description of lynched bodies, 131

Bacon, Henry (architect), 417; *see also* Piccirilli Brothers; *see also* Lincoln Memorial

Baker, John *see* "Texas Jack"

Balaskas, Peter A. (research historian), 416, 417; *see also* Piccirilli Brothers

Baltimore News, The (newspaper), reports on Rudolph Valentino's health, 391

Baltimore Sun, The (newspaper), 465

Baltimore, Maryland, 310, 465

Banco dei Medici, Florence, 355; *see also* A.P. Giannini

Banco di Napoli, Naples, 355; *see also* A.P. Giannini

Banco di San Giorgio (Bank of St. George), Genoa, Italy, 355; *see also* A.P. Giannini

Bancroft Library at University of California Berkeley, 316; *see also* Antonietta Pisanelli

Bank of America, 107, 355- 357, 358-359; as world's largest commercial bank, 359; first known as "Bank of Italy," bank note *357*; *see* A.P. Giannini

Banking, 355-358; as "Italian invention," 355-356; *see also* A.P. Giannini

Barber of Seville (opera), 272, 275, 318

Barbetta Restaurant (Manhattan), celebrates 100th Anniversary, 524; list of "firsts" into American culture, 524; as New York City's "Most Elegant Italian Restaurant," 524; transforms presentation of Italian "food," 524,

Bari, Puglia in southern Italy, 463

Baritono Brillante, 314-316; *see also* Antonio Pini-Corsi

Barone, Jerry (actor), 107; *see also Two Bits*

Barsotti, Carlo (editor), 287; *see also* Verdi Monuments

Bartholdi illustration in *Harper's Weekly*, 80

Bartholdi, Frédéric Auguste (French sculptor), 52-56, 61; visits Colossus of San Carlo Borromeo, 63, visits Florence, 61; of "Italian and German heritage," travels to New York, 61; *see also* Statue of Liberty

Barzini, Luigi (author), 466; *see also* Giovanni Schiavo

Baseball Hall of Fame, 406

Basilica of Croce, Florence, 61-62, *61*; *see also* Pio Fedi

Basilica Palladiana, 321, *321*; *see also* Andrea Palladio

Basilicate, Italy, 143

Basilio Catania, Basilio (historian), 270

Batella, Fausto, 455; *see also* Boxing

Battalino, Battling "Bat" (boxer "Christopher Battaglia"), 459

Battle of Britain, 414-415; *see also* Giulio Douhet

Battle of Lights, Coney Island (painting), *446*; *see also* Joseph Stella

Battle with the Slum, The (expose), 195-197; *see also* Jacob Riis

Beats Per Minute (BPM), 326; *see also* Italian Music

Beauty Products, 313-314; *see also* Lina Cavalieri

Beaux Arts Style (architecture), 27, 422; *27, 423*; *see also Piccirilli Brothers*

Bedloe's Island (Liberty Island), 52,

Bedloe's Island, 52, 54-55, 66; *see also* Statue of Liberty

Behring Center, division of the Smithsonian Institute as, 324

Bel Canto ("beautiful singing"), 266, 268, 280; *see also* Opera

Bel Paese, defined, 344-345; *see also* California

Bell, Alexander Graham (inventor), claims invention of telephone, 172-173; awarded patent for working telephone, 173; *see also* Antonio Meucci

Bell' Italia (Beautiful Italy), 146-147, 344; *see also* Rick Steves

Bella Tuscany, 344

Bellamy, Rev. Francis J. (author), 45-48; as author of Pledge of Allegiance, 46-48; affirms authorship of Pledge, 48; known as "Olympic Salute," 47-48; similar to "Nazi Salute," 47-48; *photo 46*; *see also* Pledge of Allegiance

Bellanca Aircraft Corporation of America, *see* Giuseppe Bellanca

Bellanca, Giuseppe Mario (aviator), 406-410, 411; *409, 419*; death of, 410; WB-2 exceeding Lindbergh's flight, 410; *see also* Giuseppe Bellanca; Enea Bossi; Paolo Invernizzi; Aviation History

Bellini, Vincenzo (composer), 268, 280, *266*; *see also* Opera

Belsom, Jack (historian), 268; *see also* Opera in New Orleans,

Bennett, Tony (Italian American singer), 302

Berkes, Anna (research historian), 518

Bernardo Winery, 345-346; *346*

Bertolino, Angelo (inventor), 173, *see also* Antonio Meucci

Bethesda Fountain (New York), 43-44; *44*, *see also* Emma Stebbins

Bexar County Court House, Texas, 364, *364*; *see also* Salvatore Lucchese

Biagi, Giancarlo (artist), 444; *see also* Cabrini Memorial; Jill Biagi

Biagi, Jill (artist), 444; *see also* Cabrini Memorial; Giancarlo Biagi

Bianchi, Giovanna (opera singer), 280; as "The Mother of Music in California," 279-280

Bible, The, 403, 404, 478

Bibliographies of Italian American writers, 205

Bicycle, and Italian immigrants, 246-247; *247*; as "dangerous for women," 246-247; social and moral concerns, 246-247; and "weaker sex," 246-247

Biden, Dr. Jill (first lady), 13

Biden, Joseph R. (president), 13

Bill, Buffalo (performer), *305*; *see also* Ned Buntline

Binder, Prof. Frederick M. (historian), xi, 502-503

Biography of Giuseppe Garibaldi, 157-158

Birds of Passage, 8

Birth Control, 244-245, *245*, *see also* Margaret Sanger

Birth of a Nation, The (movie), 23-24, 372; as first "American" made blockbuster, 372; popularity, 23-24; screened at the White House, 23

Black Death, 88-89; *see also* Lazaretto

Black Diamond, Washington, 234, 351-352

Black Face, 257; *see also* Vaudeville

Black Hand, and Italian criminals, 474-475; *see also* Prohibition

Black Lives Matter (campaign), 40

Black Race, defined by Miller and Davis, 499

Blakemore, Erin (historian), 104; *see* Hennessy murder

Blaming Columbus for Every Evil since 1492 is Easy but Wrong (article), 33-34;

Blériot, Louis (aviator), 411; *see also* Anzani Engine

Blitz, Matt (biographer), 522; *see also* Chef Boyardee

Blitzkrieg, 414-415; *see also* Giulio Douhet

Blockbuster, 372, 374; *see also* Hollywood; *Cabiria*; *The Birth of a Nation*

Blood and Sand (movie), 387; *387*; *see also* Rudolph Valentino

Bodie, Ping (baseball player), 452-453; *452*; nickname of "The Great Bambino" for Babe

Boiardi, Ettore (chef), known as Hector Boyardee, 521; *see also* Chef Boyardee

Bolden, Charles "Buddy" (musician), 324, as "first actual 'jazzman." 328

Bologna Italy, 205, 292; *see also* Guglielmo Marconi

Bolt, Rodney (biographer), 270, 271, 272; *see also* Lorenzo Da Ponte

Bonaparte, Charles Joseph (law enforcement), 461; *461*

Bonfanti, Marietta (ballet dancer), 280

Bonito, Italy, 366

Bootlegging, 474-475; *see also* Prohibition

INDEX 553

Bordoni, Faustina (opera soprano), as setting standard as "diva stereotype," 313

Borglum, Gutzon, 426-428; *see also* Mt. Rushmore

Borromeo, Cardinal Carlo, 438-439; *see also* Mother Cabrini

Borzage, Frank (director), 25

Bossi design of first all stainless steel aircraft, *412*;

Bossi, Enea (aviation pioneer), 411-412; *412*; *see also* Enea Bossi; Giuseppe Bellanca

Boston, Massachusetts; 117-121, 278, 320, 351, 366, 399; and Social Darwinism, 117-121; *see also* Mandy Tuttle

Boston Globe, The (newspaper), reports on Rudolph Valentino's health, 391

Botein, Barbara (historian), explains discriminatory reality, 111

Boxing crowd attendance, 455

Boxing, 453-459; *454, 456*

Brace, Charles Loring (journalist), 175-182, *178*; *see also* Orphan Train

Branch Banking System, 357-358; *see also* A.P. Giannini

Brent, Charles Henry (Reverand), hatred against Italians, 489

Brewer, David J. (Supreme Court Justice), 243; *see also Muller v. Oregon,*

Brief History of Italian Food in America (article), 509-510

Brinkley, Douglas (historian), 428; *see also* Luigi Del Bianco

Broadway, 371, 500; as "subversive to 100 per cent American Patriotism," 500-501

Brockton, Massachusetts, *see* Rocky Marciano

Broma Process, 354; *see also* Chocolate,

Bronx County Historical Society, 416; *see also* Piccirilli Brothers

Bronx, New York, 419, 420, 421, 441, 448-451, *see also* Piccirilli Brothers

Brooklyn Academy of Music, *277*

Brooklyn born Italian-American heritage, 14,

Brooklyn Borough Hall, 43-44; *45*,

Brooklyn Bridge, 446- 447, 448; *447*; *see also* Joseph Stella

Brooklyn College archives, 253

Brooklyn Daily Eagle (newspaper), 204, 325; *see also* Pascal D'Angelo

Brooklyn Museum, Coney Island exhibition, 446-447

Brooklyn, New York, 14, 39-40, 44, 78, 301, 433, 457, 460

Brooks, Louise (actress), "personified flapper image," 476; *476*; *see also* Flappers

Brotherhood Winery, as "oldest winery," 345

Brown, Arthur, Jr. (architect), 320-321

Brown, Tom (musician), 327-328; *see also* Nick LaRocca, Jazz

Brumidi, Constantino (artist), 155-156; discrimination due to "foreign birth," 156

Bubola and aftermath of Messina Earthquake, 72-73

Bubola, Emma (journalist), 72-73; complications of the Messina Earthquake, 72

Buckingham Palace, 335; *see also* Original Dixieland Jazz Band

Budd BB-1 first all stainless steel aircraft, 412; *photo 412*; *see also Enea Bossi*

Buntline, Ned (promoter), 304-305, 308; *photo 305; see also* Giuseppina Morlacchi

Burnett, Gene (journalist), 130-131

Burns, Ken (documentarian), 326-327, 335; incorrect reference on origin of word "Jazz," 335; undue criticism of Nick LaRocca, 327; *see also* Jazz

Business of Fireworks (article), 464

Byrne, Prof. Julie (historian), 503-504; difference between Catholic and Protestant, 504

C:

Cabiria (movie), 372-376; *374, 376*; as first movie viewed at White House, 372; as movie "epic," 374-376; *see also* Giovanni Pastrone

Cabot John (Italian explorer), 49

Cabrini Memorial in Battery Park City, 442-443

Cabrini Tomb and Statue, 441-444; *442, 443*; *see also* Mother Cabrini

Cabrini, Catholic New York City High School, 441; *see also* Mother Cabrini

Cabrini, Mother Frances Xavier (saint), 12, 437-444, *442, 443*; as "saint," 439; granted American citizenship, 440; "skeletal remains at altar of St. Frances Cabrini Shrine," 441-442; dedication to Italian immigrants in America, 439-440; memorial, unveiled on Columbus Day, 442-443; "traveled indefatigably" beyond New York, 439; travels across America, 439; as Patron Saint of Immigrants, 441-442; "mission," 437

Cadman Plaza, Brooklyn, 40

Caesar Salad, 429, 509

Caiazzo, Italy, 309; *see also* Rosa Ponselle

Calabrese, 97-98,

Calabria and Messina Earthquake, 68-69

Calabria Earthquake and Author's Grandmother, 76-79

California, 155, 307, 310-311, 317, 343-352; as "the Italy of America," 344; producing wine in the Italian tradition, 351-352

California Fruit Canners Association, 350

California Gold Rush, 343, 356, 359, 452-453,

California, wineries affected by Prohibition, 476

Callas, Maria (opera soprano), 313

Camden, New Jersey, 329; *see also* Jazz

Camille (movie), 386; *see also* Rudolph Valentino

Campbell, Frank E. (funeral director), 391-392; *see also* Rudolph Valentino

Can-Can (dance), 302-304

Candle making, 171-172; *171, see also* Antonio Meucci and Giuseppe Garibaldi

Cangiano, Victor, 429,

Cannato, Vincent (historian), 8

Cannes Film Festival, 373; *see also* *Cabiria*

Canning, 350

Canova, Antonio (sculptor), 515

Cantella, Michele (entrepreneur), 351

Canzoneri, Tony (boxer), 459

Capone, Al (gangster), as "famous celebrity," 475; *see also* Prohibition

Capra, Francesco Rosario "Frank" (director), 378

Cardini, Alex (Italian restaurateur brother), originates "Caesar Salad," 509

Cardini, Cesare "Caesar" (Italian restaurateur), originates "C aesar Salad," 509

Carmel, New Jersey, 234, *234*

INDEX

Carmen (opera), 310, 320; *see also* Rosa Ponselle

Carnegie Hall, 294

Carnera, Primo (boxer), 458-459

Carr, John (journalist), and "The Coming of the Italian," 96

Carrara marble, 287, 417, 418, 448-449; *417*; *see also* Verdi Monument New York City; *see also* Piccirilli Brothers

Carroll, Bill (researcher), 415, 416; *see also* Piccirilli Brothers

Carroll, Rory (journalist), 174; *see also* Antonio Meucci,

Carrot King, *see* Joseph Maggio

cartes de visite (CdV), 307; *see also* Carlo Gentile

Caruso, Henricus "Enrico" (opera singer), 11-12, 251, 254-255, 275, 296-297, 299-302, 309, 311-312, 322, 378, 420, 524, as clown for *I Pagliacci*, 298, *254, 298, 299, 309*, American debut, 297; birth in Naples, 297, called "Man with the Golden Voice," 300; compared to Eduardo Migliaccio, 254-255; death of, 300; "introduces Italian opera to upper and middle social class," 299; legacy, 301-302; obituary, 300; opera debut, 297; movies, 299; Lifetime Achievement Grammy Award, 300-301; recordings, 297-298; "stricken with pleurisy," 300; traditional Neapolitan working class songs, 298; vocal range described, 297; *verismo* vocal style, 298-299; as "The World's Greatest Tenor," 296; *see also* Rosa Ponselle

Caruso, Joseph (labor organizer), 235; *see also* Ludlow Massacre

Caruso, Major Adolfo (manager), 319; *see also* Josephine Lucchese

Casa dei Bambini ("Children's House"), 431; *see also* Maria Montessori

Casa-Museo Joe Petrosino di Padua, *see* Joseph Petrosino,

Caserta in Campania Italy, 414; *see also* Giulio Douhet

Casoni & Isola (sculptors), 450; *see also* Woodlawn Cemetery

Casoni, Vincenzo (sculptor), 450; *see also* Casoni & Isola,

Castellamare Del Golfo region of Sicily, 465

Castellaneta, Italy, 380; *see also* Rudolph Valentino

Castle Clinton National Monument, 52-53

Castle Clinton (immigration station), 22, 51-54, 83; map *52, 53, 54*; *see also* Immigration; Ellis Island

Castle Garden Conservancy, 53-54; *see also* Immigration

Castle, Irene (dancer), 325-326; refine "vulgar dances," 325; *see also* Vernon Castle

Castle, Vernon (dancer), 325-326; *see also* Irene Castle

Cataldo, Giuseppe (Jesuit priest), 91

Catherine de Medici, 518

Catholic Burial, 128-129; *see also* Tallulah Lynching

Catholic Church, 23, 34, 85-86, 94, 128-129, 353, 366, 401-404, 437-444, 501-504; parishes dominated by Irish priests, 503; vandalized, 94, 479; *see also* Mother Cabrini

Catholic News Agency, see Patrick Mason

Catholic Ritual and Protestant Christianity, 503-504

Cava de' Tirreni, Italy, 251

Cavalieri, Natalina "Lina" (opera soprano), 302, 310-314, 378; *311*; *313*; advertisement Columbia Records, 313; allure of celebrity status, 313; as author, 314; beauty books, 314; beauty products," 313-314; billed as "the world's most beautiful woman," 312; and Caruso perform Puccini's *Manon Lescaut*, 312; as female lead opposite Enrico Caruso, 312; as "forgotten," 312; killed in an Allied bombing raid, 314; legacy 311; as "master at self-promotion," 313-314; newspaper column, 314; opera debut, 312; "passionate" onstage kiss with Enrico Caruso, 312; recording career, 312-313; *see also* Opera

Cavatelli (pasta), 521

Celenza, Anna Harwell (cultural historian), 324, 32, 333-334, 336-337; explains jazz arrival on Italian shores, 337; on New Orleans-style jazz, 324; on role of Italian immigrants in the genesis of Jazz in U.S., 337

Cello, 340, 341; *see also* "Italian Instruments"

Center for Migration Studies of New York, 465, 503

Central Park, in New York City, 44, *44*, 162, 222; *see also* Bethesda Fountain and Emma Stebbins

Cesnola, Luigi Palma di (Union Army Colonel), 158-160, 161-162, *162*; and "archeological excavations in Cyprus," 161-162; as first Director of the Metropolitan Museum of Arts in New York, 161; *see also* U.S. Civil War

Chaffey, Don (director), 217

Champs Élysées, in Paris, 314

Changing Concepts of Education (educational thesis), 495-497

Great Arrival, 52-92

Charleston (dance), 367

Chef Boyardee, 512-522; introduces Italian food to Americans, 521-522; macaroni products, 521; *see also* Ettore Boiardi

Chiaravalle, Italian Province of Ancona, 429-430; *see also* Maria Montessori

Chiariglione, Ettore "Hector" (editor), as the "Father of Columbus Day;" 32, 34-35

Chicago and Jazz, 327

Chicago Architecture Center, 27; *see also* Architecture

Chicago Daily Tribune, The (newspaper), 216-218, 390; writes of Hull House, 220; *see also* Nora Marks

Chicago Opera, 284; *see also* Opera

Chicago White Sox (baseball team), 453

Chicago World's Fair, 463,

Chicago Herald Examiner, on Rudolph Valentino, 390

Chicago, 26, 308, 316, 327

Chicken Tetrazzini, 284; *see also* Luisa Tetrazzini

Child Labor and cruelty, *153*, *226*, *232*, *234*; *see also* Padrone System

Children's Aid Society, 175-182

China and introduces macaroni to Italian peninsular, 512, *see also* Marco Polo

Chinese Exclusion Act of 1882, 479

Chocolate, 354-355; *see also* Domenico Ghirardelli

Choi, Connie (curator), 447; *see also* Joseph Stella

Cholera Epidemic, 139, 141

Christian, Emile (musician), 334; *see also* Original Dixieland Jazz Band

Christopher Columbus Piazza, 36; *see also* Christopher Columbus

Chronicle, The (illustrated children's newspaper), *see* Nora Marks

Cimino, Dr. Teresa, (inventor), 14; *see also* Manhattan Special

Cioppino (fish stew), and Italian origin, 509-510

Ciotola, Nicholas P. (historian), 66-67, 68; *see also* Ellis Island

Cipalla, Rita (historian), 234-235, 351; wine in Walla Walla, Washington, 351-352; history of Italian immigrant workers, 352

Circolo Italo-Americano (organization), 220; *see also* Denison House

City of Dreams: The 400-Year Epic History of Immigrant New York, 198, 202

City University of New York (CUNY), 4

Civil War Italians, 45, 148, 158-161, 272, 500; *see also* Giuseppe Garibaldi; American Civil War

Civil War, U.S., 158-161; *see also* Luigi di Palma Cesnola

Civiletti, Pasquale (artist), 287; *see also* Verdi Monument New York City

Civitavecchia, Rome, 515

Clancy, Robert H. (U.S. Congress), 492-493 opposes "Shut the Door," *493*; calls Shut the Door Policy "Un-American," 494; defends Italians, 494; describes "racial discrimination at its worst," 494; support of "factual claim," 493-494

Clansman, The (novel), 23; *see also* *The Birth of a Nation*

Clark, Peter (director of archives), 312; writes of Lina Cavalieri and Enrico Caruso, 312

Clemens, Samuel; *see* Mark Twain

Cleveland, 522

Cleveland, Grover (president), 115

Clown Tradition, 255; *see also* Enrico Caruso; Eduardo Migliaccio

Coal Industry and Italians, 352

Cody, William "Buffalo Bill" (performer),304-306; *305*; *see also* Ned Buntline

Colacino, Annina "Anna" (grandmother), xiii; born during Calabria Earthquake, *79*

Colautti, Arturo (librettist), 312

Colella, Nicola (historian), 201-202; *see also* Padrone

Colombati, Virginia, (voice teacher), 318-319; opera debut, 318; *see also* Josephine Lucchese

Colorado and Ani-Italian, 35, 236, 455; first to establish Columbus Day as legal holiday, 32-33,

Colorado Loveland Reporter (newspaper), 300; *see also* Enrico Caruso

Colorado Mines, *see* Ludlow Massacre

Colossus of San Carlo Borromeo, 60-64, *64*; *see also* Statue of Liberty

Coltelli, Francesco Procopio dei, invents "first ice cream machine," 518

Columbia Records, 1922 Catalogue Cover *313*; 313, 314-315, 335; advertisement for Lina Columbia University, 271-272, 502

Columbian Exchange and Tomato, 514

Columbian World's Exposition and "The Pledge of Allegiance,"

Columbian World's Exposition and "The Pledge of Allegiance,"

Columbo, Russ (singer), 394-395; *395*; "mythical legacy," 394-395; death of, 395

Columbus, Christopher (Italian explorer), 5, 14, 20-21, 26-45, *27*, *29*, *31*, *35*, *37*, 40, *41*, 49, 90, *221*,

222-223, 274, *332*, 345, 357, 406, *image 406*, 459, 467, 514; "accusations against," 29-32; associated with pride in America, 34-35; "Blaming Columbus for Every Evil," 33-34; Columbian Exposition of 1893, 26-29; *27, 29*; as credit to Italian immigrants, 29-32, defense by historians and journalists, 33-34; dispelling accusations, 34; and early references in America, 34; as "enigma," 37-39; and exploration, 29-32; fictional image, 31; honored by New York City Department of Parks & Recreation, 223; "myth," 33-35; namesakes in America, 36-37; as "pioneer of progress and enlightenment," 105-106; protests to remove statues, 34-37; and "Quest for Jerusalem," 34; "return voyages," 33-35; Ship Replicas, 28-29; *29*; statues removed, 35-36; voyages, 28-34, 46; *see also* Frank Vittor

Columbian Exposition of 1893, 26-29; *27, 29*

Columbus Circle in Manhattan, 332; *332*

Columbus Day (holiday), 29-31, 33-39, 105-106, 221, 287, 345; *illustration 221*; as "Italian Holiday," 29-32; as Colorado official state holiday, 34-35; *see also* Verdi Monument New York City

Columbus Heritage Coalition, 40; *see also* Christopher Columbus

Columbus Italian Hospital in New York, 459

Columbus Park, New York City, 40, 222-223; *223*; *see also* Christopher Columbus

Columbus, Ohio (city), 28-37; "Leave the Name, Get Rid of the Monuments," 36-37; statue as gift from citizens of Genoa, Italy, *35*

Combattimento di Tancredi e Clorida (opera), 339

Command of the Air, The (treatise), 414-415; *see also* Giulio Douhet

Commedia dell' Arte, 255-256, *illustration 256*; 318; described, 255-256; *see also* Vaudeville

Como, Perry (Italian American singer), 302

Coney Island (painting), 446-447; *image 446*; *see also* Joseph Sella

Coney Island exhibition at Brooklyn Museum, 446-447

Coney Island in Brooklyn, 249-250, 446-447, 478; called "The World's Greatest Playground," 446-447; entertainment and attractions, 249-250

Confederacy, 159; *see also* Civil War

Congress and "The Immigration Act of 1924," 64, 479

Congressional Medal of Honor, 161, 471

Congressional Medal of Honor, 161

Congress Response to Immigration Reform, 505; response to derogatory references, 95

Connecticut History and Italian immigrants in New England, 261

Conrad, Barnaby (historian), 352-353

Constantine Panunzio Distinguished Emeriti Award, 207

Consumption of consumer goods, 210

Cookbooks, 513

Coolidge, Calvin (president), 120-121, 485; "America must be kept American," 120-121

Cooper, James Fenimore (author), 271

Coppini, Pompeo (sculptor), 450; buried in San Antonio, Texas, 450

Coppola, Francis Ford (director), 4, 5, 107-108; *see also The Godfather*

Corleone, Don Vito (fictional character), 107-108; *see also The Godfather*

Corleone, Michael (fictional character), 107-108; *see also* Al Pacino and *The Godfather*

Cornell, Bryan (historian), 328, 330, 336; *see also* Original Dixieland Jazz Band

Cornicello, see "Evil Eye," 125, *125*

Corriere della Sera (newspaper), 337

Corso, Antonio (singer), 127; *see also* Tallulah Lynching

COVID-19 Coronavirus (pandemic), 14, 72, 222, 424, 460; and aftermath of Messina Earthquake, 72; *see also* Dr. Anthony Fauci

Cowboy Boots, 363-365; *see also* Salvatore Lucchese, Tony Lama

Cowgirl Magazine, 303; *see also* Giuseppina Morlacchi

Crabtree, Lotta (entertainer), 282-284; *283*; *see also* Lotta's Fountain

Cradle of Aviation Museum in Long Island, New York, 406-407, *409*

Crawford, Joan (actress), 367-368; *368*; *see also* Salvatore Ferragamo

Cremona Violin, 342; *see also* Thomas Jefferson

Cremona, Italy, 339

Criminal Statistics, 144,

Cristofori, Bartolomeo (instrument maker), invention of *forte piano*, 339-340; *photo 340*; *see also* Piano Forte

Croatia, 315

Crosetti, Frank (baseball player), 453

Croton Aqueduct Reservoir, New York, 44; and wage rates, 94-95

Crutchfield, Will (opera historian), 7, 322, 315, 317; describes *baritono brillante*, 315; summation of Arturo Toscanini, 292

Cubberley, Ellwood P. (educator), 495-497, establishing study of "Education," 495-497; "support of Eugenic theories," 495-496

Cult of Celebrity, 396; *see also* Rudolph Valentino

Cultural Critics, 500-502; *see also* H.L. Mencken; George Nathan

Cultural distinction between Italy and Sicily, Steves described, 146, 147

Cultural Misconceptions, 97-98, 246-247, 289, 497

Culturally diverse immigrants, 97-98

Culver, Helen (benefactor), 214; offers Hull House to Addams and Starr

Cunningham, John M. (biographer), 284; *see also* Luisa Tetrazzini,

Cuomo, Andrew (New York Governor), 442-443; *see also* Cabrini Memorial

Cushman, Charlotte (actress), 42-43; *42*; *see also* Emma Stebbins

Customs Service, U.S. 52-43; *see also* Immigration and Ellis Island

D:

D'Annunzio, Gabriele (screenwriter), 372, 373-374; *375*; *see also Cabiria*

D'Angelo, Pasquale "Pascal" (poet), 201-206, *203*; death of, 204-205; "dropped off literary map," 204; gravesite *204*; literary rejections, 203; obituary, 204-205; pursues literary career, 202-204; writes autobiography, 203-204

Da Ponte, Lorenzo (librettist), 268-274; *272, 273*; arrival in New York, 269-270; birth name of "Emanuele Conegliano," 269; Catholic burial, 273; death of, 273-274; headstone 273-274, *274*; Italian contribution to American culture, 269-272; librettist for Wolfgang Amadeus Mozart, 268-274; and Mozart collaboration, 269; *see also* Mozart; Opera

Dagoes (defined), 94-95; "derogatory," 102

Daigneault, Regina "Reggie" (wine expert), 352

Dance Music, 324-325

Dancing, 476; as "wholesome recreation," 478; *see also* Rudolph Valentino

Dandini (fictional character), 315; *see also* Antonio Pini-Corsi,

Darin, Bobby (Italian American singer), 302

Dattilo, Annina "Anna" (grandmother), 531; *531*

Dattilo, Anthony (grandfather), 532; *532*

Dattilo, Antonio (grandfather), xiii

Dattilo, Phyllis (mother), xi

Daughters of the American Revolution, The; "How to be American," 120

Davenport and "stereotypes," 210-215

Davenport, William E. (journalist), "The Italian Immigrant in America," 210-211

DaVinci, Leonardo, 496

Davis, Jacob (clothier), 360; *see also* Levi Strauss; Denim Jeans

Day Show Business was Born, The, 262-263; *see also* Vaudeville

de Blasio, Bill (New York City Mayor), 442-443; *see also* Cabrini Memorial

De Luca Braun, Rosanne (documentarian), on Italians in Hollywood, 377

De Micheli, Giuseppe (director of Opera di Santa Croce), 62-63,

de Mille, Agnes (music choreographer), describes syncopation, 324-325

De Palma, Raffaele "Ralph" (race car driver), 451; *451*

Deadly Wave, A Lucky Star, A (essay), 76-78; *see also* John Bemelmans Marciano

Declaration of Independence, 12, 59; *see also* Statue of Liberty

Dedham County Court, 400; *see also* Sacco and Vanzetti

Dedham, Massachusetts Courthouse, 400, 401, *400*; *see also* Sacco and Vanzetti

Defatta, Charles, *124*; *see also* Tallulah lynching

Defatta, Frank, 123; spelling difference, *124*

Defatta, Joe, 123-126; *124*; *see also* Tallulah lynching

Del Bianco, Lou (grandson), 428; *see also* Mt. Rushmore; Luigi Del Bianco

Del Bianco, Luigi (sculptor), 426-428; *427, 428*;*see also* Mt. Rushmore

Del Monte Brand, 350

del Piombo, Sebastiano (artist), 31: *see also* Columbus Portrait

Delaney, Carol (historian), 34; *see also* "Columbus and the Quest for Jerusalem,"

Delaney, Carol (historian), 34; *see also* Christopher Columbus; and "Columbus and the Quest for Jerusalem"

DeLuca, Braun, categorizes on-screen Italian stereotypes, 377

DeMille, Cecil B., 366

DeMille, Cecil B. (director), 366, 385

Demo, Father Antonio (Italian parish priest), 438; *see also* Triangle Shirtwaist Factory Fire

Demographics and Immigration Act of 1924, 483

Dempsey, Jack (boxer), nicknamed "The Manassa Mauler," 455; loss by knockout to Andrew Chiariglione, 455

Denim (fabric), 359-361; relating to Italy, 360-361; *see also* Levi Strauss

Denison House

Denison House in Boston (social reform), as "woman-run endeavor," 220-221; modeled after Hull House, 220-221; *illustration 221*; *see also* Amelia Earhart

Denver Post, The, 34,

Denver, Colorado, 34, 36, 325

DePol, Don Juan "John" (manager), 303; *see also* Giuseppina Morlacchi

Depression 1893 to 1898, 210

Derogatory Words against Italians, 84-85, 94-95

Desnoyers, Julio (fictional character), 383; *see also* Rudolph Valentino

Di Fatta family, 128-129; *see also* Tallulah Lynching

Di Fatta, Giuseppe, "Catholic burial," 128-129; *see also* Tallulah Lynching

Diamond, Jack "Legs" (gangster), 475; *see also* Prohibition

Dillingham, William P. (senator), 485, 486

DiMaggio, Joseph Paul "Joe" (baseball player), 453

Dime Novels, 303-306; *see also* Ned Buntline

DiMucci, Dion (Italian American singer), 302

DiNino, Vittoria (mother), 327; *see also* Nick LaRocca

Dippel, Andreas (theater manager), 289

Discography of American Historical Recordings, 316

Discover Italy, 267; on non-Italian opera composers, 267-268

Discrimination

Discrimination against Italian Immigrants; 8, 23-25, 80-84, 85-86, 93-96, 111-117, 156, 201-205, 260-261, 272, 278, 316, 335-336, 389-390, 397, 401-404, 421, 437, 452-453, 456, 465-467, 488, 494, 519; *see also* Mark Twain; Piccirilli Brothers; Mother Cabrini

Disney film, 359; *see also* A.P. Giannini

Diva, 313; *see also* Faustina Bordoni

Dixieland Jass Band One-Step (song), 334, *330*: *see also* Jazz

Dixon, Thomas (author), 23; *see also The Birth of a Nation*

Dolomite Mountains, 109

Domestic Terrorists, 94-95; *see also* Ku Klux Klan

Don Pasquale (opera), 315; *see also* Opera

Donald Travis Stewart (cultural historian) *see* Trav S.D., 257-259

Donizetti, Gaetano (composer), 277; *see also* Opera

Dorgan, Dick (writer), accusation against Valentino, 389-390; *see also* Rudolph Valentino

Double Bass (musical instrument),

Double Bass, 341, *341*; *see also* "Italian Instruments"

Douhet, Giulio (Italian General), 414-415; *see also* Aviation

Drake, David (journalist), 467; *see also* Giovanni Schiavo

Drop the Hate. Seek the Truth (campaign), 39-44; *see also* Christopher Columbus

Dry's, 401-402; *see also* Prohibition

Dukakis, Michael (Governor), 401; *see also* Sacco and Vanzetti

Dundee, Johnny (boxer "Giuseppe Curreri"), 458

Dupuy, Jessica (editor), 363; *see also* Texas Wine Industry

Durante, Jimmy (entertainer), 249, 250, *251*; describes Coney Island, 250 as *"The Great Schnozzola;"* popularize "being distinctly Italian," 250

E:

Earhart, Amelia (aviator), 220-221; as *"The Flying Social Worker,"* 220-221; *see also* Denison House

Early Pianoforte, The (article), 340; *see also* Piano Forte

Earp, Wyatt (lawman), 317

Earthquakes in Italy, 68-72; *see also* Messina Earthquake

East Harlem, New York, 107; as "Italian Harlem," 224-225; *see also* Al Pacino

Easterling, J. Frank (bookkeeper), 129-130; *see also* Tampa Lynching

Ebert, Roger (film critic), writes on making of *Cabiria*, 373

Echoes of the Jazz Age (novel), 477; *see also* Jazz

Edwards, Eddie (trombonist), *329*, drafted into U.S. Army, 334; *see also* Original Dixieland Jazz Band

Effeminacy, 389-390; *see also* R*udolph Valentino*

Eggplant, and travels of Marco Polo, 513

Eiffel designs structure for Statue of Liberty, 55-56

Eiffel Tower as UNESCO World Heritage Site, 60,

Eiffel Tower, 55-56, **56***, 60*; *see also* Statue of Liberty

Eiffel, Alexandre-Gustave (engineer), 55-56; *see also* Eiffel Tower and Statue of Liberty

Electric Chair, 400; *see also* Sacco and Vanzetti

Elegant Italian Dining, 521-524

Elis Island, New York (immigration station), 5, 22, *map 52*, 65-68, *65*, 78, 86-87, *87*, 90, 109, 181, 201, 327, 353, 407, 437, 441-442, 457, 463, 470, 479, 490, 521-527, as cultural center and tourist destination, 90-91; and "The Great Arrival," immigrants arriving *87*; 65-68; "processed over 12 million immigrants," 66; medical problems and quarantine, 86; processing, 86; *87*; relocation proposed by William Windom, 83; restoration, 90; as site for the new immigration station, 52-53; revised processing system, 479; as temporary detainment center, 479; *see also* Immigration

Ellis, Havelock, 240-241, *240*; and "value of motherhood," 240

Emergency Quota Act of 1921, 485

Encomienda System and "genocidal cruelties," 33,

Encyclopaedia Britannica, 17-18, 297, 300; describes Enrico Caruso's vocal range, 297; explains Italy Geographically 17-18; praises Enrico Caruso, 300

Encyclopedia of Greater Philadelphia, 519

Enrico (fictional character), *see also* Antonio Pini-Corsi,

Enrico Caruso Museum of America, 301-302; *302*; *see also* Enrico Caruso; Major Adolfo Caruso

Enss, Chris (biographer), 303; *see also* Giuseppina Morlacchi

Entertainment, 249-263

Espionage Act of 1917, 470

Espresso, 524

Essex County in New Jersey develops first county park, 222

Ettor, Joseph (labor organizer), 235; *see also* Ludlow Massacre

Eugenics, 244, 478-488; and U.S. Army intelligence tests, 484; false idea blaming immigrants as rising threat," 480; publications promoting, 481; *racial superiority* versus *racial inferiority*, 483-484; and "superiority of the white race," 480; *see also* Adolph Hitler; Havelock Ellis; Margaret Sanger

Europe, James Reese (bandleader), 325-326; *see also* Vernon and Irene Castle

European "Garbage Ships," 80-82, *82*

Evening Picayune (newspaper), 279

Evil Eye (little horn), *photo 125*, translated as "little horn," described 124-125

Exploration of the American Colonies, 48-49; *see also* Christopher Columbus

F:

Fabbroni, Giovanni (Italian naturalist), 342; *see also* Thomas Jefferson

Factory mass production, 516

Factory, 226-231, *226, 231*, 516

Falstaff (opera), 315; *see also* Opera

Family meal, 510

Famous Players-Lasky Corporation (movie company), 299

Famous Scientists (website), 168; *see also* Antonio Meucci

Farfariello, 253-254; caricatures, 253-254; characters, *254*; *see also* Eduardo Migliaccio

Farleigh Dickinson University (FDU), 90-92; *see also* Peter and Sylvia Sammartino

Farragut Memorial, 450; *see also* Woodlawn Cemetery; Casoni & Isola,

Farrell and McGee, 62-63; link Italy and America, *see also* "Sisters in Liberty"

Fascism, 205, 314

Fauci, Dr. Anthony (medical doctor), 14, 459-460; *see also* Covid Pandemic

Fazzoni Brothers Fireworks Manufacturing Company, 464

Federal Bureau of Investigation (F.B.I.), 461; *see also* Charles Bonaparte

Fedi, Pio (sculptor), 61-62; statue of Abraham Lincoln,61-62; *62*; *see also* Statue of Liberty

Femina (French magazine), 314; *see also* Lina Cavalieri

Ferber, Edna (author), 500

Ferragamo, Salvatore (shoemaker), 310, 353, 365-369; *368, 382*; clients, 366-369; legacy, 368; living in California, 369; and *paisan* Rudolph Valentino, 379-380; path to America, 365; relocation to Italy, 369; as "Shoemaker to the Stars," 365-368, 380; *see also* Rudolph Valentino; Joan Crawford

Ferrara (bakery), 512

Ferreri, Enza (writer), 355-356; *see also* "Italy Invented Banks;" A.P. Giannini

Ferrero, Edward (Union Army General), 161; *see also* U.S. Civil War

Ficarrotta, Castenge (lynch victim), 130-133; *133*
Fiddle, differences from Violin, 340
Fiducia, Rosario, 123-126; *124*; *see also* Tallulah lynching
Fierro, Rafaele (historian), 261-262; *see also* Sylvester Poli
Fighters, *see* Boxing
Find a Grave, 351
FindAGrave.com (website), 286, 351, 450
Finelli, Filomena (grandmother), xiii
Fireman Jim Flynn (boxer), *see* Andrew Chiariglione
Fireworks by Grucci, 463-464; obituary, 463
Fireworks, 463-464
Firmani, B. G. (blogger), 204; *see also* Pascal D'Angelo
First World War, 242, 254, 399, 414, 465, 469-472, 500; *see also* World War I
Fisherman's Wharf in San Francisco Bay, 346, 355
Fitzgerald, F. Scott (author), 477
Five Fantastic Wine Regions to Discover (article), 363
Five Great Races (article), 497-499; *see also* Discrimination; Segregation
Five Points (book), 175-182; *see also* Tyler Anbinder
Flappers 476-477, *476*; criticism of, 476-477; in defiance of Prohibition, 476-477
Fleming, Renée (opera soprano), 313; *see also* Opera
Fleming, Victor (director), 368; *see also* Salvatore Ferragamo
Florence Academy of Fine Arts (*Accademia di Bell' Arte*), 168
Florence, Italy (city), 168, 310, 340, 355, 368, 430; *see also* A.P. Giannini

Florentine Medici's, 355; *see also* A.P. Giannini
Flu Pandemic, 334
Fly Girls (biography), 221; *see also* Amelia Earhart; Denison House
Foerster, Robert F. (historian), 121-123; *see also* Italian Immigration
Foerster; Eugene E. (historian), 136
Foggia, Italy, 312
Foner, Eric (historian), 243-244; *see also The Story of American Freedom*
Fontamara (article), 475; *see also* Italian Stereotypes
Fontana, Marco (entrepreneur), 350; forms Del Monte 350; *see also* Italian Swiss Colony; Del Monte Brand
Food & Wine (magazine), 363
Food in Italian Culture, 509-524
Forbes, Elizabeth (historian), cites Antonio Pini-Corsi, 315-316
Ford, Daniel (editor), 45; *see also* Francis Bellamy
Ford, Henry, 478, 496
Fort Bliss, in El Paso, Texas, 365; *see also* Tony Lama; Cowboy Boots
Fort Sam Houston, 363
Forte E Gentile, 204; *see also* Pascal D'Angelo
Forte, Fabian (Italian American singer), 302
Fortitude defined, 422; *see also Patience* and *Fortitude*
Fortunate Pilgrim, The (novel), 4, 108; *see also* Mario Puzo
Fossella, Vito (congressman), introduces House proclamation crediting Meucci, 174
Four Books of Architecture (treatise), 320; *see also* Andrea Palladio
Four Centuries of Italian-American History (book), 466; *see also* Giovanni Schiavo

INDEX

Four Horsemen of the Apocalypse (movie), 383; *see also* Rudolph Valentino

Franco-Prussian War, 61, *see also* Bartholdi

Frank E. Campbell Funeral Home, *photo 392*; *see also* Rudolph Valentino

Frank Leslie's Illustrated Newspaper, 80-81, 165; *81*; *see also* Statue of Liberty; *see also* Henry Tyrrell

Frankfurter, Felix (Supreme Court Justice), 400; *see also* Sacco and Vanzetti

Franklin Institute Museum in Philadelphia, 412; *412*; *see also Enea Bossi*

Frascella, Thomas (historian), and "perception of Italians," 21,

Fredericksburg, Texas, "boasts over 50 wineries," 363

Freedberg, David (professor), 269; *see also* Lorenzo Da Ponte

French Market in New Orleans, 100, *100*

French, Daniel Chester (artist), 417; *see also* Lincoln Memorial; Piccirilli Brothers

Frescoes, 155-156; *see also* Constantino Brumidi

Fresno News, 456; *see also* Young Corbett III

Fresno, California, 457

Funicello, Annette (Italian American singer), 302

Future Citizens" (article), 98

G:

Gallo Winery, 476; *see also* Prohibition

Gallo, Denise (curator), Italian Violin, 342

Gallo, Ernest and Julio (wine makers), 476

Gallo, Fortune (opera producer), 320; *see also* Opera

Gallo, Giuseppe "Joe" (wine maker), 476; growing grapes during Prohibition,

Galveston, Texas, 363

Gambino, Richard (historian), 101-102, 104, 113; characterizes Senator Lodge as "Italian-hating," 113; describes New Orleans Lynching, 101; *see also Vendetta*; New Orleans Lynching,

Ganassi, Silvestro (instrument maker), invents Double Bass, 338

Gandhi, Lakshmi (journalist), 30, *see also* Christopher Columbus

Gangsterism and Prohibition, 474-475, 509; *see also* Prohibition

Gangsters as "non-Italian," 475; *see also* Prohibition

Garavuso, Michael (inventor), 14; *see also* Manhattan Special

García, Manuel (opera singer), 272, 274, 275-276; called "our musical Columbus," 274; meets Gioachino Rossini, 275; proclaimed "greatest tenor of the day," 275; study in Italy, 274-275; *see also* Opera

Gardner, Albert Ten Eyck (curator), 417-418; *see also* Piccirilli Brothers

Garibaldi, Giuseppe (Italian Patriot), 61, 156-158, 165-167, 217, 418; *158, 163 164 165, 166*; 100th anniversary of birth, 165; asked by Abraham Lincoln to join U.S. Civil War, 159-160; with Antonio Meucci and candle making, 163, 171-172, 276; bust at Garibaldi-Meucci Museum, 165, *158, 165*; as "friend in exile," 171; inspires "Garibaldi Guard," 159-160, *160*; Garibaldi Guard and Italian

Immigrants, 159-161; as "Hero of Two Worlds, 156-158; Memorial, 165; monuments and statues, 162-163, *163*; "praises Lincoln for Emancipation Proclamation," 160; seeks quiet life in New York, 276; "in retirement," 159; statue in New York, 162-163; living on Staten Island with Antonio Meucci, 163; tributes across America and Italy, 162,; *see also* Antonio Meucci; Garibaldi-Meucci Museum; Piccirilli Brothers

Garibaldi Guard, 159-161, *illustration 160*; *see also* U.S. Civil War; Antonio Meucci; Garibaldi-Meucci Museum

Garibaldi Memorial, 165, *163 164 165*, *166*; *see also* Antonio Meucci; Garibaldi-Meucci Museum

Garibaldi-Meucci Museum (Staten Island), 163, 164-167; Garibaldi inscription 164; preserved as "Pantheon," 165-166; *166*; *see also* Antonio Meucci; Giuseppe Garibaldi

Garland, Judy (actress), 368; *see also* Salvatore Ferragamo

Garment factories, as "sweatshops," 227; *see also* Triangle Shirtwaist Factory Fire

Garvey, Ellen Gruber (historian), 246-247

Gates, Jr., Henry Louis (historian), and social class system, 484

Gatti-Casazza, Giulio (managing director), 288-291; *289*, *290*; 294; parody *296*; born in Udine, Italy, 289; death of, 291; at *La Scala*, 289; dinner in honor, *293*; as first Italian director of the Metropolitan Opera, 288-291; obituary, 290; on

cover of *Time* magazine, 290; retires, 291

Gatto, Marianna (historian), 34, 35, 343; explains California Italian American, 343; *see also* Italian American Museum of Los Angeles,

Gelato, 518

Gelosi Company (theater troupe), 256; *see also Commedia dell'arte*

Genaro, Frankie (boxer), 458

Genoa (Italian port), 360; *see also* Denim Fabric; Levi Strauss

Genoa Naval School of Engineering, 289, *see also* Genoa, Italy; Christopher Columbus

Genoa, Italy (city), 277, 289, 303, 345, 350, 360, 448-449

Gentile, Carlo (photographer), 307-308; *308*; adopts son, 307-308

Geography by Grades, Grade 4B: The Earth, The Continents (textbook), 498-499; *see also* Discrimination; Segregation

Gerardi, Rose (mother), 107; *see also* Al Pacino

German Opera, 277, 290-291; *see also* Opera

Germany and Nationalism, 18

Germont, Alfredo (fictional character), *see* Antonio Pini-Corsi,

Ghirardelli Chocolate Company, 354-355; *see also* Domenico Ghirardelli

Ghirardelli Square, San Francisco, 355; *see also* Domenico Ghirardelli

Ghirardelli, Domenico "Domingo," (confectioner), 353-354, 355, *354*; as apprentice, 354; changes first name, 354; immigration to America, 354; *see also* Ghirardelli Chocolate

Giannini, Amadeo "A.P." (banker), 107, 344, 353, 355-359, *358*;

INDEX

opens "Bank of Italy;" devises "Branch Banking System," 358; financing Walt Disney Company, 359; financing during World War II, 359; and Golden Gate Bridge, San Francisco, 358-359; and Hollywood, 358; honored with U.S. Postal Stamp, 359; 357; legacy, 359; as "The Peoples Banker," 359; *see also* Bank of America

Giannini, Ferruccio (singer), 321-322; as early proponent of music recording, 322

Gilded Age, 146, 503

Giordano, Domenico (author's grandfather), xiii

Giordano, Jonathan (author's son), xi

Giordano, Matthew (author's son), xi

Giordano, Ralph (author), *6*, *15*, *22*, *31*, *80*, *251*,

Giordano, Ralph (boxer), 455, 456-457, *456*, name change 456; *see also* Young Corbett III

Giordano, Thomas (author's brother), *251*,

Giordano, Tomaso "Thomas" (author's father), xiii

Giordano, Umberto (composer), 312; *see also* Opera

Giovannitti, Arturo (labor organizer), 235; *see also* Ludlow Massacre

Giuseppe Verdi Monument, Verdi Square Park, *288*; *see also* Giuseppe Verdi

Gladstone, Douglas (biographer), 428; *see also* Mt. Rushmore and Luigi Del Bianco

Goats and Lynching in Tallulah, Louisiana, 123-134; *see also* Lynching

Godfather, The (movie), 4, 106-107, 108; as a story of an Italian "family," 107-108; *see also* Stereotyping; Mario Puzo

Godfather, The (novel), 107-108; *see also* Mario Puzo

Godfather, The: Part II (sequel), 4-5,

Gold Rush of 1848-1850 (California), Rush, 279, 280, 307, 343, 346, 353, 354, 356, 359, 366, 452-453; *see also* California

Goldberg, David (historian), 480; describes quota laws, 483; *see also* Eugenics

Golden Gate Bridge, San Francisco, 358-359, *358*; *see also* A.P. Giannini

Golden Gate Park, San Francisco, 285; *286*

Golf, 210

Gordon, Linda and Ku Klux Klan ideology, 504-505; candidates elected to state and local offices, 505; *see also* Ku Klux Klan

Gorme, Eydie (Italian American singer), 302

Gothic Revival (architecture), 169

Gould Memorial Library at New York University, 449-450; *450*

Gould, Stephen Jay (historian), 484; *see also* Eugenics

Gowanus Canal, Brooklyn, 204; *see also* Pascal D'Angelo

Gramophone recordings, 316, 322

Gran Teatro de Tacón, 168; *see also* Antonio Meucci; Opera

Grand Central Terminal, 26, *26*

Grand Gallop Can-Can dance, *see* Can-Can dance

Grand Opera in the United States; *see* Opera

Grand Tour of Italy, 135-136

Grant, Madison (trustee), 480-482, 496; *481*; aligned with Adolph Hitler's *Mein Kampf*, 481-482; outlines Eugenic belief, 480; and "legalized sterilization," 480; and "racist theories," 491; *see also*

Eugenics; Segregation; Discrimination

Grant, Ulysses S. (president), 55

Graziano, Rocky (boxer), 457

Great Depression, 262, 358, 463, 490

Great Lover, The *see* also Rudolph Valentino,

Great Migration of 1880 to 1920, 2, 7, 9, 343, 504; *see also* Immigration

Green Bay Packers (football team), 387

Greenbrier Resort, West Virginia, 522

Greyfriars Bobby (novel), 217; *see also* Nora Marks

Greyfriars Bobby: The True Story of a Dog (movie), 217; *see also* Nora Marks

Griffith D. W. (director), 23-25, 366, 372; *see also The Birth of a Natin*

Griffith, D.W. and Italian Melodramas, 24-25

Grignola, John (sculptor), 449; *see also* Woodlawn Cemetery

Grossoni, Orazio (sculptor), 285; *see also* Verdi Monument

Grove Music Online (opera history), 315; *see also* Antonio Pini-Corsi,

Grucci Fireworks Company, 463-464

Grucci, Felix James (entrepreneur), 463-463; *see also* Fireworks

Guarneri Andrea (violin maker), 342; *see also* Italian Instruments

Guasti, Secondo (wine maker), 347-348; and Italian Vineyard Company, 347-348

Guglielmo, Jennifer (historian), 98

Guide to the Montessori Method, A (treatise), 434-435; *435*; *see also* Maria Montessori

Guide to the Montessori Method, The (article), 434-435; *see also* Maria Montessori; Ellen Yale Stevens

Gulick, Luther Halsey (social reformer), 477-478; on "morality," 478

Gumina, Deanna Paoli (historian), 317; *see also* Antonietta Pisanelli

Gumma (Italian mistress), 244

Guns, Goats, and Italian: The Tallulah Lynching of 1899 (article), 125-126; *see also* Lynching

Gusenberg, Frank and Peter (gangsters), 475; *see also* Prohibition

H:

Haag, John (biographer), describes Lina Cavalieri as "master of self-promotion," 313-314

Haas, Edward F. (historian), 125-127; *see also* Tallulah Lynching

Halévy, Fromental (French composer), 297; *see also* Enrico Caruso; Opera

Hammersmith Palais de Danse (entertainment venue), 334-335; *see also* ODJB; Jazz

Hammerstein, Oscar (playwright), 281, 294, 500; parody *296*; legal entanglement with Luisa Tetrazzini, 281

Hamwi, Ernest A. (concessionaire), sells ice cream at 1904 St. Louis World's Fair, 110,

Handy, WC (musician), 338

Hanna-Barbera, movie and television characters, 377-378; *see also* Joseph Barbera

Hannibal (Carthaginian general), 375; *see also Cabiria*

Hanson, Fred (journalist), 401; *see also* Sacco and Vanzetti

Hanson, Ralph (football player), 387; *see also* "Blood and Sand;" as "Ralph Sand," 387

INDEX 569

Harlem (neighborhood), as "Italian Harlem," 224-225

Harlem Hellfighters, 401; *see also* World War I

Harlem's Hidden History (article), 224; *see also* Italian Harlem

Harper's Weekly, 80; *see also* Statue of Liberty

Harris and Blanck (garment company), 228-229; *see also* Triangle Shirtwaist Factory Fire

Harris, Isaac and Max Blanck (owners), 228; *see also* Triangle Shirtwaist Factory Fire

Harris, William Julius (U.S. senator), "an amendment to shut the door," 490-491

Harrison, Benjamin (president), 31, 105-106, 142; cites Columbus as "pioneer of progress and enlightenment," 105-106; denounces New Orleans lynching in New Orleans, 105-106; nationwide celebration of Columbus Day, 105-106; World's Columbian Exposition of 1893, 31,

Harrison, Benjamin Henry and World's Columbian Exposition of 1893, 31,

Harvard Crimson, The, 122; *see also* Robert F. Foerster

Harvard Law School, 400

Hawaii, viewed Italians as "white," 96

Hennessy, David C. (police chief), murder of, 102-105; *103*; *see also* New Orleans Lynching

Henry Street Settlement, 213; *see also* Lillian Wald; Hull House

Herman, Pete (boxer "Peter Gulotta"), 458

Hero of Two Worlds, 158; *see also* Giuseppe Garibaldi

Hewlett-Packard, 359; *see also* A.P. Giannini

Higham, John (historian), 113, 115

Highbrow Culture, 7,

Hill Country, Texas, and wine industry, 362-363

Hill, Donna (movie historian), writes on *The Son of the Sheik*, 388-389

Hine, Lewis (photo journalist), 231-232; *see also* Jacob Riis

Hip Hop (music genre), 467; *see also* Giovanni Schiavo

Histories, The (journal), 377

History of Ice Cream, The (article), 518

History of the Life and Voyages of Christopher Columbus, A (article), 30, 31-32; *see also* Christopher Columbus

History.com (website), 31-32, 104, 148; and Columbus Day, 31-32

Hitler, Adolph and Eugenics, 47, 121, 481-482, 492; "and "genocidal terror," 121, Inspiration" from America 481-482; *see also* Madison Grant; Eugenics; Paul A. Offit

Hitler, Adolph (evil dictator), and 1936 Olympic Games, 47; racial policies, 47-48,

HIV/Aids, 460

HMS Republic (sailing ship) applies Marconi wireless for sea rescue, 75-76

Hockey, 460

Hodge, 125-126; *see also* Tallulah lynching

Hollywood Boot Shop, 367; *see also* Salvatore Ferragamo

Hollywood Film Industry, 358; *see also* A.P. Giannini

Hollywood Film Industry, 4-5, 23-25, 44, 262, 344, 358, 365-368, 371-378, 397, 475, 476, 477, 529; and "bootlegging," 475; and glorified media accounts, 509; influenced by Italian immigrants, 372-376; and Italian Stereotypes, 377, 475; *see also* Prohibition; *Cabiria*;

Hollywood in Italy (exhibit), 344; *see also* Salvatore Ferragamo

Hollywood, negative Italian stereotypes, 377-378

Home Music Box, 329-331; *see also* Jazz

Homosexuality, 240; *see also* Rudolph Valentino

Honolulu, Hawaii, 96

Hoover, Herbert (U.S. president), 404, 471-472; *472*

Hoover, J. Edgar (FBI director), 461; *see also* Charles Bonaparte

Hot Dog, 109,

Hot Tub, *see* Jacuzzi

Hotel Ambassador in New York City, 391; *see also* Rudolph Valentino

Hotel St. Regis in New York City, *293*

Houston, Texas, 4

How Columbus Sailed into U.S. History, Thanks To Italians" (article), 30

How Italians Became White (article), 96; *see also* Brent Staples

How the Other Half Lives (book) , 187-189; *187, 189*; Genesis of the Tenement, 188-189; *see also* Jacob Riis

How the Tomato Became Part of Italian Culture (article), 514

How to Sing (instruction book), 284-285; *photo 285*; *see also* Luisa Tetrazzini,

Huddled Masses, The: The Immigrant in American Society, 1880-1921 (book), 6

Hughes, Allen (journalist), 310; *see also* Rosa Ponselle

Hughes, Robert (biographer), 445; *see also* Joseph Stella

Hull House in Chicago (settlement house), 213-220, *214, 216*; as "Italian Neighborhood," 212-214; "weekly schedule of events," 219; *see also* Jane Addams and Ellen Gates Starr

Hull, Charles Jerald (benefactor), 214; *see also* Hull House

Human Sexuality, 240

Humanities, 205-207

Hunt, Richard Morris (architect), 57-60, *57*; design of pedestal, 57; *see also* Statue of Liberty; Architecture

I:

I Fedora (Italian Opera), 312; *see also* Opera

I Pagliacci (Italian Opera), *299*; 300, 320; *see also* Opera; Enrico Caruso

I quattro libri dell'architettura (treatise), 320; *see also* Andrea Palladio

Ice Cream Cone, 109-111, 518; patent *110*; *see also* Italo Marchiony

Ice Cream, 109-111, 518; served at the President's House, 518

Il Giardino d'Italia (restaurant), 522

Il Pomodoro (tomato), 513-514

Il Trovatre (opera), 277; *see also* Opera

Immigrants 4-6, *6*, 46-47, 51-54, 66-67, *66*, 80-89, chart *85, 87, 88*, 93, 98-99, 120-121, 175-182, 205, 327, 470, 479-480, 482-483, 490, 498, 505, 531-532; experience at Ellis Island, 4-5, *6*; laborers, 98-99; population, 85-86; chart *85*; arriving at Ellis Island, 66, *66*; at Castle Clinton, 83; "door *slammed*

INDEX 571

shut," 479-480; of the Great Arrival, 205; seeing Statue of Liberty, 54; as "threats to Nativist values," 80-84; path to New Orleans, 327; as "undesirables," 175-182; as *"wretched refuse,"* 80-84; ; *see also* Ellis Island; Immigration Act of 1924; Immigration; Italian Immigrant

Immigration, 9, 17-49, 21-22, 44-47, 51-54, 65-68, 83-85, 87-88, *88*, 117-123, 353, 398, 470, 479, 490, 525-527, 531-532; before 1880, 49, 85; to California, 343-352; end of "era of mass immigration," 479; ferry to New York and Jersey City, 87-88, *88*; limitations, 470; ports of entry, 353; processing at Ellis Island, 66-67, 83; "push and pull," 67-68; quotas, 120-121; 482-483; restrictions, 485, 479, 491, 495; restriction as "avoiding another world war," 491; three periods, 9; under William Windom's guidance, 83; *see also* Castle Clinton; Ellis Island; Immigrants; Italian Immigration; William Windom

Italian Immigration to America and Boston's North End (essay), 117-121

Italian Immigrant, 1, 5-7, 10, 34-36, 52-92, *88*, 93, 108, 117-121, 138-140, 159-161, 182-191, 205, 211-212, *211*, 244-263, 318, 377-378, 505-506, 519, 521, 437, 470-471, *183*, *184*, *191*, *234*, agricultural skill, 505-506; and "American born children," 211-212; adding to American cultural success, 260-261; arriving in America, 155; and "artistic talent," 205; and American citizenship, 470; living in America, 5; in Boston, 117-121; in Colorado, 34-35; "death and

destruction," 76-78; in Denver, 35-36; at Ellis Island, 181; entering America, 6, 7; "help launch Hollywood film industry," 372-378; and Leisure, 246-263; macaroni, 521; in Louisiana, 97-100; population chart 85; in densely populated urban areas, 182-191; in U.S. Civil War, 159-161; various trade skills, 365; violence against, 93; *see also* Immigration; *The Fortunate Pilgrim*

Italian Immigrant in America, The (article), 210-215; *211*

Italian Immigrant Population to America, chart *85*

Immigration Act of 1924 (Johnson-Reed Act), 64, 482-483, 488, 505; described by the U.S. Office of the Historian, 483; law officially repealed, 490; *see also* Immigrants; Immigration

Immigration and Nationality Act of 1965, 490; *see also* Immigration Act of 1924

Immigration Documents, 531-532; *531*, *532*; *see also* Immigration; Immigrants; Ellis Island; Castle Clinton

Immigration and Pledge of Allegiance, 46-47, *see also* Immigration; Immigrants; Ellis Island; Castle Clinton

Impresario (producer), 257, 276, 291, 316-317, 319; defined 257; *see also* Giulio Gatti-Casazza.

In Little Italy (movie short), 24; *see also* D. W. Griffith,

Indianapolis 500 (motor car race), 451

Industrial Revolution, 17-49, 152, 210-213

Industrial Workers of the World (IWW), 235

Industrialization, 210, *see also* Industrial Revolution

Ingram, Rex (director), 383; *see also* Rudolph Valentino

Innocents Abroad (book), 137-138; *138*; *see also* Mark Twain

Institute of Texan Cultures, and Italian Immigrants, 361-362

International Boxing Hall of Fame, 456-457

International Dairy Foods Association, 109; *see also* Italo Marchiony

Internet Movie Database (IMDb.com), 13, 372-373; describes plot of *Cabiria*, 372-373

Introduction, 1-15

Invernizzi, Paolo (aviator), 408; *see also* Giuseppe Bellanca and Enea Bossi

Irish Times, The (journal), 335, 401; explains Al Smith's Italian Ancestry 401; *see also* Original Dixieland Jazz Band

Irving, Washington (author), 30, 271; *see also* Columbus Day

Isola, Pietro T. (sculptor), 451; *see also* Casoni & Isola,

It (intangible element), 372; *see also* Hollywood

It's A Wonderful Life (movie), 378; *see also* Frank Capra

Italians, 207, 253, 465-467; affinity, 1; Academy for Advanced Studies at Columbia University, 269; in Agriculture, *photo 234*; as "household names in America," 302; calling themselves "American," 49; in Boston, 117-121; in California, 343-352; in the U.S. Civil War, 158-161; classified as "dagoes," 94-95; cotton and sugarcane fields, 98-100; in Detroit, 494; and fictional criminal activity, 107-109, 490; perish in Triangle Shirtwaist Factory Fire, 225-231; willing to "grow grapes," 505-506; in Hollywood, 372-378; at Hull House, 215-220; as inferior to the "white" race, 480; Italian boxers, 456-459; as cheap labor, 95, 96-97, 201-205; lynched, 123-134, *133*; awarded Medal of Honor, 161; as "Mustache Pete's," 257; myths, 4, 397; change name to avoid discrimination, 452-453; "negativity," 3; in New York City, 21-22; occupations, 225-226; in Philadelphia, 519-520; population, 525-527; as Loyal Patriots, 48; in San Francisco, 352-395; in rural settlements, 97; in lowest social class below "Negroes," 95, 96-97, 484; singers as "household names in America," 302; racially suspect," 98; in "sewing-trades," 226-228; as "Sicilian," 97-98; "slaves" in America, 198-201; and Sports, 451-459; in Texas, 361-365; on *RMS Titanic*, 74-76; in Vineland, New Jersey, 504-507; as "white," 96, 498; writers, 204-207; in World War I, 470-472, 494; working across America, 225-239

Italians Coming in Great Numbers (editorial), 489

Italian American Heritage Month, 530; *see also* Janice Therese Mancuso

Italian American Heroes of World War I, 469-472

Italian American Museum of Los Angeles (museum), 34, 94-95; *see also* Marianna Gatto

Italian American Population in America, 525-527

Italian American singers as "household names in America," 302

Italian Americans, The History and Culture of a People (book), 136

Italian Americans, The: La Famiglia (documentary), 13

Italian Americans: A History (book), 1, 4, 509; *see also* Maria Laurino

Italian Americans: The History and Culture of a People (book), 12-13,

Italian Anarchists in America, 120; *see also* Sacco and Vanzetti

Italian Ancestry and Ellis Island, 90

Italian and Sicilian Immigrants, 98-99, 336; and Sicilian immigrants, desire to work, 97

Italian Bakery, 511-512

Italian Banking System, 117-121, 355; *see also* A.P. Giannini

Italian Boxers fight under Americanized names, 458-459

Italian Clown Tradition, 255; *see also* Enrico Caruso and Eduardo Migliaccio

Italian *Commedia dell'arte*, 255-256

Italian Community in San Francisco, 320, 457

Italian Culture in America, 2, 17-21, 51-64, 135-136, 153, 205-207, 244-245, 279, 284, 351-352, 377-378, 505, 511-513; before 1880, 51, 244-245; in California, 279; clown tradition, 255; discrimination, 492-493; earthquakes, 69-71, 76-78; image and "false imagery," 94; admired by "genteel" America, 496; *Commedia dell'arte*, 255-256; image as "criminal element," 101, as portrayed by Hollywood, 377-378; and Sunday afternoon dinner, 512; and "The Mysterious Italian Genius," 205-207; connections

with Statue of Liberty, 54-64; and Thomas Jefferson, 51; wine, 84

Italian Culture In America (book), 2,

Italian Culture: Facts, Customs, & Traditions, (article), 18

Italian Emigration of Our Times, The, 121-122; summary, *see also* Robert F. Foerster.

Italian entertainment at Hull House, 217, 219; *see also* Nora Marks

Italian Explorers, 12, 33, 48-49; Italian Food, 10, 284, 349-351, 509-524; common in America, 511-514; introduced to mass market, 521-522; and "slumming," 510; *see also* Chef Boyardee Company

Italian Government denounces lynching, 105-106

Italian Historical Society of America, 21-22

Italian Imprints, 5-6

Italian Influence at the Woodlawn Cemetery, The (article), 448-449

Italian Instruments, 338-342

Italian Language of Music, 326, 338-342

Italian man and *gumma* ("mistress"), 244

Italian Market (New Orleans), 98-100, *100*

Italian Market in Philadelphia, described, 519-520; *520*

Italian Melodramas, 24-25; *see also* D. W. Griffith,

Italian music, as nucleus of American cultural music, 341-342

Italian Musical Instruments, 338-342; *339, 340, 341*

Italian Opera Company, 277-278; *see also* Max Maretzek; Opera

Italian Organ Grinders, 175-182; with monkey, *180*

Italian Presence in American Art 1760-1860, The (book), 1-2, 155-156, 205

Italian Presence in American Art 1860-1920, The (book), 3, 444-445

Italian Presence in American Art 1860-1920, The (monograph), 444-445

Italian Renaissance, 11, 44, 60, 214, 355

Italian Restaurants in America, 510-511, *511*; and stereotypical red and white checkerboard table cloth,511

Italian Sculptors, 450-451

Italian Sons & Daughters of America, 126, 316

Italian Tradition of Wine Making in America, 345-346, 347-349, 362-363

Italian Unification, "impacts U.S. foreign policy," 158-159

Italian Unification, 18-20, 118-119, 157-158, 205, 418, 514; *see also* Giuseppe Garibaldi

Italian Vineyard Company, 347-348; *see also* Secondo Guasti

Italian violin linked to "America's unique Jazz culture," 342; *see also* "Italian Instruments"

Italian Wine in Texas, 362-363

Italian Wine in Walla Walla Washington, 351-352

Italian Wine in California, 345-349

Italian Women in the workplace, 225-226,

Italian Words in the American Vernacular, 528-519

Italian-American Cultural Heritage Center, 167; *see also* Garibaldi-Meucci Museum

Italian-American Image During the Twentieth Century, The (article), 93-94

Italian-American Sports Hall of Fame, 457

Italianate Architectural Style, 214-215, *215*

Italians as "the filthy, wretched, lazy, ignorant, and criminal dregs," 83-84; *84*

Italians and "lower wages than Negroes in America," 150-151

Italians and Morality, 143-144

Italians and regional differences, 97-98

Italians and Sicilians as not "white," 100,

Italians and Sicilians, 97-98

Italian-Swiss Colony Wine, 348-349; as a cooperative, 348; *see also* Andrea Sbarbaro

Italophile, 1; *see also* Thomas Jefferson

Italy, allied with Great Britain, France, and United States, 470; and banking, 355-356; compared to California, 344; cultural differences, 496; disinformation, 2; and "extreme poverty," 150-151; as fascist, 470; as birthplace of Opera; famous Opera Houses, 268; geography, 17-18, 69-72, 139-141; 344; map *19*; earthquake history, 74-78; and natural disasters, 69-72; recognizes Meucci as "inventor of telephone," 174; regions, 17-18; as top tourist destination, 136; tradition of fishing, 355; and volcanic eruptions, 69-71

Italy in Hollywood (exhibition), 310-311; *see also* Salvatore Ferragamo Museum

Italy Magazine, and tributes to Giuseppe Garibaldi, 162

INDEX

J:

Jackson Park, Chicago, 26

Jacuzzi Airplanes, 413-414; *414*

Jacuzzi, 413-414, 429; *see also* Aviation History

Jacuzzi Rachele, "designed and built a successful wooden propeller," 413

Jaffe, Irma B. (art historian), 1, 3, 205, 444-445; biography of Joseph Stella, 444-445; and "the mysterious Italian genius," 205

Jaffee Frank, Robin (curator), 447; *see also Joseph Stella*

James Reese Europe's Society Orchestra, 325; *see also* Jazz; Vernon and Irene Castle

Jane Addams Papers Project,

Jass in Chicago, 327; *see also* Jazz

Jass, *see* Jazz

Jazz (music), 323-342, *329*; *330, 331, 332, 333*; 476-477; as "America's Gift to the World," 323, 324; across the Atlantic to Italy, 337-338; as original American cultural creation, 323; birthplace, 323-325; first commercial recording, 328; encouraging dancers, 476-477; derived from many cultural art forms, 342; and "evolution to Italian descent," 326-333; as mix of two cultures, 327; recordings, 330-332, *330, 331*; summation, 324; term origins, 326-327; *see also* "Italian Instruments;" Original Dixieland Jazz Band (ODJB)

Jazz (PBS documentary), 327, 335; *see also* Jazz,

Jazz Club, *see* Reisenweber's; Jazz

Jazz Italian Style (book), 336; *see also* Jazz

Jazz Singer, The (movie), *see also* Al Jolson; Jazz

Jefferson, Thomas (Italophile), 1, 2, 3, 9, 11, 27, 51, 59, 91, 135-136, 153, 206, 225, 320, 342, 345, 421, 427, *427*, 449, 467, 515-516, 517, 518; and "affinity for Italian culture," 51; "genius was not by accident of birth," 206; sampling of ice cream, 518; as lifelong Italophile, 1-3, 59, 345; macaroni machine, 516; and Philip Mazzei, 91; as music enthusiast, 342;favored Italian style of music, 342; in Paris, 135; as president, 342; popularizing modern violin, 342; visits Italy, 11, 135-136, 517; wine production in America, 345

Jenny Lind Theatre, 279

Jersey City Railroad Station, 88, *88*

Jersey Shore (TV series), 106; *see also* Stereotyping

Jerusalem and Christopher Columbus, 34,

Jesuit Priests, 353

Jin Crow Laws, 487

John D. Calandra Italian American Institute, 7, 153

Johnny *Blood*, 387; *see* John Victor McNally

Johnson Quota Act of 1924, 120-121, 483, 488

Johnson, Lyndon B. (U.S. president), repeals Immigration law, 490

Johnson-Reed Act, 120-121, 483, 488; *see also* National Origins Act,

Jolson, Al (singer), 330; as America's best-known entertainer, 330; *see also* Jazz

Jones, Mary Harris "Mother Jones" (social reformer), 232

José, Edward (film director), 299; *see also* Enrico Caruso

Juan Gallardo (movie character), 384-385; *see also* Rudolph Valentino

Judge (political magazine), 82-83, *82*; depicts Statue of Liberty as "future emigrant lodging house, 82; "dumping" of immigrants at Statue of Liberty, 82-83; against William Windom, 83

Julio Desnoyers (fictional character), *see* Rudolph Valentino

K:

KDKA (radio station), 293

Keepers of the Gate: A History of Ellis Island, 52-53; *see also* Ellis Island; Immigration

Kelly, Matt (researcher), 450; *see also* Woodlawn Cemetery

Kermit the Frog (Muppet), emulates Rudolph Valentino as "World's Greatest Lover;" *see also* Rudolph Valentino

Kern, Jerome (playwright), 500

Kerns, Matthew (biographer), 303, 305; writing on "Morlacchi's American Debut"

Kilpatrick, William (educator), critical of Montessori Method, 435-436; *see also* Maria Montessori; Education

King Charles I, 518

King Edward VIII, 335; *see also* Original Dixieland Jazz Band

King George V, 335; *see also* Original Dixieland Jazz Band

King Henry II, 518

King Henry III, 256

King Louis XIV, 256

King of Italian Vaudeville Entertainers, *see* Eduardo Migliaccio

King Umberto I, 514

King, Gamaliel (architect), 44; *see also* Emma Stebbins

King, Gilbert (journalist), slurs Rudolph Valentino, 389, 390; *see also* Rudolph Valentino

Kingdom of Italy, 315

Klaczynska, Barbara (research historian), 519; and Ku Klux Klan in Philadelphia, 519; *see also* Ku Klux Klan; Discrimination

Klansmen Guardians of Liberty (newsletter), 403; illustration *403*; *see also* Ku Klux Klan; Discrimination

Klaske, Elise M. (historian)," 436-437; *see also* Maria Montessori

Klemfuss, Harry (press agent), *see* Rudolph Valentino Funeral

Knights, Melanie F. (historian), 18

Kramer, Rita (biographer), *see* Maria Montessori

Kraut, Alan (historian), 6, 7

Krehbiel, Henry E. (music critic), 274

Ku Klux Klan (KKK) (terrorist organization), 23-24, *24*; 86, 94, 148, *403*, *404*; *493,* 504-507; acceptance in mainstream society, 505; as anti-Catholic, 504-507; and church membership, 502; as "secular arm of churches," 501-502; ideology, 505-506; anti-immigrant 86, 504-507; as anti-Italian, 506, 519; "legal spike in membership," 479; in New Jersey, 506-507; in Philadelphia, 519; in Vineland, New Jersey, 504-507; in Washington D.C., 506; and White Nationalists, 94-95; *see also The Birth of a Nation*

Ku Klux Klan newsletter *Fellowship Forum*, 403-404; illustration *404*; *see also* Ku-Klux Klan

Kuper, Theodore Fred (professor), 3, 517

INDEX

L:

L'America, 5, *L'America*, 72-74; *see also* Italian Immigration

L'Amico Francesco (opera), 297; *see also* Opera

L'Italia (Italian language newspaper), 285

La Bohème (opera), 315; *see also* Opera

La Carusi, 153, **153**; *see also* Frederick Douglass

La Cenerentola (opera), *see* Antonio Pini-Corsi; Opera

La donna più bella del mondo (movie), 314; *see also* Lina Cavalieri

La Guardia, Fiorella (mayor), 181, 406-407, 420, 424, 449; as aviator 407; as Congressman, 181; as interpreter at Ellis Island, 407; as New York City Mayor, 181, 407; bans organ grinders, 181; *see also* Aviation; Giuseppe Bellanca; Ellis Island; Piccirilli Brothers

La Juive "The Jewess" (opera), 297; *see also* Enrico Caruso; Opera

La Marca, Gaetano (entrepreneur), 351

La Rocca, Nick, *see* Original Dixieland Jazz Band (ODJB)

La Salle University, 257

La Scala (opera house), 280, 289, 292, 297, 303; *see also* Opera; Arturo Toscanini

La Sonnambula, 280

La Stella (Italian language newspaper), 34-35,

La Storia: Five Centuries of the Italian American Experience (book), 12, 98-99, 114, 181, 496

La Traviata (opera), 281; *see also* Antonio Pini-Corsi; Opera

La Traviata, 318

Labor Actions, 129-131; 235-239

Labor Dispute in Tampa, Florida, 129-131

Laboulaye, Édouard de, and idea for Statue of Liberty (1811-1883), 54-55; *see also* Statue of Liberty

Ladies' Home Journal (magazine), 477

Lady Gaga (entertainer), 13

Lady in Black, The, 394; *see also* Rudolph Valentino

Lady Liberty *see* Statue of Liberty

Lama, Anthony "Tony" (boot maker), 365; *see also* Salvatore Lucchese

LaMotta, Giacobbe "Jake" (boxer), 457

Landis, Charles K. (lawyer), establishes Vineland, New Jersey as "alcohol free," 505

Lansky, Meyer (gangster), 475; *see also* Prohibition

Lanzetta, Anthony (entrepreneur), 463; *see also* Fireworks

Larghetto Adagio, *see* Italian Terminology of Music

Largo, *see* Italian Terminology of Music

LaRocca, Dominic James "Nick" (band leader), 327-333, **329, 333**; defended by journalist David Norris, 336; Jazz predecessors, 328; "learning by ear," 327; legacy eclipsed, 335; pursue music career, 327; perceived racist statement, 335; slight in PBS Documentary "Jazz," 335; praised by Louis Armstrong, 338; LaRocca, receives undue criticism, 327; viewed within the social lens of the time, 336; *see also* Jazz; Original Dixieland Jazz Band

Laskin, David (historian), 470-472

Latin Lover and his Enemies, The (article), 390; *see also* Rudolph Valentino

Latin Lover, 385; *see also* Rudolph Valentino,

Laurino, Maria (historian), 3, 4, 397, 509

Lazaretto

Lazaretto in Philadelphia (immigration station), 88-89, *89*; as immigrant point of entry to Philadelphia, 88-89; as Italian word for maritime quarantine station, 89; *see also* Immigration

Lazarus, Emma (poet), 58-59; *58*, 116; *see also* "The New Colossus" and Statue of Liberty

Lazzeri, Tony (baseball player), 453

Le mie veritá "My Truths" (autobiography), 314; *see also* Lina Cavalieri

Le Procope serving ice cream in France, 518

Lebensraum ("living space"), 492; *see also* Adolf Hitler, Eugenics

Legend of Rudolph Valentino, The (documentary), 396; *see also* Rudolph Valentino

Leif Erickson Day, 36; *see also* Christopher Columbus

Leisure, 210-212

LeMay, Curtis E. (General), 414-415; *see also* Giulio Douhet

Lento, see Italian Terminology of Music

Leoncavallo, Ruggero (opera composer), 255

Leonora (fictional character), 309; *see also* Rosa Ponselle; Giuseppe Verdi

LeRoy, Mervyn (director), 475; *see also* Prohibition

Levi Strauss & Co., 360; *see* Levi Strauss; Jacob Davis

Levine, Charles (aviator), 409; *see also* Giuseppe Bellanca

Levine, Lucie (historian), 419-420, 421-422; *see also* Piccirilli Brothers

Libertas, see Statue of Liberty

Liberty Coaster Company, 463; *see also* Radio Flyer; Antonio Pasin

Liberty Enlightening the World, see Statue of Liberty,

Liberty of Poetry 3D Representation, 61-63, *61*; as influence for Statue of Liberty, 61-62; *see also* Pio Fedi and Statue of Liberty

Library of Congress, 6, 14, 20, 51, 78, 94, 155, 342; and "Attacks on Italians," 51, 94; and natural disasters, 78

Librettist, defined, 269; *see also* Lorenzo Da Ponte

Lick, James (chocolate maker), 354; *see also* Domenico Ghirardelli

Lies My Teacher Told Me (book), 33; *see also* James Loewen,

Life on the Mississippi (book), 137; *see also* Mark Twain

Lina Cavalieri: My Secrets of Beauty (book), *see* Lina Cavalieri

Lincoln Memorial, Washington, D.C., 415-416; *416, 417*; *see also* Abraham Lincoln; Piccirilli Brothers

Lincoln, Abraham (U.S. President), 61-62, 148, 159-160, 415-416, *416, 417*; 427; *427*; assassination, 62; issues Emancipation Proclamation, 160; offers Garibaldi to join U.S. Civil War, 159-160; *see also* Giuseppe Garibaldi; Piccirilli Brothers; Pio Fedi

Lindbergh, Charles (aviator), 405-406, 410, 411; *405*; *see also* Frank Vittor

L'Italo-Americano, (newspaper), on Tallulah Lynching, 126,

Literacy Tests, 120, 485; *see also* Discrimination

Literary Digest, The (journal), 485-486, 497; anti-immigrant cartoon, 485; associated with "primitives and promiscuity," 497, illustration *486*

Little Caesar (movie), 475; *see also* Prohibition

Little Chronicle Publishing Company, The, *see* Nora Marks

Little Italian Slaves, 198-201; *see also* Padrone System

Little Italy (neighborhood), 9, 181-185, *183, 184*, 224-225, 249, 251-252, 474, 510, 519, 526,; described, 224-225

Little Red Wagon, 462-463; *see also* and Radio Flyer

Livery Stable Blues – Fox Trot (song),

Livery Stable Blues (song), 330, 334; *330*; *see also* Jazz

Livy, Titus Livius (ancient poet), 372; *see also* Cabiria

Lo Cascio, Claudio (biographer), 327; *see also* Nick LaRocca

Locali Storici d'Italia, designates Barbetta Restaurant as historic, 524

Lochner v. New York - 198 U.S. 45 – 1905 (Supreme Court Decision), 242-243; limit workday for bakers, 242-243

Lodge, Senator Henry Cabot (U.S. Senator), 111-120, *112*, 136, 519; as "Italian-hating," 111-115, 120; rebuttal to Emma Lazarus poem, 116-117; and "Lynch Law and Unrestricted Immigration," 114; and "literacy test" for immigrants, 120; supports "good people of New Orleans," 114; "disciple of Social Darwinism," 119; "heightened xenophobia," 115

Loewen, James W. (historian) and Columbus, 33, 498; Columbus, 33; and segregation, 498

Lollobrigida, Gina (actress), 314; *see also* Lina Cavalieri

London Palladium, (entertainment venue), 335; *see also* Original Dixieland Jazz Band

London, 281, 334

London, 334

Long Way Home, The (book), 470; see also David Laskin

Lorenzo Da Ponte, a Bridge from Italy to New York (exhibition), 268-269; *see also* Lorenzo Da Ponte

Los Angeles Times (newspaper), 35, 36-37; *see also* Christopher Columbus

Lotha, Gloria (cultural editor), describes Enrico Caruso's vocal range 297

Lotta's Fountain,

Lotta's Fountain, San Francisco, 282-284, *photo 283*; *see also* Lotta Crabtree

Louisiana, 95-111, 268, 327; *see also* Lynching

Lowbrow Culture, 7,

Lower East Side of Manhattan, 212, 249; *see also* Jacob Riis

Lucchese™ Boot Company, *see* Salvatore Lucchese

Lucchese, Josephine (opera singer), as "The American Nightingale," 302, 318-319; *320*, 364; as cast member of San Carlo Opera Company, 319; marriages, 318; born in San Antonio, 318; voice lessons with Virginia Colombati, 318-319; *see also* Salvatore Lucchese; Lucchese Boots

Lucchese, Salvatore "Sam" (bootmaker), 318, 363-365, *364*; celebrity clients, 365; death of,

364; purchases Mexican-American theater, 364; obtains U.S. Citizenship, 364; *see also* Josephine Lucchese

Luciano, Charles "Lucky" (gangster), 475; *see also* Prohibition

Luconi, Stefano (historian), lynching of Italians, 132-133

Ludlow Massacre, Colorado, 235-239, Ludlow Massacre, *237, 238, 239*

Luftwaffe (German air force), 414-415; *see also* Giulio Douhet

Lusitania (ocean liner), 75, 469; *see also* Guglielmo Marconi

Lutes, 341; *see also* "Italian Instruments"

Luther, Martin (cleric), 502

Lynching *illustration 127*; *see also* Tallulah Lynching

Lynching of Italians, 3-4, 101,-111,123-134, *127, 133, 134*, 316, 392; and "Back-to-Back" describes bodies of Ficarrotta and Albano, 131; and "corpses were left hanging overnight;" 130-132, *133*; defined, 101; "gallows humor," 130-132; "humiliate the victims in death," 130-133; "to serve as a warning," 130-133, *133*; "Swing in Moonlight," 131; and "technology of photography," 133-134; as "a transitive verb," 101

M:

M'Guffey's Reader, 496; *see also* Segregation; Americanization

Mac and Cheese (food), 11

Macaroni Machine, 521-524; *see also* Macaroni

Macaroni, 1, 10-11, 284, 512-516, 521-524, illustration *523*; as common in American, 515-516; defined, 515; and "patriotic song," 517; recipe, 516; and tomato sauce, 512; *see also* Thomas Jefferson; Pasta

Macchietta Coloniale (fictional characters), 253; *see also* Eduardo Migliaccio

MacManus, Frank (lynch victim), **photo 134**

Madalena, Ralph J. (Valente grandson), 471; *see also* Michael Valente

Madden, Owney (gangster), 475; *see also* Prohibition

Made in Hollywood: Italian Stereotypes in the Movies, (documentary), 377,

Madison Square Garden, 457; *see also* Boxing

Maestrissimo! (article), 288-289; *see also* Giulio Gatti-Casazza.

Mafia (criminal organization), 101, 104, 113, 114, 397, 461, 466-467, 529; and "false accusations," 467; as "more fantasy than fact," 101; influence on Rap Music, 467; *see also* Henry Cabot Lodge; Giovanni Schiavo; Hollywood; Stereotyping

Maggio, Joseph (entrepreneur), as "The Carrot King," 350-351

Maioglio Brothers (restaurant), 524; *see also* Barbetta Restaurant

Maioglio, Laura (restaurant owner), 524; *see also* Barbetta Restaurant

Maioglio, Sebastiano (restaurant owner), 524; *see also* Barbetta Restaurant

Maioglio, Vincenzo (restaurant owner), 524; *see also* Barbetta Restaurant

Maisel, Max (publisher), 240; *see also* Margaret Sanger

Maison Carrée (Roman temple), 361, *361*

INDEX

Maison Carrée, 360; 361, *361*
Maloney, Wendi (historian), 323
Malthus, Thomas, 240; *see also*
Margaret Sanger
Man Farthest Down, The (book), 68,
148-149, 152, *148*; *see also*
Booker T. Washington
Mancusi, Aldo (curator), 301-302;
302, *see also* Enrico Caruso
Mancuso, Janice Therese (historian),
xi, 37-39, 430, 509-510, 530;
explains Caruso launches
phonograph industry, 300;
explains, classic Radio Flyer
wagon, 463; *see also* Italian
American Heritage Month
Mandatory education, 496
Mandatory public education for
children, 205, 432, 496-497; *see
also* Maria Montessori
Mandell, Sammy (boxer "Salvatore
Mandala"), 458
Mandolins, 341; *see also* "Italian
Instruments"
Mangione, Jerre and Ben Morreale
(cultural historians), 12-23, 98-99,
122, 496; partnership of Italian-
Swiss Colony, 348; explain misuse
of word "mafia," 114; explain
Xenophobia, 114; *see also La
Storia*
Manhattan Opera House, 281; *see
also* Opera
Manhattan Special (coffee soda), 14
Manon Lescaut (opera), 312; *see also*
Lina Cavalieri,
Marchegiano, Rocco Francis (boxer),
see Rocky Marciano
Marchione, Sister Margherita
(educator and historian), 90-92, *92*
; autobiography, 91; donates
Mazzei documents to Thomas
Jefferson Foundation, 91, as
Professor Emeritus of Italian
language, 91; publications, 91; on

Philip Mazzei, 91; *see also*
Farleigh Dickinson University;
Thomas Jefferson
Marchiony, Italo (inventor), 109-111,
110, 518; factory in Hoboken,
New Jersey, 110; first ice cream
cone, 109; invents ice cream cone,
109-111, 518
Marciano, John Bemelmans
(journalist), recalls Messina
earthquake, 76-78
Marciano, Rocky (boxer), 457
Marconi, Guglielmo (Italian
inventor), 56, 74-76, 292-294,
293, 425, 463; and "saves" Eiffel
Tower 56; Nobel Prize Award,
293; and *Titanic* 74-76; wireless
transmission, 74-76; *see also*
Radio
Mardi Gras (painting), *see* Joseph
Stella
Maremoto (tsunami), *see Messina
Earthquake*
Maretzek, Max (impresario), 276-
279, *279*; as director of traveling
opera company, 277-278; and
German Operas, 278; proposal to
rent "Forest Cottage" to Antonio
Meucci, 276; Max Maretzek
Italian Opera Company, 169; rents
Staten Island home to Meucci and
Garibaldi, 169; *see also* Opera;
Antonio Meucci
Margherita Pizza, origin, ingredients,
514
Maria Montessori Sails to America
(book),
Marinari, Maddalena (professor),
travel bans, 488-489; explains
immigration processing system,
490; *see also* Immigration
Marino Faliero (opera), 277; *see also*
Opera
Marino, Cesare (biographer), 307;
see also Carlo Gentile

Maritime Quarantine Station *see* Lazaretto,

Marks, Nora (journalist), 216-218; as "children's book author," 217; as Eleanor Atkinson, 217; enthralled with Italian culture at Hull House, 217; invited to Hull House, 217-218; as "pen name," 217; "a visit with American and Italian friends," 217; writes of evening of Italian entertainment at Hull House, 217-218; *see also* Hull House

Marsalis, Wynton (musician), 335; *see also* Jazz

Martegana, Giuseppe (artist), 157-158; *see also* Giuseppe Garibaldi Marble Bust

Martin, Dean (Italian American singer), 302

Martinelli, Giovanni (historian), 318; *see also* Virginia Colombati

Martone, Eric (historian), 13, 136

Marx Brothers (performers), 258-259; *see also* Vaudeville

Marx, Leonard "Chico" (performer), 258-259; as stereotypical Italian, 259; *see also* Vaudeville

Mascagni, Pietro (composer), 267, *267*,

Mason, Patrick (journalist), 33-34; *see also* Christopher Columbus

Massachusetts, 399-401; 401; *see also* Sacco and Vanzetti

Masses, The (magazine), 239, *239*, *see also* Ludlow Massacre

Master Carvers: Casoni & Isola (article), 450-451; *See also* Woodlawn Cemetery

Master Class, describes Italian terminology, 326

Mastrantonio, Mary Elizabeth (actress), 107; *see also Two Bits*

Mastro-Valerio, A. (editor), 217, 219-220; as "the Chicago

Garibaldi," 217; *see also* Jane Addams; Hull House

Mathis, Jane (screen writer), 394, *394*; as friend of Rudolph Valentino, 394; "temporarily loan" of burial crypt for Rudolph Valentino, 394; *see also* Rudolph Valentino

Maxim's (dance palace), 381; *see also* Rudolph Valentino

Mazzei, Philip (statesman), 51, 59, 91, 345; commitment to liberty, 59; and Declaration of Independence, 91; and wine production in America, 345; as "Zealous Whig," 91; *see also* Statue of Liberty *see also* Thomas Jefferson; Sister Margherita Marchione; Statue of Liberty

Mazzini, Giuseppe (statesman), 61, 220; *see also* Giuseppe Garibaldi

McArthur, Judith N. (biographer), 318; *see also* Josephine Lucchese

McClure, Samuel (editor), 432; *see also* Maria Montessori, *McClure's Magazine*,

McClure's (magazine), 432-434, *432, 434*; articles on Maria Montessori, 432-434; billed as "The Marketplace of the World," 432; as "influential American magazines," 432; *see also* Maria Montessori

McMahon, John R. (editor), 477; *see also Ladies' Home Journal*

McNally, John Victor (football player), as "Johnny Blood," 387

Mein Kampf (book), *see* Adolf Hitler, Paul A. Offit, Madison Grant

Melford, George (director), 383; *see also* Rudolph Valentino

Memories of the Opera (autobiography), 291; *see also* Giulio Gatti-Casazza,

INDEX 583

Mencken, H.L. (cultural critic), 501-502; *501*; *see also The American Mercury*

Mennillo, Francesco "Frank" (padrone), 381, 391; as "close friend of Valentino," 381; as "Olive King," 381; 381; at Valentino's hospital bedside, 391; *see also* Rudolph Valentino

Merola, Gaetano (conductor), 302, 310, 320; death of, 320; forms resident opera company in San Francisco, 320; *see also* Opera

Merriam-Webster (dictionary), 1, 40, 112, 303, 528; defines "American Impresario," 257; defines Can-Can dance, 303; defines "lynch," 101; defines Nationalism and Patriotism, 23; dictionary defines "Xenophobia," 112

Merry Melodies cartoon series, 180; *see also* Organ Grinder

Messina Earthquake, Italy, 68-72, 76-78, *70, 71*, "death and devastation," 70-71, *70, 71* as "most destructive to hit Europe," 68-71; Italian government response, 69-71; and resulting *maremoto* (tsunami), 68-71; recovery of the dead, *photo 70, 71*; and "residual problems," 72; survivors, 68-70; 76-78; *See also* John Bemelmans Marciano

Metropolitan Museum of Art in New York, 12, 161-162, 340, 368, 416, 417-418; and "Cesnola Collection," 162; and "oldest surviving pianoforte," 339-340; *340*; *see also* Luigi di Palma Cesnola; Salvatore Ferragamo; Piccirilli Brothers

Metropolitan Opera House in New York, 278, 288-291, 294-296, *295*, 297, 307, 312, 320, 524; orchestra, 291; *see also* Giulio Gatti-Casazza; Opera

Meucci, Antonio (inventor), 163, 168-174, *168, 170*, 270, 276-277; in Cuba, 168-169; death in obscurity, 166, 173-174; and Esterre moved to U.S., 168; financial ruin, 173-174; and Garibaldi friendship, 276; with Garibaldi in Candle making business, 171-172; house moved, 166; injured in Staten Island Ferry disaster, 171-172; injuries reported in *The New York Tribune*, 172; recognized by Italy as inventor of telephone, 174; as "inventor of the telephone," 167; laboratory, 170; on "public assistance, 174; home on Staten Island *170*; "stonewalled," 173; temporary housing in Manhattan, 168; trial on ownership of telephone patent, 172-173; *see also* Garibaldi-Meucci Museum; Giuseppe Garibaldi; Max Maretzek,

Mezzogiorno, 7, 9, 175; defined, 9

Michelangelo, 496

Middleweight Championship, *see* Boxing

Midgley, Denis (music professor), explains Monteverdi as developer of Opera, 339

Migliaccio, Eduardo "Farfariello" (entertainer), 251-255; *254*; compared to Enrico Caruso 254-255; as "Farfariello," review, 253; as "King of Italian Vaudeville Entertainers," 251-252; *see also* Vaudeville

Migliaccio, Richard (grandson), 251; *see also* Eduardo Migliaccio

Milan, Italy (city), 98, 256, 289, 297, 303, 410

Miller, Francis Trevelyan and John W. Davis (educators), 498-499; *see also* Eugenics

Milroy, Elizabeth (art historian), 42-43; *see also* Emma Stebbins

Mining in Washington State, 234-235; recruit a labor of Italian immigrants, 34,

Miscegenation, 500; *see also* Segregation

Misinformation, 497-499; *see also* Xenophobia

Mismeasure of Man, The (book), 484; *see also* Eugenics

Missionaries of St. Charles Borromeo, 438-439; *see also* Mother Frances Cabrini

Missionary Sisters of the Sacred Heart of Jesus, *see also* Mother Cabrini

Mitchell, Billy (general), 414, 415; *see also* Giulio Douhet

Moderato, see Italian Terminology of Music

Modern Language of music, 326

Modernism, 444-448; *see also* Joseph Stella

Modotti, Tina (actress), 311, 378-379; *379*; as one of "Four of the Biggest Stars of the Era," 378-379; death, 379; legacy, 311; moves to Mexico, 379; "mostly forgotten," 378; as "political activist," 379

Monkey *see* Italian Organ Grinders

Monod, David (historian), 258; *see also* vaudeville

Montesano, Giuseppe (doctor), 431; *see also* Maria Montessori

Montessori Method, "three distinct periods," 436-437; *see also* Maria Montessori

Montessori Method, The (manual), 430-435, *430, 435*

Montessori Method, The (textbook), 431-432; *see also* Maria Montessori

Montessori, Alessandro (father), 430; *see also* Maria Montessori

Montessori, Carolina (great granddaughter), 432; *see also* Maria Montessori

Montessori, Maria (educator), 418, 429-437; *430, 432, 434, 435*; birth of son, 431; critics, 435-437; death, 437; decline, 436-437; as "one of first female doctors in Italy, 430; expansion of schools applying "Montessori Method," 432-433; legacy into 21st century, 437; medical career, 431; monthly feature in *McClures*, 432-434; prominence in America, 432; schools, 429-437; schools in America, 432; textbook, 431-432; "three distinct periods," 436-437; transitions "from physician to educator," 431; visits America, 432

Montessori Movement in America, 431-434; *see also* Maria Montessori

Montessori, Mario (son), accompanies Maria Montessori to America, 434

Montessori, Renilde (mother), 430; *see also* Maria Montessori

Montessori System Examined, The (critique), 435-436; *see also* Maria Montessori

Monticello, 11; *see also* Thomas Jefferson

Montmartre area of Paris, 303

Moore, Anna "Annie" (first immigrant at Ellis Island), 66; *see also* Ellis Island

Moore, Clement C. (author), 271; *see also* Lorenzo Da Ponte

INDEX

Morality Critics, 500-502; *see also The American Mercury*

Moran, George "Bugs" (gangster), 475; *see also* Prohibition

Moreno, Barry (historian), 66; *see also* Ellis Island

Morlacchi, Giuseppina Antonia "Josephine" (ballerina), 302-307, *304, 305, 307*; death, 306; debut in New York City, 303; fame grows, 303; "first female performer in Wild West Shows," 303-307; introduces Can-Can dance to America, 302-303; *see also* Can-can Dance

Moroder, Jay (journalist), reports on Rudolph Valentino funeral, 392-393

morra (Italian game), 211

Morreale, Ben (cultural historian), 98-99; *see also* Mangione and Morreale

Morton, Jelly Roll (musician), 336; *see also* Jazz

Moses, Victoria (historian), 259; *see also* vaudeville

Moshulu (sailing ship), 5; *see also* Immigration; Ellis Island; *The Godfather*

Most Beautiful Woman in the World, The (movie), 314; *see also* Lina Cavalieri

Mother Cabrini and the Missionaries of St. Charles Borromeo, 437-444

Mother Frances Cabrini (saint), 437-444, *438, 440, 442, 443*; memorial at Castle Clinton, 441-444; *443*; statue, Battery Park City, 443

Motherhood, 244; *see also* Margaret Sanger

Motion Pictures, 372; *see also* Hollywood

Moulin Rouge, Paris, 303-304

Movie-Made America: A Cultural History of American Movies, 3880, 389

Mozart, Wolfgang Amadeus (composer), 268-274; *272*; and Da Ponte collaboration, 269; and Italian opera, 270; *see also* Lorenzo Da Ponte; Opera

Mr. Peanut (icon), 462; *see also* Amadeo Obici

Mt. Rushmore Monument, South Dakota, 426-428; *427, 428*; *see also* Luigi Del Bianco

Muffuletta Sandwich, and Italian / Sicilian origin, 509-510

Mulberry Bend Park (New York City), 40, 222-224; *223*; renamed as "Columbus Park," 224; *see also* Little Italy; Mulberry Bend Park

Mulberry Street, as "Little Italy," 40, 183, *183, 223*, 249

Muller v. Oregon - 208 U.S. 412 – 1908 (Supreme Court Decision), 242-243; women as "weaker sex," 243; *see also* U.S. Supreme Court

Muppet Show, 396; *see also* Rudolph Valentino

Murals by Constantino Brumidi, The (article), 155-156

Muscio, Giuliana (historian), reflects upon Enrico Caruso, 298; describes *verismo*, 298

Musée du Louvre, Paris, 161

Museo della Musica, Venice, Italy, collection of musical instruments, 341

Museo Ferragamo in Florence, 344

Museo Italo America, 353, 413; *see also* Jacuzzi

Museo Salvatore Ferragamo, 368; *see also* Salvatore Ferragamo

Music Trades (magazine), 319

Music Trades (magazine), 319, *319*, *see also* Josephine Lucchese

Musical Instruments, as "distinctly Italian," 11-12, 338-342

Mussolini, Benito (dictator), 205, 393; *see also* Rudolph Valentino

Muzquiz, Albert (writer), 363; *see also* Salvatore Lucchese

My Cousin (movie), 299; *see also* Enrico Caruso

My Life of Song (autobiography), 284; *see also* Luisa Tetrazzini

My Secrets of Beauty (book), 314; *see also* Lina Cavalieri

Myth Busting Italians and the Italian Mafia, 151, 398-401, 465-466; *see also* Giovanni Schiavo; Booker T. Washington

N:

Naldi, Nita (actress), 385; *see also* Rudolph Valentino

Naples, Italy (city), 3, 10, 72, 97-98, 124-125, 139-141, 143, 249, 255, 275, 297, 307, 316, 320, 366, 398, 456, 474, 514-515, as birthplace of pizza, 514; *see also* Enrico Caruso; Macaroni; Pizza; Rick Steves; Mark Twain

Napoleon Bonaparte (emperor), 18, 461; and Nationalism, 18; *see also* Charles Bonaparte

Nasaw, David (historian), xi, 23

Nathan, George Jean (cultural critic), 501-502; *501*; *see also The American Mercury*

Nation, The (news magazine), 203; *see also* Pascal D'Angelo

National Academy of Recording Arts & Sciences, 300-301; *see also* Enrico Caruso

National Air Races of 1923, 408; *see also* Aviation

National Child Labor Committee, 233

National Education Association, 232

National Endowment for the Humanities, 8

National Football League (NFL), 387, 453; *see also* Rudolph Valentino

National Football League (NFL), 453

National Football League Hall of Fame, 387

National Geographic (magazine), 142, 244; *see also* Eugene Schuyler

National Historic Landmark, 450; *see also* Woodlawn Cemetery

National Institute of Allergy and Infectious Disease (NIAID), 460; *see also* Dr. Anthony Fauci

National Italian American Foundation (NIAF), 465

National Italian American Sports Hall of Fame, 453

National League, *see* Baseball

National Origins Act of 1924, 479, 483-488; *see also* Immigrant Quota Act of 1921,

National Park Service cites Statue of Liberty Pedestal, 57

National Park Service links negative Nativists reaction against immigrants, 81-82

National Park Service, 428; *see also* Luigi Del Bianco

National Park Service, 64

National Parks Service, describes parody of Statue of Liberty, 81-82

National Register of Historic Places, 424; *see also* Piccirilli Brothers

National Restaurant Association, 510

Nationalism and Nativism respond to "New Immigration," 22-23,

Nationalism, 17-49; confused with Patriotism, 23; defined, 18, 23

Native American Indians 496; *see also* Segregation

Native American Indians, 94-95

INDEX 587

Nativism, 13, 22-24, 80, 210; 478-479, 519; blame immigrants for taking away jobs, 210; *see also* Discrimination; Ku Klux Klan; Nationalism; Segregation

Naturalization Act of 1790 (1 Stat. 103, enacted March 26, 1790), 479

Nazi Party, 47-48, *48*, 470, 481-482; *see also* Eugenics; Adolph Hitler; Madison Grant

Nazi Salute, similar to Bellamy Salute, 47-48; *48*; *see also* 1936 Olympic Games, Francis Bellamy; Pledge of Allegiance

NBC Radio Studios, 294; *see also* Arturo Toscanini

Neapolitan folk songs, 255, 317; *see also* Enrico Caruso

Neapolitan *paisan*, 251, 254-255; *see also* Enrico Caruso; Naples

Neapolitan style pizza, 511, 514-515

Neo Classical (architectural style), 27, *27*, 44, 162, 165-166, 361, *361*, 420; buildings of the White City, 27; *27*; *see also* Architecture

New Colossus, The (poem), 59; *see also* Emma Lazarus; Statue of Liberty

New Haven, Connecticut, 309; *see also* Rosa Ponselle

New Jersey, 155, 527-528

New Orleans Jazz National Historical Park, 328; *see also* Jazz

New Orleans, 3-4, 30, 101-111, 114, 123-134, 268, 323-333, 337-338, 397, 484; docks, 98-99, *99*; and Jazz, 323-342; "lynch mob," 104-105; lynching, 101-111, illustration *105*, 123-134; as "Opera Capital," 268; Muffuletta Sandwich, 509-510; musicians, 327-328; residents "in a frenzy," 102-103; *see also* Jazz; Lynching; Opera

New Wave of Immigration, 34-35,

New York Academy of Music, 277, *277*

New York Armory Show, 445-448; *see also* Joseph Stella

New York Call, The (newspaper), 239-240; *see also* Margaret Sanger

New York City, 8, 25-26; *26*, 31, 39-44, 97, 163, 184, 212-214, 222-223, 229, 239-242, 244, 249-252, 268-269, 276, 283, 287-288, *288*, **289-290,** 303, 316, 330, 334, 352, 359, 371, 385, 448-451, 478, 479, 480, 496-497, 500, 502, 503, 512, 513, 519, 526-527; honors Christopher Columbus, 223; church celebrations, 249; as "direct entry point from Atlantic Ocean, 51-53; Fire Department (FDNY), 229; marathon, 527; and "local morons," 502; neighborhoods separated by wealth, 213; Department of Parks & Recreation, 40, 222-223, 287-288; Police Department (NYPD), 393, 462, *462*; most populous city in U.S., 184; Settlement Houses, 212-214; subway, 8, 288, *288,* *see also* Ellis Island; New York City Marathon; Jacob Riis, Triangle Shirtwaist Factory Fire; Adolph Ochs

New York Evening Transcript (newspaper), 303; *see also* Giuseppina Morlacchi

New York Herald Tribune, The (newspaper), 159, 163, 174, 204, 314, 401, 450, 465; articles by Lina Cavalieri, 314; describes Garibaldi's arrival in New York, 163; "supports Lincoln's choice of recruiting Garibaldi," 159; Meucci obituary, 174; *see also* Pascal D'Angelo; Woodlawn Cemetery

New York Public Library, 422-424; *423*; *see also* Patience and Fortitude, Piccirilli Brothers

New York Review, The (literary journal), 101, 466, ; *see also* Giovanni Schiavo

New York State Athletic Commission, 454-455; *see also* Boxing

New York State Supreme Court Building, 40-42, *41*

New York Times, The (newspaper), 9, 14, 43, 68-71, 76-78, 84, 95-96, 98, 104, 108, 123, 129-130; 142, 171-172-182, 257, 282, 287, 290, 310, 320, 391, 405, 439, 455, 457, 479, 480, 489-490; "Chief Hennessy Avenged," 104; describes Italians as "the filthy, wretched, lazy, ignorant, and criminal dregs," 84; lower East Side, 175-182; Earthquakes, 69-71; false report to "weed out undesirable Italians," 490; first Italian immigrant, 9; "Five Italians Lynched," 123; tells of "illegal processing of Italians," 489; Italian Discrimination, 479; "justification of mob justice," 123; Messina Earthquake, 68-69; review of *The Fortunate Pilgrim*, 108; obituary for Young Corbett III (Giordano), 457; cites Rosa Ponselle, as "one of the greatest operatic talents," 310; prejudice editorial, 489-490; Staten Island Ferry disaster, 171-172; stereotypes against immigrants, 84, 489-490; reports on Tallulah lynching, 123; Tampa Lynching, 129-130; on Vaudeville, 257

New York Tribune, The (newspaper), 172, 174; death of Lorenzo Da Ponte, 274; Antonio Meucci's injuries, 172

New York Zoological Society, 480; *see also* Eugenics; Madison Grant

Niblo, Fred (director), 384; *see also* Hollywood; Rudolph Valentino

Niccolini, Giovanni Battista (poet and playwright), 61; *see also* Basilica Santa Croce

Night Before Christmas, The (poem), 271; *see also* Lorenzo Da Ponte

Nîmes, France (city), 361; *361*; *see also* Denim; Levi Strauss

Niña, Pinta, and *Santa Maria* (Columbus ships), 28-29; *see also* Christopher Columbus

Noakes, Jeremy (historian), describes *Lebensraum*, 492

Nobel Prize in Physics, 293; *see also* Guglielmo Marconi

Nobili, Giovanni Pietro Antonio "John" (priest), founding of Santa Clara College, 353

Noce, Angelo (editor), 34, 35, credited for Colorado state holiday of Columbus Day, 35; *see also* Christopher Columbus; Columbus Day

NonèRadio (Italian language news site), 356; *see also* A.P. Giannini

Norfolk County Courthouse in Dedham, Massachusetts, 400; *400*; *see* Sacco and Vanzetti

Normal Schools, 496; *see also* Segregation

Norris, David (journalist), defends Nick LaRocca and ODJB, 336,

North Beach, San Francisco, 317, 357

North End neighborhood and Paul Revere House (Boston), 117-121, *118*

Notes on the State of Virginia, 206; *see also* Thomas Jefferson

Nude Descending a Staircase (painting), 445; *see also* New York Armory Show

INDEX 589

Nudity in American Culture, 445; *see also* New York Armory Show

Nureyev, Rudolf (actor/dancer), 396; *see also* Rudolph Valentino

NY Review of Books, The, summary of *Second Coming of the KKK,*

O:

O'Banion, Dion (gangster), 474; *see also* Prohibition

O'Brien, Keith (author), 221; *see also* Amelia Earhart

O'Connor, Bill (New Orleans police officer), 102; *see also* David C. Hennessy

O'Connor, Francis V. (professor), 155-156; *see also* Constantino Brumidi

O'Neill, Eugene, 500; *see also The American Mercury*

Oakley, Annie, 305-306; *see also* Josephine Morlacchi

Obici, Amadeo (business owner), 462; *see also* Planters Peanuts; Mario Peruzzi

Ocean Travel, and danger, 72-76

Ochs, Adolph (editor), 69; *see also* Messina Earthquake; *The New York Times*

Office of the Historian of the U.S. Department of State, 18, 158-159, 483; describes "Unification of Italian States," 20, 158-159

Offit, Paul A. (journalist), *see also* Madison Grant, Adolf Hitler, *Mein Kampf*

Old Rhinebeck Aerodrome, New York, 405; *see also* Charles Lindbergh

Old West, 303-306, 317; *305; see also* Ned Buntline; Josephine Morlacchi

Oliver, Joseph "King" (musician), 328; *see also* Jazz

Olmstead, Frederick Law Olmstead (landscape architect), 222; *see also* Urban Parks

Olsen, Thelma Lynn, xi, 6, *6,* 15, 60, 79, 88, *511*

Olympic Games, 47-48; *48,* 460

Omohundro, "Texas Jack" (performer), 303-307, *305, 307;* death of, 306; *see also* Ned Buntline; Giuseppina "Josephine" Morlacchi

Omohundro, Rick (biographer), 303-304; *see also* Texas Jack Omohundro

One Drop Law, *see also* Miscegenation; Segregation; Virginia Racial Integrity Law

Only Way to Handle It, The (illustration), 486

Opera Buffa, 315; *see also* Antonio Pini-Corsi

Opera Companies, 294-296

Opéra de Monte-Carlo (opera house), 312

Opera House, 268, 277, 312, 320; *277, 321*

Opera, 169, 223- 255, 265-268, *277,* 279-280, 289, 291-299, 315-318, 322, 339, 364-365; in America, 280; in America before 1812, 268; appropriated by wealthy, 268; debated ancestry, 267-268; debut in San Francisco, 279-280; defined as cultural art form, 265-267; defined by Encyclopedia Britannica, 265-267; developed by Claudio Monteverdi, 339; first commercial recording, 322; German-Italian debate, 289-291; "lowbrow to highbrow," 268; in New Orleans, 268; in New York, 289; performance for an Italian audience, 317; recordings 297-298; and "riskier ventures such as

Rigoletto," 278; as favorite of working-class Italians, 223, 299;

Order of the Sons of Italy in America, 167, 459, 470

Order Sons and Daughters of Italy in America (OSIA), 525

Organ Grinder (street entertainer), 180-181, *180*, 257, and Monkey, 257; "outlawed," 181; *see also* Italian Organ Grinders

Organ Grinder, The (cartoon short), 180

Organized Crime, 465-466; *see also* Mafia

Original Dixieland Jazz Band (ODJB), 327-338, *329, 333*; as first to apply the word "Jazz," 327-333; as "first great jazz orchestra," 338; praised by Louis Armstrong, 338; "first commercial jazz recording," 334; first Jazz performance in London, 334; performs for British Royalty, 335; records in England, 335; list of recordings 331, *331*; undue criticism, 327; *see also* Jazz; New Orleans; Nick LaRocca

Orphan Train Movement, 175-182, *78*; *see also* Charles Loring Brace

Orselli, Frank, as "first Italian the Walla Walla Valley," 351

Oslo, Norway, 511, *511*

Out of Rushmore's Shadow: The Luigi Del Bianco Story (book), 428; *see also* Luigi Del Bianco; Mt. Rushmore

Outlook (magazine), 96, 150, 210; and horrors of Child Labor, 150; *see also* Frederick Douglass

Over the Rainbow (song), 368; *see also* Salvatore Ferragamo

Overman Wheel Company, 246-247; *247*; *see also* Bicycle

Owens, Jesse (athlete), 47-48; *48*; opts for American military salute, 48, *48*; *see also* Pledge of Allegiance; 1936 Olympic Games

Owens, Rev. C. A. Owens (minister), 500; *see also* Miscegenation

Oxford Standard Dictionary describes "tenor," 297

P:

Pacific Commercial Advertiser, The (newspaper), 97

Pacino, Al (actor), 107; connected to factual town of Corleone, 107; *see also The Godfather* and *Two Bits*

Pacino, Salvatore (father), 107; *see also* Al Pacino

Padrone (work boss), 198-200; 201; *see also* Pascal D'Angelo

Padrone Act of 1874 (18 U.S.C. 446), 198-201; text of the law, 200

Padrone System in New York, The (article), 198

Padrone System, 198-201, 207, 381; *see also* Pascal D'Angelo

Padua, Italy, 263

Paganini, Niccolò (composer), 267, *267*; *see also* Opera

Paglia, Camille (journalist), review of *The Fortunate Pilgrim*, 108; *see also* Mario Puzo

Pagliacci (Italian for "clown"), 255; *see also* Enrico Caruso; Eduardo Migliaccio

paisan (term of endearment), 261, 345, 369, 379-380, 444

Palermo, Sicily, 327, 363

Palladio, Andrea (architect), 27, 165, 206, 214, 320-321, *321*; *see also* Architecture

Panama Pacific International Exposition in San Francisco, 434

Panunzio, Constantine M. (author), 206-207; autobiography *The Soul of an Immigrant*, 206-207

INDEX 591

Paone, Maria (author's great grandmother), 78, 531; *531*; immigrates to America, 78

Parc Monceau (public park) *see* Statue of Liberty

Parish for Italians, 437-438; *see also* Saint Raphael Society,

Park Theater, Italian opera first performed in America, 270, illustration *276*

Parks and Playgrounds, 222-225

Parmenter, Frederick , 399; see: Sacco and Vanzetti

Parmesan Cheese; 135

Parodi, Teresa (opera singer), 277, *279*, *see also* Opera

Pasin, Antonio (business owner), 462-463; *see also* Radio Flyer; Little Red Wagon

Passing of the Great Race (book), 480; *481*, 491; *see also* Madison Grant; Eugenics

pasta al pomodoro, 513; *see also* Food

Pasta Machine, 523, *523*

Pasta, 10, 512-513, *523*; *see also* Macaroni

Pastene (tuna fish), 351

Pastene, Luigi (entrepreneur), 351

Pastor, Antonio "Tony" (impresario), 257-263; *258*; as the "Father / Dean of Vaudeville," 258; Italian heritage, 259; *see also* Vaudeville

Pastrone, Giovanni (director), 372; *375*; technical innovations, 373-374; *see also* Blockbuster; Hollywood

Pastry shop, 512

Pathé Records, 314-315

Patience and *Fortitude* (Lion Sculptures), 422-424; *423*; *see also* New York Public Library; Piccirilli Brothers

Patience defined, 422; *see also* *Patience* and *Fortitude*

Patriotism defined, 23

Patrizi, Ettore (editor), 285-286; *see also L'Italia*

Paul, Tommy (boxer "Gaetano Alfonso Papa"), 459

PBS *American Experience* (documentary), 13, 335, 359; cites Amadeo Peter "A.P." Giannini, 359; reference on the origin of the word "Jazz," 335; *see also* Jazz

Pearl Harbor, Hawaii, 414-415; *see also* Aviation; Giulio Douhet

Pechie, Joseph S. (historian), 10

Peckham, Rufus (Supreme Court Justice), 242; *see also Lochner v. New York,*

Peiss, Kathy (historian), on immigrant leisure and recreation, 212

Pellegrini Opera Company, 280; *see also* Opera

Pellegrino, Nicholas, xi

Pelosi, Nancy (Speaker of the House), 13

Pep, Willie (boxer "Guglielmo Papaleo"), 459

Peragallo, Olga (author), 205

Pergola, Italy, 318

Peruzzi, Mario (business owner), 462; *see also* Planters Peanuts; Amadeo Obici

Petrosino, Joseph (police officer), 461-462; *462*

Pezzolo, Francesco Stephano (baseball player), *see* Ping Bodie

Phelan, Mark (journalist), 401-402; *see also* Al Smith

Philadelphia Athletics (baseball team), 453

Philadelphia Lazaretto, 88-89; *see also* Ellis Island; Immigration; Lazaretto

Philadelphia, Pennsylvania (city), 5, 278, 316, 509-510, 519-520; and "tradition of English opera," 278;

"Italian Market," 520-521; Little Italy, 519-520; Philly Cheese Steak and Italian origin, 509-510

Phonograph, 208, *298*, 300, 329-331; *see also* Jazz

Photographer's Association of America, 308; *see also* Carlo Gentile

Photography and Lynching, 133-134; *133, 134*

Photoplay (trade magazine), 389-390; *see also* Rudolph Valentino

Piano di Coreglia region of Tuscany, 259

Piano Forte, 339-340, 371-372; *340*; *see also* Bartolomeo Cristofori

Piantadosi, Roger (journalist), 5, 7; *see also* Christopher Columbus

Piccirilli Brothers (sculptors and stone masons), 397, 415-426, 397, *417, 419*, *425*, 424, 494; Attilio as "foreigner in Italy," 418; Bronx studio, 418, 420, *419*; immigrate to New York City, 418; at Lincoln Memorial, 415-417; *416, 417*; select list of public works, 424, *425*; *see also* Lincoln Memorial

Piccirilli, Attilio (brother), 418; *419*; *see also* Piccirilli Brothers

Piccirilli, Ferrucio (brother), 418; *419*; *see also* Piccirilli Brothers

Piccirilli, Furio (brother), 418; *419*; *see also* Piccirilli Brothers

Piccirilli, Getulio (brother), 418; *419*; *see also* Piccirilli Brothers

Piccirilli, Masaniello "Thomas," (brother), 418; *419*; *see* Piccirilli Brothers

Piccirilli, Orazio "Horace," (Brother), 418; *419*; *see* Piccirilli Brothers

Pick and Shovel, 201-205, *202*, 470; *see also* Pascal D'Angelo

Pie definition, 515; *see also* Pizza

Pierro, Antonio, 472; *see also* Italians who served in world War I

Pilot, The (newspaper), *see* Padrone System

Pini-Corsi, Antonio (opera singer), 127, 302, 314-316, *315*; born to Italian parents, 315; debut Italian city of Cremona, 315; gramophone recordings, 316; "height of his fame," 316; *see also* Opera

Pink Powder Puffs, (article), 389-390; *see also* Rudolph Valentino

Pisan, Antonio (entrepreneur), 12,

Pisanelli, Antonietta (impresario), 316-318; as "The Italian Colony's First *Impresario*" 316; experiences tragedy, 317; appeal of Italian immigrants, 316; choice of operas, 317; *see also* Opera

Pitkin, Thomas (historian), 52-53; *see also* Castle Garden

Pittsburgh, Pennsylvania,34, 452, 463-464, 527; as "Steel City," 34; *see also Frank Vittor*

Pittsburgh Pirates (baseball team), 452

Pittsburgh Tribune-Review (newspaper), 406; *see also* Frank Vittor

Pizza, 10, 511-515, 525; traces roots to Naples, 514; Queen Margherita, 514; recognized by UNESCO, 514; *see also* Naples; Queen Margherita

pizzicato ("plucked"), 339; *see also* Claudio Monteverdi

Planned Parenthood, *see* Margaret Sanger

Planters Peanuts Company, 462; *see also* Amadeo Obici

Playground (magazine), 477

Playground Association, 477-478

Pledge of Allegiance, 46-48, *47*; adding affirmation to "God," 47; by all American school children,

INDEX 593

45-46, "Bellamy Salute," 46-47; and Congressional word changes, 46-47; original 23-word, 46; *see also* Francis Bellamy

Plessy v. Ferguson, 115, 209, 487; *see also* Segregation

Plight of Columbus and Italian Americans, The (essay), 37-39; *see also* Christopher Columbus

Po River, 135,

Poggioreale, Sicily, *see* Nick LaRocca

Polenta, 524

Poli, Sylvester Z. (impresario), 257-263, *260*; apprentice in Paris, 260; entrepreneurship, 260-261; support of Italian immigrants, 260-261; as "positive example of Italian immigrants," 261; Wonderland Theater, 260; *see also* Vaudeville

Political Cartoons, 486

Political Science Quarterly (journal), *see also* Eugene Schuyler

Pollard, Calvin (architect), 44; *see also* Emma Stebbins

Pollens, Stewart (music historian), cites Cristofori as introducing "pianoforte," 339-340

Pollock, Michael (journalist), 181

Polo, Marco (explorer), 512-513, 518; and ice cream, 518

Ponselle, Rosa (opera singer), 302, 309-310, 313; *309*; as "artistic director of the Baltimore Opera," 310; and Enrico Caruso, 309; *309*; obituary, 310; opera debut, 309; marriage, 310; praised by music critic, 310; sings at London's Covent Garden, 310; in vaudeville with sister Carmela, 310; vocal talent, 309-310; *see also* Enrico Caruso; Opera

Pont du Gard (aqueduct), 361, *361*

Ponzillo Sisters, *see* Rosa Ponselle

Ponzillo, Carmela (opera singer), *see also* Rosa Ponselle

Pope Leo XIII, 437, 439; *see also* Mother Cabrini

Pope Pius XII, 36, 442; declares Mother Cabrini as Patron Saint of Immigrants, 442; *see also* Mother Frances Cabrini; Immigrants

Popeye the Sailor Man episode "Organ Grinders Swing," 180

Population, 85-86, 184, 511; chart *85*; of Americans with Italian heritage, 511; Chart Top Three American Cities, 184

Populist movement, 23-24, 272; "growing discontent," 272

Port of New Orleans, 98-99; *see also* Immigration; New Orleans

Porter, Lewis (jazz historian), corrects reference on origin of word "Jazz," 335

Portrait of a Man, said to be Christopher Columbus (painting), 31, *31*; *see also* Christopher Columbus

Poughkeepsie, New York, 3

Prescott, William H. (historian), on Italian poetry, 271

Presley, Elvis (entertainer), 336, 467; and "Memphis Mafia," 467; *see also* Giovanni Schiavo

Press of Atlantic City, The (newspaper), 506; *see also* Vineland, New Jersey

Prestissimo, see Italian Terminology of Music

Presto, see Italian Terminology of Music

Price, Stephen (theater manager), 272; *see also* Lorenzo Da Ponte

Prima, Louis (Italian American singer), 302

Primo magazine, 40,

Prince Pasta, 351

Prisoner of Love (song), *see* Russ Colombo

Prof. Bollini the Italian Magician, 259, *259*; *see also* Vaudeville

Professional Boxing, *see* Boxing

Progressive Movement, 209, 432; *see also* Maria Montessori

Progresso Company, 506; *see also* Vineland, New Jersey

Prohibition, 362, 401, 402, 473-476, 505-506; as Anti-Italian, 473-474; and "gangland murders," 474-475; *see also* Vineland, New Jersey

Protestantism (religion), 22, 23, 232, 502

Public Education / School System, 205, 232, 498; *see also* Americanization

Puccini, Giacomo (composer), 312, 524, *267*, *see also* Opera

Puck (political magazine), 33, 294, 296, 454, *454*; parody "Grand Opera Opens," 296Pueblo and

Pueblo, Colorado (city), 34-36, *35*; and Italian Immigrants, 34-35; mining 34; statue of Christopher Columbus removed, 35, *35*; *see also* Christopher Columbus

Punic War between Rome and Carthage, *see Cabiria,*

Pushcart, 182-184, *183*, *184*, 211; and street vendors, 182-184; *see also* Mulberry Street

Puzo, Maria Le Conti (mother), 4; as inspiration for Vito Corleone, 107-108; *see also* Mario Puzo; *The Godfather*

Puzo, Mario (author), 4, 107-108, *see also Fortunate Pilgrim* and *The Godfather*

Q:

Quaker City, USS (sailing ship), 139-140; *140*; *see also* Mark Twain

Qualia, Frank (wine maker), 362-363; *see also* Val Verde Winery

Quarantine Islands, 66-67, 88-89; "contagious disease ward," 88-89; regulations, 88-89; *see also* Ellis Island; Lazzaretto

Queen Margherita of Savoy, 514; as wife of King Umberto I, 514; *see also* Pizza

R:

Racial Discrimination, 23-24, 337, 484-488, 491, 494; *see also* Discrimination; Eugenics; Madison Grant; Stereotypes

Radio and NBC Symphony Orchestra conducted by Arturo Toscanini, 294

Radio Broadcast magazine, 293; *see also* Guglielmo Marconi

Radio City Music Hall, 294

Radio Flyer Red Wagon, as part of the "American Dream," 463

Radio, 293; first radio transmitter *293*; simultaneous live broadcasting, 293; *see also* Guglielmo Marconi

Radlauer, Dave (music historian), 335, 336; *see also* Jazz; Nick LaRocca

Rag Picker, 175-182

Ragas, Henry (piano), 329, 334, *329*, dies during Flu Pandemic, 334; *see also* Original Dixieland Jazz Band

Ragtime (music), 250, 323-325; origins, 324-325; piano driven style, 324; "swept the nation," 325; called "unmusical rot," 325; *see also* Jazz

Railroads, Industry, and Immigration, 25-26

Raimondo, Gina (governor), 13

INDEX 595

Rainbow (shoe), 368; *see also* Salvatore Ferragamo

Ralph *Sand*, 387; *see* Ralph Hanson

Ralph's Italian Restaurant in Philadelphia, 510

Rambova as costume designer for Cecil B. DeMille movies, 385

Rambova as set designer, 385;

Rambova, Natacha (actress), 385-386, *385*, *386*; born as "Winifred Shaughnessy," 385; trained as ballerina, 385; *see also* Rudolph Valentino

Rap (music genre), 467; *see also* Giovanni Schiavo

Rapallo, Italy, 354

Raphael (artist), 496

Recording Industry, 322

Recreation and Leisure, 212-213, 477-478

Rector's Club, (entertainment venue), 335; *see also* Original Dixieland Jazz Band

Red Scare, 399; *see also* Sacco and Vanzetti

Red Shirts *see* Giuseppe Garibaldi

Reimers, Prof. David (historian), 502-503; difference Italian and Irish Catholicism,

Reisenweber's (entertainment venue), 330, 331-332; *see also* Original Dixieland Jazz Band; Jazz

Reisenweber's Café, 330, *332*, *333*; *see also* Jazz, Original Dixieland Jazz Band

Religion, 98, 146, 175-182, 273, 311, 365, 394, 401-404, 437-444, 476, 501-504, 519; exemptions during Prohibition, 476; during "Gilded Age," 503; and Ku Klux Klan, 501-502; as "moral morons," 501-502; *see also* Catholicism; Mother Frances Cabrini; Protestantism; Al Smith

Remarkable Carlo Gentile, The (biography), 307; *see also* Carlo Gentile

Renaissance and Enlightenment, 1, 3, 7, 18, 42, 98, 206, 320, 337, 355, 445, 496; art in Italy, 445; *see also* Joseph Stella

Restaurants in America, 510-524

Richman, Jeff (researcher), 450-451; *see also* Casoni & Isola

Rigoletto (opera), 278, 297, 318, 319, *319*; *see also* Opera

Riis, Jacob (social reformer / photographer), 175, 186-201, *187*, 239; and Theodore Roosevelt, 195-196; *see also How the Other Half Lives*

Riley & Co. Bookstore, 271; *see also* Lorenzo Da Ponte

Risorgimento and Italian Unification, 18-20, 61; *see also* Giuseppe Garibaldi

Rizzo, Vincent (wine maker), 345

Robichaux, John (musician), 328; *see also* Jazz

Robinson, J. Russel (musician), 334; *see also* Jazz; Original Dixieland Jazz Band

Rock 'n' Roll, 323, 336; *see also* Elvis Presley

Rocky (movie), 457

Rocky Horror Picture Show (movie), 529

Rogers, Francis (opera historian), 274; acceptance of Italian Opera, 274; *see also* Opera

Roman Aqueducts, 360; *361*

Roman Empire, 18, 20, 42, 98, 311, 360, 361, *361*, 372-373, 419, 420, 518

Romanesque (architectural style), 364; *see also* Architecture

Romeyn, Esther (biographer), 254-255; compares Migliaccio and Enrico Caruso, 255; *see also*

Eduardo Migliaccio; Enrico Caruso

Roosevelt, Theodore "Teddy" (U.S. President), 120, 148-149, 195-196, 210, 420, 427, *427*, 461, 498; and Boxing, 453-454, *454*; and Jacob Riis, 195-196; *see also How the Other Half Lives*

Rosina (opera character), 318; *see also* Josephine Lucchese; Virginia Colombati

Rossi, Pietro Carlo (wine maker), 348-349; tragic death of, 349; *see also* Italian-Swiss Colony Wine

Rossini, Gioachino (composer), 265, *265*, 268, 275, 315, 318; *see also* Antonio Pini-Corsi;

Rotella, Mark (author), 301; *see also* Enrico Caruso

Rothman, Lily (journalist), *see also* Mother Frances Cabrini

Rothstein, Arnold (gangster), 475; *see also* Prohibition

Rotunda at the University of Virginia, 449

Roughing It (book), 137; *see also* Mark Twain

Royal Air Force (RAF), 414-415; *see also* Giulio Douhet

Rubato, see Italian Terminology of Music

Rules for the Use of Airplanes in War (treatise), 414-415; *see also* Giulio Douhet

Ruth, Babe (baseball player), nickname of "The Great Bambino" 453, 455; *see also* Baseball; Ping Bodie

Rydell, Bobby (Italian American singer), 302

S:

S.S. Florida (ocean liner) and Italian Immigrants, 72-73; *see also*

Messina Earthquake

Sacco and Vanzetti, 120, 134, 397, *398*, *399*, 398-401, 426

Sacco, Nicola, *see*: Sacco and Vanzetti

Safety Bicycle, and "new found freedom," 246-247

Saint Ignatius College, 353

Saint Lazarus, 88-89; *see also* Lazaretto

Saint Raphael Society for Italian Immigrants, 503

Saint Raphael Society for the Protection of Italian Immigrants, 437-438, 503

Saint, defined, 439, 440; *see also* Mother Frances Cabrini

Salaparuta, Sicily, 327

Salerno, Italy, 251

Salieri, Antonio (composer), 267, *267*

Salvatore Ferragamo Museum in Florence, 310-311; *see also* Salvatore Ferragamo

Sammartino, Peter (educator), 90-92, *92*; experimental teaching concept at FDU, 90; as founder of Fairleigh Dickenson University, 90-92; as child of Italian immigrants, 90; as "personification of American Dream," 90; publications on education, 90; *see also* Farleigh Dickinson University

Sammartino, Sylvia "Sally" (educator), 90, *92*; *see also* Peter Sammartino

San Antonio, Texas, 318-319, 363, 450; *see also* Josephine Lucchese, Salvatore Lucchese

San Carlino (theater), 309; *see also* Opera; Rosa Ponselle

San Carlo Opera Company, 319, 320, *319*; *see also* Josephine Lucchese

San Diego, 345

INDEX 597

San Francisco Chronicle
(newspaper), Tetrazzini's
Christmas Eve concert, 281-282
San Francisco Earthquake, 283, 318,
357; *see also* A.P. Giannini;
Lotta's Fountain
San Francisco Italian community,
317, 346
San Francisco War Memorial Opera
House, *321*; *see also* Gaetano
Merola
San Francisco, California (city), 279-
281, 283, 285, 317-318, 320, 344,
345, 346, 350, 352-357, 358-359,
352-361, 385, 452, 453, 509-510;
and *Cioppino*, 509-510;
geographical advantage, 352-353;
Italian community, 317, 346; and
Opera 279-280; as major port of
entry, 344; *see also* Baseball;
Mauro Battocchi,
San Fratello, Sicily, 107; *see also* Al
Pacino
San Gennaro (Italian street Festival),
249, 513, 519
San Maurizio Church, 341; *341*; *see
also* "Italian Instruments"
Sanger, 239-240, 241-242, *241*, 244-
245, *245*; as opposed to Abortion,
245; opens first birth control clinic
in America, 245, *245*; "Birth
Control is NOT Abortion," 245;
and "disseminating information on
birth control," 245; "eugenic-like
statements," 245-246; and
immigrant low wages, 244;
preserving "potential
motherhood," 244; founding
Planned Parenthood, 244-245,
245;cites "ignorance of
reproduction," 244-245; and
"value of motherhood," 240-241
Sant'Angelo Lodigiano, 437; *see
also* Mother Frances Cabrini

Sant'Apollinare, Italy, 471; *see also*
Michael Valente
Santa Barbara, California, 366; *see
also* Salvatore Ferragamo
Santa Clara College, 353
Santa Maria (Columbus ship), *29*;
see also Christopher Columbus
Santa Maria da Nazareth, Venice,
see Lazaretto
Santa Rosa Business College, 347;
see also Isabelle Simi
Santa Rosa Press Democrat
(newspaper), 348-349
Sartori, Giovanni Baptiste "John"
(merchant), sale of macaroni in
America, 515-516; client Thomas
Jefferson, 515-516; as consul of
the Vatican, 515; emigrates to
Philadelphia, 515-516; as U.S.
consul at Rome, 515
Satchmo: My Life in New Orleans,
(autobiography), 338; *see also*
Louis Armstrong; Jazz
Saturday Night Live (television
show), 294; *see also* Arturo
Toscanini
Sbarbaro, Andrea (wine maker), 344;
see also Pietro Carlo Rossi;
Italian-Swiss Colony Wine
Sbarbaro, Tony (drummer), 329, *329*,
see also Original Dixieland Jazz
Band
Scambray, Ken (journalist) on
Tallulah Lynching, 125-126
*Scanland, John Milton "J.M."
(journalist),* describes opera
Italian audience, 317
Scarface (movie), 475; *see also*
Prohibition
Scelsa, Joseph, xi
Schiavo, Giovanni Ermenegildo
(professor), 205, 464, 465, 466-
467; publications, 465; as student
of Italy and Italians in America."

466-467; *see also* Italian American Studies

Schonberg, Harold C. (music critic), praises Rosa Ponselle 310

Schubert, Laura, xi, *511*

Schultz, Dutch (gangster), 475; *see also* Prohibition

Schuyler, Eugene (American Diplomat), as Diplomat in Italy, 142-145, *143*, 146; convalesce in Venice, 142; and emigration statistics, 143-144; observations in Italy, 143-144; and morality of the Italians, 144; and "worthless criminal statistics," 144

Schwarzenegger, Arnold (celebrity), 365; *see also* Salvatore Lucchese

scopa (Italian game), 211

Scorsese, Martin (director / film maker), 4, 373; praises *Cabiria*, 373

Scouts of the Prairie, The (Wild West Show), 303-307; *305, 307*

Scranton, Pennsylvania, 462

Seals Stadium in San Francisco, 456, 457, *456*; *see also* Boxing

Seattle Star (newspaper), review of *The Sheik*, 383; *see also* Rudolph Valentino

Seattle Times, The (newspaper), 235

Second Coming of the KKK, The: The Ku Klux Klan of the 1920s (book), 505

Second Industrial Revolution in America, 8, 25-26, 34-35

Second World War, 414-415, 470; *see also* Giulio Douhet

Secrets of Beauty, My (article), 314; *see also* Lina Cavalieri

Sedition Act, 470, 485

Segregation, 209, 487-488, 496-498, 499; of Music Markets, 336; "inferiority of the non-white races," 499; *see also* Discrimination

Séguin, Edouard (educator), 431; *see also* Maria Montessori

Sellaro, Vincenzo (doctor), founding of Columbus Italian Hospital in New York, 459

Seller, Maxine (historian), 280, 316-317; praise for Antonietta Pisanelli, 317; *see also* Antonietta Pisanelli

Seminara, Giuseppe (entrepreneur), 351

Sempa, Francis P. (historian), 414-415; *see also* Giulio Douhet

Serge de Nimes (fabric), 360; *see also* Denim

Setti, Giulio 291; *see also* Giulio Gatti-Casazza

Sewing Trades, 227-228, described by Jane Addams, 227-228

Shakespeare plays, 287, 318; *see also* Verdi Monument New York City

Shakspeare (New Orleans mayor), orders "arrest every Italian," 102-103; *see also* New Orleans Lynching

Shaughnessy, Winifred, *see* Natacha Rambova

Sheik, The (movie), 388-389, 458, 477; *see also* Rudolph Valentino

Shelley, Mary (researcher), 415, 416; *see also* Piccirilli Brothers

Shields, Larry (clarinet), 329, *329*, *see also* Original Dixieland Jazz Band

Shirtwaist (garment), described, 228, *228*; *see also* Triangle Shirtwaist Factory Fire

Show Business, 251-263; *see also* Vaudeville

Show People (silent film), 367; *see also* Salvatore Ferragamo

Showboat (Broadway Play), 500; *see also* miscegenation

Shut the Door, 491-494; immigration policy, 491

INDEX 599

Sicilian Immigrants, 7, 14, 18, 68-71, 100, 144, 151-152, 205, 327, 344, 347, 350-351, 474, 518; cultural distinctions, 146-147; "darker complexion," 100; "evil eye" (*malocchio*), 124-125; fishermen, 347; and "feudal system," 144; and Messina Earthquake, 68-71; and "The Mine Boys," 151-152; and horrors of *La Carusi*, 147-153; in New Orleans, 327; "a social class below African Americans," 150-151; as "not white," 100; *see also* Booker T. Washington; Rick Steves

Silent Films, 299, 367, 373; *see also* Enrico Caruso; Hollywood; Rudolph Valentino

Silver Screen (trade magazine), 372; *see also* Hollywood

Silver Screen, described, 372; *see also* Motion Pictures; Hollywood

Simi Winery, California, 347, *347*; as "oldest continuous winery in California," 362

Simi, Isabelle (wine maker), 347, *347*; as "Queen of the Healdsburg Flower Festival," 347; as supervisor of the Simi Winery347; *see also* Wine

Simms, Norman (historian), 7, 93-93, 257, 377; on negative Italian stereotypes in movies, 377 of Italian immigrants struggling to assimilate, 377; writes of Vaudeville performances, 257; *see also* Vaudeville

Sinatra, Frank (Italian American singer), 302

Singers of Italian heritage, 302

Sir Banister Fletcher's A History of Architecture, 205-206; *see also* Architecture

Sisters in Liberty (exhibition), 60-64; *see also* Statue of Liberty; Ellis Island

Sitting Abraham Lincoln (memorial) *see* Piccirilli Brothers

Sklar, Robert (film historian), 380, 389, 390-391; Sklar, Robert (film historian), 380, 389; explains legacy of Rudolph Valentino, 380; Valentino as "fulfilling fantasies of American women," explain "Valentino's passion," 389; *see also* Hollywood; Rudolph Valentino

Small, Matthew (cultural historian), 224; *see also* Italian Harlem

Smallwood, Ray C. (director), 386; *see also* Rudolph Valentino

Smith, Al (Governor), 401-404, *402*; and Election of 1928, 401-402; as Governor of New York, 401; Italian ancestry, 401

Smith, Ellison DuRant (U.S. senator), 491-493, *493*; supports "shut the door policy," 491; speaks of a "pure breed," 492

Smith, Jacob (historian), 278; *see also* Max Maretzek

Smithsonian (magazine), 2, 269

Smithsonian National Air and Space Museum, 405, 409, *409*; *see also* Charles Lindbergh

Snow White and the Seven Dwarfs (movie), 359; *see also* A.P. Giannini

Social Class System, 210, 484

Social Dancing as dance of "primitive peoples, 497

Social Darwinism and Eugenics, 117-121, 481-482, 491

Social Reform and Tenements, 186-201; *see also* Jacob Riis

Social Reform, 239-242; *see also* Jane Addams; Ellen Gates Starr; Lillian Wald

Soldier Field, Chicago, *see also* Boxing

Son of Italy (autobiography), 203-204; *see also* Pascal D'Angelo

Son of Sheik, The (movie), 380, *380*, *388*, 388-389, 391; *see also* Rudolph Valentino

Sonoma Valley, California, 345, 348-349; *see also* Wine Making,

Sopranos, The (TV series), 106; *see also* Stereotyping

Soul of An Immigrant, The (autobiography), 206-207; *see also* Constantine M. Panunzio

Soulmaker: The Times of Lewis Hine (retrospective exhibit), 231; *see also* Lewis Hine

South Braintree, Massachusetts, see: Sacco and Vanzetti

Spahr, Rob (journalist), 506; *see also* Vineland, New Jersey

Spanish Conquistadors exploring America, 514

Spanish Mission San Diego de Alcala in California, 345

Speakeasies, 474; *see also* Prohibition

Spinola, Francis B. Spinola (Union Army General), 161

Spirit of St. Louis (airplane), 405, 410; *photo 405*; *see also* Charles Lindbergh

Splendid Romance, The; (movie), 299; *see also* Enrico Caruso

Sports and Games, 211, 451-459; *see also* Baseball, Boxing

Sports Illustrated (magazine), 387

SS *Canopic* (steamship from Italy), 120,

SS *Florida* collides with *RMS Republic*, 72-74; *73*, *74*

St. Frances Cabrini Shrine, 441-442; *442*

St. Januarius (patron saint), 249

St. John's Cemetery, Queens NY, 204; *see also* Pascal D'Angelo

St. Louis World's Fair, 109-110; and "fast food," 109; serves ice cream, 518

St. Mark's Square, Venice, 19, *19*

Stanford University, 320

Staples, Brent (journalist), 95-96, 98

Starr, Ellen Gates, 213-220, *214*; visits Italy, 219-220; *see also* Jane Addams; Hull House

Stars of the San Carlo Opera Co, 318-319, *319*; *see also* Josephine Lucchese

Staten Island Advance reports on Staten Island Ferry disaster, 171-172, *172*, 527

Staten Island, New York, 163, 164, 169, 171-172, 174, 410; *see also* Antonio Meucci; Garibaldi-Meucci Museum; Giuseppe Bellanca

Statue of Liberty ("Liberty Enlightening the World"), 5, 6, *6*, 15, *15*, *55*, 54-58, *57*, *58*, 59-64, *60*, 79-83, *79*, *81*, *82*, 116-117, 463, 527; "awaiting arrival of the gift from France," 80; "born from an Italian idea." 54-64; and Declaration of Independence, 59; dedication in New York harbor, 116-117; as site for "European Garbage ships," 82, *82*; connection with immigration, 79-83; displayed at Paris Universal Exposition, 54-55, *55*; Inaugural celebration, 58, *58*; and "Italian Connection," 59-60; as *Libertas*," 59; as "Lady of the Park," 55-56, *55*; designated National Monument, 64; parodied, 81-82, *82*; assembly in Paris, 55-56, *55*; pedestal, *57*, *58*; plaque for San Carlo of di Arona, 63-64; torch, 15, *15*; as UNESCO World

INDEX

Heritage Site, 60; "welcome arrival," 57-58, *photo 58*; *see also* Gustave Eiffel; Richard Morris Hunt

Statue of Liberty, Torch, 15, *15*

Stebbins, Emma (sculptor), 39-44, *42*; death of, 43; gender and sexual orientation, 42; living in Rome, 42

Steeplechase Amusement Park, 478; *see also* Coney Island

Stein, Gertrude (author), 477

Stein, Johnny (drummer), 327; *see also* Jazz; Nick LaRocca

Stella, Giuseppe Michele "Joseph" (artist), 444-448;*446, 447*; as "American Artist," 444-448; paints *Battle of Lights, Coney Island*, 446, *446*; buried at Woodlawn Cemetery, 448; death of, 448; as a "Futurist Painter," 444-445; return to Italy, 445; expands Modernist style, 444-446; returns to New York, 445; travels to industrial cities, 445

Stereotype of Italian Americans as criminals, 113-114; arising during Prohibition, 474-476; *see Also* Discrimination; Mafia

Stereotype, 4-5, 105-106, 113-114, 180, 211-212, 257, 258-261, 289, 377-378, 462, 497-499, 509; in American Culture, 4-5; in Hollywood movies, 106

Stevens, Ellen Yale (journalist), 429-433; visits Maria Montessori in Italy, 433; *see also* Maria Montessori

Steves, Rick (cultural historian / travel expert), 145-147, *147*, 153; observations about Italy, 145-147; and "social responsibility," 145; and "Travel as a Political Act," 145

Stoddard, Lothrop (professor), 481; *see also* Eugenics

Story of American Freedom, The (textbook), 243-244

Stradivari, Antonio (violin maker), 342; *see also* "Italian Instruments"

Strait of Messina, 69; *see also* Messina Earthquake

Strando, Joseph (lynch victim), 134

Strangers in the Land: Patterns of American Nativism, 1860-1925 (article), 113, 115

Strategic Bombing in Aerial Warfare, *see* Giulio Douhet

Straton, John Roach (Reverand), 402; *see also* Al Smith

Strauss, Joseph (engineer), 358-359; *see also* Golden Gate Bridge; A.P. Giannini

Strauss, Loeb "Levi" (clothier), 359-361

Street Children, 175-182

Strikes, 235-239

Studies in the Psychology of Sex (book), 240; summarized by *Encyclopedia Britannica*, 240; *see also* Havelock Ellis; Margaret Sanger

Studio 8H, 294; *see also* Arturo Toscanini; Saturday Night Live

Sunday Afternoon Macaroni Dinner, 513

Swiss/Italian Alps, 372-373

Sylvain (French opera), 268; *see also* Opera

Syncopation, 324; *see also* Jazz

T:

Taft, William Howard (U.S. president), 210, 420

Take Down Columbus (campaign), 39-42; *see also* Christopher Columbus

Tales of Hoffmann, The (opera), 319; *see also* Josephine Lucchese; Opera

Taliaferro, William B. (Confederate General), 161

Talking Box, 329-331; *see also* Jazz

Tallulah Lynching, Louisiana, 123-134, *124*; burial site *129*; incident described, 123-124

Tamburri, Anthony (historian), 7, 153, 205

Tampa Morning Tribune (newspaper), 130, 132-133; reports on lynching of Italians, 132-133; *see also* Tampa Lynching

Tangires, Helen (historian), describes Italian ethnic enclave, 519

Tango (dance), 383; *see also* Rudolph Valentino

Tango Pirate (dancer), 381; *see also* Rudolph Valentino

Tartini, Giuseppe (composer), 267, *267*

Teatro alla La Scala in Milan; *see* Opera

Teatro dell' Opera di Roma (opera house), 268 ; *see also* Opera

Teatro della Pergola (opera house), 168; *see also* Antonio Meucci

Teatro Nuovo in Naples, 297, 315; *see also* Will Crutchfield; *see also* Opera

Teatro San Bartolomeo (opera house), 268; *see also* Opera

Teatro San Carlo (opera house), 268; *see also* Opera

Teatro Zaragoza in San Antonio, 364; *see also* Salvatore Lucchese

Teenage Mutant Ninja Turtles (fictional characters), 10; *see also* Pizza

Telephone, *see* Antonio Meucci

Telettrofono (telephone device), 168-170, *168*, 173; *see also* Antonio Meucci

Ten Metro Areas with Most Italian Americans, 525-527, chart *526*

Tenements, 181-201, *197*, 444; chart 188; *floor plan 189, 197*; history, 183-191; and Social Reform, 186-201; *see also How the Other Half Lives*; Jacob Riis

Tenor (vocal range), described, 297; *see also* Enrico Caruso

Tetrazzini, Luisa (opera singer), 280-285, *281, 284, 285*; Christmas Eve concert, 281-282; concert at Lotta's Fountain, 283; death of, 284; dedication ceremony for Verdi Monument, 284, 286; later life, 283; legal entanglement with Oscar Hammerstein, 281; "memorable performance," 282; return to San Francisco, 284; *see also* "Chicken Tetrazzini,"

Texas Hill Country, 363

Texas Jack Omohundro (performer), 305-307, *305, 307*; "America's First Cowboy Star," 305; *see also* Ned Buntline

Texas State Capitol, 450

Texas State Historical Association, 318; *see also* Josephine Lucchese

Texas Wine Industry, 362-363

Texas, and Italian Immigration, 361-365

Texas: A Wine Drive Through Hill Country (article), 363

Théâtre d'Orléans (opera venue), 268; *see also* Opera

Theodore Kosloff's Russian Ballet School, 385; *see also* Natacha Rambova

Thirty-One Days of Italians (e-newsletter), 39, *see also* Janice Therese Mancuso,

Thomas Jefferson Papers, The, 515-516; *see also* Thomas Jefferson

Thomas Jefferson Park and Community Center in Italian Harlem, 225, *225*; described, 225;

INDEX 603

Tikkanen, Amy (research historian), 69-70, 229-230, 297-298; earthquakes in Italy, 69-70; *see also* Enrico Caruso; Earthquakes; Triangle Shirtwaist Factory Fire

Time (magazine), 291, 288, *290*, 290, 292, 358, 402, 439, 440; cites Cabrini as "an American after America's heart," 439, 440; on Metropolitan Opera season, 291; *see also* Giulio Gatti-Casazza; Mother Frances Cabrini

Tirro, Frank (professor), 335

Titanic tragedy (ocean liner), 74-76; sinking and Italians onboard, 74-76; "distress calls," 74-75; *see also* Guglielmo Marconi

Title Cards, 374-375; *see also* Cabiria; Hollywood Movies; Silent Film

Tivoli Opera House, 281; *see also* Opera

Tomato Sauce, 506, 512-514; *see also* Macaroni; New Jersey; Progresso Company; Vineland

Tony Lama Boot Company,® 363, 365; as the "Ferragamo's" of the boot world, 365; *see also* Tony Lama; Salvatore Lucchese

Torremaggiore, Italy, 398

Torrio, Johnny (gangster), 474; *see also* Prohibition

Toscanini, Arturo (conductor), 11-12, 291-292, *293*, 294, 297, 524; as "most acclaimed musician," 291-292; broadcast "Studio 8H" built in Rockefeller Center, 294; dinner in honor, *293*; fame aided by radio, 292; as temporary conductor for Verdi's "Aida," 291-292; *see also* Saturday Night Live

Toynbee Hall, London (settlement House), 213; *see also* Hull House

Tozier, Josephine (journalist), 432; *see also* Maria Montessori

Traboulay, David (professor), xi, xiii

Transamerica Corporation, 359; *see also* A.P. Giannini

Trav S.D. (cultural historian), 257-259; *see also* Vaudeville

Trenchard, Hugh M. (RAF Air Force), 414; *see also* Giulio Douhet

Trenton, New Jersey, 515-516; *see also* Macaroni

Triangle Shirtwaist Factory Fire, 225-231, 438; illustrations and photos of dead *227, 229, 230, 231*; historical account summarized, 226; horse drawn fire engine, 229, *229*; newspaper stories, 229

Triumphal Arch, 419-421

Truitt's Farm, Delaware, 233

Truth About the Mafia and Organized Crime in America (book), 466; *see also* Giovanni Schiavo

Tunney, Gene (boxer), 455

Turin, Italy, 373

Tuscany, Italy (region), 287, 345; *see also* Verdi Monument New York City

Tuskegee Normal and Industrial Institute, 148; *see also* Booker T. Washington

Tuttle, Mandy (research historian), 117-121; *see also* Paul revere House

Twain, Mark (author), 128, *138*, 136-142, 153; assessment of contemporary Americans, 139; and cholera epidemic in Italy, 141; "gallows humor," 141; on Italian Natural Geography, 140; enters port city of Genoa, Italy, 138-139; in Italy, 136-142; describes everyday Italian life, 139-140; arrives in Naples, 139-140; "travel is fatal to prejudice," 142

Twenty Years at Hull House (biography), 213, 216, 220; recalls Italian celebrations at Hull House, 220

Two Bits (movie), 107-108; positive portrayal of Italian family, 107; *see also* Al Pacino

Tyrrell, Henry (journalist), 165, 167; *see also* Garibaldi-Meucci Museum

U:

U.S. Armed Forces and Italian Immigrants, 470

U.S. Capitol, 155-156, 158; *see also Constantino Brumidi*

U.S. Census Bureau reports on restaurants in America, 511

U.S. Census Statistics, 10-11, 175, 511, 525

U.S. Congress H.R. 7995, "Act to limit the immigration into U.S.," 488, *489*

U.S. Congress, 106, 20, 174, 200, 479, 483, 488, *489*, 490; and "Due Process Clause," 242-243passes Emergency Immigration Act, 120; House Resolution, 174; ends "great era of Italian immigration," 479; responds to Padrone System, 200; rejects Treaty of Versailles, 490; xenophobia, 106; *see also* Henry Cabot Lodge; Antonio Meucci

U.S. Congressional Medal of Honor, 471-472; *see also* Michael Valente

U.S. Government vs. Alexander Graham Bell and the Bell Company, 173; *see also* Antonio Meucci; Telephone

U.S. Library of Congress, 93, 94, 175, 293, 294, 323, 336, 342, 478

U.S. National Register of Historic Places, 36, 167

U.S. Patent "Making Flat Macaroni," *illustration 523*

U.S. Patent Office, 171; *see also* Antonio Meucci

U.S. Supreme Court Decisions, 209, 242-243

U.S. Supreme Court, 209,

Ullman, S. George (manager), 381, 382-383; at Valentino's bedside, 391; as Valentino's manager, 386; remembers "Rambova first met" Valentino, 386; *see also* Rudolph

Uncharted Seas (movie), 386; *see also* Rudolph Valentino

Uncle Sam, 486, *486*; *see also* Immigration

UNESCO World Heritage Sites, 60, 514

Unguarded Gates (poem), 116-117; *see also* Statue of Liberty

Unification of Italy, 496

Unification of Italy, 496; *see also* Italian Unification

United Mine Workers of America, 235; *see also* Ludlow Massacre

United States entry into World War I, 469-470; *see also* World War I

United States Senate Catalogue of Fine Art, 156

United States vs. Bell, 174; *see also* Antonio Meucci

University in Bologna, 205

University of California, Santa Barbara Library, 316

University of California, Los Angeles (UCLA), 207

University of Rome, 430; *see also* Maria Montessori

University of Texas, 450

University of Virginia Law, 401, 449; archives, 401; *see also* Sacco and Vanzetti

Up From Slavery (book), 152; *see also* Booker T. Washington

INDEX

Upham, James B. (editor), suggests "Bellamy Salute," 45; *see also* Francis Bellamy
Upright Bass (musical instrument), 338-339, *339*
Urban Parks, 222-225

V:

Val Verde (winery), 362-363; as "oldest established" winery in Texas, 362; as "Italian Texas winery," 362-363; *see also* Wine
Valente, Michael A. (Medal of Honor), 471-472, *472*; citation, 471-472; and Italian origin, 472
Valentino (movie), 396; *see also* Rudolph Valentino
Valentino as I Knew Him (biography), 382; *see also* S. George Ullman; Rudolph Valentino
Valentino, Rudolph (movie actor), 311, 369, 378, *380, 382, 383, 383*, 383-396, *385, 386, 392, 393, 394*, 458, 476-477; ballroom dancer, 389; birth name, 380; coffin, 393, *393*; as "cultural icon," 396; death of, 391; and Jack Dempsey, 382, *382*; divorce from Natacha Rambova, 386; cast as Julio Desnoyers, 383; arrested on "charge of effeminacy," 389-390; collapses 391; friendship with Salvatore Ferragamo, 379-380; "fulfilling fantasies of American women," 390-391; as "Latin Lover," 385; lavish funeral, 392, *392*; funeral mass, 393; funeral as Hollywood publicity stunt, 392-393; graveside, 394; hospitalized, 391; attacks on Valentino's masculinity, 389; and morality, 389-390; receives "Last Rites," 391; legacy, 396; mayhem at

funeral, 393; cast in *The Sheik*, 383; optimistic recovery, 391; and "sex appeal," 389; "screen image," 381; *see also* Salvatore Ferragamo; Kermit the Frog
Vamp (movie character), 385; *see also* Hollywood; Nita Naldi
Van Doren, Carl (editor), 206; *see also* Pascal D'Angelo
Vanzetti, Bartolomeo, *see* Sacco and Vanzetti
Variety (magazine) review of *The Birth of a Nation*, 23-24
Vassar College, Poughkeepsie, New York, 3
Vaudeville Theater, 251-263, *258, 260, 262*, 371; impresarios, 257-263; and Italian performers, 257-259; *see also* Tony Pastor; Sylvester Poli
Vaughn, Samantha (cultural historian), 309-310; *see also* Lina Cavalieri
Vendetta (movie), 106; *see also* New Orleans Lynching and Richard Gambino
Vendetta: The True Story of the Largest Lynching in U.S. History (book), 101; *see also* Richard Gambino; Lynching
Venereal Diseases, The (pamphlet), 244; *see also* Margaret Sanger
Veneto, Italy (region), 462
Venice, Italy (city), 18-19, *19*, 88-89, 98, 142, 256, 268, 269, 320, 462; *see also* Lazaretto
Veniero (bakery), 512
Verdi Monuments, 285-288, *288*; *see also* Giuseppe Verdi
Verdi, Giuseppe (composer), 223, *267*, 268, 277, 279, 281, 285-288, *286, 288*, 309; Monuments, 285-288; *see also* Italian Opera
Vergine, Guglielmo (voice teacher), 297; *see also* Enrico Caruso

Verismo (vocal style), described, 298-299; *see also* Enrico Caruso

Veronesi (historian), food in Italian culture, 510

Veronesi, Gene P. (historian), 510, 512-513, and "macaroni during Etruscan times," 512-513

Verrazzano Narrows Bridge, 52, 527

Vespucci, Amerigo (Italian explorer), America named after, 49,

Vesti La Giubba (song), 300; *see also* Enrico Caruso

Via Santi Quaranta, 251; *see also* Eduardo Migliaccio

Vic Damone (Italian American singer), 302

Victor Men's' Bicycle, 246-247; *see also* Bicycle

Victor Record Catalog, 252, *252*, 328, 331-334 *330, 331*; *see also* advertisement "A brass band gone crazy!" 334; *see also* Jazz; Original Dixieland Jazz Band

Victor Records, *photo 252*,

Victoria Ladies' Bicycle, 246-247

Vigilante Justice, 102-106; *see also* Lynching

Vignes, Jean-Louis (wine maker), 345

Villa Rotonda in Vicenza, Italy, 165; *see also* Andrea Palladio

Villarosa, Frederico, as "the first official Italian victim of lynch law in America," 133-134

Vinci, Count (Italian Ambassador) and correspondence on Lynching, 126-127

Vineland Historical and Antiquarian Society, 504-507, 527-528; as "hotbed of anti-Italian KKK activity, 506-507; *see also* Ku Klux Klan

Violence against Italian immigrants, 93-94

Violin (musical instrument), 340, *340*, 341-342; differences from Fiddle, 340; *see also* "Italian Instruments;" Thomas Jefferson

Violin Maker of Cremona, The (movie short), 25; *see also* D. W. Griffith

Violone (musical instrument), 339, *339*

Virginia, 21, 345, 484-488; and Racial Integrity Laws, 484-488

Vitantonio, Angelo (inventor), invents the first hand-crank pasta machine, 521, 523-524,

Vitantonio, Luigi *see* Louis De Vito

Viterbo, Italy, 311

Vittor, Frank (artist), 406, *406*; *see also* Charles Lindbergh; Christopher Columbus

Vivace, see Italian Terminology of Music

Vivacissimo, see Italian Terminology of Music

Vivaldi, Antonio Lucio (composer), 267, *267*; *see also* Opera

Viviano, Frank (journalist), 101, 133-134; writing "Atrocities America Forgot," 133-134

Vivolo, Angelo, 39-40; *see also* Christopher Columbus

Volstead Act, 473; *see also* Prohibition

W:

Wagner, Honus (baseball player), 406; *see also* Frank Vittor

Wagner, Richard (composer), 290-291; *see also* Opera

Wald, Lillian (reformer), *see also* Henry Street Settlement, 213

Waldseemüller, Martin (geographer), 49

Walker Law, 454-455; *see also* Boxing

INDEX 607

Walker, Stanley (editor), 402; *see also* Al Smith

Walla Walla, Washington, and wine industry, 351-352

Walt Disney Company, 217; *see also* A.P. Giannini

Waltz (dance), 323

Washington and Columbus connection, 6

Washington D.C. as "New Rome," 6, 417

Washington D.C., 5-6, 11, *24*, 52, 320, 417; as the "New Rome," 6, 417

Washington Post, The (newspaper), 5,

Washington Square Arch, 419-421, *421*

Washington Square Park, 163, *163*; *see also* Giuseppe Garibaldi

Washington State, agricultural fields, 234-235; among Top-Ten Wineries in America, 351-352; chart *349*; ranked second as wine producer in America, 351-352

Washington, Booker T. (Intellectual), 68, 147-153, *148*; and "Horrors of *La Carusi* in Sicily," 147-153; and "falsehoods labeled against Italian immigrants," 151; and "extreme poverty" in Italy, 150-152; observations in Italy and Sicily, 149-150; travel in Italy and Sicily, 147-153; *see also* Rick Steves; Mark Twain

Washington, George (U.S. President), 419-420; *421*, 427, *427*; *see also* Piccirilli Brothers

Wassaja (adopted son), 307-308, *308see also* Carlo Gentile

WB-2 (airplane), 410; *410*; *see also* Giuseppe Bellanca

We the Italians (newsletter), 455; *see also* Boxing

Weinstock, Herbert (music historian), 267-268; detailed explanation of opera, 267-268

Weiss, Hymie (gangster), 474, 475; *see also* Prohibition

Welch Grape Juice Company in Vineland, New Jersey, 506

Welch, Charles Edgar (son), *see also* Welch Grape Juice Company

Welch, Thomas Bramwell (minister), "unfermented wine," 506; *see also* Vineland, New Jersey

Westfield II (Staten Island Ferry), disaster, 171-172, *see also* Antonio Meucci

Wever, Walther (German General), 414-415; *see also* Giulio Douhet

What Every Girl Should Know (articles), 239-240; *see also* Margaret Sanger

White City" *see* World's Columbian Exposition

White House, 148, 372

White Nationalist, 94-95, 117-119; *see also* Ku Klux Klan

White Race, 496; defined by Miller and Davis, 499; *see also* M'Guffey's Reader

White Supremacy, 481, 492-493, 505; *see also* Discrimination; Eugenics; Ku Klux Klan, Lynching, Nativism; Populism

White, Meghan (preservationist), and characteristics of Italianate Architecture, 214-215

White, Stanford (architect), 419-420

White, Stanford (architect), 419-429, 449; *see also* Architecture

White-Wash, defined by *Encyclopedia Britannica*, 111

Whitney, Anne (sculptor), 43; *See also* Emma Stebbins

Wild West Shows, 303-307; *see also* Giuseppina Morlacchi

Wilder, Gene (actor), 396; *see also* Rudolph Valentino

Willard, Jess (boxer), 455

Wilson, Caryn A. (journalist) and Earthquakes in Italy, 69-70

Wilson, Johnny (boxer "Giovanni Francesco Panica"), 458

Wilson, Matthew R. (historian), 263; *see also* Vaudeville

Wilson, Michael (journalist), 14

Wilson, Woodrow (U.S. President), 120, 219, 372, 420, 473, 522; views Italian film *Cabiria*, 372; and Prohibition, 473

Windom, William (treasury secretary), 53, 83; parodied in *Judge* and *Puck* magazine, 83; proposes relocation to Ellis Island, 83; *see also* Immigration, Ellis Island

Wine Production, 86, 345-349; and Italian Culture, 86; oldest winery, 345; Top 10 per U.S. State (chart), 349

Winston-Salem Journal (newspaper), 500; *see also* Miscegenation

Wireless Communication,

Wireless Telegraph, 293; *see also* Guglielmo Marconi

Wizard of Oz, The (movie), 368; *see also* Salvatore Ferragamo

Wobblies, 235; *see* Industrial Workers of the World

Woke (movement), 40; defined, 40

Wolfgang, Marvin E. (professor), 466-467; *see also* Giovanni Schiavo

Woman and the New Race (book), and Virtue of motherhood," 241, 244; *see also* Margaret Sanger

Women and "Weaker Sex," 242, 246-247; *see also* Bicycle

Women, and "prevailing American cultural view of motherhood," 241-242

Women's Christian Temperance Movement (WCTM), 473; *see also* Prohibition

Wonder Worker in Education (article), *see* Maria Montessori

Wood, Steve (research historian), 464; *see also* Fireworks

Woodlawn Cemetery, Bronx New York City, 448-451; *see also* Joseph Stella

Workday Hours, 226, 241-243; regulated hours by gender, 242-243

World Columbian Exposition, 26-29; *see also* Christopher Columbus

World Heavyweight Boxing Title, 455, 457-458; *see also* Boxing

World War I , 120, 209, 325, 366, 401, 405, 407, 412, 435, 436, 469-472, 480, 484, 485, 522; and United States entry, 120; victory parade, 401

World War II, 9, 48, 205, 294, 302, 314, 359, 414-415, 482, 490, 492; and its aftermath, 302; *see also* Giulio Douhet

World's Columbian Exposition (1893), 26-32, *27*, *29*; opening day, 26-27; *see also* Christopher Columbus

World's Greatest Lover, The (movie), 396; *see also* Rudolph Valentino

Wright Aeronautical Corporation, 408; *see also* Giuseppe Bellanca

Wright Brothers, 405, 411, Wright Whirlwind Engine, 408; *see also* Aeronautics

Wright-Bellanca WB-2 (airplane), 408, 409; ***410***; *see also* Giuseppe Bellanca

X:

Xenophobia

INDEX

Xenophobia, 111-117, 477-478, 494, 500-502; defined, 112; fear-mongering warning, 111-115; first known use of the word, 112-113; *see also* Henry Cabot Lodge

Y:

Y.M.C.A., 477-478

Yankee Doodle Dandy (song), lyrics, 517; *see also* Macaroni,

Year of Italian Culture, 10

Young Corbet III (boxer), 455, 456-457, *456*; career record, 456-457; inducted into Hall of Fame, 457; as Middleweight Champion, 456; obituary, 457; wins World Welterweight title, 456, *456*; *see also* Boxing; Ralph Giordano Boxer

Youth's Companion, The (youth magazine), 46; *see also* Francis Bellamy; Pledge of Allegiance

Z:

Zambelli, Antonio (entrepreneur), 464; *see also* Fireworks

Zamboni (ice resurfacer), 429, 460; as "official ice resurfacer of the NHL," 460

Zimmer, Hans (film composer), describes Italian Terminology of Music, 326

Zimmermann, Kim Ann (freelance writer), on Italian Culture, 18

Zinn, Howard (historian), 33,

Zito, Martina (historian), 518

Ziv, Stav (journalist), 447; *see also* Joseph Stella

Zuculin, Chevalier Bruno (diplomat), describes Jazz to Italy, 337; describes two categories of jazz bands, 337; racial delineation between Jazz bands, 337

Printed in the USA
CPSIA information can be obtained
at www.ICGtesting.com
JSHW011825250324
59870JS00018B/153/J